FOURTH EDITION

ROY A. COOK
Fort Lewis College
Professor Emeritus

LAURA J. YALE
Fort Lewis College
Professor Emeritus

JOSEPH J. MARQUA
CEO/EIR
Tourism and Hospitality Development Group

Tourism
The Business of Travel

Prentice Hall
Upper Saddle River, New Jersey
Columbus, Ohio

Library of Congress Cataloging-in-Publication Data

Cook, Roy A.
    Tourism : the business of travel / Roy A. Cook, Laura J. Yale, Joseph J. Marqua. — 4th ed.
        p. cm.
    Includes index.
    ISBN 0-13-714729-5
    1. Tourism. I. Yale, Laura J. II. Marqua, Joseph J. III. Title.
    G155.A1C674 2010
    910.68—dc22   2008053052

Editor in Chief: Vernon Anthony
Acquisitions Editor: William Lawrensen
Associate Editor: Daniel Trudden
Editorial Assistant: Lara Dimmick
Production Coordination: Lisa Garboski, Bookworks
Project Manager: Kris Roach
AV Project Manager: Janet Portisch
Operations Specialist: Deidra Schwartz
Art Director: Diane Ernsberger
Cover Designer: Bryan Huber
Cover Image(s): SuperStock
Manager, Rights and Permissions: Zina Arabia
Image Permission Coordinator: Craig Jones
Director of Marketing: David Gesell
Marketing Manager: Leigh Ann Sims
Marketing Coordinator: Alicia Wozniak
Copyeditor: Nancy Marcello

This book was set in Input Field by GGS Book Services and was printed and bound by Edwards Brothers. The cover was printed by Lehigh-Phoenix Color/Hagerstown.

Pearson Education Ltd., London
Pearson Education Singapore Pte. Ltd.
Pearson Education Canada, Inc.
Pearson Education—Japan

Pearson Education Australia Pty. Limited
Pearson Education North Asia Ltd., Hong Kong
Pearson Educación de Mexico, S.A. de C.V.
Pearson Education Malaysia Pte. Ltd.

Prentice Hall
is an imprint of

www.pearsonhighered.com

10 9 8 7 6 5 4 3 2 1
ISBN-13: 978-0-13-714729-8
ISBN-10:   0-13-714729-5

To my wife, Gwen, who supported me and
encouraged me in the completion of all of my writing endeavors.

—R. A. C.

To my husband, Don, for his love and support and shutterbug skills.

—L. J. Y.

To my wife, Mary, who is the living expression of love and hospitality.

—J. J. M.

Brief Contents

Contents

Preface

The tourism industry is both dynamic and diverse. Most students come to the study of tourism full of enthusiasm and questions yet the textbooks available have been dry and/or overly focused on travel agencies and transportation modes. Often, they are full of facts with little theoretical or macro-issue discussion. As a result, students' enthusiasm soon wanes, and their interest in careers in "tourism" diminishes. We decided to write and continue to update this book to be as interesting and multifaceted as the field itself. Like the three previous editions, the fourth edition of *Tourism: The Business of Travel* features a conversational style, making it fun to read, yet provides a thorough overview of the tourism industry and gives balanced coverage to each component. The role of the travel agent and the importance of transportation modes are included, but not to the omission of significant coverage of other industry issues, such as accommodations, destinations, attractions, and food and beverage operations.

As our title suggests, we look at the tourism industry through the lens of business, specifically by considering the management, marketing, and finance issues most important to industry members. The book starts with a comprehensive model of tourism and unfolds by considering each piece of the model in succession. Students should find the book enjoyable and educational, no matter which facet of the industry they find most interesting.

ENHANCEMENTS IN THE FOURTH EDITION

We have built on the success of the previous editions of *Tourism: The Business of Travel* and created an even better learning tool in the fourth edition. We kept and expanded all the features that readers and reviewers said they liked and added topics about which they said they wanted to know more. We added a separate chapter on the impact of technology on the industry, and we have continued to integrate the importance of technology throughout the text. Another new chapter highlights the importance of sustainability issues to the tourism industry. Several important improvements are featured in this fourth edition and in the Instructor's Manual. The most significant modifications include:

- The impact of technology is highlighted in Chapter 5.
- There is expanded discussion of consumer behavior issues concerning tourism, especially as they relate to the impacts of technology, including decision making and consumer motivations.
- The importance of tours, tour operators, meeting planners, and specialized tourism segments has been emphasized.
- Chapter 13 emphasizes the importance of sustainability to the future of tourism.
- Several new readings, "Tourism in Action" segments, and "FYIs" have been added to give instructors opportunities to generate student debate and interest.
- Content, examples, facts, and figures have been updated throughout the textbook.

WHO SHOULD USE THIS BOOK

We designed this fourth edition of *Tourism: The Business of Travel* so that it can be tailored to suit a variety of needs. Its engaging writing style and hundreds of updated industry examples make it the perfect textbook for freshman and sophomore students taking their first tourism class. The thoroughness of content also makes it suitable for a similar course introducing students to the hospitality industry. To meet the advanced critical thinking needs of junior and senior students, we have augmented the text's basic content with readings and integrative cases so they can apply their knowledge and refine their problem-solving skills.

No matter how experienced the instructor or students, we believe this fourth edition is one that professors can teach with, not simply from. The various text features and teaching supplements allow each instructor to develop the course to fit his or her style and the special needs and learning styles of students.

HOW THE TEXT IS ORGANIZED

Tourism: The Business of Travel introduces students to an integrative model of tourism as a dynamic industry and then unfolds, considering each of the model's components in turn. Part I focuses on the traveling public and tourism promoters, and explains the importance of providing quality service and the critical linking role of distribution channel members. Part II familiarizes students with each of the tourism service providers, beginning with transportation and concluding with destinations and resorts. Part III elevates students' attention to macro issues facing the industry, such as the important impact tourism can have on host communities and the world. Each part of the book is followed by supplementary readings and integrative cases. Three practical application appendices are included to enhance students' professional skills.

SPECIAL FEATURES

We incorporated many features into the fourth edition of *Tourism: The Business of Travel* to make it engaging for both the instructor and the students.

- Each chapter opens with learning objectives and a detailed outline.
- Each chapter features a real-world vignette that illustrates a major component of the chapter and then is mentioned again within the chapter pages.
- All chapters include ethical/critical thinking dilemmas ("You Decide") that are useful in

generating class discussion and encouraging students to practice critical thinking skills. Each "You Decide" is written to be especially relevant to the chapter in which it appears.

- Each chapter includes many tables and figures that will help students understand the more abstract concepts and theories presented.
- For Your Information ("FYI") boxes are sprinkled throughout the chapters. These serve as examples of chapter concepts and provide helpful travel tips or useful business information.
- Each chapter includes a "Tourism in Action" topic that provides students with an in-depth industry example.
- Discussion questions at the end of the chapter are based on the learning objectives.
- "Applying the Concepts" offers professors and students a variety of thought-provoking topics to explore or to use as a blueprint for applying newly acquired knowledge.
- A glossary of terms follows each chapter's content, and there is a full glossary at the end of the book.
- The text is full of concepts and examples of organizations that will be familiar to students.
- Students are sensitized to the economic, political, social, cultural, and environmental impact of tourism.
- Readings and integrative cases follow each part of the textbook, offering the instructor supplemental material and examples for student discussion.
- Three appendices highlighting geography, tourism research, and job-seeking skills prepare students for tourism careers.

THE INSTRUCTOR'S TOOLKIT RESOURCES

To fulfill our goal of making this fourth edition of *Tourism: The Business of Travel* customizable for individual instructor needs, we have developed a comprehensive suite of instructor's toolkit of resources available for download from our

Instructor's Resource Center (www.pearsonhighered.com/irc) including an Instructor's Manual and PowerPoint slides. The toolkit includes not only the usual elements—detailed chapter outlines and a test bank—but also includes supplemental lecture material and discussion guides to support the use of the readings and cases provided in the text. In addition, discussion suggestions are offered throughout the chapter outlines to generate student debate on several of the textbook features, such as the "You Decide" chapter dilemmas. The power of the written word in our text is also supported by a set of PowerPoint slides.

ACKNOWLEDGMENTS

The number of friends, colleagues, and industry members who helped us in developing and revising this book is far too large to acknowledge individually. To each and every one of them, we offer our heartfelt thanks and appreciation.

We want to recognize our colleagues at Fort Lewis College, as so many of them offered support and special aid in producing our textbook. The following members of the FLC community deserve special mention:

Gary Linn, Dean, School of Business Administration
Leonard Atencio

Skip Cave, Dean Emeritus
James Clay
Larry Corman

Thomas Eckenrode

J. Larry Goff

Eric Huggins

O. D. Perry

Minna Sellers

Allyn Talg

Terence Tannehill

Chuck Tustin

Simon Walls

Several industry members also came to our aid above and beyond their duties:

Lisa Ball, Harrah's Entertainment Corp.

Earl Bebo, The Culinary Institute of America (retired)

Paul Clarke and Treva Ricou, Vancouver Aquarium

Paula Conkling and Jack Musiel, Holland America Cruise Lines

Tom Little, VIA Rail Canada Inc.

Peter Marshall and his staff at the DoubleTree Hotel, Durango, Colorado

R. Michael Thornton, Specialist in Hospitality and Human Resource Management

Sue Trizila, Wyndham Jade

Special thanks go to Lara Dimmick, Lisa Garboski, Dan Trudden, Nancy Marcello, and Gwen Cook for their support and dedication to excellence.

We are grateful to our photographers who provided the photographs included in the book: Dr. Cheryl Clay, Mr. Chad Cook, Mr. Terence Tannehill, Dr. John White, Ms. Janet Wolverton, Dr. and Mrs. Charles Yale, and Dr. Donald Yale.

Finally, we would like to thank those educators who reviewed our text for this fourth edition and made it better through their suggestions and constructive criticism: James D. Bigley, PhD, Georgia Southern University; D'Arcy Dornan, Central Connecticut State University; Amy Hart, Columbus State Community College; and Margaret A. Persia, East Stroudsburg University of Pennsylvania.

About the Authors

Roy A. Cook, DBA (Mississippi State University), is Professor Emeritus, Fort Lewis College, Durango, Colorado. He has written several textbooks: *Tourism: The Business of Travel, Human Resource Management, Meeting 21st Century Challenges,* and *Guide to Business Etiquette.* He has authored over one hundred articles, cases, and papers based on his extensive working experiences in the tourism and hospitality industry and research interests in the areas of strategic management, tourism, human resource management, communications, and small business management. In addition to serving as past editor of *Annual Advances in Business Cases*, he serves on the editorial boards of the *Journal of Teaching in Travel and Tourism, Annual Advances in Business Cases*, the *Business Case Journal*, and the *Journal of Business Strategies*. He is a long-standing member of the International Society of Travel and Tourism Educators, Academy of Management, and Society for Case Research (past president and currently Director of Development). Dr. Cook served as Associate Dean of the School of Business Administration at Fort Lewis College, and as Director of the Colorado Center for Tourism Research, and taught courses and consults in Tourism and Resort Management, Human Resource Management, Strategic Management, and Small Business Management.

Laura J. (Richardson) Yale, PhD, holds BS and MS degrees in Hotel, Restaurant, and Travel Administration from the University of Massachusetts at Amherst. After working in the restaurant, institutional food service, and entertainment industries, Dr. Yale began teaching at Northern Arizona University. While in Arizona, she was instrumental in developing and directing a regional tourism association and served on the Governor's Intrastate Tourism Committee. She received her PhD in Marketing from the University of California–Irvine. Dr. Yale is retired from Fort Lewis College, after years of teaching courses and conducting research in tourism and resort management and services marketing and management. She now devotes herself full time to writing and traveling.

Joseph "Jay" Marqua is Entrepreneur in Residence (EIR) for Tourism and Hospitality Development Group. He has comprehensive experience in organizational systems, service management, quality controls, e-commerce, and technology systems. He has provided leadership for more than a dozen start-up, transformation, and business development efforts. Professional relationships include Sports Express; The Culinary Institute of America; Amtrak: Acela, Auto Train, and Coast Star Light product lines; Aramark; Marriott International; Premier Resorts International; The Saint James Club; SunRay Park and Casino; G.W.C. Gaming; Sky Ute Lodge and Casino; Syndicom, The Ritz-Carlton, and Telluride Ski & Golf Resort.

PART 1

The Traveling Public and Tourism Promoters

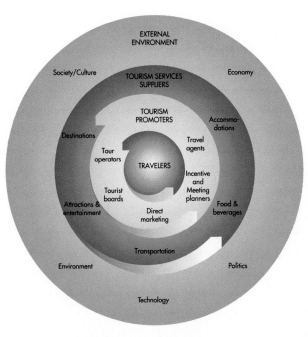

■ An Integrated Model of Tourism.

LEARNING OBJECTIVES

After you have read this chapter, you should be able to:

- Understand and explain the basic definition of tourism.
- Identify the major participants and forces shaping the tourism industry.
- Explain historical factors that encouraged the development of tourism activities.
- Explain the impact of physical, human, and regional geography on tourism activities.
- Explain why tourism should be studied from marketing, management, and financial perspectives.
- Identify future challenges and opportunities facing the tourism industry.
- Discuss career prospects in the tourism industry.

CHAPTER OUTLINE

CHAPTER 1

Introducing the World's Largest Industry, Tourism

Travel is fatal to prejudice, bigotry, and narrow-mindedness.

—Mark Twain

COULD A CAREER IN TOURISM BE IN YOUR FUTURE?

From the day he entered the hospitality management program at Central Piedmont Community College, Bruce Moss knew he wanted to be in the business of serving people. The twists and turns his career took after graduating have been as varied and exciting as the industry that became part of his life—tourism. Bruce's career began with a bang and soon skyrocketed. It started with the job of assistant manager at a 177-room Ramada Inn franchise in Charlotte, North Carolina, right after graduation. He was soon promoted to the position of general manager at another Ramada Inn with the same company in Clearwater, Florida. Based on his successful track record of profitable operations, he was recruited to open the 244-room Tampa Airport Hilton. The promotions and opportunities just kept coming.

Just six years after graduation, he was recruited to fill the position of Director of Front Office Operations of the Innisbrook Westin Resort, a four-star, four-diamond golf/tennis resort in Palm Harbor, Florida. After two short years, he was promoted to Vice President/ Resident Manager of this resort complex covering 1,000 acres with over 1,200 condominium units, three championship golf courses, four restaurants, over 60,000 square feet of banquet space, and a staff of 1,000 employees.

Like almost everyone in the tourism industry, Bruce was presented with many new and challenging opportunities on a regular basis. His next assignment found him moving from the seashore to the mountains as he accepted a transfer to Innisbrook's sister property, Tamarron Resort, high in the Colorado Rockies. "Bitten by the resort operations bug," Bruce decided to complete a four-year degree in tourism to open up even more opportunities. Armed with additional education and a broad base of operational experience, expanded career opportunities led him to General Manager positions at Purgatory Village in Durango, Colorado, and later in Jackson Hole, Wyoming.

His most recent career move finds Bruce as a business owner, serving all segments of the tourism industry. After 25 years of serving the traveling public, Bruce and his wife Lori purchased a central reservations business, which books lodging, destination activities, and vacation packages for individuals and groups traveling to the southwest Colorado region. Achieving success in this multimillion-dollar tourism operation hasn't happened by accident. Intensive employee training focused on the highest quality customer service and constant technology investments (over $100,000 in just one year) keep Gateway Reservations (http://www.gatewayreservations.com) on the cutting edge of service delivery.

As you approach the study of tourism, let your imagination soar, learning all you can to prepare yourself to grow as your career advances. Like Bruce, who earned two degrees in hospitality/tourism management and continues to maintain his Certified Hotel Administrator (CHA) designation, never stop learning. The opportunities that await you are endless.

INTRODUCTION

Welcome to the study of a dynamic group of industries that have developed to serve the needs of travelers worldwide—**tourism**! Tourism is the **business** of travel. Whether we are travelers or we are serving travelers' needs, this exciting and demanding group of visitor services industries touches all of our lives. In this book, you will explore the many and varied segments of this multifaceted industry. As you learn more about tourism, begin thinking about the future challenges and opportunities that lie ahead for all of these industries and how they may influence your life.

SERVICES AND TOURISM

Services and tourism go hand in hand. You will learn more about services in Chapter 3. However, as we begin our study of tourism, it is important to know that these activities make a significant economic impact on almost every nation in the world! Services are growing at a faster rate than all agricultural and manufacturing businesses combined. In fact, tourism-related businesses are the leading producers of new jobs worldwide.

Tourism has developed into a truly worldwide activity that knows no political, ideological, geographic, or cultural boundaries. For a long time, tourism was disparate and fragmented, but as this industry has continued to grow and mature, a sense of professional identity has emerged. It has formed lobbying groups such as the World Travel and Tourism Council, which includes airlines, hotel chains, and travel agents among its members and concentrates on making the case for tourism's global importance and economic value. The future prospects for tourism are brighter than ever as people continue to travel for work or pleasure. "Given its historical performance as a luxury good during expansions and a necessity during recessions, travel and tourism's future economic prospects look quite bright" (p. 51).[1] As we will see later, the growth and popularity of tourism activities have not been accidental.

Tourism has become more than just another industry; it has developed into an important part of the economic fabric of many communities, regions, and countries. Tourism activities have historically demonstrated a general upward trend in numbers of participants and revenues. Even during times of recession, travel and tourism expenditures continue to rise.

■| WHAT IS TOURISM?

As tourism-related activities have grown and changed, many different definitions and ways of classifying the industry have emerged. Use of the term *tourism* has evolved as attempts have been made to place a title on a difficult-to-define group of naturally related service activities and participants. As we embark on our study of tourism, it is helpful to begin with a common definition that has been accepted for decades: "the temporary movement of people to destinations outside their normal places of work and residence, the activities undertaken during their stay in those destinations, and the facilities created to cater to their needs."[2]

As our definition shows, tourism includes a wide array of people, activities, and facilities.

Although tourism is not a distinctly identified industry, most people would agree that it is a unique grouping of industries that are tied together by a common denominator—the traveling public.

Can you describe tourism in your own words? Take a moment to think about this question. You might find it easy to answer this question in general terms, but more difficult to answer if you were asked to provide specific details. In fact, you might find yourself facing a task similar to the one depicted in Figure 1.1. Tourism is much like the elephant: diverse and sometimes hard to describe, but, just like the elephant, too big to be ignored.

Specific segments of tourism, such as air transportation, theme parks, eating and drinking establishments, accommodations, and museums, have their own industrial classification codes in the **North American Industrial Classification System (NAICS)**. However, tourism does not have its own industry code. Even though tourism cannot be classified as a distinct industry, it is generally agreed that "'[t]ourism' appears to be becoming an acceptable term to singularly describe the activity of people taking trips away from home and the industry which has developed in response to this activity."[3]

The Travel Industry Association of America (TIA) has combined both of these concepts to track and report tourism trends in an effort to highlight the size, scope, and impact of this industry grouping. For reporting purposes, the TIA has taken the commmonly agreed-upon definition of tourism and restricted its scope by adding some specific rubrics, use of accommodations and distance, to highlight the significance of tourism. To accumulate statistics, it defines travel as "[a]ctivities associated with all overnight trips away from home in paid accommodations and day trips to places 50 miles or more, one way, from the traveler's origin."[4] By using this very specific definition, data are collected from 16 types of businesses providing tourism and travel-related services that can be fit into specific NAICS classifications.

Because definitions conjure up different meanings and can be used for different purposes, some critics have suggested using a term other than *tourism* to describe the industry. One of

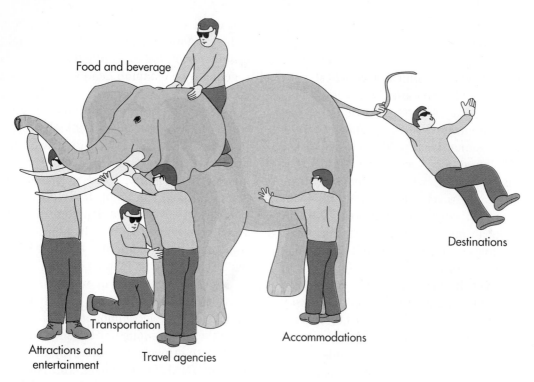

Food and beverage

Destinations

Transportation

Attractions and
entertainment

Travel agencies

Accommodations

■ **Figure 1.1**   The blind men and tourism.

these suggestions has been to use a more inclusive and descriptive term such as "visitor-service industry."[5] For convenience and ease of understanding, however, we will refer to tourism as an industry in this book.

■ A TOURISM MODEL

In an attempt to overcome some of the problems encountered in describing tourism, the **model** presented in Figure 1.2 was developed to highlight important participants and forces that shape the tourism industry. The model, like a photograph, provides a picture that begins to capture the dynamic and interrelated nature of tourism activities. This model can be used as a reference throughout the entire text. Although many of the terms in our tourism model may not be familiar at this time, you will be learning more about each one and its importance in later chapters.

As you study our tourism model, notice its open nature and how each of the segments is related to the others. Let's begin our study of tourism by looking at travelers (tourists), who

serve as the focal point for all tourism activities and form the center of our model. Radiating from this focal point are three large bands containing several interdependent groups of tourism participants and organizations.

Individual tourists may deal directly with any of these tourism service suppliers, but they often rely on the professional services provided by tourism promoters shown in the first band of our model. Tourism promoters, such as travel agencies and tourist boards, provide information and other marketing services. Moving to the next band of our model, we see key tourism suppliers who provide transportation, accommodations, and other services required by travelers.

Tourism suppliers may provide these services independently; they may compete with each other; and, at times, they may work together. For example, airline, bus, railroad, cruise ship, and car rental companies may compete individually for a traveler's business. However, they may also team up to provide cooperative packages such as fly–ride, fly–cruise, and fly–drive alternatives. Or, as airlines have discovered, they must establish strategic alliances with many other carriers to provide seamless travel

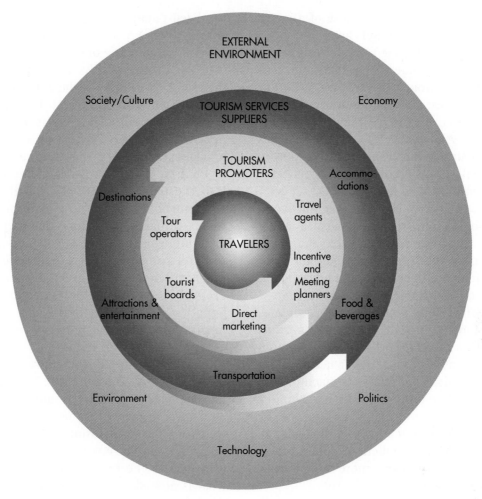

■ **Figure 1.2** An integrated model of tourism.

across states, nations, and continents. Hotels and resorts may also compete against each other for the same traveler's patronage yet cooperate with transportation providers to attract tourists to a specific location. Service providers representing all segments of the tourism industry may often work together to develop promotional packages designed to attract tourists to destinations.

How closely these individuals and organizations work together is ultimately influenced by the forces shaping the face of tourism activities. As our model shows, the tourism industry does not operate in a vacuum. All of the participants, either individually or as a group, are constantly responding to a variety of social/cultural, political, environmental, economic, and technological forces. These forces may range from subtle changes, which are noticeable only after many years, to more dramatic changes, which have

immediate and visible impacts. Examples of these forces can be found all around us.

Gradual changes may be noticed in destinations that were once fashionable but eventually faded in popularity, such as Niagara Falls on the Canadian/U.S. border and Brighton in England. Similar shifts can also be seen in transportation. Steamship passage across the North Atlantic was eclipsed by the faster and more efficient airplane, which opened new horizons for travelers. Immediate impacts can be seen in sudden shifts brought about by currency devaluations, wars, fuel shortages, and natural disasters. Rapid adoption of new technologies such as the Internet (see color insert, Figure 1.3) can have immediate and far-reaching impacts on tourism activities and service providers. A country that was once avoided may suddenly become a popular tourism destination because it is more affordable or accessible. Conversely, a once-popular destination may be avoided because of a recent natural disaster or political upheaval.

The number of travelers from nations also varies dramatically due to political and economic changes. Through the year 2020, Europe will continue to see the largest number of tourist arrivals followed by east Asia and the Pacific and then the Americas.[6] Now that China has developed a sizable middle class due to its economic growth, it has become the biggest Asian nation in terms of outbound travelers.[7]

Let's look at how our model might work. Suppose you (a tourist) want to visit a sunny beach or a snow-covered mountain. You might begin planning your trip by browsing the websites of different airlines, condominiums, hotels, and/or resorts (tourism service suppliers) searching for possible flight schedules and accommodation options. You could simply call a travel agent (tourism promoter) who would search out the best alternatives to meet your needs, rather than spending time and money contacting each supplier. Another option would be taking a "virtual trip" to your desired destination by browsing offerings on the Internet. Finally, you could contact local chambers of commerce or visitors bureaus to learn more about your preferred destinations.

As you progress through this book, we will focus our attention on specific features of our model, learning more about each component and how it interacts with other components of the tourism industry. We will begin our journey into the study of tourism by looking back in time to discover the origins of these activities and the foundations they laid for tourism as we know it today.

■| THE HISTORY OF TRAVEL AND TOURISM

Table 1.1 lists some of the milestones in the development of tourism. Long before the invention of the wheel, travel occurred for a variety of reasons. In the beginning, it was simple. As seasons changed and animals migrated, people traveled to survive. Because these early travelers moved on foot, they were confined to fairly small geographic areas. Travel may have remained a localized experience, but people by nature are curious. It is easy to imagine these early travelers climbing a mountain or crossing a river to satisfy their own sense of adventure and curiosity as they sought a glimpse of the unknown.

We can only guess at the wonder and amazement of early travelers as they made each new discovery. However, there is a rich history of people and cultures that forms the foundation of tourism. History provides important insights into the reasons for travel and the eventual development of tourism. Based on early records, we know that many cultures and nations moved great armies and navies to conquer and control resources and trade routes. Although military forces often traveled great distances, it was probably not until the emergence of the Egyptian, Eastern Mediterranean, and Roman Empires that travel began to evolve into tourism as we know it today.

Early recorded history provides a glimpse into ancient tourism activities. The Phoenicians, like many travelers, were interested in travel because of a sense of curiosity and discovery as well as a means of establishing trade routes. Although written records are scarce, other peoples such as the Mayans on the Gulf Coast of what is now Mexico and the Shang Dynasty in what is now present-day China probably traveled for many of the same reasons as the Phoenicians. Evidence of their travels can be found in the artifacts they collected during their journeys to faraway places. One thing we know for sure is that as civilizations became established and spread geographically, travel became a necessity.

The Empire Era

The point at which simple travel evolved into the more complex activities of tourism is hard to identify. However, tourism as an industry probably began to develop during the Empire Era, which stretched from the time of the Egyptians to the Greeks and finally came to an end with the fall of the Roman Empire. During this time, people began traveling in large numbers for governmental, commercial, educational, and religious purposes out of both necessity and pleasure. The Egyptian Kingdoms (4850–715 B.C.)

Table 1.1	Milestones in the Development of Tourism
Prerecorded history	Travel begins to occur out of a sense of adventure and curiosity.
4850 B.C.–715 B.C.	Egyptians travel to centralized government locations.
1760 B.C.–1027 B.C.	Shang Dynasty establishes trade routes to distant locations throughout the Far East.
1100 B.C.–800 B.C.	Phoenicians develop large sailing fleets for trade and travel throughout their empire.
900 B.C.–200 B.C.	Greeks develop common language and currency, and traveler services emerge as city-states become destinations.
500 B.C.–A.D. 300	Romans improve roads, the legal system, and inns to further travel for commerce, adventure, and pleasure.
A.D. 300–A.D. 900	Mayans establish trade and travel routes in parts of Central and North America.
A.D. 1096–A.D. 1295	European travel on failed religious crusades to retake the Holy Lands from Muslim control introduce these military forces to new places and cultures.
A.D. 1275–A.D. 1295	Marco Polo's travels throughout the Far East begin to heighten interest in travel and trade.
14th–16th centuries	Trade routes develop as commercial activities grow and merchants venture into new territories.
A.D. 1613–A.D. 1785	Grand Tour Era makes travel a status symbol for wealthy individuals seeking to experience cultures of the civilized world.
18th–19th centuries	Industrial Revolution gives rise to technological advances, making travel and trade more efficient and expanding markets; increasing personal incomes make travel both a business necessity and a leisure activity.
1841	Thomas Cook organizes first group tour in England.
1903	Wright Brothers usher in era of flight with the first successful aircraft flight.
1913	Westinghouse Corporation institutes paid vacations for its workers.
1914	Henry Ford begins mass production of the Model T.
1919	First scheduled airline passenger flight debuts between London and Paris.
1945	World War II ends and ushers in new era of prosperity, giving rise to millions of people with the time, money, and interest to travel for pleasure and business.
1950	Diners Club introduces the first credit card.
1952	Jet passenger service is inaugurated between London and Johannesburg, South Africa.
1978	Competition on routes and fares begins with signing of Airline Deregulation Act.
2001	Dennis Tito launches the advent of space tourism as he pays $20 million for an eight-day vacation aboard the International Space Station.
2001	Transportation Security Administration (TSA) is created to ensure airline passenger safety in the wake of the September 11th terrorist attacks on the World Trade Center in New York City and the Pentagon in Washington, D.C.
2002	The euro currency is introduced, signaling liberalization of travel among member nations of the European Union.

were the first known civilization to have consolidated governmental functions at centralized locations. Travel to these locations by boat was particularly easy because travelers could use the Nile River, which flowed northward but was constantly brushed by southward breezes. Because oars were not needed, travel in either direction was relatively effortless. Boats could go north with the current or south with sails.

As travel became commonplace, basic necessities such as food and lodging had to be provided. Several factors combined to encourage travel during the height of the Egyptian, Greek, and Roman Empires. Large numbers of

■ Tourism—past and present: Roman theater at Ephesus (Turkey). Photo by C. E. Yale

travelers began to seek out enjoyable experiences in new locations. The most notable group of these travelers, because of their numbers, was the Greeks.

The Greek Empire (900–200 B.C.) promoted the use of a common language throughout much of the Mediterranean region, and the money of some Greek city-states became accepted as a common currency of exchange. As centers of governmental activities, these city-states became attractions in themselves. They offered visitors a wide variety of opportunities to enjoy themselves while away from home. Shopping, eating, drinking, gaming, and watching spectator sports and theatrical performances are just a few of the many activities that grew out of travel and evolved into the more encompassing aspects of tourism.

The growth of the Roman Empire (500 B.C.–A.D. 300) fostered expanded tourism opportunities for both middle-class and wealthy citizens. Good roads (many of which were built to connect the city of Rome to outlying areas in case of revolt) and water routes made travel easy. As these roads were developed, so were inns, which were located approximately 30 miles apart, making for a day's journey. Fresh horses could be hired at the inns and at more frequent relay stations. With effort, people could travel 125 miles a day on horseback, knowing they would have a place to eat and sleep at the end of the day. These roads, which connected Rome with such places as Gaul, Britain, Spain, and Greece, eventually extended into a 50,000-mile system. The most famous road was the Appian Way, joining Rome with the "heel" of Italy.

Many of the hassles of travel to distant places were removed because Roman currency was universally accepted and Greek and Latin were common languages. In addition, a common legal system provided protection and peace of mind, allowing people to travel farther away from home for commerce, adventure, and pleasure. Just like the Greek city-states, cities in the Roman Empire became destination attractions or wayside stops along the way to a traveler's final destination.

Has this brief glimpse into ancient history taught us anything of use today? The answer is yes. Even today, tourism activities continue to flourish where individuals have free time; travel is easy and safe; there are easily exchangeable currencies; common languages are spoken; and established legal systems create a perception of personal safety. The absence of any of these factors can dampen people's desire to travel and enjoy tourism-related activities, as can be seen in the demise of travel during the Middle Ages.

The Middle Ages and the Renaissance Era

Travel almost disappeared during the Middle Ages (5th–14th centuries A.D.). As the dominance of the Roman Empire crumbled, travel became dangerous and sporadic. The **feudal system** that eventually replaced Roman rule resulted in many different autonomous domains. This breakdown in a previously organized and controlled society resulted in the fragmentation of transportation systems, currencies, and languages, making travel a difficult and sometimes dangerous experience.

As the Roman Catholic Church gained power and influence, people began to talk of Crusades to retake the Holy Land. There were nine of these Crusades (A.D.1096–1291), but each failed. In 1291, Acre, the last Christian stronghold, was retaken by the Muslims, bringing the Crusades to an end. Although conquest and war were the driving forces behind the Crusades, the eventual result was the desire of people to venture away from their homes to see new places and experience different civilizations.

After the Crusades, merchants such as Marco Polo traveled to places well beyond the territories visited by the Crusaders (see Figure 1.4). Reports of Polo's travels and adventures (1275–1295) across the Middle East and into China continued to heighten interest in travel and trade. The rebirth in travel emerged slowly during the Renaissance (14th–16th centuries). Merchants began to venture farther from their villages as the Church and kings and queens brought larger geographic areas under their control. Trade routes slowly began to reopen as commercial activities grew and merchants ventured into new territories. The desire to learn from and experience other cultures heightened awareness of the educational benefits to be gained from travel and led to the Grand Tour Era.

The Grand Tour Era

The Grand Tour Era (1613–1785), which marked the height of luxurious travel and tourism activities, originated with the wealthy English and soon spread and became fashionable among other individuals who had time and money. Travel, and the knowledge provided by these travels, became a status symbol representing the

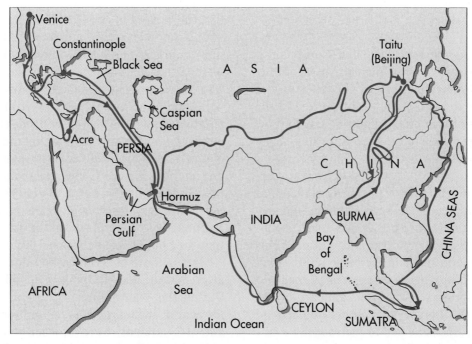

■ **Figure 1.4**   Marco Polo's travel route from his home in Venice, Italy, to China during the 13th century.

ultimate in social and educational experiences. Grand Tour participants traveled throughout Europe, seeking to experience the cultures of the "civilized world" and acquire knowledge through the arts and sciences of the countries they visited. Their travels took them to a variety of locations in France, Switzerland, Italy, and Germany for extended periods of time, often stretching over many years.

Although the desire to participate in the Grand Tour continued, the Industrial Revolution, which began c. 1750, forever changed economic and social structures. Whole nations moved from an agricultural and commercial focus to modern industrialism. People became tied to the regimented structures and demands of factory life and the management of business enterprises. Economic growth and technological advances led to more efficient forms of transportation, the integration of markets across geographic and international boundaries, and higher personal incomes for larger numbers of people. Travel became a business necessity as well as a leisure activity, and tourism suppliers rapidly developed to serve the growing needs of travelers. The days of leisurely travel over extended periods of time to gain cultural experiences faded away as fewer and fewer people were able to take advantage of these time-consuming opportunities.

The Mobility Era

Growing economic prosperity and the advent of leisure time as well as the availability of affordable travel ushered in a new era in the history of tourism. People who were no longer tied to the daily chores of farm life began to search for new ways to spend their precious leisure time away from their jobs in offices, stores, and factories.

The Mobility Era (1800–1944) was characterized by increased travel to new and familiar locations, both near and far. Tourism industry activities began to increase as new roads, stagecoaches, passenger trains, and sailing ships became common sights in the early 1800s. Great Britain and France developed extensive road and railroad systems well before Canada and the United States. The growth and development of roads and railroads helped to increase the availability of transportation alternatives and reduced

their costs, attracting more and more people to the idea of travel.

Thomas Cook (1808–1892) can be credited with finally bringing travel to the general public by introducing the tour package. In 1841, he organized the first tour for a group of 570 people to attend a temperance rally in Leicester, England. For the price of a shilling (12 pence), his customers boarded a chartered train for the trip from Loughborough, complete with a picnic lunch and brass band. The immediate success of his first venture and the demand for more assistance in making travel arrangements led Cook into the full-time business of providing travel services.

The next major steps in the Mobility Era were the introduction of automobiles and air travel. Although automobile technology was pioneered in Britain, France, and Germany, it was Henry Ford's mass production of the Model T in 1914 that brought individual freedom to travel, opening new horizons for millions of people. Winged travel was not far behind, and the time required to reach faraway places began to shrink. Orville and Wilbur Wright ushered in the era of flight with their successful test of the airplane in Kitty Hawk, North Carolina, in 1903.

The Modern Era

But the means of mobility and an interest in seeing new places were not enough. The seeds of **mass tourism** were planted during the first half of the 20th century when industrialists such as George Westinghouse created the paid vacation, believing that annual breaks from work for employees would increase productivity. The working and middle classes in industrialized countries thus were given the financial means and the time to satisfy their newfound wanderlust. Indeed, at the dawn of the 21st century, most workers in virtually all industrialized nations have several weeks of vacation time that they may choose to spend traveling.

Mass tourism received an additional boost after World War II (which ended in 1945). During this war, millions of people throughout the world, including over 17 million Canadian and U.S. citizens, were exposed to many new, different, and even exotic locations as they

All Work and No Play

Forego vacation time? You would have to be crazy, right? Well, many Americans and Brits work insane hours and frequently skip their allotted paid vacation periods. Nearly one-quarter of self-confessed workaholics in Great Britain take not a single day's "holiday" of the 24 days they earn during the year. 10 percent of workers who work over 48 hours per week also forego vacation breaks, whereas another 22% of these "long hours workers" take ten days or less. In the United States, a Harris poll revealed that 51% of Americans did not plan to take an annual vacation even though they had earned an average of 14 days. In contrast, workers in France on average forego only 3 of the 36 days they earn each year. Human resource experts believe that vacation time is necessary for workers to be productive, and they believe that the U.S. federal government should mandate paid vacation days just as many European countries do. Believe it or not, President William Taft (1909–1913) proposed that all workers should be given two or three months off each year!

Sources: All work and no holidays. (2002). *Management Services,* 46(2), 5; Bellows, Keith. (2003). Too little play time. *National Geographic Traveler,* 20(8), 18; Allegretto, Sylvia A., and Josh L. Bivens. (2006, July–August). *Foreign Policy,* pp. 26–27.

served in a variety of military assignments. Military service forced many people who had never traveled before to do so, and they were eager to share their positive experiences with family and friends when they returned home.

Following the end of World War II, several additional factors helped encourage the growth of tourism. Cars were again being produced in large numbers; gas was no longer rationed; and prosperity began to return to industrialized countries. The introduction of jet travel in the 1950s and its growing popularity in the 1960s further accelerated growth in both domestic and international travel. To grease the gears of the tourism industry even further, in 1950, the credit card was born in the form of the Diners Club card. Credit cards provided travelers with purchasing power anywhere

in the world without the risk of carrying cash and the hassle of currency exchange. In fact, credit cards are now the preferred form of international buying power because travelers can charge their purchases in the local currency. Time, money, safety, and the desire to travel combined to usher in an unparalleled period of tourism growth that continues today.

The 20th-century phenomenon that came to be known as mass tourism now includes two different groups of travelers.[8] These groups are classified as organization mass tourists who buy packaged tours and follow an itinerary prepared and organized by tour operators. The second group is classified as individual mass tourists. These travelers visit popular attractions independently but use tourism services that are promoted through the mass media.

Well into the 21st century, the tourism industry has proven to be full of opportunities and challenges. Widespread Internet access, opening of previously closed international borders, and increased wealth and mobility of citizens in increasingly industrialized countries such as China and India are opening new venues for travelers and providing millions more potential tourists. However, the future is not completely rosy for tourism. Terrorism, rising fuel prices, and health scares have discouraged travel. Increased security efforts have also meant increased hassles and time constraints for travelers at airports, borders, and attractions. Only time will tell what the future holds for us, as tourism industry members and as consumers of tourism services.

This has been just a brief journey through some of the changes that have led to the growth of tourism. In later chapters, we will explore more of the historical details and importance of each of these changes as well as some of the more recent factors that have shaped the tourism industry.

◼ BRINGING TOURISM INTO FOCUS

The continued growth in tourism and, more specifically, international travel may well make tourism the world's peace industry. "As we travel and communicate in ever-increasing numbers, we are discovering that most people, regardless of their political or religious orientation, race, or socio-economic status, want a peaceful world in which all are fed, sheltered, productive, and fulfilled."[9]

Our methods of transportation have definitely improved, and the distances we can cover in relatively short periods have greatly expanded, but the sense of curiosity and adventure found in those early travelers is still with us today. However, travel today is more than just adventure, and it has spawned an entire group of service industries to meet the needs of tourists all over the world.

Where people travel, why they choose a particular location, and what they do once they arrive is of interest to everyone in the tourism industry. These data are now collected and recorded based on the reasons given for taking trips. The primary reasons for travel can be broken into three broad categories: vacation and **leisure travel**, visits to friends and relatives (called **VFR** in the tourism industry), and **business** or **professional travel** (see Figure 1.5). Travel in all of these categories creates demands for other tourism activities.

Travel and tourism have now become so commonplace in industrialized countries that we may fail to think about what has made these activities possible. If you think about it, tourism affects all of our lives and is intertwined throughout the entire fabric of a **host community**, region, or country. Tourism can be viewed and studied from a variety of perspectives. In addition to geography and the commonly studied business disciplines of marketing, management, and finance, other disciplines often included in the study of tourism are:

- Anthropology
- Sociology
- Economics
- Psychology

Each of these perspectives provides important insights into tourism activities and raises a variety of questions. Some of the more commonly asked questions that could help us understand travel, tourism, and tourists include:

- Who are these visitors?
- Why do they travel?
- Where do they travel?
- What are their concerns when they travel?
- What are their needs when they travel?
- What forms of transportation do they use?
- Where do they stay?
- What do they do when they travel?
- Who provides the services they need?
- What impact do they have on the locations they visit?
- What types of career opportunities are available in this industry?

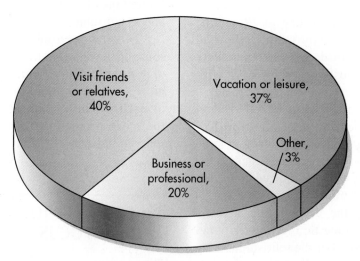

■ **Figure 1.5** Typical reasons for travel. The percentage of trips in each category may vary from year to year, but is relatively constant over time.
Source: Travel Industry of America, *Travelscope*, 2003.

These and many other questions point to the need to study tourism.

Casual or commonsense approaches to answering these questions will not prepare us to meet the needs of tomorrow's visitors. Rather than studying tourism from only one perspective, throughout this book you will have the opportunity to learn more about tourism in general, the segments of the tourism industry, and the key issues facing tourism.

Technology continues to have an unprecedented effect on the tourism industry. For example, the Internet has inexorably changed the way tourism services are sold and automation is being adapted for new uses. Throughout the chapters of this text, we will highlight how technology is affecting the service landscape. Technology plays such an important role in the tourism industry that we will take a more in-depth look at these impacts in Chapter 5.

GEOGRAPHY DESCRIBES THE TRAVELER'S WORLD

Travel is a key component in all tourism activities; therefore, a basic understanding of geography can enrich our understanding of the tourism industry. Information provided through three broad categories of geography—physical, human (cultural), and regional—will enable you to learn more about locations around the world and to provide others with that information without ever having to visit those locations. Let's look at how you might use some of these basic geographical concepts in a variety of settings. See the color insert, Figures 1.6 and 1.7, for maps highlighting these concepts. To learn more about how geography can enrich your knowledge of tourism, see Appendix A, Geography: Your Window to the World.

Physical Geography

Knowledge of **physical geography** provides the means to identify and describe natural features of the earth, including landforms, water, vegetation, and climate. When these natural features are combined, they create an environment that can either encourage or discourage tourism activities.

For example, during winter months in the Northern Hemisphere, visitors might be attracted to snow-covered mountains for skiing or to warm sun and sandy beaches for a break from the harsh realities of winter. As the seasons change, these same physical attributes could deter tourism. As the snow melts and mud appears, the mountains may lose their appeal. The same can be said for the once-sunny beaches as the rainy season arrives.

Many different types of maps have been developed to highlight significant physical geographic features. An example of one specific type of map highlighting climatic regions around the world can be seen in Figure 1.6 in the color inserts. Could a map like this help you or someone else plan travel and other tourism activities?

Locating and describing destinations requires knowledge of how to read and interpret maps. Unlocking the information contained in maps requires some basic skills. These skills include an understanding of basic **cartography** notations, that is, geographic grids (longitude and latitude), legends (symbols and colors), and indexes (locational guides). In addition to the natural features, location and accessibility are also key factors that will influence the level of tourism activity. But geography is more than just landforms, water, vegetation, and climate. It also includes people.

Human Geography

The exhilaration of experiencing other cultures is enjoyed by many through languages, foods, beverages, products, arts, and crafts that are typical to particular locations. Simply being in a different location and participating in daily activities can be an adventure in itself. An understanding of **human (cultural) geography** provides specific types of information that can enhance any tourism experience.

Human geography, which includes people and economic activities, creates the rest of the picture that can be captured and explained through maps. Culture, as expressed through language, religion, dress, foods and beverages, and other customs, plays a critical role in the popularity of many tourism destinations. Other factors such as politics and economic conditions can also play an important role in the ease of travel, especially across international boundaries. Governments can encourage or discourage tourism through passport and visa requirements as well as through policies relating to taxation or the ease of currency exchange.

For example, English is the most commonly spoken language in the industrialized world, but it may not be spoken in some locations. In other locations, Chinese, French, Spanish, Russian, Japanese, or a host of other languages may be common. Although this might create a language barrier for some, it can create opportunities for others who provide interpretation or tour services.

Human geography allows travelers to become aware of cultural norms and religious expectations so they do not commit social blunders. In some countries, it is common practice for businesses to close on certain days and times because of accepted cultural norms or for religious reasons. For example, all commercial activity ceases in many Middle Eastern countries during designated prayer times. Figure 1.7 in the color insert highlights the impact of culture by providing a map identifying the specific locations of predominant languages around the world.

Regional Geography

The level of tourism interest and activity in a specific area often depends on a combination of both physical and human geography that comes together, making certain locations more attractive than others. It may be curiosity or a combination of natural as well as developed features and attractions that meet visitor wants, needs, and expectations. **Regional geography** is a useful framework for studying the physical and human geography of a specific area or location, providing a convenient way to organize a wide variety of facts.

For example, locations near large population centers combined with access to well-developed transportation systems generally create high levels of tourism activity. Climate also influences the level and type of tourism activity. Factors such as time of year, geographic location, and proximity to major bodies of water all contribute to demand. This may explain why the most popular tourist destinations in Europe can be found along the Mediterranean Sea and in Asia around the South China Sea. We can see a similar pattern in the United States, as six of the top ten locations

■ The geography of the Rocky Mountains—sun, snow, and scenery—makes them winter's wonderland. Photo by D. A. Yale.

for domestic travelers are located near major bodies of water: Arizona, Arkansas, California, Colorado, Florida, Hawaii, Nevada, New York, Texas, and Washington, D.C.

Regions also play an important role in the development and promotion of tourism activities. The Gold Coast in Australia, the Alps, and the Rocky Mountains form natural regions of tourism activities that cross political boundaries. Smaller regions such as the wine-growing regions of California, Washington, New York, France, Germany, Italy, and Spain also attract a great deal of tourism activity and have become popular destinations. Other regions may be defined by specific boundaries such as the Valley of the Kings in Egypt, the Lake District in England, Canada's Capital Region, Chicagoland, and the French Riviera.

Geography provides a foundation to help us understand why people visit or fail to visit certain areas, but we also need to learn how to meet their needs efficiently and effectively as they travel. The three primary interrelated business functions—marketing, management, and finance—add the structure to our foundation, providing many of the tools necessary to plan and meet current and future needs of travelers. Let's look at how these business functions work together in the tourism industry.

STUDYING TOURISM FROM BUSINESS PERSPECTIVES

First, marketing concepts provide insights into why people travel as well as possible approaches to meeting their needs as they travel. Second, management concepts provide insights into the processes needed to meet societies' and visitors' current and future demands. Third, financial concepts provide the tools needed to understand, design, and supply profitable levels of visitor services. By combining knowledge from each of these perspectives, a basic understanding of tourism fundamentals can be developed.

Marketing

Studying tourism from the marketing approach provides valuable insight into the process by which tourism organizations create and individual visitors obtain desired goods and services. Everyone who has either worked in or used tourism-related services knows that customers (visitors and guests) can be very demanding. The more you know about these travelers and how to meet their needs, the more successful you will be as a tourism professional. In fact, individuals and organizations who attempt to

---

Tourism in Action

An enormous challenge to any business in the tourism industry is managing information. Who are the many different guests of the business? Where do they come from? What do they have in common and how do their needs differ? What time of year do they come and how long do they stay? What qualities and services do we have or need to develop to fit visitor lifestyles? The questions are endless and so is the amount of data generated by the answers. As introduced in this chapter, the ability to segment markets and serve them profitably are critical components to competing successfully in the global tourism industry. So how do you put all the data into clear, easy-to-use information and put it into the hands of people to use it? One answer is to use a geographic information system (GIS) for presentation and spatial

data analysis (information linked to geographic location).

A geographic information system is a set of computerized tools, including both hardware and software. GISs are used for collecting, storing, retrieving, transforming, and displaying spatial data. An easier way to think of GIS is as a marriage between computerized mapping and database management systems. In other words, anything that can appear on a map can be fed into a computer and then compared to anything on any other map, and everything on any map can have layers of data and information attached. GIS is a powerful technology and its potential uses are endless. GISs are now being used to locate park and recreational facilities as well as to generate site specific economic and environmental impact information on tourism activities.

understand and meet the needs of these visitors successfully are practicing what is called the **marketing concept,** an organizational philosophy centered around understanding and meeting the needs of customers.

Marketing theorists have coined a variety of phrases to describe the philosophy of an organization.[10] The "production orientation" organization views its mission to produce its product most efficiently and customers will simply arrive to purchase whatever is produced. In a noncompetitive, high-demand environment, this orientation works. Consider the gasoline industry. A second philosophy is the "sales orientation." Under this philosophy, an enterprise produces its product but it needs an effective (even pushy) sales force to encourage customers to buy all of the organization's production. This philosophy is frequently exhibited at large city hotels. The hotels have an inventory they need to "move," and it is the role of their sales staff to fill those beds each night and bring in those conventions and wedding receptions to fill those ballrooms!

Notice that neither of these orientations focuses on the needs or wants of the customer: The focus is on the "need" of the organization to produce and sell. A third philosophy, the heart of marketing, places the customer at the core of a firm's production or service delivery purchase. This newer philosophy is called the "consumer orientation" and requires that organizations determine what customers really want and need in a product or service so that a firm's offerings closely fit what is wanted by consumers, and therefore selling the firm's offerings becomes much easier.

Meeting visitor needs relies on a complex set of tools and techniques that is referred to as the **marketing mix.** The marketing mix consists of four variables that are often called the four Ps of marketing: product, price, place, and promotion. *Product* refers to the good or service that is being offered. *Price* is the value of the good or service. This value is the amount of money that will be paid as well as the time "given up" to obtain the good or service. *Place* includes the location and the activities that are required to make the good or service available to the visitor. Finally, *promotion* refers to all of the activities that are undertaken to communicate the availability and benefits of a particular good or service. Just think about yourself or someone else who is traveling to another city to attend a concert. How can each of the variables in the marketing mix come together to make that trip a memorable experience?

Although tourists, as a whole, are a very diverse group, they can be divided into subgroups or market segments. Market segmentation allows an organization to develop the most appropriate marketing mix to meet the needs of specifically targeted visitor segments effectively and efficiently. For example, would a young college student want the same types of experiences at Disney World as a family would want?

Each market segment contains individuals who share many of the same characteristics and common needs. For example, businesspeople may need to get to their destinations as quickly as possible, whereas the summer vacationer may want to take the most leisurely and scenic route. Young college students may need to locate inexpensive accommodations at their destinations, whereas a conventioneer may need to stay at the hotel that is hosting the convention, regardless of price. Some visitors may be seeking a variety of entertaining outdoor activities, whereas other visitors are interested in shows and shopping. This list of examples could go on, but the point should be clear: As organizations plan to meet these differing needs, they can no longer afford to try to serve the needs of all visitors. They simply do not have the resources to reach everyone and meet their diverse needs successfully.

You will learn more about the importance of marketing and its role in meeting tourists' needs in the following chapters. As we explore the many facets of the tourism industry, think about yourself as well as other specific groups of visitors who are being served and how these targeted individuals shape marketing as well as management decisions.

Management

Management furnishes additional tools and techniques to serve visitor needs successfully. Management, just like marketing, is essential to the continued success of all organizations, both public and private. The study of management provides a unified approach to planning, organizing, directing, and controlling present and future actions to accomplish organizational goals. As our model depicts, economic, political, environmental, cultural, and technological forces affect all tourism organizations and play a key role in the development of strategic plans.[11] Managers need to understand each of these forces and how they will impact decisions as they plan for the future.

Basically, management is the common thread that holds any organization or activity together and keeps everyone moving in the same direction. For example, managers working for the Forest Service must decide how many people can comfortably use a campsite and when and where new campsites should be built. Government planners and administrators must make decisions about the desirability and necessity of new or expanded highways, airports, and shopping facilities. Restaurant managers must decide how many employees are needed to provide high-quality service and, at the same time, make a fair profit. Resort managers must decide whether or not to expand and what level of service to offer. Think back to that trip you were asked to plan earlier in the chapter, and you will begin to see how all of the management functions must fit together to have a successful experience.

The process might go something like this. After you mentioned the possibility of renting a cottage at the beach to enjoy some sun, surf, and sand, several of your friends asked if they could go with you. The first management function used in putting this trip together is planning: where to go, how to get there, and how many will go. Once these decisions are made, the next function used is organizing. You are using the organizing function when you assign someone to search the Web for more information and decide who will make reservations, who will buy food and refreshments, and who will call everyone to make sure each person shows up on time on the day of departure.

The next logical step you would use in putting together your trip would be the directing function. You are directing as you answer questions and coordinate all of your planned activities. Finally, you will use the controlling function. You are controlling as you check maps, directions, itineraries, and reservations to ensure the success of your trip. Although the activities may be more complex, managers in all tourism-related activities are constantly going through the same types of processes.

Finance

Studying tourism from a financial approach provides a basic understanding of how organizations manage revenues and expenses. To continue operating and providing services, tourism organizations must strive to generate revenues in excess of expenses or effectively and efficiently use the financial resources they have been allocated. Even nonprofit and government organizations are being called on to generate more of their own funding and to gain better control of their expenses.

By definition, a business is an organization operated with the objective of making a profit from the sale of goods and services. **Profits** are revenues in excess of expenses. They are used as a common yardstick to represent financial performance and are the ultimate measure of financial success. However, some tourism organizations such as governmental agencies, museums, and visitors and convention bureaus may be classified as nonprofit. Even though they may not technically operate with a profit motive, most still strive to generate revenues in excess of expenses. For simplicity, we will use the generic term *business* in our discussion of financial concepts.

To use and communicate financial information, a common language must be spoken. That language is known as **accounting,** which is often called the "language of business." Accounting is an activity designed to accumulate, measure, and communicate financial information to various decision makers, such as investors, creditors, managers, and front-line employees. One of the purposes of accounting information is to provide data needed to make informed decisions. Examples of sources of basic financial information for specific segments of the tourism industry are shown in Table 1.2.

Table 1.2	Sources of Financial Information for Tourism Segments

The typical library has many references that can be effectively used to research financial information on the various tourism segments. Although it is not practical to list all the possible library reference works that can assist your research, the following are some of the references commonly available at public and university libraries:

The North American Industrial
  Classification System
The Department of Commerce Financial
  Report
Trade publications
Industry Norms and Key Business Ratios
RMA Annual Statement Studies
Mergent's Industry Review
Standard & Poor's Industry Surveys

Almanac of Business and Industrial
  Financial Ratios
Compact Disclosure

The Value Line Investment Survey: Ratings & Reports

Dun & Bradstreet
Mergent's Handbook of Common Stocks
Standard & Poor's Stock Reports

To measure and report financial results as accurately as possible, a standard set of procedures is followed, usually referred to as the "accounting cycle." The cycle involves several steps including analyzing, recording, classifying, summarizing, and reporting financial data. The accounting cycle reports data in the form of financial reports. There are two main categories of financial reports: internal and external. Internal financial reports are used by those who direct the day-to-day operations of a business. External financial reports are used by individuals and organizations who have an economic interest in the business but are not part of its management (see Figure 1.8).

Three basic building blocks are used to measure financial success:

1. Margin (the amount of each sales dollar remaining after operating expenses have been deducted)
2. Turnover (the number of times each dollar of operating assets has been used to produce a dollar of sales)
3. Leverage (the extent to which borrowed funds are being used)

When these three components are multiplied together, they equal **return on investment (ROI)**, which measures profit. The ability to operate profitably is critical to tourism organizations because they are typically faced with low margins, high turnover, and the need to use leverage (other people's money). As can be seen in Figure 1.9, managing these three components is a delicate balancing act, and tourism is an industry in which every nickel counts and profits depend on recognizing the importance of pennies.

Let's look at some practical examples of how these building blocks for financial success might work in specific segments of the tourism industry. In its simplest form, margin (50¢) for a food-service operator serving a hamburger and fries would be the sales price ($8.00) minus the cost of preparation, ingredients, and service ($7.50). Airlines would measure turnover by the number of times a seat was sold during a 24-hour period. Leverage is an indication of how much money has been borrowed or invested in a business. For example, a ski resort wanting to add a new gondola might go to a bank or investor to get the money needed for this expansion. We will explore the importance of finance in later chapters as we examine specific industry segments.

Remember the analogy of the elephant? Financial information is much like the elephant's nervous system. Just as the elephant's nervous system allows it to respond to its environment, an organization's financial information system allows it to read its environment and move in the direction of profitable operations.

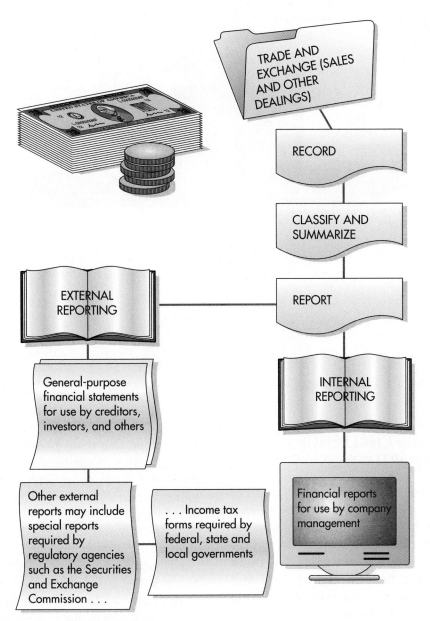

■ **Figure 1.8** The financial cycle and reporting.

Hospitality

Legend has it that New England sea captains, after returning from a voyage, speared a pineapple on the iron gates in front of their homes to let it be known that all were welcome. The pineapple has since been known as a symbol of hospitality!

Basic knowledge of geography, marketing, management, and finance concepts will provide many of the tools needed for your future success in the tourism industry. However, the importance and practice of hospitality must be added to these basic concepts. To make a profit, managers must use their marketing and management skills to extend hospitality and high-quality service that meet guests' needs. We will explore the importance of providing hospitality and delivering service quality in Chapter 3.

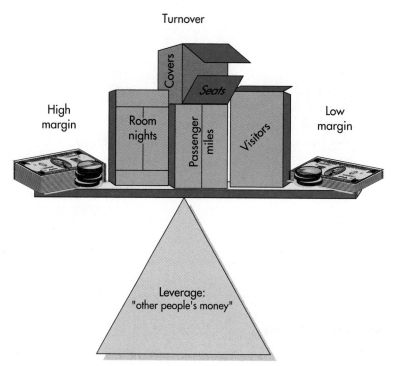

■ **Figure 1.9**   The art of finance. Finance is a matter of balancing margin, turnover, and leverage.

TOURISM'S CHALLENGES AND OPPORTUNITIES

Meeting the needs of travelers by providing tourism-related goods and services has proven to be an attractive form of economic development. Attempts to encourage the development and growth of tourism activities are often desirable because tourism creates jobs and brings money into a community or country. However, unplanned tourism growth can lead to problems.

Although tourism can create greater cultural understanding and enhance economic opportunities, it may also change social structures; may place increasing demands on transportation systems, public services, and utilities; and may lead to environmental degradation. Whether we are participants in or beneficiaries of (both positive and negative) tourism activities, we are all in one way or another affected by tourism.

Pause for a moment and consider the following examples of how tourism might affect our lives and communities. For example, tourism could create needed jobs for residents and increase business for local merchants in a small coastal town seeking economic security. However, as that town grows into a more popular destination, it can become overcrowded, and the original residents who sought increased tourism expenditures may be driven out because of increased housing costs, higher taxes, and/or changing business demands. Tourism can generate needed funds to improve the lives of an isolated native tribe in the rain forests of South America. Yet, it can also forever change the lives of these peoples as they are exposed to the cultures and habits of the tourists who come seeking what they consider to be the ultimate travel experience.

The future of tourism provides many challenges and opportunities as well as many unanswered questions:

■ Can tourism growth and development continue without creating environmental problems?

■ How will advances in technology change tourism experiences and how tourists and service providers deal with each other?

■ Will the expansion of the use of technology by tourism suppliers lead to a "low-touch" service that is less appealing to guests?

- As tourism service activities continue to grow, will an adequate workforce with the necessary skills be available?
- Will tourism change the social structure of countries and communities when they experience increased tourism activities?
- Will the threat of terrorism continue and spread around the globe, decreasing potential travelers' sense of security and thus decreasing the level of international travel?

These are only a few of the questions that may arise as plans are made to respond to the demands of tourism growth. Information presented throughout this book will provide you with the fundamental knowledge necessary to begin forming your own opinions and possible answers to many of the questions and issues that you will face as decision makers of tomorrow.

As you search for answers to the future of tourism, let your thoughts and actions be guided by ethical principles. Although most people can easily distinguish between right and wrong based on their own personal experiences, they are often faced with decisions where it is difficult to make these clear distinctions. In an effort to promote ethical behavior, organizations often publish codes of ethics to help guide individuals in their daily activities and decisions.

Even without the help of a code of ethics, there are some very simple questions you can ask yourself about any situation or problem to identify ethical and unethical behavior:

- Will someone be hurt in this situation?
- Is anyone being coerced, manipulated, or deceived?
- Is there anything illegal about the situation?
- Does the situation feel wrong to you?
- Is someone else telling you that there is an ethical problem?
- Would you be ashamed to tell your best friend, your spouse, or your parents about your contemplated actions or your involvement?
- Do the outcomes, on balance, appear to be positive or negative?
- Do you or others have the right or duty to act in this situation?
- Is there a chance that you are denying or avoiding some serious aspect of the situation?[12]

Finally and possibly the simplest, yet most thorough, ethical guideline is the Golden Rule: Do unto others as you would have them do unto you.

World Tourism Organization (WTO)

The World Tourism Organization (WTO), an agency of the United Nations, serves the world as a global source of tourism information and skill development. Headquartered in Madrid, Spain, the WTO boasts 144 member countries and over 300 affiliate members from the private sector and other tourism organizations. Begun in 1925, the WTO, through its various programs and committees, aids countries in developing tourism and its benefits. For example, the WTO was instrumental in the Silk Road Project aimed at revitalizing the ancient highway through Asia. The WTO's Business Council works hand-in-hand with private-sector members to strengthen public–private sustainable tourism efforts. The WTO also is a major publisher of important tourism resources, offering more than 250 titles in four official languages.

A critically important role of the WTO is its collection of global tourism statistics. Its international standards for tourism measurement and reporting provide a common language that allows destinations to compare tourism revenues and other data with those of competitors. The WTO is recognized as the world's most comprehensive source of tourism statistics and forecasts. In 2000, the United Nations approved the WTO's Tourism Satellite Account methodology. This method helps ensure the measurement of the tourism industry's true economic contribution in terms of gross domestic product, employment, and capital investment.

To learn more about the WTO and its structure and activities, visit its website at http://www.world-tourism.org.

◼ WHERE DO YOU FIT IN?

The prospects for the future of the tourism industry and employment in this industry are bright. Projections from the World Tourism Organization indicate that tourism will remain the world's largest "industry" through the year 2020 with travel and tourism sales growing at the rate of 4.1% a year. Employment opportunities in the United States appear to be especially positive.

Realizing the significant role tourism plays in everyone's future, we should all attempt to understand how it functions. Only through understanding the participants and forces shaping the tourism industry can we meet the expectations and desires of society. Tourism offers a world of opportunities for you to become involved as either a visitor or service supplier. Just like Bruce, whom you met in the chapter opener, you never know where a career in tourism may find you in the future.

◼ TOPICS COVERED IN EACH CHAPTER

The text, like our tourism model, is organized around meeting the needs of travelers who are discussed in detail in Chapter 2. In Chapter 3, you will learn more about travelers and how tourism suppliers identify and deliver quality services. Each of the fundamental participants and forces shaping tourism can be explored through the information presented in the remaining chapters.

Chapter 4 takes an in-depth look at the multifaceted distribution systems and sales functions that link travelers and tourism suppliers. Chapter 5 explores how technology has shaped and continues to change every aspect of the tourism industry. Chapters 6 through 10 focus on the marketing, management, and financial issues facing primary groups of tourism service suppliers—transportation, accommodations, food and beverage services, attractions and entertainment, and destinations, respectively. Throughout these chapters, we highlight the importance of maintaining a motivating environment that supports high-quality service.

Chapters 11 and 12 explore the forces that shape the current and future operating environment for every person and organization that is found in the tourism model. These forces include economic, political, environmental, and social/cultural issues. Chapter 13 is devoted to exploring how we can mantain tourism's benefits. Chapter 14 takes a glimpse into the future of tourism. Finally, selected readings have been included at the end of each major section of the book to complement and expand the information provided in the chapters. Integrative cases at the end of each major section give you an opportunity to apply your knowledge to real-world situations.

Questions and exercises at the end of each chapter will allow you to check your knowledge and apply the concepts you have learned. You will also have an opportunity to think about some of the challenges and ethical issues facing participants in the tourism industry.

Finally, you will find three appendices that support each of the chapters as well as providing guidance for your future in the tourism industry. We sincerely hope that you enjoy the journey as you study all this multifaceted industry has to offer!

◼ SUMMARY

The study of tourism will introduce you to one of the fastest-growing industries in the world. As shown in our model, tourism is a multifaceted service industry that has a rich history and exciting future marked by many challenging opportunities. The career opportunities created from serving the needs of travelers are almost limitless.

Our journey into the study of tourism began with a brief look back in history. History provides many important lessons that help explain the growth and significance of travel in world economies. In fact, the lessons to be learned from history can still be used to help serve the needs of travelers today and in the future. Travel continues to be influenced by factors such as time, money, mobility, and a relative sense of safety.

A business focus centered on marketing, management, and finance will be used as a foundation for examining the development and interdependence of the participants and forces shaping the tourism industry. Based on this foundation, and recognizing the importance of geography to travel and tourism, we will explore all of the components of the industry on an individual basis and in an economic, political, environmental, and social context.

As you learn the concepts and terminology of tourism, you will gain an appreciation for how the industry has developed and you will be equipped to gain more from your travel experiences or understand and meet the needs of others as they travel. Finally, if you decide to become a member of this industry, by practicing the art of hospitality, you can use all of your knowledge and skills to meet and exceed visitor expectations. As you explore the world of tourism throughout this book, you will be introduced to the concepts and issues facing tourism today and in the future.

■| YOU DECIDE

The idea of traveling for education and experience reached its pinnacle in the Grand Tour Era. During that time, travel to locations such as Paris, Rome, and Venice was considered to be the ultimate travel experience. Today's equivalent of the Grand Tour participant, the adventure traveler, may not have the time or money for extended trips but still seeks the same educational experiences.

Although the adventure traveler may travel to some of the same destinations that were popular on the Grand Tour, these destinations are not new or exotic. Today's adventure traveler seeking new and exotic destinations may be found trekking through Nepal, viewing wildlife on the Galápagos Islands, or braving the elements in Antarctica.

The original Grand Tour participants and today's adventure travelers may have been seeking the same benefits from travel, but their travel impacts are very different. Whereas Grand Tour participants traveled to cities to study, explore, and experience the arts, today's adventure travelers visit remote areas and cultures, seeking new experiences while generating new income sources for the native population. As they popularize these different locations, roads, utilities, buildings, and other environment-altering activities follow.

Think for a moment about the impacts Grand Tour participants had on the areas they visited while traveling throughout Europe. Are the impacts adventure travelers have on today's destinations the same? From an ethical perspective, should tourism activities be encouraged everywhere?

■| NET TOUR

To get you started exploring the world of tourism, enter the terms "tourism and travel," "history of travel and tourism," and/or "travel and tourism geography" into your favorite search engine, or use the specific links provided here to learn more.

http://www.wttc.travel

http://www.unwto.org

http://www.tia.org

http://www.mapquest.com

http://travel.state.gov

■| DISCUSSION QUESTIONS

1. Why should we study tourism?
2. History has taught us that people travel and engage in tourism activities in increasing numbers when several basic conditions can be met. Identify and describe these conditions and why they help facilitate travel and tourism activities.
3. What is geography?
4. How do physical, human (cultural), and regional geography influence tourism activities?

5. Why should we study travel and tourism from a marketing approach?
6. Why should we study travel and tourism from a management approach?
7. Why should we study travel and tourism from a financial approach?
8. What are some of the future opportunities and challenges facing the tourism industry?

■ APPLYING THE CONCEPTS

1. Ask several people of different ages, occupations, and genders to describe tourism to you. Note the differences in their descriptions. List those things that are common in their descriptions as well as some of the distinct differences.
2. Travelers are attracted to countries such as Australia, Canada, England, France, and the United States to participate in tourism activities. However, they have typically avoided countries such as Afghanistan, Cuba, and Iraq. Why are tourists attracted to some countries while they avoid others?
3. Based on your knowledge of the factors and conditions that encourage tourism, find articles that could explain the popularity of travel and tourism destinations such as Canada, Costa Rica, France, Macao, New Zealand, Spain, Thailand, and the United Kingdom. List the things that popular destinations have in common as well as the things that may be missing in less popular destinations.
4. Go to the reference section at your local library and look at the different types of maps that are available. After selecting or being assigned a nation, state, or province, make two lists of geographic features: (a) physical and (b) human (cultural). Your lists should provide an overview of significant information that would be of use to someone traveling to the destination you are describing.
5. Use your favorite search engine to find three sources of maps. Prepare a list including Web addresses showing the types of maps available and the information contained on these maps.

■ GLOSSARY

Accounting A service activity of business designed to accumulate, measure, and communicate financial information to various decision makers.

Business An organization operated with the objective of making a profit from the sale of goods and services.

Business travel Travel-related activities associated with commerce and industry.

Cartography The science or art of making maps and interpreting mapped patterns of physical and human geography.

Feudal system A system of political organization, prevailing in Europe from the 9th to about the 15th century, in which ownership of all land was vested in kings or queens.

Host communities Towns or cities that welcome visitors and provide them with desired services.

Human (cultural) geography The human activities that shape the face of a location and shared experiences, including the cultural aspects of language, religion, and political and social structures.

Leisure travel Travel for personal interest and enjoyment.

Management The distinct processes of planning, organizing, directing, and controlling people and other resources to achieve organizational objectives efficiently and effectively.

Marketing concept An overall organizational philosophy that is focused on understanding and meeting the needs of customers.

Marketing mix Those things that an organization can do to influence the demand for its goods or services. It consists of four variables, often called the four Ps of marketing: product, price, place, and promotion.

Mass tourism Twentieth-century phenomenon whereby the working and middle classes began traveling in large numbers for leisure purposes.

Model A simple representation showing how important features of a system fit together.

North American Industrial Classification System (NAICS) A classification system developed for use by North American Free Trade Agreement (NAFTA) countries, that is, Canada, Mexico, and the United States of America, to collect and report economic and financial data for similar establishments in the same industry.

Physical geography The natural features of our planet, including such things as climate, land masses, bodies of water, and resources.

Professional travel Travel by individuals to attend meetings and conventions.

Profits Revenues in excess of expenses representing the financial performance and the ultimate measure of the financial success of a business.

Regional geography The components of geography that focus on regional landscapes, cultures, economies, and political and social systems.

Return on investment (ROI) A measure of management's efficiency, showing the return on all of an organization's assets.

Services The performance of actions or efforts on behalf of another.

Tourism The temporary movement of people to destinations outside their normal places of work and residence, the activities undertaken during their stay in those destinations, and the facilities created to cater to their needs.

VFR Visits to friends and relatives.

■ REFERENCES

1. Wilkerson, Chad. (2003). Travel and tourism: An overlooked industry in the U.S. and Tenth District. *Economic Review, Third Quarter.* Federal Reserve Bank of Kansas City. Available at: http://www.kc.frb.org.

2. Hunt, J. D., and Layne, D. (1991, Spring). Evolution of travel and tourism terminology and definitions. *Journal of Travel Research,* pp. 7–11.

3. Waters, Somerset. (1990, February). The U.S. travel industry: Where we're going. *Cornell Hotel & Restaurant Administration Quarterly,* pp. 26-33.

4. U.S. Chamber of Commerce/Travel Industry of America. (2005). Definitions of the travel and tourism industry. In *Impact of travel and tourism on the U.S. and state economies.* Washington, D.C.: Author.

5. *Outbound tourism market becomes spotlight of industry.* (Retrieved 2004, July 20). Xinhua (China). Available at: http://www.xinhua.org.

6. *Tourism 2020 vision.* (2008). Available at: http://www.unwto.org/facts/eng/vision.htm.

7. *Outbound tourism market becomes spotlight of industry.*

8. Cohen, Eric. (1972). Towards a sociology of international tourism. *Social Research,* 39(1), 164–182.

9. D'Amore, Louis. (1988, Summer). Tourism - The world's peace industry. *Journal of Travel Research,* pp. 35–40.

10. Burns, Alvin, and Bush, Ronald F. (2008). *Basic marketing research* (2nd ed.). Upper Saddle River, NJ: Pearson Education, Inc.

11. Faulkner, Bill (H. W.). (2004). Developing strategic approaches to tourism destination marketing: The Australian experience. In William F. Theobald, ed., *Global tourism* (3rd ed., pp. 326–345). Burlington, MA: Elsevier Publications.

12. Code of ethics: Hospitality service and tourism industry. (1992). In Stephen S. J. Hall, ed., *Ethics in hospitality management.* East Lansing, MI: Education Institute of the American Hotel and Motel Association.

LEARNING OBJECTIVES

After you have read this chapter, you should be able to:

- Explain the importance of segmenting the tourism market.
- Identify the four major foundations for understanding tourism motivations.
- List and describe the steps involved in segmenting a market.
- Describe the major approaches that are used to segment the tourism market.
- Discuss the importance of business and professional, incentive, SMERF, mature, and special-interest travelers.
- Describe how information gained from segmenting the tourism market can be used to target and meet the wants, needs, and expectations of the traveling public.

CHAPTER OUTLINE

CHAPTER 2

Marketing to the Traveling Public

I have wandered all my life, and I also traveled; the difference between the two being this, that we wander for distraction, but we travel for fulfillment.

—Hilaire Belloc

■ The mysteries of Stonehenge attract a wide variety of tourists

A RIDE ON THE WILD SIDE!

"Let's start our own rafting business!" When Jim first mentioned the idea to Andy, they both laughed. Sure, they had been raft guides during summer breaks, but what did they really know about starting and running a business? As they stared through their dorm window at the leaves falling from the trees and thought about their summer adventures, they began to talk about the possibilities.

It had all started on a summer vacation. Like many tourists who visit the Rocky Mountains, they had taken a whitewater rafting trip. During this trip, they struck up a conversation with Casey, the owner of the company. At first, what they learned from Casey seemed almost too good to be true. Was it really possible to spend the summer months guiding people through the rapids on a beautiful mountain river and earn a living at the same time?

The lure of the outdoors, the river, and job offers to work for Casey as raft guides pulled them back to that same small mountain town the following summer. Casey, like most business owners in small tourist towns, was always looking for good potential employees. When he asked Jim and Andy to come back and work for him the next summer, they jumped at the opportunity.

Now, after two summers of experience, Jim wanted Andy to help him start their own whitewater rafting business. Once Andy said yes to the idea, things really started happening. They scanned maps of the Rocky Mountain region to locate premier rafting rivers and thumbed through every outdoor enthusiast magazine they could find. They wrote to government agencies in every location that looked interesting to find out what types of permits and licenses were needed. After months of research, they decided on the perfect location.

On spring break, they visited the town where they wanted to set up their business. It was perfect: no other rafting companies in town and a great place for rent with a barn and an old house right on the river. Everything seemed to fall into place. Jim's grandmother agreed to lend them enough money to purchase their equipment, and two of their college professors helped them to develop a business plan. Casey even offered them some words of encouragement as they prepared to launch their new business.

After graduation, Jim and Andy were ready to put their knowledge and experience to work. They moved in, hung up their sign, opened the doors, and waited for the customers to come to their new business, A Ride on the Wild Side! June was a great month, but July and August were even better! In fact, business was so good and they were so busy, they almost didn't notice a story in the local paper announcing the granting of a permit for another rafting company.

When the rafting season was over, Jim and Andy stored their equipment, counted their profits, discussed their successes and mistakes, and began to think about next year. What would the new competition mean for them? There had been plenty of customers this year, but what about next year? Would there be enough business for two companies? Who were their customers? Where did they come from? How did they find out about A Ride on the Wild Side? Would they return? Would they tell others about their experiences?

To continue their success and prosper with new competition on the horizon, they needed to know more about marketing and customer service. As they thought about the future, they realized many of the lessons they had learned about business in their college courses would be useful.

INTRODUCTION

In the first chapter, we presented a model highlighting the scope and complexity of the tourism industry. Referring back to this model, notice that the center is the focal point and primary reason for all tourism activities: travelers. In this chapter, we will learn more about these travelers (tourists) and how we can plan to meet their wants and needs successfully. Take a minute to look around and notice all the different types of people at your college or university. The diversity of this group may be similar in many ways to the diversity of guests being served in the tourism industry. Because these tourists are at the heart of the industry, we need to know more

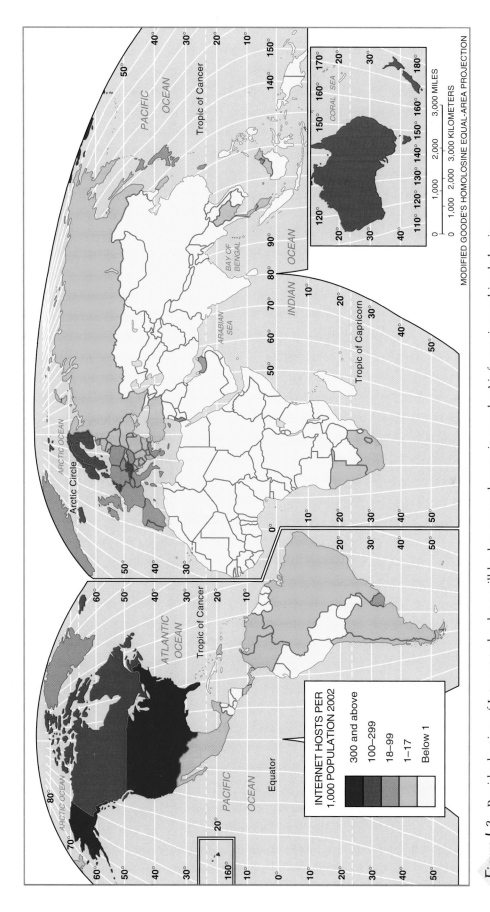

Figure 1.3 Rapid adoption of Internet technology will lead to many changes in travelers' information seeking behaviors.
Source: Rubenstein, James M., *Cultural Landscape, The*, 8th Ed., © 2005. Reprinted by permission of Pearson Education, Inc.,
Upper Saddle River, NJ.

INTERNET HOSTS PER
1,000 POPULATION 2002

300 and above
100–299
18–99
1–17
Below 1

MODIFIED GOODE'S HOMOLOSINE EQUAL-AREA PROJECTION

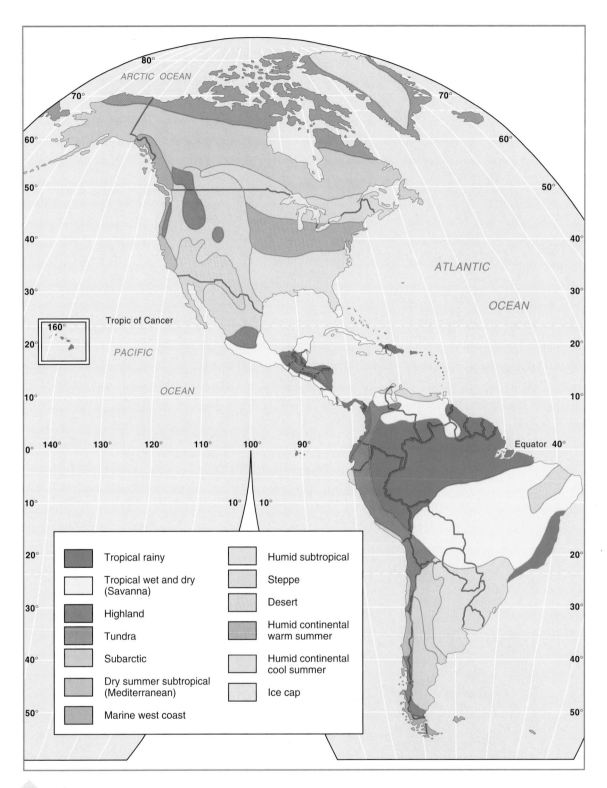

Legend:

- Tropical rainy
- Tropical wet and dry (Savanna)
- Highland
- Tundra
- Subarctic
- Dry summer subtropical (Mediterranean)
- Marine west coast
- Humid subtropical
- Steppe
- Desert
- Humid continental warm summer
- Humid continental cool summer
- Ice cap

Figure 1.6 Climatic regions of the world. Climate is the long term condition of the atmosphere. Although there are many elements of climate, most classifications use only the two most important: temperature (level and seasonality) and precipitation (amount and seasonality).

Source: Clawson, David L. and Johnson, Merrill L., editors, *World Regional Geography: A Development Approach,* 8th Ed., © 2004. Reprinted by permission of Pearson Education, Inc., Upper Saddle River, NJ.

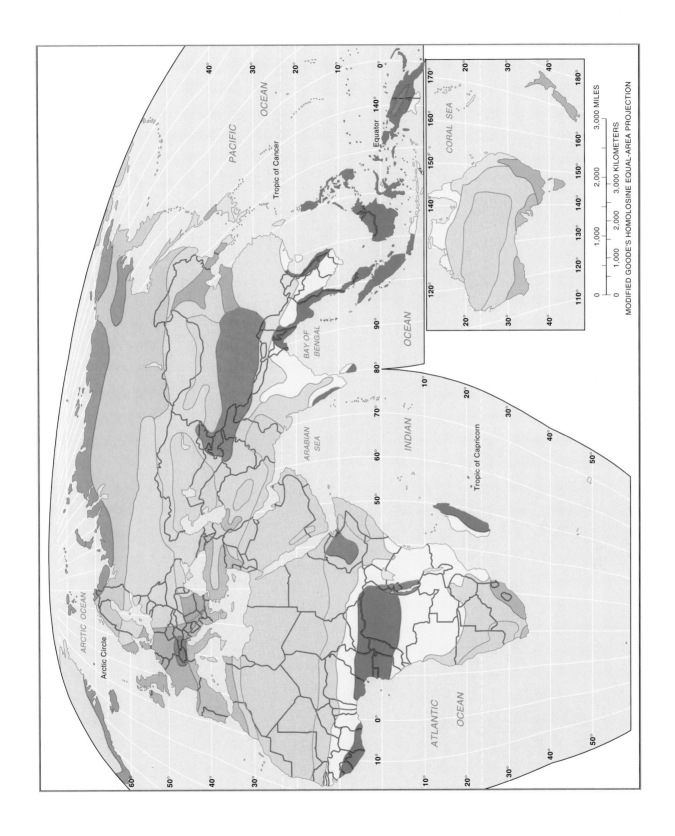

MODIFIED GOODE'S HOMOLOSINE EQUAL-AREA PROJECTION

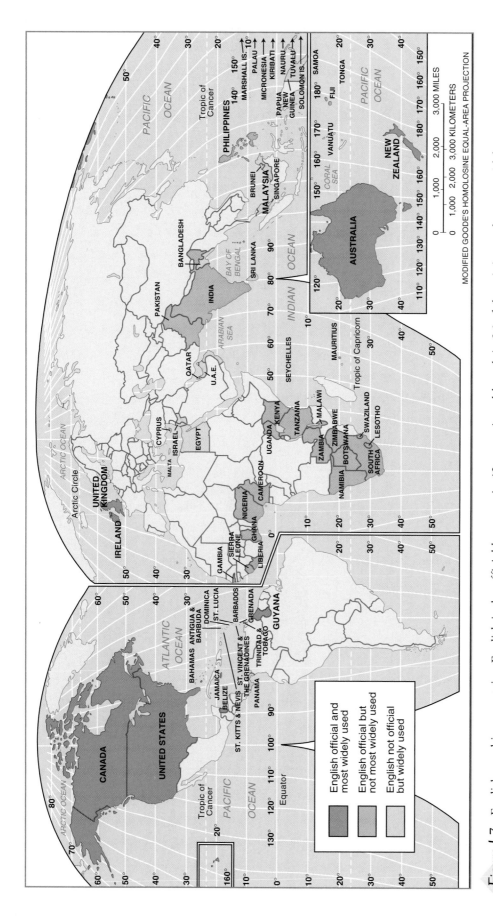

Figure 1.7 English-speaking countries. English is the official language in 42 countries, although in 26 of these it is not the most widely used language. English is also understood by a significant number of people in several other countries that were once British colonies. *Source:* Rubenstein, James M., *Cultural Landscape, The*, 8th Ed., © 2005. Reprinted by permission of Pearson Education, Inc., Upper Saddle River, NJ.

about who they are, why they travel, and what they expect during their travels.

Any number of activities, including seeking the assistance of a travel agent, flying to another city, or walking through the gates of a theme park, change a person into an active participant using tourism services. As consumers of these tourism services, we have sometimes similar, as well as different, needs. In response to the tasks of understanding consumers, their needs, and the actions they take to satisfy these needs, a whole branch of marketing, **consumer behavior**, has developed.

Consumer behavior is the study of consumer characteristics and the processes involved when individuals or groups select, purchase, and use goods and services to satisfy wants and needs. How we behave as consumers is determined by a variety of interpersonal influences (for example, we learn how to make shopping decisions from our parents) and by our individual characteristics (gender, age, personality, etc.). Consumers will continue to return and use goods and services as long as their needs are met. Consequently, we need to learn more about who these consumers are and what they need and want.

■ DECISIONS, DECISIONS, DECISIONS

Think of the number and variety of decisions that go into a vacation. First, you have to decide in a general way that you want to spend a period of time away from your home area. That time period may run the gamut from a quick overnight escape to a full year's travel to "find yourself." You then have to consider where you might want to go, your destination. Will you travel to a single destination, such as Ogunquit, Maine, and stay put for a relaxing long weekend, or will you travel continuously during your vacation using a multi-destination itinerary? Will you rely on a travel professional to help in your planning, or will you do all the "legwork" yourself? Will you make lodging reservations and buy attraction tickets in advance, or will you simply wing it? Will you stick to your original plans and choices, or will

you make modifications as your trip progresses? As you read this section, look at Figure 2.1 to aid your understanding.

The previous paragraph hints at the endless number of decisions leisure travelers need to make. How and when do travelers make decisions? How much information do they gather prior to selecting their choice? The depth of information search conducted and the timing of that information gathering are of substantial importance to tourism suppliers. They want to provide the information that tourists desire at the time they most desire it. Consumer research has proven that we will most notice and remember advertising messages and other forms of information when we are actively seeking information to make a certain decision. This information receptive mode is called selective attention.[1]

Information Seeking

When we are in the midst of making a decision regarding a trip, we have a variety of information sources available. First, we have our own memory, including our existing base of knowledge and experiences. This form of memory reliance is called internal information search. Imagine Kurt and Sharon who are thinking about going on a weeklong family vacation. They recall the terrific time their kids had at that great RV resort at Lake George in upstate New York and simply decide to make that trip again.

Frequently, we feel the need to gather additional information; this is termed external information search. These external sources are grouped into two types, personal sources and nonpersonal sources. Personal sources are individuals who provide us with information. A friend who recommends a rafting company that offers Colorado River trips through the Grand Canyon would be an example of a noncommercial personal source. Your trusted travel agent who helps you decide which cruise best fits the true you is an example of a commercial personal source. And, finally, the front desk clerk who suggests a fun nightspot where locals party is also a personal source of information.

Nonpersonal sources of information are all other forms of information available to you,

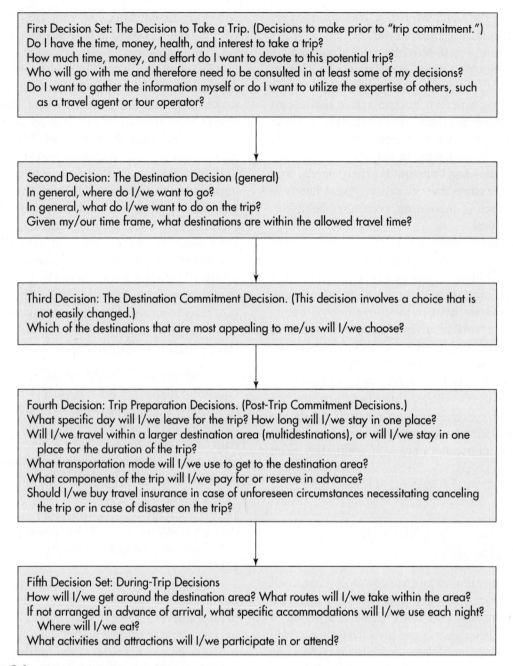

First Decision Set: The Decision to Take a Trip. (Decisions to make prior to "trip commitment.")
Do I have the time, money, health, and interest to take a trip?
How much time, money, and effort do I want to devote to this potential trip?
Who will go with me and therefore need to be consulted in at least some of my decisions?
Do I want to gather the information myself or do I want to utilize the expertise of others, such
     as a travel agent or tour operator?

Second Decision: The Destination Decision (general)
In general, where do I/we want to go?
In general, what do I/we want to do on the trip?
Given my/our time frame, what destinations are within the allowed travel time?

Third Decision: The Destination Commitment Decision. (This decision involves a choice that is
     not easily changed.)
Which of the destinations that are most appealing to me/us will I/we choose?

Fourth Decision: Trip Preparation Decisions. (Post-Trip Commitment Decisions.)
What specific day will I/we leave for the trip? How long will I/we stay in one place?
Will I/we travel within a larger destination area (multidestinations), or will I/we stay in one
     place for the duration of the trip?
What transportation mode will I/we use to get to the destination area?
What components of the trip will I/we pay for or reserve in advance?
Should I/we buy travel insurance in case of unforeseen circumstances necessitating canceling
     the trip or in case of disaster on the trip?

Fifth Decision Set: During-Trip Decisions
How will I/we get around the destination area? What routes will I/we take within the area?
If not arranged in advance of arrival, what specific accommodations will I/we use each night?
     Where will I/we eat?
What activities and attractions will I/we participate in or attend?

■ Figure 2.1   The travel decision-making process.

from travel magazine ads to resort brochures to billboards along your trip route. Tourism suppliers can control to a large extent the information in nonpersonal sources, such as websites and pop-up ads. However, one form of tourism information often consulted by long-trip-duration travelers are published travel guidebooks, which frequently include opinions and impressions from the authors/editors. Travel guides such as Frommer's and Lonely Planet are viewed as neutral sources of information because the author is usually not being compensated to make the recommendations included in the guide. Many travelers are also turning to blogs, which may or may not contain reliable and unbiased information. We will explore the impact of blogs on the tourism industry when we turn our attention to technology issues in Chapter 5.

Although business and professional travelers will have a set plan and reservations for almost all components of their trips, leisure travelers have a full range of planning options. As suggested earlier, after deciding to travel, the next decision a traveler faces is where to go. And with the endless possibilities out there, that is often not a simple choice. Leisure travelers often spend hour upon hour gathering information about various destinations to find the one that most tickles their fancy. The conclusion to the destination decision may be very specific—"I'm going to Disney World!"–or it may be very general, such as Southeast Asia.

After the decision of "where" is made, travelers will differ on how much information they collect before making other decisions. A portion of vacationers will turn most of the information gathering and decision making over to others, by using a travel agent and purchasing a tour package. Package tours allow the traveler to trust the judgment of a tour wholesaler to piece together the necessary services so that decision making by the traveler is minimal.[2]

However, most travelers are independent travelers, those who do not leave the planning to someone else. Specifically, independent travelers do not book a transportation and accommodations package. These travelers have many decisions to make, both before (pretrip planning) and during their trip. Independent travelers tend to have more flexibility in their itineraries, in terms of where they go, how long they spend at any one place, where they stay, and what they do at each locale. Travel planning by independent travelers can be thought of as a continuum. Travelers may make virtually all decisions prior to departure regarding route, duration of stays, where to stay, and what they will do each day. On the other extreme of the continuum is the traveler who does virtually no pretrip planning and allows his or her trip to evolve spontaneously.[3] For example, in studies of visitors to New Zealand (NZ), Tourism New Zealand researchers have found that more than 40% do absolutely no preplanning before their arrival on NZ shores.

By now, you realize that travel decision making involves a series of choices concerning many facets of a trip. "Compared to most other examples of consumer decision making, vacation decision making is a particularly complex and multi-facetted matter, involving a series of decisions on multiple elements of the vacation itinerary" (p. 20).[4] What factors make pretrip planning more likely or less likely? Research conducted in a variety of countries indicates that certain characteristics of a trip lead to greater information search by leisure travel consumers. These characteristics are lack of experience with the destination, longer duration of trip, farther away from home (especially international), commercial accommodations (rather than staying with friends or relatives), larger group size, and multiple destinations.

It's All in the Details

Logically, the length of a trip will play a role in determining how much pretrip planning occurs. For short-term domestic trips, most tourists will plan many elements of the trip ahead of time, such as dates of the trip, destination, accommodations, and travel route. For such a trip, even the attractions to attend and other activities are likely to be planned ahead, although travelers will allow some flexibility in these areas.[4]

Trips of longer duration allow travelers the opportunity to have multiple destinations. Multi-destination trips tend to be less rigidly planned and allow for more spontaneity. Travelers who take long multidestination trips tend to utilize guidebooks and on-site information sources for help in making decisions as they travel. Locals and other travelers met along the way are important personal sources of information regarding what to do, where to stay, and where to dine. Typically, the sequence of decision making for multidestination, long-duration trips tends to be subdestination decisions, followed by travel route (how to get from A to B), concluding with decisions concerning attractions and activities to attend/participate in.

Personality type and demographics also impact how much information search and trip planning a traveler will perform. Think of two very different friends of yours. One is a planner, a clock-watcher, and a deliberate thinker. The other is spontaneous, ready to drop everything and go where the wind blows him. Your first friend likely would enjoy pretrip planning and view this information-gathering step as part of the challenge and fun of travel. Your other friend would view such planning as confining and ruining the surprise of a vacation. Generally speaking, older travelers tend to plan more, along with those who perceive substantial risk, such as those traveling in a country whose people do not speak the traveler's language.

Finally, think of the type of information travelers may want. In choosing a destination, travelers may seek general information to get a "feel" for the look, culture, and possible activities of the location. They may also seek more specific information once they have narrowed their focus to a few destinations, their choice set, so they can compare the possibilities in more detail. For example, Jo may want to take a fun-in-the-sun break from winter and decides from all the possibilities that she will go to one of the islands of the Caribbean. She needs detailed information about the islands she finds most intriguing. Once she chooses an island destination, St. Lucia, she will need information about resorts on the island to make an advance reservation. Finally, while at the destination, she will need to collect information to make individual decisions to satisfy her day-to-day needs for food, entertainment, local transportation, and the like.

Tourism suppliers therefore vary in the type of information they need to provide prospective customers. At the macro level, destination marketing organizations, such as British Columbia SuperNatural, need to entice visitors to their region by providing general information in an appealing format. At the micro level, individual hotels need to have websites that can be accessed directly or that are linked to the destination marketing site or will be listed when a traveler conducts a Web search. Small-scale area attractions, such as that of Jim and Andy from the chapter opener, need to have attractive brochures available in local area shops, restaurants, and the local visitors center. From this discussion of decision making and information gathering, we hope you now have a better understanding of the challenges facing tourism suppliers in getting the right information to the right people at the right moment in time.

FOUNDATIONS FOR UNDERSTANDING TOURIST MOTIVATIONS

In Chapter 1, you learned that humans have traveled away from their homes throughout history. What has motivated people to leave familiar surroundings and travel to distant places? In this section, we will consider what psychological reasons compel individuals to travel. Psychologists have long studied motivations for a variety of human behaviors including the drive to travel. We will discuss four of the most well-accepted theories for tourist motivations: push and pull motivations, Maslow's hierarchy of needs, Pearce's leisure ladder, and Plog's psychocentric–allocentric continuum.

Push and Pull Motivations

For decades, tourism researchers have grouped tourist motivations as push or pull factors. The notion is that travelers are both "pushed" to travel by personality traits or individual needs and wants, and "pulled" to travel by appealing attributes of travel destinations. "Traditionally, the push motivations have been thought useful for explaining the desire for travel while the pull motivations have been thought useful for explaining the actual destination choice" (p. 32).[5] Table 2.1 lists many of the push and pull factors proposed and examined by tourism motivation researchers.

This "theory" of travel motivation highlights the fact that tourists are pushed (motivated) to travel by many factors simultaneously, and destinations pull (attract) visitors with a combination of resources. For instance, a tourist generates the desire to escape from his mundane day-to-day routine and seeks a destination that seems to offer the "ticket" to that escape. Research has shown that push and pull factors are matched by travelers. For example, studies have found a large percentage of travelers are motivated to travel by a desire to be pampered, comfortable, and entertained. Destinations that generate the most "pull" for this group of travelers are cities and beach resorts.

Table 2.1	Push and Pull Travel Motivations
Push	*Pull*
Desire for escape	Beaches
Rest and relaxation	Recreation facilities
Health and fitness	Historic sites
Adventure	Budget
Prestige	Cultural resources
Social interaction	Undisturbed nature
Novelty seeking	Ease of access
Exploration	Cosmopolitan environment
Enhancement of relationships	Opportunities to increase knowledge
Evaluation of self	Opportunities to experience a different culture
Regression	
Learning new things	
Desire for pampering/comfort	
Being entertained	
Hobbies	

Several of the "push" factors listed in Table 2.1 are identified and researched personality traits (e.g., novelty seeking). An additional and particularly appropriate personality trait theory that relates to tourism is optimal arousal theory. Briefly, the core of this theory is that each of us has some optimal level of arousal at which we feel most comfortable. For some, that level is quite low, leading to a relaxed, slower-paced lifestyle, whereas for many, the optimal arousal level is very high, driving individuals constantly to seek new and challenging activities. A person who is stressed out by work may desire to reduce arousal by seeking a quiet seaside resort to spend some quiet time with a loved one. Another who is bored by the routine of his job and life may instead decide to travel to Europe and test his mettle on the ski slopes of the Alps.

As mentioned in Chapter 1, other factors also play a role in the desire to travel. In addition to the push and pull factors, there are inhibitors to travel. Travel requires time, money, energy, and security. Work and school demands on time may keep a person from traveling. Lack of funds may restrict travel opportunities, and failing health prevents travel altogether for some. Family situations, for example, a new baby or caring for an elderly parent, may limit opportunities to travel. Finally, due to worldwide political unrest, uncertainty about personal safety while traveling has made many hesitant to travel. The extra security now mandated at many borders, attractions, and events has dampened the carefree attitude some may have had prior to the increase in terrorist attacks on civilians, especially travelers, around the globe.

Maslow's Hierarchy of Needs

Abraham Maslow provided a good general framework for describing human needs in his classic model depicting the hierarchy of needs.[6] This hierarchy, as can be seen in Figure 2.2, begins at the bottom with basic physiological needs and progresses upward through safety, belongingness, esteem, and self-actualization needs. Maslow further grouped these needs into two broader categories: lower-order and higher-order needs. He believed that this hierarchy of needs was shared by everyone. Although the hierarchy of needs model was developed to explain human behavior and motivation in general, we will see later in the chapter how these same concepts can be applied specifically to tourists.

To understand an individual's behavior, we begin at the bottom of the hierarchy and move upward. As each level of needs is satisfied, individuals move up to the next level of needs. At

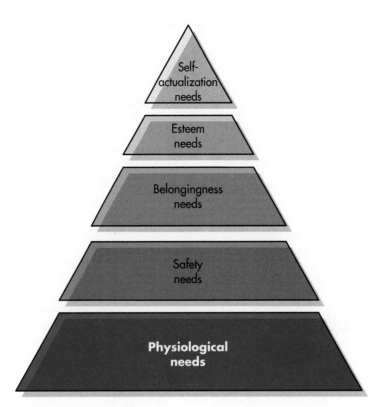

■ **Figure 2.2**   Maslow's hierarchy of needs.

the lowest levels are basic physiological and safety needs. Basic physiological needs consist of food, water, clothing, shelter, and sleep. Next are safety needs, which consist of protection, security, and the comfort we seek from familiar surroundings. In the advanced economies of developed countries such as Australia, Canada, Great Britain, Japan, and the United States, most consumers' lower-order physiological and safety needs have been met. Because these needs have been satisfied, they are no longer motivators. Individuals often strive to fulfill their higher-order needs through travel.

These higher-order needs include belongingness, esteem, and self-actualization. Belongingness needs include love, friendship, affiliation, and group acceptance. Esteem needs include the desire for status, self-respect, and success. The highest level in Maslow's hierarchy of needs is self-actualization or the desire for self-fulfillment.

Travelers may be seeking to fulfill more than one need when they participate in a tourism activity. Let's put the ideas in Maslow's hierarchy of needs into practice by looking at specific examples in the tourism industry.

Physiological
■ Tour packages that offer frequent rest stops
■ Easily accessible food outlets in theme parks
■ Sleeping shelters strategically located along the Appalachian Trail for overnight visitors

Safety
■ Reservation service provided at government-approved agencies or locations
■ Cruise ship lines providing medical facilities and doctors as part of their standard services
■ Tour guide services provided in exotic or unfamiliar locations

Belongingness
■ Group tours with people having similar interests and/or backgrounds
■ Group recognition gained by belonging to frequent-user programs provided by airlines, hotels, restaurants, and car rental companies
■ Trips made to explore one's ancestral roots

Esteem

- Elite status in frequent-user programs such as gold, silver, or bronze "memberships"
- Incentive travel awards for superior company performance
- Flowers, champagne, and other tokens provided to guests in recognition of special occasions

Self-Actualization

- Educational tours and cruises
- Trekking through Nepal, a personal challenge to one's physical limits
- Learning the language and culture before traveling to another country

The hierarchy of needs model provides a good foundation as well as a brief glimpse into the fundamentals of motivation. Can you think of other examples?

The Leisure Ladder Model

The leisure ladder model developed by Pearce[7] is similar to Maslow's hierarchy of needs, but it goes further by providing more detailed insights into specific tourist behaviors. The leisure ladder model attempts to explain individual behaviors on the basis of stages in a tourist's life cycle. When you think about tourist life cycle stages, it may be helpful to remember that they are very similar to the stages individuals experience in their working careers. Just as a person tentatively enters a career and eventually becomes more proficient and effective based on experience, so do tourists as they venture into leisure activities.

According to Pearce, tourists move through a hierarchy (or series of steps) similar to the one depicted by Maslow. They must first take care of relaxation and bodily needs before they can move up to the successively higher rungs of stimulation, relationship, self-esteem and development, and fulfillment on the leisure ladder. Figure 2.3 shows an example of the various levels on this leisure ladder as applied in a theme park setting. Further attempts to understand and broadly describe the differing wants and needs of tourists have resulted in a widely used model developed by Stanley Plog.[8,9]

The Psychocentric–Allocentric Model

Based on observable and consistent patterns of behavior, it is possible to use personality characteristics to understand tourists' behavior patterns further (see Table 2.2). Plog accomplished this task by originally classifying tourists along a continuum with **allocentrics** anchoring one end and **psychocentrics** anchoring the other.[10] In an update, Plog suggested the terms **venturers** and **dependables** were better descriptors for the end points. In general, venturers are seeking adventure through travel, whereas dependables are seeking the comforts of familiar surroundings in their tourism experiences. However, as the model shows, most travelers fall between these two extremes and would be classified as near-venturers, midcentrics, and near-dependables.

The venturer found at one extreme of Plog's continuum (see Figure 2.4) would be referred to by marketers as an "innovator." These innovators seek out new locations and activities before they are discovered by others. As more people become aware of these locations and activities, information about them is communicated or diffused to more and more people. Interest in traveling to these new locations or experiencing new activities passes from the venturer to the midcentric and eventually to the dependable as these locations or activities become commonplace.

The dependable found at the opposite extreme of Plog's continuum would most likely be tradition bound and tend to be uncomfortable with new and different activities and/or locations. These individuals would be interested only in visiting popular locations and participating in customary activities. They desire predictability and the comforting reassurance that other visitors have enjoyed the same experiences.

Dependables can enter a McDonald's restaurant throughout the world and find a familiar atmosphere and menu. On the other extreme, venturers may be drawn by the allure of seeking out unique travel and tourism experiences that have previously gone unnoticed. Taking a rubber raft down the headwaters of the Amazon River or trekking among the highland villages of Nepal might appeal to the venturesome travelers today,

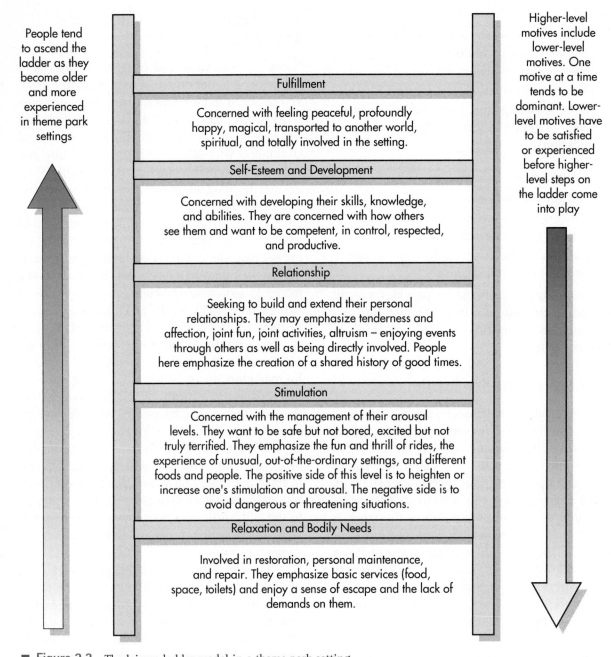

People tend to ascend the ladder as they become older and more experienced in theme park settings

Higher-level motives include lower-level motives. One motive at a time tends to be dominant. Lower-level motives have to be satisfied or experienced before higher-level steps on the ladder come into play

Fulfillment

Concerned with feeling peaceful, profoundly happy, magical, transported to another world, spiritual, and totally involved in the setting.

Self-Esteem and Development

Concerned with developing their skills, knowledge, and abilities. They are concerned with how others see them and want to be competent, in control, respected, and productive.

Relationship

Seeking to build and extend their personal relationships. They may emphasize tenderness and affection, joint fun, joint activities, altruism – enjoying events through others as well as being directly involved. People here emphasize the creation of a shared history of good times.

Stimulation

Concerned with the management of their arousal levels. They want to be safe but not bored, excited but not truly terrified. They emphasize the fun and thrill of rides, the experience of unusual, out-of-the-ordinary settings, and different foods and people. The positive side of this level is to heighten or increase one's stimulation and arousal. The negative side is to avoid dangerous or threatening situations.

Relaxation and Bodily Needs

Involved in restoration, personal maintenance, and repair. They emphasize basic services (food, space, toilets) and enjoy a sense of escape and the lack of demands on them.

■ **Figure 2.3** The leisure ladder model in a theme park setting.
Source: Pearce, Douglas G., and Butler, Richard W., eds. (1993). *Tourism research critiques and challenges.* London: Routledge.

but they will be looking for something new and different tomorrow.

The creators of the Disney mystique may be catering to a broad cross section of visitors. For dependables, a Disney theme park assures them of similarity and consistency in operations. However, Disney is continually adding new attractions and entertainment to appeal to a broader market group of visitors. How would you classify yourself along this continuum? To

find the answer, log on to BestTripChoices.com and take a short quiz.

■ SEGMENTING THE TOURISM MARKET

The old saying "You can't please all the people all the time" certainly holds true for tourism service suppliers. Because you can't please

Table 2.2	Psychocentric–Allocentric Personality Characteristics
Psychocentrics/Dependables	*Allocentric/Venturers*
Prefer familiar travel destinations	Prefer non-"touristy" destinations
Like commonplace activities at destinations	Enjoy discovering new destinations before others have visited them
Prefer relaxing sun-and-fun spots	Prefer unusual destinations
Prefer low activity levels	Prefer high activity levels
Prefer driving to destinations	Prefer flying to destinations
Prefer heavy tourist accommodations, such as hotel development, family-style restaurants, and souvenir shops	Prefer services such as adequate to good accommodations and food, and few developed tourist attractions
Prefer familiar rather than foreign featuring a full schedule of activities atmospheres	Enjoy interacting with people from different cultures
Prefer purchasing complete tour packages	Prefer tour arrangements that include basics (transportation and accommodations) and allow for considerable flexibility

Source: Plog, Stanley C. (1974, February). Why destinations areas rise and fall in popularity. *Cornell Hotel & Restaurant Administration Quarterly,* pp. 55–58; Plog, Stanley C. (2002). The power of psychographics and the concept of venturesomeness. *Journal of Travel Research,* 40, 244–251.

everyone, whom should you please? One common approach to answering this question is to focus marketing efforts by segmenting potential customers into groups with fairly similar wants and needs.

Identifying tourism customers and deciding how to meet their wants and needs is a basic task facing everyone in the tourism industry. In large organizations, this task is often given to marketing professionals. In smaller organizations, such as Jim and Andy's A Ride on the Wild Side!, this responsibility might remain with the owner or manager.

As we discussed in Chapter 1, the marketing concept creates a customer-oriented philosophy that is essential to meeting visitors' wants and needs. Let's think about the questions raised by Jim and Andy as they considered the future of

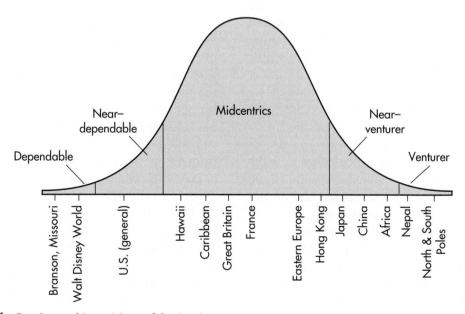

■ **Figure 2.4**   Psychographic positions of destinations.

■ An African photo safari fulfills the venturer traveler's needs. Photo by Cheryl D. Clay.

their rafting business. They both agreed on the importance of knowing more about marketing, sales, and customer service, but they weren't sure where to start.

The starting point for any organization planning to implement the marketing concept is to learn more about its customers. But, who are these customers? Although it may sound appealing to think of everyone as a potential customer, marketers have learned that this usually does not lead to a high level of customer satisfaction. A common example with which we can all identify will help explain this statement.

Imagine for a moment you are the president of a major lodging company. You decide that it would be profitable to come up with the perfect hotel—a hotel at which everyone would want to stay. Is such a dream possible? If you designed the "average" hotel—rooms, a restaurant, and a swimming pool—do you think every potential guest would be equally satisfied with this hotel? Of course not. Some guests want inexpensive accommodations and have no need for any amenities other than a clean, comfortable room for the night, whereas others want to

be pampered and select from a large variety of services, room types, and amenities. With this in mind, could you design an "average" hotel that would satisfy everyone? Probably not, because trying to meet everyone's needs and wants with the same services would prove to be an impossible task.

The task of meeting diverse needs and wants led to the idea of **market segmentation**. Instead of trying to meet everyone's needs and wants with a single product or service, marketers divide the large, **heterogeneous** market for a good or service into smaller but more **homogeneous** market segments. A heterogeneous market is one composed of people having differing characteristics and needs, whereas a homogeneous market is one with people of similar characteristics and needs.

The task of grouping millions of travelers into groups with similar needs and wants may appear to be a bit complex at first. However, this process can be simplified if we begin to think of the tourism market as a large jigsaw puzzle. Each piece of this puzzle (i.e., each consumer) is unique. Once several pieces are put together, they begin to form similar-looking sections (market segments). Finally, when all of these sections of the puzzle are put together, they form the whole picture (the market).

As you saw in Chapter 1, it is possible to begin segmenting the tourism market by using the broad reasons people give for traveling: vacation and leisure, visiting friends and relatives, and business and professional. Although these broad reasons for travel may provide some initial insight into potential tourism market segments, they do not provide the level of detail needed to understand specific consumer needs. What are needed are segmentation approaches that clearly describe travelers and that can be used as a basis for planning to meet their needs and wants.

Common approaches (called "bases") to segmenting markets can be achieved by grouping customers according to the following variables:

1. Geographic characteristics
2. Demographic characteristics
3. Psychographic characteristics
4. Product-related characteristics

These segmentation variables provide a good starting point as we begin to fit the pieces of the tourist jigsaw puzzle into a meaningful picture. Each of these segmentation approaches also serves to highlight the breadth, depth, and differences to be found among individuals and groups of tourists. However, as we begin to study groups of travelers, do not lose sight of the importance of meeting individual needs. Remember, Maslow, Pearce, and Plog showed that although we may behave in similar ways, we are all still individuals! The brand boom taking place in the hotel industry demonstrates the importance of serving the needs of varying segments of travelers. With over 350 brands, and many of them part of the same parent company, there is a hotel to cater to everyone's needs.[11] We will explore hotel brands in more detail later in this chapter and also in Chapter 7.

Geographic Segmentation

Geographic segmentation, grouping potential tourism customers based on their location, is the oldest and simplest basis for market segmentation. Even though people in the same geographic location do not usually have similar wants and needs, their location often has an important impact on their selection of tourism goods and services. Commonly used geographic segmentation variables include nations, regions, states/provinces, counties/parishes, cities, and even neighborhoods.

Geographic segmentation has proven especially useful in segmenting the traveling public. Many tourism facilities and attractions market their services regionally, recognizing that the time and money involved in traveling makes them more attractive to consumers within a certain defined geographic area. For example, the Walt Disney Company advertises Disneyland, located in California, heavily in the Western United States and the Pacific Rim countries (such as Japan), whereas it markets Walt Disney World, located in Florida, more heavily in the Eastern United States and Europe. On a smaller scale, Killington Ski Resort in Vermont is promoted to skiers in northeastern North America, whereas Durango Mountain Resort outside Durango, Colorado, tries to attract skiers primarily from the southern and western United States. Would geographic segmentation provide useful information to Jim and Andy about their potential customers?

Demographic Segmentation

Although geographic segmentation is the simplest and oldest approach to grouping tourists, **demographic segmentation** is the basis most commonly used for market segmentation. Using this approach, consumers are grouped according to variables that define them in an objective, easily measurable way. These variables include classifications such as gender, age, ethnicity, occupation, education level, income, household size, and family situation. **Demographics** are frequently used by marketers because information about people's objective characteristics is routinely collected and widely available. A gold mine of segmentation information for marketers who know how to use it can be found in data gathered and reported by Statistics Canada and the U.S. Census Bureau.

Examples of tourism organizations using demographic segmentation abound. Club Med is using demographic segmentation when it attempts to serve the needs of two distinct upscale market segments. One segment is composed of young singles and the other of high-income married couples with children. Tour operators and cruise lines are using demographic segmentation when they develop special tours or cruises featuring nostalgic, educational, religious, or ethnic experiences. Can you think of other examples?

Psychographic Segmentation

Geographic and demographic variables provide easy approaches to segmenting travelers, but we all know that people are much more different than these simple pieces of information might suggest. For example, most of us listen to music. And, even though age is an important factor in determining the type of music different people enjoy, you probably know people of similar ages who have different tastes. Some twentysomethings enjoy rap music while some enjoy old-fashioned rock and roll and still others prefer the sounds of the forties-era swing bands. These differences come from what marketers call "**psychographic** variables."

Psychographics were developed by marketing researchers to try to link personality to product or brand usage. Originally these researchers relied on standard psychological personality measurement.[12] Personality refers to a person's unique psychological composite that compels a person to react in consistent ways to his or her environment. Examples of personality traits that

are commonly measured by psychologists are introversion/extroversion (outgoingness), need for cognition (think and puzzle things out), and innovativeness (degree to which a person likes to try new things). To better capture a person's "consuming" self, researchers added to personality concepts the measurement of activities, interests, and opinions, called AIOs.

Psychographic segmentation involves grouping people on how they live, their priorities, and their interests. Put all this together and you have a description of a person's lifestyle and personality. Psychographic segmentation has been used by cruise lines and resorts to target individuals with similar hobbies, sports preferences, and musical interests.

Sometimes, psychographic segmentation is called lifestyle segmentation. A **lifestyle** is broadly defined as a way of living identified by how people spend their time (activities), what they consider important (interests), and what they think of themselves and the world around them (opinions). Some examples of activities, interests, and opinions that might be important to those working in the tourism industry are included in Table 2.3.

The idea of segmenting travelers based on activities, interests, and opinions might seem familiar, because this approach was popularized by Stanley Plog in his psychocentric–allocentric continuum. More recently, three large psychographic segments have been identified in the American travel market. In a proprietary (privately funded) study based on survey information collected from thousands of travelers, a

Table 2.3	Psychographic Lifestyle Dimensions	
Activities	*Interests*	*Opinions*
Work	Family	Themselves
Hobbies	Home	Social issues
Social events	Job	Politics
Vacation	Community	Business
Entertainment	Recreation	Economics
Club membership	Fashion	Education
Community	Food	Products
Shopping	Media	Future
Sports	Achievements	Culture

Source: Wells, William D., and Tigert, Douglas J. (1971). Activities, interests, and opinions. *Journal of Advertising Research,* 11, 27–35.

research firm developed segments by associating values expressed by the survey respondents and the type of vacations they preferred.

The largest segment the study identified is termed the "family getaway traveler" (38% of American travelers). This segment values family time above all else and seeks activities that all members of the family can enjoy together. The second segment is called the "adventurous/ education traveler" (31%). This type of traveler values physical activity and challenge, and enjoys interacting with nature. Segment three is composed of "romantics" (28%). As the name suggests, these travelers value intimate companionship and have a primary desire for comfort and relaxation. Do you see yourself fitting into any of these categories?

The United States Tour Operators Association (USTOA) now includes psychographic segmentation on its website. Website viewers are encouraged to take a "vacation personality quiz" online. The test includes 15 sets of statements that link to personality type and activities, interests, and opinions. For example, when taking the test you will be asked to check which of the following three statements best fits you:

> Bungee jumping would be exciting.
> I would never fall for bungee jumping.
> I might enjoy watching friends go bungee
> jumping.

After you complete the test, the computer "analyzes" your results and then tells you which of the three types of tour packages offered by member companies will be best for you. By using psychographics, the USTOA better targets its members' products to potential clients. To learn more about psychographic or lifestyle segmentation, consult any consumer behavior textbook.

Product-Related Segmentation

The previously mentioned bases for segmentation—geographic, demographic, and psychographic—are all used to help marketers move closer to the goal of developing product offerings that better satisfy potential tourism consumers. However, in all these cases, we are indirectly grouping people based on characteristics we assume are related to

their needs and wants. Because assumptions can sometimes get us into trouble, marketers often try to segment less indirectly and more directly: They attempt to group potential buyers directly from what people indicate they need or want in a particular good or service. These product-related variables include:

1. The benefits people seek in the good or service (for example, the ability to guarantee the availability of a room at a hotel)

VALS (Values and Lifestyles)

The most widely used psychographic segmentation system, VALS, was developed by a California firm, SRI International, in 1978. Using a survey of about 1,600 households, researchers grouped consumers into nine values and lifestyles segments. Since its development, the system has been updated (VALS 2, which uses eight groupings) and modified for use in countries the world over. If you would like to determine which VALS 2 segment fits you, visit SRI's website at http://www.sric-bi.com and take the test!

Lifestyle measurement has gone global. In addition to the "internationalization" of VALS 2 by SRI, Backer Spielvogel Bates Worldwide is one company that annually surveys thousands of consumers around the globe to monitor changes in the world's psychographic segments. The company's effort, called Global Scan, groups respondents into the following five major segments.

Strivers—young people on the run
Achievers—slightly older, affluent opinion-
    leaders
Pressureds—largely women, facing economic
    and family concerns that drain them
Adapters—contented older people that still
    find newness fun and challenging
Traditionals—conservative older people who
    prefer the good old days and ways

Source: Boone, Louis E., and Kurtz, David L. (2009). *Contemporary marketing* (13th ed.). Mason, OH: South-Western Cengage Learning.

2. The amount of good or service used (light users such as occasional leisure travelers versus heavy users such as business travelers)

3. The degree of company loyalty shown by the consumer in relation to the specific good or service (participation in frequent-user programs)

In Chapter 1, we mentioned that travelers are frequently grouped into leisure versus business categories. These groupings serve as good examples of **product-related segmentation.** Tourism suppliers know that travelers seek different benefits based on the purposes of their trips. Think about the benefits a businessperson seeks in accommodations compared to the benefits desired by a person traveling on a holiday or vacation. How would these benefits differ?

Business travelers tend to be the "heavy users" of many tourism services, especially air transportation, hotels, and rental cars. Airlines, hotels, and rental car companies have responded to these needs by developing services and forms of promotion that appeal especially to these busy frequent travelers. Services such as ticketless travel, hotel rooms wired for all types of technology, and the computerized check-in kiosks at many airport rental car locations were all developed to appeal to this special group of travelers. Finally, in a special appeal to this group, frequent-user programs were developed expressly to encourage and reward loyalty and repeat patronage.

Putting Segmentation Knowledge to Work

Now that you know some of the basic approaches to market segmentation, you are faced with yet another challenge: when to segment. It would be nice if we could neatly categorize and slice up all travelers into distinct market segments. However, we can encounter several problems in attempting to segment markets. For example, some markets might be too small to segment. In addition, each of us can be classified as members of many different markets, which tends to complicate the segmentation task.

There are almost as many potential market segments as there are groups of people. In fact,

many market segments that were not even considered a few years ago, such as travelers with disabilities and volunteerism travelers, are growing in size and importance.

The task of deciding when to segment can be clarified by answering the following questions:

■ Can the market segment be relatively easily identified and measured in both purchasing power and size?

■ Is the segment large enough to be potentially profitable?

■ Can the segment be reached efficiently and effectively through advertising and other forms of promotion?

■ Is the segment interested in the service offered?

■ Is the segment expected to be long term and will it grow or shrink in size?[13]

Although this list of questions helps narrow the range of potential segments, the most important reason for segmenting should not be forgotten. Segmenting permits tourism service suppliers to better meet specific customer needs and wants while attempting to increase their satisfaction. Once a segmentation approach has been selected, the next task is to decide which of these segments to target.

Marketers use a five-step approach to accomplish this market segmentation decision process. In Step 1, they choose one or more of the segmentation approaches we have previously described for grouping individuals. Even though we introduced each basis for segmentation separately, most organizations tend to use a combination of these approaches. For example, the Vancouver Aquarium in British Columbia might define its market in terms of geographic location and demographic profile. The aquarium's marketing team might break the potential market for its educational and entertainment services into two geographic segments, such as people within a 200-mile radius of Vancouver and those living more than 200 miles away, and then further group potential visitors by age and family situation.

In Step 2, each segment is profiled in as much detail as is cost effective. This greater amount of detail provides a more accurate understanding of the needs of the segments and

■ Market segmentation helps satisfy differing visitor needs. Photo by C. A. Cook.

is used in developing a basic outline of the marketing mix that each segment would require. Continuing with our example, management of the Vancouver Aquarium may decide to conduct a comprehensive consumer research study to gather detailed information about the visitors to the aquarium. The decision makers can then develop more thorough profiles of the various segments. In acquiring this consumer information, the research team would need to survey consumers who visit the attraction at different times of the year. Visitors during July may tend to be international travelers from the United States and Japan, whereas visitors in December may tend to be Vancouver locals and other British Columbians.

In Step 3, forecasts are developed for the market potential of each segment being considered. All segments will not be the same in terms of number of potential buyers and amount of purchasing power, nor will they be equally likely to desire the good or service.

In Step 4, an "educated guess" about the share of each segment's business that the organization is likely to be able to achieve is prepared. Some segments are likely to find the organization's offerings more appealing than are other segments.

In Step 5, the decision is made as to which segment or segments will be targeted, that is, for which segments a specific marketing mix will be developed. These segments then become the organization's **target markets.** Returning to our example, although school trips to the aquarium are plentiful and acquaint thousands of area youngsters with its marine species, this segment does not bring in large revenues to cover the cost of operations. Other segments with more purchasing power will also need to be attracted to generate the money necessary to keep the aquarium "afloat."

Based on the information gathered in this five-step process, as shown in Table 2.4, marketers are able to develop sets of "product, place, promotion, and price" that they hope will be attractive to the segments they have chosen to target. As an illustration, the marketing director of the Vancouver Aquarium may decide that the "within 200-mile radius, environmentally concerned, married retiree" segment has great potential during the fall. She may therefore develop a

Table 2.4	The Segmentation Process
Step 1.	Select segmentation approach.
Step 2.	Create detailed profile of segments.
Step 3.	Forecast market potential of each segment.
Step 4.	Estimate likely market share of each segment.
Step 5.	Decide which segment or segments to target and design appropriate marketing mix.

marketing package that offers these consumers special guided tours (including lunch) on Tuesdays during September and October for one all-inclusive price. She may advertise this package on area radio stations that feature swing-era music.

The process of segmenting larger markets and then targeting these specific segments furnishes tourism organizations with the tools to focus their attention on providing appropriate levels of service to their most likely customers. Just like the time and effort it takes to put together an intricate jigsaw puzzle, it may also require time and commitment to identify potential groups of tourism consumers, but the effort will be worth it. When wants and needs are identified and met, tourists will return and often tell others who share similar characteristics about their positive experiences.

SPECIALIZED TOURIST SEGMENTS

Five large and distinctive segments of tourism consumers deserve special discussion because of their size and importance to the industry. These segments are business and professional travelers (product-related segmentation), incentive travelers (product-related segmentation), SMERF groups (psychographic segmentation), mature travelers (demographic segmentation), and special-interest travelers (psychographic segmentation). Let's take a brief look at the size, importance, and common characteristics of each of these segments.

Business and Professional Travelers

Business travel is considered to be the backbone or "bread and butter" of the tourism industry because businesspeople are often required to

travel as a part of their day-to-day activities. Because travel is a part of their jobs, the amount of money they spend on tourism services tends to stay fairly constant, and they are not as price sensitive as vacation and leisure travelers. Therefore, the demand for business travel services is fairly inelastic. When demand does not significantly change with price fluctuations, it is said to be inelastic. In contrast, when demand changes substantially as price fluctuates, it is referred to as elastic. The demand for vacation and leisure travel and tourism services is elastic because it can be significantly influenced by changes in prices.

The prices travelers pay for airline tickets provide an excellent example highlighting differences between inelastic and elastic demands. When looking at airfares, you may have noticed the least expensive airfares are the ones booked the farthest in advance of the scheduled departure date, or the last-minute sales of distressed inventory. Because businesspeople typically have to travel on short notice at specific times and to specific destinations, they are willing to pay higher fares to obtain needed services (inelastic demand). However, because leisure travel is elastic and these individuals can plan their trips in advance or on the spur of the moment, they are attracted to lower airfares and are often willing to travel to bargain destinations just for the fun of the experience. How would the concepts of inelastic and elastic demand work for a downtown commercial hotel experiencing heavy demand from business travelers during the weekdays while attempting to fill the rooms with leisure travelers on the weekend?

Business travel expenses are also one of the largest and most controllable expense categories in any organization. Because these travelers are so important to the profitability and potential success of most tourism service suppliers, it is

Table 2.5	Business Traveler Profile	
Seventeen percent of frequent business travelers take 64% of all business trips.		
Average number of trips		7
Average number of nights per trip		3.2
Average miles per trip		1,128
Traveled by car		60%
Traveled by air		38%
Used a rental car during business trip		25%
Stayed in hotel		65%
Combined vacationing with business trip		62%
Male		57%
Female		43%

Source: Miller, Richard K., and Washington, Kelli D. (2005). *The 2006 travel & tourism market research handbook.* Loganville, GA: Richard K. Miller & Associates.

important for us to know more about these individuals. The task is made easier because there are several characteristics that are common to many business travelers, as can be seen in the information provided in Table 2.5.

Business travelers will continue to become more demanding of tourism service suppliers as they come to expect the current level of services and benefits as a standard level of performance. The challenge of retaining and satisfying these individuals will depend on identifying the aspects of the travel and tourism experience that can be modified or improved to truly delight these demanding tourists.

Professional travelers are similar to business travelers in many ways, although this type of travel is more elastic than business travel. Professional travel is built around the meeting and convention markets. These markets have grown as transportation, especially by air, has become more available and affordable. As professional travel continues to grow, new and expanded meeting and convention facilities have been developed to satisfy this increasing demand. Along with this growth, new management challenges have arisen to serve this specialized market. Some of the key market segments for meeting participants or attendees are associations, businesses, exhibitions and trade shows, religious organizations, political parties, and governments.

For many years, forecasters have predicted the demise of business and professional travel based on the increasing availability and sophistication of electronic communication technology. However, the importance of face-to-face interaction remains important in maintaining business relationships. Many futurists have also predicted a decline in business and professional travel with the introduction of **teleconferencing**. Although teleconferencing serves to introduce people to each other electronically, they will eventually want to meet in person to interact and network. This need for personal contact and interaction has allowed the business travel market to grow even in the face of advancing technology.

In response to the needs of the business travel segment, tourism service suppliers have offered a wide array of services and benefits. Airlines instituted frequent-flier programs and service **upgrades** including business class and have provided corporate pricing, discounts and rebates, travel lounges, and preferred check-ins. Amtrak developed club service with reserved seating, snack and beverage service, telephones, and conference rooms on some trains. Car rental companies, following the lead of airlines, established frequent-renter programs that provided corporate pricing, discounts, rebates, upgrades, and special check-in procedures. Hotels and other lodging properties have provided similar benefits to business travelers including corporate pricing, discounts, and rebates; special floors and sections including business centers; frequent-stay programs; and upgrades.

The Marriott Company provides a good example of how one company has used consumer behavior information to further segment the business and professional travel market successfully. It has designed multiple types of lodging facilities to serve six distinct segments. The first is the full-service Marriott Hotel that is targeted to the business traveler who wants all the facilities needed while on business trips, such as secretarial support, room service, conference rooms, a variety of restaurants, and other services. The second is the JW Marriott Hotels & Resorts and the Renaissance Hotels brands that are targeted to the upscale business market. The third, Courtyard by Marriott, was designed expressly with the "limited expense account" businessperson in mind. This type of traveler wants the basics of a business hotel but doesn't have the budget to pay for the extras not used. The fourth concept is the Fairfield Inn. It was designed to appeal to the traveler who is simply looking for a clean, comfortable room for the night with none of the extras. The fifth concept contains the Residence Inns, Spring Hill Suites, and Towne Place Suites, which were designed to meet the wants and needs of the business traveler seeking the comforts of home for an extended stay. Finally, Marriott Vacation Club offers vacation ownership opportunities for the leisure market.

Originally, these styles of lodging had been built separately and usually at quite a distance from their sister hotels. In an intriguing move, Marriott renovated the 782-room Miami Airport Marriott into three hotels: a 365-room, full-service Marriott, a 125-room Courtyard by Marriott, and a 285-room Fairfield Inn. The original hotel had three parts—a main tower and two low-rise buildings in the back. Management realized there was a demand for a Courtyard and a Fairfield Inn, but no available area to build on. Vóila! The two lower buildings were converted to appeal to the unserved segments.[14] Catering to a variety of needs has become even more important, as there is a growing trend for business travelers to combine pleasure trips with business demands.

Incentive Travelers

One of the faster-growing segments of the tourism industry is **incentive travel**, which generates over 11 million trips annually worldwide.[15] Employee productivity and motivation are a concern for all organizations, and incentive travel awards are an attempt to achieve higher levels of both. Incentive programs are designed to create competition, with the winner(s) receiving many different types of awards, including complete holiday getaway packages. The good news for the tourism industry is that, in general, if properly planned, people will work harder to receive an incentive trip than any other type of reward, including cash.[16] Incentive programs can be designed and purchased through a variety of sources, as shown in Table 2.6.

■ Identifying and meeting the needs of various market segments. Courtesy of Marriott Lodging at Miami International Airport.

Table 2.6	How Travel Awards Are Purchased*	
Corporate travel agency		29%
Direct purchase—airline, hotel, etc.		31%
Retail travel agency		18%
Incentive company/incentive house		18%
Sales promotion/advertising agency		15%

*Percentages will add to more than 100% as respondents could choose more than one category.
Source: 2003 Incentive Federation Survey.

Planning incentive travel awards requires creating a party format for celebrating achievement, so the settings for celebrating these successes are spectacular by design. Typical destination locations for recipient awards include Hawaii, Europe, and the Caribbean Islands. Trips to these locations often involve recognition award banquets and many other special activities where the recipients can be honored and pampered.

All aspects of incentive travel are structured so that everything is first class, filled with pleasant surprises, and arranged so that participants never have to pay for anything. The incentive travel segment demands the best in service and, at the same time, is willing to pay **incentive tour operators** top dollar for these services. Companies such as BI, Maritz, and Wyndham Jade provide organizations with a one-stop shop for motivation and loyalty enhancement programs designed around rewarding people with incentive travel. These programs can be designed to reward individuals or groups by providing everything from transportation, lodging, food, activities, to entertainment. BI's efforts to continuously improve its internal processes and customer satisfaction recently garnered the coveted Malcolm Baldridge National Quality Award. BI joins only one other tourism service provider, the Ritz Carlton Hotels, to have achieved this distinction of excellence.

SMERFs

SMERFs are not those little blue creatures that became popular Saturday morning cartoon icons in the 1980s but is an acronym for a very large, but hard to define and reach, group of travelers.

SMERF stands for Social, Military, Education, Religious, and Fraternal. Even though these groups are hard to define and reach, their importance to the tourism industry cannot be overlooked. They are a large market in terms of potential revenue; they tend to hold events on weekends, which creates traffic when business travel volume is at its lowest point; and contrary to popular opinion, they are not always price sensitive.

Estimates have placed the market value of these groups of travelers at anywhere between $18 billion and $90 billion annually and growing. Because of the size, growth, and need for personalized service, this market segment is proving to be very attractive to tourism service providers, especially travel agents, tour operators, cruise lines, hotels, and resorts. Because SMERF groups are typically run by volunteers, they pose some unique marketing challenges both in identifying the specific groups and in creating service offerings that cater to their needs. Social groups such as vacation clubs, reunions, weddings, and girlfriend get-togethers may be the hardest of all the SMERFs to identify and target, but they have proven to be the least price sensitive.[17]

Mature Travelers

Another large and growing segment of tourism consumers is **mature travelers**. The face of the industrialized world's population is changing. Although it is probably a mistake to lump all mature travelers together into a single market, it is important to understand the immense size of this market. The United Nations estimates that the number of senior citizens in the year

2025 will be 1.1 billion worldwide.[18] By 2050, this group will make up over 21% of the world's population.[19] A good idea of the changes taking place in the mature segment of the tourism market can be seen by looking at the changes taking place in the United States. The American population is aging and will continue to increase as a percentage of the total population. This segment will grow seven times faster than all other age segments.[20] Similar demographic shifts are taking place in many countries throughout the world.

The number of senior citizens in the United States who compose the market segment called mature travelers has been growing at double-digit rates. This rapid growth provides many opportunities for firms who recognize and plan to meet the needs of these travelers. The mature traveler market segment is especially important because these individuals spend 30% more than younger travelers and account for 80% of all commercial vacation travel.[21]

Other significant facts about this group of travelers in the United States that may have gone unnoticed or unappreciated are as follows:

- They are the fastest-growing segment of the travel market.
- They control over three-quarters of the United States' disposable wealth.[22]
- They control over 50% of the United States' **disposable income.**

Findings from two recent surveys (see Table 2.7) of travelers over the age of 50 provide useful insights into the needs and expectations of this growing market.

Many mature visitors have the time, money, and energy to travel and enjoy family, friends, new sights, adventures, and active lifestyles. Several researchers have found that most mature travelers fall into one of three segments. The first tend to be sightseers, preferring package tours to cities with a wide variety of urban attractions. They do not like surprises nor the party scene and are very concerned for their safety while they travel. The second segment are enthusiastic participators, who tend to be younger, better-educated seniors, and they seek adventure and new experiences. They enjoy exploring on their own and mingling with the local population at destinations. The third segment of mature travelers are family focused, preferring travel that results in family time and interactions. They tend to be less affluent and less educated than the other two segments.[23]

Mature travelers are increasingly traveling with their families, at least on some of their trips. Because families are scattered across a country (or even around the globe), more and more families

Table 2.7	Profile of Mature Travelers
Value excellent food while vacationing more than any other age group	
Less interested in bars and nightlife activities than other age groups	
Age group most likely to take cruise vacations	
Age group most likely to visit casinos	
Travel primarily for pleasure: 37% to visit friends and relatives, 32% to seek entertainment	
Travel primarily by car, truck, or recreational vehicle: 75%	
Take long trips: 5.3 nights	
Take the longest pleasure trips of all age groups: 948 round-trip miles (avg.)	
Age group most likely to purchase package tours	
Account for 32% of visitors to historic sites	
Account for 33% of visitors to cultural events	
Least likely to use the Internet for travel planning and/or to make reservations	

Sources: The 55+ traveler. (1995). Washington, D.C.: Travel Industry Association of America; Morrison, Alastair, Yang, Chung-Hui, O'Leary, Joseph T., and Nadkarni, Nandini. (1994). A comparative study of cruise and land-based resort vacation travelers. In K. S. Chon, ed., *New frontiers in tourism research.* Harper Woods, MI: Society of Travel and Tourism Educators; Hsu, Cathy H. C., Cai, Liping A., and Morrison, Alastair. (1995). Relationships between sociodemographic variables, travel attitudes, and travel experiences. In K. S. Chon, ed., *New frontiers in tourism research.* Harper Woods, MI: Society of Travel and Tourism Educators; Travel Industry Association of America, *Fast facts*, 1998.

Tourism in Action

Developed in 1974 to fulfill the educational and travel needs of the increasing senior citizen population, Elderhostel has long focused on the mature traveler segment of the tourism market. Pioneered at five New Hampshire colleges and universities, the nonprofit Elderhostel organization developed into a nationwide network on college campuses that used dormitories and classrooms during the summer months. The programs provided inexpensive, residential educational programs for persons 60 years of age and over. In 1995, the eligibility age was lowered to age 55.

Since its humble beginnings, the Elderhostel concept has expanded to include programs at over 8,000 different locations in 90 countries. Responding to the expanding affluence and sophistication of the retiree population, Elderhostel now offers travel adventures that are far from two weeks on a traditional New England college campus. International Elderhostel programs span the globe from Antarctica to Iceland and can range from single-site one- or two-week educational tours to four-week treks through several countries.

For example, Elderhostel offers such exotic programs as a four-week train journey studying Australia's human and natural landscapes, a two-week expedition to the Cook Islands in the Pacific Ocean, and a three-week journey into the heart of Asia. Participants in any of these programs may extend their travels and adventures by purchasing pre- and posttour packages to the areas they are visiting.

Elderhostel has served the educational and travel adventure needs of over 4 million seniors throughout the world. Given the growth in size and financial resources of the mature traveler segment, Elderhostel should continue to expand and thrive in the 21st century. The overriding objective of Elderhostel has always been the self-actualization of older adults, that the "sky is the limit" when it comes to personal potential—at any age!

Source: Elderhostel brochure and catalogs. Elderhostel, 75 Federal Street, Boston, MA 02110. Available at: http://www.elderhostel.org.

---

are using vacations as a time for family togetherness, including grandparents and other extended family members on the trip. This emerging segment is called intergenerational or multigenerational travel. These family groups tend to take vacations to destinations that offer a wide variety of activities so everyone, no matter one's age, can find something exciting to do. Las Vegas, Hawaii, and cruises have proved to be popular destinations for these family "reunions."[24]

Special-Interest Travelers

Over the past 50 years, tourism has evolved as tourists have become more sophisticated and more discriminating in their tastes and jealous of their limited free time. Originally, tourism was characterized by general-interest tourism (GIT). The destination and its variety of attractions were the most important components of the tourism product and the primary motivators for leisure travel. Today, more and more travelers are focusing their vacation attention on activity and are selecting a destination based on

the ability to participate in one or more of their favorite pastimes. This selective form of tourism is now called **special-interest tourism (SIT)**. SIT is "defined as tourism undertaken for a distinct and specific reason; thereby indicating that the special interest tourist has a specific interest-based motivation for his/her travel to another destination" (p. 12).[25] Table 2.8 shows the evolution of this tourism transition.

Special-interest travelers come in all shapes and sizes. Tour operators, for example, are now offering tours for the wine aficionado, the opera buff, gardeners, and amateur photographers.[26] These groups are particularly appealing to tourism suppliers for a number of reasons. Often they travel in small groups on very specific itineraries, so they see the planning and knowledge benefits of using a travel agent or specialty tour operator. They highly value education and skill enhancement, so many of these travelers prefer to hire the services of guides. They frequently travel during shoulder or off-season periods, providing revenue when businesses need it the most. Because their special interest is central to

■ Train enthusiasts travel worldwide to board the many historic trains still riding the rails. Photo by D. A. Yale.

their lives, they typically spend above-average amounts on their trips. Take a look at Table 2.9 for a sampling of some typical special-interest trips often taken with tour groups. Have you ever taken a special-interest tourism trip? One of the larger and faster-growing special-interest groups of travelers is **sport tourism visitors,** so we will take a closer look at this group.

Rather than traveling for rest and relaxation, more and more of the world's population is traveling for sport-related reasons. Sport tourism has exploded in the last ten years and is now seen as a major form of special-interest tourism. Sport tourism is "travel away from home to play sport, watch sport, or to visit a sport attraction including both competitive and noncompetitive activities" (p. 2).[27] Think of the vast array of travel that is included in this definition. Sport team members traveling to out-of-town tournaments are included; booster and alumni clubs trekking to "bowl" games are included; golf fans traveling to the British Open are included; a snowboard/ski club traveling to the Rockies for spring break is included!

Sport tourism is not a new phenomenon. The first Olympic Games occurred nearly 3,000 years ago. In 1852, a New England railroad company sponsored the Harvard–Yale crew competition in part so ridership would increase dramatically. The Northern Pacific Railroad developed the Sun Valley ski resort to generate passengers during the company's slow season! As sport participation, spectatorship, and team affiliations have increased with the world's increased affluence and health consciousness, sport tourism has exploded as a segment of the tourism market.

Table 2.8	Evolution of Special-Interest Tourism	
General-Interest Tourist	*Mixed-Interest Tourist*	*Special-Interest Tourist*
Where would I like to go?	Where do I want to go and what activities can I pursue there?	What interest/activity do I want to pursue, and where can I do it?

Table 2.9	Examples of Special-Interest Trips	
Archeological	Bird watching
Culinary	Dark
Educational	Genealogical
Heritage	Mystery
Railroad	Shopping
Sports	Winery

Table 2.11	Sport Tourism Event Participation Percentages
Baseball/softball	17%
Football	15%
Basketball	9%
Auto/truck racing	8%
Golf tournament	6%
Skiing/snowboarding	5%
Soccer	5%
Ice hockey	4%
Other	13%

Source: Getz, Donald. (2003). Sport event tourism: Planning, development, and marketing. In Simon Hudson, ed., *Sport and adventure tourism* (pp. 49–88). New York: Haworth Press.

Sport tourists are primarily of two types, participatory sport tourists and spectator sport tourists, and these two types can be further grouped (see Table 2.10). Participatory sport tourists tend to be physically active, college educated, relatively affluent, and young (18–44 years old). This type of traveler also tends to participate in more than one activity; for example, a skier by winter may be a golfer by summer.

However, even the least physically active among us can be a sport tourist. Millions upon millions of travelers worldwide are following "their team" or their favorite athlete, and they spend billions for tourism and other services. Travel Industries Association of America estimates that nearly 40% of U.S. adults are sport event travelers, and the percentage in the industrialized world is likely to be high as well.[28] Many of these trips are families traveling to watch a family member compete in a sporting event, so sport tourism is now a major component of family travel. Table 2.11 lists the most popular types of sport tourist events. Sport event travel is about evenly split between professional and amateur sporting events, and summer is the peak season for such travel, although autumn is also a popular sport tourism season. Many cities, states/provinces, and even countries have specially designated sports commissions whose primary role is to attract sport tourism events.

DELIVERING HIGH-QUALITY SERVICE

Simply identifying and attracting targeted customers is not enough. Tourism organizations must then meet customer expectations by satisfying

Table 2.10	Types of Sport Tourists
A.	Outdoor/Nature Sport Tourists—Usually must travel substantial distance to participate in chosen sport, as many sports are dependent on a natural resource (e.g., a mountain, a river, a wilderness area). Most of these sports are nonteam and noncompetitive, but some require substantial skill. Frequently, participants return to the same destination many times throughout the year.
B.	Resort Sport Tourists—Travel typically to highly developed luxury resorts to participate in such sports as golf and tennis. Some skiers also fall in this category.
C.	Amateur Team Sport Tourists—Travel to participate in a team sport or travel to watch, coach, or support team members. Travel is usually to urban or suburban locations.
D.	Athletic Spectators—Most often travel with group of friends or family members. Travel is to high-profile events (e.g., NASCAR race) or to scheduled professional or high-profile sport team game.

Based on Weed, Mike, and Bull, Chris. (2004). *Sports tourism: Participants, policy and providers*. Oxford: Elsevier, Butterworth-Heinemann.

their wants and needs. Every component of the tourism industry is service oriented. Therefore, providing consistently high-quality service is the key to establishing and maintaining a successful operation.

Because the tourism market has become more competitive, service quality has become critical for tourism suppliers. It is no longer

good enough simply to provide today's demanding traveler with adequate service. Travelers now expect consistency in service, if not superior service. Delivery of superior service requires understanding travelers' needs and expectations. We will talk about the specific knowledge and skills needed to deliver service quality in Chapter 3.

■ SUMMARY

We continue our journey through the dynamic world of tourism by starting at the center of the tourism model, where we focus on the millions of people who travel away from home each day. Because it is impossible to serve all of their wants and needs, we learned more about who these travelers are, their reasons for travel, and how we can meet their needs. As we learned more about these travelers, we could begin segmenting them into groups based on some similar characteristics.

Common approaches to segmenting markets include classifying consumers based on geographic, demographic, psychographic, and product-related characteristics. There are several very large market segments such as business and professional, incentive, SMERF, mature, and special-interest travelers that are particularly important to the future of the tourism industry.

Segmentation and target marketing are used to focus marketing efforts on groups of individuals with

common wants and needs. A segment can then be seen as a distinct target that can be served with its own unique mix of services, prices, locations, times, and promotional activities. When customer wants and needs are properly identified and customer expectations are met, travelers will often tell others about their experiences and return.

Providing service that, at a minimum, results in satisfaction and strives truly to delight customers should be the goal of all tourism organizations. Remember, tourism is a business dependent on human relations and shared experiences. People like to be served and feel that they are welcome, that their business is important, and that service providers care about their experiences. By identifying the specific needs of individuals and groups of guests and visitors, it is possible to meet and exceed their expectations.

■ YOU DECIDE

Event tourism ranging from art shows and music festivals to athletic tournaments and food fairs are becoming a large and growing travel industry entertainment component. Communities that host these events have been, for the most part, receptive because of their apparent economic benefits. These events provide a variety of leisure opportunities for participants, as well as needed traffic for local tourism service providers. In fact, many of these events are intentionally scheduled during traditionally slow tourism periods to provide an extra boost to the local economy.

Although local residents may greet special events enthusiastically, one event, the motorcycle rally, seems to polarize communities along emotional lines: equally vocal supporters and detractors. Why do these events generate so much local interest? A quick look at their history gives a good indication as to why.

The first recognized motorcycle rally was held in Sturgis, South Dakota, in 1940 and attracted about

200 people. However, today, this sleepy little mountain town "welcomes" over 200,000 rally enthusiasts to this event each year. The success of the Sturgis rally has spawned other rallies in places such as Bainbridge, Georgia; Hollister, California; Daytona Beach, Florida; and Laconia, New Hampshire.

Many of these Sturgis copycat rallies were promoted because the economic benefits could be enormous, but there are other impacts to be considered. Just think about the thundering sounds and raucous partying that occur as thousands of motorcyclists descend on these many annual gatherings. Motorcycle rally participants are a far cry from the genteel crowds that come together for a spring flower show!

Whereas members of the tourism community, from lodging facilities and restaurants to attractions and retailers, who benefit directly from increased expenditures are supporters, local governmental agencies from law enforcement to sanitation are not always quite as enthusiastic. They are the ones who must provide extra services at additional costs, which may not be offset by increased tax receipts. And although local residents may enjoy many of the event activities, they may resent the noise, wild party antics, and other inconveniences created by a sudden influx of revelers.

Governmental officials and local tourism service suppliers face a variety of issues when making decisions regarding endorsing or encouraging the creation and/or continuance of these events. They must weigh the potential economic benefits against the costs and inconveniences they create. If your hometown was presented with the opportunity to host a motorcycle rally, what would you recommend?

■ NET TOUR

To get you started on exploring Internet links for this chapter, please see

>   http://www.ustoa.com
>
>   http://www.nbta.org

http://www.elderhostel.org

http://www.sric-bi.com

■ DISCUSSION QUESTIONS

1. What do we mean when we refer to segmenting a market?
2. Why do we segment the tourism market?
3. Identify and provide examples of the common approaches to segmenting the tourism market.
4. Why are business travelers so important to the tourism industry?
5. How do SMERF groups complement the business travel market?
6. Why are mature travelers so important to the future of the tourism industry?
7. Why are special-interest travelers becoming more important to tourism service suppliers?
8. Why are incentive travelers so important to the future of the tourism industry?
9. Why are special-interest travelers so important to the future of the tourism industry?
10. Why should the topic of customer service be important to tourism service suppliers?

■ APPLYING THE CONCEPTS

1. Collect several advertisements for tourism-related goods or services. Based on the content of these advertisements, describe the customer segment you believe is being targeted.
2. Browse the Internet and find three tourism supplier home pages. Which segments do you think each is targeting based on the information provided on the home pages?
3. Interview the head of a tourism service supplier's marketing or sales department to find out the segments targeted and the relative importance of each of these segments to overall profitability.
4. Interview a member of one of the specialized tourist segments introduced in this chapter.

Develop a profile of this segment's travel behaviors. Examples of questions you might ask include: Where do you travel? How frequently do you travel? When do you travel, how do you travel? What do you enjoy doing when you travel? With whom do you travel? What types of service suppliers do you select to meet these needs?

5. Based on what you know about market segmentation, help Jim and Andy by preparing a list describing some of the common characteristics of the people who might be potential customers for their whitewater rafting business.

GLOSSARY

Allocentrics   *See* Venturers.

Consumer behavior   The study of consumer characteristics and the processes involved when individuals or groups select, purchase, and use goods, services, or experiences to satisfy wants and needs.

Demographics   Characteristics used to classify consumers on the basis of criteria such as age, education, income, gender, and occupation.

Demographic segmentation   Dividing consumer markets based on demographic data such as age, education, income, gender, religion, race, nationality, and occupation.

Dependables   Travelers who seek the comforts of familiar surroundings.

Disposable income   Household income after paying taxes that is available for personal use.

Distressed inventory   Tourism services that have not been sold as the date of use approaches.

Elastic demand   A change in the quantity of goods or services used in a proportion that is greater than changes in prices.

Geographic segmentation   Dividing consumer markets along different geographical boundaries such as nations, states, and communities.

Heterogeneous   Having differing characteristics and needs.

Homogeneous   Having similar characteristics and needs.

Incentive tour operators   Tour operators who specialize in organizing, promoting, and conducting incentive tours.

Incentive travel   Motivational programs designed to create competition, with the winner(s) receiving travel awards.

Inelastic demand   A change in the quantity of goods or services used that is not in direct proportion to changes in prices.

Lifestyle   A mode of living that is identified by how people spend their time (activities), what they consider important in their environment (interests), and what they think of themselves and the world around them (opinions).

Market segmentation   Dividing a broad market into smaller and distinct groups of buyers—each group with similar needs, characteristics, or behaviors.

Mature travelers   People aged 55 and older; also called "senior citizens."

Product-related segmentation   Dividing consumer markets according to characteristics such as the amount of use or benefits consumers expect to derive from the service.

Psychocentrics   *See* Dependables.

Psychographics   Consumer psychological characteristics that can be quantified, including lifestyle and personality information.

Psychographic segmentation   Dividing consumer markets into groups based on lifestyle and personality profiles.

SMERF   An acronym for the market comprising social, military, educational, religious, and fraternal groups.

Special-interest tourism (SIT)   Tourism undertaken for a distinct and specific personal reason.

Sport tourism visitors   People who travel to participate in or view sporting activities.

Target market (target segment)   A group of people sharing common characteristics that an organization attempts to serve by designing strategies to meet the group's specific needs.

Teleconferencing   A meeting that allows people to remain in several locations but come together and communicate through a combination of television and telephone connections.

Upgrades   Receiving a better class of service or facility than was paid for, such as moving from coach to first class.

Venturers   Travelers who seek adventure.

REFERENCES

1. Schiffman, Leon G., and Kanuk, Leslie Lazar. (2007). *Consumer behavior* (9th ed.). Upper Saddle River, NJ: Pearson Prentice Hall, Inc.
2. Bieger, Thomas, and Laesser, Christian. (2004, May). Information sources for travel decisions: Toward a source process model. *Journal of Travel Research*, pp. 357–371.
3. Hyde, Kenneth F., and Lawson, Ron. (2003, August). The nature of independent travel. *Journal of Travel Research*, pp. 13–23.

4. Jeng, J. (1997). Facets of the complex trip decision making process. In *28th Travel and Tourism Research Association annual conference proceedings*. Norfolk, VA: Travel and Tourism Research Association.

5. Baloglu, Seyhinus, and Uysal, Muzaffer. (1996). Market segments of push and pull motivations: A canonical correlation approach. *International Journal of Contemporary Hospitality Management,* 8(3), 32–38.

6. Maslow, Abraham. (1954). *Motivation and personality.* New York: Harper & Row.

7. Pearce, P. L. (1991). *Dreamworld.* A report on public reactions to Dreamworld and proposed developments at Dreamworld. Townsville, Australia: Department of Tourism, James Cook University.

8. Plog, Stanley G. (1974, February). Why destination areas rise and fall in popularity. *Cornell Hotel & Restaurant Administration Quarterly,* pp. 55–58.

9. Plog, Stanley C. (2002). The power of psychographics and the concept of venturesomeness. *Journal of Travel Research,* 40, 244–251.

10. Plog, Stanley G. (1974, February). Why destination areas rise and fall in popularity. *Cornell Hotel & Restaurant Administration Quarterly,* pp. 55–58.

11. Chipkin, Harvey. (2008). Brand proliferation hotels respond to consumers' demand for the new and different. *HSMAI Marketing Review,* 25(1), 36–40.

12. Solomon, Michael. (2008). *Consumer behavior* (8th ed.). Upper Saddle River, NJ: Pearson Prentice Hall, Inc.

13. Boone, Louis E., and Kurtz, Daniel L. (2009). *Contemporary marketing* (13th ed.). Mason, OH: South-Western Cengage Learning.

14. Richards, Rhonda. (1995, August 15). Business travel. *USA Today,* p. 8B.

15. Sheldon, Pauline J. (1995, Spring). The demand for incentive travel: An empirical study. *Journal of Travel Research,* pp. 23–28.

16. Snyder, Michael. (2006-2007). Trends in incentive travel award programs. *HSMAI Marketing Review,* 24(1), 81–84.

17. Rogers, Beth. (2007). SMERF: A multi-billion dollar market worth pursuing, *HSMAI Marketing Review,* 24(2), 22–26.

18. United Nations' Third International Conference on Senior Tourism Brochure. (1999).

19. Population Division of the Department of Economic and Social Affairs of the United Nations Secretariat. (2002).

20. *2004 Domestic outlook for travel and tourism.* Proceedings of the Travel Industry Association of America's Twenty-ninth Annual Marketing Outlook Forum. Austin, TX, October 20–22, 2003.

21. Conaway, Frank. (1991, May). Targeting mature markets: Segmenting will unleash mature market potential. *Public Relations Journal,* pp. 18–19.

22. Badinelli, Kimberle, Davis, Nigel, and Gustin, Libby. (1991, September 9). Special report: Senior traveler study. *Hotel & Motel Management,* pp. 31, 33–34.

23. Horneman, Louise, Carter, R. W., Wei, Sherrie, and Ruys, Hein (2002). Profiling the senior traveler: An Australian perspective. *Journal of Travel Research,* 41(1), 23–37.

24. Exploring the niche. (2001). *Travel Weekly,* 60(12), 27.

25. Brotherton, Bob, and Himmetoglu, Bulent. (1997). Beyond destinations - Special interest tourism. *Anatolia: An International Journal of Tourism and Hospitality Research,* 8(3), 11–30.

26. Surge in special-interest breaks. (2004, February 16). *Travel Weekly,* p. 50.

27. Delpy-Neirotti, Lisa. (2003). An introduction to sport and adventure tourism. In Simon Hudson, ed., *Sport and adventure tourism* (pp. 1–25). New York: Haworth Press.

28. Getz, Donald. (2003). Sport event tourism: Planning, development, and marketing. In Simon Hudson, ed., *Sport and adventure tourism* (pp. 49–88). New York: Haworth Press.

LEARNING OBJECTIVES

After you have read this chapter, you should be able to:

- Describe how services are different from goods.
- Explain how a service is like a play.
- Explain the different factors that affect a guest's service experience.
- Explain how a person develops expectations of a service and how tourism organizations can meet or exceed these expectations.
- Name and describe the five service quality dimensions.
- Explain how a comparison of service expectations with the actual service encounter can give rise to three possible satisfaction levels.
- Explain what tourism managers can do to ensure high-quality service.
- Explain how negative "breaks from the script" should be handled in order to "turn a frown upside down" and create guest loyalty.
- List the important aspects of a service guarantee.

CHAPTER 3

Delivering Quality Tourism Services

We have 50,000 moments of truth out there every day.

—Jan Carlzon, President, Scandinavian Airlines

■ Towel animals add a personal touch to the cruise experience.

ALL'S WELL THAT ENDS WELL?

After a short night's sleep, six hours of air terminal waits and airline flights, and a hectic taxi ride, Jamal and Kayla Johnson were ready for the peace and quiet of their hotel room. However, when they arrived at the Town Center Hotel to begin their vacation in Vancouver, things got off to a bad start. Although they had received an email confirmation of their room reservation two months ago, the Town Center was completely full for that night.

The Johnsons were furious! They showed Mike an email copy of their reservation confirmation. Mike apologized sincerely, admitted the mistake, and explained that several guests had stayed over unexpectedly, so there were no available rooms. Mike next picked up the phone to find the Johnsons suitable accommodations nearby. Although the city was virtually full due to a major conference in town, Mike was able to obtain a suite for the Johnsons at a hotel nearby and explained that the Town Center Hotel would pay for the suite to compensate the Johnsons for their trouble.

To keep their inconvenience to a minimum, Mike also arranged for a taxi to take the Johnsons to their new hotel. To ensure that friends and relatives could contact them if need be, they would be listed in the Town Center database so any calls could be forwarded to their new hotel.

The next day, a room at the Town Center was available for the Johnsons. Mike welcomed them as they returned the next afternoon and again apologized for the inconvenience. As they were escorted to their room by a bellman, Mike thought, "I'll call the Johnsons in about an hour just to check and make sure they are settled in and satisfied." It was an unfortunate situation, but he was certain the Johnsons would forgive the error and give the Town Center another chance the next time they came to Vancouver.

INTRODUCTION

As you learned in Chapter 1, services are the fastest-growing industry in the world, and tourism is the fastest-growing segment in the service industry. Most of us easily recognize and know where to purchase goods such as cell phones, textbooks, and toothpaste. However, in the tourism industry, we deal mainly with services, not goods. We may find it difficult at times to describe these services, know where to purchase them, or even make clear distinctions between services and goods. Even these distinctions may at times become blurred because some tourism organizations are involved primarily in the delivery of services, whereas others deliver both services and goods.

These differences can be seen in the services/goods continuum shown in Figure 3.1. At one end of the goods/services continuum, you will find organizations such as travel agencies and convention and visitors bureaus that primarily provide services. In the middle, you will find organizations such as restaurants that provide both goods and services. On the opposite end, you will find organizations such as retail shops that provide primarily goods and some services.

But wait a minute. Didn't we just say that tourism is a service? Yes, but services are often accompanied by something called a facilitating good. **Facilitating goods** are tangible items that support or accompany the service being provided. For example, if you were to call the Israel Government Tourist Office located in Chicago, Illinois, and ask questions about the types of documentation needed for travel into Israel, the answers you received would be a service. If you

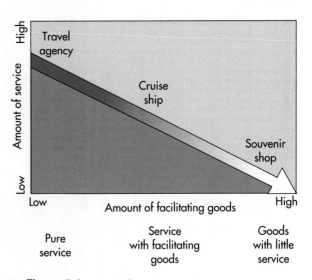

■ **Figure 3.1**   Goods/services continuum.

requested brochures, then you would be receiving both a service and a facilitating good.

Services provided by these and other tourism organizations are called "intangibles" because they cannot be placed in inventories and pulled out of warehouses or off of shelves like a can of beans or a compact disk. Services are not only intangible but also highly perishable. Tourism services perish or lose their value with the passage of time just like fresh fruits and vegetables that eventually spoil and must be thrown away. Think about the airplane that has just left the gate, the cruise ship that has just been pushed away from the dock, or the fireworks show that marks the end of a concert. In each of these situations, the opportunity to generate revenue from the seat, cabin, or concert has disappeared forever.

Services are also different from goods because they are actions performed by one person on behalf of another. Sometimes we are merely the recipients of services, but at other times, we become actively involved in the service delivery process. For example, once we call a travel agency to book a flight, we are through with active participation. The travel agent finds the best route and the best flight and reserves seats for us. However, some tourism organizations may actively involve customers in the service delivery process: Airline passengers check in via self-service kiosks or pick up box lunches before boarding; hotels allow guests to check in electronically or check out over the telephone or through the television without ever going to the front desk; and restaurants invite guests to serve themselves at salad bars. The Internet also allows passengers to check on current flight status, find frequent-flier mileage, and confirm upgrades without ever having any human contact in person or on the phone.

QUALITY

Quality. Hospitality. In the case of tourism, these two words are inseparable. When thinking about a high-quality experience in any tourism service, whether a restaurant meal, a hotel stay, an airline flight, or a guided tour, most people think of friendly, helpful personnel who treat them with concern and kindness. The concept of quality with its important hospitality component is the focus of this chapter.

As the tourism marketplace becomes more competitive, quality becomes more crucial for continued financial success. Consumers are more critical and demanding today than they have ever been. Simply providing guests average service is not good enough in this competitive environment. In a market full of tourism suppliers, a company needs to offer more and better service because guests can always take their business elsewhere.

"Virtually every survey of restaurant guests tells a similar story. If a property [hotel] has great service, the guests will come back even if the food is mediocre. Reverse the situation and the opposite occurs: Great food with bad service, and guests will most likely not return. The bottom line? Great service is a necessity."[1] Therefore, to be successful, every organization in the tourism industry needs to understand what quality means to prospective customers and strive to improve the service quality offered so customers keep coming back again and again.

Take a moment to think back on a memorable tourism service experience that you would label as very high in quality. What were the circumstances? Why is this encounter more memorable than others? What aspects of it make you recall it as high quality?

As we have already suggested, different travelers have different needs and wants. What is "high quality" to one may be perceived as entirely unacceptable to another. Think of Mexican food. Some restaurant patrons believe that high-quality Mexican food must make you perspire and set your tongue on fire. Many other fans of South of the Border fare like their food much less combustible and prefer milder versions of Mexican classics. Those red chili burritos may be delicious to you, but to a friend born and raised in Santa Fe, New Mexico, they may seem bland and tasteless. So, quality is a complex concept, difficult to define in terms on which all can agree.

Defining Quality

As Figure 3.2 shows, quality can have several definitions. Most of us probably think of quality as synonymous with "excellence." Technically,

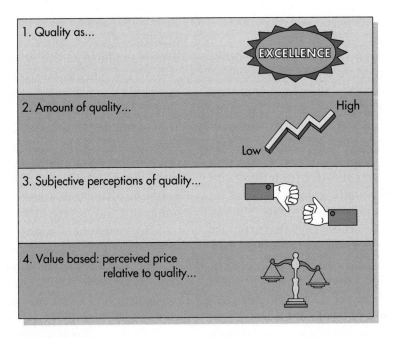

1. Quality as...   EXCELLENCE

2. Amount of quality...   High   Low

3. Subjective perceptions of quality...

4. Value based: perceived price relative to quality...

■ **Figure 3.2**   Quality definitions.

from a management and marketing perspective, quality represents a form of measurement like a thermometer or ruler. Products have some amount of quality: We talk of high quality or bad quality, good quality or poor quality. Quality is both objective and subjective in nature. Objectively, we can measure some aspects of quality because they involve objective, or measurable, amounts of certain attributes or ingredients. A spacious hotel room would be rated as higher quality than a smaller one simply based on the measurable dimensions of the two rooms. Likewise, a flight that takes off on time and arrives ahead of schedule would be thought of as higher in quality than a late flight, based on the quantifiable aspect of time as measured in minutes.[2] However, this measurable concept of quality is not the complete picture of quality. Much of quality is subjective—in the "eye of the beholder."

In addition to these objective versus subjective concepts of quality is the idea of value. The value-based definition of quality incorporates the notion of a trade-off: the trade-off between service attributes and service performance with the price paid for the quality received. Even if you are an infrequent flier, you no doubt have recognized the objective quality differences between first or business class and coach. In

first class, passengers sit in leather-covered, spacious "lounger"-style seats with more leg room between the rows. In addition, they receive bountiful amounts of food and beverages served on fine china. But do you believe the quality received in first class is worth the difference in price?

First- and business-class airfares are often three to five times as expensive as coach-class fares, yet everyone takes off and arrives at the exact same time in the exact same place. In the case of air travel, the value-based concept of quality therefore involves a person's perception

Tips

One commonly used but often misunderstood measure of service quality is tipping. Although many employees rely on tips to supplement their income, they may fail to recognize the origin of the term *tips*. TIPS is actually an acronym for the phrase "*To Insure Prompt Service*." Tips are not automatic; the amount (if any) a guest leaves is often a pointed comment on the service received.

of the best use of his or her travel and time budget. For example, frequent business travelers value the quiet time and space for relaxing or working that is provided in first-class seating. The values of leisure travelers vary. If you believe that "getting there is half the fun," you may decide to spend the extra money to enjoy the benefits of first-class travel. But if you believe that the plane ride is simply transportation to be endured in order to get to where the fun starts, you are more likely to save those travel dollars to spend at your destination.

Why is quality so important? Higher quality can result in three important benefits for companies. First, when consumers perceive a company's product as superior in quality, they are willing to pay higher prices, which can translate into higher profits. Second, superior quality can lead to increased **market share**.[3] Third, superior quality can generate truly brand-loyal customers. These are customers who will accept no substitutes, do not respond to competitors' promotions, and pass along positive word-of-mouth messages, enhancing a company's reputation even further. Can you think of a local tourism provider in your area that has a superior quality reputation? Keep this business in mind throughout the rest of this chapter and see whether the ideas we present explain why this business is such a success.

Quality Differences

Quality in services, including tourism services, is more difficult to define and measure than in hard goods. When manufacturers design and build hard goods, they engineer in a specified quality level. In some instances, the specification **standards** are very high, as in the case of BMW automobiles, but in most cases, manufacturers focus on the value component of quality. How much quality is the customer willing to pay for? The GM Saturn is perceived by most consumers as a high-quality car because the value trade-off is positive. For a modest price, the car buyer receives a comfortable, stylish, and reliable automobile. Both BMW and the General Motors Company design a car with certain **specifications** that are then met in virtually every model that rolls off the assembly line.

Unfortunately, we do not manufacture services. Remember, services are actions performed on behalf of a customer. In most cases, human beings perform at least part of the actions, and therefore consistency in actions is much lower than if a machine performed the actions over and over. Machines can be programmed to repeat the same action thousands of times. People are far less consistent than machines. In addition, tourism services frequently necessitate the input and participation of the consumers themselves. For example, when you go hiking, you are intimately involved in the "production" of that tourism service. Things you control and don't control, from your skill and decisions about which trails to hike as well as the weather and your companions, play a large part in determining how much enjoyment and "quality" you perceive during your trip.

SERVICE ENCOUNTERS

The tourism industry is one of close customer contact, and every interaction between a service employee and a customer becomes a **service encounter**.[4] Both tourism customers and tourism supplier personnel bring to each encounter expectations about what will occur during the interaction. As customers and suppliers, we learn what to expect in tourism encounters from past experiences and from the experiences of others that we observe. In a sense, we all perform an important role in a service encounter "play." As customers or suppliers, we both have role expectations of each other that dictate appropriate behavior for each party.

In Table 3.1 and Figure 3.3, we extend this theater metaphor for services a little further. Most tourism services have a backstage area that the audience (guests) does not usually see. Managers of these services must be careful in their choices of props and sets onstage, those service areas guests experience. Services even have two types of employees, backstage hands, those who work behind the scenes to ensure a smooth running "show," and front stage actors, those employees who directly interact with guests.

Although we can think of service encounters as little plays that involve **service scripts**,

Table 3.1	Services as Theater: Everyone Has a Role
Services Terminology	*Theater Terminology*
Employees	Cast
Customers	Audience
Physical facilities	The set
Uniforms	Costumes
Front stage	Those areas that the audience sees
Backstage	Those areas that the audience seldom sees
Manager	Director
Service encounter	Performance
Personal front/"character"	Face/role that cast assumes when front stage (allowed to "break character" when backstage)

Source: Grove, Stephen J., and Fisk, Raymond D. (1983). The dramaturgy of services exchange: An analytical framework for services marketing. In L. L. Berry, G. L. Shostack, and G. D. Upah, eds., *Emerging perspectives on services marketing.* Chicago: American Marketing.

we all realize that they do not involve a rigid, prerehearsed set of lines. After all, a stay at Motel 6 is not expected to be as well rehearsed and performed as a Broadway production. Each encounter will be somewhat similar to but also different in some ways from every other encounter, depending on the individual customer and the individual service employee. These service encounters are frequently called "moments of truth" because it is through these encounters that customers derive their quality impressions about a service.[5]

Take a careful look at Figure 3.3 while thinking about your favorite full-service restaurant. What are the backstage parts of the service theater, such as the kitchen, that guests do not usually see but that are important in determining the experience any guest will have? What "staged" areas of the restaurant, from the parking lot to the "powder room," will the guest encounter that can affect how she perceives the restaurant? Which restaurant employee "actors" is she likely to see and/or interact with whose appearances and actions can influence her quality perception? Finally, think about how other members of the audience can influence the guest's enjoyment of her meal. If she is dining with her fiancé, she is probably hoping for a quiet, intimate dinner experience. If the hostess seats a family with three overtired children at the next table, our guest and her date are likely to have a lower-quality restaurant encounter than they had originally hoped for.

This preliminary discussion of service quality and service encounters should help you realize that quality assurance in tourism services is quite a challenge. Management of all the factors that affect service quality requires skilled planning, organizing, staffing, directing, and juggling.

SERVICE QUALITY MODEL

The diagram in Figure 3.4 begins with the factors that lead to quality expectations of a service.[6] When you go to a water park for the first time, do you have some idea of what benefits you will receive from that particular attraction? Of course you do. And how did you develop these **service expectations**? You may have talked with friends who had been to the water park (word-of-mouth communications). You may be going to the water park because you believe it will be fun and provide relief from the heat (personal needs). You may have been to other water parks and therefore have a general impression of what water parks are like (past experience). And, finally, you may have seen commercials on TV giving you an impression of the park (**marketing communications**). These factors combine and lead to expectations about the type of experience you will have during this tourism service encounter.

Once you enter the park, what elements of the experience will be important in shaping

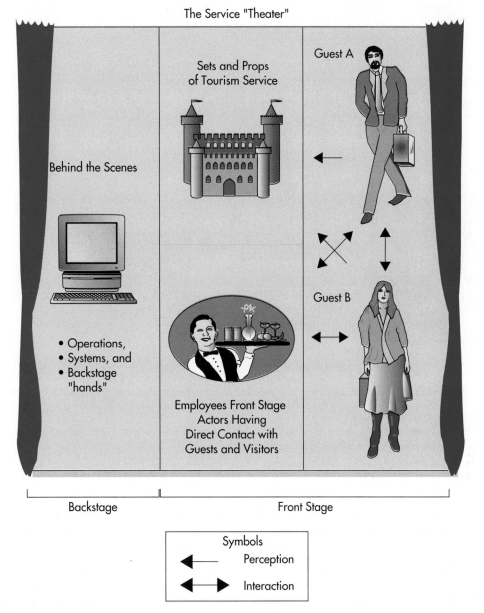

■ **Figure 3.3** The service encounter as theater.

Developed from ideas originally discussed in E. Tangeard, J. Bateson, C. Lovelock, and P. Eiglier. (1981). *Marketing of services: New insights from consumers and managers;* Report No. 80–104; Cambridge, MA: Marketing Sciences Institute; and Grove, Stephen J., and Fisk, Raymond D. (1983). The dramaturgy of services exchange: An analytical framework for services marketing. In L. L. Berry, G. L. Shostack, and G. D. Upah, eds., *Emerging perspectives on services marketing.* Chicago: American Marketing.

your perception of the quality of this park? People generally consider five dimensions when judging the quality of a service. In Figure 3.4, these dimensions link to the expected and perceived service boxes.

Tangibles are those physical aspects of the service that we can see and with which we interact—the physical appearance of the facilities, the equipment we use or that service employees use for us, the appearance and uniforms of the employees, and any signs or other communications materials that are provided. For instance, in our water park example, you may be provided with a brochure that includes a map and information about support facilities such as lockers and places to buy a snack or soft drink.

Reliability refers to the ability of service personnel to perform the promised service accurately

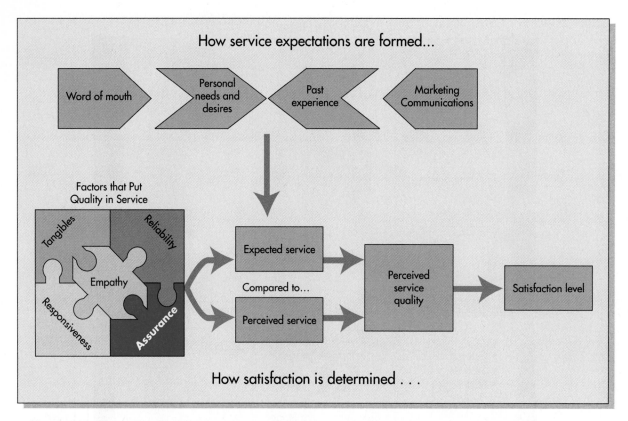

How service expectations are formed...

Word of mouth

Personal needs and desires

Past experience

Marketing Communications

Factors that Put Quality in Service

Tangibles

Reliability

Empathy

Responsiveness

Assurance

Expected service

Compared to...

Perceived service

Perceived service quality

Satisfaction level

How satisfaction is determined . . .

■ **Figure 3.4**   Service quality model.

Source: Adapted from Parasuraman, A., Zeithaml, Valarie, and Berry, Leonard. (1985). A conceptual model of service quality and its implications for future research. *Journal of Marketing,* 49, 41–50.

and consistently. For example, if the water park provides you with the opportunity to learn how to snorkel, do the instructors teach you well enough so that you can snorkel without drinking half of the pool?

Responsiveness involves service employees' willingness to help customers and their promptness in providing service. You expect snack bar personnel to wait on you as soon as possible and to provide your food without unnecessary delay.

Assurance is a catch-all quality dimension that involves the faith we have in the service personnel. Do they seem well trained? Are they knowledgeable about the park as a whole? Do they seem trustworthy? After all, lifeguards at a water park literally have guests' lives in their hands.

Finally, *empathy* is the "warm, fuzzy" piece of service quality, the part of quality that is heartfelt. Empathy is the quality element that

shows that service personnel care about you and understand your needs and frustrations. It involves setting operating hours for the convenience of guests, not management or employees. It includes caring about waiting times and fairness in waiting line systems. For example, our hypothetical water park's management realizes that many people will be waiting in lines in their bare feet on hot pavement. For guest comfort, they have located shade trees and shade umbrellas over the line areas so that you can jump from one shady area to the next while waiting your turn.

Empathy is also the element of a service that makes us feel special, when service providers recognize that we are individuals. It is the care and individualized attention that is (or is not) provided to us. When a water park "host" suggests that you might need to reapply your sunscreen because your skin is beginning to turn pink, he is showing empathy.

Cab Drivers

Many cities are realizing that visitors begin their journey to satisfaction or dissatisfaction immediately on arrival at the air terminal. Who, then, represents the first "ambassador" of a city? The cab drivers! Singapore has had special educational and licensing programs for cab drivers for many years. The drivers must learn guest relations skills and then pass rigorous tests to become officially licensed cab drivers. These skills include proficiency in English, safety, and knowledge of a wide variety of locations.

In the never-ending quest toward continual improvement, the taxicab industry in Singapore has put itself to the test by becoming part of the country's National Customer Satisfaction Index. Based on the survey results compiled to produce this index, taxicab companies can view their ratings and see where they can improve. National Trades Union Congress secretary-general Lim Swee Say noted that "we must never neglect that improving quality service is a daily event, it's a daily challenge."

Over $1.7 million was raised to fund the first year of this service improvement initiative, which included additional training for 5,000 taxicab drivers, mystery shoppers, and training courses on the finer points of service. The goal is to train 5,000 drivers each year. Cities from London to New York are keeping an eye on these programs with a view toward improving their services.

Sources: Kotler, Philip, Haidera, Donald H., and Rein, Irving. (1993). *Marketing places.* New York: Free Press; Almenora, Maria. (2008, February 23). Taxi industry aims to up service standards. *The Straits Times* (Singapore).

QUALITY AND CUSTOMER SATISFACTION

How are expectations of the service received and service quality factors linked? Figure 3.4 shows that customers compare their prior expectations of the service to their "during service" judgments of the five service quality elements—their overall quality perception of "actual quality." The result of this comparison of **expected quality** to perceived **actual quality** is the customer's level of satisfaction. Figure 3.5 shows the three possible satisfaction outcomes customers can have. If a customer perceives that the quality of the service actually received (after-the-fact perceptions) was better than expected, the guest will be pleasantly surprised and highly satisfied. On the other hand, if the guest perceives the service actually delivered to have fallen short of before-the-fact expectations, the guest will be unpleasantly surprised and therefore dissatisfied.[7]

A third quality comparison is also possible. The third possible outcome is that expectations are met exactly. If the service quality actually received is almost identical to expectations, the guest will likely be "just" satisfied. The guest received the service quality expected and so is neither pleasantly nor unpleasantly surprised.

If meeting a customer's expectations yields satisfaction, organizations should determine exactly what customers expect and then deliver it, right? Not usually. In many services, such as most tourism services, there are major added benefits to delivering *more than is expected* so that the customers are delighted, not simply satisfied. As some airlines discovered, simply relying on statements that showed customer satisfaction can lead to trouble. Airline customers indicated they were satisfied with the present level of service, but they were eager to switch to carriers that provided improved quality service.[8]

Empathy

A great example of the empathy–quality dimension is provided at the Old Faithful Lodge in Yellowstone National Park. Fishing is one of the most frequently experienced recreational activities enjoyed by visitors to the park. But what can a hotel guest do with a fish he or she catches? Bring it to dinner! Guests can deliver their personal "catch of the day" to the main dining room at the lodge, and chefs will prepare it for the guests to eat as their entrée for dinner.

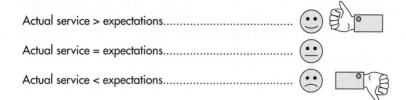

Actual service > expectations.......................................
Actual service = expectations.......................................
Actual service < expectations.......................................

■ **Figure 3.5**   Satisfaction equations.

Studies have found that customers who are highly satisfied become more valuable customers. First, delighted customers tend to pass along many more positive word-of-mouth messages than do customers who are just satisfied. Second, these highly satisfied customers are also more likely to purchase again and spend more in the future than are customers whose expectations were met but not exceeded. Finally, highly satisfied customers are unlikely to pay attention to competitors' advertising and promotional offers. Customers who are merely satisfied are more willing to try out a competitor's service to see whether it might just be better than the service they have been using.[9]

So, now that we have discussed how expectations about services are formed, how can this information be used to improve service and ensure that guests are delighted? Keep reading and you will discover the answers to this question.

■ HUMAN RESOURCES: THE KEY TO HIGH-QUALITY SERVICE

Guest services almost always require active guest involvement. Service organizations depend on everyone from the front line to the boardroom to deliver customer satisfaction. Guests will perceive, judge, and value their experiences based on the culmination of dozens, even hundreds, of one-on-one service encounters over the course of a visit. Although management must always remain focused on price, market share, and cost savings strategies, it is now more dependent than ever on everyone in the organization to deliver on its behalf.

Shaping organizational culture and implementing change are now central to highly satisfying hospitality experiences. Human resource

■ The well-trained Disney character cast members interact with guests, personalizing the guests' theme park experience.

professionals must become change agents and employee champions in this process by creating **learning organizations** dedicated to continuous improvement and organizational effectiveness. The demand for organizational excellence translates into:

- Encouraging employee participation and commitment to delivering value at every level
- Developing and expanding employee commitment, capacity, and innovation
- Creating a workplace environment where everyone is motivated to excel and is accountable for organizational success

One of the primary functions of human resource departments in today's service environment is to implement best practices through effective recruitment, selection, training, retention, and team-building programs. These efforts, combined with clear communication of an organization's vision and programs designed to generate and reward desired employee behaviors, create an environment where customer satisfaction can be measured and achieved.

Understanding and Meeting Guest Needs

Table 3.2 provides a quick list of the methods needed to ensure high-quality service. The first step in delivering high-quality service is to learn and fully understand what customers want in a particular tourism service. Tourism managers can uncover specific needs and expectations of customers in a number of ways. First, marketing research can be used to gather information from potential and existing customers. Many companies regularly survey members of their target market to better understand the changing needs and desires of segments they hope to serve. For example, when PepsiCo acquired Taco Bell, management conducted a study of fast-food customers (any fast-food customer, not simply customers who liked Mexican food). From this survey, PepsiCo concluded that fast-food customers had expectations about four things, which can be remembered by the acronym FACT. Customers wanted their fast food really *F*ast; they expected their orders to be *A*ccurately delivered; they wanted the premises to be *C*lean; and they expected foods and beverages to be served at appropriate *T*emperatures. With this knowledge, top management redesigned

Table 3.2	Management Methods That Ensure High-Quality Service	
Learn and Understand Customer Wants	*Emphasize Team Goals*	*Select and Train the Right People*
1. Regularly survey customers.	1. Actively participate, support, recognize, and reward teams in achieving goals.	1. Reinforce basic skills and abilities.
2. Frequently interact with customers.	2. Recognize, reward, and reinforce individual behaviors that support and further team progress.	2. Select employees with the following character traits: ■ Positive and willing service attitudes ■ Flexible and team-based behaviors
3. Actively seek and listen to front-line employee opinions.	3. Give teams the training, tools, and technology needed to achieve the organization's goals.	
4. Reduce the number of management levels.	4. Train and empower team members to make decisions, solve problems, and make process and service improvements.	

the entire Taco Bell system to better deliver these expected qualities.[10]

Management can also learn about customer expectations and experiences by communicating frequently with customers and by welcoming suggestions from front-line employees who deal on a one-on-one basis with customers every day. At times customers may not know what they want, so efforts should also be made to uncover unknown customer needs. This flow of communication from customers to management is more likely to occur if there are fewer levels of bureaucracy through which the information must pass. After making the restaurant manager's job more customer and employee interactive, Taco Bell has been able to streamline its organization. Taco Bell has eliminated two levels of bureaucracy so that all members of the organization are closer to the customer.

In addition to understanding the customer's needs and expectations, tourism managers must be able to hire the right people and train them well. To delight guests, tourism employees must have a positive service attitude; they must have the necessary abilities to learn and perform jobs well; and they must be flexible enough to meet different customers' needs and expectations. Management must decide on proper training for employees and set standards and policies that result in high quality and high satisfaction. However, management needs to remember that customer expectations will differ and quality perceptions will vary, so employees need to be able to make judgments and adaptations to best satisfy each guest. Remember, one of the key elements to service quality is empathy, and empathy means understanding and appreciating each customer's specific needs. Employees who are trained to follow policies strictly cannot empathize with customers and meet their needs. Managers are learning that delivering successful customer service requires allowing employees to "think while doing."

Building Service Teams

In addition to individual efforts, employees must also work together as a team. If you have worked in any tourism industry job, you already know that delivering good service is a team effort. Imagine two different restaurants. One features servers who have a "that is not my table" attitude. The other has servers who constantly help each other out by refilling water at any table needing it and by delivering meals to any table when the meals are ready to come out of the kitchen. The second restaurant is obviously the higher-quality one and demonstrates the benefits of teamwork.

Allowing employees to think as they serve and building teams are not easy managerial tasks, but the rewards are worth the effort. Recognizing individual efforts that lead to team success promotes employee involvement and commitment. When employees understand organizational goals and how to measure their performance in accomplishing these goals, the foundation for improving service delivery has been laid. Understanding the importance of their individual and team efforts leads to organizational success. Promoting teamwork also serves as a powerful tool for overcoming problems created by cultural differences as well as generating shared understandings, building appreciation across functions and between individuals, and increasing skill and knowledge levels.

■ Tangibles enhance the theme and ambiance for restaurant guests.

Teams can be developed and supported by management in a variety of ways. First, management can convey team spirit by being an active member of the team. Employees should be hired, trained, and supported so that all team members know their jobs and can carry their shares of the load to achieve the team's common goals. Second, team members also need to be supported with well-maintained and appropriate technology. Finally, team members should be able to make decisions without constantly having to check with a supervisor.

Some companies allow employees to make decisions using their own best judgment. Other firms train employees to handle a wide variety of customer scripts and problem situations. Put this all together and more in hotel companies such as Joie de Vivre Hospitality and Four Seasons, and you discover the benefits of focusing on employees that ranges from lower employee turnover (less than half of industry standards) to intense customer loyalty.[11,12] Management in these and other successful organizations has discovered the benefits of taking on the role of coach rather than boss so that the entire team can win.[13] After all, management is ultimately responsible for continually improving the service quality delivered to guests.

Ramada Inns has been recognized for its innovative program to create high-quality service and employee satisfaction. This program, called Ramada's Personal Best, has "four major components: (1) a predictive prescreening test for selecting employees, (2) a training program that uses an interactive CD, (3) an employee reward program, and (4) an independently administered monthly survey of guests' satisfaction with employee service" (p. 56).[14]

The Ritz-Carlton Company is the gold standard of service quality, having won the prestigious Malcolm Baldridge National Quality Award twice. See Table 3.3 for the philosophies by which company employees serve.

Service Mistakes

As illustrated in the chapter opener, although management and employees may want to delight guests in each and every service encounter, problems can occur. Fortunately, most consumers are willing to forgive "service mistakes" when appropriate responses to them occur. What constitutes a service mistake that can result in a guest's being dissatisfied? In simple terms, a mistake occurs when the customer's expectations are not met—when a customer's "service script"[15] is broken. We have learned that customers' script expectations develop from word-of-mouth and marketing communications, from personal needs, and from past experiences. When customers experience an unexpected change from their **expected script,** we call this a "break from the script."

A tourism-focused research study investigated these breaks from customers' scripts.[16] Interestingly, the researchers found that there were

Table 3.3	The Ritz-Carlton Hotel Company, L.L.C. Service Philosophies

Motto
"We Are Ladies and Gentlemen Serving Ladies and Gentlemen"
Credo
"The Ritz-Carlton Hotel is a place where the genuine care and comfort of our guests is our
   highest mission.
We pledge to provide the finest personal service and facilities for our guests who will always enjoy
   a warm, relaxed yet refined ambience.
The Ritz-Carlton experience enlivens the senses, instills well-being, and fulfills even the unexpected
   wishes and needs of our guests."
Three Steps of Service
1. A warm and sincere greeting. Use the guest name, if and when possible.
2. Anticipation and compliance with guest needs.
3. Fond farewell. Give them a warm good-bye and use their name, if and when possible.

Source: 1992 The Ritz-Carlton Hotel Company. All rights reserved. Reprinted with the permission of the Ritz-Carlton Hotel Company, L.L.C.

two categories of breaks from a script. The first type of break is a positive change from what the customer expects. For example, a particularly cheerful and efficient front desk clerk who provides a suggestion for a good, inexpensive place to dine that evening might be perceived as a pleasant change from the expected script–a "positive break" from the script. Positive breaks lead to highly memorable and highly satisfying service encounters that guests enjoy recounting to friends.

Unfortunately, the opposite type of break also can occur. When a change from the expected script is negative, the customer will be dissatisfied. If a front desk clerk doesn't look up from the computer screen when a guest approaches the desk, the guest is likely to perceive this behavior as a negative break from her expected script and be more than a little annoyed at the lack of service!

Mistakes Happen

Researchers have found that common negative breaks from the script occur from (1) failures in the core service (a broken-down mattress in a hotel room; an overdone, cold steak; or a bus that breaks down midtour); (2) unwillingness to accommodate a customer's special need or request (to locate an elderly guest on the ground floor of a hotel, to modify an entrée to fit a patron's special dietary needs); and (3) unsolicited tourism employee actions (inattention, rudeness, or thievery on the part of an employee). What was the negative break from the script the Johnsons faced in the chapter opener?

Fortunately, the research team discovered that all is not lost when a negative break from a script occurs. Customers will often give tourism providers a chance to make things right. When a tourism encounter is less than satisfactory, the tourism employee can right the situation and "turn the guest's frown upside down." This reversal of a service problem is called service recovery.[17] However, if a mistake is made and the employee does not make a sincere effort to better the guest's situation, highly memorable dissatisfaction occurs.

So, the bad news is that mistakes are inevitable in tourism businesses. The good news is that, with proper handling, a negative break

from the guest's script can be reversed and turned into an extra-satisfying, memorable service encounter. Keep in mind that satisfied guests represent potential future flows of revenues and profits, whereas dissatisfied guests represent future losses because they fail to return and they pass negative word-of-mouth comments to their friends.

Be a Can-Do Problem Solver

Most service unreliability is rooted in poorly designed service processes, inattention to detail, and simple carelessness. The tourism service team members need to have a "do-it-right-the-first-time" spirit. All team members, managers, and front-line employees should constantly search for fail points–steps in the process that are vulnerable to failure. Attention to these details and suggestions on improvements should be paramount in the minds of all team members. But we know that sometimes service will fail. What can be done then to try to retain the customer? Thankfully, there are several things.

When a customer complains or a service employee somehow senses that a service mistake has occurred, what happens next is critical to customer satisfaction. If the problem is ignored, the customer is likely to be furious and subsequently spread negative comments about the company. If the problem is handled but not to the customer's complete satisfaction, the customer is still likely to be dissatisfied and also speak ill of the experience. However, if the problem is solved, the guest is likely to be pleased and recount the story of the incident to friends. In this way, tourism service providers can take a bad situation and make it positive.

How can tourism managers ensure that problems are handled and their guests leave smiling? To solve problems, employees must know problems exist. Therefore, managers must encourage customers to voice their problems immediately so that employees can solve them. Because most guests are hesitant about voicing complaints, employees should also be trained to recognize problem situations so that they can fix the problem. And the problem solution needs to occur immediately. This quick response handling is most likely to occur when management

Laugh

Need help remembering the problem solution steps? Just LAUGH. Each letter of the word *laugh* stands for a step on the road to turning a dissatisfying encounter into a satisfying one. *L*isten. Let the guest relate the problem in detail and really listen to what is said. *A*cknowledge that the problem really is important. *U*nderstand. Indicate that you understand the situation by reviewing with the customer what has occurred. *G*ive solutions. Provide the guest with a variety of solutions to the problem, and allow him or her to choose the preferred solution. *H*it home with a follow-up. When possible, contact the guest a short time after the problem is solved to make sure that the guest is now satisfied.

gives employees the knowledge and authority to solve problems on their own, without having to check with supervisors.

"Making things right" for most customers simply involves doing a few simple things. Customers want acknowledgment that the problem exists. They also like to be told why the problem arose in the first place. Next, they want a sincere apology. Finally, customers want to be made "whole" again. In other words, they want some form of compensation that will lessen the cost of the problem to them. They need to be compensated for any bother or annoyance they perceived or experienced because of the problem. Which of these steps did Mike use in the chapter opener to make things right for the Johnsons?

Think of a recent situation in which you were less than satisfied with the service you received and voiced your dissatisfaction. What happened? Did the service employee respond appropriately, as we have just outlined? Did you leave frowning or smiling?

Correcting the immediate mistake and satisfying the customer are a great start to creating a truly service-oriented organization, but there is still more to do. Steps should be taken to make sure that the problem does not recur. This requires figuring out why the mistake happened and making operational or training changes so that it does not happen again. These changes could be very simple or creative. One example of a creative solution to a service problem comes from a theme park in South Korea. Managers were having trouble with employees sticking their hands in their pockets during work. The solution: Sew up the pockets until employees broke this annoying habit.

SERVICE GUARANTEES

One way to instill more confidence in guests regarding quality of service is by guaranteeing it. You are probably familiar with guarantees for hard goods. When a good you purchase, for example, a cell phone, proves to be unsatisfactory, producers frequently guarantee your satisfaction by offering you one or more options. In the case of dissatisfaction with a cell phone, the manufacturer may replace it, repair it, or refund your money. In the tourism service environment, it is more difficult to use these options. How does one "replace" an unsatisfactory visit to a theme park? How does management "repair" an unpleasant stay at a motel? You could get your money back, but that may not fully satisfy you. In most tourism services, one other important difference exists. You must complain face-to-face to another human being to get your money back or have your problem solved. Many of us do not like the confrontational nature of such direct complaining. Our server may "complain" back or become overly embarrassed by our complaint.

So how can a tourism service provider guarantee service quality? By using a customer satisfaction guarantee that has five important features[18]:

1. The guarantee should be unconditional with regard to the elements that are under the control of management and the employees. Airlines and other transportation providers cannot control the weather, but they can control most other aspects of your flight or ride experience.
2. The service guarantee should be easy to understand and communicate to guests.

It should be brief and worded very simply. Fine print and legal language should not be used to confuse the customer.

3. The guarantee should be meaningful, guaranteeing an important quality aspect to guests. For example, if speed of service (responsiveness) is an important element of quality to lunchtime restaurant patrons, the restaurant might use the following guarantee: "Your meal in just 5 minutes or it's free!"

4. The guarantee should be easy to collect. The customer should not have to "jump through hoops" to collect, and no guilt should be heaped on the guest for asking for the guaranteed **restitution**.

5. Compensation should be appropriate. How does management decide what is appropriate compensation for a service failure? Management needs to consider the price of the service to the customer in money but also the seriousness of the failure in inconvenience or other bother. Finally, but probably most important, what does the customer think is fair given the problem?

Companies that are excellent at problem solving give the customer a list of problem

Service Guarantees

Service guarantees come in many different forms. Some are in the form of a commitment. For example, management at the Best Rest Inn in Boise, Idaho, uses its welcome sign, "We delight every guest, every day, one guest at a time," as a statement of its service commitment. The Hampton Inn chain uses the slogan "Get what you expect—guaranteed!"

Others are more direct and detailed. For example, Holiday Inn calls its service guarantee its Hospitality Promise. The promise is prominently displayed in each guest room. It reads, "Making your stay a complete success is our goal. Just let our Manager on Duty or front desk staff know if any part of your stay isn't satisfactory. We promise to make it right or you won't pay for that part of your stay."

solution choices or ask the customer what would make him or her happy. In that way, the customer decides what the guarantee payout should be.

■ SUMMARY

Quality, hospitality, and satisfaction are all crucial concepts in tourism. To a large extent, quality is like beauty: It is "in the eye of the beholder." The marketing and management challenge lies in identifying how guests judge quality and then measuring these factors so service delivery can be continually improved. Guests judge the quality of a tourism service by five factors: (1) the tangibles of the tourism service, (2) the reliability of the service performance, (3) the responsiveness of employees, (4) the assurance they feel from the tourism provider, and (5) the empathy they are shown during their tourism experience. These five factors combine and yield a guest's overall quality perception.

Guests have expectations of tourism services that they compare to the actual service they receive. This comparison determines the level of satisfaction they feel. Guests can be highly satisfied, just satisfied, or dissatisfied with a tourism service. Quality is more variable in tourism services than in manufactured goods because so many factors can change the quality of the service, from the weather to the mood of the service employee. When guests are dissatisfied with a service, problem handling becomes paramount. Every effort should be made to fix the problem and satisfy the guest.

Tourism managers can ensure high-quality service and guest satisfaction by researching guest expectations, by acting on employee suggestions for improvements, by hiring and training employees well, and by emphasizing a team approach in service delivery. Providing guarantees for services is also an effective way to reassure customers and to focus employees' attention on the important aspects of service quality.

YOU DECIDE

What does quality mean to you? Does it mean the same thing to you as to everyone else? Do you expect the same level of service when dining at an upscale sit-down restaurant as you would expect at a quick-service restaurant? Your answer is probably no. The same comparison question could be asked about almost any group of tourism service providers and your answer would be similar.

However, in one segment of the tourism industry, this question has become an important issue for airline passengers in recent years. As the industry has struggled with profitability concerns and competitive pressures, it has become apparent that one size definitely does not fit all passengers when it comes to choices in air travel. If it doesn't matter how you get from point A to point B, all you need is a ticket. However, if you buy a ticket without knowing anything about the airline, you could find yourself flying on anything from a 400-passenger jet flying a nonstop route with snacks and in-flight movies to a 19-passenger turboprop with no service making multiple stops.

Low-cost carriers such as AirTran, Frontier, JetBlue, Southwest, and Ted think that their customers will define quality based on low price, frequency of flights, and on-time performance. And, they market their services as no-frills experiences. On the other hand, larger carriers such as American, Lufthansa, Singapore, Qantas, and United think that their customers will define quality in terms of a larger bundle of services such as in-flight meals, airport lounges, and extensive route systems. And, they market the expansiveness of their services. To add to this potentially confusing array there are also regional airlines such as Mesa and SkyWest that fly routes for many of the major airlines under something called code-share agreements. So, you could find yourself flying with a company that you might never have heard of.

These differing levels of marketed services have created a dilemma for both the airlines and their consumers. When customers see a particular brand, should they expect a specific level of service? As the airlines struggle to remain profitable, they have begun to blur not only the service lines between brand names but also who provides the service for their brand, as many carriers may be subcontracting these services to other independent carriers under code-share agreements.

Do customers make a conscious quality distinction between these brands or for that matter between carriers in general? What obligation do the airlines have to communicate these distinctions to their customers? What level of service do you think passengers expect or should expect when they purchase their tickets on any of these flights?

NET TOUR

To get you started on exploring Internet links for this chapter, enter the phrase "tourism service quality" into your favorite search engine, or please see

http://www.quality.nist.gov
http://corporate.ritzcarlton.com
http://fourseasons.com

DISCUSSION QUESTIONS

1. Define quality using the many meanings the word can have.
2. Explain why the quality of tourism services is harder to define and manage than the quality of hard goods.
3. How are expectations of a tourism service formed?
4. What is a break from the service script? How do breaks from the script affect customer satisfaction?
5. What should a tourism service employee do to "turn a frown upside down"?
6. What can management do to ensure high-quality service?

■ APPLYING THE CONCEPTS

1. Use an airline flight to illustrate the service as theater concepts highlighted in Figure 3.3.
2. Choose a local tourism supplier and rate it on the five dimensions of quality. Why does it rate high, average, or low on each dimension? Be detailed in your answers.
3. Describe a recent tourism service encounter in which a service mistake was handled to your satisfaction or dissatisfaction. What was done, or could have been done, to turn your frown upside down?
4. Develop a service guarantee for a tourism service with which you are familiar. Critique your guarantee using the five important features of service guarantees.

■ GLOSSARY

Actual quality   The level of quality a consumer perceives following the consumption of a good or service.

Expected quality   The level of quality that a consumer predicts he or she will receive from a good or service.

Expected script   The set of steps and statements that a guest expects to occur during a service encounter.

Facilitating goods   Tangible items that support or accompany a service being provided.

Learning organization   An organization committed to identifying best practices and creating systems to achieve high-quality standards.

Marketing communications   Any communication between a marketer and a consumer.

Market share   The percent of the total market for a good or service that a single company has.

Restitution   An amount of money or other item given to make up for some mistake or wrongdoing.

Service encounter   A single episode during which a customer and service personnel interact; often also called a "moment of truth."

Service expectations   The quality level of the five dimensions of service expected by a customer.

Service recovery   The process of reversing a service problem.

Service script   Learned patterns of behavior that guide interactions during a service encounter.

Specification   A detailed written description of a procedure or ingredient.

Standard   A predetermined procedure or amount of an ingredient.

■ REFERENCES

1. Dorn, Charles C. (2008, February). Breakfast . . . it's not just bacon & eggs anymore. *AAHOA Lodging Business*, pp. 34–36.
2. Lovelock, Christopher H., and Wirtz, Jochen. (2007). *Services marketing* (6th ed.). Upper Saddle River, NJ: Prentice Hall, Inc.
3. Buzzell, Robert D., and Gale, Bradley T. (1987). *The PIMS principles: Linking strategy to performance.* New York: Free Press.
4. Solomon, Michael R., Surprenant, Carol, Czepiel, John A., and Gutman, Evelyn G. (1985). A role theory perspective on dyadic interactions: The service encounter. *Journal of Marketing*, 49, 99–111.
5. Bateson, John E. G. (1995). *Managing services marketing: Text and readings* (3rd ed.). Fort Worth, TX: Dryden Press/Harcourt Brace College Publishers.
6. Parasuraman, A., Zeithaml, Valarie, and Berry, Leonard. (1985). A conceptual model of service quality and its implications for future research. *Journal of Marketing*, 49, 41–50.
7. Oliver, Richard L. (1980). A cognitive model of the antecedents and consequences of satisfaction decisions. *Journal of Marketing Research*, 17, 460–469.
8. Jones, Thomas O., and Sasser, W. Earl, Jr. (1995, November–December). Why satisfied customers defect. *Harvard Business Review*, pp. 88–99.
9. Zeithaml, Valarie, Parasuraman, A., and Berry, Leonard L. (1990). *Delivering quality service.* New York: Free Press.
10. Schlesinger, Leonard. (1991). *Taco Bell Corp. Harvard Business School case.* Cambridge, MA: Harvard Business School Publishing.

11. Dvorak, Phred. (2007, December 17). Hotelier finds happiness keeps staff checked in. *Wall Street Journal,* p. B3.

12. O'Brien, Jeffery M. (2008). A perfect season. Fortune, 157(2), 62–66.

13. Berry, Leonard L., Zeithaml, Valarie A., and Parasuraman, A. (1990). Five imperatives for improving service quality. *Sloan Management Review,* 31, 29–38.

14. Enz, Cathy, and Siguaw, Judy A. (2000). Best practices in human resources. *Cornell Hotel & Restaurant Quarterly,* 41(1), 48–61.

15. Solomon, Michael R., Surprenant, Carol, Czepiel, John A., and Gutman, Evelyn G. (1985). A role theory perspective on dyadic interactions: The service encounter. *Journal of Marketing,* 49, 99–111.

16. Bitner, Mary Jo, Booms, Bernard H., and Tetreault, Mary Stanfield. (1990). The service encounter: Diagnosing favorable and unfavorable incidents. *Journal of Marketing,* 54, 71–84.

17. Hart, Christopher W. L., Heskett, James L., and Sasser, W. Earl. (1990). The profitable art of service recovery. *Harvard Business Review,* 68, 148–156.

18. Hart, Christopher W. L. (1988). The power of unconditional service guarantees. *Harvard Business Review,* 66, 54–62.

Tourism's History

Many factors of the Greek Empire combined to make tourism possible.
Nigel Hicks © Dorling Kindersley

Venice, Italy—a primary stop during the Grand Tour era.
Demetrio Carrasco © Dorling Kindersley

The Traveling Public

The beauty and mystery of the Taj Majal in India attracts near, allocentric travelers.
Photo by C. E. Yale.

London is a favorite city for a variety of tourist segments.
Photo by D. A. Yale

Quality Hospitality

Old Faithful geyser in Yellowstone National Park—always true to its name!
Andy Holligan © Dorling Kindersley

Careful attention to the dimensions of quality
yields highly satisfying service encounters.
Linda Whitwam © Dorling Kindersley

Bringing Travelers and Tourism Suppliers Together

Bus tours offer travelers an informative travelogue of a new city.
Gunter Marx © Dorling Kindersley

Hong Kong serves as China's window to the world. *Chris Stowers © Dorling Kindersley*

LEARNING OBJECTIVES

After you have read this chapter, you should be able to:

- Explain the importance of intermediaries in the distribution of tourism services.
- Identify and describe the three different types of distribution channels that are used for tourism services.
- Describe the roles of travel agencies in bringing tourists and tourism providers together.
- Describe the roles of tour wholesalers in bringing tourists and tourism service providers together.
- Explain how and why the Internet has changed the distribution of tourism services.
- Identify and describe how travelers access information for tourism services.

CHAPTER OUTLINE

CHAPTER

4

Bringing Travelers and Tourism Service Suppliers Together

There are no such things as service industries. There are only industries whose service components are greater or less than those of other industries. Everybody is in service.

—Theodore Levitt Former Editor, *Harvard Business Review*, In *The Marketing Imagination*, Free Press, 1986

■ Tour guides add a personal touch to the travel experience.

ONE STOP DOES IT ALL!

Kristin Hatten has just stepped into the office and already the phone is ringing and the message light is blinking. This workday will probably be just like every other workday in her life as a travel agent—always different. The demands of the day will require that she be a true multiprocessor, handling several tasks at once, from answering the phone to entering, retrieving, and verifying data from a sophisticated computer reservation system, searching the Internet, and responding to a multitude of emails. At the same time, during all these tasks she must focus her attention on the ultimate goal of providing high-quality customer service. As a travel agent, Kristin serves as an important link between suppliers in the tourism industry and her clients.

As a front-line service employee, Kristin faces a demanding public that often does not understand the constantly changing industry rules and prices with which she must work. On any given day, she may receive information about changing regulations and prices as well as invitations for seminars and **familiarization trips** from airlines, hotels, resorts, cruise lines, rental car companies, and a host of other tourism service suppliers. Kristin must sort through this information to learn more about the services that will meet the needs of her clients.

Kristin will spend most of her day answering the phone and serving customers who walk through the door seeking help with their travel plans. She will deal with a wide variety of customers, ranging from her regular business clients who know what they want to first-time customers who have little knowledge about travel and tourism in general. The uncertainties that fill each day can make her job stressful, but the opportunity to learn more about the world and help others meet their travel needs keeps Kristin going.

At the end of a particularly hectic day, she takes a moment to think about her list of appointments and calls to be made the next day. Most of the calls are from her typical leisure customers and require only providing information on basic scheduling options. As she continues reviewing the list, Kristin notices one appointment that she is particularly looking forward to. Mr. and Mrs. Gildea phoned last week to discuss an upcoming trip they were planning from Lethbridge, Canada, to Hawaii. After obtaining some brief information about the Gildeas and their needs, Kristin scheduled an early morning appointment.

Looking at the notes she took during that phone conversation, Kristin begins thinking about the types of information and services the Gildeas might want. The Gildeas, a recently retired couple, have always wanted to visit Hawaii and return home with pictures and stories they could share with friends and relatives. They have been reading extensively about the attractions and have some ideas of where they want to go and what they want to see and do, but they are interested in any suggestions Kristin might offer. Before she leaves for the day, Kristin prints out several different itineraries and gathers brochures, Web addresses, and other information that she feels will help the Gildeas in making their plans for an unforgettable experience.

INTRODUCTION

When people travel, they need a whole range of tourism services. These services may include airline tickets, car rentals, places to stay, places to eat, places to shop, tickets and admissions to attractions, and information about things to do and see. In this chapter, we will explore the basic concepts of services and how marketing, management, and finance decisions have an impact on the way travelers access the services of tourism suppliers. The success and profitability of tourism service suppliers depend on their ability to reach and meet targeted customers' needs effectively and efficiently.

As you learned in Chapter 2, by dividing the larger tourism market into distinctive groups, we can plan and provide services that are targeted to the needs of a specific segment of the tourism market. Once these target customers and their needs have been identified, the goal of service suppliers becomes reaching, serving, and satisfying their needs profitably. This is not an easy task because "competition today demands that service be delivered faster, cheaper, and without defects."[1] By referring to our model of tourism in Figure 1.2, you will see that many different organizations and approaches have been developed to accomplish this task. In this chapter, we will explore the basic concepts of services and discover how travelers obtain information about and access to tourism services.

SERVING TRAVELER NEEDS

Remember Thomas Cook, who organized and conducted the first large **tour** in 1841? He used a variety of marketing, management, and financial skills as he packaged, sold, and escorted that first organized tour. Cook negotiated reduced fares on a train trip between Loughborough and Leicester, England, and arranged for picnic lunches and afternoon tea for almost 600 people. He was serving as an **intermediary**. As an intermediary, he did not work for the railroad company or the bakery, but he sold their services and goods. His clients benefited from his efforts because he took care of their needs while saving them money; the suppliers benefited from his efforts because they received increased revenues without having to spend additional monies attracting more customers.

Once an organization has developed a service offering, it must be made available for customer use. Consumers are often unable to sample or even see services before purchasing, so they rely primarily on information to make their purchase decisions. Determining how this information will be made available and how travelers will obtain the services they need involves a variety of decisions. For example, should the organization deal with customers directly, or should it rely on others to attract and inform customers about its services? How much money should be spent on attracting customers? Does the organization have the people and talent to distribute information about its services efficiently and effectively, and, at the same time, achieve the desired levels of profit, service quality, and satisfaction?

In answering these questions, managers need to consider two key issues. The first deals with who should be involved in bringing travelers and tourism service suppliers together, and the second deals with how to manage these activities. A simple example will help highlight these issues.

Consider for a minute a small coastal resort located in South Carolina. It would probably not have the money or the marketing staff to reach all of its desired target customers effectively. Rather than attempting to accomplish this task alone, the manager of the resort could rely on the help of others. The state tourism office, local visitors bureau, membership in a regional reservations system, cooperative brochures including other local attractions, an interactive website, participation in a referral system, and a listing in *Hotel & Travel Index* would provide just a few possibilities for informing and attracting potential guests. However, even with all of these efforts, the resort may still not reach enough of its targeted audience to be profitable. To close this information loop, the resort might rely on the professional services of travel agents such as Kristin Hatten, whom we met in the chapter opener. As you will see in this chapter, these are just a few of the alternatives a manager should consider when attempting to reach potential customers.

Travelers need access to a wide variety of tourism services. These services may be as simple as having questions answered about the availability of services or as complex as purchasing an **all-inclusive** prepackaged tour. No matter how simple or how complex the needs are, there are several types of distribution channels that can be used to access tourism services and information about these services. These channels may range all the way from one-level direct access to more complex three-level arrangements involving several intermediaries. Figure 4.1 shows typical one-, two-, and three-level distribution channels for tourism services.

WHY USE INTERMEDIARIES?

Although tourism service suppliers such as airlines, theme parks, and restaurants may reach some of their customers directly, they can also use the distribution services provided by one or more intermediaries. Intermediaries perform a vital

One-level   Two-level   Three-level

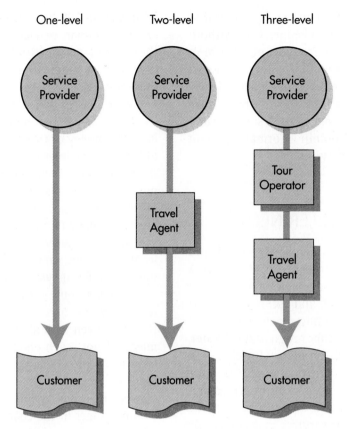

■ **Figure 4.1** Distribution channels.

function for tourism service suppliers by making the suppliers' services available to large numbers of potential customers in a cost-effective way. These services may be as simple as providing directions for a motorist at a welcome center to more complex service activities such as packaging, selling, and then escorting tour groups.

Intermediaries in tourism distribution channels perform a variety of value-adding functions. Examples of just a few of these distribution functions are:

- Providing information about the types and availability of service offerings
- Contacting current and potential customers
- Making reservations and other travel arrangements
- Assembling services to meet customer needs
- Preparing tickets and/or providing confirmations
- Providing extensive marketing data to tourism suppliers through databases

containing targeted consumer behavior information
- Reducing costs of acquiring new customers
- Encouraging repeat use of supplier channels
- Marketing excess inventories
- Risk taking by buying or booking large quantities of services in advance and then reselling them to individuals and groups

The expenses of selling services through an intermediary typically occur in the form of **commissions** and do not arise until the services have been sold or used. The company providing the final service such as the cruise line, hotel, resort, or attraction pays the commission on each ticket sold or reservation used. Increasingly, users are paying some type of service fee to compensate for the demise of commissions. Services may also be purchased in large quantities at reduced costs and resold at higher prices called markups.

Credit card companies are becoming important intermediaries in the distribution of tourism services. Companies such as American Express provide an array of services such as reserving theater tickets and golf tee times for groups of travelers that frequently purchase travel services. In addition to these services to travelers, they also can provide key marketing information to suppliers through their data mining capabilities. Specific service offerings can then be targeted to meet customer needs.

ONE-LEVEL (DIRECT) DISTRIBUTION CHANNELS

One-level distribution channels are the simplest form of distribution, providing travelers with direct access to tourism suppliers. In this type of distribution channel, suppliers deal directly with travelers without the assistance of intermediaries. Airlines, car rental companies, passenger railroads, lodging facilities, resorts, restaurants, theme parks, and attractions all engage in promotions and advertising to encourage people to purchase their products and services directly. These advertising and promotion programs also serve to generate business for other travel intermediaries, such as travel agencies and tour operators.

Information technology offers another promising format for bringing service suppliers and customers together through the touch of a keyboard or the click of a mouse. Services such as electronic travel brochures and basic information about airlines, international rail service, passenger bus lines, car rental companies, cruise lines, hotels/motels, and resorts can be accessed through a variety of online services and Internet connections.

The future holds many exciting challenges and opportunities for tourism marketers and service suppliers. How we access and use tourism information is changing radically as information technologies develop and improve. Advances in computer technology have made it possible for travelers to visit faraway places without ever leaving their homes or offices. They can connect to reservation systems through their personal computers, search for related travel information, book flights, and make other travel arrangements and reservations. We will take a more in-depth look at the transformational role of technology in the tourism industry in Chapter 5.

Airlines have encouraged many of these changes because they help reduce operating expenses and develop brand loyalty. "The Internet has brought fundamental change to the economy and to how commerce is conducted. Many businesses use the Internet as a way to bypass product and service intermediaries to deal directly with consumers."[2]

Traditional channels of distribution of tourism services have evolved to incorporate Internet technologies. Although direct channels, especially **call centers,** have been used by many tourism suppliers in the past, the increased use of the Internet makes the direct channel a more feasible and cost-effective option for suppliers to reach their consumers. As travelers have become comfortable with information technology and power of the Internet, they view it as a do-it-yourself means to search for tourism service information and for the booking and purchase of travel services.

TWO-LEVEL DISTRIBUTION CHANNELS

Two-level distribution channels are more complex than one-level direct-access channels. In a two-level channel, **travel agents** or planners serve as intermediaries bringing suppliers and consumers together. Bringing another person or organization in between tourism service suppliers and the traveler may at first seem a bit more complex than the one-level approach to distribution that we just described. However, it can simplify the travel process for consumers and it is often more efficient and effective for tourism suppliers.

Travel Agencies

Although technology has changed, travel agencies still provide important sales and information links between tourism service suppliers and the traveling public. One of the most popular forms of purchasing tourism services is still through travel agencies led by American Express, Navigant, Travel Leaders, and World Travel Partners.[3] However, the form of travel agency being used is changing from brick and mortar to online. Whether through a personal touch or online point-and-click interfaces, travel agencies act as focal points for many of the sales and reservation activities in the travel industry. Although the Internet has created an environment where various transactions bypass them, many travel arrangements, especially those involving high-end or complex arrangements, still involve this intermediary function.[4] In addition, with the phenomenal growth of the big three Internet travel agencies—Expedia, Travelocity, and Orbitz—travel agencies have now become the department stores of the tourism industry.

One segment of the tourism industry, cruise lines, has developed and nurtured a close working relationship with travel agents. "There are good reasons 90% of cruises are still booked with agents. A ship can have 35 different room types and a myriad of onboard charges. An experienced agent can help navigate the complexities and may be able to snag fare discounts, cabin upgrades and other perks."[5]

Individuals filling the travel agent role offer a wide variety of services, including providing information to travelers, making reservations, and securing other services and travel-related documents. Individual travelers can perform many of these same functions themselves through Internet travel agencies, also called online travel agencies. However, no matter which type of agency is used, these agencies do not take title to (own) the services they are selling. Figure 4.2 shows the flow of payments, information, and delivery of services that are purchased and consumed by travelers through travel agencies.

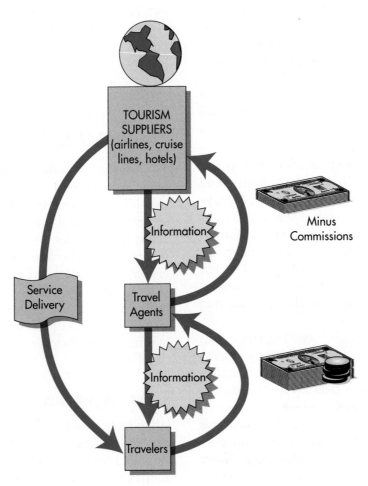

■ **Figure 4.2** Flow of payments, information, and service delivery.

Travel agencies serve as sales outlets and are compensated on a markup or commission basis by most of the service suppliers with the exception of airlines. Commissions are based on the level of sales, which are referred to as "bookings." **Markups** are the difference between the price for which travel agencies can obtain the service and the price they can charge when selling the service. As you will see later, the commissions that travel agencies can earn are being reduced or eliminated. Service suppliers sometimes view them as expenses to be controlled, and customers sometimes think it is quicker and cheaper to deal directly with the service supplier. However, because travel agencies, especially Internet-based agencies, continue to play a critical role in facilitating the distribution process, let's take a more detailed look at their operations.

The beginning of travel agencies goes back to the glory years of railroads and steamship lines, when agents sold tickets for these carriers and received a commission for their efforts. Thomas Cook, whom you read about previously, started the concept of the travel agent. By making travel arrangements simple and affordable, he was able to attract growing numbers of people to explore places away from their homes and villages.

By the late 1800s, the idea of seeking help for travel arrangements had made its way to the States. A gift shop owner in St. Augustine, Florida, can be credited with starting the idea of a travel agency in the United States. Although he probably never planned to be a travel agent, his knowledge of geography, rail schedules, and hotels soon led him to be the local source for travel information. When anyone had a question about travel, he or she was sent to "Ask Mr. Foster." In 1888, Ward G. Foster turned his love of geography and his hobby of studying maps, transportation, and destinations into Ask Mr. Foster Travel. Ask Mr. Foster continued to grow and eventually became part of one of the largest travel agencies in the world, Carlson Wagonlit Travel, now Travel Leaders.[6]

From these small service-oriented beginnings, travel agencies have evolved and adapted to an electronic world to become an integral link in the tourism distribution system. These agents are no longer just order takers who spend the entire business day making bookings at the client's direction. In fact, only a small portion of an agent's day is spent actually making reservations. Travel agents, as consultants, spend much of their time researching travel products and conferring with clients.[7]

Many travel agencies, brick and mortar as well as online, specialize by focusing their efforts on large target markets such as business or leisure customers, whereas others serve a general group of customers, or a specific market niche such as cruise-only customers. Even though there are many types of agencies (see Table 4.1) serving different types of customer needs, they all typically provide a common group of services called a "product mix." These services include providing an **itinerary**; airline, rail, and cruise reservations with ticketing confirmations; car rental, accommodation, and activity reservations; **tour packages**; travel insurance; theater and event ticketing; and general travel information from necessary travel documents to current weather information. As a consumer, recognize the professional status of travel agents and focus your attention on the questions shown in Table 4.2.

The growth in Internet agencies has continued to encroach on the traditional brick-and-mortar customer base. Whereas in the past, a travel agency was largely limited in clientele to its small geographic territory, the Internet has made possible the servicing of clients who are thousands of miles away. Through the use of websites and electronic mail, agents now compete with virtually all other agents, regardless of where they are located. And, Internet-based agencies are beginning to look a bit more like traditional storefront travel agencies as they attempt to move from promoting the lowest possible prices to planning and customizing trips based on individual interests by adding more planning tools for customers.[8]

Maintaining profitability within the highly competitive travel agency business requires a combined effort focused on generating sales, offering high-quality customer service, and controlling operating costs. Remember that travel agencies depend on their marketing abilities and programs to generate sales for other tourism suppliers and receive only a portion of these sales in the form of commissions or markups. So,

Table 4.1	Travel Agency Types

Independent agencies—small agencies, privately owned, unaffiliated with any larger organization; less than 40% of all travel agencies; traditionally serving clients from a walk-in office location or over the telephone.

Agency chains—wholly owned—mega-agencies that have dozens to hundreds of branch offices throughout a region, country, or worldwide.

Agency chains—franchises—semi-independent agencies affiliated with each other through franchise agreements.

Consortium-affiliated agencies—independent agencies that link together through a consortium to gain the financial benefits of a chain but have lower fees and commissions.

Specialty agencies—agencies that offer limited services, such as cruise-only agencies.

Corporate travel agencies—agencies that provide services to business clients but not regularly to the general public. A corporate travel agency is a private enterprise that specializes in business clientele and may have branch offices on-site at major clients' locations. These agencies are frequently compensated by management fees rather than commissions on the travel services they sell.

Corporate travel department—similar to a corporate travel agency but agents are employees of the organization in a department that handles most if not all of the travel needs of the organization's employees.

Home-based agencies—agents who conduct their services from their homes, using electronic technology, rather than from an office location in which clients meet with the agent in person; may be independent or affiliated with some organization (e.g., consortium or chain).

Internet agencies—either opaque (hiding service supplier, e.g., Priceline) or transparent (showing service supplier, e.g., Travelocity). Other agencies in this category may be home based, serving clients primarily through the Internet, and use telephone, fax, and postal communications to a lesser degree than traditional agencies.

a small travel agency that generates $1 million in sales may receive only $80,000 in commissions and markups to cover operating expenses and earn a profit. As commissions continue to dwindle, brick-and-mortar travel agencies must rely on increasing service fees (see Table 4.3). In contrast, online travel agencies rely mainly on markups for their profitability.

Table 4.2	Four Questions to Ask a Travel Agent

1. *What are your qualifications?* Expect an agent to have credentials just as you would an accountant or other advisor. What certifications does the agent have? What industry affiliations does he or she hold? Is the agency part of a greater network of agencies? Is the agent a specialist or expert in a particular industry sector (e.g., cruises) or area of the world (Asia)?

2. *What are your relationships with specific industry members?* Special relationships with a certain airline, cruise line, or hotel chain can work for and against the agency's clients. Links to a cruise line, for example, may result in stateroom upgrades for the agency's clients but may also mean that the agency will "push" the cruise line rather than recommending one that better matches your needs or personality.

3. *What will you charge and what will I receive for your fee?* Ask what fees will be charged and determine whether the expertise of the agent is worth the money. An expert on Africa who has booked many trips in the last six months is assuredly worth a $100 fee.

4. *What are your phone numbers?* Agents should return calls promptly and should be available in emergencies to solve problems. The agents who are most worth their salt are those who will go to bat for you when trouble arises while you're halfway around the world from their office.

Source: Based on Loftus, Margaret. (2003, March). The new travel agent. *National Geographic Traveler*, p. 18.

Table 4.3	Ideas for Service Fees

1. Get a commitment deposit, which applies to the cost of the trip.
2. Charge a consultation fee of $50 to $75 for cruise bookings.
3. Charge fees of at least $10 to $15 for booking hotels and rental cars.
4. Corporate agents should use a fully unbundled approach to selling products and services. Services that can be unbundled include document delivery, management reports, and 24-hour emergency services.
5. Corporate agents should charge a "success fee" for vendor negotiations. (For example, if the fee is 25%, agents can earn $250 if they save the client $1,000 during a hotel negotiation.)

Source: Agent life. (2004, January 5). *Travel Weekly,* p. 24.

Because the most efficient brick-and-mortar travel agencies are able to make only a few pennies of profit on each sales dollar, maintaining the financial health of the business by controlling expenses such as salaries and benefits, rent, computer reservation systems, advertising and promotion, utilities, repairs and maintenance, insurance, and other miscellaneous items becomes an important managerial task. Online agencies may have fewer personnel and office costs, but they face higher technology costs as systems must be upgraded constantly and maintained 24 hours a day, seven days a week.

Airline deregulation and the subsequent elimination of commissions on airline ticket sales have brought about many changes in the operation of travel agencies. Although airlines no longer pay commissions, they do allow large-volume travel agencies to earn **overrides** and frequently provide them with "conversion ability" for large volumes of business to their routes. This is the ability to convert a regular full-economy-priced airline reservation to a discounted fare price when all discounted seats are sold out. These two factors have encouraged agency owners and managers to seek affiliation through a **franchise** or a **consortium** to gain the necessary volume of business that can lead to improved profitability.

The Internet also has made the at-home agent more competitive with the in-office agent because the Web client need never know that there is no office (and all its associated expenses) at the other end of the phone or Internet communication link. Some larger agencies are outsourcing to small home-based agencies to serve clients better by offering after-hours reservations, service recovery assistance, information, and so on.

Internet and online agencies have forever changed the role of today's travel agent (see Table 4.4). The typical travel agent role was very transactional—processing reservations—and focused on a few sequential travel logistics—for the most part air, car, and hotel. Today's travel agent has expanded greatly on that traditional role. Travel agents have adopted a much more consultative role, serving as a travel concierge, and go to great lengths to influence the travel guest's overall experience. They are arranging to have their travel guest's luggage delivered door-to-door, making theater and dinner reservations, setting up golf tee times, and arranging for spa treatments. Travel agents are increasingly expected to be subject experts on destination markets, and so we see these travel experts focusing on markets where they have the ability to make informed recommendations on shopping, night life, and even where the "locals" eat. Experienced travel agents having specific knowledge of where to find or avoid travel services such as singles-only, gay, nude, and seniors-only hotels, resorts, and cruises can make or break a vacation.

Although many predictions were made about the demise of the travel agent in an Internet era, the reverse has happened. After a prolonged dip in revenues, travel agencies began to grow as customers sought service. Travelers soon discovered they did not have the time or did not care to invest the effort in finding the best deal. They also were seeking to talk to a person rather than punching buttons to work their way through an automated call system only to be put on hold. With airlines scaling back on staffing in call centers, travel agents have gone back to

Table 4.4	Travel Agents' Changing Role

Travel Agents	
Pre-Internet Role	*Post-Internet Role*
■ Transactional focus ■ Process transactions and concentrate on travel logistics ■ Book air, lodging, and car ■ Majority of compensation from suppliers through commissions ■ Little or no follow-up with clients	■ Travel experience focus ■ Manage overall travel experience ■ Book air, car, and hotel ■ Majority of compensation from markups and service fees Concierge orientation: ■ Door-to-door delivery of sports equipment and luggage ■ Theater tickets ■ Restaurant reservations ■ Golf tee times ■ Spa treatments, etc.

the basics of providing customer service. The result? Many travel agencies are now experiencing double-digit growth.[9]

Improving Service Delivery Through Cooperative Systems

The majority of all travel agency business is conducted through **global distribution systems (GDSs)**, which provide access to a wealth of data about tourism service suppliers. GDSs allow travel agents as well as the general public to obtain online information on space availability, schedules, rates, and fares. They also provide the means of booking reservations and printing itineraries, tickets, and invoices. **Computer reservation systems (CRSs)** linked to Sabre or Travelport serve as databases for tourism services and travel information as well as reservation systems. Information and reservations for tourism services such as hotels, rental cars, cruises, tours, and more are now standard features.

Because the majority of travel agency revenues are derived from overrides; commissions on hotels, tours, and cruise line reservations; and service fees, appointment and accreditation by two key agencies are critical to continued success. The **Airlines Reporting Corporation (ARC)** and the International Airline Travel Agency Network (IATAN) operate the financial networks and clearinghouses that allow travel agencies to sell airline tickets. ARC accreditation is the most important because it handles transactions for domestic airlines, many international airlines, and Amtrak and Britrail as well. IATAN handles transactions for the international airlines that are not processed through the ARC system.

Whereas airlines have virtually reduced commissions to zero, hotel companies, especially Marriott, seem to be taking a different approach. By passing a product knowledge test and being certified as a Preferred Travel Agency, Marriott guarantees agencies a full 10% commission plus other money-saving and educational benefits. Travel agencies that do not participate in the program will see their commission rates reduced to 8%. The program called Hotel Excellence! is available in ten languages and teaches travel planners how to sell hotel services.

The equivalents to the ARC in the accommodations sector of the tourism industry may be Hotel Clearing Corporation's Pegasus Solutions. Pegasus serves thousands of hotel properties and travel agencies around the world by collecting and consolidating hotel commissions.[10]

THREE-LEVEL DISTRIBUTION CHANNELS

Three-level distribution channels involve many of the same activities and characteristics found in the previously described two-level or indirect-access channels. However, they bring in another layer of intermediaries, such as **tour operators** and convention and visitors bureaus, who market tours and facilitate the process of bringing travelers and tourism suppliers together. Many travel agencies are also becoming active participants in these distribution channels as they package and sell tours, especially in the motorcoach market.

Tour operators serve to both create and at the same time anticipate demand by purchasing or reserving large blocks of space and services to be resold in the form of tours at reduced rates in packages. Tour operators do not typically work on a commission basis like travel agents but on a markup basis. They buy large blocks of services such as airline seats and hotel rooms at very favorable prices by guaranteeing minimum levels of revenues or by making nonrefundable deposits and then resell these services at a higher price. Tour operators are a particularly significant intermediary in the tourism industry because they supply packages for travel agencies to sell, as well as buying services from airlines, cruise lines, hotels, resorts, car rental companies, and many other tourism suppliers. "Traditionally, wholesalers have provided 60 to 70 percent of all room revenue for tourism-driven destinations such as Hawaii, the Caribbean, and Europe. Large wholesalers such as Happy Tours, Blue Sky Tours, and Classic sell exclusively to retail travel agencies, who in turn market directly to the client."[11]

Tours

The word *tour,* as defined by the United States Tour Operators Association (USTOA), "encompasses a broad and varied array of products, ranging from highly structured escorted packages to a collection of independent components travelers piece together themselves." Tour packages include at least two of the following elements: transportation, accommodations, meals, entertainment, attractions, and sightseeing activities. Packages vary widely in the number of elements included and in the structure of the itinerary. Listed here are some of the more common types of tour packages.

■ **Independent tour**—the least structured tour package. Hotel "escape" weekends featuring accommodations, some meals, and possibly

a rental car qualify as independent tours, as does Disney's Resort Magic package, which includes car rental, accommodations, and entrance to all of the Walt Disney theme and water parks. Purchasers of independent tours set their itineraries themselves.

■ **Foreign independent tours (FITs)/domestic independent tours (DITs)**—customized tours including many elements designed and planned to fulfill the particular needs of a traveler. FITs and DITs may be designed by a travel agent or by a wholesaler in consultation with the traveler's agent.

■ **Hosted tour**—provides buyers with a number of tourism supplier elements plus the services of a local host who is available to give advice, make special arrangements, and iron out any problems that may occur.

■ **Escorted tour**—the most structured of tour types and usually the most complete in the elements included for the package price. An escorted tour begins and ends on a set date and follows a specific, detailed itinerary. A tour escort accompanies tour members throughout the tour. Most escorted tours use motorcoaches with experienced drivers to transport travelers for all or part of the tour. Escorted tours are very popular with tourists traveling to exotic locations or in areas of the world where few members of the native population are likely to speak the traveler's language.[12]

Why would a traveler prefer to purchase a tour package rather than buy from individual tourism suppliers? The reasons are many but benefits include:

1. *Convenience.* Purchasing a package allows the decision-making process to be shortened so that the traveler does not need to spend a lot of time deciding what to do and which supplier to use. Often all the details including **ground transfers,** tipping, and baggage handling are included, alleviating worry about the little things.

2. *One-stop shopping.* The buying process is also made easier; one payment covers the cost and paperwork of two or more

services. All-inclusive tours can be virtually cash free and allow the traveler to know how much the trip will cost without the fear of being "nickeled and dimed" along the way.

3. *Cost savings.* In most cases, tour packages are less expensive than the cost if the tourist were to purchase all of its elements separately. Tour wholesalers are able to take advantage of volume discounts and usually pass on some of the cost savings to tour purchasers.

4. *Special treatment.* Because of the volume of business tour operators represent to service suppliers, tour members tend to receive preferential treatment. For example, tour group members rarely stand in long lines or park far away from entrances to attractions.

5. *Worry free.* When traveling on a hosted or escorted tour, tourists are able to concentrate on the experiences and new world around them, leaving problems and details in the hands of tour personnel. In addition, as a participant of an escorted tour, travelers have a ready-made group of new friends accompanying them, increasing the fun.[13]

Tour packages are usually sold through retail travel agents who are typically paid a 10%

commission for the selling efforts they provide the tour wholesaler. Travel agents distribute tour brochures and consult various sources, such as the *Official Tour Directory* and *Jax Fax Travel Marketing Magazine,* published monthly to match client desires to available tours.

Tour Operators

Tour operators are, by definition, business organizations engaged in planning, preparing, marketing, and, at times, operating vacation tours. The terms *packager, wholesale tour operator, tour operator, tour wholesaler,* and *wholesaler* often are used interchangeably. In almost every case, the company acting as a wholesaler also operates the tours it creates or packages.[14]

Although there are many different names that can be used to describe this distribution function, for simplicity, we will use the term *tour operator.* Tour operators may work with all segments of the tourism industry to negotiate rates, block space, and coordinate the myriad details found in a tour package at an inclusive price. Some of the larger well-known wholesalers and operators are listed in Table 4.5.

The tour business holds a certain mystique for many people who like to travel and think that they would like to arrange and package travel

Dynamic Packaging

The Internet has permanently altered the way vacation packages are created, marketed, and priced. The newest technology being leveraged throughout the travel industry is **dynamic packaging**. Consumers can now purchase packages from a variety of sites including online agencies, hoteliers, and airlines. The choices and types of options have never been so broad. Internet travel continues to grow rapidly, and package sales have emerged as one of the leading growth categories. The role of dynamic packaging technology is to bundle all the components chosen by the traveler to create one reservation. Regardless of where the inventory originates, the package that is created is handled seamlessly as one transaction and requires only one payment from the consumer. It automatically applies rules defined by the suppliers and the travel

marketer to build and price travel packages. This package configuration process determines which components are used, what combinations of components are allowed or required, and handles inclusions such as taxes, fees, or additional package features. Rules also determine how the final retail price is computed.

For suppliers and distributors, dynamic packaging facilitates dynamic pricing. It applies pricing to a "package," thereby allowing greater margins to be realized by travel marketers and sellers than can be realized by individual pricing of every component within a package for consumer comparison. Comparison shopping forces suppliers into the uncomfortable position of commodity pricing. Dynamic packaging allows travel suppliers and sellers to sell instead on value, features, and benefits.

Table 4.5	Do You Recognize the Names of Any of These Tour Operators?
Abercrombie & Kent International Certified Vacations Collette Travel Service Dertravel Services Globus & Cosmos	Gogo Worldwide Vacations Holland America Line–Westours Japan & Orient Tours Tauck Tours Trafalgar Tours/Contiki Holidays

and tourism services for others. However, the tour business is extremely risky. Both tour operators and wholesalers are an unregulated segment of the industry because there are no entry requirements for licensing, bonding, or insurance. Although every segment of the tourism industry deals with highly perishable services, the problem of perishability is compounded in the tour business. Once a tour has departed, there is no way to sell additional seats on the tour and receive revenues for services that have already been reserved and, in most cases, paid for in advance.

In addition, tour wholesalers and operators often must commit to prices for services far in advance and are therefore faced with the potential problems of inflation and foreign currency fluctuations that may reduce their profit margins. If that weren't enough, there are the additional problems of natural disasters, political unrest, and changing consumer tastes, which are all outside the control of the tour operator.

Realizing all of these potential problems, it becomes critical for successful tour operators to control costs, competitively price the packages they offer, and market these packages to the appropriate target market(s). Assembling a package that interests consumers and then pricing it competitively becomes a tricky issue because tour operators must work with a very thin markup, usually 20% or less. Getting out the word on tour packages is also a challenge because most tour operators must develop their marketing campaigns on limited budgets. Therefore, market segmentation and targeting are essential to continued success.

Another specialized layer of the tourism distribution channel is the **receptive service operator (RSO)**. A receptive service operator is a local company that specializes in handling the needs of groups traveling to its location. The RSO coordinates (and is often in charge of

booking) the local suppliers serving the needs of the group. In other words, the RSO is in charge of handling the land arrangements for the group and is therefore sometimes termed a **ground operator**. RSOs may work with travel agents in developing packages for groups, and they also may subcontract with wholesalers in providing better service to tour groups.

Consolidators and Travel Clubs

Consolidators and **travel clubs** are very special combinations of wholesalers and retailers who perform unique tourism distribution functions. Consolidators buy excess inventory of unsold airline tickets and then resell these tickets at discounted prices through travel agents or, in some cases, directly to travelers. Travel clubs also provide an inexpensive and convenient outlet for members to purchase unused seats at the last minute. Both consolidators and travel clubs perform a win–win function as intermediaries in the distribution channel. They help the airlines sell a highly perishable service and often provide consumers with some real bargains in the process.

Where travel agencies are the department stores of the tourism industry, consolidators and travel clubs are to the airline industry what factory outlet stores are to clothing manufacturers. They are an efficient way to move highly perishable inventories of services to shoppers who have the flexibility to adjust their travel schedules to take advantage of lower prices on scheduled flights for which airlines have not been able to sell all of their available seats. Although there may be restrictions and the frequent fare wars that airlines wage may make the savings differential smaller, bargains can be substantial. Travel clubs also perform the additional function of selling accommodations, car rentals, and other tourism services at reduced rates.

The Internet provides consolidators with more market opportunity to sell their inventories. For example, Travelocity's Special Deals icon links Web surfers to consolidators such as Cheap Tickets, Inc. Other service providers such as Priceline and Hotwire offer airlines a simple way to move distressed inventory.

Meeting Planners

Meeting planners, sometimes called event or convention planners, are another important tourism intermediary. The size and scope of their activities in this $82.8 billion industry segment may go unnoticed, but their impact is tremendous.[15] For example:

- Meetings represent $1 out of every $4 spent on air travel.
- In the United States, meetings represent $23 billion of the hotel industry's operating revenue (36% of all hotel room income), and an even higher percentage among the business hotels.
- Almost 4 of every 10 room nights is used in conjunction with a meeting.

- Professional and vocational associations represent 70% of the billions of dollars spent on meetings.
- The number-one factor that associations consider when selecting a meeting site is quality of service.

Meeting planners are employed by corporations, associations, and others who need their specialized services. The main function of a meeting planner is the detailed planning of business meetings, incentive travel, educational meetings, conventions, trade shows, sales meetings, tournaments, executive retreats, reunions, and association gatherings. Meeting planners, like travel agents, handle many tasks at once. Take a moment to review Table 4.6, which shows just a sample of the decisions that need to be made by meeting planners on a daily basis.

One of the most pressing responsibilities of meeting planners is to control costs for the organizations they serve. As a result of corporate "belt tightening," the need for meeting planners is predicted to expand, and the destinations and number of sites (both domestic and international) they select will continue to grow.

■ Meetings and conferences require coordination of efforts of many tourism suppliers.

Table 4.6	A Small Sample of Decisions Made by Meeting Planners

How many people will attend the meeting?

What city of destination will you choose to host the meeting?

What types of transportation services will clients need?

What types of food functions must be planned?

- Meeting catering
- Reception catering
- Event/program catering
- Banquet catering
- Festival catering
- Cocktail receptions

What types of support services will be needed?

- Message and paging service
- Welcome banners
- Registration assistance
- Welcome packets
- Room blueprints

What types of facilities equipment and supplies will be needed?

- High ceilings (for projections)
- Light controls in each space
- Variety in table size
- Overhead projection
- Flip charts
- Portable computer stations
- Teleconferencing
- Simultaneous translation
- Projection screens
- Overhead computer panels
- Video conferencing

What types of activities need to be planned outside of meeting times?

- Tennis
- Horseback riding
- Golf
- Shopping
- Sightseeing
- Tours

Once again, technology is playing a key role in improving efficiencies when it comes to managing these functions strategically. Companies such as StarCite provide a suite of e-products serving the needs of both suppliers and buyers to reduce expenditures and increase return on investment.

The meetings planned are usually high profile or of strategic importance to the organization the meeting planner serves, so planning professionals are scrutinized for the level of service, hospitality, and spirit experienced by the meeting participants. This means the meeting planner must walk a tightrope, balancing cost constraints with the desires of the meeting attendees.

TAPPING THE POWER OF DUAL DISTRIBUTION

The Internet and other changes in information technology are allowing tourism service suppliers to utilize more channel structures to sell their products, a tactic called dual distribution

Trip-Cancellation and Trip-Interruption Insurance

Trip-cancellation and trip-interruption insurance policies will provide reimbursement for financial losses you might suffer if you can't begin and must cancel a trip or it is interrupted while in progress. This insurance will cover such things as missing a flight due to an automobile accident, a sudden illness, injury, or death, but it doesn't cover changing your mind. Should you buy trip-cancellation insurance? The answer to this question could be yes, no, or maybe. If you are making a large deposit, if you are paying in advance for an expensive tour package or cruise, or if you have purchased any type of expensive nonrefundable ticket, then the answer is yes. In all other situations, read the fine print and decide for yourself.

in marketing. For example, Carnival is actively developing and using at least five different channels in attempts to generate enough demand to fill its expanding supply of cabins:

1. Direct channel using Carnival's Internet site
2. Direct channel using mall locations
3. Indirect channel using traditional travel agents
4. Indirect channel using Internet-based cruise-only agents
5. Indirect channel using last-minute fire sale agencies to fill cabins close to sailing dates

In addition, other cruise lines such as Princess and Norwegian are using tour packagers to move their inventory. For example, both are now featured occasionally in direct mail catalogs sent by Grand Circle Tours to its huge list of likely travelers. According to one industry expert, "While the number of brick-and-mortar agencies has continued to decline . . ., the travel generated by the agency community continues to be strong. And although some of the Internet-based agencies are among the largest in the country in terms of sales, there is clearly room in the marketplace for agencies of all types. This

will remain the case as the industry continues to evolve."[16]

TOURISM INFORMATION SOURCES AND SERVICES

As we have noted, travelers need access to information before and during their trips. Marketing communications through websites, directories, advertising, blogs, public relations, and **personal selling** can all be used to provide travelers and tourism intermediaries with information they need about benefits, prices, and availability.

During the trip planning phase, it has become popular to rely on blogs for travel and destination insights. However, a note of caution is in order. Anyone can post to a blog, and governmental entities as well as private organizations often pay to receive positive comments. Some high-profile examples of sponsored bloggers include The Netherlands Board of Tourism & Conventions, Visit Milwaukee, and Pennsylvania's "Roadtripper" project. They are fun to read and provide some useful information to a consumer, but don't rely on the information contained in just one blog. At the same time, if you are a tourism service provider, don't overlook the power of having your organization's name in the blogging world.[17]

When tourists are seeking general information about travel and locations *en route* to their destinations, they often rely on the services of tourism offices. These offices may range from national tourism offices (which we will learn more about in Chapter 11) to local chambers of commerce. These information sources help promote tourism activities on both the individual and the group level by providing information and other services. In addition, national, state, provincial, and local tourist offices can be accessed to obtain information and updates on currency, transportation, restaurants, and more. Many of these offices also provide toll-free telephone access to improve customer service.

Because tourism is an important economic activity, state, provincial, and local governments are often actively involved in providing tourist information. In fact, tourist information centers appear to be one of the more important information sources that visitors use in accessing general information about destinations.[18] We will explore more about the roles that governments play in encouraging tourism expenditures in Chapter 11.

Central reservations offices, which are operated by government agencies or contractors, play a critical role in promoting destinations, educating travelers on the destinations, and connecting area travel suppliers with the destination traveler. Typical services provided by the central reservations allow travelers to book everything from accommodations to golf tee times, browse virtual tours, view maps of the area, get weather reports, access local restaurant and events listings—everything travelers need to know or need for travel to the destination is put at their fingertips.

The role of central reservations offices also often encompasses cooperative marketing, inquiry fulfillment, domestic and international advertising, industry relations, domestic and international advertising, public relations, research, sales promotion, and welcome centers. For example, if you are from Connecticut and want to ski Steamboat in Colorado next year for the first time, where are you going to start? Answer: Steamboat Central Reservations. It will educate you on all Steamboat has to offer and then connect you with the appropriate travel suppliers to meet your budget, needs, and preferences.

The amount of money spent at the local level helps to determine the type of organization that will provide general tourist information. In large metropolitan areas or in cities where tourism is an important economic activity, you will find convention and visitors bureaus. These offices are often funded by lodging, restaurant, or other tourism-related use taxes. In smaller cities, these same information functions would be provided by the local chambers of commerce. No matter where the operation is located, the primary functions are providing information for visitors and serving as facilitators in bringing together individual tourists and groups of tourists with tourism suppliers.

The best way to gain information and become familiar with a particular location and all it has to offer is actually to visit the location. Familiarization trips (also called "fams" or "fam trips") are offered to tourism intermediaries by a variety of tourism-related organizations such as governmental agencies, hotels, resorts, convention and visitors bureaus, and tour operators at low, or no, cost. These trips are designed to promote tourism in general and acquaint participants with the specific capabilities of tourism service suppliers. In addition, annual travel trade shows provide continuing education, promotional, and selling opportunities for industry participants. Some, such as TIA's International Pow Wow, which is billed as the travel industry's largest international marketplace, are designed to bring travel organizations together. And Pow Wow does this in a big way, bringing together over 1,000 U.S. travel organizations and close to 1,500 buyers from over 70 countries.[19] Others such as ITB Berlin, the world's

The Internet: It's Not One-Stop Shopping

Need to book a flight or a hotel room? It's simple—just hop on the Information Superhighway and you're through, right? Better slow down; the 'Net isn't the place to practice one-stop shopping. Your first stop might be one of the three "omnibus" travel sites (i.e., Expedia, Travelocity, and Orbitz), but these sites often don't offer the best deal out there. Check out sites such as Kayak.com and Sidestep.com as well as consolidator sites such as Hotels.com and discount sites such as Hotwire.com.

Next, try destination sites such as Vegas.com for special deals. Consider airfare/hotel/rental car package deals, too, because suppliers often will price services superlow if they don't have to disclose the actual price being offered. And, if you don't travel much or if you enjoy the personal touch of service, you may still want to maintain a good relationship with a travel agent. Many agents, due to expertise and experience, can find even more and better deals than you can on your own.

largest travel trade show, are designed to bring service suppliers and consumers together. ITB Berlin does this in a huge way, hosting almost 11,000 travel-related companies and well over 100,000 attendees each year.[20]

SELLING ADDS A PERSONAL TOUCH

No matter which channels are used to distribute tourism services, personal selling skills provide a key ingredient to creating customer satisfaction by adding the personal touch. Personal selling is a communication process that includes discovering customer needs, finding the appropriate services to meet these needs, and then persuading the customer to purchase these services. Effective salespeople are more than just order takers; they cultivate long-term customer relationships as part of a process called *customer relationship management,* creating win–win situations for both customers and suppliers. According to one customer care specialist, "[m]aking the first sale to a new customer costs five times more than making a follow-up sale to an existing customer,"[21] so know your customer.

Most airlines, car rental services, hotel/motel chains, resorts, convention centers, and cruise lines maintain their own sales force and reservations staff. These individuals either actively solicit business or engage in **missionary sales** efforts. Missionary salespeople call on travel agencies and other tourism service suppliers, such as tour operators, to answer questions, provide brochures, and offer other information services—in short, to educate others about their company's services so those services may be sold more effectively. Let's take a closer look at what it takes to create a successful sales effort.

Close your eyes for a moment and think about some very special place you have visited. Now, think about how you would describe this place to your best friend, using just words, no pictures allowed. Could you paint a vivid verbal picture that would excite your friend's imagination? The ability to connect with customers through visual images is a key ingredient to successful selling and it begins with product knowledge. A Louis Harris Travel Agency Marketing Survey revealed that "consumers want a travel counselor who's an expert, an opinion broker and a trusted ally who can provide insider knowledge and wise counsel that's difficult or impossible for them to match, even through a guidebook or Internet research" (p. 9).[22] In addition to being customer oriented and acquiring detailed knowledge of the services they are selling, effective salespeople must also be likable, dependable, and honest.

Acquiring Product Knowledge

The ability to excite, give details, and help others envision places near and far, known or unknown, is one of the first skills you will need in selling tourism services. Customers must have confidence in your ability to assess their needs and make recommendations that will not only satisfy those needs but also delight them so they return again and again. It's hard to sell an experience if you don't have extensive product knowledge. A successful salesperson is constantly gathering additional knowledge that will be useful to existing and potential clients.

Approaching the Client

Armed with the confidence of product knowledge, salespeople are prepared to serve their clients. The approach begins with the salesperson's first contact with a client. This contact may be over the phone, through email, or in person. No matter how the contact is initiated, the salesperson has a responsibility to create a positive and professional impression through common business courtesies. When clients contact or approach you, stop what you are doing and focus all of your attention on them.

Qualifying the Client

Clients come in many varieties, ranging from casual information seekers to qualified buyers. Although a plethora of information is available through the Internet, people continue to seek the personal touch that can come only from human interface. Many of today's clients will have already completed much of their basic homework, thanks to the Internet. They will be familiar with schedules, prices, and service offerings, meaning they will be shopping for a "deal." They know what they want and are only looking for help and, they hope, a better price, using the salesperson as a facilitator in this process. Others will rely on your knowledge, skills, and ability to identify and satisfy their individual wants and needs, taking them through every step of the process.

Whether these contacts are made over the phone, through the Internet, or in person, your task is to identify and serve each client's need. Qualifying the customer entails asking questions to discover his or her specific needs, budgetary considerations, and the necessary personal information that can be used to make the sales presentation. Qualifying clients allows you to determine whether or not you have a product or service to meet their needs and then tailor your presentation to meet those needs. You should not waste time on unqualified clients, but don't be rude. Even if they don't make a purchase today, treating everyone with courtesy today may result in sales or positive comments to potential clients tomorrow.

Making the Sales Presentation

Your assessment of clients' intentions won't always be perfect, but with a little practice, your skills in dealing with clients will improve. Sales presentations provide opportunities for the salesperson to present the features and benefits of a service or package of services that will meet the client's needs. This may be as simple as making a recommendation as to the best airline schedule or as complex as presenting a complete sales proposal for a major convention. The sales tools used in the presentation may include brochures, videotapes, PowerPoint presentations, DVDs, testimonial letters from satisfied clients, reprints of travel articles, or virtual tours through websites.

Successful selling means that you will adapt your presentation to meet your clients' needs by selling benefits rather than features. Always deal with clients on the basis that you will make the sale whether today or in the future. Make your contacts and presentations personably and enthusiastically, building the foundation for long-term relationships.

■ Professional sales training adds knowledge and polish to the sales force. Photo by Joanne Giampa.

Closing the Sale

Clients may be ready to purchase when the presentation is made, but it may also be necessary to overcome objections or resistance. Negotiations involve responding to objections or concerns and discovering how to meet client needs. Many objections can be cleared up through active listening and clarification. However, salespeople should anticipate possible objections such as mismatches between brand-quality and price perceptions, time of year, or seasonality concerns. Remember, special requests should be met whenever possible.

Be prepared to counter or overcome these resistance points effectively to close the sale. The sale is formally closed when payment is made; the reservation is confirmed; a deposit is made; and/or the contract is signed. Don't make the common mistake of continuing to sell after the sale has been made. This may result in losing the sale. Always look for verbal and nonverbal signals, as shown in Table 4.7, that a client is ready to commit.

Following Up

Follow-up is the final step in the selling process. Providing service after the sale creates customer loyalty and satisfaction. Salespeople can create repeat business by letting their clients know they truly care about them as individuals. Personalization can even be achieved in telephone interactions. Smile when you talk on the phone and use your customer's name. Your personal warmth will come through to the person on the other end of the call.

Follow-up is a team effort, requiring everyone in the organization to pitch in, not just members of the sales staff. Tourism is a people business, and everyone in the industry who has contact with customers is a salesperson, whether he or she knows it or not. Even if your job is not specifically sales related, you are still responsible for building customer relations, which can lead to future sales. The Walt Disney Company epitomizes this philosophy by training all employees (cast members), even park cleaners, that they are always "on stage" as customer service representatives. When they step into the "park" in uniform, they are there not only to do their jobs but also to help customers by answering questions and providing directions. The same roles should be played in every tourism setting by everyone who serves in supporting roles for those who actively sell the experience.

Building Relationships

In addition to following the steps of the selling process, a good salesperson provides consistent high-quality service to clients. Returning phone calls and emails promptly, solving problems, providing thank-you cards, or notifying clients of special sales or special offers as simple tokens of appreciation can all go a long way toward creating customer loyalty.

Even if you never plan a career in sales, sooner or later, you will be in a selling situation. From landing your first professional job or asking for a promotion to making a transfer request or asking for a raise, you are selling your most valuable asset—yourself! To improve your chances for success, you need to create powerful first

Table 4.7	Common Closing Signals
Stop talking. If the clients don't have any more questions, ask for their business.	
When clients begin asking specific questions that personalize the conversation, make the assumption that they are ready to buy!	
When clients agree with how your product or service descriptions meet their needs, they are probably ready to buy.	
When clients ask about forms of payment, deposit requirements, or making reservations, it is time to close.	
Pay particular attention to body language and voice tone. Any of these cues may signal it's time to close: smiles, nods, relaxation, friendly voice tones.	

impressions. Always be prepared to put yourself in a positive spotlight, creating a powerful and lasting impression every time you meet someone.

Whether you like it or not, you are judged by the way you look and how you present yourself in person, on the phone, and in written communications. Long before you utter a word or extend your hand, opinions have been formed.

Paying attention to details in all of these areas no matter what type or in which setting you find yourself, from formal to informal, will set you apart as a professional. For more information and specific recommendations for successfully navigating the complexities of the business landscape, see *Guide to Business Etiquette*.[23]

SUMMARY

Tourism is a service-oriented industry that focuses on meeting the needs of the traveling public. The success and profitability of tourism service suppliers depend on their ability to reach and meet the needs of selected target markets effectively and efficiently. With changes in technology and challenges to the commission system for intermediaries, the distribution landscape is continuously evolving.

As channel relationships change, suppliers in the tourism industry face many new and unique marketing challenges. The number of options for reaching customers with information about service offerings and booking reservations continues to grow. However, the fact that the services they provide are highly perishable and cannot be placed in inventory remains the same. In addition, with some tourism services often involving a great deal of customer involvement and employee contact, the need for well-trained employees remains a constant management challenge.

Although providing profitable levels of customer service is important, it is equally important to make sure that these services reach the intended markets. There are several types of distribution channels for providing consumers with access to the suppliers of tourism services, ranging from direct access, travel agents, and tour operators to more complex multi-level channels involving several intermediaries. The majority of all of these travel reservations are facilitated through global distribution systems that provide access to a wealth of data about tourism service suppliers.

Tourists need information to make informed buying decisions, and there is no shortage of available information thanks to the Internet. This information may range from general facts about a location to specific details concerning schedules and availability. Organizations such as conventions and visitors bureaus and local chambers of commerce have been developed to provide general tourism information. Tourism service suppliers are learning to utilize a combination of information sources from the personal touch of salespeople to the 24/7 availability of online information to supply the specific information needs of the traveling public. With improvements in information technology, the ways we access and use tourism information have changed radically and will continue to evolve.

YOU DECIDE

Brenda Baumgardner, manager of Discovery Travel, looked at the letter one more time. The offer sounded too good to pass up! Five all-expense-paid days at the Canyon Fire Resort and an opportunity to generate more business for her travel agency. It would be similar to a fam trip, only she would be hosted by a client rather than a group of tourism service suppliers.

The letter had come from John Smithers, Corporate Director of Marketing at a local manufacturing company. He had invited Brenda to accompany him on the company's annual incentive award trip. The January date was perfect for Brenda. Business was usually slow at that time of year, and the chance to leave the snow behind for the warmth of the desert was appealing. Besides, the enclosed itinerary of activities looked interesting.

John had indicated in the letter that he was considering having his office coordinate some of the travel and meeting planning activities for this annual event. He had typically turned this task over to an incentive travel company, but recent budget cuts might force him to scale back the program or consider other travel awards. John stated that his staff could handle some of the administrative details, but he might need Brenda's agency to help coordinate travel and accommodation needs for future meetings. John had closed the letter by asking Brenda to call him with an answer by the end of next week.

Brenda had visited Canyon Fire on previous occasions and looked forward to a chance to return and enjoy a little fun in the sun. Although she wanted to experience the pampering of an incentive trip firsthand, she was a bit troubled by the invitation. Brenda's agency handled many of the travel arrangements for John's sales managers, who had

told her that the company was considering establishing an in-house travel agency.

Although Brenda wanted to accept the invitation, she was concerned from both a personal and business perspective. How would her staff and friends view the personal invitation? Would accepting the invitation create a sense of obligation and limit her negotiating abilities in future business dealings with John? Would the sales managers for John's company understand that she was on a business trip and not simply there for pleasure? If you were Brenda, what would you do?

NET TOUR

To get you started on exploring Internet links for this chapter, please see

    http://www.astanet.com

    http://www.arccorp.com

http://www.ustoa.com

http://icccaworld.com

DISCUSSION QUESTIONS

1. Describe how services are different from goods.
2. Explain the functions of intermediaries in tourism distribution channels.
3. What are the differences in one-level, two-level, and three-level tourism distribution channels?
4. Why have travel agents remained an important link in the distribution of tourism services?

5. How has the Internet changed the distribution of tourism services?
6. Explain the functions of tour operators and wholesalers.
7. How is information about tourism services made available to the traveling public?
8. Why have personal selling skills remained important for tourism services professionals?

APPLYING THE CONCEPTS

1. Make an appointment with a travel agent at his or her place of business to discuss the impact of the Internet on his or her travel agency. Also ask what type of education and training will be necessary to be successful in the future. While you are at the agency, ask for a demonstration of how the GDS/CRS is used to make reservations with tourism suppliers.
2. Look for the following headings in the Yellow Pages or business section of your phone book: "Tourist Information" and "Tours." Call or visit one organization. Prepare a brief outline describing the information you received from your contact.

3. Find an article describing how consumers can use information technology to access tourism information. Prepare a brief (half-page) summary and copy of the article.
4. Using the Internet, perform the necessary steps to make airline and hotel reservations at the destination of your choice. Write down the steps and Web addresses you visited in completing this task.
5. Find a brochure or a website that describes an all-inclusive tour package. List all of the tourism suppliers that have been linked together to make this tour package possible.

GLOSSARY

Airlines Reporting Corporation (ARC) The clearinghouse for receiving commission payments for airline ticket sales.

All-inclusive Single price for all or nearly all major services provided in a tour, resort, or cruise package.

Call centers Centralized locations designed and managed to handle large volumes of incoming telephone inquiries, in many cases on a 24/7 basis.

Commissions The percentage paid to a sales agent (travel agent) by tourism suppliers for booking travel arrangements.

Computer reservation systems (CRSs) Computer hardware and software that allow travel agents to tap into global distribution systems.

Consolidators Wholesalers who buy excess inventory of unsold airline tickets and then resell these tickets at discounted prices through travel agents or, in some cases, directly to travelers.

Consortium An affiliation of privately owned companies to improve business operations and gain the necessary volume of business that can lead to improved profitability.

Domestic independent tour (DIT) Customized domestic tour including many elements, designed and planned to fulfill the particular needs of a traveler; may be designed by a travel agent or by a wholesaler in consultation with the traveler's agent.

Dynamic packaging The ability to aggregate multiple tourism service supplier offerings (e.g., air, hotel, and car) in real time into a package.

Escorted tour An all-inclusive tour with a structured itinerary and a guide who accompanies the guests.

Familiarization trips (also called "fams" or "fam trips") Trips offered by governmental tourism agencies, hotels, resorts, and tour operators at low or no cost to acquaint travel salespeople (typically travel agents) with the products and services they offer.

Foreign independent tour (FIT) Customized foreign tour including many elements, designed and planned to fulfill the particular needs of a traveler; may be designed by a travel agent or by a wholesaler in consultation with the traveler's agent.

Franchise A license to operate a tourism service business such as a travel agency or hotel with the benefit of trademarks, training, standardized supplies, operating manual, and procedures of the franchiser.

Global distribution systems (GDSs) Worldwide interorganization information systems that travel agencies use in selling tourism services.

Ground transfers Short-distance transportation between service providers, most frequently provided as part of a tour.

Hosted tour A tour in which a host is available at each major tour destination to welcome guests, solve problems, and answer questions.

Independent tour A tour that allows the flexibility to travel independently while taking advantage of pre-arranged services and rates based on volume discounts.

Intermediary Firms that help tourism suppliers locate customers and make sales to them, including tour operators and travel agencies.

Itinerary A detailed schedule of a trip.

Markup Adding a percentage to the cost of a good or service to arrive at a selling price.

Meeting planner An individual who specializes in planning and coordinating all the details of meetings, conferences, or events.

Missionary sales Sales calls made by individuals to retail travel agencies and other tourism industry intermediaries to answer questions and educate them about the company's services so that they may be sold more effectively.

One-level distribution channels The simplest form of distribution, in which the supplier deals directly with the consumer without the services of intermediaries.

Overrides Additional bonuses offered to travel agencies beyond their usual commission to encourage the agency to sell more tickets.

Personal selling A communications process that includes discovering customer needs, finding the appropriate services to meet these needs, and then persuading customers to purchase these services.

Receptive service operator (RSO) (ground operator) A local company that specializes in handling the needs of groups traveling to its location.

Three-level distribution channels Distribution channels in which two or more channel members, such as tour operators or wholesalers, serve as intermediaries between the supplier and the consumer.

Tour A product that includes at least two of the following elements: transportation, accommodations, meals, entertainment, attractions, and sightseeing activities. It can vary widely in the number of elements included and in the structure of the itinerary.

Tour operator   A business entity engaged in the planning, preparing, marketing, making of reservations, and, at times, operating vacation tours.

Tour package   Two or more travel services put together by a tour operator, such as air transportation, accommodations, meals, ground transportation, and attractions.

Travel agent   A sales specialist in tourism services.

Travel clubs   Membership organizations designed to serve the needs of last-minute leisure travelers at bargain prices.

Two-level distribution channels   Distribution channels in which an additional channel member, such as a travel agent, serves as an intermediary between the supplier and the consumer.

■ REFERENCES

1. Goeldner, C. R. (1995, Winter). Conference report: The 1995 travel outlook. *Journal of Travel Research,* pp. 45–48.
2. Upheaval in travel distribution: Impact on consumers and travel agents. (2002, November 13). *Report to Congress and the President.* National Commission to Ensure Consumer Information and Choice in the Airline Industry, pp. 21–35.
3. Agencies, corporate owned. (2004, May 24). *Business Travel News,* p. 4.
4. Bellstrom, Kristen. (2007, May 17). Travel agents are staging a comeback. Available at: http://www.smartmoney.com.
5. Cruising Europe. (2008, April). *Money,* pp. 111–113.
6. Name change: Carlson Wagonlit Travel now Travel Leaders. (2008, August 22). *Atlanta Business Chronicle.* Available at: http://www.bizjournals.com/atlanta/stories/2008/08/18/daily75.html.
7. Schultz, Christopher. (1994, April). Hotels and travel agents: The new partnership. *Cornell Hotel & Restaurant Administration Quarterly,* pp. 45–50.
8. Higgins, Megan. (2007, February 11). Practical traveler: Online travel agencies. *New York Times,* p. 6.
9. Ellin, Abby. (2007, July 3). Happy returns for travel agents. *The New York Times Online.* Available at: http://www.nytimes.com.
10. Chipkin, Harry. (2000, March). In search of lodging's Holy Grail. *Lodging,* pp. 56–62.
11. Hilton Hotels: Friend or foe? (2003, July 7). *eTurboNews Global Travel Industry News.*
12. Semer-Purzycki, Jeanne. (2000). *Travel vision.* Upper Saddle River, NJ: Prentice Hall, Inc.
13. *Dictionary of hospitality, travel and tourism* (3rd ed.). (1990). Albany, NY: Charles J. Metelka, Delmar Publishers.
14. Meeting industry statistics. (1999, September 27). *Meeting Professionals International.*
15. Meeting industry statistics. (1999, September 27). *Meeting Professionals International.*
16. Miller, Jeffrey. (2004, May 10). Storefront or Internet? *Travel Agent,* p. 16.
17. Elliott, Christopher. (2007, January–February). Blogs: The caveat. *National Geographic Traveler,* pp. 22–24.
18. Fesenmaier, Daniel R. (1994, Summer). Traveler use of visitor information centers: Implications for development in Illinois. *Journal of Travel Research,* pp. 44–50.
19. Meetings & events. Retrieved March 28, 2008, from http://www.tia.org/powwow/General_Information.html.
20. ITB Berlin. (2007). Retrieved October 16, 2008, from http://www1.messe-berlin.de/vip8_1/website/Internet/Internet/www.itb-berlin/englisch/index.html.
21. Gebhart, Fred. (2002, October 21). Who are you? *Travel Weekly,* Section 2, p. 2.
22. Marriott International, Inc. (1999). *Hotel Excellence!* p. 9
23. Cook, Roy A., Cook, Gwen O., and Yale, Laura J. (2005). *Guide to business etiquette.* Upper Saddle River, NJ: Prentice Hall, Inc.

LEARNING OBJECTIVES

After you have read this chapter, you should be able to:

- Describe some of the technological trends that are shaping operating practices of tourism service suppliers.
- Describe how technology can enhance productivity.
- Describe how technology can improve both internal and external communications.
- Describe how technological changes will have an impact on the future of the tourism industry.
- Describe how technology can enhance customer service.
- Describe how the Internet has changed tourism operations.
- Describe how revenue management has improved the financial performance of tourism service suppliers.

Capturing Technology's Competitive Advantages

Technology makes the world a new place.

—Shoshana Zuboff

CHAPTER OUTLINE

■ Self-service kiosks enhance customer convenience.

STAYING ON THE CUTTING EDGE

How do travel service companies stay on the cutting edge of technology? Technological innovation and customer service have been the answers for Wyndham Jade, a leader in travel services. With offices in Dallas, Phoenix, New York City, Baltimore, Chicago, Atlanta, Washington, D.C., and Rockford, Iowa, Wyndham Jade charts new courses by staying on the cutting edge of technology to maintain a leadership role in the delivery of travel services in the incentive and meeting markets, convention housing and registration markets, and corporate travel management markets.

Organizations from around the world utilize Wyndham Jade's convention planners to recommend destinations, handle negotiations, organize travel and hotel requirements, and provide a wide range of on-site support services. For large national and international meetings and conventions, Wyndham Jade offers its convention housing and registration services. Meeting attendees and exhibitors are able to register, book hotel reservations, and make travel arrangements all at the same time online via the Web . . . 24 hours a day . . . from anywhere in the world. These services are enhanced through ONEsystem+, an Internet engine designed to provide rapid and flexible reporting for event management.

Corporate travel clients receive 24-hour full-service personalized travel agency services combined with travel management analysis and reporting. In-house technology development and support programs have allowed Wyndham Jade to remain competitive with Internet vendors while adding the all-important human touch desired by the most demanding corporate travel management clients.

Incentive and meeting services clients have come to expect turnkey support from concept development to program fulfillment in a variety of performance enhancement programs designed to drive results. These fun, results-oriented programs are made possible by the same level of commitment to technological innovation and customer service that drives all of the company's other innovative programs. What are the results of all these efforts? A client list that reads like the who's who of corporate America.

How does Wyndham Jade stay on the cutting edge? By combining the skills of seasoned travel industry professions, challenging the status quo, and tapping the benefits of the latest in communications technologies, it draws on the creative talents of its diverse team to provide tomorrow's travel service needs today in one convenient virtual location.

INTRODUCTION

Technology, which we broadly define as the use of new knowledge and tools to improve productivity and systems, has created both challenges and opportunities for tourism service providers. Nowhere have technological advances been more evident than in computing capabilities. As **data** storage capacities expand, processing speeds seem to grow exponentially, all at lower and lower costs, permitting the power of **information technology** to be within the reach of almost every organization. The same technology that is driving the information revolution has spawned other innovative uses from **point-of-sale systems (POSs)** to **enterprise resource planning systems (ERPs).**

In this chapter, we will explore the challenges posed by technological advances and innovations as well as the benefits being derived as they are adopted by tourism service suppliers, both large and small. For a glimpse at how technology affects these suppliers, take a look at Figure 5.1.

Even with the demonstrated benefits of technological advancements, some tourism service providers have been reluctant to embrace new technologies. Fears of losing human connectivity that has historically been the foundation of hospitality, learning new skills, and the costs of technological applications have been the typical reasons voiced for this reluctance. Although early adopters did experience some of these problems, they soon progressed through the **learning curve** (slowly at first and then more rapidly with time and experience) and

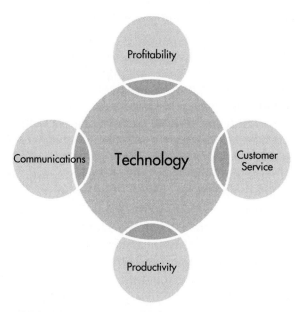

■ **Figure 5.1** Technology's impact on tourism service suppliers.

achieved many benefits, both financial and operational, from their commitment and investment. The outcome from these investments? Enhanced productivity, improved communications, and enhanced customer service leading to improved profitability and a competitive advantage. Let's take a look at how the technological revolution is transforming the tourism industry.

IMPROVING OPERATING EFFICIENCY AND EFFECTIVENESS

In the face of rising wages, increasing input costs, and intensifying competition, tourism service suppliers have been forced to make cuts in staff size, increase productivity, and rethink marketing efforts. Doing things the same old traditional ways no longer seems to be working. For example, food-service operators who traditionally planned for and staffed stand-alone kitchens have now adopted the use of central kitchens, allowing a single large operation to provide a variety of menu items to several satellite dining locations with fewer preparation and production employees, less equipment, and centralized purchasing and production planning.

RFIDs

Radio frequency identification devices (RFIDs) are being used to control hotel guest room locks, to track inventory, and for a variety of other uses for which low-cost tracking and security are needed. RFIDs use radio waves to identify people or objects automatically. These tags are different from the bar-coded tags currently being used by airlines to track the location of baggage. RFIDs do not require a direct line of sight to be read, and multiple tags can be read at one time, creating opportunities for ticketing, identification verification, and something as complex as tour group coordination.

Staffing programs allow supervisors to schedule employees in key time slots to meet peak customer demands while limiting coverage during slack times. Advances in communication technologies make internal ordering and inventory stocking more efficient by allowing employees to communicate through remote devices. Dining room and housekeeping employees can transmit orders, rooms' status, and inventory needs through wireless headsets and handheld order-entry equipment. These and many other technological innovations have evolved as tourism service suppliers search for solutions to enhance customer service, respond to operational demands, and improve profitability.

Management Information Systems

Management information systems (MIS) provide the backbone for operational decisions. They are computer-based systems designed to collect and store data and then provide information for planning, decision making, and problem solving. Deciding what information systems to use, whether to develop applications in-house or buy them, and then whether they should be centralized or dispersed to the property or store level are only a few of the decisions facing chief information officers and information technology professionals.

Think back to the chapter opener on Wyndham Jade, and you can see how one tourism services provider is dealing with these questions. To see where other participants in the tourism industry might be heading as they grapple with these questions, we can once again turn to the pioneering work of the airlines. By necessity, most of the information management functions for the airlines and other transportation service providers were centralized for operational efficiencies and profit improvement. However, many of the management information systems for restaurants, hotels, and car rental companies were initially implemented at the local level with the same profit motive, but with an eye toward enhancing productivity and improving customer service.

Points of data input for these systems may be found at the time reservations are made, when orders are entered into a point-of-sale device, or when guests check in. Point-of-sale systems for restaurants, with intuitive touch screens, reduce training time for servers and cashiers, reduce input errors and waste, and improve customer service. These same systems, designed to record and track customer orders, process debit and credit cards, manage inventory, and provide data to other networked systems, freeing up time once devoted to report preparation and analysis.

Retrieving information from any of these input points can aid in *property*- (a term used to describe individual hotels, motels, and resorts) and *store*- (a term used to describe individual food service units) level decision making, but aggregating these data across local and regional boundaries can also improve financial, management, and marketing decisions. Each of these functions can be thought of as a module. For example, reservations management systems, back office accounting systems, and human resource management systems have been in use for years. Today, lodging companies are attempting to centralize programs, moving them from individual properties to corporate offices. This allows software updates to be made once, instead of at various times in locations that may be spread around the world.[1] Table 5.1 provides just a few examples of the many individual tasks that can be accomplished with integrated data retrieval and analysis programs.

For hotels and resorts, bringing each of these functions and other applications together into a unified program creates a **property management system (PMS)**. Similar integrated management systems are available for restaurants, casinos, cruise lines, car rental agencies, and theme parks. Total integration through enterprise resource planning systems takes the concept of management information systems to the final level of integration by combining all information sources, subsystems, and processes into one unified system. For example, an ERP system would incorporate everything listed in Table 5.1 and more, allowing every department and function within a hotel or resort, even an entire chain in diverse geographic locations, to store and/or retrieve information on a real-time basis. Everything from purchasing and warehousing to payroll and sales and marketing would be managed by one system.

Table 5.1	Examples of Management Information System Features
Accounts receivables	Auditing and analysis
Climate control	Customer problems
Customer profiles and preferences	Customer relations
Financials	Food production management
Housekeeping	Maintenance
Reservations and table management	Retail outlets
Revenue management	Sales and catering
Security	Staffing
Standing orders and preorders	Telephones and televisions
Web ordering	Web reporting

Providing Customer Convenience and Service

The do-it-yourself approach to customer service met with some initial resistance, but once customers became comfortable with on-demand services, these technologies spread rapidly. Once again, we can thank the airlines for inaugurating what began as a labor-saving technology solution. Labor cost savings were realized, but ultimately customer service was improved. Shorter waits in line, reduced transaction times, and the ability to make changes without explaining the rationale for the changes were just a few of the improvements.

In addition to the ubiquitous airline counter kiosks that heralded the self-service concept, similar kiosk applications can now be found at car rental locations and hotels; kiosks at restaurants can't be far behind. Handheld devices and laptops are also aiding employees in the service delivery process. Airlines began using these devices to track baggage, but their use in many other customer service applications has led to

Pick Your Seat

Next time, before you fly, log on to http://www.seatguru.com. Select the airline on which you will be flying, and you will find a graphic seating chart for your plane, including detailed information about the location and quality of your assigned seat. If you book early enough, you may be able to select a perfect seat. Seatguru also provides information on meals, entertainment options, luggage, and other airline policies.

their widespread adoption by other tourism service suppliers. Restaurants, always keen on finding new ways to improve customer service and reduce costs, are finding handheld POS devices to be an invaluable asset. The use of these devices to place an order can save an average of four minutes over the traditional POS system, freeing more time to focus on the customer.[2]

■ Global positioning technology provides tourists with an onboard navigator on unfamiliar roads. Photo by John B. Yale.

Database marketing, also called **data mining,** is aiding tourism suppliers in targeting microsegments of their markets and customizing marketing mixes to fulfill the needs of specific travelers. Because computers can store and rapidly sift through vast amounts of information, marketers can build immense databases to provide them with extremely detailed profiles of prospective consumers.

For example, Harrah's created individualized promotion packages to tempt players to come to its casinos more often. Using information collected from its Total Gold frequent gambler cards, Harrah's began testing different promotions and learned which promotions worked best in bringing back gamers. Marketers for the chain determined that different players responded better to different promotions, such as free room nights, whereas others returned when offered free gaming tokens. Now, when a player has not come to Harrah's within a set time period, for example, two weeks, that player receives a promotion tailored to his or her tastes. This use of data mining has increased the response rate for Harrah's mailed promotions from 3% to 8%.[3]

■ CHANGING COMMUNICATION AND DISTRIBUTION CHANNELS

All travel distribution channels and sectors were fundamentally changed by the advent of the Internet. But one segment of the tourism industry has been affected more than others, the airlines. "Historically, the travel distribution channel was the domain of large suppliers. Reservation systems were complex and unwieldy, requiring significant investments in hardware, software and connectivity."[4] Conceivably, it is because airlines had traditionally relied on travel agents to be the primary intermediary in the distribution of their services that this shift in distribution had such a profound effect. The Internet introduced online distribution channels, in effect furthering competition by expanding distribution and bringing transparency to airline inventory and pricing.

Before online distribution channels, consumers bought airline tickets via the airlines and travel agencies. Both points of distribution used mainframe or "green screen"–based reservation systems such as American Airlines' Sabre and United Airlines' Apollo systems. For a number of years, airlines owned these proprietary systems, which listed available air inventories based on schedules with price being a secondary, hidden factor. Naturally, this scenario created demand for schedule-based inventory and caused airlines to deepen their commitment to operational efficiency. Airlines eventually sold off these reservation systems, but the basic schedule-based inventory practices continued.

The introduction of the Internet expanded travelers' choice for points of purchase, thereby creating price competition for airline inventory. Travel marketers created online booking engines that allowed travelers to compare available airline inventories by both price and schedule.

Tourism in Action

An interactive tabletop menu is more than just a gimmick; it serves as a means for bringing foods and beverages to life. The touchable tasting menu at New York City's Adour restaurant in the St. Regis Hotel sports an interactive wine bar. Customers can search and display a menu of wines by the glass or bottle, reds or whites, and even a selection of bar foods. After an initial selection, the menu allows users to drill down into wine regions of the world complete with producer information for each selection along with tasting notes.

This user-friendly format, freed from the clunkiness of a mouse or keyboard, brings wine selection down to a personal, even a social, level. The touchable menu provides more involvement than kiosks and simple touch-screen interactions. It is like having your own personal sommelier. New applications are sure to follow as technology giants such as Microsoft are bringing similar innovations to market for use in hotels and casino restaurants and lounges.

Source: Spencer, Ante E. (2008, January 28). The touchable tasting menu. *Business Week Online,* p. 13.

It quickly became apparent to online travel bookers that price was the result of many factors—day of week, time of day, time between connections, and number of connections. All of these are controllable factors for leisure travelers and many business travelers as well.

The Internet expanded point-of-purchase competition and changed demand for best-price rather than schedule-based airline inventories. "Carriers' full-service web sites now handle between 20 percent to 30 percent (for major carriers) and 70 percent (for low-cost carriers) of their total transactions."[5] The only segment of the tourism industry that is not following a similar shift is the cruise lines.

Internet as a Travel Tool

The Internet exploded onto the scene in the last years of the 20th century and changed the tourism industry forever. As online users have become more comfortable, confident, and convinced of the security on the Internet, more and more travelers are relying on this medium for their travel needs. Research has demonstrated that in addition to booking, online leisure travelers use the Internet for three purposes: ideas, inspiration, and information. And where are their searches taking them? In descending order of importance, they are seeking information on accommodations, attractions, where to visit, when to visit, and sample itineraries for their visits.[6]

The Internet affects our travel habits in other ways as well. We routinely turn to the Web as a source of customized maps to our destination and for on-the-go directions on how to get from place to place at our destination. We also use weather sites for up-to-the-moment travel weather reports before and during our trips. And we rely on the 'Net to check the on-time status of flights and trains, and traffic congestion on our driving routes.

The Internet has become a major source of information about travel products and destinations. Many potential travelers routinely turn to their computer whenever they have a travel need or question. Guidebooks will come in downloadable form and be carried on a personal digital assistant (PDA) or an interface converter unit (ICU).[7]

With the use of email, cell phones, and other personal technologies, we can "get away from it all" while still staying in frequent contact with others. Cyber cafes have already cropped up on cruise ships, and Wi-Fi access is available in tourist destination areas where, for a nominal fee, one can jump online and retrieve and send email. Most hotel rooms are equipped with Internet access, if not full-technology suites. The postcard may become extinct as vacationers use their digital cameras to download and email images to friends and loved ones who "wish they were there."

The Internet as a Communications Medium

Internet access has become ubiquitous. To understand the reach of this information and communications medium, refer back to Figure 1.3 in Chapter 1 to see the extent of the diffusion of this technology around the world. Take a look at Tables 5.2 and 5.3 to see the phenomenal growth, penetration, and usage of the Internet and cell phones. Between 2000 and 2008, worldwide Internet usage grew by 290% with

Table 5.2	Top Internet Usage Around the World
Country	*Number of Internet Users*
United States	210,000,000
China	131,100,000
Japan	90,900,000
India	67,600,000
Germany	50,300,000

Source: Worldwide Internet users top 1.2 billion in 2006. (2007, February 12). *Computer Industry Almanac, Inc.* Available at: http://www.c-i-a.com/pr0207.html.

Table 5.3	Internet and Cell Phone Usage and Growth		
	1990	*2000*	*2010 Projections*
Internet Users per 1,000 People			
United States	7.2	477	839
Western Europe	0.5	244	788
Asia-Pacific	0.03	34	193
Worldwide	0.4	69	262
Cell Phone Subscribers per 1,000 People			
United States	21.1	388	946
Western Europe	9.1	634	1,008
Asia-Pacific	0.4	71	379
Worldwide	2.1	123	478

Source: Europe #1 in per capita cell phone usage. (2006, February 28). *Computer Industry Almanac, Inc.* Available at: http://www.c-i-a.com/pr0206.html.

the fastest growth occurring in the Middle East and Africa as these regions catch up to the rest of the world.[8]

Even these projections may prove to be severely understated, as cellular phones are overtaking personal computers as the dominant platform to access the Internet. In countries such as China, Japan, France, South Korea, and the United Kingdom, this is already a reality.[9]

The Power of User-Generated Content

User-generated content, made possible through Web 2.0 and facilitated through **social networking** and We(b) logs, **blogs**, found its way into the world of tourism and hospitality and is having a profound impact on the entire tourism industry. "User-generated content, because it is genuinely one traveler speaking to another, offers the sense that what you see (or read) is really what you want to get: an experience that is authentic and out of the mainstream."[10] This new media format, like all technological innovations, has created both opportunities and challenges for tourism service suppliers. Opportunities are presented as awareness and interest can be created by posting positive comments. However, challenges arise when negative comments appear. Because information will be created and disseminated at lightning-fast speeds, organizations must now monitor what is being said and distributed about them.

There is more being written about some locations, hotels, restaurants, and local "hot spots" than could ever be read by one person. In fact, "[d]ue to the high volume of user-generated content typically found on social media and networking sites, it is difficult for each travel supplier to absorb it all."[11] Like any technological advance, decisions will have to be made on how to monitor and respond to the information that is being created. This monitoring function is especially important, as anything can be posted, true or untrue, requiring the need for rapid response to legitimate customer complaints and to correct false information.

IMPROVING PROFITABILITY

Revenue management (which is also called **yield management**), a foundational component of almost every management information system for tourism service suppliers, was developed by Bell Laboratories in 1988 and initially used as a scheduling tool for the airline industry. However, its effectiveness in addressing a host of marketing, management, and financial issues soon expanded its use to other tourism service providers such as hotels/motels, resorts, restaurants, cruise ships, golf courses, and car rental companies. Basically, revenue management requires allocating capacity to customers at the right price and at the right time to maximize revenue or yield, enhance customer service,

Biometrics

Fingerprint scans are only the tip of the iceberg when it comes to enhanced security and service. Both employees and guests will find biometrics incorporated into the workplace and the guest experience. For safety and security concerns, even in the face of privacy concerns, operators are turning to **biometrics**: fingerprint scans, handprint scans, facial scans, and iris scans. With these new technologies, there is no more need for time clocks, keys, or entry cards. With the scan of facial features, the blink of an eye, the press of a finger, or the wave of a hand, entrance is approved and a time record is established. Once an individual's personal profile (face, eye, finger, or hand) has been entered into a computer system, entry, checking in or checking out, and security are easily managed.

Sources: Kirby, Adam. (2008, January). Buying into biometrics. *Hotels*, pp. 49–50; and Yu, Roger. (2008, February 5). Some guests can open doors in a blink. *USA Today*, p. 4B.

improve operating efficiency, and increase profitability under the following conditions.[12]

- *When capacity is relatively fixed.* For example, when demand increases, airlines cannot simply add more seats; hotels cannot add more rooms; and rental car companies cannot quickly enlarge fleets at specific locations.
- *When demand can be separated into distinct market segments.* For example, tourism service providers can segment demand based on specific customer profiles and needs.
- *When inventory is perishable.* For example, as we have previously mentioned, once a plane has left the gate, there are no more opportunities to fill its seats with revenue-paying passengers on that flight.
- *When services can be sold well in advance.* For example, reservation systems allow leisure travelers to save money by making advance reservations with specific time restrictions.

- *When demand fluctuates substantially.* For example, during periods of high demand, higher rates can be obtained, but during periods of lower demand, lower rates may be necessary to attract customers.
- *When marginal sales costs are low and marginal capacity costs are high.* For example, the cost of selling an additional reservation for an airplane seat or a night's lodging is minimal, but the cost of purchasing a larger airplane or adding rooms to an existing hotel would be very expensive.

"One of the underlying principles of revenue management is to understand what customers value and develop products that enable those customers that value a particular attribute to obtain what they want; albeit, having them pay for that privilege."[13] Technological advances now allow tourism service suppliers from airlines to rental car companies to sell everything efficiently from empty seats to unrented cars through global distribution systems, through their own Internet sites, or via intermediary Internet sites, such as Travelocity, Expedia, and Orbitz at the best possible price.

Operational Considerations

Although revenue management holds the promise of maximizing revenues, it, like most other quantitative management tools, should not be used blindly. Factors such as desired market position, customer satisfaction, employee morale, and demand for related goods or services must be considered. As competition among transportation services increases and more governments privatize or eliminate subsidies to their airlines and passenger rail systems, revenue management techniques will grow in importance.

Mere possession of a revenue-management system does not guarantee success. For a company to be successful with revenue management, it must have a clear understanding of the needs and price sensitivity of its various market segments; it must be able to fully integrate its revenue management system with other computerized systems; it must be able to properly train and motivate its employees and mangers; and it must be able to quickly respond to competitive pressures.[14]

Additional benefits can be obtained from revenue management when it is combined with dynamic packaging and suggestive selling. Look at the benefits already gained from this approach by an innovative marketing leader in Web selling, Amazon.com. Any time you search for or purchase an item on Amazon, a message appears saying, "Other people who bought this item also bought. . . ." Tourism service suppliers are beginning to use this same idea of suggestive selling, but the full potential of this sales tool along with cross-marketing and dynamic packaging have yet to be fully embraced.

Revenue Management in Practice

The following example will highlight the importance of revenue management techniques as they are used to enhance revenues and potential profitability in an airline setting. This same approach can be used by every other tourism service supplier. For ease of understanding, we will use a smaller 37-seat aircraft in this example. The principles will remain the same for larger aircraft as well as in other settings where tourism service providers are seeking to enhance revenues.

On a 250-mile flight between cities A and B, we know from past reservation data that we can sell all 37 seats on our flight to leisure travelers. These travelers would be willing to purchase all seats for advance purchase excursion ticket fares of $89 each way ($89 fare × 37 passengers = $3,293). We also know that we could sell 15 full-fare coach tickets to business travelers for $225 each way ($225 fare × 15 passengers = $3,375). If this were an either/or decision, we would choose to sell only full-fare coach tickets because it would result in $82 more in revenue ($3,375 − $3,293); we could focus more attention on each passenger with the same required flight crew; and we would save fuel with a lighter load.

However, neither one of these choices will allow us to maximize revenues for this flight. What we need to do is hold back enough seats in the full-fare ($225) category to serve our business customers who need to travel at scheduled times and do not make their travel decisions solely on price. At the same time, we still want to fill the plane to generate as much revenue as possible. We could sell all of the remaining 22 seats at the $89 advance purchase excursion fare. However, this choice would still not maximize revenues.

Based on information provided from our revenue management system, we decide to sell seven seats at $89 each if they are reserved more than 30 days in advance, 18 seats at $109 if they are reserved more than 14 days in advance, and hold 12 seats at the $225 fare that can be sold up to the time of departure. By making these decisions, we have begun the process of maximizing revenues.

Our true yield for this flight will be based on the number of revenue-paying passengers who actually fly on the day of departure. Passengers buying discounted tickets know that these fares are nonrefundable and have restrictions. Therefore, they typically arrive for the flight, claim their reservations, and board the plane. On the other hand, passengers who have paid full fare may not claim their reservations, because they can be canceled and/or changed without penalties. Knowing this, we might overbook the flight, realizing that based on historical information, a certain percentage of passengers holding reservations will not show up to claim their seats.

Figure 5.2 shows a seating configuration for a 37-passenger airplane and how these seats might be filled with revenue-paying passengers in our example. By managing our seats to meet the needs of specific target groups, we will generate $5,285 in total revenue if all passengers honor their reservations. Remember that for the sake of simplicity in our example, we used a smaller aircraft flying a direct route. As the size of aircraft increases, we add in a round trip, and the number of **legs** multiplies; revenue management calculations can become very complex, requiring sophisticated computer hardware and software programs.

There are several other key statistics that can be generated from the data that are gathered

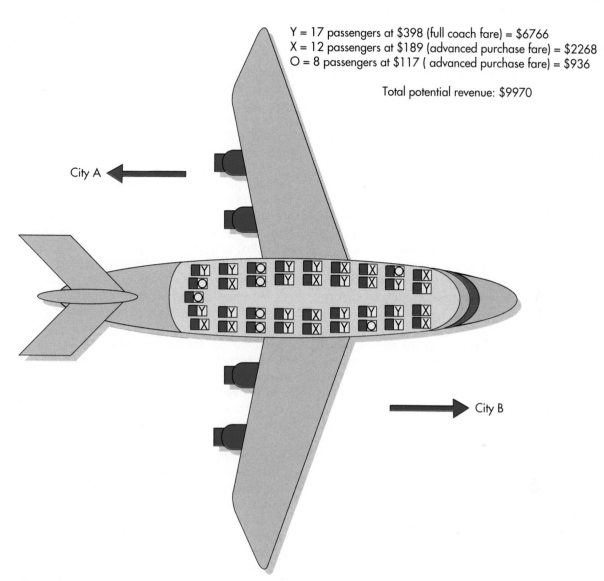

Y = 17 passengers at $398 (full coach fare) = $6766
X = 12 passengers at $189 (advanced purchase fare) = $2268
O = 8 passengers at $117 (advanced purchase fare) = $936

Total potential revenue: $9970

City A ←

City B →

■ **Figure 5.2**   Revenue management example for one leg of flight.

to maintain our revenue management system. These data include **available seat miles (ASMs), revenue passenger miles (RPMs)**, and **load factor**. In our flight example, we had 9,250 ASMs (250 miles × 37 seats, which generated 7,500 RPMs (250 miles × 30 revenue passengers), resulting in a load factor of 81% (7,500 RPMs ÷ 9,250 ASMs).

Airlines have continued to expand the capabilities of revenue management. Not only are they using it for its original intent, but they are also expanding its use to generate other operating efficiencies. Everything from flight planning and crew management to group sales management and cargo sales are being incorporated into an integrated system.[15]

Technology will definitely change the face of the tourism industry. Where and when these changes will occur is anybody's guess. What we do know is that technological advances will change how operators deliver services and how customers access and enjoy these services. When you reach Chapter 14 we will share with you some of our expectations for the future impacts of technology on tourism and hospitality.

SUMMARY

In response to the need for information to improve planning and decision making, management information systems designed to collect, store, and interpret data have evolved to support every function found in tourism and hospitality operations. Staying on top of the technological advances that make these support systems can be an expensive and time-consuming proposition, as change is a constant when it comes to technology. Not only is it expensive to incorporate each new technological advance, but it can also require a significant commitment in training and education for both employees and customers. In addition to time and resource commitments, there can also be reluctance to adopt changes owing to fears of losing the human connection that has historically been the foundation of hospitality.

In spite of these concerns, technology is revolutionizing the tourism industry. In the face of rising wages, increasing input costs, and intensifying competition, doing business the same old traditional ways no longer seems to be working. Technological innovations ranging from fairly simple handheld input devices to complex property management systems are improving operations, profitability, and customer service.

All travel distribution channels and sectors were fundamentally changed by the advent of the Internet. The introduction of the Internet expanded travelers' access to information and choices for points of purchase, intensifying competition. In response, travel marketers created online booking engines that allowed travelers to compare available inventories by both price and availability. As online users have become more comfortable, confident, and convinced of the security of the Internet, more and more travelers are relying on this medium for their travel needs.

Creating and accessing user-generated content found its way into the world of tourism and hospitality and it, like the Internet, has created even more changes for marketing managers. This new media format, like all technological innovations, has created both opportunities and challenges as information, both positive and negative, is created and disseminated at lighting-fast speeds, requiring constant monitoring. Handheld devices and laptops are also aiding employees in the service delivery process.

Revenue management, a foundational component of almost every management information system for tourism service suppliers, was initially used as a scheduling tool for the airline industry. However, its effectiveness in addressing a host of marketing, management, and financial issues soon expanded its use to other tourism service providers such as hotels/motels, resorts, restaurants, cruise ships, golf courses, and car rental companies as part of more complex management information systems. Although revenue management holds the promise of maximizing revenues, it, like most other quantitative management tools, should not be used blindly. Revenue management and all of the other technological innovations discussed in this chapter will definitely change the face of the tourism industry. Where and when these changes will occur is anybody's guess.

YOU DECIDE

Frequent travelers love them. The more you fly, rent, stay, play, and dine, the more you earn. And, the more you earn, the higher your status and prestige with the airline, car rental company, hotel, casino, or restaurant. What are they? Points!

The benefits that flow from points range all the way from upgrades to free flights, rental, stays and more. So it's no wonder that travelers are willing to give up a host of personal information to tap into these loyalty programs.

Think for a moment about the types of information these program participants willingly share with their travel service providers. Depending on which travel service provider is concerned, your personal profile could contain credit card numbers, driver's license number, your mother's maiden name, or even information about other travel service providers you frequently use.

Once a traveler becomes active in a program, other information may be collected ranging from birthdays and anniversaries to spending patterns and leisure versus business activities. All of these specifics provide the key pieces of information needed for creating effective targeted marketing communications. With ever-expanding databases and software enhancements, the depth and breadth of information that can be collected are limited only by the imagination of the data acquirer.

Although these programs have been designed to capture customer loyalty and enhance service delivery and satisfaction, a question of how much information is enough, arises. What types of information is it ethical to acquire and store on loyal customers? How should this information be used? How long should it be retained? Can it be shared with other entities in the same organization and/or related travel partner organizations? Where should the lines be drawn on information collection?

NET TOUR

To get you started on exploring Internet links for this chapter, please see

http://www.tripadvisor.com

http://www.pegs.com

http://www.radiantsystems.com

http://www.micros.com

DISCUSSION QUESTIONS

1. What technological advances have made the most significant changes in the tourism industry?
2. How can technology be used to enhance productivity?
3. How can technology be used to improve both internal and external communications?
4. How has the Internet changed the delivery of tourism services?
5. How can technology be used to enhance customer service?
6. How can revenue management be used to improve financial performance?

APPLYING THE CONCEPTS

1. Make an appointment to visit the manager of a local hotel, resort, or restaurant. During your visit, find out how technology is being used. Make a list of the names of products, systems, and/or programs being used and describe the functions they perform.
2. Browse the Internet for point-of-sale suppliers. Develop a list from your search of three companies that supply this technological application along with a description of the services they offer.
3. Browse the Internet for property management systems. Develop a list from your search of three companies that supply this technological application along with a description of the services they offer.
4. Using your favorite search engine, type in "travel blog." Based on the results, select one blog and summarize your findings for that site.
5. Using Expedia, Travelocity, or Orbitz, search for airfares between Atlanta and Los Angeles on three different dates. The first date for your search should be at least 30 days from today's date. The second date should be 15 days from today's date. Your third date should be 5 days from today's date. Prepare a list of flights and rates. Are the prices the same? If they are different, explain why there is a difference.

GLOSSARY

Available seat miles (ASMs)   The distance traveled multiplied by the number of seats available.

Biometrics   Technologies for identifying and verifying an individual's physiological characteristics such as fingerprints, handprints, facial features, and irises.

Blogs   Online journals composed of links and postings in reverse chronological order.

Data   Facts and figures.

Data mining   Analyzing information stored in computer databases with the help of statistical techniques to uncover hidden relationships and patterns.

Enterprise resource planning system (ERP)   A system designed to combine all information sources, subsystems, and processes from various locations into one unified system.

Information technology   Computer systems that provide for the storage and retrieval of data.

Learning curve   The rate at which people learn over time.

Leg   The segment of a flight between two consecutive stops.

Load factor   The number of revenue passenger miles (RPMs) divided by the number of available seat miles (ASMs).

Management information systems (MIS)   Computer-based systems designed to collect and store data and then provide information for planning, decision making, and problem solving.

Point-of-sale systems (POSs)   Systems designed to record and track customer orders, process debit and credit cards, manage inventory, and connect to other systems in a network.

Property management system (PMS)   A unified system used to manage sales and marketing, reservations, front office operations, point-of-sale systems, telecommunications, back office operations, and revenue management.

Revenue management (yield management)   The process of allocating the right type of capacity to the right kind of customer at the right price so as to maximize revenue or yield.

Revenue passenger miles (RPM)   One seat on an airplane, railroad, or motorcoach traveling one mile with a revenue-producing passenger.

Social networking   Individuals tied together by a common interest or theme who share bookmarked Web links and conversations.

Technology   The use of new knowledge and tools to improve productivity and systems.

REFERENCES

1. Haussman, Glenn. (2007, July 3). Lodging cos shifting to centralized tech. *Hotel Interactive.* Available at: http://www.hotelinteractive.com.
2. Courtney, Manion. (2004). Handheld wireless point of sale systems in the restaurant industry. *Journal of Foodservice Business Research,* 7(2), 103–111.
3. Binkley, Christina. (2000, May 4). A casino chain finds a lucrative niche: The small spenders. *Wall Street Journal,* pp. A1, A10.
4. Offutt, Bob. (2007, August 14). *Five predictions about the future of the Long Tail in travel.* Available at: http://www. hotelmarketing.com/index.php/content/article/070814.
5. Global travel trends. (2007). *BDC white paper.* Available at: www. bdctravel. com.
6. Travel Industry of America. (2007, February). *2007 Outlook for travel & tourism.* Washington, D.C.: Author.
7. Pizam, Abraham. (1999). Life and tourism in the year 2050. *International Journal of Hospitality Management,* 18(4), 331–343.
8. Internet usage statistics. (2008). Available at: http://www.internetworldstats.com/stats.html.
9. Wright, Adam. (2006, April 18). *Mobile phones could soon rival the PC as world's dominant Internet platform.* Available at: http://ipsos-na.com/news/pressrelease.cfm?id=3049.
10. User-generated content more than just hype. (2007, October). *Tourism, Canada's Tourism Business Magazine,* p. 11.
11. Green, Cindy Estes. (2007). Social media and networking. *Hospitality Upgrade,* 13(2), 156, 158.
12. Brotherton, Bob, and Mooney, Sean. (1992). Yield management—Progress and prospects. *International Journal of Hospitality Management,* 11(1), 23–32.
13. Liebermann, Warren H. (2007). From the back seat to the driver's seat. *Journal of Revenue & Pricing,* 6, 300–303.
14. Kimes, Sheryl E. (2003, October-December). Revenue management: A retrospective. *Cornell Hotel & Restaurant Administration Quarterly,* pp. 131–138.
15. Michels, Jennifer. (2008). Saudia chooses Sabre for four business programs. *Aviation Daily,* 371(7), 5.

PART 1

Readings

American Society of Travel Agents (ASTA) Code of Ethics (May 1, 2008)

◾ PREAMBLE

Travelers depend on travel agencies and others affiliated with ASTA to guide them honestly and competently. All ASTA members pledge to conduct their business activities in a manner that promotes the ideal of integrity in travel and agree to act in accordance with the applicable sections of the following Principles of the ASTA Code of Ethics. Complaints arising under this Code should be filed in writing with the ASTA Consumer Affairs Department.

ASTA has the following categories of membership: Travel Agent, Premium, International Travel Agency Company, International Travel Agent Associate, Allied Company, Allied Associate, Travel School, Senior [terminating 12/31/08], and Honorary.

◾ RESPONSIBILITIES OF TRAVEL AGENT, PREMIUM, INTERNATIONAL TRAVEL AGENCY COMPANY, AND INTERNATIONAL TRAVEL AGENT ASSOCIATE MEMBERS

1. *Accuracy.* ASTA members will be factual and accurate when providing information about their services and the services of any firm they represent. They will not use deceptive practices.
2. *Disclosure.* ASTA members will provide in writing, upon written request, complete details about the cost, restrictions, and other terms and conditions, of any travel service sold, including cancellation and service fee policies. Full details of the time, place, duration, and nature of any sales or promotional presentation the consumer will be required to attend in connection with his/her travel arrangements shall be disclosed in writing before any payment is accepted.
3. *Responsiveness.* ASTA members will promptly respond substantively to their clients' complaints.
4. *Refunds.* ASTA members will remit any undisputed funds under their control within the specified time limit. Reasons for delay in providing funds will be given to the claimant promptly.
5. *Cooperation.* ASTA members will cooperate with any inquiry conducted by ASTA to resolve any dispute involving consumers.
6. *Confidentiality.* ASTA members will treat every client transaction confidentially and not disclose any information without permission of the client, unless required by law.
7. *Affiliation.* ASTA members will not falsely represent a person's affiliation with their firm.
8. *Conflict of Interest.* ASTA members will not allow any preferred relationship with a supplier to interfere with the interests of their clients.
9. *Compliance.* ASTA members shall not have been convicted of a violation of any federal, state, and local laws and regulations affecting consumers. Pleas of nolo contendere, consent judgments, judicial or administrative decrees, or orders, and assurances of voluntary compliance and similar agreements with federal or state authorities shall be deemed convictions for purposes of these provisions.

◾ RESPONSIBILITIES OF ALL MEMBERS

1. *Notice.* ASTA members operating tours will promptly advise the agent or client who reserved the space of any change in itinerary, services, features or price.
2. *Delivery.* ASTA members operating tours will provide all components as stated in

their brochure or written confirmation, or provide alternate services of equal or greater value, or provide appropriate compensation.

3. *Credentials.* An ASTA member shall not, in exchange for money or otherwise, provide travel agent credentials to any person as to whom there is no reasonable expectation that the person will engage in a bona fide effort to sell or manage the sale of travel services to the general public on behalf of the member through the period of validity of such credentials. This

principle applies to the ASTA member and all affiliated or commonly controlled enterprises.

CONCLUSION

Failure to adhere to this Code may subject a member to disciplinary actions, as set forth in ASTA's Bylaws.

Reprinted by permission from the American Society of Travel Agents.

Motorcoach Tours Had Modest Start in New England in 1925

BY EVA HODGES WATT

This fall, motorcoaches will once again wend their way along New England's country roads, framed by hillsides aflame with fall's spectacular colors.

The popular leaf-peeping tradition may well trace its genesis to the day a young New England bank teller spilled a cigar box of coins down the building's dumb waiter.

Arthur Tauck helped the bank manager pick up the coins from the basement's greasy floor and was then fired for his trouble. But if they took Tauck for a milquetoast, they were mistaken. The young New Englander promptly invented a brick-shaped metal tray to hold coins, still in use today.

The bank rehired him, but he soon realized there was more money to be made traveling the New England countryside and upstate New York in his newfangled automobile, selling the metal tray to banks.

In the fall, he was dazzled by nature's wondrous array of crimson, burgundy, and golden leaves quilting the hillsides.

Tauck found most automobilers were businessmen like himself, driving alone. The few tourists he saw seemed to be bumbling about aimlessly. He began inviting friends with him on his trips.

And then—his family believes—Arthur Tauck invented the motorcoach tour in 1925.

"Who else thought of taking out an ad in the Newark Evening News and then driving guests on a 1,100-mile trip, 900 of them on dirt roads?" asks his granddaughter Robin Tauck, who with her brother, Peter, is co-president of Tauck World Discovery.

Arthur, who was 24 when he began his tours, promised his guests the best hotels and an exciting journey through New England and even into Canada. There were six passengers on the first tour. His fledgling business flourished, and in 1927 Arthur Tauck bought buses.

In 1935, License No. 1, the first tour broker's license in the travel industry, was issued to Tauck Tours by the newly formed Interstate Commerce Commission. Today, Tauck World Discovery tours circle the globe with more than 90 itineraries.

We took the "original" (updated, of course) 11-day Autumn Foliage Tour, which left from New York's Waldorf-Astoria Hotel on a crisp, sunny day in late September.

As our motorcoach traveled through the scenic Hudson River Valley, our guide, Joemy Wilson (her parents named her "Poem"), read us poet Robert Frost's homage to birches bending over water like

girls on hands and knees
that throw their hair
Before them over their heads to
dry in the sun,

just as the graceful trees we were viewing bowed over the river.

Our first two nights were spent at the magnificent Mirror Lake Lodge at Lake Placid. Daytime tours took us to see Olympic hopefuls ski-jumping down steep slopes into large tanks of water and for a cruise on Lake Placid ringed by "camps," as they call the often elaborate summer homes of wealthy owners such as the late singer Kate Smith and the millionaire who invented the spout for milk cartons.

The next day, after ferrying across Lake Champlain, we followed the turning of the leaves—glorious flashes of brilliance on the green hillsides—as we made our way through Vermont. The early French explorer Samuel de Champlain is said to have exclaimed on first seeing the countryside in the early 1600s, "ah, vert mons"—"ah, green mountains."

We paused to visit the Shelburne Museum, a large park dotted with period buildings filled with artworks and crafts, then traveled to Stowe for a buffet lunch at the Trapp Family Lodge (owned by the family featured in "The Sound of Music") and visited apple cider and maple syrup operations.

On ensuing days, we rode through picturesque villages—towns with pristine Victorian, Federalist, and Colonial homes painted white or in pastel hues (by community mandate), all centered about churches with slender spires and looking as perfect as Hollywood sets. We passed into the White Mountains of New Hampshire, where the fall hues intensified.

Traveling the rocky coast of Maine, we saw lobstermen, boatyards, and fine summer homes, including that of former President George Bush of Kennebunkport.

Our travels toward Massachusetts inspired recollections of the Revolutionary War and the heroism of the ill-clad, ill-equipped Colonial volunteers against superior British forces. Tactfully,

Joemy reminded our seven passengers from Great Britain that "these rebels weren't 'Americans' at that time, they were British citizens."

For a change of pace from our rural ramblings, we spent two nights at the Boston Marriott Copley Place. A city tour took us to Boston Common, Back Bay, Beacon Hill, Charles Street, and Faneuil Hall. Our passengers also fanned out to visit the Boston Museum of Art, which has the second largest collection in the country; to follow the well-marked Freedom Trail, or even to an opera performance of Wagner.

Then it was on to Plymouth, with a stop to peer at the much diminished Plymouth Rock (visitors chipped away at it for more than 200 years before it was fenced off) and to tour Plimoth Plantation, a fine re-creation of the 17th-century village, where, in each of the tiny homes, local people were costumed as the original residents and spoke to us in the dialect and context of their times.

As we rode toward Newport, R.I., Joemy read to us from Edith Wharton's novel "The Age of Innocence" about well-to-do New Yorkers preparing for their annual migration to the upscale resort to enjoy the summer social season at the turn of the century.

The next morning we viewed many of the splendid Newport mansions on an oceanside drive. We toured The Breakers, the 73-room Vanderbilt marble "cottage" and its magnificent grounds, as well as Auchincloss Farm, where President John F. Kennedy often vacationed at his in-laws' digs. There, from the desk in his cliffside office, he could look out to sea.

We also explored Newport by foot, and that night we walked from the Newport Harbor Hotel and Marina to a nearby restaurant for a final lobster dinner and farewell party.

En route to New York City, a visit to Mystic Seaport, Conn., was our last adventure. An entire village of lovingly preserved old ships, homes, and shops gave us an excellent feel for Mystic's heyday as a great whaling port.

Arthur Tauck survived the Great Depression thanks to his savvy business acumen in promoting his motorcoach tours to and from the 1933 Chicago World's Fair. Until then, the only overland link between Chicago and New York was by rail.

Tauck died in 1961. Today, Arthur Tauck, Jr. is chairman of the family-held company's board. His children, Peter and Robin, began their careers in the mailroom at early ages, Peter when he was 7, Robin a couple of years later.

Arthur, Jr. proved to be as visionary as his father, first creating new itineraries that combined air and motorcoach travel throughout the western United States with an emphasis on the national parks. The business continued to expand, by helicopters, sea, and land, in the alpine areas in the Canadian Rockies, in Hawaii, Europe, the Mediterranean, and Asia.

All this has not gone unnoticed by the travel industry. Tauck's testimonials include receiving the American Automobile Association's best customer satisfaction award the last four years.

Reprinted by permission of Eva Hodges Watt.

The Art of Travel Writing

BY WILLIAM R. GRAY

Over the past three decades or so, travel writing—like other nonfiction—has undergone a transformation from a more reportorial style to one that is propelled by the literary voice of the author. This approach is personal and features the active participation of the writer in the subject matter—and thus is highly involving for readers, who feel they are being taken on a journey of discovery.

Writers such as Edward Abbey, John McPhee, William Least Heat-Moon (particularly in *Blue Highways*), and Paul Theroux were in the vanguard of this approach to nonfiction writing, and today there are literally platoons of excellent writers following their lead. And the great travel magazines overflow each issue with generally superb writing.

In teaching my writing courses—including travel writing—and speaking at conferences, I try to instill the key elements that contribute to quality nonfiction writing, and all of these apply most emphatically to travel. Focusing on these attributes helps elevate the quality of the writing, the personal involvement of the author, and draws readers in—and as writers we always need to keep our readers in the forefront of our minds.

- *Keen Observer:* always seek the descriptive element, the penetrating detail that truly brings your subject to life and illuminates its uniqueness. When interviewing someone, avoid the obvious descriptors such as color of hair and eyes; instead focus on timbre of voice, tilt of head, the gesture or mannerism that reveals character, the way light and shadow play across the face. Likewise with place, use imagery to evoke essential qualities; atmospherics and color are integral—the play of clouds, the tone of wind; use color dramatically—a cobalt sky; a sunset the color of apricots.

- *Active Participant:* be both dynamically and intimately involved with your subject; follow every lead and participate in every activity appropriate to the place you are writing about. Get up early, stay up late, and experience new things all day long.

- *Depth of Feeling:* develop empathy for your subject; seek to experience it emotionally and do not hesitate to reveal something of yourself—how events and people affect you.

- *Openness to Experience:* seek the harrowing, the exhilarating, the unusual. Canoe through the crocodile-infested waters; climb the treacherous cliff; stay up all night with the raucous carnival celebrants. In other words, be open to doing everything that might contribute to your understanding of the place you are writing about. Be spontaneous—one of these activities may form the basis of the lead to your story.

- *Desire to Seek Knowledge* and *Understanding:* strive to know your subject deeply; it's the way it is today because of the confluence of history, geology, exploration, warfare, cultural traditions, racial configuration, tourism, and a dozen other factors. Understanding these elements will give perspective to your writing and help make it insightful and profound.

- *Desire to Seek a High Level in the Craft of Writing:* use a strong first person point of view and a clear literary style to elevate and distinguish your writing. Begin with an effective, original lead and end meaningfully. Always be aware of diction, sentence variety, and quality of transitions. Write so creatively and imaginatively that you leave your readers impatiently waiting to devour your next piece of writing.

William R. Gray traveled the globe for 33 years as a writer, editor, and publishing executive with the National Geographic Society. He took an early retirement and moved to Durango, Colorado, with his family in 2002, where he has resumed his magazine and book writing career, teaches several writing *and* editing courses—including travel writing—and launched a publishing consulting business.

PART 1

Integrative Cases

Elite House: Using e-Service Recovery to Deal with Brick and Mortar Failure

100% Satisfaction Guaranteed

Elite House: Using e-Service Recovery to Deal with Brick and Mortar Failure

MICHAEL R. LUTHY, BELLARMINE UNIVERSITY

CURT RICHARDS, BELLARMINE UNIVERSITY

INTRODUCTION

When consumers report critical incidents to companies, both positive and negative ones, they are providing the organizations with significant information concerning how effective and how efficient they are in serving their customers and markets. While a single negative incident reported by a lone consumer seemingly holds little value, good organizations acknowledge that each notification of a failure (whether perceived or actual) may represent the "tip of the iceberg," highlighting an issue or process that a great many more customers may be experiencing without taking the time and effort to report it; and that it may be a sign of a deeper rooted issue for the organization. The communications presented here are actual e-mail messages exchanged between a consumer and the Elite House Hotel chain through their corporate website. The consumer's initial e-mail message is sent to both the hotel property (Elite House) website and corporate (Elite House International) website simultaneously.

Tuesday, March 13, 9:59 A.M.—Initial E-Mail Complaint

> To: EliteHouseNet/Subject: Guest Relations—Inside the U.S. Hotels
>
> To: Internet Help Desk/Subject: Guest Relations—Inside the U.S. Hotels

(1) Last week (March 7–10), I stayed at the Elite House in Atlanta as part of the Southern Business Association (SBA) conference. The organization has held its annual meetings there for many years and generally things go well. This year, however, I experienced a number of minor and not so minor problems that made the stay as much frustrating as enjoyable. In the lobby, as well as on the 5th floor, Elite has placed several terminals that offer 10 minutes free Internet surfing. On at least four separate occasions during my stay, I tried to take advantage of this to check for e-mail messages. I provided my name, e-mail address, and other personal information but was never connected to my school's website. My 10 free minutes just ran out—every time. I finally broke down and went to the Elite business center where I was able to use the service—for a $5.00 minimum fee. As I look back on this now, I wonder what will happen to the information I provided and why this occurred.

(2) One morning, I decided to splurge and order breakfast from room service using the card left on my bed. I checked the 6:00–6:20 A.M. delivery time box and left it hanging on my door. The food was delivered almost 10 minutes before this, causing me to scramble a bit since I was not expecting it to come before then.

(3) A minor but irritating issue was the soft drink machine on my floor (the 18th). Rather than raid the room's mini-bar for a $2.25 can of pop, I went to buy one for $1.75 on my floor's machine. After trying for several minutes to get it to accept my various dollar bills without success, I admitted defeat and went downstairs to the lobby to get quarters. Given the delay with the elevators (see next note), this wasn't a quick trip. Upon returning to the 18th floor I found that the machine wouldn't take my quarters either. They just kept falling through the machine. I ultimately went up to the 19th floor and that machine wouldn't take the quarters either. Fortunately, it took my dollar bills. (Gunga Din didn't have as much trouble finding water.)

(4) During my stay a bank of elevators in the hotel was out of service. Because the floor I was on (and many others from the conference) was only serviced by one set of three elevators, some of the waits were interminable. Twenty to thirty minutes wasn't too uncommon and I believe quite a few complaints were lodged with the Elite

House staff. After a while, a passing staff person told us that we could use the freight/service elevators. Over the next two days, more and more of us did this after a ten-minute wait. While the staff riding with us was generally quite nice, some were heard muttering under their breath that they weren't too happy that we were increasing their wait time for an elevator. I thought this was particularly ironic considering the signs I saw in the service elevator area stated that guest satisfaction was priority #1. Ultimately, what I'm asking for is an explanation from Elite House why these things happened and why it believes treating guests in this manner is appropriate. Thank you./Sincerely, Dr. Matthews.

Wednesday, March 14, 3:32 A.M.—Initial Response (Automated)

Elite's Internet Help Desk in Seattle, Washington, has just received your e-mail for processing. We thank you for taking the time to send us your comments! I have taken the liberty of forwarding your message to the Guest Relations Department for their attention. Please note that all e-mail is processed in the order of which it is received. We thank you for your patronage! Regards/Lorri M./Internet Coordinator/Seattle, WA.

Thursday, March 15, 12:01 P.M.—Initial Response (Real Person)

Burt Garry, General Manager of the Elite House, is in receipt of your e-mail dated March 14th in reference to your recent visit to the hotel to attend the Southern Business Association conference. He was extremely concerned to learn of the difficulties you experienced during your stay with us and asked me to convey his apologies.

There is simply no excuse for the myriad of small problems that plagued you during your visit and you may be certain that these issues have been addressed and corrective measures have been initiated. With regard to the lengthy elevator delays you experienced, we are currently undergoing a project to modernize our elevator cabs, which entails taking two cars out of service at a time. Unfortunately, during your stay with us, two additional cars malfunctioned resulting in the delays you describe. As you indicated, our service elevators were made available to our guests to expedite their movement through the hotel. We do regret you were subjected to any inappropriate comments from hotel staff regarding the elevator situation.

Dr. Matthews, as you mentioned, guest service is our number one priority and we are concerned with the overall impression you have formed of the hotel based on your recent experience. We would certainly welcome the opportunity to regain your goodwill and, with that in mind, would be pleased to provide you with complimentary accommodations for one evening during your next visit to Atlanta. This invitation is based upon hotel availability and is valid until March 15, [one year from time of previous stay]. Please contact me directly so that I may handle your reservation requirements. We look forward to the opportunity to serve you in the true spirit of hospitality for which Elite House Hotels are known. Sincerely/Susan Henry/Executive Office/Elite House.

Thursday, March 15, 1:15 P.M.

Dear Ms. Henry, I appreciate you responding to my message, and for doing so, so quickly. While your offer of a complementary night's stay to regain my goodwill is a generous one, it puts me in the position of having to return to Atlanta within the next year in order to take advantage of it. I would like the decision of whether to return to the Elite House and when to be a nonconditional one. In that spirit, I would like to request a credit to my American Express card for the cost of one of my recent nights' stay during the conference (when the problems occurred). Please let me know what you decide.

Friday, March 16, 12:37 P.M.

Dr. Matthews, we would be happy to refund your room and tax charges for one night. We have instructed our Finance Department to process a credit to your American Express account in the amount of [$184.99]. Susan Henry/Executive Office/Elite House.

◼ QUESTIONS

1. How would you characterize the tone and content of the original (Tuesday March 13th) letter written by the consumer? Is he a crackpot? What is he asking for? And is it reasonable? Explain.
2. What is your analysis of the company's initial (March 15th) response to the consumer?
3. After reading the remaining communications, have your opinions of the parties involved or their positions changed?

4. How much would the organization's first offer cost them? How does it compare to what they finally agreed to for Dr. Matthews?

Note: This case was developed as the basis for class discussion rather than to illustrate either effective or ineffective handling of a customer service situation. The identities of individuals, the company, and locations have been disguised.

100% Satisfaction Guaranteed

After a particularly frustrating business trip, Sales Representative Dan O'Brien sent the following letter to the president and CEO of El Primo Inns, Inc.

Dear Mr. Simmons,

As a long-time El Primo customer, I am very disappointed with the way I was treated on my most recent visit. You advertise a 100% Satisfaction Guarantee. However, I left your hotel nothing close to 100% satisfied.

I made a reservation through your reservation system for the airport location because my flight was not scheduled to arrive until 10:30 P.M. Your reservation clerk assured me that the hotel had airport shuttle service available at that time. I gave the airport location to my boss as he was to meet me the morning after my arrival.

Due to weather, my flight was over an hour late. After collecting my luggage, I called the hotel to request the shuttle. The clerk at the hotel could not find my reservation and asked for my confirmation number. Upon receiving it, he informed me that my reservation was at another El Primo property about 6 miles away. I called that property for shuttle service and was told that the service stopped running at 10 P.M. Therefore, I was forced to pay $16 for a cab to take me to the hotel.

Upon checking in, I asked the clerk to call the airport hotel location and leave a message so that my boss could find me at this other location. Her response? "It's not my problem."

The next morning, I tried to explain the problems I had to the general manager. His only reaction? "I'm sorry." Is this all your managers are authorized to do when confronted with a dissatisfied customer?

When I checked in, the rate I was given was $69, the rate I was quoted by your reservation clerk. When I checked out the next morning, the rate had increased to $79. When I brought this discrepancy to the clerk's attention, he said that the night audit system automatically posts the rate of $79 unless the night auditors override the system. He then corrected the amount. Again, I talked with the general manager and his response again was simply, "I am sorry."

These are the facts. Your 100% Satisfaction Guaranteed slogan doesn't really seem to mean very much. I look forward to your response.

Sincerely,
Dan O'Brien

Based on the above information,

1. What should a "100% Satisfaction Guarantee" mean in the case of a hotel? What did it appear to mean in the case of El Primo Inns?
2. How many breaks from the service script occurred according to Mr. O'Brien's letter?

3. What service recovery measures should have been taken?

4. If you were Mr. Simmons, what would your response(s) be in this situation?

5. Should Mr. Simmons follow up on his letter to Mr. O'Brien? If so, what kind of follow-up? What should he say?

This critical incident was prepared by Roy A. Cook, Laura J. Yale, and John E. Cave of Fort Lewis College and is intended to be used as a basis for class discussion rather than to illustrate either effective or ineffective handling of the situation. The name of the organization, the individuals, and locations have been disguised to preserve the organization's desire for anonymity. Copyright © 2001 by Roy A. Cook, Laura J. Yale, and John E. Cave.

PART 11

Tourism Service Suppliers

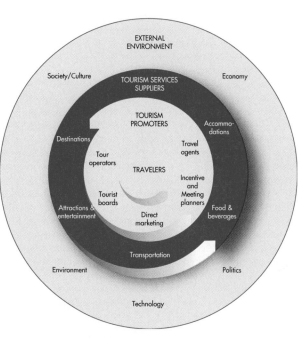

■ An integrated model of tourism.

LEARNING OBJECTIVES

After you have read this chapter, you should be able to:

- Explain the importance of transportation to the tourism industry.
- Identify and describe the major components of the tourism transportation system.
- Explain the differences between passenger railroad operations within and outside the United States.
- Explain the importance of automobiles and motorcoaches to the tourism transportation system.
- Describe the role and importance of water transportation in the movement of travelers.
- Describe how airlines operate in a deregulated and competitive environment.

CHAPTER OUTLINE

CHAPTER 6

Transportation

For my part, I travel not to go anywhere, but to go. I travel for travel's sake. The great affair is to move.

—Robert Louis Stevenson

■ Ferries form one of the many links in the transportation system.

THE GRADUATION GIFT

When Shawna opened the envelope at her graduation party, it seemed too good to be true: a trip to Europe! Her grandparents had often discussed the benefits of travel and encouraged Shawna to travel to learn more about the world around her. They had taken Shawna with them on some of their journeys and she had also traveled with her parents on summer vacations and business trips. These trips had allowed her to see some beautiful and exciting places, but now she was going to faraway places to do things she had only dreamed about.

After the excitement of the graduation party was over, Shawna settled down to carefully read the letter her grandparents had written describing their travel gift. They were going to buy her a round-trip airline ticket from her home in Montgomery, Alabama, to her choice of either London or Paris. They also were going to give her the money to buy a Eurailpass and her choice of a ticket to travel on the Eurostar through the Chunnel between London and Paris or a ticket on one of the ferries that cross the English Channel. In addition, they had included a check for $1,000 to help pay for some of her other expenses.

Shawna knew it was late, but she couldn't wait to call her grandparents and thank them for the gift. When she asked them what airline to call and which one of the channel-crossing options to take, they simply told her that the experiences to be gained from planning her travels were part of the gift. With this in mind, Shawna contacted Derik, her mother's travel agent, for help in designing her itinerary.

During her first meeting with Derik, she learned that she would be using many different types of transportation while on her trip. She could begin by driving, riding a bus, or flying on a small commuter airline to Atlanta. Once there, she could fly directly to either London or Paris. After arriving in Europe, Shawna would have several choices of air, rail, and bus transportation. In addition, there was still the question of how she should cross the English Channel between England and France. Derik answered all of Shawna's questions, but his answers led her to ask only more questions.

Shawna soon began to realize that there were several ways to meet her travel needs and she wanted to know more. Provided with a whole new understanding of transportation options, she and Derik began to discuss and plan the details of her upcoming trip. Her grandparents were right; planning her trip was a learning experience.

INTRODUCTION

Although we may not think about it, the tourism industry would cease to function without an efficient and effective transportation system; trains, automobiles, and airplanes are just a few of the more obvious parts of this system. The importance of all of these transportation modes to both travelers and tourism suppliers was vividly demonstrated as the air transportation system was shut down in the United States following the September 11, 2001, terrorist attacks. Every segment of the tourism system was adversely affected.

There are many other modes of transportation in addition to planes, trains, and automobiles from which to choose. The components of this system can be conveniently classified and placed into two broad categories: surface (land and water) and air. As Figure 6.1 shows, transportation is often **intermodal**, with travelers relying on several different modes of transportation to reach their final destinations. How did this system develop and how does it function today?

Modes of transportation evolved slowly until the 19th and 20th centuries; then, as Table 6.1 shows, things really began to happen. By this time, railways criss-crossed the continents of Europe and North America; gasoline-powered cars became a common sight as highways were developed; steamships plied the waters across major trade routes; and the possibility of flight became a reality. Transportation has now become so efficient that we often think of travel in terms of time rather than distance.

The international standard for transportation timetables is the 24-hour clock. Figure 6.2 presents a visual example of the 24-hour clock. Notice

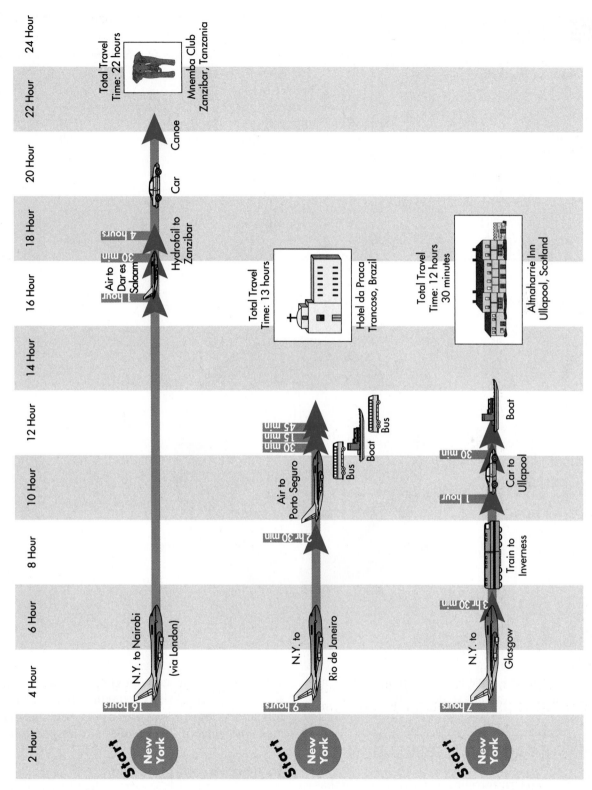

■ Figure 6.1 Intermodal transportation and times.
Adapted from *Condé Nast TRAVELER* (1996, March), pp. 106–107.

Table 6.1	Trends in Travel Time	
Year	*Method*	*Elapsed Time in Days*
Around the World		
1889	Sailing ship–Nellie Bly	72.00
1924	U.S. Army aircraft	35.00
1929	*Graf Zeppelin* dirigible	30.00
1947	Pan American Airways Constellation	4.00
2006	Suborbital passenger spacecraft	0.50
Across the Atlantic *(New York to London)*		
1905	Sailing ship–*Atlantic*	12.00
1938	Steamship–*Queen Mary*	4.00
2005	QE2	6.00

■ Figure 6.2   The 24-hour clock.

that by using this style of timekeeping, there is no need for either A.M. or P.M. designations.

SURFACE TRANSPORTATION

Just like modern travelers, early travelers probably used both land and water. Modern modes of surface transportation were ushered in with the development of sailing vessels and then passenger railroads, and grew with increased personal ownership of automobiles, availability of rental vehicles, and the convenience of motorcoach services. We will briefly examine important historical developments as well as key issues associated with each of these modes of transportation.

Plying the Waves

The power of the wind behind a good sail moved passengers across countless miles of water to many locations for business and pleasure. However, no matter how sleek or fast these ships, they were always subject to the vagaries of the wind. With a favorable wind, it truly was "smooth sailing." But when the wind died and the sails went slack, there was little for passengers and crew to do other than sit and wait for the wind to return.

With the introduction of steam power, regularly scheduled passenger service on primary water routes became a reality. Like most of the early technological innovations in transportation, steam-powered ships originated in Europe. In 1838, two passenger ships (the *Sirus* and the *Great Western*) crossed the Atlantic from Ireland and Great Britain to the United States. By today's standards, and even compared with the speed of clipper ships, their 19- and 15-day crossings were slow. But they ushered in a new age of dependable scheduled service whereby travelers had some assurance that they would arrive at their destinations on time.[1]

Transatlantic passenger traffic grew rapidly until 1957 when another technological innovation—the jet engine—heralded the demise of **point-to-point** ocean crossings. Although Cunard Lines still runs scheduled routes between Southampton, England, and New York City, and some cruise ships at times carry passengers on point-to-point crossings, ocean-going transportation is now limited. Long-distance cruise ship crossings are typically restricted to **repositioning cruises**, in which cruise ships are being moved from one location to another. For example, a cruise line will move ships from the Caribbean to the Mediterranean to take advantage of seasonal changes and passenger demands.

Mention water transportation, and most people think about cruise ships or a brief hop on a ferry when they cross a river, lake, or other short distance on a waterway. Water transportation, especially ferry services, is still an important link in the total transportation system. Passenger ferries have evolved over time and have become more sophisticated, offering a wide range of services. They are now designed to do more than just carry passengers and vehicles. Some ferries also offer sleeping cabins, restaurants, lounges, casinos, movie theaters, shops, and child care services.

Passenger ferry routes have been designed to tie in with rail and road systems to facilitate intermodal transportation. These routes create

important links in the transportation system for many residents and visitors in North American locations such as Alaska, British Columbia, Newfoundland, Nova Scotia, and Washington State. British Columbia, for example, has an extensive system of ferries calling on 42 coastal ports.[2] For the millions of people who travel throughout Asia and the European community, water transportation is not a luxury but a necessity.

Technological advances in ferry design and construction have increased both speeds and operating efficiencies. These high-speed ferries are particularly noticeable in high-traffic tourist areas such as the Bahamas, Catalina Island, Hong Kong, and along the Massachusetts coastline. These locations are all served by high-speed catamarans that can transport passengers at speeds of up to 42 miles per hour.

Riding the Rails

Passenger rail service had its origins in Europe. The first railway service for passengers was inaugurated in Europe on September 17, 1825, when the Stockton and Darlington Railway began offering regularly scheduled service in England. Passenger rail service arrived in North America in 1829, when the South Carolina and Canal Railroad began carrying passengers between Charleston, South Carolina, and Hamburg, Georgia, with steam-powered locomotives. Transcontinental service in the United States began in 1869 and in Canada in 1885.

Long-distance rail travel was given a boost in the United States when George Pullman developed the Pullman coach, with sleeping facilities for overnight travel. The addition of dining cars and legitimate food and lodging facilities pioneered by Fred Harvey heralded the golden age of passenger railroad service in the United States. Dissatisfied with poor food and service, Harvey arranged in 1875 to provide food service for the Atchison, Topeka, and Santa Fe Railroad at its Topeka, Kansas, depot. He became so well known for quality and service that the railroad eventually awarded him all of its dining car services.

Passenger rail service flourished and was an important form of domestic transportation in

Canada and the United States until the 1940s. In fact, railroad transportation was so prominent that lodging facilities were developed at major destinations along the rail lines such as Banff, Alberta, Canada, and White Sulphur Springs, West Virginia. However, the forces of change eventually led to the decline of passenger rail service in North America. First, automobile ownership as well as the number of miles traveled by car increased. Then, the Trans-Canada Highway Act of 1949 and the U.S. Federal Aid Highway Act of 1956 enabled provinces and states to begin constructing major highway systems. Both of these factors facilitated long-distance automobile travel. Second, domestic jet passenger service became available. Third, the railroads did not adequately maintain their tracks or customer services. The final blow to U.S. passenger rail service came in 1967 when the post office announced that it would no longer ship mail by train. Without this government subsidy, passenger services became unprofitable, and the railroads began to concentrate on moving freight.

AMTRAK AND VIA RAIL CANADA SERVICES

Rail passenger service followed similar tracks of decline in both Canada and the United States until public interest in salvaging long-distance passenger train service resulted in government intervention. **Amtrak** was formed in 1971 and **VIA Rail Canada** in 1978 to reduce the number of routes and points served while upgrading the remaining passenger rail systems. Although in different countries, there are many similarities between these two passenger-rail-operating companies.

Amtrak is the marketing name for the National Railroad Passenger Corporation, which is a combination of the passenger rail services of U.S. railroads. Amtrak trains now serve 45 states, with stops in hundreds of communities. (Note: The popular Alaska Railroad is not part of the Amtrak system.) VIA Rail Canada is the marketing name for Canada's passenger train network, which links over 400 communities throughout the country. Although they both receive governmental financial support, neither Amtrak nor VIA Rail Canada is a government

agency; they are corporations structured and managed like other large businesses.

Passenger rail service in Canada and the United States, where passenger and freight trains share the same rails, still faces an uncertain future and will probably continue to rely on some form of government subsidies. However, with increased urban growth and new airports being constructed farther and farther from city centers, rail service may grow in importance. Because train terminals were originally built in the center of cities, they now provide a convenient central location and, in many cases, faster and easier transportation in crowded corridors. This is especially true between major cities in close proximity to each other, such as Montreal and Toronto, New York and Boston, Kansas City and St. Louis, and Los Angeles and San Francisco.

Recent improvements in Amtrak service can be attributed to several factors: introduction of improved service and scheduling in the high-traffic Northeast corridors, aggressive marketing and packaging of vacation trips including rail passes (All Aboard America Fares) and fly/rail packages, membership in the Airlines Reporting Corporation (ARC), and listings on airline computer reservation systems. Amtrak service has been further enhanced by the addition of high-speed trains (top speeds of 150 mph) on major passenger routes and routes that serve as feeders to major hub airports. In fact, in some city pairs, transit time is shorter via Amtrak service than by air service. See Table 6.2 for some examples.

Similar steps such as rail passes (**CANRAIL-PASS**), fly/drive packages, special tour packages, and lodging partnerships have been taken by VIA Rail Canada to enhance customer service and ridership.

More generous government support has also enhanced Canadian rail service. "Subsidized by the Liberal Canadian government to the tune of $170 million a year (43% of VIA's budget compared with the 39% Amtrak gets from U.S. taxpayers), VIA whooshes through some of North America's most spectacular wilderness scenery in charmingly retro style."[3] Amtrak is also finding new market niches as it has partnered with Grand Luxe Rail Journeys to offer regularly scheduled luxury private rail services.

■ Passenger rail service varies in importance as a transportation mode from country to country.

Table 6.2	Comparison of Travel Times Between Washington, D.C., and Chicago, Illinois
Mode of Transportation	*Travel Time*
Airplane	4 hours
Bus	17 hours
Car	11 hours
Train	18 hours

Note: The above time estimates factor in check-in lead times and transportation to terminals.
Source: Clark, Jane. (2008, January 18). The deal's on the bus. *USA Today*, pp. 7D–8D.

■ INTERNATIONAL PASSENGER RAIL SERVICE

Although train travel has declined in Canada and the United States, it has continued to be an important mode of intercity transportation in Europe and Asia. At present, the countries with the largest number of train passengers are Japan, Russia, and India. Heavy population concentrations and attention to roadbeds and tracks dedicated solely to passenger traffic have led to the development of high-speed rail service. China, Japan, Korea, France, Great Britain, Italy, Germany, Sweden, and Spain are just a few of the countries where passengers can travel by train at speeds averaging up to 220 miles per hour (350 kilometers per hour). The technology for high-speed rail travel is continually evolving, and trains that can travel at speeds of up to 270 miles per hour are being put into service.[4]

Between major population centers within European countries, train travel has become so fast and efficient that it is often more convenient and less expensive than travel by plane when travel to the airport, check-in, and baggage handling times are considered.[5] As you look at the expansiveness and complexity of the European Rail System, which also includes ferry links as shown in Figure 6.3, think back to the limited service provided by Amtrak or VIA Rail Canada. Examples in Table 6.3 compare the competitive nature of train and air travel between key European cities.

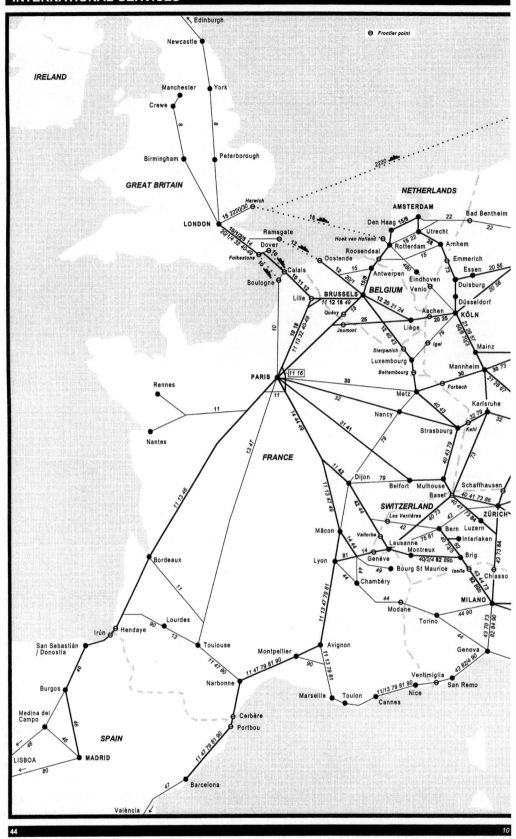

■ **Figure 6.3** Example of rail and ferry service in Europe. This is a map of the main international rail and ferry services in Europe, representing only a fraction of the full rail network of Europe.
Reproduced by permission of Thomas Cook Publishing from *Thomas Cook European Timetable,* published monthly. Available from Thomas Cook Publishing or in North America from Rail Europe Inc., White Plains, New York.

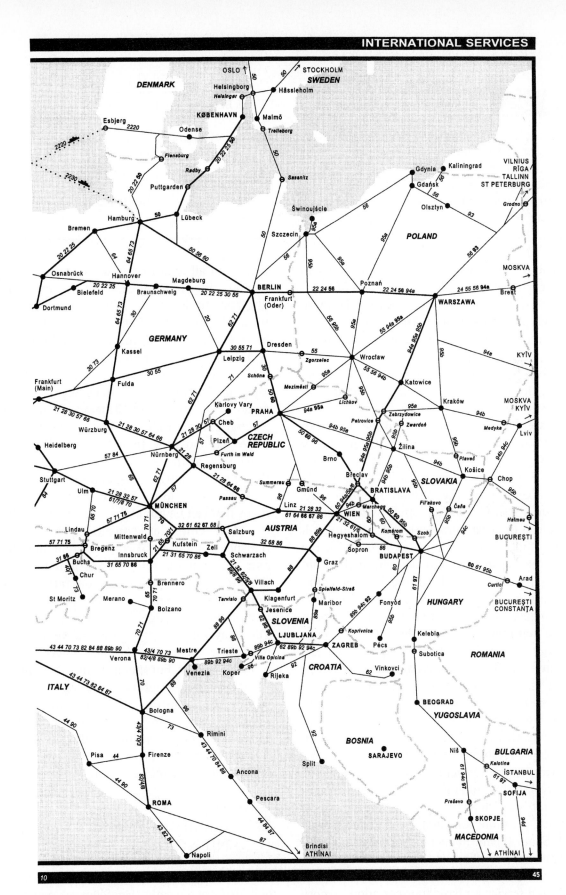

■ Figure 6.3 (continued)

Table 6.3	Comparison of Train and Air Travel Times Between Key European Cities	
	By Rail	*By Air*
London to Edinburgh	4 hr	1 hr 15 min
Paris to Marseilles	4 hr 15 min	1 hr 20 min
Madrid to Seville	3 hr 30 min	55 min
Hamburg to Munich	6 hr	1 hr 15 min
Rome to Milan	4 hr	1 hr 5 min

One of the most exciting developments in rail transportation was the inauguration of high-speed passenger rail service between London, England, and Paris, France. The Eurostar, which travels through the channel tunnel or "Chunnel," allows passengers to make the entire trip in just under two hours at speeds of close to 200 mph, cutting the time in half when compared with ferry crossings.

Passenger rail service in Europe has been further enhanced through expansion of the **Eurailpass.** A number of European countries—Austria, Belgium, Denmark, France, West Germany, Italy, Luxembourg, the Netherlands, Norway, Portugal, Spain, Sweden, and Switzerland—introduced the first Eurailpass in 1959. Finland, Greece, and Ireland were added later. With the fall of the Berlin Wall and the end of the Cold War, the pass became valid throughout the entire German Republic as well as the Czech Republic and Hungary. Trains have become so significant in Europe that they move more than 40 times more passengers every day than in the United States.[6]

The Eurailpass is used as a marketing tool to attract international visitors from outside the European community because it is available only to non-European tourists. Pass holders are allowed unlimited travel for varying periods of time throughout Western Europe, with the exception of Great Britain. Recognizing the importance of rail travel to their total tourism package, individual countries such as Great Britain (Britrail pass), Germany (German Railpass), Switzerland (Swiss Pass), Spain (Spain Railpass), and Greece (Greek Railpass) are providing similar services.

In addition to the ready availability of passenger rail service for basic transportation in most developed countries, there are also several specialty trains with particular appeal to tourists. The Orient Express is without a doubt the most famous of all luxurious or scenic trains. With its magnificently restored cars, it runs from London, England, to Istanbul, Turkey. Another classic train, the Blue Train, can be found traveling between Cape Town and Johannesburg, South Africa. With its gold-tinted windows and fine dining, the Blue Train is also renowned for its mystique and romanticism. China's Sky Train carries passengers across the Tibetan Plateau from Xining, China, to Lhasa, Tibet, using three locomotives to cross the 16,640 Tangula Pass.[7] Other trains such as the Copper Canyon in Mexico, the Palace on Wheels in India, and the Indian-Pacific in Australia are just a few of the many specialty trains that can be found throughout the world.

Most countries consider passenger rail transportation to be of vital national importance and continue to retain government control. Therefore, information on operating results (other than ridership) and the financial condition of most passenger railroads is not available. This may all change in the future as a trend toward private ownership and reduced subsidies has emerged in European countries, especially Great Britain and Germany. Managers there find themselves venturing into unfamiliar territory, requiring marketing skills to maintain and increase ridership and financial skills to attract the necessary capital to maintain and improve service quality while controlling costs.

CRUISING THE HIGHWAYS AND BYWAYS

The term *highway* came into use as roads were built up from the paths they followed to raise them out of the mud and make them usable on a year-round basis. Innovations in road construction that were pioneered by the French and English soon spread throughout the world.[8] Road construction has continued to progress and now plays a central role in the transportation systems of all developed countries. For example, the first multilane highway, the Autobahn, built in Germany during the 1930s, still serves as a vital link in that country's transportation system. These improvements in road systems allowed travelers to move from horses and carts and stagecoaches to automobiles and motorcoaches.

Automobiles

Nowhere in the world is the love affair with the automobile stronger than in North America. Much of the credit for this attraction goes to the pioneering genius of Henry Ford, who ushered in the age of mass automobile travel with his famous Model T. Between 1908 and 1923, fifteen million of these affordable cars were produced. The car is now more than simply transportation for most Americans; it is a symbol of freedom and individualized lifestyles.

The availability of affordable automobiles and an expansive highway system have made automobile travel the most popular form of transportation in Canada and the United States. As Table 6.4 shows, the vast majority of domestic trips in the United States were taken over the highways. In addition, 84% of all overnight weekend travelers drove to their destinations.

Both Canada and the United States have focused government attention and resources on the development of highway systems rather than rail systems. The Trans-Canada Highway spans 4,860 miles between Victoria, Vancouver Island, British Columbia, and St. John's, Newfoundland. The interstate highway system in the United States has resulted in an intricate web of 42,800 miles of divided highways connecting every

Table 6.4	Modes of Transportation for U.S. Trips
Auto	75%
Airplane	16%
Rental car	3%
Other	6%

Source: Travel Industry Association of America. (2003). *National travel survey* and *Travelscope*

major city in the country. This system is truly remarkable because it accounts for only 1% of all roads in the United States but carries over 20% of all highway traffic.

Why do travelers rely on their personal motor vehicles for so many of their trips? Reasons vary but include the relatively inexpensive cost of vehicle travel compared with that of other modes, especially for families. In addition, cars, trucks, and recreational vehicles offer the convenience of having a vehicle at the destination, the ability to alter the route and pace, and the opportunity to explore new places "up close."

Supporting all of these over-the-road travelers is the American Automobile Association, commonly known as AAA. The association is a network of 86 independent auto clubs in the United States and Canada. AAA boasts 47 million members in North America and is affiliated with over 100 million members in 120 countries through its reciprocal agreements with 212 auto clubs throughout the world. Services provided by AAA to its members include emergency road service, travel insurance, access to professionally trained travel agents and counselors, trip routing and mapping services, and assistance with travel documents.

Although automobiles may be the desired form of personal transportation in the United States, less than 20% of the population has ever rented a car. Growth in the rental car business has historically paralleled or exceeded the growth in air travel, with almost two-thirds of car rental revenues being derived from airline passengers.[9]

This growth has been dominated by a few large companies as this industry segment has gone through a significant consolidation period. Enterprise (with the acquisition of Vanguard, the parent company of Alamo and National) has the largest rental car fleet, followed by the combination of Avis and Budget into the Avis Budget Group, and Hertz, respectively. At present, the primary users of rental cars are business travelers, who rent over 75% of all vehicles, but car rental companies are beginning to turn some of their attention to leisure travelers. Hertz and Enterprise serve to highlight the differences in marketing strategies among the rental car companies. Hertz controls the largest market share at most major airports whereas Enterprise has chosen

Renting a Car

Although renting cars in the United States is fairly straightforward, except for those under 25 years of age, renting outside the United States can be a more complicated adventure. There can be a variety of charges added to the basic cost of rental, including mileage, insurance, drop-off charges, and airport fees. The list goes on, so it pays to ask questions and shop around as well as to use the services of your travel agent.

Check the restrictions on your credit card coverage before you rent. Most credit cards provide supplemental collision-damage waiver or loss-damage waiver (CDW/LDW) coverage, but only for damages not already covered by your personal automobile or other insurance. If you do decide to rent a car as you travel abroad, take the time to get an international driving permit.

to service a broader range of customers by delivering cars directly to customers from less expensive off-airport sites.[10]

The range of variables managers must deal with in this industry is staggering. "Picture an industry where costs have more than doubled in just four years, where repeated attempts to raise prices have failed, and where demand is largely determined by demand for a rival product [scheduled airline service]."[11] To deploy fleets of cars ranging in average age from 8 to 12 months across broad geographic areas and achieve maximum **fleet utilization**, managers must anticipate a wide variety of customer demands, including car types, rental periods, insurance, fuel options, and

pickup and return locations. Like other tourism service suppliers, rental car companies have a slim profit margin. For example, "the profit margin on a $50 rental is around $5."[12] Just think about what happens to that margin if a renter brings the car back with less than a full tank of gas.

Logistics also play a key role in successful car rental operations in getting the right cars to the right place at the right time. Recent software developments provide the necessary information for employees and managers to know when to refuse a short-term rental based on the probability that the same vehicle can be rented for a longer term to a different customer.[13] Can economies of scale make a difference? The answer is yes, as demonstrated by the dominance of Enterprise and the Avis Budget Group in the business and leisure markets shown in Table 6.5.

In this highly competitive industry, price is important, but it is often the little things, such as how quickly you get your car, that make a difference.[14] Surveys show that customers want to cut as many hassles out of rental car returns as possible. Car rental companies are responding to these requests by enhancing their services to include valet delivery and parking services to avoid shuttle buses, equipping cars with onboard computerized navigation systems, providing drop boxes for the return of keys and rental forms, and equipping service personnel with handheld computers to complete rental transactions at the point of return.[15]

Motorcoaches

Motorcoaches have come a long way since their predecessor (stagecoaches) bounced across the countryside. There are now two primary categories

Table 6.5	Major Business and Leisure Rental Car Suppliers in the United States	
Company	*Cars in Service*	*Number of Locations*
Enterprise Rent-A-Car	876,181	6,793
Avis Budget Group	347,800	2,050
Hertz	327,200	2,850
Dollar Thrifty Automotive Group	167,000	606
Advantage Rent-A-Car	20,000	108

Source: 2007 U.S. car rental market. (2008, April 8). *Auto Rental News*, Retrieved May 24, 2008, from http://autorentalnews.com, statistics, p. 6.

of motorcoach (often called bus) transportation—scheduled intercity travel and charter/tour groups. Intercity bus travel, like rail travel, has continued to command less and less of the scheduled travel market in the United States. As with railroads, the importance of scheduled bus service in the United States peaked in the 1940s, and the decline continues today. In 1980, bus travel accounted for 12% of all interstate travel, but it now accounts for only about 6% of that market segment. Although the number of passengers utilizing interstate buses has continued a gradual downward trend, this mode of transportation still provides a vital link in domestic and international transportation systems.

In the United States, schedules, fares, and routes of intercity buses were closely regulated by the Interstate Commerce Commission (ICC) until passage of the Bus Regulatory Reform Act of 1982, which eliminated most regulations except those pertaining to safety. In this deregulated environment, intercity bus lines have continued to consolidate and pare their schedules and now focus primarily on trips of less than 250 miles. Greyhound Lines is now the dominant intercity bus service provider in North America with over 40,000 daily departures in Canada, Mexico, and the United States. Although the primary market segment served remains visiting friends and relatives, several diverse target markets, including lower-income groups and riders under the age of 24 or over the age of 65, are proving to be fertile ground for future growth.

New life is being breathed into the North American market by upgrades at Greyhound and a variety of start-up carriers serving paired cities like New York–Washington, D.C., Los Angeles–San Francisco, and Chicago–Milwaukee. Using concepts such as yield management and hub-and-spoke systems, bus companies are finding new niches and growth opportunities.[16]

Although intercity bus travel in the United States has declined, motorcoach usage in general has increased owing to its popularity among tour and charter operators because of flexibility and economy of operation. In addition, intercity bus travel remains an attractive alternative to rail travel in many countries with high population densities.

Additional growth opportunities for motorcoach travel can be found in the mature traveler market segment. "During the next two decades, the first wave of baby boomers will begin to enter their senior years, making them a prime target for the domestic motorcoach market."[17] Their primary considerations in selecting motorcoach tours will be service, quality, and comfort. Motorcoach executives predict that health, spa, special event, entertainment, and golf and ski packages will be the primary tours sought by these demanding groups in the future.[18]

As profiles of individuals using motorcoaches have changed, so have the motorcoaches. "Seats are wider. Views are better. There's stereo music and often an integrated video system showing the latest movies, just like the airlines. Increasingly, there's a hot beverage service or even a full galley with a microwave oven."[19] The standard motorcoach has grown from 40 feet to as much as 45 feet in length, and passenger capacity has increased from 47 to 55. Motorcoach operators such as Gray Line highlight their ability to provide a wide range of ground transportation services especially suited to motorcoaches, from sightseeing tours and charter services to airport services on six continents at 150 destinations.

Motorcoach operations, whether intercity (bus) or charter (tour operators), have many of the same operational concerns that face every participant in the tourism industry. Because operators in this industry are privately owned, financial data are not available.

Competition and government involvement in intercity bus transportation varies widely outside the United States. In some countries, such as Spain, bus transportation is more important than rail transportation; in other countries, such as Iceland, there is no train service, only bus service; and in Japan, the Japan Rail Pass includes unlimited travel on the bus as well as the train. Therefore, because of the country-specific nature of intercity bus transportation, we will leave the investigation of availability and operations in specific geographic locations up to your exploration.

Motorcoaches usually serve many more locations than trains, which are confined to specific routes because of their fixed tracks. They are frequently less expensive to ride and can often take you to places not served by trains, although they are generally slower. However, there are several exceptions to this general rule. In southern European countries, including Portugal, Greece, Spain, and Turkey, bus service may be faster but more expensive than trains.[20] The long-distance bus networks of Great Britain, Ireland, Portugal, Morocco, Greece, Turkey, and the Czech Republic are more extensive, more efficient, and often more comfortable than trains. The Eurobus programs provide direct competition to train-pass programs, with two months of unlimited travel on buses accompanied by an English-speaking driver and guide. Destinations in continental Europe include Paris, Amsterdam, Cologne, Prague, Munich, Venice, Rome, and Milan. As with rail passes, passengers get on and off at their leisure.[21]

IMPORTANT TRANSPORTATION LINKS

The final link in the surface transportation system is composed of many modes such as subways, trolleys, intracity buses, and light-rail systems. Although each of these forms of transportation is important to the overall transportation system,

we will not examine them in this book because they are used primarily for daily commuting to and from work and do not fall within our definition of tourism. However, they do fill an important transportation need for many individuals who do not want to be burdened with automobiles as they travel.

If short distances are involved and/or individuals do not need a car while at their destination, then they may rely on taxi, limousine, or shuttle services. Taxis fill an important transportation function by efficiently moving large numbers of people within cities, especially in crowded urban areas, as well as to and from airports and railway stations. One of the most significant changes in the tourism industry has been the intermodal tour that combines motorcoach, air travel, railroad, and water travel.[22]

A highly valued transportation link for air travelers is transport to and from the air terminal. In 1983, SuperShuttle pioneered door-to-door ground transportation by offering shared ride vans for travel to the Los Angeles airport. Today, SuperShuttle provides service for over 20,000 air travelers a day. Reserving a ride on one of SuperShuttle's blue vans is as easy as picking up the phone or clicking on its website.

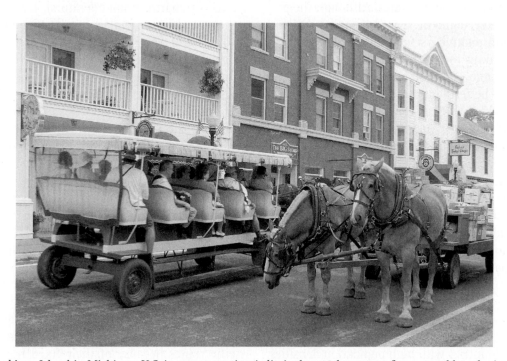

■ On Mackinac Island in Michigan, U.S.A., transportation is limited to 19th-century forms to add to the journey-to-the-past experience. Photo by Janet Wolverton.

Consider Your Options

Traveling from Boston to New York? Your options are numerous!

Luxury bus	Called the LimoLiner, this luxury bus costs about $140 round-trip, takes 4 hours, and features such amenities as reclining leather seats, free sandwiches, and movies.
Bus	Greyhound offers round-trip express service for $50 with a trip time of about 4 hours and 20 minutes. Standard motor-coach amenities are offered.
Train	Amtrak provides round-trip service for around $140, and the rail journey takes about 4 1/4 hours. Seats offer more legroom and you can get up and walk around. Café cars sell snacks and drinks. No reservations are required. Just show up and buy a ticket.
High-speed train	Amtrak's Acela is priced between $170 and $200, and the special train shaves nearly an hour from the duration of the regular train's trip. Amenities include extra legroom in comfy seats and power outlets for computers, phones, and DVD players. Foods offered are also a cut above its traditional counterpart.
Airplane	Several airlines offer shuttles between cities. Advance-purchase tickets can often be had for about $120, whereas walk-up fares may be as high as $360. But the flight is short (about 1 hour). US Airways even offers a special expedited security check so passengers can arrive just 20 minutes before take-off.

Source: Hamashige, Hope. (2004, April). Plane, train, or bus. *National Geographic Traveler, 21*(3), 26.

▉ SOARING THROUGH THE SKIES

The first scheduled passenger flight debuted in Europe on August 25, 1919, with a route between London and Paris, and jet passenger service was inaugurated on May 2, 1952, with a flight between London and Johannesburg, South Africa. However, in the United States, passenger service did not begin until April 17, 1926, with an inaugural 6.5-hour flight between Los Angeles and Salt Lake City. Domestic jet passenger service did not appear until 1958, with scheduled service between New York City and Miami.

With a long and meaningful history, domestic (U.S.) cooperation between airlines has been accomplished through the **Air Transport Association (ATA)** and international cooperation through the **International Air Transport Association (IATA)**. Formed in 1936, ATA serves as a united voice for the airline segment of the tourism industry and provides a format for the discussion of safety and service issues and the promotion of technological advancements. IATA, which is composed of almost all major international airlines, was formed in 1919 and reorganized in 1945. Its purpose is to facilitate the movement of passengers and freight across a combination of route structures and international boundaries. Through these cooperative agreements, passengers are able to buy a single ticket based on one currency that is valid for travel throughout an air system that may involve many carriers and cross many national boundaries.

As with all tourism service providers, competition among airlines is intense. In an attempt to attract more customers and to develop brand loyalty, American Airlines pioneered a frequent-flier marketing program in 1981. This program was soon copied by other major carriers. These programs have increased customer loyalty, with passengers often going out of their way or taking inconvenient flights to obtain frequent-flier miles, yet few actually cash in their mileage for awards.[23] Airlines are also partnering with a multitude of other organizations both inside and outside the tourism industry by offering miles for purchase to generate additional revenues, increase brand awareness, and heighten customer loyalty.

The Marketing Power of Frequent-Flier Miles

Frequent fliers are finding some new ways to earn additional miles even when they are not in the air. Airlines are selling frequent-flier miles to just about any organization from banks and retailers to charities that are willing to buy them. Purchases can be made for about two cents per mile. The airlines gain added revenue and the purchasing organizations obtain attractive promotional incentives.

Source: In terminal decline. (2005, January 8). *Economist*, 374(8708), 14.

"Airlines have always had a love–hate relationship with their programs—they love the loyalty they instill in passengers, but they hate the fact that people collect so many miles. According to an estimate by *Inside Flyer* magazine, there's a backlog of about eight trillion unredeemed frequent-flyer miles."[24] This accumulated mileage could be a financial liability for some airlines, where revenue-paying passengers could be displaced by non-revenue-paying frequent-flier awardees. Recognizing this potential liability, airlines have increased the number of miles required to obtain frequent-flier awards and restricted the number of seats available for these awards, especially on popular routes.

Airlines, like most other service providers in the tourism industry, operate on very thin profit margins. Therefore, controlling costs and

Tourism in Action

Talk about intermodal transportation! Look at a large group of tourists who gather in Iowa at the end of July each year and you will find people who have come from all over the world. Who are these intrepid travelers? Bicyclists! Once they arrive via planes, trains, automobiles, tour buses, and recreational vehicles, they quickly revert to an age-old mode of transportation: pedal power. Just imagine thousands of bicycle riders who throng to Iowa each year to participate in the Register's Annual Great Bicycle Ride Across Iowa (RAGBRAI).

These riders soon get a firsthand, up-close lesson in Iowa geography. "The RAGBRAI route averages around 467 miles and is not necessarily flat. It begins somewhere along Iowa's western border on the Missouri River and ends along the eastern border on the Mississippi. . . . Eight Iowa Communities along the RAGBRAI route serve as 'host communities' for overnight stays" (RAGBRAI XXIII).

RAGBRAI began almost accidentally in 1973 when John Karras and Don Kaul, columnists for The *Des Moines Register,* decided to do a 6-day, cross-Iowa bike ride to rediscover the state's roots. Through a story in the paper, they issued an invitation for people to join them. To their astonishment, about 300 did . . . . Today, admission is by lottery with only 7500 riders accepted out of the 10,000 who apply. Even so,

organizers estimate that 9000 cyclists participate, since many unregistered riders join in. . . . Thanks in part to RAGBRAI's success, big multi-day tours have boomed. Now cyclists can dip their wheels into an alphabet soup of cross-state trips: BRAN (Nebraska), BRAT (Tennessee), BRAG (Georgia), PALM (Michigan), RAM (Minnesota), RAIN (Indiana), CAM (Maryland), BAMMI (Illinois), NYRATS (New York), and so on" (*Bicycle Touring*).

And it's not just the cyclists who converge on these events. Their support teams (mostly family and friends) create moving cities of recreational vehicles and tents that creep across the countryside and fill every motel room in sight, eating tens of thousands of meals and buying everything from necessities to souvenirs. Events like this and bicycle touring throughout the world highlight the economic benefits of recognizing the power of pedaling enthusiasts around the globe. No matter what your skill level, there is a bicycle tour to meet your needs. From rides like RAGBRAI to reliving the Tour de France, cycling organizers and tour companies have packaged something for everyone.

Sources: RAGBRAI XXIII. (1995, July 23–29). *Des Moines Register;* Martin, Scott. (1992). Iowa's rolling party turns 20. *Bicycle Touring,* 10(2); *Commerce Research.* (1992, Spring), pp. 5–8; Round and round. (2007, July 14). *Wall Street Journal,* p. R5.

maximizing revenues are major concerns and absolute necessities for survival and profitability. As can be seen in Figure 6.4, the most significant expenses as a percentage of sales in the airline industry are operating costs and equipment. Because costs other than labor are difficult to control, airline companies attempt to maximize revenues. This can be accomplished by obtaining the highest possible load factor per revenue passenger mile on each flight.

In the United States, the leader in low-cost airlines, Southwest, has achieved what seems to be an amazing operational cost per seat mile flown of six cents. However, Air Asia has eclipsed this efficiency benchmark by flying its planes at a cost per seat mile of three cents.[25] Combining low cost with maximizing available seat miles (ASMs) has led to profitability in an industry filled with competition that struggles even to achieve break-even.

Operating in a Deregulated Environment

The Airline Deregulation Act of 1978 is still shaping the landscape of the domestic (U.S.) airlines. Prior to the passage of the Act:

1. Airlines did not compete on price.
2. Airlines wanting to begin services to new cities had to apply to the Civil Aeronautics Board (CAB).

3. Airlines had to apply to the CAB 90 days in advance and receive formal approval to discontinue service to a city.
4. Airlines were prohibited from entering the tour business.

The crafters of the Deregulation Act envisioned the creation of a freely competitive market that would provide needed air service more efficiently. The passage of this act may seem like ancient history, but even after 30 years, airlines are still grappling with this evolving competitive marketplace.

To facilitate the move to a competitive market, the CAB and its regulatory capacities were eliminated, and the **U.S. Department of Transportation (DOT)** assumed the responsibilities for overseeing operational issues such as the overselling of tickets, smoking on flights, and potentially deceptive advertising practices, as well as competitive concerns such as mergers and acquisitions. Air routes were made available to all carriers who could meet safety and service standards, and new carriers were encouraged to provide a variety of low-priced services. The **Federal Aviation Administration (FAA)** has responsibility for the safety of air transportation carriers.

Deregulation removed all the previously listed operating constraints that restricted airline operations. Pricing became very complex. Rather than a simple three-tier structure (economy,

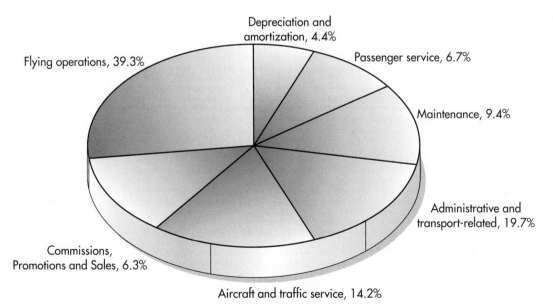

■ **Figure 6.4** U.S. airline expenses.
Source: Air Transport Association. Available at: http://www.airlines.org

coach, and first class), there are multiple prices, and airlines change these prices hundreds of thousands of times each day. Sometimes, very low prices on a particular route may be available for only a few minutes. All these changes are being made as airlines attempt to meet customer needs, maximize load factors, and increase revenues through their revenue management systems. Today, there is little to keep a carrier from entering a new city other than airport safety and capacity constraints.

Airlines may now function as tour operators, providing packaged tours directly to the public. In addition, they may own and operate travel agencies, and they may develop new methods of selling tickets other than directly and through the existing travel agency system. This latter change has resulted in satellite ticketing terminals that operate in a manner similar to automatic teller machines and other forms of electronic access, including ticketless travel.

Deregulation made the **hub-and-spoke system** the primary route pattern in the United States. Airlines select hubs near major metropolitan areas, where passenger, administrative, and maintenance activities can be concentrated and quickly rerouted to their final destinations. By designating primary hubs (see Table 6.6), airlines are able to funnel traffic into these centers to feed their **trunk routes** from smaller markets along **spoke routes**. This system allows the airlines to capitalize on **economies of scale** and match the size of the aircraft serving a market to the demand from that market. An example of a hub-and-spoke system is shown on the map in Figure 6.5.

Regional/commuter airlines, which fly domestic passenger miles on spoke routes, typically operate on a **code-share** basis. In a code-share agreement, a regional/commuter airline will share the same two-letter identification code of a major airline in the computer reservation system and usually paints its planes the same color.

The term *code* refers to the flight number that is used in flight schedules. Under a code-sharing agreement, participating airlines can present a common flight number for connecting flights. Although obviously and importantly this portrays a simple and seamless picture to the travel buyer, it is not the only benefit. Cooperating airlines also strive to synchronize their schedules, to maximize passenger transfers between connecting flights, and consolidate the cost of both airlines' flying the same route. Code sharing allows carriers who do not operate their own aircraft on a given route to gain exposure in the market through display of their flight numbers and the ability to offer those markets to their customer base.

Code-sharing agreements have also been established between airlines and rail lines. They involve some integration of both types of transport, for example, in finding the fastest connection, allowing exchange between an air ticket and a train ticket, or a step further, permitting an air ticket to be valid on the train, and so on. Examples of such code-sharing arrangements are Amtrak out of Newark Liberty International Airport in Newark, New Jersey; Deutsche Bahn out of Frankfurt International Airport in Frankfurt am Main, Germany (AiRail Service); and Swiss

Table 6.6	Primary Hubs	
Carrier	*Hub Cities*	
Air Canada	Montreal, Toronto, Vancouver	
Air China	Beijing, Chengdu	
American Airlines	Dallas/Fort Worth, Chicago–O'Hare, San Juan, Puerto Rico, Miami, St. Louis	
British Airways	Heathrow (London), Gatwick, Glasgow	
Lufthansa	Frankfurt	
Qantas	Sydney, Melbourne, Singapore	
Singapore Airlines	Singapore	
United Airlines	Chicago, Denver, Los Angeles, San Francisco, Washington Dulles	
Varig-Brazilian Airlines	Rio de Janeiro, Sao Paulo	

■ **Figure 6.5** Hub-and-spoke system.
Airline Route Map Courtesy of Frontier Airlines.

Rail out of Zurich International Airport in Zurich, Switzerland.

In theory, by utilizing the hub-and-spoke system, **legacy carriers** such as American and United are able to increase operating efficiency through scheduling arrivals and departures in **banks of flights.** Banking flights is the process of coordinating flight schedules to maximize the use of ground crews and equipment as waves of flights are scheduled to arrive and depart at very close to the same time. In addition, the shorter the period of time that an aircraft remains on the ground, the more time it can spend in the air earning money. Some regional/commuter airlines are able to turn their aircraft around or **push** them in 15 minutes or less, whereas major carriers may take as long as 45 minutes to do the same tasks.

Deregulation and the growth of passenger air service in general have created several potential problems. The hub-and-spoke system has created bottlenecks at hub airports and increased travel times. The management teams at airline companies are addressing these problems through the designation of secondary and **rolling hubs** and instituting more direct flights to pair cities. Traditionally, hub-and-spoke carriers would feed hub operations all at once during peak travel periods with short connect times so as to speed passengers to their final destinations. For example, rather than flying from Indianapolis to Chicago and then on to their final destination in St. Louis, passengers can fly directly from Indianapolis to St. Louis.

Service to secondary and feeder cities in North America and Europe is improving as larger, more fuel-efficient regional jets (also called RJs) that can seat up to 76 passengers are being added to airline fleets. RJs are ideal for serving long, thin routes from an airline's hub. Most of these smaller planes are being operated by code-share carriers. With the addition of RJs to their fleets, many code-share carriers not only are flying routes to hubs but also are flying more point-to-point routes in secondary markets. That means more service to cities that support small, 37- to 100-seat planes, not larger jets, as these smaller planes can operate at a much lower break-even point than larger planes. Finding new efficiencies is critical to financial survival in an industry in which pricing has become transparent and consumer demand is driven by low price.

Rolling-hub operations have eliminated peak departure hours by more evenly spreading flights throughout the day, using more regional jets, and ratcheting down mainline operations. The effect for passengers is longer, more random connections, causing passengers longer layovers and total travel time, but allowing for lower fares. For hub-and-spoke operators, it means less expensive operations and the ability to meet consumer price demands. Low-fare airline operations, pioneered by Southwest Airlines, have focused their flight schedules on point-to-point systems. These systems fly directly between pair cities, avoiding the transfers involved in hub-and-spoke systems. The Southwest model of operation is attracting a great deal of attention as airlines around the world attempt to mimic its success. From Ryanair in Europe to Virgin Blue Airlines in Australia, carriers around the globe are drawn to an operating model that holds the possibility for profitability by slashing operating costs.

Decoding the Language of the Airline World

All participants in the tourism industry have their own particular set of terms they use to describe operating issues, but the airline industry has more than most. To understand the airline industry, it is important to be familiar with some of the more common terms.

1. Every airline has its own two-letter identification code. Examples of these codes for the largest airlines in the world are American Airlines (AA), Air Canada (AC), Air China (CA), British Airways (BA), Lufthansa (LH), Qantas (QF), Singapore Airlines (SQ), and United Airlines (UA).

2. Every city with scheduled passenger service has its own three-letter **airport code** to identify the airport that is served. Examples of these airport codes are Albuquerque, New Mexico (ABQ); New York/Kennedy International Airport (JFK); Orlando International, Florida (MCO); Omaha, Nebraska (OMA); Orly, Paris, France (ORY);

What Happens When There's No Room on the Plane?

Because it is a common practice for individuals to make airline reservations and not show up for their scheduled flights, airlines overbook in order to fly at capacity. Federal regulations require them to make amends to passengers who are **involuntarily denied boarding (bumped)** because of **overbooking**. The airline must first ask for volunteers to give up their confirmed reserved space on the flight for some form of compensation.

If there are insufficient volunteers, then the airline will involuntarily deny boarding based on its established policies. Passengers who have been denied boarding are entitled to compensation of up to 200% (or a maximum of $400) of the value of their remaining flight coupons. This amount may be reduced by the airline if comparable transportation can be arranged that will allow passengers to arrive at their scheduled destinations within two hours of their originally scheduled arrival time on domestic flights (four hours on international flights). Other types of benefits offered may include phone calls and/or free or reduced-cost lodging and meals if an overnight stay is required.

Narita, Tokyo, Japan (NRT); and Toronto, Ontario, Canada (XYZ).

3. Every airline uses codes to identify class of service. Examples: First Class (F), First Class Discounted (D), Business Class Premium (J), Business Class (C), Coach and Economy Class (Y), Non-Refundable Coach (Q), and Advance Purchase Excursion (APEX).

4. Airline service is also classified as **nonstop, direct** or through, and **connecting.** Nonstop flights are from the point of origin to a destination with no intermediate stops. Direct or through flights are from the point of origin to a destination with one or more intermediate stops. Connecting flights require passengers to change planes to a connecting flight between the point of origin and final destination.

5. There are also several types of trips that passengers can book. Examples: **one-way**—a trip from origin to destination without a return to origin; **round-trip**—a trip from origin to destination with a return to origin; **circle trip**—similar to a round-trip except that either the outbound or the return trip will follow a different route and possibly use a different airline; **open-jaw**—a round-trip that allows the passenger to utilize different points of origin or departure.

■| SUMMARY

Passenger transportation, whether on land, over the water, or in the air, is the lifeblood of the tourism industry. Water transportation was the first mode of transportation to move travelers rapidly over long distances, but many other modes have since evolved to meet time and distance requirements. Geography and governmental policies and subsidies combined to create a host of transportation alternatives that vary greatly by country and location.

When it comes to transportation, travelers have the choice of plying the waves, riding the rails, cruising the highways, or soaring through the skies. Which one they choose will depend on where they are going, their budget, and the amount of flexibility they desire.

Ocean-going passenger service, which was once popular crossing the Atlantic, declined as jet air service increased. However, water transportation alternatives, including ferry services, which are designed to carry everything from passengers to trains, motorcoaches, and automobiles, are still very important in many parts of the world.

Land transportation revolves around rail service, automobiles, and motorcoaches. Passenger rail service, which originated in the European countries, has continued to improve in efficiency and still meets the needs of those travelers, but it is also popular in other countries, especially those in Asia, with high population concentrations and large cities located in close proximity to each other. In other countries, such as Canada and the United States, automobiles account for the majority of all travel away from home. Taxis, shuttles, limousine services, and light-rail systems fill important transportation needs for travelers everywhere. In addition, the flexibility and economy of operations of motorcoaches that can serve scheduled routes as well as organized tours continue to meet the needs of travelers worldwide.

Air transportation has proven to be the driving force behind the explosive growth in domestic and international travel. As governmental regulations are removed from air transportation, international barriers fall, and major airlines vie for an increasing number of passengers, competition as well as passenger traffic will continue to increase. Airlines, like most other service providers in the tourism industry, are being forced to rely on more sophisticated marketing and management techniques to achieve profitability and deliver high-quality service.

■| YOU DECIDE

Too many calls and not enough time! As Meredith Carpenter, national sales manager for Park Plaza Hotels, reviewed her schedule for the upcoming week, she began to wonder if she had built in enough flexibility. Being pressed for time was nothing new, but five clients in three cities in one week would be pushing it. On top of that, she was hoping to squeeze in a few cold calls as she prospected for new business.

Meredith knew it would be hectic but worth it if she beat her quota and qualified for her incentive bonus.

Meredith had worked closely with her travel agent to develop an itinerary that would allow her as much time as possible in each city. The itinerary was set up so that she could catch the last scheduled flight as she moved from city to city. This schedule looked good at the time she arranged it, but she was now beginning to think about how inflexible it might be. What if her appointments ended early or she was unable to connect with decision makers on her cold calls? Would she be wasting time in one city when she could be more productive in the next one?

Just before leaving, Meredith decided to make some contingency plans in case her business needs changed. Using her laptop computer, she made reservations on a different airline for an early afternoon flight from each city. In addition, she tucked several pocket-sized airline timetables into her briefcase. Having these schedules with her, she could make last-minute changes and book even more convenient flights if necessary.

It would be hectic, but she was prepared. Armed with two reservations for flights from each city and information at her fingertips for alternative flights, Meredith was prepared for any contingency. If her plans changed and she finished early, she could cancel her reservation for the later flight. However, if her sales calls went as planned, she would simply do a "no-show" for the earlier flights and use her original reservations. After all, Meredith thought, airlines always overbooked and no one would be hurt by either a last-minute cancellation or a no-show. Do you think Meredith did the right thing?

NET TOUR

To get you started on exploring Internet links for this chapter, please see

http://www.eurail.com

http://www.iata.org/index.htm

http://www.supershuttle.com

http://transtats.bts.gov

DISCUSSION QUESTIONS

1. What are the major modes of transportation, and why is each of these modes important to the current and future success of the tourism industry?
2. Who do many travelers, especially based on geographic location, rely on water transportation to meet their transportation needs?
3. Why is passenger rail service more efficient and effective outside Canada and the United States?
4. Why are automobiles the dominant form of tourism traffic in North America?
5. Why are motorcoaches experiencing renewed growth as a transportation source?
6. Discuss some of the many changes that have occurred since deregulation of the U.S. airline industry.

APPLYING THE CONCEPTS

1. Take on a planning task similar to the one faced by Shawna in our chapter opener. Select three major cities that are serviced by scheduled airlines. One city should serve as your reference point for departure and the other two cities should be two different destinations. One destination city should be in an adjacent province or state and the other city should be located in a different country. Prepare a table showing the following information:

    a. The types of transportation you could use to reach each of your selected destinations.

    b. The distance between each city in air miles and surface miles.

    c. The estimated time it would take to reach each of your selected destinations by both air and surface travel.

    After you have developed the table, explain the pros and cons of each of the available transportation alternatives.

2. Select one mode of transportation that is particularly interesting to you and learn more about it. Either schedule an interview with an employee of a representative company or collect copies of newspaper and magazine articles about the industry and companies in the industry. Based on the data you obtain, write a short report discussing important information you learned from your interview or research containing facts about the industry, the company, and the person's job.

3. Using the resources that are available in your local library, develop a list of companies, along with their phone numbers, that are supplying transportation services in your region.

4. Browse the Internet for intercity bus transportation information for three different countries. Describe the information that is available on each site.

5. Choose a long-distance city pair (the origin and destination cities for a trip), and interview a travel agent or access information using the Internet to determine the variety of fares and transportation alternatives available between them.

■ GLOSSARY

Airport code A three-letter designation used to identify specific airports.

Air Transport Association (ATA) A domestic association that provides a format for discussing safety and service issues and promotes the advancement of technology.

Amtrak The marketing name for the National Railroad Passenger Corporation, which is a combination of the passenger rail services of U.S. railroads.

Banks of flights The process of coordinating flight schedules so that aircraft arrive and depart during similar time periods.

Bumping The process of denying boarding to airline passengers with confirmed reservations due to overbooking (overselling) the flight.

CANRAILPASS Allows 12 days of economy class travel within a 30-day period anywhere VIA Rail goes in Canada.

Circle-trip flight A flight plan that includes return to city of origin but via different routing or airline.

Code share An agreement allowing a regional/commuter airline to share the same two-digit code of a cooperating primary carrier in the computer reservation system.

Connecting flight A flight plan that includes a change of aircraft and flight number.

Direct flight A flight plan that includes one or more intermediate stops but no change of aircraft or flight number.

Economies of scale Savings in time, money, or other resources organizations enjoy as the result of purchasing and/or selling in large quantities, specialization at a particular job or function, and the use of specialized machinery.

Eurailpass Allows unlimited travel for non-European tourists for varying periods of time throughout Austria, Belgium, Denmark, Finland, France, Germany, Greece, Ireland, Italy, Luxembourg, the Netherlands, Norway, Portugal, Spain, Sweden, and Switzerland.

Federal Aviation Administration (FAA) Agency within the DOT charged with ensuring air safety and promoting the growth of aviation.

Fleet utilization Percentage of time transportation vehicles are used for revenue-producing purposes.

Hub-and-spoke system The primary airline route pattern in the United States. By designating primary hubs, airlines are able to funnel traffic into these centers to feed their trunk point-to-point routes between major market cities.

Intermodal A trip requiring the use of two or more forms of transportation.

International Air Transport Association (IATA) Association for airlines offering international air service that provides a means of resolving problems for mutual benefit.

Involuntarily denied boarding A situation that occurs when airline passengers with confirmed reservations are denied boarding on scheduled flights due to overbooking. Passengers may either voluntarily give up their reserved space or be involuntarily denied boarding in exchange for compensation.

Legacy carrier A carrier offering varying classes of services with global networks that include alliance partners, which allow passengers to earn and redeem frequent-flier miles across these networks.

Nonstop flight A flight between two cities with no intermediate stops.

One-way flight A flight plan that includes no return to city of origin.

Open-jaw   An air travel trip that includes intermediate surface transportation between point of origin and point of destination, often used by cruise and rail passengers.

Overbooking   Accepting more reservations than there is capacity to serve those customers making the reservations (e.g., accepting reservations for more passengers than there are available seats on an aircraft or for more rooms than there are in a hotel).

Point-to-point   Direct travel between two destinations.

Push   The act of pushing an aircraft away from the gate for departure. The term is used to indicate the length of time necessary to unload, fuel, service, and reload an aircraft between time of arrival and departure.

Repositioning cruise   The transfer of a ship from one cruising area to another to take advantage of the seasonality of demand.

Rolling hubs   Connecting flights are spread over longer periods of time to reduce congestion and facility and equipment demands.

Round-trip flight   A flight plan that includes return to city of origin via identical routing.

Spoke routes   Air service provided from smaller secondary markets to feed passengers into primary hub markets.

Trunk routes   Point-to-point air service between primary hub markets.

U.S. Department of Transportation (DOT)   Organization within the U.S. government charged with establishing the nation's overall transportation policy, including highway planning, development, and construction; urban mass transit; railroads; aviation; and waterways.

VIA Rail Canada   The marketing name for Canada's passenger train network, which is a combination of the passenger rail services of Canadian railroads.

■ REFERENCES

1. Ridley, Anthony. (1969). *An illustrated history of transportation.* New York: The John Day Company.

2. Sharp, Duane. (1994, March). Ferry service promising users a better route with integrated POS solution. *Computing Canada,* p. 20.

3. Adams, Susan. (2006, January 30). Through the Rockies in style. Forbes, pp. 129–130.

4. Stroh, Michael. (2003). Speed vs. need. *Popular Science,* 262(4), 42.

5. Matlack, Carol, and Djemai, Karim. (2002, November 11). See Europe—At 217 miles an hour. *Business Week Online.*

6. Europe's trains—Fast and fun for '04. (2003, December). *Travel Wire News.*

7. Great rail journeys of the world. (2007, August). Encompass, pp. 16–17.

8. Ridley, Anthony. (1969). *An illustrated history of transportation.* New York: The John Day Company.

9. Driven into the ground. (1996, January 30). *The Economist,* pp. 64–65.

10. *Auto Rental News.* Available at: http://www.fleet-central.com/arn/stats.cfm.

11. Driven into the ground. (1996, January 30). *The Economist,* pp. 64–65.

12. Renting a car becoming a bumpy road. (2007, October 7). *Post Courier* (Charleston, SC), Section F, pp. 1, 5.

13. Driven into the ground. (1996, January 30). *The Economist,* pp. 64–65.

14. Customers rank rental cars. (2004). *Office Pro,* 64(4), 7.

15. Carroll, Cathy. (1994, October 31). Rental firms singing those low-down, abandoned car blues. *Travel Weekly,* pp. 1, 4.

16. Spiffy new wheels. (2006, September). *National Geographic Traveler,* p. 32.

17. Spritzer, Dinah A. (1992, November 26). Motorcoach firms: Future clients will be a more demanding lot. *Travel Weekly,* pp. 15–16.

18. Spritzer, Dinah A. (1992, November 26). Motorcoach firms: Future clients will be a more demanding lot. *Travel Weekly,* pp. 15–16.

19. Field, Mike. (1993, March 29). Riding in style. *Travel Weekly,* pp. 8–10.

20. van Itallie, Nancy, ed. (1994). *Fodor's 95 Europe.* New York: Fodor's Travel Publications, Inc.

21. Fox, Declan, ed. (1995). *Let's go Europe 1995.* New York: St. Martin's Press.

22. Bowden, Bill. (1991, July). Tour directors: A changing role. *Courier,* pp. 33–34.

23. Blyskal, Jeff. (1994, May). The frequent flier fallacy. *Worth,* pp. 60–68.

24. Christopher, Elliott. (2003). End of the free flight? *National Geographic Traveler,* 21(1), 18.

25. Proletariat capitalism. (2007, June 18). *Forbes,* pp. 128–130.

LEARNING OBJECTIVES

After you have read this chapter, you should be able to:

- Explain the importance of accommodations to the tourism industry.
- Identify and describe the major classifications of accommodations.
- Identify and describe the primary ownership patterns of lodging properties.
- Describe the basic organizational structures in lodging properties.
- Describe the differences between front-of-the-house and back-of-the-house operations.
- Identify and describe key marketing, management, and financial considerations in lodging operations.
- Demonstrate knowledge of basic accommodation terminology.

CHAPTER 7

Accommodations

A guest never forgets the host who had treated him kindly.

—Homer

CHAPTER OUTLINE

■ The Banff Springs Hotel, Alberta, Canada, just one of many lodging choices.

▮ EXPECT THE UNEXPECTED

The alarm went off at 5:00 A.M., but David knew he couldn't hit the snooze button. It was going to be a busy day and he wanted to be at work by 6:30 A.M. The hotel was full, and a large convention group was checking out with an even bigger group checking in that afternoon. As the assistant general manager of a large downtown hotel, David prided himself on the quality of service his staff delivered to each guest every day. Although his employees were well trained, he liked to be on hand, especially on busy days, to help out where needed.

As he rubbed his eyes and looked out the window, he stared in disbelief and his mind began to race. It was snowing and the parking lot in front of his apartment was covered with snow. If he had been living in the North, where snow was common, this would not have been a problem, but he lived in Georgia, where snow was a novelty. Could he get to work? Could his employees get to work? Would the airport be open?

The drive to the hotel that morning was a little nerve-racking, but he made it. While he listened to the radio on the way to work, he groaned. The city buses would not be running today, and unseasonably cold weather was still in the forecast. Everyone was being encouraged to stay home, and several "fender benders" had already been reported.

When he arrived at the hotel, he was relieved to see that some of the kitchen staff had made it. He asked the night auditor and front desk employees if they would stay a few extra hours and help out. Several other employees had arrived after braving the slick streets and sidewalks, but the calls were starting to come in from many more employees who were not able to get to work. By 7:00 A.M., the lobby was beginning to fill with guests, and a line had formed in front of the coffee shop.

This may not be a typical day in the life of a hotelier, but David had learned to expect the unexpected. The day was still young, and there were sure to be many more challenges. Solving problems, meeting needs, training employees, and being an active part of the community kept his job from being anything but dull.

▮ INTRODUCTION

"Come in; please be my guest." For years, these words of welcome have greeted weary travelers seeking shelter for the night. Providing travelers with temporary shelter is an age-old profession that can be traced through recorded history to the inns of biblical times. In fact, the term *hostel* (meaning inn) can be traced back to the Middle Ages.

The inns of old, usually no more than simple structures, offered meals and a bed in a room shared with other travelers seeking safety and shelter for the night. By today's standards, these early inns were very crude. They usually had one or maybe two rooms with several beds in each room. The innkeeper would put two, three, or perhaps even four people in a bed. Although many early innkeepers were not always the most reputable lot, they did provide an important service by meeting travelers' basic needs for shelter and food.

Most early inns looked like any other home along the roadside and could be recognized only by special signs hung by their front doors. As lodging facilities became more sophisticated, they often added taverns, which served as gathering spots for locals. Because these inns and taverns were usually built around courtyards, they became natural entertainment areas for speakers and traveling minstrels and troubadours.

Early "hotels" were usually just overgrown inns. However, it didn't take long for large structures specifically designed for lodging to appear. Most of these hotels were originally built in or around seaports and train depots as well as at major spa resort destinations in Canada, England, France, Germany, and the United States. In fact, development of lodging facilities closely followed improvements in transportation, particularly steamships and railroads. From these modest beginnings a variety of accommodation choices have emerged to meet the needs of today's travelers. "It is difficult to imagine how today's fast-paced, globalized economy could function at all without countless hotels around the world offering shelter and services to a burgeoning clientele of international business and leisure travelers."[1]

OH, SO MANY CHOICES!

Think for a minute about some of the accommodation options from which you can choose when planning a trip. Where will you spend the night(s) on the way to your destination? Where will you stay once you reach your destination? You can probably think of alternatives ranging all the way from staying with friends and relatives to pampering yourself at a luxury hotel. Over the years, a wide range of facilities have been developed to meet travelers' accommodation needs. Just like inns of old, these facilities become a focal point for community gatherings and social activities. In addition, they attract visitors and create opportunities for these guests to spend more time and money in the area.

Although accommodations can be found in many shapes and sizes, these facilities have commonly been grouped under the umbrella term **lodging**. The accommodations segment of the tourism industry consists of many popular alternatives such as bed and breakfasts, condominiums, timeshares, conference centers, hotels, and motels, as well as recreational vehicle parks and campgrounds.

If you think back to the transportation service providers we studied in Chapter 6, you will also find that many of them that travel over long routes, such as passenger trains, ferries, and even airplanes, often include **accommodations** as part of their total service packages. In addition, resorts provide extensive lodging facilities, and some of the newer mega–cruise ships are often referred to as *floating resorts*. We will not discuss resorts or cruise ships in this chapter but, more appropriately, in Chapter 10 as we explore destinations. As you will begin to see, the range of available accommodation alternatives is extensive.

With so many choices, attracting and retaining guests requires attention to their needs. Marketers have zeroed in on this important group of potential frequent stayers by fine-tuning strategies to meet their specific needs. As Table 7.1 illustrates, a broad array of strategies are needed to attract and retain a loyal following. In addition to targeting frequent stayers, marketers have recognized and developed varying brands within hotel chains to meet the needs of specific market segments (see Table 7.2).

No Two Are Exactly Alike

The bed-and-breakfast (B&B) concept began in the small towns and rural areas of Europe where a family would open its home to travelers. Known as **pensions,** these original B&Bs were probably a lot like the inns of biblical or medieval times: a room or two with a shared bath down the hall and a homemade breakfast served before departure.

The idea of B&Bs may have started in small towns and rural areas, but this concept has spread across the world and can be found anywhere someone wants to be his or her own boss. In fact, after the fall of communism, some of the first businesses to appear in the former Eastern European Bloc countries were B&Bs. However, it should be noted that in the United States, and probably other countries, very small B&B homes are generally operated for supplemental income, tax benefits, and as a means of defraying utility costs rather than as an investment or sole source

Table 7.1	Strategies for Developing Loyal Guests
Strategy Type	*Example*
Social	Frequent communications with former hotel guests
Emotional	Use of guest's name to provide sense of recognition
Experiential	Provide special-touch extra services (e.g., turndown service)
Functional	Provide extra amenities such as Internet access
Temporal	Offer guest time savings via quick check-in/out
Financial	Offer guest discounts or free services

Source: Based on Shoemaker, S., and Lewis, R. (1999). Customer loyalty: The future of hospitality management. *Hospitality Management*, 18, 345–370.

Table 7.2	Hotel Companies' Global Reach
InterContinental Hotels Group (Properties in 100 Countries)	
InterContinental Hotels & Resorts	Holiday Inn Express
Hotel Indigo	Staybridge Suites
Holiday Inn	Crowne Plaza Hotels & Resorts
Candlewood Suites	
Accor (Properties in 100 Countries)	
Novotel	Ibis
Mercure	Etap
All Seasons	Formule 1
Sofitel	Motel 6
Suitehotel	Studio 6
Accor Thalassa	
Starwood Hotel & Resorts Worldwide (Properties in 100 Countries)	
Sheraton Hotels/Inns/Resorts/Suites	St. Regis
Westin Hotels & Resorts	W Hotels
Le Meridien	The Luxury Collection
Four Points Hotels aloft	Starwood Vacation Ownership Element
Best Western (Properties in 80 Countries)	
Hilton Hotels (Properties in 77 Countries)	
Hilton Hotels	Conrad Hotels
Embassy Suites Hotels	Hilton Garden Inns
DoubleTree	Scandic
Homewood Suites	Hilton Grand Vacation Club
Hampton Inns & Suites	The Waldorf Astoria Collection
Marriott International (Properties in 68 Countries)	
Marriott Hotels & Resorts	Marriott Conference Centers
Courtyard by Marriott	Springhill Suites by Marriott
Fairfield Inns by Marriott	TownePlace Suites by Marriott
Residence Inns by Marriott	Marriott Vacation Club
Renaissance Hotels & Resorts	JW Marriott Hotels & Resorts
Choice Hotels International (Properties in 40 Countries)	
Comfort Inn	Comfort Suites
Quality	Sleep Inn
Clarion	Cambria Suites
MainStay Suites	Suburban
EconoLodge	Rodeway Inn

of income.[2] No matter what the setting or operator, research has shown the successful B&B operators are those providing guests with the same positive experience again and again.

"[T]he typical American B&B is located in a small town (under 10,000 population), with six or seven rooms, five or six baths and ten parking spaces."[3] Young innkeepers are taking over B&Bs in record numbers, with a quarter of inns now run by under-40 owners, according to a survey by BedandBreakfast.com.[4]

Today, B&Bs come in a wide variety of sizes and service offerings. You can now find Bed & Breakfast Homes (1 to 3 rooms), Bed & Breakfast Inns (4 to 20 rooms), and Bed & Breakfast Hotels (over 20 rooms and sometimes a small restaurant). If you travel to southern Europe or perhaps Quebec, rather than finding B&Bs, you might find

■ Accommodations can be found in many shapes and sizes depending on the location. Photo by C. A. Cook.

pensions, which offer similar accommodations. As B&Bs have grown in numbers, government-sponsored as well as independent reservation and **referral organizations** have evolved to assist owners in marketing their services to travelers seeking the "comforts of home." B&B owners have found the Internet to be an especially effective marketing tool for **booking** reservations.

Even though B&Bs may look different, personal attention and breakfast in the morning are common themes that tie all B&Bs together. One reason some travelers prefer bed-and-breakfast lodgings to hotel accommodations is that a $100 room in a B&B is a better buy than a $100 hotel room. A B&B operator rarely adds on parking, telephone connection, or other charges, and many offer afternoon snacks and wine in addition to a hearty breakfast. With the ready availability of the Internet, it is just easy, and more personal, to book a stay at a bed and breakfast virtually anywhere in the world.

Other than the differences in sizes and names, you might also notice that the breakfast foods offered will vary from country to country. For example, a breakfast in England might include

stewed tomatoes, beans, and eggs. In Germany, you could be served an assortment of cold meats, hard breads, and cheeses, whereas in Canada, you might be served cereals, toast, and fruit.

Same Time, Same Place?

Timeshares at condominium properties usually have the same **amenities** found in a typical luxury apartment setting. Condominiums (condos) and other types of accommodations are often marketed as timeshares. The idea of owning timeshares (vacation or fractional ownerships), especially in resort locations, is very appealing to individuals who can plan their travel activities in advance and want to be assured of accommodations at set times and in specific locations.

Historically, buying a timeshare unit (typically 1/52 or 1/26, one or two weeks) meant purchasing fixed weeks at a single-site location on a **fee simple** or **right-to-use** basis. This ownership assured the purchaser of having specific accommodations for a set time and place each year. Through companies such as Resort Condominiums International and Interval International, purchasers could exchange their units and times with other owners at participating locations. Timeshare companies now offer flexibility through multisite programs, global exchanges, point systems, and vacation clubs. The point system or vacation credits are the up-and-coming way timeshare resorts are being marketed and sold. Resort developers assign a point value to each season, week, unit size, and type. Owners then can use their points to exchange vacation times and locales.[5]

Not surprisingly, the most popular locations for the millions of timeshare owners are in locations that are not subject to seasonality. In the United States the most popular timeshare properties are found at destinations such as Florida, California, Hawaii, Arizona, and Nevada. The same holds true for international destinations, with the most popular locations being the Caribbean, coastal Europe, Mexico, and Australia.[6]

Just as there are popular locations, there are also different times of the year that are more popular than others. These time periods are classified by colors indicating the level of demand. Low-demand weeks are classified as "blue," medium-demand "white," and high-demand "red."[7] For example, a week during Christmas in Orlando, Florida, would probably be more desirable than a week in February in Okoboji, Iowa.

The allure of timeshare ownership is especially strong in the United States, where purchases are growing at an 8% compounded annual rate.[8] The United States leads the world in the timeshare market, with over 3.2 million owners, and Americans are also active buyers of timeshares in other countries (see Table 7.3). The popularity of timeshares is expected to continue growing as more and more baby boomers enter the prime age for buying second homes (ages 45 to 64), and more hotel companies begin supplying the timeshare market. Hotel companies such as Disney, Fairfield, Hilton, Hyatt, Intercontinental, Marriott, and Starwood Hotels are being attracted to this industry segment because occupancy rates average almost 94%.[9] With over 5,000 properties worldwide and many easily recognized brand names, timeshare ownership should continue its pattern of rapid growth. Vacationers desiring ownership for longer periods of time turn to condominiums.

In a condominium development, individuals buy units for their own use. In contrast to a fractional ownership plan, the units are frequently made available for rental when not being used by their owners. These units may be managed under a straight rental agreement or be placed in a **rental pool**.

In a straight rental agreement, condo owners receive a portion of the rental revenues based on the rental income received for their units. In a rental pool, all condominium owners share in rental income based on the square footage of their units. In either situation, the owners typically pay for all taxes, utilities, and general maintenance expenses. In return, they receive a percentage of the rental income (usually 49%), and the management company retains the remainder (usually 51%) as compensation for operating and maintaining the property when owners are not using their allotted times

Table 7.3	Profile of Timeshare Owners

Married, well-educated baby boomer with children
Much more likely to fly domestically (3X) and internationally (2X) and to have taken a cruise (4X) than general population
Average household income $103,000 compared to $51,000
1999 domestic trips—9.7 compared to 3.3 general population
88% owned computer compared to 52%
More likely to (1) travel for leisure, (2) travel with family, and (3) stay longer than non-timeshare travelers
Travel farther, and more likely to participate in skiing, golfing, swimming, and sightseeing
California and Texas the top two owner states
Florida and California the top two property states

Source: Yetzer, Elaine. (2000). Timeshare surveys reveal mobile sector. *Hotel and Motel Management, 215*(8), 3, 68.

or units. One industry leader in vacation rentals, ResortQuest, provides an

> extensive marketing plan [that] also includes web-based initiatives and a number of alliances and programs with travel agent firms and consortia. More than 1,000 travel agents have signed up for the company's ResortQuest Specialist Program, an online and print course that teaches and certifies agents to sell their unique aspects of the product.[7]

For those wanting a special touch in vacation ownership, fractional ownerships are just the ticket. Fractional ownership plans, typically providing high-end accommodations, can be purchased for one to three months of usage periods. Premier properties in breathtaking locations with hotel-like amenities take away the hassles of being confined to one destination and add the benefits of multiple vacation home ownership destinations. Companies such as Exclusive Resorts and Storied Places are finding demand is high for their exclusive offerings. To meet this demand, condo hotels, such as the condominium tower at the Fontainebleau Resort in Miami Beach, Florida, are entering the lodging market.[8]

Your Attention, Please!

Providing accommodations built around a setting specifically designed, equipped, and staffed to host meetings creates the unique environment of a conference center. The first of these facilities was established by former President Dwight D. Eisenhower when, as president of Columbia University in 1950, he opened Arden House, a 30-bedroom house on a country estate outside New York City.[9] Today, there are over 300 conference centers in the United States, including the original Arden House and a host of other locations such as the Scanticon Conference Center in Princeton, New Jersey; the Macklowe Conference Center in downtown New York City; and the Inn and Conference Center at the Biosphere in Oracle, Arizona.

With an employee:guest ratio of from 1:0.5 to 1:2.5, conference center managers can focus their attention on the specific needs of each group and excel at providing the desired experience of living, learning, and leisure. Extra service touches such as rearranging housekeeping schedules to clean guest rooms when attendees are in meetings or adjusting foodservice schedules based on changing group needs highlight the flexibility provided in conference centers. Extremely strict guidelines established by the International Association of Conference Centers must be achieved and adhered to if the facility is to be classified as a conference center

Enjoying the Great Outdoors

Campers have traditionally been viewed as families or individuals wanting to save money or get close to nature and experience the great outdoors. However, with advances in technology, more people are being drawn to camping as they realize that the outdoor experience can be achieved without "roughing it." It is not uncommon to find swimming pools, cable TV hookups, convenience stores, and even restaurants as part of the operations of commercial campgrounds and recreational vehicle (RV) parks. As the levels of convenience have increased, so has the number of people who camp as well as use RVs to take a bit of home along with them.

Campgrounds and RV parks fill a special need in seasonal recreational areas, as they can add significantly to the accommodation base. From an economic perspective, government-funded as well as privately developed campgrounds have essentially shifted capital investment needs to campers who bring along their tents, camper trailers, trailers, and RVs. Rather than investing in expensive buildings that could remain empty for a large part of the year, limited investments can be made in support facilities when travelers bring along their own accommodations.

In response to the growing popularity of RVs, many lodging facilities, especially when associated with casinos, are providing parking spaces for these vehicles. Nowhere is the mutually beneficial relationship between traditional lodging facilities and recreational vehicles more evident than at Walt Disney World or in Laughlin, Nevada. Specifically designed campgrounds and parking spaces with full RV hookups are adding to the accommodations base. In addition, whole communities of travelers can be found springing up on a "temporary" basis in Arizona, Florida, and south Texas during the winter months or in the mountains of Alberta, British Columbia,

■ Rooms on wheels meet seasonal accommodation needs. Photo by Laura J. Yale.

Colorado, New Mexico, Montana, Washington, and Wyoming during the summer months.

ROOMS, ROOMS, AND MORE

From some of the more specialized and unique types of accommodations, we now move to hotels and motels that meet the majority of travelers' lodging needs. The history of hotel development centers largely in the United States, as this is where the hotel concept originated.[10] The construction of the 170-room Tremont House in Boston in 1829 technically marked the beginning of the hotel segment of the tourism industry in the United States. Services and conveniences such as a "rotunda man" (bellhop) to carry guest bags because there was no elevator, a restaurant featuring French cuisine, private rooms with locks, soap and pitchers of water in each room, and indoor toilets made the Tremont a special place to stay. The opening of the Brown Palace Hotel in Denver, Colorado, in 1892, with its distinctive atrium design, marked another significant milestone in lodging history.

The next major change in the development of modern lodging occurred when Ellsworth M. Statler opened the Buffalo (New York) Statler Hotel in 1908. This hotel truly revolutionized the industry because it was designed and operated with guest comfort, convenience, and safety in mind. Each room had an electric light just inside the doorway, a private bath with tub and toilet, and a pitcher of iced water. In addition, free morning newspapers were delivered to each room. The hotel also had fire doors and a host of other standard features.

The Buffalo Statler Hotel ushered in a new era of lodging growth, and the industry continued to flourish in the early 1900s as hotels, designed to be the biggest and best, sprouted up across Canada and the United States. This boom stopped abruptly with the Great Depression (which began in 1929), when nearly 85% of all hotels in the United States went bankrupt as business and leisure travel came to a screeching halt.

Prosperity finally returned with the end of World War II, but the focus shifted to motels rather than hotels. With improvements in road construction and maintenance, increased automobile traffic, and the desire and ability to travel, the motel segment flourished. As families began using automobiles for vacation travel, the old practice of sleeping in cars or camping beside the road no longer met their needs.

In response to changing needs, small wooden structures (the forerunner of the modern motel) were built beside major highways to serve this growing group of automobile travelers.

> The first use of the term "motel" occurred at the Milestone Mo-Tel, built in 1925 in San Luis Obispo, California. Strategically located adjacent to the then-youthful Pacific Coast Highway (later U.S. 101) at the base of the Cuesta Grade near the foot of the Santa Lucia Mountains, the motel was a popular stop for modern motorists exploring this ruggedly beautiful country in their automobiles.[11]

The idea of "tourist courts" for the motoring public caught the eye of another lodging pioneer, Kimmons Wilson. Wilson believed consistent marketing programs and operating procedures could lead to financial success by fulfilling an unmet need: standardized facilities, service, and quality at the end of each day. His answer to meeting this need was Holiday Inns, the first of which was opened on the outskirts of Memphis, Tennessee, in 1952.

Based on the promise of providing standardized facilities, Holiday Inns soon grew into a successful chain of motels stretching across the United States. One room looked just like another and travelers always knew there would be free parking, a telephone, air conditioning, a swimming pool, and free ice. In addition, children under the age of 18 could stay free with their parents wherever they found the distinctive Holiday Inn sign.

Hyatt Hotels ushered in the renaissance of downtown hotel properties when it agreed to take over a yet-to-be-completed hotel construction project that other companies had shunned in Atlanta, Georgia. Architect John Portman had designed the hotel with an open atrium where conventional wisdom would dictate that another 500 rooms could be built. Hyatt Hotels took on the challenge of what most hoteliers considered to be an unworkable design and successfully opened the first major downtown atrium hotel since the historic Brown Palace debuted in

Old Faithful Lodge

Old Faithful Lodge, the grand dame of the U.S. National Park lodge system, turned 100 in June 2004. Incredible as it may seem, the old lady almost didn't make it. Not only was she threatened by blazing forest fires, but in the late 1970s, there was talk of tearing her down to be replaced by more modern accommodations. Thankfully, those with a preservationist bent prevailed and she was updated and renovated, including a new roof and sprinkler system that saved her "life" in 1988 from the devastating North Fork Fire. Today a team, termed the historic restoration crew, works every day replacing deteriorating timbers and maintaining her for generations to come. Volunteer tour guides offer free 45-minute tours of the old lady daily throughout the season, May to October.[12]

Source: Fanselow, Julie. (2004, April–May). Still faithful. *American Heritage,* pp. 54–57.

Denver, Colorado, in 1892. The atrium concept is now widely accepted and can be found in a wide variety of lodging properties and most of the newer mega–cruise ships.

Recent decades have been marked by high periods of growth and profitability for the hotel industry. In addition, companies continue to add new brands of properties to better target specific segments, such as extended-stay travelers (see Table 7.4). As the consolidation and the brand boom continue, a handful of mega-operators dominated by Accor, Marriott International, Choice Hotels International, Hilton Hotels Corp., InterContinental Hotels Group, Best Western International, and Starwood Hotels and Resorts Worldwide are emerging.

Making Sense of Classifications and Ratings Systems

A wide variety of lodging **properties** and amenities developed to meet the needs of specific market segments. For example, business travelers expect to find computer connectivity in their rooms as well as larger desks, better

Table 7.4	Profile of Extended-Stay Guests

Stay for five or more consecutive nights
Bring personal items, such as photos, slippers, and pillows
Set up a workstation within the room
Kitchen an important room amenity
Work in their rooms so place extra importance on space, lighting,
    comfortable chair, and handy telephone
Take baths (to relax) in addition to showers

Source: Rowe, Megan. (1998). The nesting habits of extended-stay guests. *Lodging Hospitality,* 54(3), 10.

lighting, seating, irons and ironing boards, and hair dryers. As these features and other amenities such as shampoo, lotion, in-room coffee, and free morning newspapers became standard, travelers began to expect even more. As lodging properties race to meet customer needs, differences between traditional lodging property classifications such as hotels and motels have begun to blur. To clarify this situation and more clearly communicate the differences in facilities and services among properties, organizations developed standardized classification and reporting systems.

Based on the American Hotel & Lodging Association system, individual lodging properties can be classified into the following seven categories based on the distinct market segments served (examples of brand names in each category are shown in parentheses):

1. *Limited-service budget motels.* Simple, basic, clean rooms with no amenities other than clean towels, linens, and soap. (Sleep Inns and Microtel)

2. *Limited-service economy motels.* Upgraded room decor with color television, telephone, vending machines, and generally located close to restaurants. (Motel 6, Super 8, and Red Roof Inns)

3. *Full-service, midpriced hotels and motels.* 24-hour front desk, upgraded interior and exterior decors, limited food service, extra room amenities, and other services. (Courtyard by Marriott, Four Points Hotels, and Holiday Inns)

4. *Full-service, upscale hotels.* Better quality and more luxurious, upgraded food service, and usually **concierge service.** (Canadian Pacific Hotels, Delta Hotels, Hyatt Hotels, Hilton Hotels, and Westin Hotels)

5. *Luxury hotels.* Lavish guest rooms offering the ultimate in room amenities. Noted worldwide for service and surroundings. (Ritz-Carlton and Four Seasons Hotels)

6. *All-suite hotels.* Separate sleeping and living quarters, limited kitchen facilities, and complimentary food and/or beverage service in morning and evening. (Embassy Suites and MainStay Suites)

7. *Extended-stay hotels.* Apartment/studio living quarters targeting travelers seeking accommodations for five or more nights. (Residence Inns, Hyatt Summerfield Suites, Studio 6, and Staybridge)

Other organizations such as Smith Travel Research use classifications such as upper upscale, upscale, midscale with food and beverage, midscale without food and beverage,

Motel 6

Motel 6 took on its rather distinctive name from its original pricing strategy. When the chain was first developed, each of the motels offered rooms for only $6 a night! Several similar motel chains followed suit with names such as Super 8 and National 9. In Asia and Europe, the owner of Motel 6, Accor, provides lodging with the same pricing philosophy under the name Formule 1.

and economy to differentiate properties based on room rates.[16] Historic hotels (independently owned properties that are over 50 years old) occupy a special category in the classification system. They not only fulfill all the requirements of a typical full-service hotel but also have a unique character created through restored architectural structures and collections of antiques and other memorabilia. Each of these classification systems provides managers with reference groups and **benchmarks** against which they can evaluate performance and plan for the future. Best practices have been identified for a variety of hotel operations including check-in, housekeeping, maintenance, food and beverage, marketing, and information technology. For example, the Newark Gateway Hilton and the Ritz-Carlton Dearborn designed processes to speed up the traditional check-in process, and Motel 6 achieved excellence by creating a cohesive, chainwide promotional campaign.[17,13]

Rating systems can be just as confusing as classification systems. There are literally hundreds of rating systems, both public and private, in every country. With published guides, blogs, and tourism sites boasting individual rating services, it is easy for the consumer to become confused. The three time-honored standbys for rating lodging properties are the Michelin Guide (started in 1900), the Mobil Travel Guide (started in 1958), and the AAA Guide (started in 1963). All of these rating organizations use standardized rubrics and annual visits by anonymous inspectors to classify properties.

Lodging Lexicon

Some lodging terminology (see Table 7.5) is very specific and may sound almost like a foreign language the first time you hear it. For example, terms such as *occupancy rates*, *average daily rates*, *RevPAR* (revenue per available room), and *RevPAC* (revenue per available customer) carry specific meanings and are frequently used to measure financial performance and make comparisons among similar classifications of lodging properties. However, other lodging terminology is more variable and at

Diamonds Aren't Forever

Diamond Ratings

A diamond rating is assigned to a property based on the conditions noted at the time of the inspection. All physical attributes and the quality of services are considered.

One Diamond Properties provide good but modest accommodations. Establishments are functional, emphasizing clean and comfortable rooms. They must meet the basic needs of comfort and cleanliness.

Two Diamond Properties maintain the attributes offered at the one-diamond level while showing noticeable enhancements in room decor and quality of furnishings. They may be recently constructed or older properties, both targeting the needs of a budget-oriented traveler.

Three Diamond Properties offer a degree of sophistication. Additional amenities, services, and facilities may be offered. There is a marked upgrade in the physical attributes, services, and comfort.

Four Diamond Properties are excellent and display a high level of service and hospitality. These properties offer a variety of amenities and upscale facilities in the guest rooms, on the grounds, and in the public areas.

Five Diamond Properties are renowned. They exhibit an exceptionally high degree of service, striking and luxurious facilities, and many extra amenities. Guest services are executed and presented in a flawless manner. The guest is pampered by a professional and attentive staff. The property's facilities and operation help set the standards in hospitality and service for the industry.

Source: Lodging listing requirements and diamond rating guidelines (1998). Heathrow, FL: American Automobile Association. © AAA, reproduced by permission.

times causes some confusion. Therefore, it is always advisable to seek clarification when using these terms to ensure effective communications. Figure 7.1 illustrates how some of the more typically used terminology can be applied to a guest room.

Table 7.5	Hotel Terminology
Single	Room with one twin bed
Twin	Room with two twin beds
Double	Room with one double bed
Double double	Room with two double beds
Murphy	Room with a Murphy bed (a bed that folds out of a wall or closet)
Suite	Room with one or more bedrooms and a living area
Connecting	Rooms that are side by side and have a door connecting the two rooms
Adjoining	Rooms that are side by side but do not have a connecting door between the rooms
European plan (EP)	Room only, no meals
Continental plan (CP)	Continental breakfast (juice, coffee, roll, pastry) included in the room price
Modified American plan (MAP)	Continental or full breakfast and dinner included in the room price
American plan (AP)	Continental or full breakfast, lunch, and dinner included in the room price

ORGANIZING FOR SUCCESSFUL OPERATIONS

Lodging facilities are typically marketed and managed under one of the following ownership patterns: independent properties, franchise properties, management contract properties, or chain properties. With the possible exception of very small **independent properties**, some type of formalized management structure, training programs, property management systems, and standard operating procedures will be found in most lodging properties. Property management systems manage all of a property's financial reporting and a variety of other tasks such as pricing and travel agent commissions. These tasks are often offered through an Internet platform.[14]

At first, most hotels and motels were operated as independent properties. However, between 1960 and 1990, the trend moved toward **franchise** affiliations and **chain operations**. These affiliations have proven to be profitable because "[t]hree-quarters of business travelers and two-thirds of leisure travelers claim to be brand-conscious."[15] Today, the trend is for larger properties operated under **management contracts**, although it appears that more and more property managers are once again deciding to go it alone.[16]

Going It Alone

Independent properties are lodging facilities owned and operated as single units with no chain affiliation or common identification. Managers of independent properties have many of the same advantages and disadvantages as the sole proprietors of B&Bs. They are not bound by corporate policies, so they are free to be creative and respond quickly to the needs of their guests and communities. The price they pay for this freedom, however, is a lack of marketing, management, and financial support and other resources that are typically provided through larger, multiproperty organizations such as franchises or chains. The epitome of these independent hotels is referred to as a *boutique* hotel with unique architecture and décor, offering a high level of service and typically having fewer than 150 rooms.[17]

Franchising

Franchise agreements provide owners/operators (franchisees) with the use of a recognized brand name, access to central reservation systems, training programs, documented operating procedures, standardized computer software, quantity purchasing discounts, and technical assistance from the parent company (franchiser) in return for **royalties** and fees. Examples of franchise

Connecting rooms
Rooms that are side by side and have a door connecting the two rooms

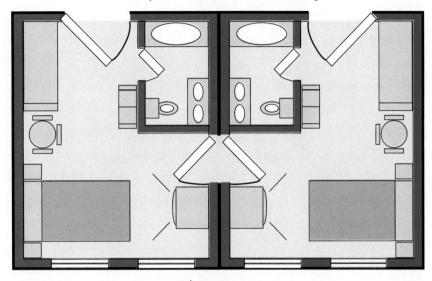

Adjoining rooms
Rooms that are side by side but do not have a connecting door between them

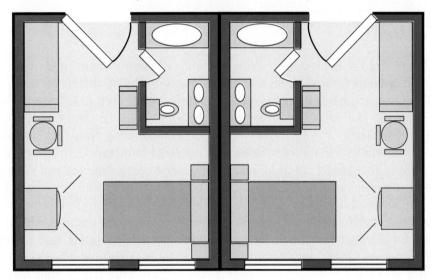

■ **Figure 7.1**   Room layouts demonstrating lodging terminology.

operating fees and requirements are shown in Table 7.6.

In return for the benefits received from the franchiser and in addition to the required franchise fees, franchisees must give up some of their operational flexibility and follow standardized operating procedures and purchasing requirements as outlined in the franchise contract. Although franchising has been favorably received in the United States, it "has not been a great success in Europe and it's been even less successful in Asia, especially where there are

not enough operations in a single country to establish the brand or to require the services [assistance and support] of the franchiser."[18]

Management Contracts

The idea of operating hotels under management contracts was born in the 1950s with the Caribe Hilton in San Juan, Puerto Rico. "The Puerto Rican government's development agency wanted a modern hotel to encourage tourism and attract industry. [The government] was so anxious to

Table 7.6		Franchise Requirements and Operating Fees		
Company	*Minimum # of Rooms*	*Annual Franchise Fee*	*Marketing/ Reservations Fee*	*Application Fee*
Days Inns Worldwide	40	5.0% of revenues	3.8% marketing/ reservations	$35,000 or $350 per room plus $1,000 application fee
Hilton	120	5% of revenues	4% marketing/ reservations	$85,000 minimum
Holiday Inn Express	70	6% of revenues	3% of revenues	$500 per room, $50,000 minimum
Motel 6	60	4% of revenues	3.5% of revenues	$25,000
Preferred Hotels & Resorts	100	$300 per room per year, $25,000 minimum	$20,000 per year	$35,000 to $50,000

Source: Franchise fact file. (2007). *Lodging Hospitality*, 63(17), 124–130.

attract a name brand and the management skills needed that it offered to build, furnish and equip the hotel."[24] Hilton was approached and agreed to market and manage the property under a profit-sharing lease agreement.

Management contracts, like franchises, allow lodging chains to expand aggressively into new markets without having to make capital investments in physical facilities. Under a management contract, hotel operating companies act as agents for the owner of the property. The owner of the property "hires" the operating company to fulfill all of the management and marketing functions needed to run the property. The property owner continues to retain all financial obligations for the property, and the management company is responsible for all operating issues. For their operating expertise, management companies receive anywhere from slightly under 3% to almost 6% of either total revenues or room revenues.

Chain Operations

Chain operations refer to groups of properties that are affiliated with one another and have common ownership and/or management control

and oversight. Chain operations can be created in a variety of different ways. For example, many chains such as Interstate Hotels & Resorts, Inc. and John Q. Hammonds Hotels have been developed using franchise agreements or management contracts. In other cases, such as Extended Stay America and Walt Disney Resorts, all properties within the chain are owned and managed by a single company. However, the most common structure is a blend of ownership, management contracts, and franchises, which is used by both Hilton and La Quinta Inns & Suites.

Parent companies may own, franchise, or contract to manage any or all of the properties they operate. Interstate Hotels, Inc. provides an interesting example of how these combinations can be put together. Interstate operates franchises under the Marriott, Hilton, Westin, and Hampton names as well as other properties under management contracts. The use of different brand names allows Interstate to target travelers in a variety of market segments.

Chain operations provide many management, marketing, and financial benefits. These benefits include increased purchasing power, lower costs of operations, common signage and advertising, expanded access to centralized reservation systems, and greater support from professional staff functions such as sales and marketing, finance and accounting, and human resource management. Marketing synergies are also gained through shared database information on customer preferences and usage patterns, providing opportunities for cross-selling brands.

Strength in Numbers

Can property owners retain operating autonomy and still reap some of the benefits that go along with franchise affiliations or chain ownership? This question may seem like asking for the best of both worlds, but the answer is yes. Membership in referral associations allows property owners to "go it alone" and still share the benefits that come from "strength in numbers."

Referral associations come in all sizes, meeting many different marketing needs. You may already be familiar with Best Western, but not Utell. Best Western claims more than 4,000 properties in over 80 countries; the Best Western logo can be found on all types of properties ranging from airport and convention center hotels to roadside motels and resorts.[25] In contrast, Utell is less well known but represents over 6,400 properties linked to over 450,000 travel agent terminals worldwide. Whereas some referral organizations such as REZolutions, Inc. serve a wide variety of properties, others such as the Historic Hotels of America Association and Preferred Hotels and Resorts Worldwide serve the needs of property owners catering to specific market niches.

There is no need for members to meet standardized design specifications or change time-tested operating procedures. In fact, membership requirements are straightforward and the benefits can be numerous. After meeting established quality standards and paying an initiation fee, the benefits can begin. The marketing power of instant name recognition, a centralized reservation system, and widely distributed membership directories are just the beginning. Additional benefits can come in the form of cooperative purchasing agreements, access to training information, and the ability to share ideas with other managers.

■| IT ALL BEGINS WITH SALES

Lodging properties rely on a steady flow of new and repeat guests to remain financially healthy. Even before a property opens for business, sales and marketing efforts often begin and should never end. These efforts may range from simply operating under a recognized brand name with a toll-free reservation system to a complete in-house staff dedicated to selling and marketing an individual property or an entire chain of properties. No matter how simple or complex the marketing effort, the ultimate goal is to attract future bookings of both individual and group business.

To generate reservations, hotels have a variety of options. Think back to Chapter 4 and the channels of distribution we presented. Hotel reservations can be made directly by travelers or via travel agents or through other intermediaries such as tour operators. For example, you might pick up the phone and call your hotel of choice directly to book a room. Or you could stop in and see your travel agent who could use her CRS to reserve your room. If you were attending a large convention, you might call the convention and visitors bureau or a convention housing services firm to reserve your room. Table 7.7 provides a list of many of the sources used by hotels to fill their rooms.

Too often, employees fail to recognize that they are an important part of these sales efforts. Just as employees must be trained to deliver high-quality service, they must also be trained to anticipate guest needs and serve as sales ambassadors. For example, when checking in, guests' comments that they are tired and hungry provide opportunities to recommend room service. Or when checking out, guests who mention that they will be returning in a month provide an opportunity to ask whether they would like to make a reservation now for their next visit.

Providing a Home Away from Home

Lodging properties are more than just mortar, bricks, and sticks. Once the physical facility has been constructed, a staff must be hired, trained, organized, and motivated to meet guest needs.

Table 7.7	Sources of Room Reservations

Direct telephone number to the individual property
Central reservation telephone number for the chain or other referral system
Local visitors bureau reservation service telephone number
Property sales staff
Corporate sales staff
Proprietary website for hotel property or chain
Intermediary websites, such as Travelocity and Expedia
Auction-style websites, such as Priceline.com
Travel agents
Hotel room consolidators, such as Hotel Reservations Network
Conventions/other meetings
Presold room blocks through tour operators or preferred partners

This task often begins long before reservations are made or guests arrive. Depending on the size of a property, guests may encounter a whole host of service employees.

Basic operating functions that must be performed in all properties include administration (general management), guest contact services (such as front office reception, cashiering, and housekeeping), and guest support services (such as groundskeeping, engineering, and maintenance). In a small motel, inn, or B&B, there may

Traditions Are Important

Two important traditions are typically performed when new lodging properties are constructed. First, when the final floor is completed, an evergreen tree is placed on the top of the building. This act signifies that the building will rise no higher. It also symbolically ties the building safely to the ground through the "roots of the tree."

The second important tradition is performed when the ceremonial ribbon is cut on opening day. At that time, the key to the front door is symbolically thrown onto the roof because it will never be used again. This is a symbol signifying that the building is more than just a building. It has become a place that will always be open to those who are seeking a room for the night or more appropriately a "home away from home."

be only one or a few employees performing all of these functions. However, owing to the size and complexity of many lodging properties (some with thousands of rooms and employees), additional managers, support staff, and hourly employees performing a variety of specific functions may also be required to ensure effective and efficient operations.

No matter how large or small the property, the ultimate responsibility for property management remains with the general manager. General managers hold uniquely important positions, as they are the focal point for employees, guests, and the community. As the top manager of a property, they perform many different but interrelated roles. These roles include providing leadership, working with the community, gathering and distributing information, allocating resources, handling problems, and coordinating a wide variety of activities and functions.

As properties grow, the primary administrative and senior management duties are typically divided between the front office manager, the director of food and beverage, and the director of housekeeping, who report to the general manager. It is also common in many properties to find the front office manager and the director of housekeeping reporting to the rooms manager. These duties are further divided between front-of-the-house positions (guest contact services) and back-of-the-house positions (guest support services). For all but the smallest properties, front-of-the-house rooms duties are performed in the front office and by guest service employees such as the bell, concierge, and valet parking staff. Back-of-the-house rooms duties are typically performed by the housekeeping department. You will learn more about food and beverage operations in Chapter 8.

Larger and more complex properties will require additional functions such as marketing (sales), accounting (controller), human resource management (HR), building maintenance (engineering), purchasing, and security services. An example of a traditional organizational structure for a large lodging property can be seen in Figure 7.2. No matter what

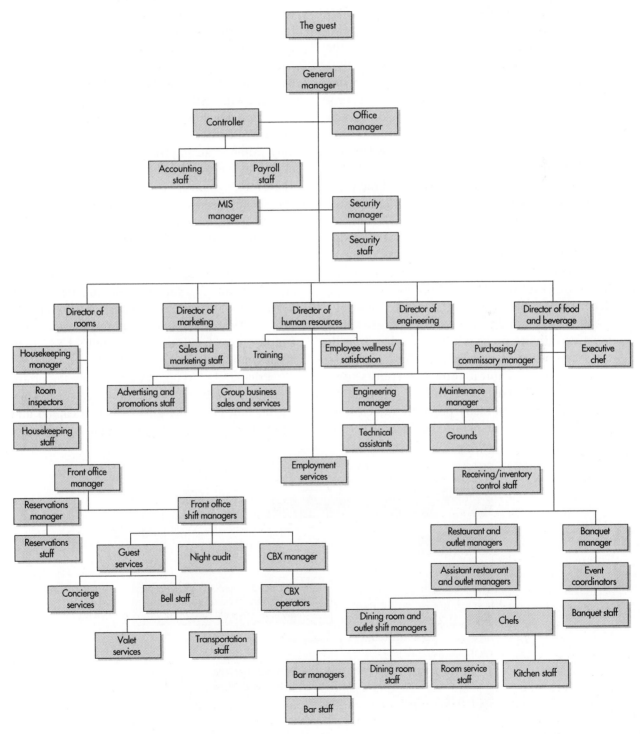

■ **Figure 7.2**   A typical lodging property organizational chart.

brand or management structure, "[t]he modern guest is looking for environments that are refreshing, colorful, creative, and connective, not just efficient and tasteful."[19]

Meeting Guests' Needs

The front office serves as the "heart" of all lodging properties as well as the first and last point for guest contact. Front office operations are the nerve center and focal point of all guest activities and many employee contacts. Front office employees are charged not only with meeting and greeting guests but also with fielding their inquiries about other available services and serving as the point of exchange for most financial transactions. Other special assistance that may be provided under the direction of the front office includes bell service, concierge service, and valet parking.

A key back-of-the-house guest service support group that is critical to guest satisfaction is housekeeping. In addition to ensuring the cleanliness of all guest facilities, the housekeeping department typically has the largest number of employees in a lodging property. Housekeeping must coordinate its activities very closely with the front office as it maintains the cleanliness and readiness of guest rooms, corridors, and common public areas in addition to managing laundry facilities in many properties. Each time guests check in, their rooms should appear as if

no one else had ever used them. In fact, complaints about housekeeping are the number-one concern for travelers.[20]

Achieving Profitable Operations

Figure 7.3 provides a brief glimpse of the major revenue sources for hotels as well as average levels of profitability. The financial performance of lodging properties has been historically cyclical. When the economy grows, the demand for overnight accommodations also tends to grow. This growth results in higher **occupancy rates**, attracting developers who build more properties. This building boom finally slows when the economy softens, causing travel to slow or the supply of new rooms to exceed demand for these rooms. Therefore, construction and pricing decisions should be based on the ability to achieve and exceed **break-even** occupancy levels. To achieve long-term profitability, hotel developers use the following rule of thumb: For every $1,000 in construction costs, $1 in room revenue must be achieved.[21] So, for example, on the average per-room construction cost of approximately $120,000[22] for a midscale hotel without food and beverage facilities, a room rate of $120 per night would need to be generated.

Pricing and occupancy are doubly important to lodging facilities, which are noted for operating on thin profit margins owing to capital and labor intensiveness. Building and equipping a

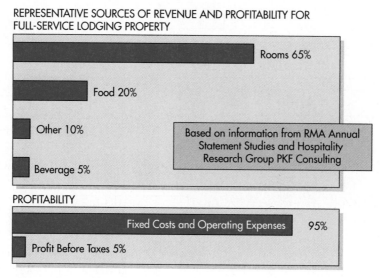

REPRESENTATIVE SOURCES OF REVENUE AND PROFITABILITY FOR
FULL-SERVICE LODGING PROPERTY

Rooms 65%

Food 20%

Other 10%

Based on information from RMA Annual
Statement Studies and Hospitality
Research Group PKF Consulting

Beverage 5%

PROFITABILITY

Fixed Costs and Operating Expenses   95%

Profit Before Taxes 5%

■ **Figure 7.3**   Typical financial performance of U.S. hotels.

■ Beach resorts abound with a wide range of accommodation types and styles.

lodging facility is very expensive and requires a long-term commitment of financial resources or capital. Once constructed, the daily, weekly, and monthly costs of providing adequate staffing continue to be incurred.

The rooms side of hotel/motel operations provides the main source of income and operating profits for lodging properties, typically generating over 60% of revenues and yielding a departmental margin of approximately 70%. A great deal of management and marketing effort is focused on maximizing occupancy levels and room rates by monitoring the rate or pace of future room reservations. To achieve the maximum occupancy at the best price, hotels and motels have relied on establishing several different rates and borrowed the concept of revenue management from the airline industry. These systems help managers achieve the maximum amount of revenue from a variety of available rates. If you were to walk in off the street, you would probably receive the **rack rate,** the standard and most expensive quoted rate for one night's lodging.

The rack rate that is offered to transient guests is the most profitable rate for a property.

The least profitable are long-term contracts with preferred customers, such as airline crews, that guarantee a minimum number of paid stays per year. These contract rates may result in prices that are only one-quarter of the rack rate, but hotel operators are willing to forgo higher rates in exchange for guaranteed consistency in occupancy and revenues. For competitive reasons, slight discounts of 10% are offered to certain groups of travelers such as senior citizens, club members, and frequent stayers. Because these guests are dealing directly with the hotel or the hotel's central reservations system, the hotel saves on paper handling costs and commissions that would be paid to a travel agent or intermediary. Room rates may be further reduced when travel agents and tour operators are extended commissions of 20% or more to generate business during slow periods. Other groups offered prices below rack rates are government employees and convention attendees. Government employees may be offered significant discounts because they frequently are limited in how much they can pay by their **per diem** rates. Conventioneers also receive reduced rates that have been negotiated based on the total volume

Tourism in Action

Going Green: Doing Good and Doing Well

When hotels "go green" by instituting conservation measures, they benefit in two ways. The measures can save the earth's resources and reduce costs at the same time. Here are a few examples:

Conservation Measure	Eco-Benefits	Cost Savings
Energy-saving light-bulbs and "smart" thermostats	By using more efficient lightbulbs and allowing high-tech thermostats to regulate heat and air conditioning when a room is empty, hotels reduce the energy they demand from their regional power grid, freeing up this power for other users.	By reducing energy usage, the hotel saves on its energy bills, usually by tens of thousands of dollars per year for medium to large properties.
Towel and linen reuse	By allowing guests to choose to reuse towels and bed linens, hotels cut their water consumption and reduce the use of chemicals by about 10%.	Hotels not only save costs associated with water and sewer bills and detergent and bleach but also cut labor costs. Housekeepers can clean more rooms when they do not have to change sheets and towels in each room assigned.
Refillable shampoo dispensers	By dispensing with all those little plastic bottles, hotels free up space in area landfills.	Complimentary shampoo can be provided at a reduced cost because most of the cost of such small-size grooming products is represented in the packaging. Hotels find they can offer higher-quality shampoo to guests at a lower cost to the hotel when going "green."

Source: Based on Rosenthal, John. (2003, January–February). Why hotels go green. *National Geographic Traveler,* 20.

of business the convention will bring to a property.

For revenue management systems to work in lodging properties, "the problems of multiple-night stays, the multiplier effect of rooms on other hotel functions (such as food and beverage), the booking lead time for various types of rooms, the lack of a distinct rate structure and decentralized information systems" must all be addressed.[23] Failing to understand and adjust for these multiple variables can lead to the problem of **overbooking.** Even when manual systems are used, overbooking can occur.

When a property is overbooked and everyone holding confirmed reservations shows up, some guests must be relocated or "walked" to other accommodations, which costs money and creates guest dissatisfaction. Because a lodging

Transportation

Boats called tenders provide ship-to-shore transportation for cruise passengers.
Photo by D. A. Yale.

The front seat on a helicopter tour provides panoramic views.
Photo by D. A. Yale

Accommodations

Atriums, now common in lodging properties, are appearing in cruise lines' megaships.
Photo by D. A. Yale.

Lodging options abound at Waikiki Beach in Hawaii, USA.
Photo by D. A. Yale

Food and Beverage

New Orleans attracts visitors from far and wide with its renowned cuisine.
Photo by C. E. Yale.

Presentations excite the mind and the palate.
G. Huntington

Attractions and Entertainment

Butchart Gardens (Victoria, British Columbia) offer guests a bountiful bouquet of color.
Photo by C. E. Yale.

Kruger National Park in South Africa affords many species a safe haven.
Photo by Cheryl Clay

Checkout Penalties

If you've made a reservation with a major hotel chain such as Hilton, Hyatt, or Westin for three days and decide to check out after the second day, don't be surprised to find a $25 penalty added to your bill. In an attempt to control room availability and better serve their guests, these and many other hotel chains are adding a checkout penalty when guests fail to honor the full length of their reservations.

point for accumulated data and integrate a variety of activities at the property level such as:

- Reservations
- Pricing and revenue management
- Guest profile
- Electronic keys
- Telephone, messaging, and television activation
- Maintaining guest **folios**
- Updating housekeeping data
- Combining **night audit** information and reports
- Maintaining employee payroll records
- Updating inventory records
- Creating financial statements
- Tracking the effectiveness of marketing programs

reservation is a binding contract, lodging property managers should be prepared to provide alternative accommodations free of charge plus transportation and a long-distance phone call when there is "no room at the inn."

Even though properties may grow in size and complexity, the basic business operations remain the same. Providing accommodations to the traveling public continues to be a 24-hour-a-day, 7-day-a-week task that demands dedication to detail and a strong desire to welcome and serve each guest as if that guest were the first and most important person of the day.

■ USING TECHNOLOGY TO TIE IT ALL TOGETHER

Property management systems combine computer hardware and software into an integrated information system. These systems provide a central

These systems have been further enhanced by another important development in the use of management information technology—**enterprise systems**—that combine information for multiple properties. Enterprise systems present a new model of corporate computing. They allow companies to replace their existing information systems, which are often incompatible with one another, with a single, integrated system. An enterprise system enables a company to integrate the data used throughout its entire organization. By streamlining data flows throughout an organization, these management information systems are delivering dramatic gains in operational efficiency and profitability. The information generated from these databases can be mined and used for a variety of marketing programs as shown in Table 7.8.

Table 7.8	Examples of the Uses of Data-Mining Information in Hotel Marketing
Create direct-mail campaigns	
Plan seasonal promotions	
Plan the timing and placement of ad campaign	
Create personalized advertisements	
Define which market segments are growing most rapidly	
Determine the number of rooms to reserve for wholesale customers and business travelers	

Source: Magnini, Vincent P., Honeycutt, Earl D., Jr., and Hodge, Sharon K. (2003, April). Data mining for hotel firms: Use and limitations. *Cornell Hotel & Restaurant Administration Quarterly,* pp. 94–105.

SUMMARY

Accommodations create temporary living quarters for guests through a variety of sources, including bed and breakfasts, condominium properties, timeshares, conference centers, hotels, motels, recreational vehicle parks, and campgrounds. Lodging properties, which provide the bulk of overnight accommodations, can be traced to biblical times but did not develop into a significant segment of the tourism industry until rail and oceangoing transportation systems improved and automobile travel became convenient and popular.

Growth in the number of lodging facilities has resulted in the development of several classification schemes that can be used for reporting and comparison purposes. These classification schemes show that lodging facilities come in many sizes and types and therefore require varying levels of staffing and managerial expertise for successful operations. Basic functions that must be performed in all lodging properties include administration, front office, housekeeping, and maintenance.

The necessary staffing requirements of properties change as they grow in size and complexity.

Additional line functions such as food and beverage and support staff functions such as accounting, engineering, human resource management, security, and purchasing are added as needed. Because some of the terminology concerning lodging and other accommodation facilities is often loosely used, it is important to seek clarification when talking with guests or other individuals in these establishments.

Providing accommodations to the traveling public requires training, dedication to detail, and a strong desire to welcome and serve each guest. To meet and serve the diverse needs of travelers, a wide variety of accommodations has been developed. Although much of our attention has been devoted to lodging properties, other specialized forms of accommodations such as campgrounds and recreational vehicle parks can significantly increase the number of guests who can be served in any one location.

The statement, "Come in; please be my guest," is more than just words. It is both an invitation and a statement of dedication to provide hospitality to the weary traveler.

YOU DECIDE

"It just doesn't make any sense, Nancy. We've been underbid on four of our last five convention proposals. Worse yet, each time we've been underbid, it's been by the City Center Hotel, and they've beat us out by almost 5% on the total value of the contract.

I want some answers before we submit another bid. It seems to me that we are either totally out of touch with the realities of our marketplace or there are some serious operational problems in your office."

As a downtown hotel that targeted business travelers and convention business, the Forest Park Hotel had traditionally been very successful in following up and capturing its fair share of leads that were developed by the local convention and visitors bureau. Because of these past successes, Rich Edwards, general manager of the hotel, was particularly disturbed by the failure of Nancy Peak, director of sales, in securing some key convention groups for the hotel.

A heated meeting with Rich was always an uncomfortable situation, but Nancy was particularly troubled by this encounter because she had no immediate answers. After an early-morning conference

with her sales staff, she was confident they could find the cause of the bidding failures.

Less than two weeks had passed when Harvey Zoller sheepishly walked into Nancy's office. He said that he felt he may have found the source of the bidding problem. He had been tossing draft copies of his estimates and proposals into the trash. Somehow, these papers must have been finding their way into the hands of the City Center Hotel employees, because there were suspicious parallels between the contract proposals he had developed and the final bid proposals submitted by the City Center Hotel.

After a thorough investigation, Nancy concluded that although disposal procedures were normal, they were inadequate in this situation. Further investigation confirmed that the night custodians working for a contract-cleaning firm had been taking discarded worksheets and proposals from the office wastebaskets. Nancy reported her finding to Rich and assured him that adequate control procedures had been implemented to prevent future problems.

However, Nancy failed to tell Rich that she had instructed Harvey to create fictitious worksheets and proposals to be discarded on a current bid proposal. A few weeks later, Nancy was informed that Forest Park Hotel's bid had been accepted and it would serve as the host hotel. She felt that it was poetic justice that the bid proposal submitted by the City Center Hotel had been 5% less than the fictitious work discarded by Harvey but 2% over the actual bid she had submitted. Did Nancy make the right decision?

◼ NET TOUR

To get you started on exploring Internet links for this chapter, please see

http://www.arda.org

http://www.Marriott.com
http://www.ahma.com

◼ DISCUSSION QUESTIONS

1. Identify and describe each of the major types of accommodations.
2. Explain how timeshares (vacation ownerships) operate.
3. Describe the differences among independent, franchise, management contract, and chain properties.
4. Explain the importance of this statement: "It all begins with sales."
5. Identify and describe key front-of-the-house and back-of-the-house functions.
6. Describe how different rates can affect hotel revenues.

◼ APPLYING THE CONCEPTS

1. Although several hotel pioneers were mentioned in this chapter, there are many other individuals who have had a significant influence on the lodging industry. After selecting or being assigned one of these pioneers, briefly describe the contributions that person made to the industry.
2. Arrange to visit a lodging property and schedule an interview with the manager. Your interview should include questions about how the property is marketed, what types of standard operating procedures are followed, and how financial performance is measured.
3. Select one of the hotel management companies listed in this chapter. Using your local library or other sources, list the sizes (number of rooms) and brand names of properties this company manages.
4. Choose four different lodging properties in your area. Based on your knowledge of these properties, assign a classification or rating based on the standardized system described in this chapter. Provide a brief rationale for why you arrived at each of your decisions.

◼ GLOSSARY

Accommodations   Loosely defined as establishments engaged primarily in providing lodging space to the general public.

Amenities   Goods and services provided with accommodations that contribute to guest comfort.

Benchmarks   Performance measures that are used by similar types of businesses to monitor key operations.

Booking   A reservation.

Break-even   The level at which total sales equals total costs.

Chain operations Groups of properties that are affiliated with one another and have common ownership and/or management control and oversight.

Concierge services Services provided by employees who specialize in meeting the special requests of guests and provide guest services such as making reservations and supplying information.

Enterprise system Management information systems that combine data from multiple properties.

Fee simple Right of ownership evidenced by the transfer of a certificate of title. The buyer has the right to sell, lease, or bequeath the property or interest (as in a timeshare).

Folio Record of an individual guest's charges, including nightly room charge, telephone charges, food and beverage charges, dry cleaning, parking, etc.

Franchise A contractual agreement providing for the use of a recognized brand name, access to a central reservation system, training, documented operating procedures, quantity purchasing discounts, and technical assistance in return for royalties and fees.

Independent properties Facilities that are owned and operated as single units with no chain affiliation or common identification.

Lodging Facilities designed and operated for the purpose of providing travelers with a temporary place to stay.

Management contracts Operating agreements with management companies to conduct day-to-day operations for a specific property or properties.

Night audit Nightly accounting process that reconciles all property income, including rooms, telephone, food and beverage outlets, catering, gift shop, parking, etc.

Occupancy rate Ratio comparing the total number of rooms occupied for a given time period to the total number of rooms available for rent.

Overbooking Confirming more reservations for rooms than can be provided during a specified time period.

Pension A small inn or boarding house similar to a bed and breakfast.

Per diem Maximum travel expense amount that will be reimbursed on a per day basis.

Properties Individual accommodations and lodging facilities.

Rack rate The standard quoted rate for one night's lodging.

Referral organizations Associations formed to conduct advertising and marketing programs and generate reservations and referrals for member properties.

Rental pools Groups of condominium units that are released by their owners for rental purposes and are managed by lodging companies.

Right-to-use A type of lease in which legal title does not pass to the buyer. The buyer has the right to occupy and utilize the facilities for a particular time period.

Royalties Payment (usually a percentage of sales) for the use of a franchiser's brand name and operating systems.

Timeshare Either ownership or the right to occupy and use a vacation home for a specific period of time.

REFERENCES

1. Sandoval-Strausz, A. K. (2008, January). The hotel. *United Hemispheres,* pp. 52–54.
2. Poorani, Ali A., and Smith, David R. (1995). Financial characteristics of bed-and-breakfast inns. *Cornell Hotel & Restaurant Administration Quarterly,* 36(5), 57–63.
3. Emerick, Robert E., and Emerick, Carol A. (1994, Spring). Profiling American bed and breakfast accommodations. *Journal of Travel Research,* pp. 20–25.
4. Fong, Mei. (2002, September 13). Inns turn a new leaf. *Wall Street Journal,* p. W1.
5. Baumann, M. A. (2000). Points offer consumers flexibility, variety. *Hotel & Motel Management,* 215(9), 18.
6. Interval International sponsored study shows huge jump in familiarity with timesharing amongst U.S. leisure travelers. (2007). *Vacation Ownership World,* 240, 18.
7. Bouillon, Marvin L., and Wang, Jennifer. (1990, Spring–Summer). Time-share performance: A survey of financial data from developers. *Real Estate Issues,* pp. 44–47.
8. Vacation-ownership net sales increase 7.6 percent in 2002. (2004, May 17). *Hotel & Motel Management,* p. 36.
9. Next stage of 2002 timeshare research complete. (2002, November 13). ARDA press release. Available at: http://www.arda.org/Pressroom/pr2020/nov13b.htm.

7. Watkins, Ed. (2002). Lodgings' last frontier. *Lodging Hospitality,* 58(12), 20–24.

8. Palmeri, Christopher. (2005, December 9). Checking out—and into—condo hotels. *BusinessWeek,* p. 2.

9. Szathmary, Richard. (1991, November). The case for conference centers. *Sales and Marketing Management,* pp. 101ff.

10. Sandoval-Strausz, A. K. (2008, January). The hotel. *United Hemispheres,* pp. 52–54.

11. Leach, Sara Amy. (2000, September). On the highway of life. *Lodging,* p. 120.

12. Smith Travel Research. (1997). 105 Music Village Blvd., Hendersonville, TN 37075.

16. Smith Travel Research. (1997). 105 Music Village Blvd., Hendersonville, TN 37075.

17. Siguaw, Judy A., and Cathy Enz. (1999). Best practices in hotel operations. *Cornell Hotel & Restaurant Administration Quarterly,* 40(6), 42–53.

13. Siguaw, Judy A., and Cathy Enz. (1999). Best practices in marketing. *Cornell Hotel & Restaurant Administration Quarterly,* 40(5), 31–43.

14. Marta, Suzanne. (2003, February 21). Dallas-based Pegasus has solution for hotel managers. *Travel Wire News,* p. 1.

15. Travel and tourism: Home and away. (1998, January 10). *The Economist,* p. 7.

16. Gillette, Bill. (1996). Going it alone. *Hotel & Motel Management,* 211(9), 22–23.

17. Anhar, Lucienne. (2001, December 12). The definition of boutique hotels in recent years. *HVS International Newsletter,* p. 1.

18. Bell, Charles A. (1993). Agreements with chain-hotel companies. *Cornell Hotel & Restaurant Administration Quarterly,* 340(1), 27–33.

19. Attracting your guests from the outside. (2004, May). *AAHOA Lodging Business,* p. 22.

20. Cheers and jeers from hotel travelers. (2003, March). *American Demographics,* p. 15.

21. Chittum, Ryan. (2007, July 25). Living like Eloise: More hotels add condos. *Wall Street Journal,* pp. B1, B8.

22. Sahlins, Elaine. (2008). The cost of hotel development. *AAHOA Lodging Business,* 7(3), 52–58.

23. Kimes, Sheryl E. (1989). The basics of yield management. *Cornell Hotel & Restaurant Administration Quarterly,* 30(3), 14–19.

24. Bell, Charles A. (1993). Agreements with chain-hotel companies. *Cornell Hotel & Restaurant Administration Quarterly,* 340(1), 27–33.

25. Top brands. (2007). *Lodging Hospitality,* 63(3), pp. 30–31.

LEARNING OBJECTIVES

After you have read this chapter, you should be able to:

- Explain how travel and other events in history have influenced the growth and acceptance of different foods and beverages.
- Discuss the impact of science and technology on foods and beverages.
- Explain the importance of rhythm, timing, and flow in foodservice operations.
- Discuss the importance of a menu and its impact on production and service delivery.
- Identify the important operational and financial concerns faced by foodservice managers.
- Describe how foods and beverages can add value to other tourism services.

CHAPTER OUTLINE

CHAPTER 8

Food and Beverage

There is no love sincerer than the love of food.

—George Bernard Shaw

■ Food presentations should be designed to please all of our senses.

◼ SOMETIMES IT'S MORE DIFFICULT THAN IT SEEMS

What had begun as an exciting sale soon turned into an important learning experience. It was Carrie's first big sale and she could hardly contain her excitement. As the newest employee on the catering and sales staff at the River Front Hotel, she was anxious to pull her weight and be a productive member of the team.

After dealing with several small groups, Carrie had been assigned to work with Marge Lundstrum of Getaway Tours. Marge had already reserved space for a lunch stopover on their Fall Foliage Tour, and the only remaining detail was to select a menu. After a few qualifying questions, Carrie learned that there would be three busloads consisting of 125 to 150 older men and women.

Marge said that they had been served chicken salad in pineapple boats their last two fall seasons, but this time they wanted something different. She also stated that they didn't want to spend much more than they had in the past. Following a brief discussion, Carrie and Marge decided on bacon, lettuce, and tomato sandwiches (BLTs) with garnish to be accompanied by a fruit salad with poppy seed dressing.

As Carrie reviewed the proposed menu at the weekly staff meeting, the food and beverage director, Martin Yantis, listened in disbelief. The thought of toasting 450 slices of bread would prove to be a logistical nightmare with the other daily activities taking place in the kitchen.

Although Martin thought about having Carrie call Marge to offer her some other alternatives that would be just as appealing and easier to prepare, he decided to turn this potential problem into a learning experience. On the day of the luncheon, Carrie was given the opportunity to work with the preparation staff in the kitchen.

She soon discovered how difficult it was to make so many BLTs. Carrie learned that preparing and serving large meal functions required a team effort and consideration of the physical and human capabilities of the kitchen and staff. Carrie now knew her job was more than just sales and decided to learn more about all of the different aspects of food and beverage marketing, management, and finance.

◼ INTRODUCTION

Just think of the lasting memories and friendships that you have developed while sharing your favorite foods and drinks. As we learned in Chapter 2, all of us share some of the same needs. Foods and beverages are not only instrumental in filling a number of basic human needs, but they also fill special tourism needs. **Culinary tours** have recently emerged as a significant component of the overall tourism industry. Research has shown that **culinary tourists**, those who travel to participate in cooking classes, dine out in unique locations, sample wines, and attend food festivals and farmers' markets, are younger, better educated, and more affluent than other travelers.[1] Meeting the needs of these special travelers as well as those seeking to fulfill basic physiological and social needs creates a variety of opportunities for tourism service providers to satisfy their guests and build lasting relationships.

Tourists provide an important source of revenue to many, but not all, foodservice operations. "Roughly half of all travelers report that they dine out when they travel, and that doing so is the most important activity planned after tourists arrive at a destination."[2] Some operations such as Hard Rock Café and Bubba Gump Shrimp Company Restaurant and Market rely on a steady stream of tourist traffic, whereas others cater mainly to local clientele. Location and target segments will determine the relative importance of tourists versus local patronage in an operation's financial success. Research has shown that foodservice providers seeking to cater to tourists can target marketing efforts on one or more of the segments shown in Table 8.1.

Because food and beverage experiences are very personal, the thought of pleasing all these different tastes may seem like a difficult task. What may be pleasing and desirable to you may be completely unappealing to someone else. The good news is that there are fundamentals that can be followed to provide successful food and beverage (F&B) services. In this chapter, you will learn about these principles as well as some of the marketing, management, and financial decisions that combine to create the dynamic and fast-paced working environment of food and

Table 8.1	Restaurant Selection Factors
Value seekers	Tourists seeking restaurants providing food value for money expended
Service seekers	Tourists seeking quality service, availability of healthy choices, and a convenient location
Adventurous seekers	Tourists seeking local, new, and interesting food as well as convenient locations
Atmosphere seekers	Tourists seeking a festive and social atmosphere conducive to good times
Healthy food seekers	Tourists seeking restaurants offering healthy food choices

Source: Yüksel, Atila, and Yüksel, Fisun. (2002). Measurement of tourist satisfaction with restaurant services: A segment-based approach. *Journal of Vacation Marketing*, 9(1).

beverage operations. You will also discover in Appendix B that manners matter and should be practiced in every professional and social setting.

MAJOR INFLUENCES ON THE DEVELOPMENT OF FOOD AND BEVERAGE SERVICES

We can trace the most important influences on the development of foods and beverages to travel experiences and innovations in science and technology. Throughout history, travel has introduced visitors to new tastes, and these discoveries continue today. Visiting new locations allows us to enjoy unfamiliar foods. It also allows us to expand our understanding and appreciation of new cultures, ceremonies, and traditions. In fact, throughout history, foods and beverages have often been at the center of social gatherings and celebrations.

Travel and Discovery

The quest to explore and conquer new lands that encouraged early travel also led to the spread of different food and beverage offerings. The importance of foods and beverages to the development of travel and tourism can be seen all the way from the expansion and conquests of the Greek and Roman Empires to the travels of Marco Polo.

Precious metals and land were not the only treasures sought by these early adventurers—so, too, were flavorful spices and herbs. The Greeks brought home food-related "treasures" from their travels in Egypt, Persia, Babylon, and India. These **culinary** treasures were later passed on to the Romans. In fact, at the height of the Roman Empire, the typical Roman cook was a male slave brought from overthrown Greece, where cooking skills and **cuisine** were highly developed. The Romans' appetites for pleasurable indulgences placed these cooks in high demand and raised the status of cooking to an art form.[3]

As the world moved into the so-called Dark Ages, travel began to diminish. The art of cooking, however, was preserved during this period because most of the rich cooking styles and the books that discussed foods and beverages were guarded in monasteries. Outside monastery walls, people continued to prepare rough, simple dishes that had been passed down unchanged for generations. The revival of travel by the wealthy during the Grand Tour Era after the end of the Middle Ages had a significant impact on food and beverages. When the noble classes began to expand their travels into new territories, they encountered and brought home many new foods, beverages, and methods of preparation.[4]

As Europeans began to travel to the Americas and West Indies, they returned with many native foods from those regions such as chocolate, chilies, beans, corn, tomatoes, and potatoes. Some of these items were initially avoided and treated with suspicion because they looked different and were often regarded as poisonous. Through the efforts of pioneers such as French agronomist Antoine-August Parmentier and American scientist George Washington Carver, deep-seated fears and misconceptions about different foods were dispelled. Parmentier successfully spearheaded a campaign begun in 1774 that made potatoes a staple on the French dinner table.[5] Research efforts led by Carver resulted in over 300 products including cheese, milk, flour, and coffee made from peanuts.

Once people began emigrating from Europe to the "New Worlds" of North America, they brought along their favorite drinks, breads, desserts, herbs, spices, and fruits. These old favorites were combined with new foods, creating distinctive regional cuisines from New England clam chowder to hominy grits. Now, at the dawn of the 21st century, the majority of people in industrialized countries can afford to travel for pleasure and, through tourism, enjoy new foods and dining experiences. These experiences continue to influence the development of menus and service styles for food and beverage operations as international and regional cuisines are blended together.

In the same way that travel has driven their development, foods and beverages now drive many travel choices. Food and beverage events attract tourists in increasing numbers to resorts, festivals, theme parks, casinos, and many other destinations. For example, travelers come from all over the world to enjoy the sights, sounds, and delights of Oktoberfest celebrations throughout Germany or Fiesta Days in San Antonio, Texas. In fact, pleasant memories of foods and beverages enjoyed as part of a trip often linger and are remembered more often than any other part of the travel experience.[6] Just as travel and the quest for new experiences have awakened our taste buds, science and technology have continued to advance, so we can enjoy these newfound treats wherever and whenever we desire.

Science and Technology

Now more than ever before, food and beverage professionals can deliver on the promise "your wish is my command." If a meeting planner wants to arrange a closing celebration banquet for a sales conference in Arizona in January with live lobster and fresh corn on the cob, no problem! Scientific advances and new technologies have made it possible to transport highly perishable foods safely over great distances. Products such as strawberries and asparagus can now be enjoyed anywhere and at any time of the year. Advances in farm technology have increased the quantity, quality, variety, and availability of foods, expanding menu choices all over the world. For example, **aquaculture** now brings high-quality seafood such as shrimp, salmon, and oysters to the kitchens of the world 365 days a year.

Refrigeration and freezing technologies, along with the use of irradiation,[7] also allow foods to be stored longer and transported over greater distances without affecting quality. Continuing technological advances have also led to an array of computerized equipment such as internal temperature probes, which can be accurately programmed to regulate oven cooking and holding temperatures. These advances ensure the greatest **yields** and the highest-quality food products. In addition, information and new ideas about food and beverage preparation and presentation are now freely shared. Featured food sections in magazines and newspapers, special television programs, attractive websites, professional publications, and a cable channel dedicated to food have heightened both awareness and appreciation of this segment of the tourism industry.

■ BUILDING A CULINARY HERITAGE

Creating the foods we enjoy involves a combination of technology, science, and a great deal of culinary and service talent. This talent can be

---

Tourism in Action

Wine tasting trips offer so many benefits, but one really does need a designated driver to enjoy them all. There are several ways to travel from winery to winery without DWI worries: chauffeured limousine, bus tour, or cruise. CRUISE? Yes, cruise. Because wineries tend to be located along rivers, two American cruise companies offer small-ship itineraries through Napa Valley. American Safari Cruises provides a luxury cruise from San Francisco upriver on its 22-passenger yacht. Cruise West offers a similar route aboard its 102-passenger *Spirit of Endeavor*. What a way to go!

found in many different types of food and beverage operations. The most common are commercial restaurants serving the general public and travelers who dine for reasons that range from need and convenience to entertainment and pleasure. Commercial restaurant operations vary all the way from fast-food (quick service) and take-out to elegant, full-service, sit-down operations. Whereas restaurants are the most typical food and beverage (F&B) operation, they represent only one of many types of food and beverage services. Others can be classified into employee food service, recreational food service, transportation food service, lodging properties, banquet/meeting and catering facilities, and institutional foodservice establishments. Most of these foodservice operations touch travel and tourism in some way.

The Beginnings of Modern Foodservice Practices

Independent eating and drinking establishments were the first food and beverage operations to evolve, and today, they still generate the majority of all food and beverage revenues. It all began in Paris, way back in 1765 when Monsieur Boulanger served a typical peasant's dish: sheep's feet (also known as trotters) in a white sauce as a restorative along with ales in his tavern. In fact, the word *restaurant* comes from the French word *restorante*, which means "restorative." Tavern keepers in Boulanger's time were limited to serving beers and ales only in accordance with the controls imposed by the medieval guild system. These controls were designed to maintain standards and restrict competition. Because Boulanger was limited by law to serving beers and ales only, he was brought to court to stop the practice of serving food in his tavern. He won the case and the rest is history; the door was opened for restaurants to serve food and drink together.

The French Revolution marked another important milestone in the growth of these new eating establishments. Chefs, who had previously worked for the monarchy or nobility under the constant threat of losing their heads in the guillotine, fled to the countryside and opened restaurants.[8]

Foodservice operations have come a long way from the pioneering days of Monsieur Boulanger. As societal norms, customs, and economies evolved, so, too, did the entire food and beverage industry. The first disciplined approach to the culinary arts was captured through the grande cuisine instituted by Marie-Antoine Carême. His cooking style, along with recipes describing dishes and sauces of the grande cuisine, were collected and published in *La Cuisine Classique* (1856) and other books that followed. Although these books were popular in the kitchens of the nobility, they were slow in finding their way into the fledgling restaurants, which offered a simple **table d'hôte**. This type of menu provided little if any choice. Carême's grande cuisine created a new style of service and range of menu choices. Menus expanded through the offering of a "carte" or list of suggestions, giving rise to the *à la carte* restaurant.

The next major step in the development of modern foodservice operations was marked by the opening of the Savoy Hotel. It opened in London in 1898 under the direction of Caesar Ritz and George Auguste Escoffier. Grande cuisine was still the exception, but it was embraced by these two foodservice pioneers who ensured that their *à la carte* presentations were an event. Diners enjoyed the best of food and service as well as the ambiance of elegant surroundings.

Escoffier was the most famous chef of his day and is considered by many to be the father of modern-day chefs. Escoffier revolutionized the methods of food service and kitchen organization during his years of managing the kitchens at the Savoy and later the Carlton Hotel. He expanded and refined the idea of *à la carte* service by establishing carefully planned sequences of courses. For example, a typical sequence of courses for today's full-service casual American-style restaurant might start with an appetizer and then be followed by soup, salad, entrée, and dessert.

Escoffier also reorganized tasks and activities in the kitchen, eliminating duplication of effort and improving efficiency in operations by creating and defining the work of **stations**. More than anyone else, Escoffier helped to focus foodservice providers on the important task of

Tapas

It will always be difficult to categorize every type of foodservice operation. Differences arise owing to variations in service goals, the number and profiles of people served, menus, atmosphere, seasons, and production techniques. One example of a unique type of foodservice operation that originated in Spain is a tapas bar or café. The service goal of these operations is to provide guests with a wide variety of foods in appetizer portions. They are most commonly found in the heart of theater districts, restaurant groupings, and other areas of a city where late-night activity thrives. A tapas kitchen will often stay open much later than other foodservice operations. Tapas bars also serve as a meeting place for guests wanting a drink and an appetizer before going elsewhere to dine. Because of this practice, tapas bars often thrive when surrounded by restaurants.

catering to guests' needs and desires by making dining a memorable experience. This was only the beginning, as others contributed to the constantly evolving developments in foods and beverages. Table 8.2 traces the historic evolution of foods and preparation methods from the Egyptian Kingdoms to Ray Kroc's brainchild, McDonald's.

Planning to Meet Guest Expectations

Foodservice operators are not simply in the business of providing food and beverages; they are in the business of creating guest enjoyment. Achieving this goal requires attention to detail and preparation that begins well in advance of welcoming the first guest. The guest experience is determined by a variety of interrelated factors from menu design and place settings to **plate presentation** and style of service. Each of these factors plays a significant role in achieving guest satisfaction and must be made within the physical and human constraints of the operation. Issues such as size of storage areas, production and service areas, types of equipment,

and the capabilities of preparation, production, and service personnel must all be considered.

Armed with an understanding of these constraints and capabilities, the first step in preparing to welcome guests is designing the menu. Effective menu design begins with identifying target segments and planning to meet their desires. This requires asking some basic questions. What image should foodservice operations support? How many items should be offered on the menu? How diversified should the offerings be and how seasonal should they be? What impact will different menu items have on preparation, production, presentation, and service? The answers to these questions may result in a variety of menu offerings and styles of service ranging from quick-service snacks to full-service formal dining.

The second step involves the design and presentation of the menu itself. Seemingly simple things such as deciding what type of menu board should be placed above an ordering station or selecting the paper stock, graphics, color, font, and layout of a menu take on new importance. These decisions communicate an image to guests even before the food is presented.[9] A theme-park guest wanting a restful break will have different expectations than a businessperson on an expense account entertaining clients. The design and presentation of the menu sets the stage for the next important decisions.

The third step involves a variety of decisions that range from selecting service ware to designing place settings. These decisions may be driven by the functional demands of serving as many guests as inexpensively as possible or a desire to create an aesthetically pleasing atmosphere. Plastic or paper with self-service areas for condiments may be the best selection for guests in a hurry, but the same choice would not be suitable in a fine-dining situation.

Designing the actual plate presentation is the fourth and possibly most artistic step in the process. Attention to detail in the previous steps comes to life when guests receive their selections. Once the order is delivered, whether hot dogs and fries or chateaubriand, the eyes always take the first taste. Even with simple dishes, the presentation should be designed to fill our senses through a thoughtful combination of color, texture, shape, aroma, and arrangement. Think for a moment

Table 8.2	A Food and Beverage Timeline
4850 B.C.–715 B.C.	Egyptian kingdoms—travel became popular; people sought new foods and experiences.
900 B.C.–200 B.C.	Greek Empire—Greeks traveled to Egypt, India, Persia, and Babylon and brought back knowledge of various cooking methods.
500 B.C.–A.D. 300	Roman Empire—Romans conquered the Greeks, bringing back Greek slaves and their knowledge of food and preparations. The Romans' appetite for indulgence elevated cooking to the status of an art form.
5th–14th centuries	Dark Ages—travel all but disappeared; the spread of cooking knowledge and skills stopped and even began to diminish.
A.D. 1275–A.D. 1295	Travels of Marco Polo to the Middle East and China brought spicy new "treasures" such as salt and pepper to Europe, renewing interest in travel, trade, and desire to discover new foods.
14th–16th centuries	Catherine de Medici, an Italian princess who married a French prince, introduced etiquette such as the use of a fork and napkin as well as the Italian Florentine style of cooking.
16th–17th centuries	European travel to the Americas and West Indies added new foods such as chocolate, chilies, beans, corn, tomatoes, and potatoes.
	Ann of Austria, a member of the Spanish Hapsburg family, married Louis XIII. Her Spanish chefs introduced sauce *espagnol* and the use of roux as a thickener for sauces.
1651	Pierre Francois de la Varenne published the first cookbook, *Le Vrai Cuisinier François,* which detailed the cooking practices of the French nobility.
1765	M. Boulanger, a Paris tavern keeper, started the first restaurant.
1789–1799	The French Revolution—chefs who were classically trained and had worked in royal households began to work for wealthy "nonnoble" families. The exchange between classically trained chefs and domestic chefs produced a number of culinary innovations and refinements.
1856	Marie-Antoine Carême established the grande cuisine and published *La Cuisine Classique,* systematizing culinary techniques.
1898	The Savoy Hotel opened in London under the direction of Caesar Ritz and George Auguste Escoffier.
19th–20th centuries	George Auguste Escoffier introduced the "brigade system."
	Soldiers returned from each of the world wars with appetites for the traditional foods of Italy, Germany, France, and Asia.
1955	Ray Kroc opened the first McDonald's, revolutionizing ideas about franchising and customer service.

Sources: Labensky, Sarah R., Hause, Alan M., Labensky, Steven R., and Martel, Priscilla. (2007). *On cooking: A textbook of culinary fundamentals* (4th ed.). Upper Saddle River, NJ: Prentice Hall, Inc.; The Culinary Institute of America. (2006). *The professional chef* (8th ed.). Hoboken, NJ: John Wiley & Sons, Inc.

about how many different ways a chicken breast can be prepared and presented. Does your choice encourage the guest to sample and savor or simply eat because it is there and he or she is hungry?

The fifth and final step in planning to meet guest expectations is accomplished when the type of service is selected for delivering menu items. Service may range from moving down a cafeteria line to formally orchestrated **Russian service.** Whatever the selection, the ultimate goal is meeting guests' needs. Proper planning, as shown in Table 8.3, sets the stage for enjoyable dining experiences.

It All Comes Down To Rhythm, Timing, and Flow

Developing menus and having the right equipment, ingredients, and talent to produce these items is only the beginning of a successful

■ The view from the restaurant atop Auckland's Sky Tower makes it a favorite of international visitors to New Zealand. Photo by D. A. Yale.

Table 8.3	Menu Planning Essentials
Step 1.	Decide on items to include on the menu.
Step 2.	Design menu appearance.
Step 3.	Select appropriate service ware and place settings for menu items.
Step 4.	Determine plate presentation for all menu items.
Step 5.	Select appropriate level of service for menu items.

foodservice operation. Just like the conductor of an orchestra who brings a musical score to life, food and beverage managers bring menus to life. The **brigade** system, developed by Escoffier, was designed to make this task possible. Under this system, each position has a station (assigned workplace) and clear-cut responsibilities. For example, one station in the kitchen makes all of the **stocks** and **reductions** needed for the bases of soups and sauces instead of having each station make its own. Although the brigade systems (see Tables 8.4 and 8.5) were originally designed for use in fine-dining establishments, they are flexible and can be modified for use in any size or style of foodservice operation.

Professionally planned menus, a properly designed and equipped kitchen, well-trained employees, and effective preparation and production systems make up the basic ingredients for delivering high-quality food and service. However, it takes more. A dedicated team constantly striving to balance the rhythm, timing, and flow of production and service delivery adds the final ingredients that bring the dining experience to life. To achieve this balance, managers must focus on being team leaders or coaches for their employees and move away from the authoritarian approach that has been traditionally used by foodservice managers.[10]

■ Rhythm is the coordination of each required task and activity.

■ Timing is the sequencing of each task and activity to produce desired results.

■ Flow is the combination of rhythm and timing resulting in a smooth, efficient operation.

To understand the importance of rhythm, timing, and flow, imagine the following setting. You and your friend have just been seated and presented with menus in a full-service American-style restaurant. The typical sequence of courses in this style of restaurant would be appetizer, soup, salad, entrée, and dessert.

As you review the menu, you look around and notice that the dining room is full, and there are customers still waiting to be seated. You see a busser (back waiter) moving a high chair toward a table; the captain (host/hostess) reseating guests who did not like their table; a waiter (front waiter) stopping to answer a guest's question; and you just heard the captain take a special request from the guests at the table next to you. While you are watching all of these activities your water glasses have been filled, and your waiter has already taken and served your drink orders.

Table 8.4	Typical Stations and Responsibilities in the Classical Kitchen Brigade System
Station	*Responsibilities*
Executive chef or *chef de cuisine*	Responsible for all kitchen operations, including ordering, supervision of all stations, and development of menu items.
Sous (under) *chef*	Second in command, answers to the chef, may be responsible for scheduling, fills in for the chef, and assists the station chefs (or line cooks) as necessary.
Station chefs or *chefs de partie*	Line cooks, often with specialized functions such as banquet chef.
Sauté station or *saucier*	Responsible for all sautéed items and their sauces.
Fish station or *poissonier*	Responsible for fish items, often including fish butchering, and their sauces.
Roast station or *rotisseur*	Responsible for all roasted foods and related *jus* or other sauces.
Grill station or *grillardin*	Responsible for all grilled foods and often broiled foods as well.
Fry station or *friturier*	Responsible for all fried foods. This position is often combined with *rotisseur.*
Vegetable station or *entremetier*	Responsible for hot appetizers, and often egg dishes. Frequently this station has responsibility for soups and vegetables, starches, and pastas. In the traditional brigade system, soups are prepared by the soup station or *potager* and vegetables by the *legumier.*
Roundsman or *tournant*	Swing cook; works as needed throughout the kitchen.
Pantry chef or *garde manger*	Responsible for cold food preparations, including salads, cold appetizers, and patés.
Butcher or *boucher*	Responsible for butchering meats, poultry, and occasionally fish.
Pastry chef or *patisser*	Responsible for baked items, pastries, and desserts.
Expediter or *aboyeur*	Accepts orders from the dining room and relays them to the various station chefs.

Source: The Culinary Institute of America. (2006). *The professional chef* (8th ed.). Hoboken, NJ: John Wiley & Sons, Inc.

Table 8.5	Typical Stations and Responsibilities Under the Dining Room Brigade System
Station	*Responsibilities*
Dining room manager or *maitre d'hôtel*	Trains all service personnel, oversees wine selection, works with the chef to determine the menu, and organizes seating throughout service.
Wine steward or *chef de vin/sommelier*	Responsible for all aspects of restaurant wine service, including purchasing wines, preparing a wine list, assisting guests in wine selection, and serving wine properly.
Head waiter or *chef de salle*	Generally in charge of the service for an entire dining room.
Captain or *chef d'étage*	Deals most directly with the guests once they are seated.
Front waiter or *chef de rang*	Ensures that the table is properly set for each course, that the food is properly delivered to the table, and that the needs of the guests are promptly and courteously met.
Back waiter or "busser" or *demichef de rang*	Clears plates between courses, fills water glasses and bread baskets, replaces ashtrays, and assists the front *commis de rang* waiter and/or captain as needed.

Source: Meyer, Sylvia, Schmid, Edy, and Spuhler, Christel. (1991). *Professional table service.* New York: Van Nostrand Reinhold.

When your waiter takes your orders, you notice that each appetizer and entrée will have to be prepared differently. The shrimp cocktail and the mozzarella cheese sticks, just like the grilled salmon and the fettuccini Alfredo, will all come from different stations in the kitchen.

Your waiter passes through the kitchen doors and you hear a muffled burst of activity before the doors quickly close. When the rhythm, timing, and flow of all of these activities occurs as planned, the dining experience can be as pleasurable as listening to a well-rehearsed symphony. *Bon appetit!*

Adding Value to Food and Beverage Experiences

Successful food and beverage operators are quick to point out the need for differentiating their operations from those of their competitors. Operators strive to distinguish themselves by focusing on guest service, adding value through quality or pricing, providing unique atmospheres and dining experiences, or offering innovative foods, beverages, and services. Any of these approaches when successfully implemented may attract new guests as well as encourage loyal supporters to come back time and time again and bring their families and friends.

With many smaller food and beverage operations, managers are usually in close contact with the entire operation, enabling them to gain personal insights into guests' needs. As operations become more complex in settings such as hotels and resorts and the number of outlets increases, the need for formal planning processes and procedures becomes more important. There are two typical designs or approaches to planning and delivering food and beverage services in these large "property" settings. The approach chosen usually depends on factors such as the number of foodservice outlets, services provided (for example, room service, event catering, poolside service, etc.), and the property's overall marketing strategy for attracting and serving guests.

At one location, food and beverage facilities may be designed to provide service to a captive audience of guests, whereas at another location, facilities may be designed to attract guests. Let's consider a ski area's approach to its food and beverage operations. There may be thousands of skiers on the mountain and many more guests in the base area. Most of the skiers are planning to take a break from skiing between 11:30 A.M. and 1:30 P.M. to have lunch. They expect conveniently located restaurants with a layout that

allows traffic to flow smoothly (the skiers want to move about without feeling as if they are stuck in a crowd). They expect to be able to order, receive, and pay for their food without long waits. They expect hot food and beverages to be served hot, and cold items to be served cold. They might expect prices to be a little higher on the mountain because of location and the desire for convenience, but they still expect good food quality. Other guests who have decided not to ski and are staying in the base area or village want the same quality and convenience, but they may desire a larger selection of food and service options.

To run the ski resort's F&B operations successfully, managers must pay close attention to a number of things. For example, organized **commissary** operations will be important to make sure each restaurant has everything it needs. Accurate tracking systems of food and supplies from the commissary to each restaurant will also be needed. By tracking food and supplies accurately, managers know how much it costs to run each foodservice outlet. Watching the costs of each of these outlets helps managers to identify and respond to potential problems quickly. Items on the menu for these types of foodservice operations are usually the result of needing to please the "mainstream" desires of guests by providing items quickly and in large quantities.

At another property, such as a destination resort, the typical approach for food and beverage operations might be quite a bit different from the one we just discussed. In this type of situation, foods and beverages may be used to support a property's overall marketing strategy. For example, an oceanside resort in Monterey, California, may use distinctive food and beverage offerings as marketing tools to attract guests and to distinguish itself from competitors. These types of properties tend to use their food and beverage operations for three special reasons:

■ *Creating a desired public image and defining their place in the market.* F&B operations can have a significant impact on a property's image in the marketplace by serving as a center for community groups and organizations, causing the property to be perceived as a point of pride in the community.

The National Restaurant Association's Ongoing Research Reveals That . . .

In the United States:

- 42% of adult females and 31% of adult males have worked in food service at some time.

- Saturday is the most popular day to eat out, followed by Friday and Sunday. Monday is the least popular.

- More than 7 of 10 operators report purchasing products made from recycled materials for their restaurants, and roughly three out of four have a recycling program.

- Foodservice companies are increasingly entering foreign markets, with operators citing the Pacific Rim and Southeast Asia as offering the best opportunities for foreign expansion.

- Chinese, Italian, and Mexican are the most popular ethnic cuisines.

Source: National Restaurant Association.

- *Attracting desired business.* F&B operations can be used to add quality or value to a property's overall image by attracting individuals such as travel agents and meeting planners who influence travel decisions. These operations are often used to attract group business by discounting F&B items, which adds value to the total meeting package and obviates the need to discount sleeping room prices. Actions like this can increase overall profitability because rooms have a greater **contribution margin** than does F&B.

- *Creating new business opportunities.* By producing events, a property can use F&B operations to create new business opportunities. Wine tastings, celebrations, theme dinners, balls, brunches, and other combinations of food, beverage, and entertainment often entice people to visit a property. Once there, they may stay longer to enjoy the guest rooms, restaurants, lounges,

pools, spas, and golf and tennis facilities. These marketing strategies can be especially effective for generating business during **shoulder seasons**.

In properties that use food and beverage as part of their overall marketing strategy, the F&B director is expected to run the operations in a way that will best benefit the entire property. In other words, the F&B director should be more concerned with the overall profitability of the property and meeting guests' needs rather than simply the profitability of F&B operations. This approach can be seen in operations in which attention to little details and customer service are the norm. Little things like responding to a guest request for an item not on the menu, such as a peanut butter and jelly or grilled cheese sandwich, or grander gestures, such as hosting a "no charge" cocktail reception as a kickoff to a three-day conference, create lasting and positive impressions.

Other tourism suppliers face similar types of decisions. Should foods and beverages simply be provided to fill a basic human need or should they be used as a valuable addition to the marketing mix? To answer that question, think about the approaches taken by two different airlines. Singapore Airlines is noted for its high-quality foodservice operations and uses this as a marketing tool, whereas Southwest Airlines flies only short legs, choosing to avoid the costs and challenges associated with foodservice operations.

From Ten to Ten Thousand

How many did you say we should expect? Feeding small and large groups of guests on a one-time basis creates some unique challenges for foodservice operators. Meeting these special needs ranges from simple to complex. It may be as simple as reserving a special section in a restaurant for a tour group as they step off the bus to enjoy a relaxing lunch, or it may be as complex as serving multiple meals at scattered sites across a broad geographic setting such as at the Summer Olympics.

Whether it's providing breakfast, lunch, dinner, or refreshment breaks for groups, foodservice teams must be prepared to meet their needs and budgets flexibly. There are a variety of facilities either specifically designed for **banquets** or that can be easily converted to meet **catering** needs. Most large hotels and resorts and many smaller properties have multipurpose rooms that can be used for both meetings and food functions, and convention centers and even sports arenas can be converted to feed tens of thousands of guests. The task of planning, setting up, and serving these functions falls in the capable hands of catering (also called banquet) managers and their supporting service teams.

Catering sales managers work with clients to discover their needs for such things as meeting and exhibit space as well as food and beverage requirements. These requirements are then described in great detail for internal use for kitchen and service employees on a catering contract or **banquet event order (BEO)** form. The BEO serves as an internal form of communication that provides specific timing and instructions for the banquet service team to meet guest expectations. This level of detail becomes especially important when dealing with groups requiring a variety of services over multiple days. For example, at a four-day conference, meeting goers will likely be served breakfasts, lunches, dinners, refreshment breaks, and cocktail parties. These may range from a formal dinner-dance banquet to a self-service continental breakfast.

FYI

Tourism Traffic Builders

- Give tourists a taste of regional specialties.
- Train staff to answer questions about area attractions.
- Add evening entertainment to attract visitors looking for things to do.
- Place coupons on the back of tickets for local tourism attractions.
- Invite front desk staff and concierges from nearby hotels to dine so they can make firsthand recommendations.
- Advertise in visitor guides and other tourism publications.
- Place mini-menus with discount coupons at tourism and visitor centers.

Source: National Restaurant Association.

BUILDING PROFITABLE OPERATIONS

"Mention food and beverage, and most hotel owners and managers want to run for the exits. Restaurants, and to a lesser extent bars and lounges, are hard to conceive, staff, operate, and certainly profit from."[11] Competition in the food and beverage industry is fierce, with owners and managers facing the added problem of operating on very thin profit margins, so it is not surprising that a 60% failure rate for restaurants has been reported.[12]

Why is this failure rate so high? People seem to become financially involved in food and beverage establishments naively or for many of the wrong reasons. Some are motivated to own or invest in a restaurant because they crave social recognition, whereas others like to dine out and think they know how to deliver the dining experience. Still others venture into this line of business because they have gained status as accomplished cooks from dinner parties put on for friends. Such experiences lead many to believe falsely that they have the necessary skills to be good food and beverage operators.

Even if they do have the necessary talent, they may often fail to realize that foodservice operators are faced with working long hours and then dealing with many complex problems in today's competitive environment.[13] Profit margins are shrinking, and controllable costs, such as payroll, employee benefits, food costs, and taxes, are being forced up by inflation and governmental regulations, and foodservice patrons are unwilling to accept higher menu prices. In fact, F&B operations require a great deal of attention to detail, and they are a business in which every nickel counts, and profits are often measured in pennies.

According to one industry expert, there are a number of steps restaurant operators can take to ensure success. Table 8.6 lists those factors that can make the difference between success and failure.[14] "Whether in a quick service environment or a five-star resort, just the right amount of planning will increase the likelihood of success exponentially."[15]

Table 8.6	Recipes for Restaurant Success
Recipe	*Ingredients*
#1	Operating costs are high and profit margins are low, so budgets, costs, and portion controls are a must.
#2	Labor is a significant cost and a time-consuming issue; be sure to focus on effective selection, training, and retention.
#3	Prepare a good business plan and have sufficient cash flow and capital to make it through slow times.
#4	You must have a passion for the business and develop as well as practice strong internal controls. Not only must you interact with customers; you have to be involved in the day-to-day business to avoid fraud and theft as well as supervising profit margins and negative signs that could infer problems.
#5	Pay attention to the number-one customer demand—quality.
#6	Monitor the marketplace. Keep your concepts current and fresh. Plan for change; don't wait for sales to slow before you implement changes.

Source: Kahan, Stuart. (2003, December). Food for thought. *Practical Accountant,* pp. 49–50.

Some of the more common performance measures that are used to evaluate performance in foodservice operations include sales per seat, sales per employee, and the number of times a **seat or table turns over** in one day. Table 8.7 provides common ratios showing how much of every sales dollar is spent on food, supplies, labor, and occupancy costs in full- and limited-service restaurants. It is important to note that these benchmarks and ratios will vary depending on the type of restaurant. As you think about these benchmarks, refer back to Figure 1.9 and remember the importance of leverage, turnover, and margin in achieving profitability.

Rather than face the complexities of foodservice operations alone, tourism service suppliers (especially small lodging properties) are turning in increasing numbers to the expertise provided through branded concepts. Guest needs can be met, kitchen and customer-service labor costs can be substantially reduced, and marketing efforts can be minimized by putting together well-known fast-food franchises into a food court setting.

Balancing Payroll Costs with Productivity

As Carrie learned in the chapter opener, producing some menu items can be very complicated as well as labor intensive and costly. Labor and food costs are the largest controllable expenses for F&B operations. High **employee turnover**, the availability and quality of new employees, and the

Table 8.7	The Restaurant Dollar	
	Full-Service Restaurants	*Limited-Service Restaurants*
Where it came from:		
Total sales	100%	100%
Where it went:		
Cost of sales	31%	30%
Salaries, wages, and benefits	33%	30%
Restaurant occupancy costs	5%	7%
Other	27%	25%
Income before taxes	4%	8%

Source: The National Restaurant Association, 2003.

constant need for training all combine to create significant operating costs. Consequently, F&B managers must constantly focus their efforts on making employees more productive through education, training, and technology enhancements. In response to continuing labor shortages, most foodservice operations are buying some ingredients that have been either partially or fully prepared. This allows managers to hire fewer employees and reduces culinary training needs.[16]

Increasing employee productivity typically involves investing for future profitability. Keep in mind that recruiting, training, and retaining skilled employees, as well as equipping them with the best tools and technology, will be costly decisions. These decisions are often difficult because the paybacks in efficiencies may be more long term than immediate. Other approaches such as reminding food servers of a simple slogan such as "hands-full-into-the-kitchen and hands-full-out-of-the-kitchen" can do wonders to increase productivity and employee satisfaction.

Food Quality and Food Costs Are the Results of Effective Purchasing

As important as controlling labor costs in F&B operations is the challenge of controlling the cost of food. Therefore, just as much attention should be paid to purchasing, receiving, and storing these products as is paid to controlling labor costs. Purchasing is much more than simply ordering and receiving food and beverage products. The greater the food knowledge and skills of the purchasing agent, the more effective the purchasing processes will be. For example, the purchaser must understand the impact that the menu, preparation methods, ingredients, shelf life, storage facilities, equipment, skill level of the staff, and guest expectations have on production and service delivery. Without this knowledge, problems are sure to occur. In addition, no matter how good the purchasing processes are, they can be made totally ineffective by poor receiving and storage procedures. Simple mistakes such as failing to verify amounts and weights or not checking product specifications against the **purchase order,** as well as using newer items before older items, can have an adverse impact on profitability and quality.

Be Your Own Restaurant Inspector

No matter where you travel, from Augusta, Maine, to Zhenghou, China, you can protect yourself from food-borne illnesses. In addition to watching what you eat and drink, be your own restaurant inspector. Practice these simple rules:

- Follow your nose's cues. If there are funny smells emanating from the restaurant, stay away.
- Look for cleanliness. Check out the back door and trash areas. If they are neat and clean, then the restaurant probably is clean also.
- Before you are seated, check out the restrooms. This is a good indication of the importance placed on sanitation.
- Notice your servers. Have they taken care with their appearance? Do they appear to be clean? How do they handle plates and service ware? If the servers are dirty or careless, it's time to move on.
- Check for general cleanliness. This doesn't mean just the tables, chairs, floor, and uniforms; check also for dead bugs and soiled menus.

Don't run the risk of spoiling your travel fun. When in doubt, leave; there is always a good place to eat if you look!

Source: Noonan, Peggy. (2001, November 2–4). Dine out safely. *USA Weekend,* p. 10.

As in many competitive industries, foodservice operators are finding it beneficial to create partnership relationships with their suppliers. These suppliers are called **purveyors** in the foodservice industry and the relationships they are creating are called **prime vendor agreements.** In a prime vendor agreement, foodservice operators agree to direct a large portion (typically up to 80%) of their orders to a specific purveyor. In return, the purveyor agrees to categorize purchases into broad groupings, such as meats, poultry, shellfish, and canned goods, and then negotiate prices for items in each category based on a set percentage markup above cost. Other incentives such as providing training or lending specialized equipment may also be offered by the purveyor to obtain additional business.

Using Technology to Improve Service Delivery[17]

Point-of-sales systems (POS) are being integrated into management information systems to improve foodservice efficiency and profitability at a staggering pace. They are no longer just glorified cash registers. Computer software suppliers are constantly updating their systems, and foodservice operators are eagerly embracing and purchasing system enhancements. Touchscreen and wireless systems are quickly becoming the standard, allowing food servers to enter customer orders without having to make unnecessary trips to the kitchen. The kitchen staff notifies the server via a vibrating pager with a digital readout when orders are ready. Newer advances allow servers to place orders using handheld devices, and server voice recognition systems have already been prototyped. These new systems will make it possible for servers to remain in the dining area to provide customers with more personalized attention.

In addition to improving the flow of information from the wait staff to the kitchen production staff, the real-time data also improve purchasing and inventory controls. Wider wireless local area networks are giving properties with multiple food service outlets the ability to integrate information and consolidate operations. Consolidated data accumulated by a chain or a POS provider are available via an Internet site. Profitability as well as enhanced food quality is achieved by keeping inventories lower through rapid turnover. The leading POS systems offer an instant multilocation interface, so that sales, labor, inventory, and purchasing information can be shared on demand.

This easy access of information creates a cost-saving environment through centralized data storage. These databases create powerful tools for making improved marketing, management, and financial decisions.

 ## AN OUNCE OF PREVENTION IS WORTH A POUND OF CURE

Foodservice operators also invest a great deal of time and money in training and technology for reasons other than improving service and profitability. In the same way an airline captain is charged with the safety of crew and passengers, so, too, are foodservice managers with their employees and guests. They must ensure that safe and proper sanitation practices and procedures are always given priority in daily operations. As you consider the following information, think about the potential dangers that could be created if sanitation were not maintained as a high priority.

Food-borne illnesses concern both consumers and suppliers. When asked what factors influenced their confidence in food safety, consumers resoundingly said cleanliness of plates and silverware, tables and tablecloths, and restrooms (81%, 77%, and 72%, respectively). How have foodservice operators responded to these concerns? See Table 8.8 for a list of action steps.[18]

Scientific developments may have increased our understanding of food processing, improved our methods of preparation, and allowed us to improve sanitation and food storage techniques, but common sense is still needed. In the past, traditional safety and sanitation practices focused mainly on the external cleanliness of food production areas and equipment, leaving invisible

Table 8.8	How Foodservice Operators Are Addressing Sanitation Concerns

- 96% have trained kitchen staff in food-safety topics.
- 88% have audited food handling, preparation, or storage procedures.
- 85% have trained waitstaff in food-safety topics.
- 66% have purchased insurance to cover food-safety losses.
- 61% have required food suppliers to submit proof of liability insurance.

Source: Perlik, Allison. (2004). To protect and serve. *Restaurants and Institutions*, 1114(5).

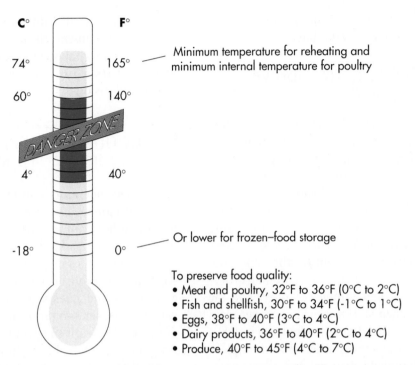

C°   **F°**

74° — 165° — Minimum temperature for reheating and minimum internal temperature for poultry

60° — 140°

DANGER ZONE

4° — 40°

-18° — 0° — Or lower for frozen–food storage

To preserve food quality:
• Meat and poultry, 32°F to 36°F (0°C to 2°C)
• Fish and shellfish, 30°F to 34°F (-1°C to 1°C)
• Eggs, 38°F to 40°F (3°C to 4°C)
• Dairy products, 36°F to 40°F (2°C to 4°C)
• Produce, 40°F to 45°F (4°C to 7°C)

■ **Figure 8.1** The Bacterial Red Zone. Time and temperature are two very important variables that must be carefully monitored. Food properly maintained at specific temperatures for certain lengths of time can enhance food quality, or, if improper time and temperatures are used, can breed disease, causing microorganisms to grow in food.

contaminants free to grow into illness-causing hazards. Most bacteria grow or multiply rapidly when products are held at temperatures between 40°F and 140°F, which is known as "The Bacterial Red Zone" (see Figure 8.1). Knowledge of how and when bacteria can grow and cause food-borne illnesses as well as the practice of basic sanitation techniques provides the foundations for protecting guest and employee safety and health.

Frequent hand washing, frequent sterilization of foodservice equipment, and careful use of cutting boards can go a long way toward preventing future problems. For example, cutting boards can be color coded and dedicated for use with a specific product. One color would be used only for cutting raw poultry, another only for fresh vegetables, and another for breads. This helps to prevent the danger of cross contamination when handling different types of foods.

BEVERAGES

The distillation, fermentation, and compounding of spirits is surrounded by a history as long and rich as the history of food. No one really knows who the alchemist was who invented the distillation process, so it is no wonder that many people through the centuries have referred to it as a gift from the gods. It was the Arabs or Saracens who gave us the words *alcohol* and *alembic*, the latter word meaning a still. In fact, the word *alembic* is used in all but the English-speaking countries even today.[19]

Beers, wines, and spirits can enhance foods and add to the overall dining experience. However, a lively bar will seldom complement a candlelit dining experience, just as a great selection of wines will do little to enhance a hot dog stand on the beach. Beers, wines, and spirits not only make a good companion for a dining experience, but they are often the predominant flavor in a sauce, entrée, or dessert. They can also be used in food preparations to season and tenderize foods.

When alcoholic beverages are used in hot food dishes, the alcohol quickly evaporates, leaving only the flavor. In dessert recipes in which an alcoholic beverage is not heated and cooked off, the practice is often referred to as *perfuming*. In short, the relationship between foods and beverages is a marriage made in heaven and there are many cultures who take the relationship for granted. For example, in Germany, you can order a beer with your Big Mac and, on a trip to Japan, you can find vending machines offering not only food but also cold beer or hot sake.

Beverage Operations

Successful beverage operations depend on many of the same fundamental business principles that we previously discussed in developing efficient, profitable, and safe foodservice organizations. In addition, beverage operations also require a great deal of attention to detail because they represent a substantial investment in equipment, furniture, décor, and inventory.

Books, television, and movies have all painted a picture of the bartender full of character, serving the guest whose stress is lifted away with a warm greeting. At the guest's request, the bartender reaches for a bottle or pulls the tap. That practice is called "free-pouring," and it is fading away to be recalled as a thing of the past. Today, it is common to see the increasing use of technology in bar operations in response to dramatic drops in profit margins. The causes of these drops are heavy taxes on alcoholic beverages and a change in consumption behaviors, as people are

drinking less but ordering more premium products. These changes along with guests' intolerance of higher prices are leading to narrower profit margins.

Today, instead of allowing the bartender to free-pour, automated systems strictly control the amount of alcohol poured and electronically transmit information to the computerized cash register system that rings up the sale and updates the bar's **perpetual inventory**. Although these systems are practical, many guests find them to be impersonal, and many professional bartenders dislike their inflexibility. Some guests

Categories of Alcoholic Beverages

1. Fermented beverages, made from agricultural products such as grains and fruits
2. Distilled or spirit beverages, made from a pure distillation of fermented beverages
3. Compounded beverages, made from combinations of either a fermented beverage or a spirit with a flavoring substance(s)

■ Pubs remain favorite gathering spots for locals and visitors. Photo by C. O. Tustin.

and bartenders perceive the bar as a place for relaxed, social exchanges where technology should be forgotten and handshakes remembered.

Keeping Spirits Under Control

Establishments serving alcoholic beverages face a unique set of legal and social challenges. "Many states have Dram Shop or Civil Liability Acts which impose liability on the seller of intoxicating liquors (which may or may not include beer), when a third party is injured as a result of the intoxication of the buyer where the sale has caused or contributed to such intoxication."[20] In addition, society's demand for more responsible drinking and stricter drinking-and-driving laws are creating additional demands on operators who serve alcoholic beverages.

These legal and social concerns are being met with strong industry support for responsible serving practices. Training programs that focus on recognition and service support for customers who have enjoyed too much of a good time are now the industry standard. Simple tactics for bartenders and waitstaff that include slowing down the speed of service, keeping "munchies" on the table, and offering appetizer menus and water are just a few approaches to responsible alcohol service. More drastic measures such as denying service, having a guest escorted to his or her room, or calling a taxicab may also be required.

The laws defining legal levels of blood alcohol before driving impairment occurs vary (typically .08% to .10% in the United States). So, can a person drink and still drive? The answer is yes, not much, or maybe not at all. A good rule of thumb to follow in the United States is that a person can drink one ounce of distilled spirits, one beer, or one glass of wine an hour and still be capable of driving legally. However, countries in Europe have much stricter laws. In the United Kingdom, alcohol is limited to 0.4 mg per liter of blood, and falls to 0.25 mg in most other countries including Germany and France, but the limit in Norway is 0.1 mg. Gibraltar is the strictest country of all; any trace of alcohol is considered a violation.[21] Paying attention to customers' needs and enjoyment can go a long way toward protecting the customer, the establishment, and the general public.

■ SUMMARY

Travel has expanded our awareness and desire for foods and beverages from all over the world while advances in science and technology have also increased the ways that foods and beverages are produced and prepared. The growing desire to experience new and tantalizing foods and beverages has created a separate category of travelers: culinary tourists.

There are many types of food and beverage operations designed to serve the public. The most common are commercial restaurants, but dozens of other styles of food service exist. No matter thesize or type of operation, all foodservice organizations are driven by the menus they offer. In delivering their menus, they must integrate the concepts of rhythm, timing, and flow to best serve their guests.

Foodservice operations range from the ubiquitous fast-food franchises that rely on drop-in customers to on-site amusement park snack bars and five-star gourmet dining rooms that serve captive audiences. No matter where they are located or whom they serve, these operations can achieve a competitive, advantage by focusing on guest service, adding value, providing unique dining experiences, or offering innovative foods and beverages.

The food and beverage sector of the tourism industry is exceptionally competitive, and profit margins are small, making controlling labor and food costs an everyday challenge. Successful foodservice operators must train and retrain their employees as well as carefully monitor purchasing and inventory control procedures. In addition, food and beverage providers must guard the safety and health of their guests and employees by using wise food-handling practices. Managers of beverage operations are also faced with many of the same challenges and opportunities that are found in foodservice operations. By paying attention to details and keeping customer service in mind, we can create pleasurable memories and lasting relationships.

■ YOU DECIDE

Jim Barnes always made it a point to go to the Bull & Bear Restaurant whenever his business trips took him to the Saskatoon area. After a busy day, he enjoyed the ambiance and the service for which the Bull & Bear had become famous. Everything was the same this time except for a new computerized cash register system that had been installed since his last visit.

As Jim scanned his guest check at the end of another enjoyable meal, he noticed something else that was different. In the past with the handwritten checks, the waiter had given Jim a receipt showing his total bill only. However, this time, the guest check showed bar, food, and tax.

Jim's company reimbursed meal expenses only, not bar expenses. Because his previous guest checks had always been handwritten, he asked his waiter if he could have a handwritten guest check showing the total amount rather than the computer-generated guest check.

His waiter apologized for any inconvenience, but said they were no longer allowed to handwrite guest checks. Undaunted, Jim decided to ask the cashier for a receipt showing the total bill only. When the cashier hesitated, Jim told her that if she would not give him the receipt, he would have to find another restaurant that appreciated his business. Would you honor Jim's request?

■ NET TOUR

To get you started on exploring Internet links for this chapter, please see

http://www.restaurants.org
http://www.darden.com
http://www.wacs2000.org

■ DISCUSSION QUESTIONS

1. How has travel expanded our acceptance of different foods and beverages?
2. How have scientific and technological advances increased the availability and variety of foods and beverages?
3. Why are the concepts of rhythm, timing, and flow important in foodservice operations?
4. How can food and beverage operations be used as a marketing tool?
5. Why must foodservice operators pay attention to detail and watch every penny?
6. Why is sanitation such an important issue in foodservice operations?

■ APPLYING THE CONCEPTS

1. Look up restaurants in the Yellow Pages of your local telephone directory. What categories are used to group the restaurants? Select one category and identify the chapter issues that are particularly related to that category of restaurant.
2. Visit two different foodservice operations in your area and compare their décor, hours of operation, staffing, menu offerings, and prices. What are the key differences and what are the similarities in these operations?
3. Make an appointment with a manager/supervisor at a local restaurant, airport caterer, hotel, motel, resort, amusement or theme park, or other location that serves food to tourists. Discuss with this manager what he or she likes and dislikes about the work as well as what types of education and training are necessary to be successful in the industry.
4. Select an article from a travel magazine or the travel section of the newspaper describing foods and/or beverages. Make a copy of the article and prepare a brief summary of the key points.

GLOSSARY

à la carte   A menu in which each item is priced and prepared separately.

Aquaculture   The farming and cultivation of water plants, fish, and crustaceans, such as kelp, salmon, catfish, oysters, and shrimp, in large quantities for human consumption.

Banquet   A food and beverage function designed, priced, and produced for a client usually for a single event or occasion.

Banquet event order (BEO)   A contract for a meeting or other special occasion that details the date, the sequence of events, special needs, foods and beverages, prices, and guaranteed quantities.

Brigade   A team of foodservice employees, for example, the service brigade (all service personnel) or the kitchen brigade (all kitchen personnel), in which each member is assigned a set of specific tasks.

Catering   A department within a restaurant, hotel, or resort property that is charged with selling and planning special meetings and food and beverage events.

Commissary   Central storage area where food and supplies are received and kept until requisitioned.

Contribution margin   What is left of the sales price after deducting operating costs.

Cuisine   A French term pertaining to a specific style of cooking (such as Asian cuisine), or a country's food in general (such as Mexican cuisine).

Culinary   The creative arts and crafts of preparing foods.

Culinary tourists/tours   Travel for unique eating and drinking experiences in the context of the local culture.

Employee turnover   The number of employees who leave their jobs because they intentionally miss work, quit, or are terminated.

Perpetual inventory   A system of tracking inventory on a continual basis so that current information on the level of stock is always available.

Plate presentation   The process of arranging menu offerings in a visually appealing fashion.

Prime vendor agreements   Agreements directing a majority of purchases to one purveyor.

Purchase order   A contract that specifies the item(s) wanted, including a brief description of quality and grade, the number desired, and the price.

Purveyors   Food-service supplier.

Reduction   The result of boiling a liquid (usually stock, wine, or a sauce mixture) rapidly until the volume is reduced by evaporation, thereby thickening the consistency and intensifying the flavor.

Russian service   A style of service in which the entrée, vegetables, and starches are served by the waitstaff directly from a platter to a guest's plate.

Seat (table) turnover   The number of successive diners sitting in one seat or at one table during each dining period, breakfast, lunch, and dinner.

Shoulder season   The period of time between high and low or closed seasons when demand for services decreases.

Station   A designated work area or department in a kitchen.

Stock   The strained liquid that is the result of cooking vegetables, meat, or fish and other seasonings and ingredients in water.

Table d'hôte   French term referring to a menu offering a complete meal at a fixed price (prix fixe).

Yield   The amount or quantity produced or returned after the preparation, processing, or cooking of a product or recipe.

REFERENCES

1. Keefe, Cathy. (2007, February 14). *Comprehensive travel survey provides insights on food and wine travelers.* Washington, D.C.: Travel Industry Association.
2. National Restaurant Association. (2008). *Travel and tourism facts.* Available at: http://restaurant.org.
3. Mizer, David A., Porter, Mary, and Sonnier, Beth. (1987). *Food preparation for the professional.* New York: John Wiley & Sons, Inc.
4. The Culinary Institute of America. (2006). *The professional chef* (8th ed.). Hoboken, NJ: John Wiley & Sons, Inc.
5. The Culinary Institute of America. (2006). *The professional chef* (8th ed.). Hoboken, NJ: John Wiley & Sons, Inc.
6. *Outlook for travel and tourism.* (1997). Washington, D.C.: Travel Industry Association of America.

7. Skerrett, P. J. (1997). Food irradiation: Will it keep the doctor away? *Technology Review*, 100(8), 28–36.

8. Labensky, Sarah R., Hause, Alan M., Labensky, Steven R., and Martel, Priscilla. (2007). *On cooking: A textbook of culinary fundamentals* (4th ed.). Upper Saddle River, NJ: Prentice Hall, Inc.

9. Kelson, Allen H. (1994). The ten commandments for menu success. *Restaurant Hospitality*, 78(7), 103–105.

10. Mills, Susan F., and Riehle, Hudson. (1993). Foodservice manager 2000. *Hospitality Research Journal: The Future Issue*, 17(1), 147-159.

11. Watkins, Ed. (2004, January). Expotel Hospitality uses F&B as its competitive edge. *Lodging Hospitality*, pp. 26-28.

12. Parsa, H. G., Self, John T., Njite, David, and King, Tiffany. (2005). Why restaurants fail. *Cornell Hotel and Restaurant Administrative Quarterly*, 46(3), 304–322.

13. Ranti, David. (1996, March 10). Out of business as usual. *News and Observer* (Raleigh, NC), pp. 1, 2F.

14. Kahan, Stuart. (2003, December). Food for thought. *Practical Accountant*, pp. 49–50.

15. Simon, Lee. (2007, June 19). The simplest kitchen on Earth. *Hotelinteractive.com*.

16. Kitchen helpers. (2000). *Nation's Restaurant News*, 4(1), 24–26.

17. Powering the point of sale. (2000). *Nation's Restaurant News*, 34(21), S16–S20.

18. Perlik, Allison. (2004). To protect and serve. *Restaurants and Institutions*, 1114(5), 42-44.

19. Grossman, Harold J. (1983). *Grossman's guide to wines, beers and spirits* (7th ed.) (revised by Harriet Lembeck). New York: Charles Scribner's Sons.

20. Black, Henry Campbell. (1979). *Black's law dictionary with pronunciations* (5th ed.). St. Paul, MN: West Publishing Company.

21. Archer, Jane. (2003, November 14). Hazards of driving abroad. *Travel Weekly: The Choice of Travel Professionals*, p. 65.

CHAPTER 9

Attractions and Entertainment

LEARNING OBJECTIVES

After you have read this chapter, you should be able to:

- Describe the major classifications of attractions and entertainment in the tourism industry.
- Understand the differences among heritage attractions, commercial attractions, and live entertainment.
- Identify key marketing, management, and financial issues facing attractions and entertainment operations.
- Describe major types of heritage attractions.
- Describe major types of commercial attractions.
- Describe major types of live entertainment alternatives.

The World is a book, and those who do not travel read only a page.

—St. Augustine

■ Chichen Itza on the Yucatan Peninsula of Mexico, a popular heritage attraction.

SO MANY THINGS TO DO AND SO LITTLE TIME

One week was just not enough, but Marie had packed in an exciting agenda of attractions and entertainment during her brief stay in London. When she and her friends first planned to visit London, one week seemed long enough for this tourism mecca. However, once they arrived, everything was so much better than the guidebooks had described that their itinerary quickly expanded. Sure, it had rained, but the rain just added to the atmosphere.

The adventure began as they boarded a flight from Toronto for Heathrow Airport. After getting their bags, clearing customs, and taking an express train to Paddington Station, they were in the heart of London. They had agreed to find a bed and breakfast (B&B) to use as a "home base" and meet there each night to discuss the different activities of the day and plan for the next. Finding a B&B was easy compared with fighting the urge to sleep.

For her first day, Marie decided to take a nonstop tour aboard one of London's famous double-decker tour buses to get a feel for the city. A side benefit of the tour was being able to stay awake by riding on the top in the open air. The tour gave Marie an overall view of London and some ideas for scheduling her time. After a fish and chips dinner, she returned to her B&B for a good night's sleep.

Day two began with a typical English breakfast: eggs, sausage, bacon, juice, toast, butter, jelly, and coffee. Marie decided to spend this day learning more about the history of London. The Tower of London, Westminster Abbey, Parliament, Buckingham Palace, and Cleopatra's Needle were just a few of the stops on this busy day. Day three was filled with shopping: Covent Garden, Oxford Street, and, finally, Knightsbridge and Harrods. Day four was supposed to be museum day, but, when the sun finally came out that morning, plans changed. A boat ride on the Thames and a visit to Hyde Park and Kensington Gardens seemed like better choices. She also visited Madame Tussaud's Wax Museum and ended the day with a visit to one of London's many theaters.

The weather on her last day was a bit gray and drizzly, so museums were back on the itinerary. There was no shortage of choices, but she finally decided to visit the Natural History Museum and the British Museum. As there were still a few empty spots in her luggage, quick trips to local shops for some last-minute souvenirs for friends and family back home topped off the day.

The plays, the shopping, the museums, the historic sights, Big Ben, the Tower of London, Westminster Abbey, Buckingham Palace, Harrods, and that chance visit to the British Museum! The days had flowed into one another as she enjoyed the delights of one of the world's premier tourism destinations. A rich history combined with a wide array of attractions and entertainment options made London the perfect tourist playground. There had been so many things to see and do that Marie had not had time to record any of her whirlwind week in her diary. Settling back in her seat for the flight home, she pulled out her diary to record the highlights of her trip.

INTRODUCTION

People have always been attracted to new, unusual, or awe-inspiring attractions and events in every corner of the world. In the days before recorded history, travelers may have journeyed for miles just to experience the beauty of the setting sun across a mountain valley or to participate in a religious festival in honor of bountiful harvests. Today, we may expect more, but we are still inspired to travel by the appeal of special attractions and events. No matter whether it is the chance to attend a rock concert, to witness Shakespeare being performed in the rebuilt Globe Theatre, to climb to the top of the Eiffel Tower, or to view the solitude and majesty of Ayers Rock, tourists are constantly seeking new sights, sounds, and experiences as well as the opportunity to participate in a variety of **leisure activities.**

Whether traveling or staying close to home, just how do people spend their leisure time? The types and varieties of activities in which we choose to participate are as varied as the seasons and the locations to which we travel. Natural attractions such as volcanoes, mountains, caves, seashores, and waterfalls; and festivals, such as planting and harvesting celebrations, served as attractions for early visitors and are still popular today. However, times have changed and, although these natural attractions and festivals are still popular, even wider varieties of alternatives have evolved to fill our leisure time. Figure 9.1 provides a brief glimpse at some of the attractions and entertainment alternatives North Americans find most attractive.

Tourists, whether visiting friends and relatives, traveling for pleasure, conducting business, or attending a professional meeting, tend to seek out a variety of attractions and entertainment alternatives to fill their leisure time. When traveling, we may continue to participate in many of our favorite leisure and **recreational activities,** but we also seek to see, do, and experience new things. Table 9.1 shows why attraction and entertainment venues are positioned for continued growth.

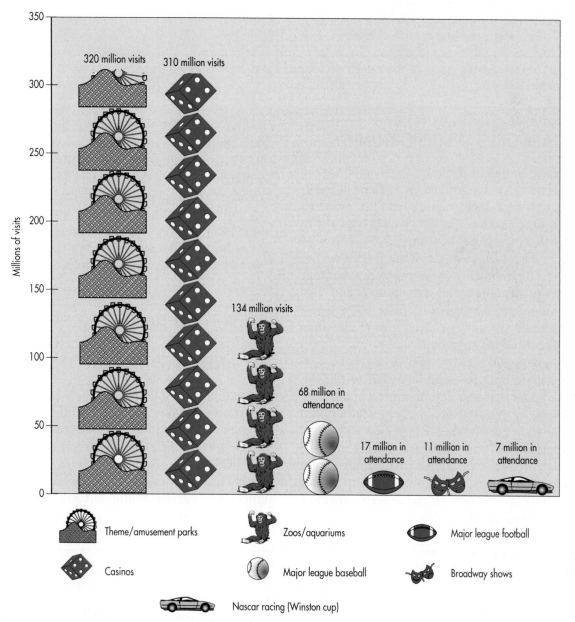

■ **Figure 9.1**   Entertainment activities enjoyed by North Americans.
Sources of 2003 attendance figures: International Association of Amusement Parks and Attractions. American Gaming Association. American Zoo and Aquarium Association. Major League Baseball. National Football League. League of American Theatres and Producers. NASCAR.

| Table 9.1 | Foundations for Attractions and Entertainment Growth |

- Increased disposable income
- More leisure time in terms of paid holidays, a two-day weekend for most people, and the ability to build up extra holiday through "flextime" systems
- Developments in technology, leading to sophisticated reservation systems and better aircraft
- The growth of personal mobility through mass car ownership
- Education
- The media, which provide images and information about destinations and attractions
- Increased marketing of destinations and attractions as governments and private companies recognize the economic benefits of tourism
- The rise of the package holiday, which helped make travel affordable for most people and took the fear out of traveling in other countries

Source: Swanbrooke, John. (2002). *The development and management of visitor attractions* (2nd ed., p. 18). Oxford: B-H Publishing.

A WORLD OF OPPORTUNITIES

As Marie soon found out in the chapter opener, the menu of attractions and entertainment possibilities travelers face is almost limitless. Selecting which ones to discuss in this chapter is almost as difficult as deciding how to spend our leisure time as we travel. To organize this discussion, we will use the following broad categories: heritage attractions, commercial attractions, and live entertainment. As shown in Table 9.2, each of these broad categories can be further classified into more specific subgroups.

As you can see, this is only a sample, and many more options could be added to the list. These attraction and entertainment opportunities may be selected as simply a sideline on a trip or they may be the main reason for travel. In Chapter 10, you will learn more about the important role many other leisure-time recreational activities, such as golf, tennis, and water and snow sports, play in the overall appeal of tourism destinations.

What would you add to this list? The Philadelphia Flower Show, the Carnival of Venice, the Calgary Stampede, Golden Days in China? Remember, things that interest you and your friends may be totally different from what others might seek to experience or enjoy. Each of these attractions or live entertainment opportunities has its own special appeal and place on the menu of leisure-time offerings.

FOUNDATIONS FOR UNDERSTANDING ATTRACTIONS AND ENTERTAINMENT

Attractions are similar in some ways to live entertainment alternatives. Visiting attractions or enjoying entertainment opportunities requires travelers to make choices about how they will use their leisure time. Some attractions are planned around historic sites and natural settings, whereas others are designed and constructed around planned activities, themes, and events. Depending

| Table 9.2 | An Attractions and Entertainment Sampler |

Heritage Attractions	*Commercial Attractions*	*Live Entertainment*
Museums and historical sites	Amusement and theme parks	Sporting activities
Zoos and aquariums	Gaming	The performing arts
Parks and preserves	Shopping	Fairs, festivals, and events
Can you think of other attraction or entertainment alternatives?		

on the purpose or setting, they may be controlled and operated by not-for-profit organizations that are dedicated to preservation and interpretation or by commercial organizations dedicated to meeting guests' needs while making a profit. Live entertainment opportunities may also be found in these same settings and may be operated on a not-for-profit or a for-profit basis. However, there are some key differences between attractions and live entertainment **venues.**

Attractions are natural locations, objects, or constructed facilities that have a special appeal to both tourists and local visitors. In addition to these attractions, tourists and other visitors are also drawn to see and be part of a variety of live entertainment opportunities. Although most attractions are permanent, entertainment alternatives are often temporary. In contrast, **events** such as fairs and festivals are temporary attractions that include a variety of activities, sights, and live entertainment venues. In addition, visitor attendance as well as the financial fortunes of almost all attractions are influenced by seasonal changes, whereas entertainment venues can be planned to take advantage of seasons and tourism flows. As can be seen in Figure 9.2, even at a popular location such as Disney World, there are definite highs and lows in attendance patterns.

Although many heritage attractions as well as amusement and theme parks are heavily used during the summer months, they may experience much less traffic in the winter months and so they close down. Even commercial attractions that were originally intended to be open year-round, such as Sea World in San Antonio, Texas, saw their visitor numbers drop so much during the colder months that it was no longer profitable to operate on a year-round basis. Yet, these attractions may still have very appealing shoulder seasons, which can meet the needs of many visitors and still generate sufficient revenues to cover operating expenses and/or generate a profit.

This seasonality of demand raises some key operating concerns for attractions. First, from a marketing perspective, how can more visitors be

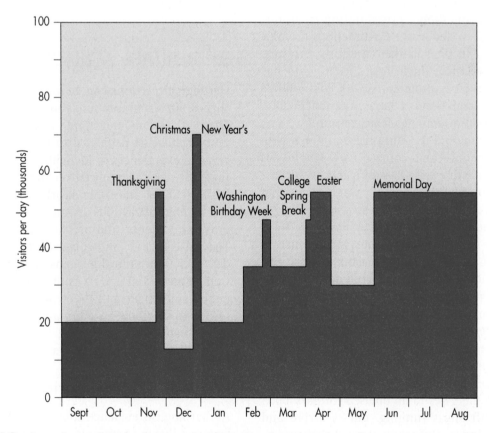

■ **Figure 9.2** Annual attendance patterns at the Magic Kingdom. Attendance figures represent weekly averages.
Source: Sehlinger, Bob, with Testa, Len. (2008). *The unofficial guide to Walt Disney World.* Hoboken, NJ: John Wiley & Sons, Inc.

attracted during less popular shoulder seasons and how can they be encouraged to spend more time and money during their visits? Second, from a management perspective, how can large numbers of employees be recruited and trained to deliver high-quality customer service? Finally, from a financial perspective, how can cash flow be managed so that enough money is available to meet payroll and other operating expenses during the busy periods while retaining enough funds to meet maintenance and administrative expenses that occur on a year-round basis? Attraction operators address these concerns through a variety of activities.

To generate shoulder season attendance, marketing efforts have been altered to target groups of potential visitors with flexible schedules such as mature travelers and families with students on year-round education calendars. In addition, activities have been added to match the seasons. For example, winter snow sport resorts have added mountain biking and alpine slides to attract summer visitors, and amusement and theme parks are hosting large groups at special promotional prices during traditionally slow shoulder seasons. Attractions are also cooperating in their marketing efforts. "To help boost attendance, the Toronto Metro Zoo has entered into cross-promotions with Paramount's Canada's Wonderland, a large amusement park located about 30 minutes from the zoo."[1]

Attracting and retaining the traditional pool of high school- and college-aged employees through the entire busy season has been accomplished through implementing wage scales that increase as the season progresses and the payment of completion bonuses if an employee stays through a specified target date. In response to fluctuating demand, many seasonal operations are also finding it helpful to recruit older workers, especially retirees who still want to be active in the workforce or simply want to supplement their incomes. No matter what the source of employees, managers must maintain a continuous recruiting and training process to fill vacant slots created by employee turnover.

When the gates to an amusement park open or a ski lift starts running, guests arrive and expect to find a staff ready to meet their needs. They also expect the same array of foods, gifts, and other goods and amenities that they would find if they had arrived a month later when the season was in full swing. Because most attractions operate on a cash basis from admission receipts, initial payroll and supply expenses must be paid before revenues are received. Planning and creative thinking are required to ensure that adequate funds are available at the start of the busy season as new employees are hired and supplies are received in anticipation of arriving guests. Selling season passes at a discount at the end of the season or before the season begins and negotiating a **line of credit** and extended payment terms with suppliers can help to ease the cash flow squeeze. As you will soon see, these are just a few of the problems and solutions facing tourism service suppliers in this segment of the industry.

In the following sections, we will describe and explore many of the heritage attractions, commercial attractions, and live entertainment alternatives that are available for people to enjoy as they travel. You may be amazed by the variety of opportunities available in each of these categories.

■ HERITAGE ATTRACTIONS

Heritage attractions can be found in a variety of shapes, sizes, and locations throughout the world. These attractions may range from a small community museum dedicated to preserving memories and experiences to incredible feats of human ingenuity and determination such as the Great Wall of China and other **World Heritage Sites**. But heritage attractions are more than just museums, monuments, and archaeological treasures. They also include showplaces for natural wonders such as **botanical gardens** and aquariums as well as parks and preserves that are dedicated to public enjoyment and the protection of natural resources. In addition, fairs and festivals create special venues for celebrating and sharing a variety of accomplishments and cultural activities.

Museums and Historical Sites

Archaeological evidence shows that once people began to live in communities, they began collecting, preserving, and displaying various items of interest from a cultural and historical perspective. These collections have provided a means of displaying history and passing on important information to future generations as well as "outsiders." Our continuing fascination with the past has created a growing demand for museums and cultural heritage sites. Although the majority of these sites are operated on a nonprofit basis, they serve as major tourist attractions, generating important cultural and economic benefits.

Today people are attracted by the diverse cultures of other people and the past that are displayed in **museums**. The number, types, and locations of museums can be counted in the hundreds of thousands, and the list of people who visit these museums each year can be measured in the millions. "Those who haven't been to a museum in a while will hardly recognize the institution. In the past decade, museums have transformed themselves, constructing eye-catching new buildings at a feverish pace, replacing dusty artifact cases with high-tech interactive exhibits, and dramatically expanding restaurants and museum shops. The goal: getting more people to come, stay longer, and spend more money."[2]

"Tourists love museums. In cities like Paris, London, Amsterdam, and New York, museums have long been major draws for out-of-town tourists. Many people will plan entire trips around a must-see exhibition; many more merely find museums a convenient place to spend a rainy afternoon. A single spectacular museum has transformed the Basque city of Bilbao from an industrial backwater into a premier tourist destination."[3] The number of available museums throughout the world continues to grow. For example, in Europe, for every museum that existed in 1950, there are now more than four. The list of museum types is extensive, but the following list provides some examples of the more common options from which visitors can choose: general, art, history, science and technology, military, and natural history. Whether there are too few or too many museums is the subject of much debate. However, as societies grow and change, museums provide a valuable foundation for studying the past and thinking about what the future may hold.

You may have heard of or even visited Colonial Williamsburg, Virginia, or Old Quebec

The Museums of Ottawa, Ontario

- Canadian Museum of Civilization
- Canadian Museum of Contemporary Photography
- Canadian Museum of Nature
- Canadian War Museum
- Central Experimental Farm
- Currency Museum
- Fort Henry
- Laurier House
- Mackenzie King Estate
- National Archives of Canada
- National Aviation Museum
- National Library of Canada
- National Museum of Science and Technology
- Royal Canadian Mint
- Upper Canada Village

Source: Ottawa, Canada's Capital Region. *Destination Planners' Guide.*

and recognize that they are major historic attractions. These are just two examples of historic sites, yet there are many other places beckoning tourists and dependent on tourism revenues to continue preservation activities. Figure 9.3 shows the brochure map provided to visitors to Historic Deerfield (in western Massachusetts), one of the oldest communities in North America.

Sites such as Historic Deerfield and others throughout the world are attracting record numbers of visitors, especially international tourists. More and more communities and countries are taking steps to preserve historic treasures and attract visitors through active restoration and interpretive programs. New life and uses are even being found for old industrial sites. "The owners of the Dürnberg salt mine in Hallein, Austria, which has been hosting visitors since at least 1700, decided in 1989 that salt was no longer profitable and closed down the mine. But it still earns money from 220,000 visitors each year, taking them on rides on the steep, long

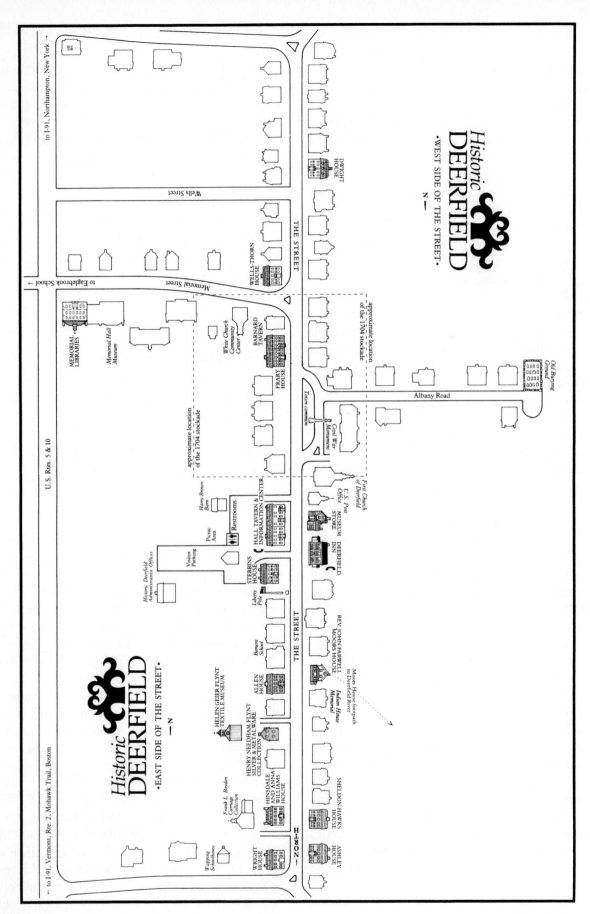

■ **Figure 9.3** Historic Deerfield map.

Map provided courtesy of A. W. Bell Design for Historic Deerfield, Inc.

wooden slides that were built to transport miners."[4] These museums and heritage sites are managed by professional **curators**, and interpretive programs are frequently conducted by **docents** who volunteer their time or work for very little pay.

Zoos and Aquariums

Large collections of animals, which were originally called *menageries*, have served as magnets for visitors since the times of the ancient Chinese, Egyptians, Babylonians, and Aztecs. Modern zoos (sometimes referred to as *zoological parks*) now come in many sizes and can be found throughout the world. The Philadelphia Zoo was the first (1859) location in the United States dedicated to the large-scale collection and display of animals. Although this facility is still of great importance, it has been eclipsed by more spectacular zoos such as the Bronx Zoo and the San Diego Zoo. Other notable zoos around the world can be found in Montreal, Vancouver, Frankfurt, London, Paris, Moscow, New Delhi, Tokyo, and Sydney. Historically, most zoos were established as not-for-profit organizations, but that form of operation is changing as over half of all the zoos in the United States now operate as for-profit organizations or only partially depend on government funding.[5]

Some of these zoos are very large, creating a great deal of public interest and publicity as well as generating significant international tourism traffic. This interest and traffic is based on unusual exhibits, collections of animal species, and efforts to re-create the natural setting found in the wild. Even the Walt Disney Company is banking on the continued draw of zoos. In the summer of 1998, Disney unveiled its Animal Kingdom theme park, which features a blend of live displays of existing animal species and animatronic displays of species from the past, such as dinosaurs.

The first public aquarium was established in London at Regents Park in 1853. It eventually failed because of poor design and management, but the idea of a preservation attraction devoted to water life has proven to be successful. Although aquariums are only about half as popular as zoos and wild animal parks combined, they are increasing in number, size, and attendance. The huge Oceanarium in Lisbon, Portugal, which opened as the flagship attraction of Expo '98, represents Europe's largest and possibly the most spectacular of the world's hundreds of aquariums. The Manila Ocean Park in the Philippines, which opened in 2008, combines not only an expansive oceanaruim but also shopping and food to round out its attractiveness to visitors.

Many aquariums are supported and managed as not-for-profit foundations, such as Canada's largest, the Vancouver Aquarium. Others have been developed as for-profit enterprises, such as the chain of Sea World Parks. Recently, many cities, such as Camden, New Jersey, and Long Beach, California, have funded aquariums to help revitalize waterfront areas by attracting tourists and residents to oceanside regions of these cities. One of the most successful aquariums, Baltimore's National Aquarium, helped ensure the success of that city's redeveloped Inner Harbor.

Parks and Preserves

Every park and preserve is a little bit different. They may range from famous urban parks such as Central Park in New York City or Hyde Park in London to forests and preserves such as Prince Albert National Park in Canada and Nairobi National Park in Kenya. Although they may be different in appearance and purpose, they are dedicated to protecting the natural beauty of landscapes, plants, and animals for future generations as well as providing visitors

Vancouver Aquarium Mission Statement

"The Vancouver Aquarium, Canada's Pacific National Aquarium, is a self-supporting, non-profit association dedicated to effecting the conservation of aquatic life through display and interpretation, education, research and direct action."

Reprinted with permission of Vancouver Aquarium.

with open spaces for rest, relaxation, and recreation. Achieving this balance requires meeting the needs of visitors while maintaining the resources contained within the lands that have been set aside for public use. To serve all these needs, the potential impacts of all activities must be monitored and managed. For example, day-use areas and campsites that are accessible by motorized vehicles and have full sanitary facilities require more upkeep and labor than wilderness areas that are accessible by foot or on horseback only.

The importance of parks as major tourist attractions was ushered in with the dedication of Yellowstone National Park in 1872. The U.S. National Park System has now expanded to include a variety of sites dedicated to the preservation of nature and heritage. The 379 units within the park system are grouped into 20 designations (see Table 9.3) including **national park, national monument, national scenic trail,** and **national preserve.** The idea of national parks soon spread north to Canada, where in 1887, the first national park was established with the opening of Banff National Park. National parks can

now be found throughout the world as countries strive to preserve and protect their more pristine natural treasures. The grandeur and importance of some of these national parks, such as Jasper National Park in Canada and Grand Canyon National Park in the United States, have become legendary and draw millions of visitors each year to enjoy their breathtaking beauty.

Some attractions such as Nairobi and Tsavo National Parks in Kenya and Serengeti National Park in Tanzania have gained such international acclaim that they serve as some of these countries' primary tourist attractions. Although people from around the world are drawn to these well-known national parks, there are also millions of acres of land that have been set aside for public enjoyment on the state, provincial, and local levels. From these giant parks to the small pocket parks tucked away in the corner of a city, not a day goes by that visitors and locals alike are not relaxing or taking in a little bit of nature.

The U.S. National Park System is a large operation in itself, with over 20,000 employees and 90,000 volunteers, and spending over $2.1 billion to serve almost 290 million visitors a year.[6,7] As a not-for-profit government agency, the National Park Service depends on **appropriations** as well as other sources of revenues. These other sources include admission (user) fees as well as revenues generated from over 650 **concessionaires** that supply a wide range of goods and services from food and lodging to transportation and souvenirs. However, the majority of operating funds (65% in 2008) still come from appropriations. Figure 9.4 shows how these funds are spent.

Botanical gardens are another important part of the tourism attraction mix for many communities. Some botanical gardens are renowned for their magnificent displays, and they draw visitors from all over the world. The oldest botanical garden was established at the University of Pisa in Italy in 1544. The Royal Botanical Gardens in Edinburgh, the Munich Botanical Gardens, the Montreal Botanical Gardens, and the Missouri Botanical Gardens in St. Louis are just a few examples of some of the more popular and frequently visited botanical gardens.

Table 9.3	Units in the U.S. National Park System
International Historic Site	1
National Battlefields	11
National Battlefield Parks	3
National Battlefield Site	1
National Historic Parks	38
National Historic Sites	77
National Lakeshores	4
National Memorials	28
National Military Parks	9
National Monuments	73
National Parks	54
National Parkways	4
National Preserves	16
National Recreation Areas	19
National Reserves	2
National Rivers	6
National Scenic Trails	3
National Seashores	10
National Wild and Scenic Rivers	9
Parks (other)	11
Total	**379**

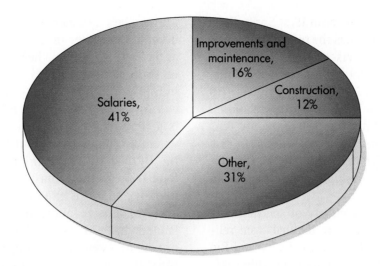

■ **Figure 9.4** U.S. National Parks expenditures.
Source: Statistical abstract of the United States 2008. Washington, D.C.: U.S. Government Printing Office.

Fairs and Festivals

Fairs and **festivals** hold unique positions in the attractions and entertainment segment of the tourism industry because they are a little bit of everything—heritage attractions, commercial attractions, and live entertainment. A fair was originally a temporary marketplace set up with the idea of stimulating commerce by creating an event that would bring together buyers and sellers. You might recognize the modern-day version of the original fair as a flea market. Festivals, on the other hand, were gatherings devoted to times of celebration.

Up through the Middle Ages, there were fairly distinct differences between fairs and festivals. However, over time, many of the same types of activities such as food, shows, and musical entertainment could be found at both fairs and festivals. The idea of having fun at these events is probably not surprising because the word *fair* comes from the Latin word *feria*, meaning "holiday."

As commerce grew, so did the idea of fairs that were designed to be large and last for longer periods of time, maybe as long as several months. Many major exhibitions highlighting achievements and industries were held before the first "World's Fair." Two of these were the Paris Exhibition of 1889 and the 1904 Louisiana Purchase Exhibition in St. Louis, Missouri.

The idea of these very large fairs that bring together exhibitors and visitors from all over the world proved to be so popular that international leaders decided to bring some uniformity to the concept. With the signing of a diplomatic convention in Paris in 1928, 43 countries agreed to the frequency and basic operational goals of events that would officially be recognized as World's Fairs. This agreement created the International Bureau of Exhibitions (BIE), which divided the world into three zones: Europe, North and South America, and the rest of the globe. It also stipulated that fairs would not be held in consecutive years in any one country and that no fees would be charged for the exhibits of foreign governments. Since its formation, there have been a number of notable World's Fairs including the New York World's Fairs (1934 and 1964); Brussels Universal and International Exhibition (1958); Expo '67 in Montreal, Canada (1967); Expo '70 in Osaka, Japan (1970); Expo '86 in Vancouver, Canada (1986); World Expo '88 in Brisbane, Australia (1988); Expo '92 in Seville, Spain; Expo 2000 in Hanover, Germany; and Expo 2005 in Aichi, Japan. Future BIE-sanctioned exhibitions will be staged in Shanghai, China (2010) and Milan, Italy (2015).

Another very popular visitor attraction is the regional, state, or county fair. Most of these have evolved around the display of agricultural and livestock exhibits, but they often include industrial exhibits and many other entertainment activities. The Eastern States Exhibition, or "The Big E" as it is called, is an annual regional

10-day fair held each summer in West Springfield, Massachusetts; it celebrates the crafts, industries, and agricultural products of the northeastern states of the United States. Some of these fairs, such as the Canadian National Exhibition in Toronto, the State Fair of Texas, and the National Western Livestock Show in Denver, draw tens of millions of visitors. However, whether it is a World's Fair, state fair, or county fair, people still travel from all over to exhibit and participate in the festivities.

Festivals celebrate a variety of special occasions and holidays. Some are derived from religious observances, such as New Orleans' and Rio de Janeiro's huge Mardi Gras festivals. Other festivals focus on activities as peaceful as ballooning (the Albuquerque Balloon Festival) or as terrifying as the running of the bulls in Pamplona, Spain. Often, festivals center on the cultural heritage of an area, such as the clan festivals that are prominent in the North Atlantic province of Nova Scotia. Seasons are also reasons for festivals such as the Winter Carnival held in Quebec City or

Milwaukee's Summerfest. More recently, food has become the center of attention at locations such as the Taste of Chicago, the National Cherry Festival in Traverse City, Michigan, or the Garlic Festival in Gilroy, California.

Any time people visit a fair or a festival, it is a time of celebration, and what celebration would be complete without fun and food? From the Oktoberfest in Munich to Hawaii's oldest food festival, the Kona Coffee Cultural Festival, tourists and locals can expect to find a tempting array of music, foods, and drinks. Community leaders have discovered that tourists can be drawn to even the smallest communities for fun-filled events. The National Cluck-off held during Chicken Days in Wayne, Nebraska, and the Oatmeal Cook-off held at the Oatmeal Days in Oatmeal, Texas, attest to people's desires to attend and be a part of festivals from the sophisticated to the seemingly silly.

In addition to these many heritage attractions, culture provides innumerable other methods to attract visitors. For further discussion of the importance of culture's role in tourism, turn to Chapter 12.

Experimental Aircraft Association's (EAA) International Fly-in and Sport Aviation Exhibition

The International Council of Air Shows estimates that approximately 450 air shows are held each year, but one of these shows is special. One week each summer, hundreds of thousands of aviation enthusiasts from all over the world converge on Oshkosh, Wisconsin, for the biggest air show this side of Paris, France. The location of this event is special. In addition to its being the busiest airport in the world for one week, Wittman Air Field is also home to a historic airport hangar filled with antique planes and is a short hop away from the EAA Aviation Center and Air Museum. The EAA festivities come complete with an opening parade, exhibits, acrobatic demonstrations, flybys, and shopping booths. So many people attend that every available form of accommodations from campgrounds and dormitory rooms at nearby University of Wisconsin, Oshkosh, to hotels is used every year.

COMMERCIAL ATTRACTIONS

In addition to the heritage attractions just discussed, a host of commercial attractions have been developed to meet travelers' leisure-time needs. Whether it's the thrill of the roller-coaster plunge, the excitement of gaming, or the joy of an armload of boxes after a day at the mall, both tourists and locals welcome the opportunity to visit and enjoy these attractions.

Amusement Parks

The first amusement parks, which were called *pleasure gardens*, were built in England and France. Some of the largest and most popular amusement parks such as Gardaland on Italy's Lake Garda and Tivoli in Denmark attract millions of visitors each year. As the name *pleasure garden* implies, these attractions began as manicured gardens designed to provide a temporary escape for city dwellers from the everyday drudgeries of life. Rides such as carousels, games,

■ Ever-more-gravity-defying roller coasters are the hallmark of a major amusement park.

weekend periods. As automobiles and buses replaced trolleys, these and other amusement parks faded in popularity as their captive audiences disappeared. However, the concept of family fun and amusement was kept alive during the first half of the 20th century by traveling carnivals that moved across the country as a source of entertainment at many fairs and festivals until a landmark event that occurred in 1955. That year marked the opening of Disneyland in Anaheim, California.

Disneyland was much more than an amusement park. Although it drew on some of the basic attributes of an amusement park, Disneyland was the first theme park, and its opening served to rekindle respectability and interest in amusement parks.[8] Since that time, the operations of amusement parks have become more sophisticated, with technology playing a far more important role. However, the basics of fun, excitement, and fantasy remain the keys to amusement park successes.

Amusement parks, family entertainment centers, and water parks serve as important

and food and drink stands were added to these pleasure gardens to meet guest needs.

The idea of parks with rides and other entertainment activities soon found its way to the United States. Interest in amusements in the United States heightened when the Ferris wheel was introduced at the 1893 Chicago World's Fair. The name for this new amusement that became the centerpiece of most early amusement parks was taken from its inventor, George Washington Gales Ferris.

Lights, sounds, rides, games of chance, food, and a flurry of activities proved to be natural draws for those early thrill-seeking visitors to such places as Coney Island in Brooklyn or the Steel Pier in Atlantic City. Many smaller amusement parks in the United States were originally located at the edge of town, where the trolley lines stopped. These amusement parks, called "trolley parks," were established as marketing tools to encourage ridership during the slow

Roller Coasters

Cedar Point Amusement Park in Sandusky, Ohio, has done it again! In 2003, the wildest roller coaster of them all opened, named the Top Thrill Dragster. What a thrill it is! As the first "strato-coaster," breaking the 400-foot barrier, it rises 420 feet into the air. Designers claim a 120-mph top speed and a 90-degree ascent and descent—that's straight up and straight down, putting 6 Gs on the riders for one second

Track length: 2,800 feet

Lift height: 420 feet

Angle of lift: 90 degrees

Angle of descent: 90 degrees

Speed: 120 mph

Ride capacity: Approximately 1,500 per hour

Source: http://www.cedarpoint.com/public/park/rides/coasters/top_thrill_dragster/index.cfm.

recreational outlets for their host communities and also attract considerable tourism interest from the region. Some of the larger amusement parks that may be recognizable to you include Six Flags/Elitch's Garden in Denver; Kentucky Kingdom in Louisville; Kennywood Park (one of the original trolley parks) in West Miffin, Pennsylvania; Grand Slam Canyon in Las Vegas; and Cedar Point in Sandusky, Ohio (the largest in North America). Like so many tourism service providers, there is no industry-specific classification system for these entertainment attractions.

Theme Parks

The distinction between amusement and theme parks is beginning to blur, but there are several unique characteristics that set them apart. Theme parks create a destination in themselves. By combining entertainment, food, and beverages and an environment different from that found outside the gates, visitors are allowed to escape reality as they enter. Through the magic of technology and elaborate staging, theme parks can replicate almost any location in the world. As visitors are transported into this simulated environment, they are afforded the luxury of being in another location without the expense or any of the potential problems of faraway travel.[9]

In addition to providing a theme around which a park operates, such as the Dark Continent (Africa) at Busch Gardens in Tampa, Florida, or Ocean Park in Hong Kong, successful parks also meet several other basic requirements. These requirements include:

- A sufficient target market of day-trippers who have the necessary disposable income to visit and enjoy park attractions
- A site of at least 100 acres or more of rolling or well-drained land for the park, parking, buffer areas, room for future expansion, and easy highway access
- Access to a large pool of prospective part-time employees
- A minimum of 140 rain-free days between April 1 and November 1
- Access to large quantities of water because most theme parks usually contain popular water attractions[10]

There may be a tendency on the part of North Americans to think that they are the center of amusement park attractions. However, remember that the idea was imported from Europe and a trip to that continent will show that it has not lost its place in the theme park spotlight. Blackpool Pleasure Park in Blackpool, England; Parc Asterix and Disneyland Paris just outside Paris ("the single biggest tourist attraction in Europe"); Port Aventura on Spain's Costa Dorado; Efteling Leisure Park in Kaatsheuvel, Netherlands; LEGOLAND in Billund, Denmark; and Phantasialand between Cologne and Bonn, Germany, are just a few of Europe's premier parks.[11] Other park locations around the world, such as Tokyo Disneyland in Japan; Dreamworld at Coomera on Australia's Gold Coast; Lotte World in Seoul, Korea; La Ronde in Montreal, Quebec; and Burlington Amusement Park on Prince Edward Island, Canada, serve to highlight the international appeal of these attractions.

"The contemporary American typically associates theme parks with concepts of permanence, gardened park-like settings and single price admission" (p. 51).[12] Theme parks meeting these criteria range from elaborate parks such as Disney World in Florida and Canada's Wonderland in Toronto to local and specialty theme parks such as Worlds of Fun in Kansas City, Missouri, and Six Flags over Georgia, in Atlanta, providing a wide range of choices for the consumer. To differentiate product offerings and compete successfully, theme park operators must become more aware of consumer perceptions and concerns. There are several core conditions that must be met by theme park operators to retain repeat patronage and attract new patrons.

From an operating point of view, parks must create a family atmosphere and be clean and visually pleasing. Park designers must provide a wide variety of rides, especially roller coasters and water rides, while reducing the perception of crowding. In addition to activities with an educational focus, new rides and features must be added on a periodic basis to maintain guest interest and ensure repeat patronage. To fund these changes, parks rely on six major sources of revenue (see Table 9.4). As operators of theme parks such as Cypress Gardens in Florida have learned, they must appeal to a

Table 9.4	Amusement/Theme Park Revenue Sources

Revenue Sources in U.S. Dollars	*Mean Percentage of Total Revenue*
Admissions	50%
Food	19%
Merchandise	11%
Games	7%
Parking	3%
Other	10%
Total	100%

Source: International Association of Amusement Parks and Attractions. (2000). *Amusement industry abstract.* Alexandria, VA: Author.

broad demographic range to attract sufficient numbers of visitors to achieve profitability.[13]

GAMING

Casino gaming has always been popular and available in many parts of the world, but it has experienced explosive growth in popularity and availability in the United States, Macao, and Canada during the past few years. When gaming was legalized in Nevada in 1931 to attract tourists during the Depression, few would have envisioned that some type of gaming operation would one day be found within easy access of so many people in so many locations. The same type of phenomenon happened in Macao in 2003 when China eased visa requirements, and gaming exploded as tourists flooded in.

The increasing availability and ease of access to gaming locations just in the United States has resulted in more Americans visiting casinos than attending major league and collegiate football games, arena concerts, symphony concerts, and Broadway shows combined.[14]

From New Mexico to Connecticut, casinos all over the country are in the midst of a high-stakes gamble: remaking themselves into full-service, if not luxury, vacation destinations. Taking their cue from Vegas, they're throwing up plush hotels, high-end shopping malls and even kiddie amusement parks, all in an unprecedented bid for the family-vacation dollar. [15]

Five basic factors combine to explain the current success and future prospects of the gaming industry. First, voters have been increasingly willing to approve new gaming alternatives because these activities have come to be viewed as a "voluntary tax"[16] or form of economic development while politicians have been unwilling or unable to pursue new taxes.[17] Second, more people than ever before are choosing casino gaming as an acceptable leisure activity. Four out of five adults now report that they consider casino gaming to be a "fun night out."[18] Third, retirees constitute the single largest segment of the casino market,[19] and their numbers continue to grow. Fourth, casinos have devised marketing programs to attract the previously ignored "low roller,"[20] and fifth, expanded availability of gaming opportunities is attracting many individuals who have never before visited casinos for entertainment.[21]

With the advent of more locations, accessibility, and new technologies, the characteristics of gaming as a leisure-time activity have changed. Currently, there are four broad categories of gaming alternatives:

- Traditional, full-scale casino gaming, including well-established locations in Atlantic City, Las Vegas, London, Macao, and Monte Carlo
- Historic, **limited-stakes** operations such as those in Colorado's mining towns
- "Dockside" (riverboat) casinos, such as those operating in Missouri and Illinois, and on the Mississippi Gulf Coast
- Gaming on Native American reservations varies all the way from limited-stakes,

small-scale operations such as the Sky Ute Casino in Ignacio, Colorado, to large-scale Vegas-style operations such as Foxwoods on the Mashantucket Pequot reservation in Connecticut

Table 9.5 highlights some of the milestones in the growth and availability of gaming activities throughout North America.

Casino gaming is one of the most regulated businesses in the United States. Gaming businesses must comply with local, state, and federal regulations. These include complying with tax laws, treasury department regulations, and rules governing alcohol consumption, types of games allowed, and sizes of bets. The size of casino operations is measured by **gross gambling revenues (GGR)**. GGR is the amount wagered minus the winnings returned to players.

Gaming Segments

The development of new games and expanded gaming availability have given rise to several gaming segments, each with a profile somewhat different from the others and each with different benefits sought from gaming. Four broad segments appear to be emerging:

1. *High rollers.* This segment is composed of sophisticated gamblers (both domestic and foreign), to whom traditional gaming was originally targeted. These gamers tend to be wealthy, older, and male. High rollers tend to play games of skill rather than luck.[22] Gaming venues outside of the United States have been especially adept at serving this segment.

2. *Day-trippers.* Retirees dominate this segment. These gamers make several short-duration trips to operations within easy driving distance and wager relatively significant amounts per trip but tend to play slots and other video gaming options.

3. *Low-stakes/new adopters.* Gamers in this segment have discovered and accepted gaming as an interesting day or evening diversion when it is close to home or when traveling. Members of this segment include the growing cadre of aging baby boomers and their retiree parents, with the time and money to enjoy the entertainment associated with gaming. Other gamers in this segment are younger adults who grew up with computers and playing video games.[23]

4. *Family vacationers.* Owing in part to the development of complementary tourism attractions such as theme parks, this

Table 9.5	Milestones in Gaming's History and Growth
Year	*Event*
1931	Gambling legalized in Nevada.
1969	Casino gambling legalized in Canada.
1978	Gambling legalized in Atlantic City.
1988	Indian Gaming Regulatory Act made gaming possible on tribal lands in almost every state.
1989	Limited-stakes gaming in Deadwood, South Dakota; Central City, Cripple Creek, and Black Hawk, Colorado.
	Limited-stakes riverboat gaming legalized in Iowa (limits removed in 1994).
	Government-operated Crystal Casino opened in Winnipeg, Canada.
1990	Riverboat gaming legalized in Illinois.
1991	Riverboat and dockside gaming legalized in Mississippi.
1992	Cruise ships permitted to operate gaming activities on the high seas.
1993	Gaming legalized in New Orleans.
	Riverboat gaming legalized in Louisiana.
2003	China eased visa restrictions on mainland Chinese travelers, and Macao boomed as a gaming destination.
2008	Indian gaming facilities were operating in 28 states in the United States.

segment tends to gamble as an offshoot of a family vacation.

Through the use of customer loyalty programs, casinos are collecting marketing data to target each segment and cross-sell related products and services.

Place Your Bets

The availability of new and expanded gaming opportunities for tourists to try their hands at "Lady Luck" are likely to continue to grow. Although many present and future gaming locations do not have the marketing advantages of destinations such as Macao, Monte Carlo, or Las Vegas, they do have one factor in common with already well-established and successful operations in places like Hull, Ontario; Atlantic City; and Laughlin, Nevada: a location within easy driving distance of a large population base. This ease of access, combined with the social acceptance and novelty of gaming as recreation, has attracted many first-time gamers and should continue to generate repeat visits.[24]

Serving this growing market for locals and tourists who are seeking the excitement and entertainment of gaming is creating attractive investment and employment opportunities. In contrast with other segments of the tourism industry that operate on very thin profit margins, gaming generates margins of up to 35%.

Gaming opportunities continue to grow as visitors can choose from a variety of venues including riverboats, Indian reservations, destination resort casinos, and the traditional casino meccas of Las Vegas and Atlantic City. International destinations such as Macao, Isla De Margarita off the Venezuelan coast, and Bermuda tempt tourists to gaming tables from around the world. Table 9.6 shows the diversity and size of gaming venues in the United States, the largest gaming market in the world.

Most of this growth can be attributed to the attractiveness of slot machines, which generate over 70% of casino revenues. The average quarter slot gamer feeds $2,500 into machines within a three- to four-hour playing session. Nevada state law requires that casinos yield a minimum 75% payout, but most of the casinos entice players with much higher payouts. New casinos will frequently offer the highest payouts, often returning 93.4% to players, whereas the payout may drop to 87% at the more established casinos. These figures represent the average of all of the slot machines within each casino. Each machine is programmed to set different yields, so a machine may pay out higher or lower.[25] "Today's computerized slot machines generate thousands of random numbers every second, even when nobody is playing them. . . . Press a button 1/100th of a second sooner or later, and the number is different."[26]

	Major Casino Markets Based on Gross Gambling Revenue
Location	*2006 Gross Revenues*
Las Vegas, Nevada	$6.7 billion
Atlantic City, New Jersey	$5.5 billion
Chicago, Illinois/Indiana area	$2.6 billion
Connecticut Indian	$1.7 billion
Detroit, Michigan	$1.3 billion
Tunica, Mississippi	$1.2 billion
St. Louis, Missouri/Illinois	$1.0 billion
Reno, Nevada	$0.9 billion
Boulder Strip, Nevada	$0.9 billion
Shreveport, Louisiana	$0.8 billion

Source: American Gaming Association. (2008). Top 20 U.S. casino markets by annual revenue. Washington, D.C.: Author.

SHOPPING

Shopping may be part of the travel experience or it may be the primary focus of travel. Shopping is an activity that crosses all market segments. "As long as cities have existed, the pattern of 'going into town' has included a leisure experience, and visiting towns is an essential part of the tourist market."[27] Whereas some visitors simply pick up necessities or a souvenir as a reminder of their travels, others may travel to specific locations for the primary purpose of shopping. "Nearly nine out of ten, or 89%, of overseas travelers report that they shopped during their visit to the United States, according to a study conducted by the U.S. Department of Commerce and Taubman Centers Inc."[28]

"Shop till you drop." This statement applies to more than just local shoppers as more and more malls are turning to tourists in search of new customers and growth. For some travelers, a visit to a mega–shopping mall has become reason enough to take a trip, especially as these malls are transforming themselves into tourist destinations by adding amusement parks and other cultural attractions and entertainment activities.[29] The success of Canada's West Edmonton Mall in attracting tourists to the shopping experience, with over 800 stores and a variety of attractions, has not gone unnoticed.

In fact, the number-one tourist attraction in Minnesota is a shopping mall. The Mall of America in Bloomington, Minnesota, attracts over 43 million visitors a year. Based on its resounding success as a tourist attraction, plans are underway to more than double the size of the mall by adding more retail, office, and entertainment opportunities as well as additional hotel rooms.[30]

What brings visitors from far and wide to these shopping meccas? It's more than just the wide array of retail shopping alternatives. For example, the Mall of America comes complete with an 18-hole miniature golf course, a 14-screen theater, and nine nightclubs. But as successful as the retailing and attraction mix is at the Mall of America, management is not counting on its past decisions for future success.

Additions like Underwater World, a 1.2-million-gallon walk-through aquarium, provide just one more reason for shoppers to plan a trip to experience a unique mall environment.

Other malls such as Woodfield Mall in Schaumburg, Illinois, and Gurnee Mills Mall in Gurnee, Illinois, do not rely on added attractions to draw in visitors, just good, solid shopping opportunities. And does this work? The answer is a definite yes, as these two malls are Illinois' number-one and -two tourist attractions, drawing in over 28 million visitors a year. Marketing efforts that provide incentives to tour operators and support from tourist bureaus keep the shoppers coming back in record numbers.

All of these malls pale in comparison to the roster of megamalls that dot the Asian continent. Nine of the ten largest malls can be found on this continent. Based on leasable space, only the West Edmonton Mall can be found in the top ten. The others are located in China, Malaysia, the Philippines, and Turkey. In addition to shopping, these attractions include everything from casinos and human-made beaches to theme parks and IMAX theaters.

When you think of a trip to the Big Apple you probably imagine visiting its famous sites, such as the Empire State Building and the Statue of Liberty. But international visitors think of New York City as a shoppers' paradise. Shopping is the number-one activity for overseas visitors to New York City, who account for over 70% of visitor retail sales.[31] In fact, Bloomingdale's claims that it is the city's third largest tourist attraction.[32]

When it comes to shopping, the motto "build it and they will come" works! Ontario Mills Mall, located 60 miles east of Los Angeles, California, attracts over 20 million shoppers each year. About 40% of these shoppers are tourists, coming from as far away as Australia, Hong Kong, Japan, Malaysia, and the Philippines, while tour buses, approximately 2,000 a year, bring in the not-so-distant tourists. All of this tourist traffic doesn't just happen by accident. The mall has an office of tourism and marketing staff targeting not only countries but also tour operators, airlines, and other travel industry representatives.[33]

Tourism in Action

A mall is a mall is a mall. Not so! Imagine a shopping and entertainment paradise that covers over 110 acres and attracts over 20 million visitors a year. Now, imagine this attraction sitting on the plains of Canada in the city of Edmonton, Alberta. If you have not visited this "shopping center," then you have missed seeing and experiencing one of the biggest malls on Earth—West Edmonton Mall. This mammoth package of tourist services attracts people from all over the world in record numbers.

The West Edmonton Mall is not like most other malls: It is massive in size and excites the imagination. Sure, it has shops, shops, and more shops. In fact, it has more than 800 stores. But the mall has more than shops and shopping to attract visitors. Almost 40% of the mall's space is dedicated to attractions as well as a hotel and more than 100 food outlets, and it is all under one roof. It takes over 15,000 employees to accomplish all of the administrative and operating duties to keep this giant enterprise ticking.

The Fantasyland Hotel has 355 guest rooms, but 127 of these rooms have been specially "themed" and decorated to fulfill guests' desires for travel adventures. When it's time to take a break from shopping there are a number of things to do and see, including Galaxyland Amusement Park, World Waterpark, Ice Palace, Europa (miniature) golf course, Deep Sea Submarine Adventure, Dolphin Lagoon and Sea Life Caverns, a full-scale casino, a bowling emporium, three cinema complexes, and a replica of one of the ships of Christopher Columbus.

Deciding what to do can be as difficult as deciding what to buy. Viewing the many animal attractions exhibiting more than 200 species of animals such as dolphins, fish, exotic birds, and a colony of breeding penguins takes you back to nature. A ride on the Mindbender roller coaster will find you dropping 14 floors at over 70 mph, while the tranquility of the submarine ride will transport you to exotic coral reefs. Or, you can splash down into the water park that covers an area the size of five NFL football fields.

The success of West Edmonton Mall and Mall of America as retailing and tourism magnets has set the stage for even bigger and better venues. Consider the South China Mall in Dongguan, China, with 7.1 million square feet; the Golden Resources Shopping Mall in Beijing, China, with 6 million square feet; and the SM Mall of Asia in Pasay City, Philippines, with 4.2 million square feet; and the West Edmonton Mall begins to look small.[34] What marketers at each of these and other megamalls have learned is that tourists are drawn to a shopping experience where they have the option of staying overnight while enjoying themed attractions, dining, and entertainment options.

Sources: http://westedmall.com; Carlisle, Tamsin. (1997, March 7). Gamble by the world's biggest mall pays off. *Wall Street Journal*, pp. B1, B18; World's ten largest shopping malls. (2008, January 30). *Forbes.com.*

◼ LIVE ENTERTAINMENT

Visiting heritage and commercial attractions and participating in activities at these locations could easily be classified as entertainment. However, live entertainment opportunities fill a special need for travelers and others seeking additional leisure-time activities. The choices of live entertainment venues can run from the deafening crowds at hallmark sporting events such as the World Cup or the Super Bowl to the serene pleasures of the ballet.

Sporting Activities

As highlighted in Chapter 2, sports have drawn visitors to scheduled events from near and far for thousands of years. Over 3,500 years ago, the Greeks initiated the idea of staging athletic competitions. The most famous of these competitions were the Olympic Games held in Olympia. The competitions began as part of their religious festivals and were staged in towns throughout Greece and Italy. The original competitions in Greece were organized as contests, but the Romans expanded the idea and staged them as games for public entertainment. Although the grand athletic competitions and festivals such as the classical Olympic Games faded and disappeared under Roman rule, the idea did not go away. With the formation of the International Olympic Committee (IOC), the modern-day Olympic Games were reborn and a new athletic tradition began in Athens, Greece, in 1896. This first modern Olympic competition was held in the summer and drew fewer than 500 athletes from 13 nations.[35] In contrast, the 2008 Summer Olympics held in Beijing, China, drew over 10,000 athletes from 205 nations and territories.[36] The Winter Olympic Games were not added until 1924, with the competition first staged in Chamonix, France.

Modern-day professional and intercollegiate sporting events such as football, soccer, baseball, basketball, and hockey draw millions of visitors each year to regularly scheduled games and playoffs. Special sporting events such as the Super Bowl, the Stanley Cup Championship, the World Cup, the Pro Rodeo Championship, the Indianapolis 500, and the College World Series, to name just a few, attract international attention and vast numbers of spectators to host communities each year. These same sports are often played at local and regional levels and, although they may not draw the same crowds, they are just as important to the participants and spectators who are attracted to the excitement of the event. In addition to team sports, a wide array of sporting activities such as golf, tennis, swimming, hiking, biking, fishing, rock climbing, and snowboarding/skiing round out the list of alternatives from which travelers can choose.

The National Basketball Association (NBA) was the growth sport of the 1980s, whereas the National Association for Stock Car Racing, better known as NASCAR, was the fastest growing spectator sport in the United States during the 1990s. Which sport has taken over the title of fastest growing spectator sport of this decade? The answer is, Professional Bull Riders (PBR). From 80,000 during the founding year in 1994, attendance at PBR events had grown to over 1 million in 2006. And, the sport is expanding globally with events in Canada, Mexico, Brazil, and Australia.[37]

The Performing Arts

The performing arts have been a popular form of entertainment for thousands of years. For some areas, such as Branson, Missouri, they

■ Live performances enhance the visit of any traveler.

serve as primary tourism revenue generators; for other areas, such as Las Vegas, they serve as one more ingredient in the menu of attractions and entertainment that the area can boast of to interest visitors to encourage them to extend their stay. Live entertainment has always been a draw for travelers. For some it may be the opportunity to select from a wide variety of plays in London's theater district; for others, it is a chance to attend a concert featuring the newest entertainment idol. For still others, it can be the opportunity to attend a country jam or an opera performance.

The classical performing arts include theater (live stage plays, not the movies), ballet, opera, concerts, and the symphony. Contemporary performing arts include stand-up and improvisational comedy, rock concerts, and even the band that is playing in your favorite local "hot spot." Performing arts entertainment, especially the classical forms, are frequently offered in locations such as concert halls (the Lincoln Center in New York City, the Athens Concert Hall in Athens, Greece, and the Forbidden City Concert

Hall in Beijing, China) developed for the express purpose of showcasing the art form.

Theaters, concert halls, and other large-seating-capacity facilities exist in almost all cities throughout the world and each, no matter how plain or impressive, serves as a draw for visitors. Some, such as the Sydney Opera House, are even renowned as landmarks. Many performing arts companies, whether a repertory acting group or symphony orchestra, have a season (a few months each year) when they stage productions and perform for the public. For example, the Desert Chorale is a classical choir that performs each summer in Santa Fe, adding to the entertainment options offered in that renowned arts city.

Think for a moment of all the performing arts productions you have enjoyed in the past year. Which were of the classical form and which would be considered contemporary? Maybe you even have experience as a participant in the performing arts? Band? Chorus? Local theater? We will discuss other cultural aspects of tourism in Chapter 12.

SUMMARY

So many things to do and so little time sums up the delightful dilemma travelers face when selecting from the menu of attractions and entertainment options. How we choose to spend our leisure time while traveling can find us seeing and doing things ranging from the simple to the exotic. Sometimes we look for the comfort and convenience of the familiar, and at other times we seek new or unusual sights, sounds, and activities.

The list of leisure-time alternatives from which visitors can choose can be conveniently classified into three broad categories: heritage attractions, commercial attractions, and live entertainment. Each of these categories contains even more choices, ranging from museums and zoos to gaming and shopping, and the list goes on. Attraction and entertainment alternatives are limited only by our curiosity, imagination, ingenuity, and resources.

Heritage attractions provide a unique two-way window that allows us to peer into the past for a fleeting glimpse of what the future may hold. Whereas heritage attractions meet our needs for

self-fulfillment and education, commercial attractions can transport us to lands of make-believe for excitement and enjoyment. When live entertainment is added to the mix of other attraction and entertainment opportunities, travelers are faced with a broad menu of choices for filling their leisure time.

Whether our leisure-time choices are simply a sideline along the way or the main reason for a trip, attractions and entertainment add special spice and memories to our travels. Although the goals of providing visitors with self-fulfillment and enjoyment may be common threads that tie attractions and entertainment together, there are a variety of business decisions that make these operations challenging. They may be operated on either a for-profit or a not-for-profit basis, creating the need to look to different funding sources. They are typically affected by dramatic shifts in seasonal demand, creating the need for skillful marketing, management, and financial decisions for continued success.

YOU DECIDE

The following letter is mailed to leaders of senior citizen clubs and organizations by the Pot O' Gold Casino.

Dear Group Leader:

Great group leaders are hard to find. That is why we wanted you to know about our group leader commission rates. The Pot O' Gold Casino offers one of the best leader incentive programs in the business. We pay you a commission based on a minimum five (5)-hour Casino stay.

On your group's arrival, a Lucky Leprechaun hostess will greet your group, verify group size, collect $10 from each group member, and give each member a $10 cashback coupon that can be exchanged for a roll of quarters at the cashiers' cages. In addition, each member receives a Gold Funbook, which contains $10 worth of coupons that can be used for food, beverages, keno play, and gift shop discounts. We also provide your group with bus transportation to the casino!

As leader of the group, you will be paid the following commission in cash on your arrival:

Group Size	Commission Rate
10–15	$3 per person
16–25	$4 per person
26–39	$5 per person
40+	$6 per person

So call our Tour & Travel department at 1-800-POTGOLD today!

Sincerely,

Etta Tsosie

Tour and Travel Coordinator

Note: Some group leaders donate their commission payment to their organization; others do not.

Why does the casino provide a free bus to the casino for groups? (Hint: minimum stay) Should this type of marketing be allowed by casinos?

NET TOUR

To get you started on exploring Internet links for this chapter, please see

http://whc.unesco.org/en/35

http://www.americangaming.org

http://www.discoverhongkong.com/eng/shop

DISCUSSION QUESTIONS

1. Why are attractions and entertainment important components of the tourism industry?
2. How does seasonality create marketing, management, and financial challenges for attraction and entertainment operators?
3. Explain the similarities and differences between heritage attractions and commercial attractions.
4. Why has gaming experienced a surge in growth and participation?
5. How have shopping malls been turned into tourism attractions?

APPLYING THE CONCEPTS

1. Ask several people of different ages, occupations, and both genders to describe their favorite leisure-time activities while traveling. Make a list of these activities and note the similarities and differences depending on whether they are traveling on business, for pleasure, or to visit friends and relatives.
2. Prepare a list and a basic description of attraction and entertainment alternatives that are available in your area. Limit yourself to 10 entries, but be

sure to include at least one location or event from each of the major categories: heritage attractions, commercial attractions, and live entertainment venues. After you have prepared your list, fill in the hours of operation, admission or entry fees (if any), services offered, and whether operations are for-profit or not-for-profit.

3. Arrange to visit an attraction or entertainment location in your area and schedule an interview with the manager or local administrator. Your interview should include questions about the typical marketing, management, and financial issues this person faces in completing his or her job duties.

4. Browse the Internet for locations or organizations mentioned under the headings of heritage attractions, commercial attractions, and live entertainment venues in this chapter (limit your search to one per heading). Describe the information that is available on each site.

GLOSSARY

Appropriations   Funding provided through governmental entities.

Attractions   Natural locations, objects, or constructed facilities that have a special appeal to both tourists and local visitors.

Botanical gardens   Gardens dedicated to the preservation, display, and study of growing plants.

Concessionaires   Individuals or companies who have been granted the right to provide a particular service, such as food service, guide service, sanitation service, or gift shop.

Curator   Person in charge of a museum.

Docent   A museum guide.

Events   Special occasions and scheduled activities.

Fairs   Temporary gathering places for the exhibition of products and services, often accompanied by entertainment and food and beverage services.

Festival   A time of celebration, with scheduled activities.

Gross gambling revenues (GGR)   The amount wagered minus the winnings returned to players.

Heritage attractions   Places, structures, and activities with historical and cultural significance.

Leisure activities   Activities performed during one's free time away from work.

Limited stakes   Legislative limits placed on the dollar amount that can be wagered on any single bet (typically $5).

Line of credit   An agreement with a bank in which loans are automatically made up to an established limit.

Museum   According to the International Council of Museums: a non-profit-making, permanent institution, in the service of society and its development, and open to the public, which acquires, conserves, researches, communicates, and exhibits, for the purposes of study, education, and enjoyment, material evidence of humans and their environment.

National monument   A landmark, structure, or other object of historic or scientific interest.

National park   A large natural place having a wide variety of attributes.

National preserve   An area in which Congress has permitted continued public hunting, trapping, and oil/gas exploration and extraction.

National scenic trail   A linear parkland.

Recreational activities   Activities and experiences people pursue for personal enjoyment.

Venue   The location of an event or attraction.

World Heritage Sites   Sites identified for preservation because of special cultural or heritage interest by the United Nations Educational, Scientific and Cultural Organization (UNESCO).

REFERENCES

1. Roberts, Russell. (1996, November). Zoos off the endangered species list. *Funworld,* pp. 60–65.
2. Quintos, Norie. (2002). Smart traveler: The new museum. *National Geographic Traveler,* 19(4), 12, 14.
3. Gauthier, Natasha. (2003, October). Museums and tourism. *Tourism: Canada's Tourism Monthly,* p. 6.
4. Kurlansky, Mark. (2002). *Salt: A world history.* New York: Walker and Company, p. 440.

5. Roberts, Russell. (1996, November). Zoos off the endangered species list. *Funworld,* pp. 60–65.

6. U.S. Department of Interior. (2004). National Park Service. Available at: http://www.nps.gov.

7. *The world almanac.* (2003). New York: World Almanac Books.

8. Foden, Harry G. (1992, Fall). Destination attractions as an economic development generator. *Economic Development Review,* pp. 69–72.

9. Milman, Ady. (2008). Theme park tourism and management strategy. In Arch G. Woodside and Drew Martin, eds., *Tourism management: Analysis, behavior, and strategy.* Cambridge, MA: CABI Publishing.

10. Foden, Harry G. (1992, Fall). Destination attractions as an economic development generator. *Economic Development Review,* pp. 69–72.

11. Prada, Paulo. (2001, June 21). Ja, ja, Americana's fabulosa. *Wall Street Journal,* pp. B1, B6.

12. Thach, Sharon V., and Axinn, Catherine N. (1994, Winter). Patron assessments of amusement park attributes. *Journal of Travel Research,* pp. 51–60.

13. Schneider, Mike. (2004, March 21). Cypress Gardens, jewel of Florida tourism, to reopen. *Denver Post,* p. 5T.

14. *Harrah's survey of U.S. casino entertainment.* (1995). Memphis, TN: Harrah's Brand Communications.

15. Barnes, Brooks, and Guzman, Rafer. (2002, September 15). Vegas nation. *Wall Street Journal,* pp. W1, W4.

16. Worsnop, Richard L. (1990, November 9). Lucrative lure of lotteries and gambling. *Editorial Research Reports,* pp. 634–646.

17. Kleinfield, N. R. (1993, August 29). Legal gambling faces higher odds. *New York Times,* p. E3.

18. *Harrah's survey of U.S. casino entertainment.* (1997). Memphis, TN: Harrah's Brand Communications.

19. Witham, Glen. (1988, November). Doing well, thank you. *Cornell Hotel & Restaurant Administration Quarterly,* p. 93.

20. Kristof, Nicholas D. (1985, November 28). Strategy part of comeback. *New York Times,* p. D1.

21. Troy, Timothy N. (1994, February 1). Getting in while the gaming's good. *Hotel & Motel Management,* p. 24.

22. Lam, Desmond. (2005). Slot or table? A Chinese perspective. *UNLV Gaming Research & Review Journal,* 9(2), 69–72.

23. Cauchon, Dennis. (2008, January 10). Slots fill niche, deal blow to table games. *USA Today,* p. 3A.

24. Cook, Roy A., and Yale, Laura J. (1994). Changes in gaming and gaming participants in the United States. *Gaming Research and Review Journal,* 1(2), 15–24.

25. Koeppel, Dan. (2003, April). Las Vegas for free (well, almost). *Travel Holiday,* 186(3), 64–68.

26. Cauchon, Dennis. (2008, January 10). Slots fill niche, deal blow to table games. *USA Today,* p. 3A.

27. Jansen-Verbeke, Myriam. (1991, March). Leisure shopping: A magic concept for the tourism industry? *Tourism Management,* pp. 9–14.

28. Knight, Mary Beth. (1999). America's tourist attractions. *Chain Store Age,* 75(3), 64–66.

29. Tarlow, Peter E., and Muehsam, Mitchell J. (1992, September–October). Wide horizons: Travel and tourism in the coming decades. *Futurist,* pp. 28–32.

30. Gibson, Richard. (1999, December 30). Mall of America considers expansion that would more than double space. *Wall Street Journal,* p. C15.

31. Dillard, Sandra C. (1999, November 21). Shop until you drop while in New York—please. *Denver Post,* p. 4T.

32. Beck, Rachel. (1998, August 19). Shopping malls reinvented as major tourism attractions. *The Durango Herald,* pp. 3B, 4B.

33. Van Riper, Tom. (2008, January 18). World's largest malls. *Forbes.com.*

34. Eventov, Adam. (2002, February 12). Tourists flock to giant Southern California mall. *Durango Herald,* pp. 4C–5C.

35. Glesson, Patrick C., and Arbes, Tina P. (1996, June). Economic impact on the state of Georgia of hosting 1996 Olympic Games. *Government Finance Review,* pp. 19–21.

36. Figure it out. (2008, August 31). *Philippine Daily Inquirer* (Manila, Philippines). Available at: http://www.inquirer.net/specialfeatures/olympics/view.php?db=1&article=20080831-157840.

37. Halliday, Jean, and Cuneo, Alize Z. (2006). The next NASCAR? *Advertising Age,* 77(18), 18.

LEARNING OBJECTIVES

After you have read this chapter, you should be able to:

- Explain how destinations combine many of the suppliers in the tourism industry.
- Describe the similarities and differences among destination resorts, resort areas/communities, and urban tourist destinations.
- Identify the major classifications of destination resorts.
- Identify the types of services and facilities that may be included in resort operations.
- Identify the recreational amenities that guests may encounter at resort locations.
- Explain why cruise ships are considered floating destination resorts.

To many people holidays are not voyages of discovery, but a ritual of reassurance.

—Philip Andrew Adams

CHAPTER OUTLINE

■ Many different sights found in Sydney, Australia make it a unique destination.

DREAMS CAN COME TRUE

The brochures answered most of their questions, but it was Richard and Connie's first time and they were still a bit nervous. Had they forgotten anything? Had they picked the right time and place? Would they really have as much fun as their friends had said? Would it be anything like the *Love Boat?*

With a little encouragement from their friends and a lot of help from their travel agent, Vanessa, Richard and Connie were set to take their first cruise! Still, there were many questions and uncertainties as they prepared to board the plane to Miami.

Connie had always wanted to take a cruise because she thought it would be relaxing and romantic: no meals to prepare, no dishes to wash, being waited on hand and foot, sitting by the pool and reading, moonlight walks on deck, and dancing the night away! However, Richard was easily bored and he had dreaded the thought of being "stuck" on a ship in the middle of nowhere with nothing to do.

When Connie met with Vanessa to book her dream vacation cruise, she shared some of Richard's concerns. As Vanessa described the different cruise ships, ports of call, and onboard activities that would meet their needs, Connie knew it would be everything she had imagined. And there would be more than enough opportunities for Richard to be entertained for four days.

Their cabin was smaller than a hotel room, but it didn't matter because they were seldom there. With gourmet meals, 24-hour buffets, shows, games, dancing, gambling, shopping, and shore excursions, there just weren't enough hours in a day. It seemed as if the staff had thought of everything! There was even an afternoon on the ship's own private island, complete with beachcombing and snorkeling lessons. The activities were endless.

As Richard and Connie prepared to disembark, the only thing they knew for sure was that four days just had not been long enough. They were ready for another cruise; but the next time, Richard said, the cruise should be for a full seven days! There had been too many things to do and not enough time!

INTRODUCTION

Up to this point, our journey through the tourism industry has introduced you to a variety of tourism suppliers. Each of these suppliers, from those providing transportation to those providing entertainment, plays an important role in meeting specific needs. However, as you will learn in this chapter, when the services of these suppliers are brought together in one location, we have arrived at another important stop on our journey—tourist destinations. These destinations can be found in locations ranging from rural retreats to bustling cities.

Destinations can be popular tourist cities and communities like Paris, France; Vienna, Austria; San Diego, California; and Branson, Missouri. They can be attractive geographic regions like the Napa Valley in northern California or the Costa del Sol in Spain. Or they can be the final stop on a trip to visit friends and relatives. In fact, the final stopping place on any trip can technically be considered a destination, but in this chapter, we are interested in the locations, communities, properties, and, yes, even ships that have evolved or been developed primarily to serve the needs of vacationers.

In a hectic world, filled with time pressures and a multitude of demands, people often want to "escape" daily routines. Destination locations provide the perfect setting for a brief change of pace or a more extended stay accompanied by a variety of activities. Destination locations can come in all sizes and shapes and are found almost everywhere, from mountaintop resorts to cruise ships sailing the high seas to artificially engineered environments such as Dubailand.

As we learned in Chapter 1, geography plays an important role in the development of tourism activity. People are naturally attracted to areas with pleasing natural beauty such as the snow-white sands of Destin, Florida, or the majesty of the Austrian Alps. They are also attracted to areas that have developed as entertainment magnets such as Las Vegas, Nevada, and Orlando, Florida. And areas with mild climates, such as the island paradises of the Caribbean and the Canary Islands off the coast of Africa, have been consistently popular with tourists.

As destinations grow in popularity, so do the services needed to meet visitors' needs. Airport services are enhanced; accommodations are improved and/or expanded; restaurants, retail shops, and visitor information services are added to deal with growing popularity. At some destinations, such as the islands of Hawaii, these services and facilities have often been added with little planning or consideration for the scenic beauty of the location. At other destinations, such as Cancun, Mexico, the national government has developed underutilized natural resources, beautiful beaches, and a near-perfect climate into a tourist destination.

All of the examples just mentioned have another important destination component in common: ease of access. Even locations that may not be pristinely beautiful can develop into popular destinations if they are easily accessible and close to heavily populated areas. For example, the gravel beaches on the cold English Channel at Brighton have become a popular summertime destination. With over 9 million potential visitors living in London, only a short train or car ride away, it is no wonder that Brighton has become a vacation playground.

■ FROM RESORTS TO URBAN DESTINATIONS

The Romans were the first to enjoy the pleasures of resorts, which were built around public baths located at natural mineral springs like those found in Bath, England. Visiting these natural hot springs baths and enjoying the relaxing atmosphere of the destination became the primary reason for travel. However, with the fall of the Roman Empire, travel for pleasure and leisure pursuits disappeared. When travel once again became safe and practical during the Industrial Revolution, the popularity of visiting resorts for enjoyment and pampering once again spread throughout Europe. With newfound wealth and leisure time, members of the upper classes sought pleasurable places outside of the industrialized cities to enjoy the sun, sea, sand, snow, and more.

The first resorts in America, like their European counterparts (especially those found in the Czech Republic), were built around spas and focused on health and escape from the daily rigors of life. Many of these early spas, such as The Greenbrier at White Sulphur Springs, West Virginia; The Homestead at Hot Springs, Virginia; Ein Bokek near the Dead Sea; and Karlsbad in the Czech Republic have since grown into world-class destinations. Although these early resorts were built around spas and the idea of rest, relaxation, and rejuvenation, later resorts began to expand by appealing to a broader cross section of market segments. To these new resort-goers, recreation became more important than simply a restful break, and a wider variety of activities was added to the mix of facilities and services provided, including retail shops, recreational facilities, and casinos.[1]

Resorts are now much more than just health spas or locations with a single purpose, catering to a single target segment. "Through the concentration of facilities, the resort acquires an identity and character, it becomes a specific place to enjoy in its own right in addition to serving as a gateway to other resources" (p. 62).[2] In fact, both **resort destinations** such as Tuscany, Italy, and Vail, Colorado, and **destination resorts**, such as Disney World and the Palm Island Resort off the coast of Dubai, now appeal to very diverse market segments ranging from individuals and families to conventions and corporate meeting groups. As can be seen in Table 10.1, most of these resort locations have certain characteristics in common.

You can find settings that fit the description of resort destinations in communities and small towns such as Jackson Hole, Wyoming, as well as in destination locations such as Mackinac Island, Michigan. Visitors also enjoy self-contained resort properties such as Marriott's Tan-Tar-A Resort, Golf Club and Spa at Lake of the Ozarks, Missouri, and Sheraton's San Marcos Resort near Phoenix, Arizona. Certain cities around the world have even developed into urban tourist destinations. Hong Kong, Paris, Rome, Vienna, San Francisco, San Antonio, Seattle, Singapore, and Vancouver can all claim to be great destinations that encourage and promote **urban tourism**. Whatever the location, tourist destinations are special places that meet guests' desires for rest, relaxation, fun, excitement, and entertainment even when visits

Table 10.1	Common Characteristics of Resort Locations

Attractive natural settings and recreational opportunities.

Easy accessibility for visitors.

Lack of or only limited manufacturing facilities.

Major employment opportunities center on service-oriented tourism-related businesses.

Large number of residents employed out of the resort area and commute to nearby cities.

Very large proportion of the population (with the possible exception of snow holiday resorts) is retired.

Typically seasonal employment opportunities and tourism activities, with periods of intense activity followed by periods of little or no activity.

Resort towns are typically small.

Source: Robinson, H. (1976). *A geography of tourism.* Estover, Plymouth, UK: MacDonald and Evans.

■ The soothing waters of spas served as destinations during the Roman Empire and continue to attract visitors in the 21st century.

are combined with the demanding schedules of business and professional meetings.

CLASSIFYING DESTINATIONS

There are several different types of locations and properties that can be classified as destinations. Although each of these locations may share some of the same activities, facilities, and amenities, the operational issues they face, such as staffing, meeting varying guest expectations, and managing cash flows, will differ depending on geographic location, size, markets served, and primary season of operation.

Operational issues were probably not on the minds of early resort developers, because many resorts and destinations were simply developed in locations with natural beauty, favorable climates, and easy transportation access. In fact, one popular classification system that has been used to describe resorts relies on the historically seasonal operational patterns that defined the markets of many resorts. Using this system, Northern Hemisphere resorts can be classified as summer resorts (beach and mountain locations operating Easter through Labor Day), winter resorts (northern and eastern locations operating November through April), winter vacation resorts (southern and southwestern locations operating January through April), and four-season resorts (mountain locations or in mild climates).[3]

For many resort properties and tourist destinations, the luxury of being open for operation during only one season is proving to be financially impractical. In today's highly competitive economic environment, investors, lenders, and governmental agencies are no longer willing to commit to financing large capital expenditures for airports, hotels, conference centers, and other facilities that may be used for only a few months during the year. As resorts and other tourist destinations have responded to these financial demands and broadened their market appeal, other classification approaches have appeared. One such approach relies on identifying the type of trip being taken. By using trip types, destinations can be conveniently grouped into categories such as cruise, beach, casino, ski, and summer country.[4] Another approach has relied on broader categories to bring several different types of resorts and destinations under common umbrella classifications. These groupings have resulted in categories such as integrated resorts, town resorts, and retreat resorts. Integrated resorts are self-contained developments planned around natural settings or recreational activities; town resorts are communities that primarily focus on resort activities; and retreat resorts are small-scale operations located in remote areas.[5]

Separating and classifying the final stopping points on trips from true destination locations may seem difficult, but there is help. Figure 10.1 introduces you to many of the different types of popular tourist destinations that include attractions, entertainment, and all of the supporting facilities needed to draw and host visitors. It provides a convenient approach to classifying these destinations based on seasonality and level of commercial development.

As we discussed in Chapter 9, seasonality is frequently a major concern for managers of attractions. The same is true for destinations. It is obvious that snow resorts in the Northern Hemisphere will experience the peak of their season during the winter months. To the contrary, similar resorts in South America see their greatest demand during June through September. However, seasonality is a more complex concept than simple weather conditions at destinations. Seasonality is also a factor, because of the weather conditions and life patterns of people's hometowns. If you live in the northern part of the Northern Hemisphere, such as Saskatoon, Saskatchewan, during the winter, you may dream of a vacation to Florida, the south of Spain, or the Caribbean to escape the cold. A resident of Phoenix, Arizona, or Houston, Texas, may save up vacation time to travel to the Rocky Mountains during August, fleeing the sweltering heat or humidity of the dog days of summer. So, in addition to the direct effect of weather on a

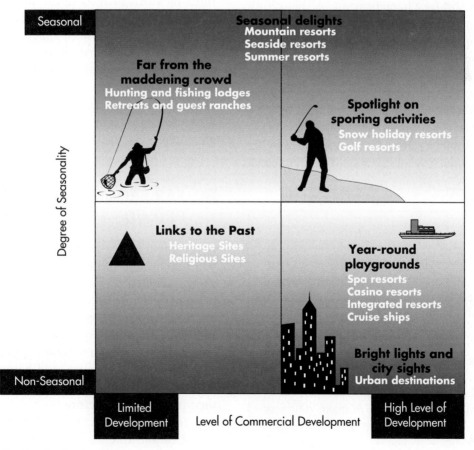

■ **Figure 10.1**   Tourist destinations.

destination, weather also has an impact on a destination because of its effect, especially if it is predictable, on the travel desires of potential customers in important geographic market areas. Hawaii has beautiful weather all year long, but its primary season is winter because that is when potential visitors are most likely to want to travel to Hawaii to escape the cold.

Interestingly, sometimes neither the weather at the destination nor in primary geographic market areas explains the ebb and flow of demand to the destination. Sometimes it is simply that one season is traditional for travel to that destination. Look back at Figure 9.2. Note the peak periods for Walt Disney World. What is the single unifying reason for the ups and downs of visits? School and work vacation periods. Although the weather in Florida is less than ideal during the summer, Disney World experiences its longest sustained peak season during the summer months, because families can travel then.

Using a concept called **strategic grouping**, we can categorize these destinations into groups that share similar characteristics. Although all destinations will not easily fit into a grouping, these groupings provide a useful framework for understanding the similarities and differences among types of destinations.

As you look at the following list, notice that although there may be some overlap and gray areas between the groups, six groupings emerge when the primary influences of seasonal weather patterns and the level of investment in commercial facilities are taken into consideration. We have chosen to label these groups using the following descriptive phrases:

- Far from the Maddening Crowd
- Links to the Past
- Seasonal Delights
- Spotlight on Sporting Activities
- Year-Round Playgrounds
- Bright Lights and City Sights

As we explore each of these destination groupings, see whether you can think of specific examples that would fit in each category.

Before we move on, consider the following two brief examples that show how Figure 10.1 can be used to place different types of destinations into strategic groupings. Winter snow holiday resorts (Spotlight on Sporting Activities) are obviously affected by seasonal changes that bring snow, and these locations also require significant commercial investments in ski lifts and snowmaking equipment as well as other mountain operations facilities such as restaurants, retail shops, and base-area accommodations. However, megacruise ships (Year-Round Playgrounds) are not significantly influenced by seasons, because they can be moved to take advantage of seasonal changes, yet they are very expensive to build and require significant capital investment. Now, let us take a more in-depth look at each of these strategic groups.

FYI

"At Your Service"

Resort destinations excel at delivering memorable experiences. During your stay, you are the center of attention. In the spirit of hospitality, resort employees are constantly searching for ways to make your stay special. Help them out. When making reservations or checking in, don't be shy about telling resort personnel you are celebrating a special occasion. You'll be helping them find that special way to make your stay memorable. So let them help you relax, enjoy, and celebrate!

◼ FAR FROM THE MADDENING CROWD

In the upper left-hand corner of Figure 10.1, you will see a group of destinations that are significantly affected by changes in seasonal weather patterns, yet have little in the way of commercial development when compared with other destinations. Traveling to destinations and taking advantage of seasonal weather patterns along with the solitude, beauty, and bounty of nature have a long history that can be traced back to the Romans, if not before.

You will find two types of destinations in this classification. One includes hunting and fishing lodges, and the other includes retreats and guest ranches. These destinations have limited levels of commercial development. Development is usually a lodge with guest rooms and common areas and a few other support buildings, built and operated to be open only during set time periods each year. For example, dude ranches in Arizona are open primarily in the winter and spring, whereas fishing lodges in Alaska and Canada serve visitors during the summer and fall. Or think about the other extreme–ice, snow, and frigid temperatures. "Imagine a hotel which is built from scratch each year, A new design, new suites, a brand new reception–in fact, everything in it is crisp and new. Well, there is such a hotel: the Ice Hotel, situated on the shores of the Torne River, in the old village of Jukkasjärvi in Swedish Lapland."[6]

Destinations that are grouped in this category face many of the same challenges as those faced by seasonal attractions, which were discussed in Chapter 9. For example, managers must hire and train a staff in a very short time and then bring all systems into operation by opening day each season. Taking care of the basics such as ordering supplies, manicuring the grounds, and deep-cleaning guest rooms are routine operations that can be easily scheduled. However, other tasks can become more difficult because facilities are often located in out-of-the-way places where there is limited access to potential employees and other services. Just think about how difficult it might be to find on short notice a plumber or an electrician for a remote fishing lodge in Manitoba.

■ LINKS TO THE PAST

Dropping down the left-hand side of Figure 10.1, we see a collection of destinations that have been attracting travelers for hundreds, even thousands, of years. The primary designations of destinations in this category are religious and heritage sites.

These locations may or may not be affected by the seasons. Some are affected by religious holidays, such as the Vatican City at Easter. Others may be affected by season of the year. For example, the pyramids of Egypt experience a reduction in visitor traffic during the scorching summer months. By definition, there is little, if any, recent commercial development at these

sites, because they have been classified as heritage locations. Some, such as the Petra archaeological site in Jordan, the Mnajdra prehistoric temples in Malta, or the Itum Monastery in Katmandu, are rapidly succumbing to the ravages of time and the stresses of Mother Nature.[7]

Travelers have been embarking on journeys called **pilgrimages** to religious sites for centuries. Greeks and Romans traveled to worship their gods, and Jews still journey to Jerusalem, Muslims to Mecca, and Hindus to Varanasi. These well-known, as well as other lesser known, sites are so popular they attract hundreds of thousands of pilgrims each year. One popular pilgrimage site that draws almost half a million people a year is Santiago de Compostela in Spain. The focus of this pilgrimage is the central marble pillar of the Gloria Portico, where St. James is depicted welcoming the tired pilgrim. This pillar has been etched with deep finger marks where untold numbers have touched it over the years.[8]

The other destinations found in this grouping feature primarily heritage attractions. These sites are dedicated to preserving and passing on the natural or cultural heritage to future generations. Several sites worldwide–such as Angkor, Cambodia; Machu Picchu, Peru; and Gettysburg, Pennsylvania–have been recognized for their unique heritage appeal to travelers. "Heritage tourism, or visiting an area's historical sites, is the hottest trend in the travel industry today. Tourists, these days, want more out of travel than visiting a park or a mountain range. They want to experience unique places, traditions, and history and learn about their roots" (p. 8).[9] As mentioned in Chapter 9, designations as World Heritage Sites are bringing increasing attention to cultural preservation and the importance of tourism management practices.

■ SEASONAL DELIGHTS

Moving toward the middle of Figure 10.1, you will find destinations that are still affected to some degree by seasonal weather patterns but that also have a greater degree of commercial development. In this strategic grouping you will find mountain, seaside, and summer resorts that have served through time as traditional destinations for tourists seeking a place to play in the water or escape the heat of summer. In fact, "[t]he resort hotel in America was traditionally a summer operation which offered, besides a comfortable room and good food, a seaside or mountain location with scenic, historical, recreational, or therapeutic advantages" (p. 23).[10] Today, these resorts have been developed not only to take advantage of the best Mother Nature has to offer during the primary season of operation but also to attract visitors during other seasons.

Mountain, seaside, and summer resorts may be found in different geographic locations, but they offer one thing in common—escape from summer's sweltering heat and a variety of warm-weather recreational activities. Depending on the location, hiking, swimming, boating, golf, tennis, and just lying in the sun or relaxing in the cool breezes head the wish list of seasonal activities visitors expect to find at these destinations during their primary operating season. Add other activities such as biking and horseback riding, and it is easy to see why vacationers are attracted to warm-weather paradises. As the following example shows, in addition to having a primary operating season, these destinations are also expanding the number and types of activities and facilities to attract visitors during **secondary seasons.**

The Wisconsin Dells (the "Dells") provide an excellent example of an area that began as a summer holiday refuge and developed into a major resort destination. Visitors still come in large numbers during the summer months to enjoy the natural beauty and warm-weather attractions that have been developed along this stretch of the Wisconsin River. However, they also come at other times of the year because of the commercial development that has taken place in the area.

> Packed in a lush "North woods" geographic area of a bit more than 3 by 5 miles are examples of just about any type of attraction ever established to entertain tourists. More than 700 amusement parks, beaches, family entertainment centers, museums, lodgings, restaurants and other attractions [from golfing and snow skiing to horseback riding and sleigh rides] in the area cater to a mix of visitors ranging from "day-trippers"
>
> with children to empty-nest couples spending busy weeks in local resort accommodations. (p. 27)[11]

Over 3 million visitors a year come to this resort area that is located midway between Chicago and Minneapolis. The total area encompasses two towns, Wisconsin Dells and Lake Delton, which have a year-round population of about 3,500 people. During peak seasons, this population temporarily swells with nearly 6,000 housing units ranging from B&Bs to condos and luxury hotels plus campsites and RV parks.

Through active support of the Dells Visitor and Convention Bureau, businesses in the area reap the benefits of a coordinated marketing campaign and a five-state employee recruiting effort. Marketing efforts range all the way from responding to requests for information (almost half a million per year) to creating major promotional campaigns. In addition to the recruiting campaign, joint customer-service seminars (area businesses employ about 6,000 seasonal workers) are conducted to prepare employees for the seasonal summer surge in visitors. This high level of cooperation continues to pay off, as can be seen by the astounding number of repeat visitors (78%). Increased marketing efforts have also attracted additional visitors during the secondary fall and winter seasons to enjoy the fall colors, hunting, and winter sporting activities.[12]

SPOTLIGHT ON SPORTING ACTIVITIES

In the upper right-hand corner of Figure 10.1 is a group of destinations that not only are affected by seasonal weather patterns but also are highly developed with specific recreational activities. Destinations in this grouping offer recreational activities, primarily participation sports, such as skiing, golf, and tennis.

Destinations that specialize by offering these activities share two things in common. First, they are affected by weather patterns that dictate primary operating seasons. For example, although golf can be played year-round in Arizona, winter and spring are much more attractive than summer, when temperatures soar to

Tourism in Action

Looking for a summer place to unwind, rest, relax, and recharge your batteries? To experience the hospitality and delights of a true summer resort destination, take a trip back in time to Mackinac Island. Take a look at the home page for Mackinac Island (http://www.mackinac.com), which contains the following statement, and begin preparing for a unique adventure:

> Welcome to the breathtaking beauty of Mackinac Island, one of Michigan's most photographed and talked about travel destinations. Located between Michigan's upper and lower peninsulas, the Island offers you unforgettable natural and historic treasures surrounded by the sparkling blue waters of the Great Lakes.
>
> There are only two ways to get to this picturesque island destination. One is by airplane and the other is by boat. Scheduled ferry service runs from April through December. For a brief period of time each winter, those hearty souls who can brave the bitter cold and winds travel to the island by snowmobile across the natural ice bridges that form in the strait.
>
> After you have made the journey across the Straits of Mackinac and arrive on the Island, what is there to do? First, don't plan on renting a car because the only forms of personal transportation allowed on the Island are bicycles and horse-drawn carriages. But, don't worry if you want to travel the entire distance around the Island (8.3 miles); it only takes about an hour on bicycle.

You could stay at the historic Grand Hotel (where *Somewhere in Time* was filmed) or at any of the Island's other accommodations ranging from small hotels to B&Bs. After checking in, you can join the bustle of activity surrounding the shopping district by the commercial docks or explore the many natural wonders and historic sites, like Sugar Loaf and Fort Mackinac.

If exploring is not to your liking, then try out your golf game at either of the Island's two courses. Whatever you decide to do, you must stop at one of the many confectionery shops and indulge yourself. Mackinac Island is famous for its fudge. Thousands of pounds of natural ingredients are mixed together in huge copper kettles, cooled on marble slabs, and cut into delectable rectangles for tourists every summer. The fudge and the tourists are welcomed sights each summer on Mackinac Island.

---

well over 100°F for most of the day. Second, these destinations are easily identified by their high levels of commercial development, such as ski lifts, snowmaking equipment, golf courses, tennis courts, and other supporting facilities.

Snow Holiday Resorts

Wherever they are located, all snow holiday resorts need the same natural wonders (steep slopes and snow) to attract winter snow-sports enthusiasts, and all have the same operational problems that accompany these snowy remote locations. The continued problem of unpredictable weather patterns has required large investments in snowmaking and grooming equipment to start, maintain, and extend ski seasons. Snowmaking not only costs money but also raises environmental concerns. Snowmaking draws heavily on available water supplies during typically dry times of the year, and additional grooming requires an increase in exhaust-producing grooming vehicles to be placed on the mountainside. Furthermore, the demographic shifts resulting from an aging population are reducing the potential number of skiers. Efforts to expand existing ski areas are being met with tough opposition from environmental groups, resulting in extensive environmental impact assessments and challenges to the use of government lands for single-season recreational use.[13]

Managers at mountain snow holiday resorts, like managers at other seasonal operations, must cope with seasonal changes to survive and succeed. Table 10.2 provides some examples of challenges faced in these types of seasonal destinations. Think about seasonal resorts with which you are familiar. Do they face the same, similar, or different problems?

Snow holiday resorts were originally developed to serve the snow-sports public. Subsequently, they have expanded facilities to appeal

Table 10.2	Factors That Have an Impact on the Survival and Success of Snow Holiday Resorts

Capital intensive, yet produce extreme fluctuations in cash flow to pay for these necessary investments.

Labor intensive and seasonal, resulting in the need to both hire and lay off large groups of service employees.

Weather dependent, resulting in the need to invest in expensive snowmaking equipment and draw heavily on an area's water resources.

Sensitive to economic fluctuations, because they are relatively expensive, and thus they must attract consumers with adequate discretionary income.

Located in remote locations, which creates potential transportation problems for both guests and employees.

to cross-country skiers, snowboarders, tobogganers, tubers, and ice skaters. However, to smooth cash flows, appeal to a broader market, and position themselves as year-round destinations, many traditional warm-weather activities such as golf and tennis have been added to their product offerings to appeal to a broader variety of market segments. The increasing popularity of mountain biking has also improved revenue potential. By offering bikers a "lift" up the mountain and providing trails for the way down, many traditional snow holiday resorts have substantially boosted the number of summer visitors.

Golf Resorts

No one is really sure where the game of golf began, but it has been a popular recreational sporting activity throughout the world for years. The origins of the game may have come from the Romans, but St. Andrew's Golf Club in Scotland, which was first used in the 16th century, is the oldest golf course in the world. The first permanent golf club did not appear in North America until 1873, when the Royal Montreal Club was founded in Canada.

Golf has continued to grow in popularity throughout the world. In the United States alone, there are over 40 million current or potential golfers.[14] With all of these golfers, it should be no surprise that golf is an especially attractive destination amenity, and the development of new golf courses is not keeping up with demand. In fact, at the current growth rate of participation it has been estimated that a minimum of 100 new golf courses must be built each year in the United States to keep up with growing demand.[15] On a national level, both France and Thailand are

using affordable and accessible golfing destinations as key marketing year-round draws.[16,17]

The only significant sports activity that meeting planners say influences their decisions in selecting a resort destination is golf. Why is it that meeting planners and others look to golf when making travel plans? Golf is both a recreational activity and a social event. The majority of the time spent golfing is more than just for sport. It is also social activity and an opportunity to enjoy the natural surroundings. The manicured landscaping and natural settings provide the perfect environment for socializing and relationship building.

A good golf course does more than present a pretty picture. It is designed and operated with the players and employees in mind for enjoyable play and ease in maintenance. The usual layout is in loops, so that the finishing hole is near the beginning one. A golf course at a resort location must be designed with the average player in mind but still be challenging enough to be interesting. It may be pretty to look at, but if it is too difficult to play, guests will become frustrated and not return.[18]

Building a golf course is a major financial undertaking, because it costs between $3 million and $5 million to build a basic course. World-class resort-style golf courses can easily approach $50 million in design and construction costs.[19] Designing a course that will meet player and employee needs as well as create the desired image for the resort requires several key ingredients. First, a regulation-length 18-hole course requires 140 to 160 acres of preferably rolling and interesting natural terrain or vegetation. Second, the design requires laying out a functional routing plan with existing topography and player

■ Golf resorts combine solitude with luxury. Photo by Shaen Adey © Dorling Kindersley.

comfort in mind. Third, to ensure player enjoyment, a rotation in pars should be planned so that each hole is "followed by one of a different par, such as 4-5-4-3-" (p. iii).[20] Each individual hole should be a complete picture within itself, with each area of the hole being a unified part of the total effect. Tee design; contouring throughout the entire length of the hole; mowing patterns at tee, fairway, and green; tree types and locations; water courses and lakes; and perhaps the most important part of the whole picture, the individual design of each green, together with locations of those seemingly necessary, but oh, so troublesome cart paths; all are part of the picture to be developed (p. iv).[21]

The greens fees generated by golf courses are an important resort revenue center. In addition, supporting services and facilities such as lessons, driving ranges, cart rentals, restaurants, and retail shops generate additional cash flows that enhance the financial attractiveness of golf course operations. However, golf resorts are more than just golf courses and related services. They must also cater to other guests and golfers when they are not on the links. These needs are being met with the addition of tennis, swimming, fitness centers, meeting rooms, shopping, dining, and more.

■ YEAR-ROUND PLAYGROUNDS

Located in the middle right-hand side of Figure 10.1, you will find a group of destinations that are highly developed commercially and only slightly affected by changes in seasonal weather patterns. What visitors experience at these types of destinations is a complex blend of facilities and services that you can see listed in Table 10.3. They may be spread across hundreds of acres or confined to the dimensions of a cruise ship. From a management viewpoint, each of these components should be planned with ease of maintenance and guest service, safety, security, and satisfaction in mind. We will explore each of the destinations in this group, but we will focus the majority of our attention on cruise ships.

Spas

Technically, the word *spa* means "mineral spring," but the use of this term has been expanded in recent years to describe a place where people go to rejuvenate bodies and minds. Guests can choose to visit either a spa that is part of a complete resort package or a **spa resort**, which is designed for the total spa experience (for example, The

■ Because of their mobility, cruise ships are floating, year-round resorts. Photo by D. A. Yale.

Table 10.3	Components of Resort Developments	
Accommodations		Conference and meeting facilities
Restaurants and lounges		Parking and/or transportation services
Entertainment and recreational facilities		Storage and maintenance facilities
Retail shopping facilities		Public information/administrative facilities

Oaks at Ojai, California, or Lake Austin Spa Resort, Texas). Although they may differ in their operating focus, the same basic ingredients will be found in either spa type: healthy food, exercise classes, baths, massages, herbal treatments, and educational training programs. The locations chosen will depend on each guest's personal desires. Guests may choose to visit spa resorts to experience the spa itself, or they may choose to enjoy the services and other recreational and social activities offered at the resort.[22]

The facilities and services provided through spas are now an important addition to the entertainment, shopping, and recreational activities found at many resorts. Through effective marketing programs and efficient management practices, spas can be an attractive revenue generator or profit center for resort properties. Marketing efforts may be focused on the individual *à la carte* user or packaged as an incentive along with other

resort activities. Just as you learned in Chapter 8 that food and beverages can be used as a marketing tool in resort properties, so, too, can spa services. Building and equipping the spa with customer satisfaction in mind is a must, but it takes more. A staff well trained to pamper guests ensures that the goal of total customer satisfaction will be achieved (see Table 10.4).

Cruise Ships

Cruising is booming as record numbers of vacationers select cruise vacations. And why not? Cruising is fun! Cruises of all durations have been experiencing growth, with the largest increase recorded in the 2- to 5-day category.[23] Very long cruises, 18 or more days in length, are also proving to be very popular. The Caribbean continues to be the favorite cruising venue, and the Mediterranean and other European routes

Table 10.4	Staffing a Spa

Massage therapists who can perform different types of massages and some body treatments

Cosmetologists who can style hair and perform manicures, pedicures, and makeup

Aestheticians who can perform facials, depilatory waxing, and makeup

Fitness employees who can teach classes, do one-on-one personal training, conduct fitness evaluations, and coordinate certain recreational activities

Spa assistants or attendants who can supervise the locker room, maintain cleanliness, and perform some body treatments

Front-desk people who can meet and greet guests, act as concierges, and schedule all guest services

Source: Monteson, Patricia A., and Singer, Judith. (1992, June). Turn your spa into a winner. *Cornell Hotel & Restaurant Administration Quarterly,* p. 42.

are the second most popular cruising itineraries. Alaska and the coast of Mexico also remain popular with cruise passengers.

Expanded fleets of ships combined with new amenities and effective marketing efforts have helped to reposition the cruise experience in consumers' minds as destination resorts rather than as transportation. Growth in the number of cruises has led to other changes as cruise line operators continue efforts to improve service and expand their marketing reach.

The number of ports and the quality of facilities where passengers may **embark** and **disembark** has grown and improved. Cruise-line companies have also expanded the number of available cruising options and targeted specific market segments. Because of the flexibility provided in cruise-line operations, each cruise can be designed to meet the tastes and needs of a specific cruising audience, with focused activities such as fitness, big band or rock music, and mystery parties.

Cruise ships come in a variety of types and offer different experiences. Cruising was originally available on classic ocean liners, such as the *Queen Mary* and the *Queen Elizabeth* (*1* and *2*). But most cruising now takes place on vessels that fit one of the following categories.[24]

1. *Megaships.* Most of the ships are extremely large, weighing up to 160,000 **gross registered tons (GRT)**, carrying up to 4,000 passengers or more, and having 12 or more **decks.** These ships are virtually floating resorts, usually offering an array of entertainment and dining options onboard.

2. *Midsize ships.* Luxury ships, older cruise ships, and ships that primarily sail select regions, for example, Europe and the Mediterranean, accommodate 200 to 1,500 passengers. These ships offer amenities but on a smaller scale than those featured on the megaships.

3. *Small ships.* Carrying 200 or fewer passengers, these ships offer a more intimate, less frenzied cruise experience. Most are used for niche markets, such as education-based, ultraluxury, or adventure cruises.

4. *Sailing ships.* Serving a distinct market segment, masted ships provide passengers with the opportunity to cruise in the original style—using wind power! Frequently, passengers act as part of the crew and aid in the sailing of the vessel.

5. *Riverboats.* An additional style of nostalgia cruising is provided by the riverboat. In the United States, riverboats designed to look like Mark Twain paddle wheelers ply the Mississippi, the Missouri, and the Columbia rivers. In Europe, modern riverboats, built low to the water to glide under bridges, travel rivers such as the Danube and the Rhine.

6. *Multipurpose ships.* Some ships, like those that transit the Scandinavian fjords, carry leisure travelers along with cargo and/or local commuters.

7. *Superyachts.* These large luxury yachts, also called megayachts, are usually over 24 meters in length and can reach up to 110 meters. Typical occupancy onboard is approximately 200 passengers, and all cabins are classically well-appointed suites or estate rooms.

The variety of jobs onboard cruise ships is even greater than the types of ships. Obviously, ships require a crew to guide them efficiently and safely through their itineraries. In addition, cruise ships carry a large staff, over 1,300 for some megaships, in charge of hotel operations. Included among these employees are the hotel manager, purser, shore excursion manager and staff, cruise director and cruise staff, housekeeping staff, executive chef and kitchen staff, *maitre d'* and dining room staff, and food and beverage manager and lounge staff. Onboard cruising operations are supported by large land-based marketing, management, and finance staff, which means that employment opportunities abound.

Cruise ships have an operational advantage over destinations that are anchored to a specific geographic location and must suffer through changing weather patterns. Sailing itineraries can be changed through repositioning cruises to take advantage of the best seasonal patterns and passenger demand anywhere in the world. In addition, "Cruise ships are an operator's dream. They run at 95% of capacity or higher, when hotels are pressed to manage 70%. And cruise passengers, unlike hotel guests, cannot wander off to eat their dinner elsewhere."[25]

With the flexibility to meet vacationer and meeting-goer needs, cruise lines are now targeting many of the same people and groups who previously stayed in traditional destination resorts. The primary geographic markets for U.S. cruise-line passengers are California, Florida, New York, Illinois, Pennsylvania, and Texas; and the primary ports for cruise ships serving U.S. and Canadian markets are located in Miami, New York, Port Everglades, Los Angeles, San Francisco, Seattle, and Vancouver. Most cruise ships sailing from these ports go southward to Mexico, the Caribbean, and the Panama Canal or northward to Alaska. Figure 10.2 shows a typical cruise ship itinerary.

Today, cruise-line passengers come from a wide range of income levels and ages. However, the fastest growth in cruisers is in the 25- to 40-year-old and family segments, which has caused the median age of cruisers to drop from 58 to 43. "At long last, cruises are being perceived as a 'hip' vacation alternative, one that appeals to a group of vacationers whose diversity is matched only by the cruise industry's diversity. We have 150 vessels visiting nearly 2,000 ports, and itineraries ranging in length from three days to three months—the possibilities are endless."[26] These new and expanding groups of cruisers are not only selecting cruise ships based on sailing itineraries, activities, and length of time at sea, but they are also changing the way in which they incorporate cruise ships into their travel plans. Today, the usual pattern involves a fly–cruise package.

These efforts are proving successful, as cruise lines can offer many of the same features as, if not more than, a traditional resort (see Figure 10.3) at an **inclusive price**. In fact, there are activities galore. Everything from rock climbing and golf lessons to ice skating and dancing. Even the amount of tips for onboard service personnel is clearly communicated to all guests in information brochures.

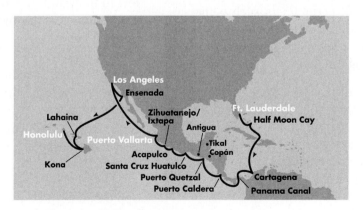

■ **Figure 10.2** Map of cruise ship itinerary for MS *Maasdam.*
Reprinted by special permission of Holland America Cruise Lines.

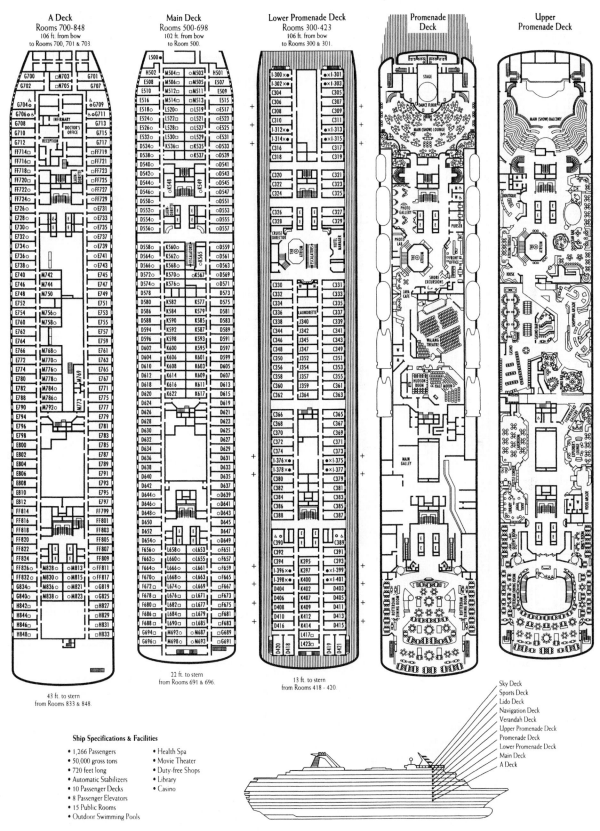

■ Figure 10.3 Exploring Holland America's MS *Maasdam.*
Reprinted by special permission of Holland America Cruise Lines.

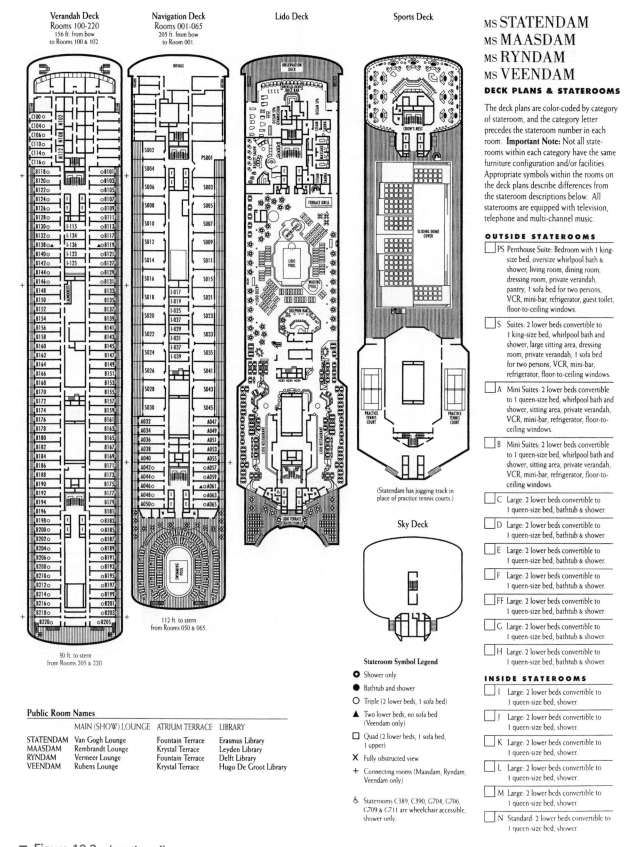

Verandah Deck
Rooms 100-220
156 ft. from bow
to Rooms 100 & 102.

Navigation Deck
Rooms 001-065
205 ft. from bow
to Room 001.

Lido Deck

Sports Deck

(Statendam has jogging track in
place of practice tennis courts.)

Sky Deck

30 ft. to stern
from Rooms 205 & 220.

112 ft. to stern
from Rooms 050 & 065.

MS STATENDAM
MS MAASDAM
MS RYNDAM
MS VEENDAM

DECK PLANS & STATEROOMS

The deck plans are color-coded by category
of stateroom, and the category letter
precedes the stateroom number in each
room. **Important Note:** Not all staterooms within each category have the same
furniture configuration and/or facilities.
Appropriate symbols within the rooms on
the deck plans describe differences from
the stateroom descriptions below. All
staterooms are equipped with television,
telephone and multi-channel music.

OUTSIDE STATEROOMS

PS Penthouse Suite: Bedroom with 1 king-
size bed, oversize whirlpool bath &
shower, living room, dining room,
dressing room, private verandah,
pantry, 1 sofa bed for two persons,
VCR, mini-bar, refrigerator, guest toilet,
floor-to-ceiling windows.

S Suites: 2 lower beds convertible to
1 king-size bed, whirlpool bath and
shower, large sitting area, dressing
room, private verandah, 1 sofa bed
for two persons, VCR, mini-bar,
refrigerator, floor-to-ceiling windows.

A Mini Suites: 2 lower beds convertible
to 1 queen-size bed, whirlpool bath and
shower, sitting area, private verandah,
VCR, mini-bar, refrigerator, floor-to-
ceiling windows.

B Mini Suites: 2 lower beds convertible
to 1 queen-size bed, whirlpool bath and
shower, sitting area, private verandah,
VCR, mini-bar, refrigerator, floor-to-
ceiling windows.

C Large: 2 lower beds convertible to
1 queen-size bed, bathtub & shower.

D Large: 2 lower beds convertible to
1 queen-size bed, bathtub & shower.

E Large: 2 lower beds convertible to
1 queen-size bed, bathtub & shower.

F Large: 2 lower beds convertible to
1 queen-size bed, bathtub & shower.

FF Large: 2 lower beds convertible to
1 queen-size bed, bathtub & shower.

G Large: 2 lower beds convertible to
1 queen-size bed, bathtub & shower.

H Large: 2 lower beds convertible to
1 queen-size bed, bathtub & shower.

INSIDE STATEROOMS

I Large: 2 lower beds convertible to
1 queen-size bed, shower.

J Large: 2 lower beds convertible to
1 queen-size bed, shower.

K Large: 2 lower beds convertible to
1 queen-size bed, shower.

L Large: 2 lower beds convertible to
1 queen-size bed, shower.

M Large: 2 lower beds convertible to
1 queen-size bed, shower.

N Standard: 2 lower beds convertible to
1 queen-size bed, shower.

Public Room Names

	MAIN (SHOW) LOUNGE	ATRIUM TERRACE	LIBRARY
STATENDAM	Van Gogh Lounge	Fountain Terrace	Erasmus Library
MAASDAM	Rembrandt Lounge	Krystal Terrace	Leyden Library
RYNDAM	Vermeer Lounge	Fountain Terrace	Delft Library
VEENDAM	Rubens Lounge	Krystal Terrace	Hugo De Groot Library

Stateroom Symbol Legend

● Shower only

● Bathtub and shower

○ Triple (2 lower beds, 1 sofa bed)

▲ Two lower beds, no sofa bed.
(Veendam only)

□ Quad (2 lower beds, 1 sofa bed,
1 upper)

X Fully obstructed view

+ Connecting rooms (Maasdam, Ryndam,
Veendam only)

& Staterooms C389, C390, G704, G706,
G709 & G711 are wheelchair accessible,
shower only.

■ **Figure 10.3** (continued)

Although cruising itineraries can be commonly found in 2-, 3-, 4-, 7-, and 14-day (or more) lengths, short cruises are proving to be the most popular and fastest-growing segment of this industry group. As was the case with Richard and Connie in our chapter opener, first-time cruisers are especially attracted to shorter cruises to test the waters and sample the cruising experience before committing to a longer itinerary. In addition, there are other factors contributing to the popularity of shorter cruises. Families and two-income households are finding short cruises to be attractive as they try to coordinate busy and often conflicting schedules that interfere with attempts to take extended vacations. Workers in pressure-filled jobs are seeking shorter and more frequent stress-relieving breaks to rest, relax, and recharge.[27]

Whether it is the inclusive pricing policies, one class of service (everyone receives the same service no matter how much he or she paid for the cabin), close attention to service details, or convenient itineraries, people seem not only to enjoy but also to praise their cruising experiences. "The satisfaction rating for cruises is the highest in the travel business: over 85% are 'extremely' or 'very satisfied.'"[28] Cruises are able to achieve these high levels of satisfaction because they can deliver high-quality service in addition to effectively combining two important characteristics of a good trip. First, passengers see and experience new activities, sights, and cultures through onboard activities and different ports of call. Second, passengers enjoy these experiences with a feeling of safety, security, and comfort in familiar surroundings, established schedules, and attentive service.

Once onboard a cruise ship, everyone, no matter how much the passenger paid for the cruise or where his or her cabin is located, has arrived at his or her destination and is treated the same. One class of service and variable pricing levels mean the cruise lines depend on high occupancy levels. Cruise lines depend on generating additional high-margin revenues to achieve profitability. Some of these profit centers include spas, beauty salons, gaming, alcoholic beverage service, shopping, and shore excursions plus pre- and postcruise packages. Other activities such as excursions to company-owned islands help to control the destination concept of the cruise and

What Is Not Included in Cruise Prices?

- Transportation between the passenger's home and port of embarkation, although it is included in some package prices.
- Port taxes and personal expenditures, including medical expenses, gambling chips, some sports activities, use of special services such as beauty salons and spas, alcoholic beverages, and shore excursions.
- Tips (gratuities). The amounts will vary. On some ships there is "no tipping" (tips are built into the package price). On others, the tips are automatically added for services. Still other ships may post guidelines in cruise-line brochures and have them explained by **cruise directors**. As a matter of professional respect, it is important to remember to tip only **hotel personnel**, never **ship personnel**.

Note: Purchases for goods and services not included in the cruise price can be charged while onboard and then settled with the **purser** at the end of the cruise by using a credit card or personal check.

generate additional revenues.[29] None of these goods and services is included in the all-inclusive pricing structure.

Trends in cruise-line operations include the building of new ships of all sizes from yacht-like vessels to superliners, new programs and itineraries, and new onboard facilities. Yet, even with all of this growth, it is still estimated that less than 10% of the adult population in the United States has cruised, leaving plenty of room for growth. Cruise-line companies are purchasing or leasing private islands for the exclusive use of their passengers, and the addition of free-style dining options will entice even more cruisers onboard. In addition, new cruise itineraries will bring back seasoned cruisers. Consider this developing route. "The Great Lakes have all the ingredients needed for successful cruising: magnificent scenery, waterfront cities with well developed tourism facilities, and a rich mix of cultural and historical institutions" (p. 13).[30]

Casino Resorts

Casino resorts constitute a large and growing segment of the tourism industry. Travelers who participate in gaming activities are demanding more when they visit these resort destinations. They are no longer satisfied with finding gaming and lodging at their destination; they want a total entertainment experience. And their demands have been met, first with a wide array of dining and entertainment alternatives and then with a menu of activities that range all the way from golf to theme and water parks.

As you learned in Chapter 9, gaming locations continue to spread across the United States and Canada. What visitors will find at any one location is limited only by the imaginations and financial resources of the developers. Casino resorts located in Nevada provide some excellent examples of the diversity that can be found in successful casino resorts that have broadened their appeal to attract the family market.

At **megaresort** theme park/casinos such as New York, New York, Bellagio, Mandalay Bay, Paris, and the Venetian located in Las Vegas (an urban tourism destination itself), complete leisure and entertainment facilities have been created to appeal to our fantasies and provide a little something for everyone. At other, more out-of-the-way desert locations, such as Players Island in Mesquite, Nevada (which is on the Utah border), visitors are tempted with spas, golf, tennis, dining, entertainment, gaming, and more to fill their days and nights. Or high in the Sierra Nevada Mountains, visitors can combine water sports, golf, and tennis in the summer or skiing in the winter with gaming, dining, and entertainment. Other locations, as diverse as

Foxwoods in Connecticut or The Wyndham Nassau Resort and Crystal Palace Casino in the Bahamas, provide all the excitement and amenities found at the Las Vegas megaresorts.

Integrated Resorts

Integrated resorts (also called "four-season resorts") are similar to other tourism destinations we have been studying. They provide many of the same facilities, activities, and entertainment opportunities that you would expect to find at any resort location. However, they are different from other destinations because they are located in settings where they can offer guests the same menu of leisure-time activities on a year-round basis. For example, see Table 10.5 for all the Atlantis Resort in the Bahamas has to offer. Even less temperate destinations, such as Kaisenbaeder in Germany, or arid destinations, such as Dubailand, have developed an array of offerings to meet seasonal demands while serving a variety of tourist segments.

However, even year-round resorts experience operational problems that result from fluctuations and spikes in demand. Integrated resorts are designed to serve a demanding group of vacationers each of whom has his or her own ideas about the meaning of rest and relaxation. Whereas one guest may describe the perfect four-season resort destination as a "haven for peace and quiet, calm, rest, and relaxation," another guest might describe it as a "giant country club with rooms" so integrated resorts must create settings that meet a diversity of needs.

Travelers are now comparing the services and amenities they receive on cruise ships with what they receive at integrated resorts. Both

Table 10.5	What Will You Find at the Atlantis Resort?

Location: Paradise Island, Bahamas
Accommodations: 2,300 rooms
Food and beverage facilities: 38 restaurants and lounges
Recreation: Golf course, sports center, spa, Caribbean's largest casino, snorkeling lagoon, tennis courts, retail shopping complex, marina, Discovery Channel camp, plus 11 million gallons of water activities including 34-acre Atlantis waterscape, the largest tropical marine habitat
Meeting facilities: 86,000 square feet, including 3 ballrooms

Source: Atlantis Resort.

types of destinations are designed to be self-contained vacation retreats. As you learned in the section on cruise lines, most services on a cruise are provided at an inclusive price. Integrated resorts are responding to this benchmark in hassle-free experiences by instituting strategies such as marketing themselves as nontipping properties and offering inclusive pricing for the use of spa facilities, golf, and other activities.

■ BRIGHT LIGHTS AND CITY SIGHTS

The final destination grouping we will discuss is located in the lower right-hand corner of Figure 10.1. This group is composed of urban areas that have developed into unique tourist destinations. Most cities will attempt to attract tourists because of the economic benefits these travelers bring to the local economy. However, travelers do not consider all cities to be tourist destinations. What is it that sets some large urban areas apart from others and makes them stand out as special tourist destinations? It is a strong desire on the part of city planners, civic leaders, and businesses to attract and serve the needs of visitors.

Using a research technique that is popular among marketers, the Canadian Tourism Commission, through the help of **focus groups,** has identified what tourists consider to be some of the key attributes of a destination city:

> For some people it was a feeling, a flavor, or an image, that made the city a beloved destination. For others it was something more concrete: an ocean or a waterfront setting, beautiful architecture, great food, a sense of history, or friendly people that give a city its appeal. . . . For many people it's the range of interesting things to see and do that makes a city a great destination. (p. 8)[31]

What we can learn from this research is that tourist destination cities have their own unique character. Tourists are attracted to these locations because they are special places to visit and enjoy, and they offer a wide variety of accommodations, attractions, entertainment, restaurants, lounges, and other activities and amenities that tourists desire. Many cities are tapping the benefits of potential increased tourism traffic by building

major league sports stadiums. The local and visitor traffic they generate helps bring restaurants, theaters, and excitement back to city centers.

■ BUILDING ON SUCCESS

As the opportunities for leisure travel for workers in industrialized countries grow and the number of mature travelers continues to increase, travel to resorts and other destinations will continue to grow in popularity. To remain competitive and attract more guests, these destinations may need to focus on attracting more than one market segment as well as increasing or improving their service offerings. To meet these needs, indoor resorts, such as Ocean Dome in Seagaia, Japan, create an endless summer environment, whereas Ski Dubai creates a variety of ski terrains in the midst of an arid desert climate.[32]

Through market segmentation, resorts are meeting this challenge by developing packages that appeal to a variety of specific guest segments. At the same time, destination resorts are focusing efforts on specific segments such as group tour business, incentive travel, meetings, and conferences. Many resorts are also breaking these focused markets into smaller segments. For example, a property might focus first on attracting association meeting business in general and then target members of one association such as the American Association for Retired Persons. These efforts are generating more year-round business and leveling out the traditional seasonal fluctuations in cash flows.[33]

The complex task of developing, marketing, and managing tourist destinations goes well beyond the physical location itself. Other concerns, such as employee housing and labor availability, capital investment requirements, recreational and attraction development, infrastructure requirements, social and cultural effects, environmental impacts, land use, tax receipts, and other public benefits and problems must be considered by private developers, citizens, and government officials. Tourist destinations thrive on positive relationships between residents and visitors, and these relationships must be encouraged and sustained for future success. We will be exploring these issues in greater depth in future chapters.

■ SUMMARY

Bringing together all of the components provided by tourism suppliers into one location creates the potential for a tourist destination. Destinations are the final stopping points of trips where tourists seek to "escape" their daily routines and enjoy rest, relaxation, recreation, and entertainment. These destinations can be found anywhere in the world and range all the way from quiet and secluded guest retreats to those floating resorts we call cruise ships. No matter where they are located or how attractive the destinations might be, tourists will not come unless the facilities and activities they desire are provided.

Spas were the original destination "resorts" built by the Romans, but the types of destinations from which travelers can choose today are numerous. Although each destination has its own unique appeal to tourists, destinations often share many similarities based on seasonal demand and the level of commercial development needed to meet guests' needs. These shared similarities allow us to classify destinations into the following strategic groups: Far from the Maddening Crowd, Links to the Past, Seasonal Delights, Spotlight on Sporting Activities,

Year-Round Playgrounds, and Bright Lights and City Sights.

Destinations that are grouped in each of these categories face similar marketing, management, and financial opportunities and challenges. Some destinations face dramatic seasonal shifts in demand, but others experience more consistent demand throughout the year. Shifting patterns in demand can affect a variety of decisions, including marketing plans, staffing patterns, cash flow projections, and capital expenditure plans. Steps are therefore being taken at most tourist destinations to attract additional visitors during less popular time periods.

Tourist destinations continue to grow in popularity and so do the choices travelers face when selecting their perfect destination. It can be a fishing lodge, a snow holiday resort, a seaside resort, a golf resort, a spa resort, a cruise ship, an urban tourist mecca, or (you fill in the blank). As the choices grow and the opportunities for leisure travel increase, tourist destinations must focus on meeting a variety of guest needs while continuing to improve service offerings for future success.

■ YOU DECIDE

Cruises are one of the best buys in vacationing today. Prices have remained fairly constant, and the amenities onboard have improved year after year. And the service is second to none. Passengers are pampered by employees at every turn: by the pool, in the many dining rooms, in the casino, and in their cabins, with a steward on call 24 hours a day.

How can cruise ships afford to provide so much personal attention and service? One way is by controlling labor costs. Nonprofessional cruise employees work 70 hours a week for an average starting pay of $2,000 a month. The vast majority of their earnings come from tips, which can add from $1,000 to $2,500 per month to their income. Cruise workers not only work long hours but also are generally at sea on five- to eight-month contracts, receiving two days off per month. They do spend six weeks onshore between contracts. Employees, of course, receive room and board, medical care, and airfare to and from home between contracts in addition to their pay and tips; and benefits are generous by international standards.

Most cruise-line employees come from Third World or former Soviet-bloc nations. Although many are college educated, they are unable to find well-paying employment in their home countries. Cruise-line personnel agencies are virtually flooded with applicants from around the globe, from Honduras to Romania. The demand for cruise ship jobs is high because wages in most nonindustrialized countries are so low.

Cruise lines can decide how much to pay employees because they are not subject to the employment regulations of industrialized countries, such as minimum wages, maximum working hours, and overtime pay. They are able to avoid these regulations by registering their ships abroad in countries such as Panama and Liberia. Should cruise lines be pressured to comply with employment laws in developed countries?

Sources: Allerton, Haidee E. (2003). Crewse. *T + D*, 57(4), 87–88.; Keedle, Jayne. Wish you were here. (2008). *Career World*, 36(5), 21–23.

NET TOUR

To get you started on exploring Internet links for this chapter, please see

http://www.scantours.com/ice_hotel.htm

http://www.wisdells.com

http://www.cruising.org

http://www.atlantis.com

http://www.dubailand.ae

DISCUSSION QUESTIONS

1. Describe the various tourism supply components that must be brought together to create a successful tourist destination.
2. What are the major classifications of tourist destinations and the similarities and differences among these classifications?
3. Why are tourist destinations attempting to attract more visitors outside of their prime seasons?
4. Describe the factors that have an impact on the survival and success of a seasonal tourist destination such as a winter snow holiday resort.
5. Why are cruise ships called "floating resorts"?
6. What is it that sets some large urban areas apart from others and makes them stand out as special tourist destinations?

APPLYING THE CONCEPTS

1. Select one type of tourist destination that is particularly interesting to you and learn more about it. Either schedule an interview with an employee or representative of the destination, or search for articles in the library about that type of destination. Based on the information you obtain, write a short report discussing important facts you learn from your interview or research.
2. Select an article from a travel magazine or the travel section of the newspaper describing two different cruise ships and itineraries. Make copies of the articles to include with your report describing the similarities and differences between the two vacation options.
3. Browse the Internet for resort information in a location that you may want to visit someday (use search terms such as "Manitoba and resorts" or "Florida and resorts"). Prepare a list showing the type of information that is available for the area along with specific information on one property at the destination.
4. Can your hometown be classified as a tourist destination? Using the information from this chapter as a guideline, prepare a list of all of the attractions and activities that would appeal to visitors. Once you have collected the information, prepare a one-page flier that highlights the best of what your hometown offers tourists.

GLOSSARY

Cruise director   The person who plans and operates passenger entertainment and activities onboard a cruise ship.

Deck   The equivalent on a ship to a floor or story of a hotel.

Destination resorts   Properties that are relatively self-contained and provide a wide range of recreational and other leisure-time activities.

Disembark   To go ashore from a ship.

Embark   To go onboard a ship.

Focus group   An in-depth interview about a topic among 8 to 12 people, with a researcher (called a "moderator") leading the discussion.

Gross registered tons (GRT)   A measure of the interior size of a ship determined by volume of public space.

Hotel personnel   All individuals responsible for the care and service of cruise ship passengers.

Inclusive price   A single price for a package of services such as accommodations, food, and activities.

Megaresort   A destination resort containing multiple facilities and world-class attractions and entertainment venues. Each revenue center at these destinations could operate as a separate business venture.

Pilgrimage   Travel to a holy place or shrine.

Purser   A ship official responsible for papers, accounts, and the comfort and welfare of passengers.

Resort destinations   Communities or areas that contain attractions, entertainment, and supporting facilities needed to draw and host tourists.

Resorts   Destination locations that are distinguished by the combination of attractions and amenities for the express purpose of attracting and serving large numbers of visitors.

Secondary seasons   Periods when tourism activities are either increasing toward peak levels or declining from peak levels; also called "shoulder seasons."

Ship personnel   All individuals responsible for the safety and navigation of cruise ships.

Spa resorts   A resort property dedicated to fitness and the development of healthy lifestyles.

Strategic grouping   Groups that share common interests.

Urban tourism   Tourism that takes place in large cities, where hotels and other facilities and services have become an integral part of urban activities.

REFERENCES

1. Gee, Chuck Y. (1988). *Resort development and management* (2nd ed.). East Lansing, MI: Educational Institute of the American Hotel and Motel Association.
2. Baud-Bovy, Manuel, and Lawson, Fred. (1977). *Tourism and recreation development*. Boston: CBI Publishing Company.
3. Gee, Chuck Y. (1988). *Resort development and management* (2nd ed.). East Lansing, MI: Educational Institute of the American Hotel and Motel Association.
4. Morrison, Alastair, M., Yang, Chung-Hui, O'Leary, Joseph T., and Nadkarni, Nandini. (1994). A comparative study of cruise and land-based resort vacation travelers. In K. S. (Kaye) Chon, ed., *New frontiers in tourism research: Proceedings of research and academic papers* (Vol. VI). Lexington, KY: The Society of Travel and Tourism Educators Annual Conference.
5. Inskeep, Edward. (1991). *Tourism planning: An integrated and sustainable development approach*. New York: Van Nostrand Reinhold.
6. Scantours. (2008, April 10). *The Ice Hotel Sweden*. Available at: http://www.scantours.com/ice_hotel.htm.
7. Sevick, Kimberley. (2001, September). Now you see it . . . *Travel + Leisure*, pp. 200–204.
8. Lausway, Edward. (1991). *Tourism planning: An integrated and sustainable development approach*. New York: Van Nostrand Reinhold.
9. Cass, Ginny, and Jahrig, Sharon. (1998). Heritage tourism: Montana's hottest travel trend. *Montana Business Quarterly*, 36(2), 8–18.
10. Gee, Chuck Y. (1988). *Resort development and management* (2nd ed.). East Lansing, MI: Educational Institute of the American Hotel and Motel Association.
11. Whitworth, A. W. (1996, October). Area profile. *Funworld*, pp. 26–35.
12. Whitworth, A. W. (1996, October). Area profile. *Funworld*, pp. 26–35.
13. Clifford, Hal. (2002). *Downhill slide: Why the corporate ski industry is bad for skiing, ski towns, and the environment*. San Francisco: Sierra Club Books.
14. Smith, Alan D., and Marco, Gayle. (2004, September). Strategic perspectives associated with the golf industry. *Journal of American Academy of Business*, Cambridge, pp. 367–373.
15. Bergsman, Steve. (1990, November 5). Company sees profit on resort golf greens. *Hotel & Motel Management*, pp. A118–A119.
16. Drive to boost business. (2003, July). *Travel Trade Gazette*, p. 39.
17. Street wise: More golfers to tee off. (2004, April 15). *The (Thailand) Nation*. Available at: http://www.nationmedia.com.
18. Course corrections. (2003, Winter). *Forbes FYI*, pp. 45–47.

19. Kalosc, Lou. (1999, September 17). Pro golfer making mark on Arizona. *Destination Golf, The Business Journal,* p. 17B.

20. Snyder, Arthur Jack. (1989). A good golf course (what is it?). In J. C. Wright, ed., *Golf courses: The complete guide* (pp. iii–iv). Oakland, CA: Lanier Publisher International.

21. Snyder, Arthur Jack. (1989). A good golf course (what is it?). In J. C. Wright, ed., *Golf courses: The complete guide* (pp. iii–iv). Oakland, CA: Lanier Publisher International.

22. Monteson, Patricia A., and Singer, Judith. (1992, June). Turn your spa into a winner. *Cornell Hotel & Restaurant Administration Quarterly,* pp. 37–44.

23. Cruise Lines International Association (CLIA). (2006). Cruise industry overview. Fort Lauderdale, FL: Cruise Line International Association, Inc.

24. Mancini, Marc. (2004). *Cruising: A guide to the cruise line industry* (2nd ed.). Albany, NY: Delmar Thomson Learning.

25. Travel and tourism: Home and away. (1998, January 10). *The Economist,* p. 14.

26. Godsman, James G. (2000, March 7). President of Cruise Lines International Association.

27. Wellner, Alison Stein. (2000). The end of leisure? *American Demographics,* 22(7), 51–56.

28. Booth, Cathy. (1992, February 17). Against the tide. *Time,* pp. 54–56.

29. Weaver, Adam. (2005). Spaces of containment and revenue capture: "Super-sized" cruise ships are mobile tourism enclaves. *Tourism Geographies,* 7(2), 165–184.

30. Re-floating a cruise-ship industry. (2003, March). *Tourism: Canada's Tourism Monthly,* p. 13.

31. Reflections on what makes a great city destination. (1997, Spring). *Americas Bulletin,* pp. 7–9. Ottawa, Ontario: Canadian Tourism Commission.

32. Thorne, Patrick. (2006, May). Outside. *Hemispheresmagazine.com,* pp. 60–63.

33. Macdonald, Julie. (1992, November 2). Resorts pursue travelers' needs. *Hotel & Motel Management,* pp. 97, 107–108.

Readings

The Hub-and-Spoke System Remodels the Airways

You're driving to Grandma's. Is there an interstate from your driveway directly to her? Not unless you have unusual connections.

Instead you travel an interstate to a hub city, take a state highway, and proceed to her town on smaller roads built to handle local traffic. Express and local train services use this same idea. It's called hub-and-spoke.

Aircraft move around the country in much the same way. But it wasn't always so.

Under the old regulatory model, carriers were forced to fly directly to remote or small markets, even with regular flights that were routinely nearly empty. These were, in effect, "unusual connections" directly from Grandma's driveway to yours. That was convenient for an isolated few, but grossly inefficient for millions of others.

Airlines obviously lost money on these routes, because the cost of any given flight is about the same whether it's empty or full. Every vacant seat at takeoff is literally lost money.

Basic economics says that every empty seat raises the "break-even" price—the point at which the airline stops losing money on each seat sold and begins to show profit instead.

Spreading those numbers across an airline's complete fleet makes it clear that half-empty flights to Grandma's front door drove costs sky-high, systemwide. In a deregulated market, such routes simply have to be dropped if there's not enough traffic to render them at least marginally profitable.

This reality is compounded by the fact that airline fleets are finite. When one of these multimillion-dollar planes flies half-empty, an airline's primary business asset—the craft and crew—is diverted from serving routes where paying customers are standing in line for seats.

Airlines are businesses. Business obeys supply and demand. And market forces insist airlines supply seats where customers demand them most often.

The industry has found that the hub-and-spoke system has enormous advantages. "Hub-and-spoke" is hugely efficient—the best method known for reaching a maximum number of destinations using a limited number of aircraft—and its efficiency becomes obvious when compared with the old "direct-line" system.

Using the old system, ten planes can deliver customers to ten destinations. But a hub-and-spoke system, with the same ten planes, can offer exponentially more routes (the exact number depends on the particular hub/spoke configuration used).

The result? More service and options to customers systemwide—not only from hubs but also at hundreds of spoke cities as well.

Normally, fierce interhub competition among carriers creates even more choices. For instance, a customer flying from Los Angeles to Hartford can choose to route through 16 hub cities: Atlanta, Baltimore, Charlotte, Cincinnati, Cleveland, Dallas/Fort Worth, Denver, Detroit, Houston, Minneapolis/St. Paul, Newark, Philadelphia, Pittsburgh, St. Louis, San Francisco, or Washington, D.C.

Hub-and-spoke routes reduce transfers. The percentage of flights during which customers change planes only once is about the same today—roughly one-third—as in 1979. But today, two-transfer flights are all but eliminated. Meanwhile, no-transfer flights have increased; and 99 of 100 transfers are to the same airline. In 1978, 14 percent of customers had to change carriers entirely.

Hubs are powerful economic engines. Transportation hubs have always sparked growth. For example, Chicago's population in 1850 was 30,000. In 1848, Chicago began railroad service, and by 1856, the city was a hub serving a dozen railroad companies. By 1860, the population had tripled, to more than 100,000.

In the same way, today's air service makes a community more attractive to businesses, investors, and tourists alike and plays a key role in economic decision-making. Hub-and-spoke also drives the economic engines for smaller communities, since they can be linked to national and international destinations with just one transfer or fewer.

The hub-and-spoke system does not increase fares. Average ticket prices at hubs are

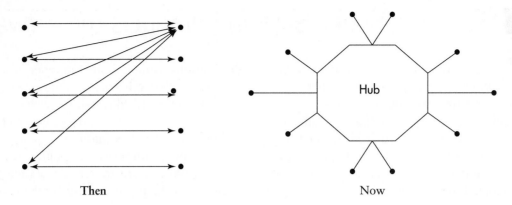

Then   Now

■ Hub-and-spoke deploys fleets efficiently.
Source: Adapted and used by permission. Anonymous.

approximately five percent higher than similar tickets at spokes. This so-called hub premium reflects the often-ignored fact that the average ticket price reflects the higher percentage of business customers who travel from hubs. Of course, most hub cities are commercial centers and enjoy a robust business base. Fares used by the business traveler generally are higher because they are booked later and have fewer if any restrictions. Although average ticket prices at hub airports may be higher, customers at hub cities have the benefits of far more service options. They enjoy

the convenience and flexibility of high frequency and nonstop service; both are important factors to the business traveler. Airlines have to cover the cost of providing this service and the large operation to support this schedule.

In sum, the hub-and-spoke system uses common sense to serve as many communities as possible, as efficiently as possible.

And it has been applied for efficiencies from everything to air transport to overnight package and mail delivery, by diverse industries, all for a very good reason: It works.

Winter Snowsports Resorts: Destinations at a Crossroads

BY TERENCE M. TANNEHILL

The American snowsports industry can trace its origins to the Scandinavian and European immigrants who came to the United States in the 1800s. The first uphill ski lift, a mine bucket tramway in 1880, was devised by miners in Johnson City, CA (Clifford, 2002). The 1932 Winter Olympics in Lake Placid, NY, initiated a new interest in winter sports. In 1936, skiing got a boost when Averell Harriman, Chairman of the Union Pacific Railroad, founded Sun Valley, ID, as the first destination ski resort, hoping the resort would increase utilization of his railroad. From these modest beginnings, the number of ski resorts grew rapidly through the 1970s but then slowed through the 1980s and 1990s. From

2000 through 2007 the industry has seen a substantial increase in skier/boarder visits with average visits 16.9% above the 1980–1999 levels. Tamarac Resort, ID, which opened in 2004, is the first major ski resort developed since Deer Valley, UT, began operations in 1983.

In the boom times of the 1960s and 1970s, skiers were satisfied with natural snow, ski lifts (rope tows, t-bars, j-bars and poma lifts were in the majority), a scattering of double chairlifts and the occasional signature gondola or tram. As competition increased and annual skier visits flattened in the 1980s, ski resorts responded with expanded snow making, improved snow grooming, high speed detachable quad chairlifts and

Table 1	The "Big Four of Snowsports Operations"		
Intrawest	*Vail Resorts*	*Booth Creek Holdings*	*Boyne USA*
Cooper Mt., CO	Vail Mt., CO	Mt. Cranmore, NH	Big Sky, MT
Snowshoe Mt., WV	Beaver Creek, CO	Northstar at Tahoe, CA	Boyne Mt., MI
Whistler/Blackcomb, BC	Breckenridge, CO	Sierra at Tahoe, CA	Boyne Highlands, MI
Mt. Tremblant, QB	Keystone Mt., CO	Waterville Valley, NH	Brighton, UT
Winter Park, CO	Heavenly Ski Resort, CA		Crystal Mt., WA
Stratton Mt., VT			Cypress Mt., BC
Steamboat Springs, CO			Loon Mt., NH
			Sugarloaf, ME
			Sunday River, ME
			The Summit, WA

Note: American Ski Company, which operated 11 ski resorts in the 1990s and 2000s, filed for dissolution in February 2007.

increased skiing and snowboarding terrain. All of these improvements have come at very high capital costs, often reaching into the millions of dollars. Colorado resorts reported investing $233 million in capital investments in 1999.

With significant investments in infrastructure there has been a significant increase in ski industry consolidation causing a 31% decrease in ski resorts since 1985. Now the industry, as shown in Table 1, is dominated by a few large corporations. With significant investments in infrastructure, corporate ski resorts are seeking new revenue sources other than just on-mountain snowsports activities. Real estate (sales and rentals), another traditional revenue source, grew in importance along with other non-snowsports activities. In fact, Canada's Whistler/Blackcomb, which has over 2.2 million skier/rider visits in the winter, is now experiencing more customer visits in the summer and fall than in the winter months.

THE CHANGING FACE OF WINTER SNOWSPORTS ENTHUSIASTS

Take a look at the demographic profiles of today's skiers and snowboarders shown in Table 2. Do you see any differences between these two groups?

Because skiing has been a sport for a much longer time than snowboarding, it is not surprising to find that, skiers are on average older and have higher incomes than snowboarders. Though both market segments average almost the same number of days on the slopes, skiers bring along their children and females account for a greater portion of the larger skiing segment than they do in the smaller boarder segment. A significant number of skier households earn incomes over $50,000 (83.4%) and include children under 18 (86.2%). The newer snowboarder segment, registering 68% under age 25, are primarily the trend-setting, thrill-seeking Echo Boomers (ages 10–27).

Marketing to both these diverse segments will be a major challenge for years to come. The Baby Boomers (ages 40–58) have been the core skier segment while Echo Boomers comprise most of the boarder segment. Somewhere in the middle is Generation X (ages 28–39) who introduced the sport of snowboarding and kept it going until the Echo Boomers could take over.

The challenge lies in the differing needs of these segments. According to Armstrong and Kotler,[1] Echo Boomers have developed a very programmed lifestyle no doubt in part because

[1]Armstrong, Gary, and Kotler, Philip. (2005). *Marketing, an introduction* (7th ed.). Upper Saddle River, NJ: Prentice-Hall.

Table 2	Skier/Snowboarder Profiles*		
		Alpine Skiers	*Snowboarders*
Total Participants		7.4 million	5.6 million
% of US Population		2.9%	2.2%
Average # of Days		9.1	8.9
Male		60.7%	77.0%
Female		39.3%	23.0%
HH Income $50,000+		83.4%	65.1%
Median Age–Male		30.2	22.0
Median Age–Female		29.2	23.5
Age 25 or Older		71.7%	32.4%
HH with children under 18		86.2%	NA
20+ Days		15.6%	17.6%
5–19 Days		31.3%	33.5%
2–4 Days		53.2%	48.9%

* National Ski Areas Association: *A Blueprint for Growth*, Fall 2002.

of their latch-key upbringing. In addition, this group has a strong influence on the younger generation born after 1994 and represents the future. Sporting activities that are enjoyed by this boarding culture include skateboarding, wakeboarding and all-terrain boarding. They also indulge in downhill biking, street lugeing, river running, and sky surfing. Obviously, they like extreme sports and risk taking.

Although they are the smallest of the three market segments, Generation Xers represent a significant amount of spending power. By the year 2010, they will have replaced Baby Boomers as the primary market in most categories.

The US Census Bureau estimates that by 2050 whites will make up roughly half the population; with the fastest growing segments made up of Asian Americans and Hispanics. This will present a significant challenge to the

snowsports industry as currently Caucasians still comprise 86% of ski resort visitors. Several West Coast ski resorts have developed specific programs to attack these nontraditional skiers such as Spanish-language brochures, Spanish speaking instructors, Asian-language television and print ads, ski reports on Hispanic and Asian television outlets and working with Asian college groups. Mountain High Resort outside Los Angeles states that more than half of its visitors are nonwhite.

About the Author: Terence M. Tannehill is a Visiting Instructor of Management at Fort Lewis College in Durango, Colorado. He combines over twenty-five years as a corporate executive with extensive experience as an entrepreneur in tourism and resort management. For ten years he owned and operated Whitneys' Inn and Black Mountain Ski Resort in Jackson, New Hampshire. He also directed a not-for-profit organization which conducted wildlife conservation programs in East Africa.

Great Place to Stay (Employed)

BY STEPHANIE SMITH

This is one of the best places to work in the United States?

Consider:

Front desk clerk Adam Kaufman, 25, listens calmly as a guest launches into a five-minute tirade over $17 in long-distance charges on a hotel bill that tops $3,000.

Kaufman deletes all of the offending phone charges. The guest continues carping, this time about the $15 daily valet parking charge. Kaufman stays polite and pleasant, but can't budge on those.

Not to be outdone, the guest's wife, who was hanging back during the confrontation, picks up a pear from the hotel's counter.

"Too hard," she complains. She keeps the fruit.

Kaufman works at the Four Seasons Resort in Palm Beach. The 420 employees at the 210-room hotel, owned by part-time Palm Beach residents Lyon Sachs and Bob Malesardi, aren't required to bow and scrape. But they come close.

Pool attendants spritz water every hour on guests lounging at the pool. Joggers are greeted on their return with chilled towels and bottled waters.

Guests at the five-star, five-diamond oceanfront resort expect a lot, and often gripe a lot. After all, they're paying $500 or more a night.

Despite the challenges for employees, their employer, Four Seasons Hotels and Resorts, has made *Fortune* magazine's list of the 100 best companies to work for in America three years running. This year, the Toronto-based luxury hotel management company ranked No. 48, up from No. 70 in 1999.

Four Seasons is a top employer because it offers rapid advancement, profit sharing and a 401(k) plan, travel opportunities, tuition reimbursement, free meals, free uniforms and more.

"The luxury hotel chain retains employees by treating them like guests," Fortune said.

Nicola Blazier, a Toronto-based company spokeswoman and a 19-year employee, said Four Seasons is a great employer not because of any single benefit, but "the respect the company gives its employees."

That shows in Four Seasons' employee turnover rate—24 percent, well below the industry standard for luxury hotels of about 40 percent.

The local Four Seasons turnover rate once was 40 percent largely because the hotel's workers tended to migrate with tourists, traveling to the Northeast during the summer and returning to Palm Beach in winter, local officials said.

But the local rate is dropping, said Four Seasons General Manager Harry Gorstayn, who came from the company's Regent Beverly Wilshire in 1998.

The resort is doing more of a year-round business by booking corporate meetings during the summer, he said.

Kaufman, the patient young man who's been at the Palm Beach resort's front desk for 2 1/2 years, has stuck with a job that can burn out most in a year because he's treated well and believes it will help him reach his goal—management.

Like many Four Seasons employees, Kaufman doesn't list money as his top reason for staying. That makes sense, according to Mark Lunt, a hospitality industry analyst with Ernst & Young in Miami.

Even in luxury hotels and resorts such as the Four Seasons, Ritz-Carlton and The Breakers, wages range from about $8 an hour for the lowest positions to a maximum of about $45,000 a year for most department heads.

"Not only do you have a challenging environment where you're face to face with customers, but you're not paid as much as comparable jobs in some other fields," said Lunt.

But, he added, Four Seasons respects its employees—and promotes the good ones quickly.

The local Four Seasons opened in December 1989 as the Ocean Grand. It became a Four Seasons–managed resort in 1994—after a relatively small improvement project to make employees more comfortable.

"Four Seasons wouldn't take over unless we promised to put in air conditioning in the laundry room," said Diane Yost, the resort's sales and marketing director.

The work was done.

Four Seasons Hotels and Resorts operates hotels under the Four Seasons and Regent names. Its 24,344 employees work at 47 hotels in 19 countries. Four Seasons has partial ownership of some of the hotels it runs, but it no longer owns any outright, a spokeswoman said.

The company (NYSE: FS), which opened its first Four Seasons Motor Hotel in Toronto's red light district in 1961, still is controlled by founder Isadore Sharp and his family. They own 67 percent of the company's voting stock.

Sharp, who is called "Izzy" by his employees, believes if the company treats employees well, they will treat guests well.

The company backs that up with anonymous employee surveys every year that go directly to headquarters.

Four Seasons also offers job security.

Once an employee reaches five years with the company, he or she can be fired only by a vice president in the company's corporate office.

"The philosophy is if you've worked here for five years, you must be pretty good," said

Shelley Komitor, human resources director at the Palm Beach resort.

Another benefit that's unique to the chain: Any full-time employee, not just executives, can receive from five to 20 free nights a year at any Four Seasons resort and a 50 percent discount on food and drink.

Four Seasons also offers profit sharing, automatic contributions to a 401(k) plan equal to 3 percent of employees' salaries, tuition reimbursement, health and dental insurance after six months of full-time employment, disability insurance, free meals at the employee cafeteria, locker rooms stocked with toiletries and free uniform maintenance that includes dry cleaning and mending.

"It makes employees work even harder when they're treated (well)," said local benefits manager Danielle Olson.

At the nation's top hotel school at Cornell University in Ithaca, New York, more graduates want to work for Four Seasons than any other company, said Millie Reed, who heads the university's student career development program.

"They were actually the top hirers of our students, and our students go into consulting and real estate and investment banking and brand management," Reed said.

Cornell graduates pick Four Seasons not only because it's a first-class hotel management company, but because of its reputation as an employer, she said.

"They're looking for a culture within a company," Reed said.

Probably the most attractive part of working for Four Seasons is the reward for a job well done: promotion.

Good employees move up fast, said Lunt, the hotel analyst and Cornell graduate who spent five years working in hotels. They often can choose jobs in such places as Paris, Milan, Tokyo, Kuala Lumpur, Hong Kong, Nevis in the West Indies and Sydney, Australia.

"They are better places to work, more fun," Lunt said of Four Seasons. "It's more attractive to work in Maui and Palm Beach. If you work for Marriott or Hyatt, where's the worst place they can put you? Detroit?"

Employees also have a direct financial stake in their hotels. They receive up to 5 percent of their salaries annually in a profit-sharing plan.

The local Four Seasons is pretty open about how it's doing. Minutes of department meetings are posted on employee bulletin boards along with the count and cost of lost laundry.

On the laundry room door are notices that in six months, 5040 wash cloths disappeared at a cost of $3,830.40, along with 4880 white napkins costing $5,807.20.

Helga Aquilina, the evening housekeeping supervisor, said she has a personal stake in the resort's finances.

"Whenever anybody breaks anything, we go, 'Look out. There goes my profits,'" said Aquilina, 64, who went to work at the hotel cleaning up the construction mess before it opened in 1989.

She expects to retire from the Four Seasons.

"I love the hotel," Aquilina said. "I've seen it from the dirt up."

When she decides it's time to quit working, Aquilina still will get free stays at any Four Seasons in the world.

Company policy.

Source: Smith, Stephanie. (2000, March 6). *Palm Beach Post,* p. 1D.

Inviting the Media to Dinner: How, When, and Why to Stage a Media Dinner/Event

BY KATHLEEN CASSEDY

The cultivation of favorable media coverage is a requisite part of marketing. "Media stories generally carry more weight than advertising because people tend to trust third-party endorsements more," says Cindy Kurman, president of Kurman Communications, a Chicago-based marketing public relations firm representing city hotels and restaurants.

Restaurants can attract publicity by hosting media dinners or luncheons to introduce the restaurant, chef, and menu. A press dinner must be planned to perfection since every aspect of the experience will be noted and scrutinized by the journalists. And while a good review can make a restaurant, a bad review can destroy it.

Consider this event. About 40 journalists who cover food and restaurants for magazines, newspapers, online publications, and radio and television shows were invited to a press dinner at a prestigious hotel in Washington, D.C. The purpose was to introduce the chef's new menu and how it could be paired with Meritage wine. After a cocktail reception, guests sat down to assigned seating. Wine was poured, and an appetizer was served. It was clear the general manager and hotel's publicist had put forth considerable effort to create this event, even to the extent of placing a cooking utensil as a favor at each setting.

With great fanfare, plates of steaming food came out of the kitchen and were placed before guests. Each person was presented with a different dish. No one, however, had chosen a particular entrée. One woman who was allergic to seafood received a crab dish; a non-meat eater was given veal; and another guest received salmon who had just eaten it earlier that day. The journalists' countenances showed surprise and, in some cases, disappointment, as they covetously eyed their neighbors' meals. Clearly, their host wanted to expose them to the full menu, but were they expected to share food from each other's plates? Eventually, some entrées were exchanged, and after more imbibing of wine, confidences were discreetly shared about the perplexing presentation.

"You should not play Russian roulette with the food," say Deborah Parker Wong, a former restaurant and hotel publicist in the San Francisco Bay area. "Most people you invite to press dinners are foodies, and foodies do not want to receive food randomly.

"The press should get the white kid glove treatment," she says. "You're hosting a press dinner to impress people. These people are jaded. They are plied constantly with invitations to these types of events, but if you go that extra mile to ensure your event is exceptional, they'll never forget it, no matter how jaded they are."

The most common mistakes are erratic service and running out of food, say both food journalists and publicists. Geneva Collins, who reviews restaurants for several publications, recalls a press dinner hosted by an inn in Maryland. The meal comprised 11 courses, each one featuring crabmeat. The inn's restaurant clearly meant to impress its guests, yet after the third course, service halted for more than an hour. Collins guesses the staff revolted. During this hiatus, journalists shuffled off on a makeshift tour of the crabs' shedding pans. The experience, however, was not a total disaster. Her exposure to Mayland seafood cuisine was used in subsequent stories.

Presentation provides the restaurant an opportunity to show off its level of service. The entire dining experience should be thought out and examined for weaknesses before it occurs, Parker Wong says.

Press dinners typically do not generate immediate media coverage. While some journalists write about a new restaurant, often the event and meal are filed away and retrieved later for a food or restaurant story unrelated to the press dinner. Publicists agree that the main objective for hosting a press dinner is to build and maintain media relationships. Each press dinner has its own purpose, which may be to publicize a restaurant opening or to renew visibility for an established venue. "You fabricate a reason to have a party," Parker Wong says. "If you have some new, wonderful seasonal dishes you can invite the press to enjoy or try them."

Tom Walton, a principal of Fortune Public Relations, representing dozens of San Francisco restaurants, aims to keep his clients top in journalists' minds. "When a restaurant is always competing with the new hot place, you need to wave that flag a little with free food to provide a chance for networking, and occasionally some [food] education," he says.

If the press dinner's goal is to introduce a new restaurant, Kurman believes the restaurant should wait until its staff is trained and the service has been finely honed. "Don't do practice meals on the press," she says. She and other publicists recall hosting dinners where the kitchen was slammed, and journalists waited 20 to 30 minutes for courses. Rather than have a huge press party, Kurman prefers to hold a series of smaller events, where journalists can experience the food and service in their most favorable light.

Generally, a magazine's or newspaper's main food critic does not attend media dinners but dines incognito several times, before reviewing a restaurant. These publications often have other critics and food writers who cover trends, restaurant openings, chefs, and attend media dinners.

Thirty journalists typically is the largest group a restaurant can handle at a media dinner. Which journalists are invited depends on the dinner's objectives, say Lisa Robinson, public relations director for the Monarch Hotel and its Bistro restaurant in Washington, D.C. If the dinner is to introduce a restaurant, the publicist invites national press and travel and food writers. If the dinner introduces a menu, publicists concentrate on local food media. Journalists also are invited based on an interest in the restaurant's chef or as required by assignment, says Parker Wong. "If the journalist has never met the chef, we ensure that the individual has a one-on-one time with the chef or is seated at a table where he or she can get the most out of the experience," she says.

Generally, invitations are sent out with a three-week lead time. The chef develops a menu and sometimes invites journalists to small gatherings, such as a chef's table. Parker Wong says she used to attend the chef's menu review held for staff. "I knew more about the food, ingredients, and wine than almost anyone at the table," she says. If a publicist cannot answer journalists' food questions, an expert is sought, she says. Unfortunately, some public relations people are brought on as an afterthought or their work is considered ancillary to restaurant operations, so they do not have intimate knowledge of the chef, service, or entire experience, she says. Optimum events occur when an in-house PR person works with an independent consultant; one brings outside objectivity to the table and the other has the inside track, Parker Wong says.

Media dinners can have a set menu, a tasting menu, or the regular restaurant menu from which guests order. A set menu, however, can be easier to prepare for large dinners. A tasting menu is a succession of small courses, each one in harmony with the next. Menus often include wine pairings.

Kurman likes to present tasting menus that showcase the entire menu. After hosting a tasting menu media dinner at which the food ran out for one popular "taste," she urges clients to prepare for voracious guests. "Don't skimp," she says. "I don't care what it costs. This is an event that will pay off for a year or more as stories find their way into print."

When the Monarch's Bistro hosts media dinners, large groups are served a set menu, and smaller groups order from the regular menu. If the dinner has a set menu, Robinson provides either printed material that describes the meal, or the chef comes out to introduce the meal. The chef or sommelier also describes the wine paired with each course. The Bistro occasionally hosts a chef's table for six to 10 journalists, who can interview the chef as he or she prepares their meal.

The Kimpton Hotel and Restaurant Group, which manages more than a dozen San Francisco restaurants, hosts media at a chef's table during celebrity dinners, attended by paying guests. "I believe the press likes to see who is from the community—they like to take in the whole picture," say Vanessa Bortnick, publicist for Kimpton's restaurants.

Most media dinners are held in a private dining room or secluded corner of the restaurant. Publicists are careful not to seat journalists with their competitors. When VIPs attend media dinners, Kurman escorts them to different tables for introductions. Kurman also prepares the journalists' dossiers containing clips of their reviews and stories, which she uses to prep clients about their guests.

"It's flattering when someone says to a journalist, 'I read that story and it was fabulous,'" Kurman says.

During dinner, the publicist should interact with all the guests and remember journalists' comments about the meal and the restaurant, says Parker Wong. (She recalls rushing to the restroom to secretly write herself reminder notes.)

"Anything publicists say or do should be to position themselves as resources to help journalists meet their deadlines," she says. "You want your work to look as effortless and flawless as possible, just like the restaurant wants to be perceived." Journalists often want copies of a restaurant's menus, including the wine list. These items can be contained in a media kit.

Parker Wong often sent media kits and menus with dinner invitations. When she followed up with phone calls, she often suggested story ideas about how the dinner's theme or an interview with the chef could work into a food column.

Robinson makes sure to send journalists thank-you notes for attending the press dinner, but never presses for coverage. "If journalists think your restaurant is worthy of writing about, they do it," she says. However, a publicist needs to be a bit of a salesperson and suggest angles for stories, she adds.

"The important thing is that you expose writers to your product and keep them informed about what is going on," Robinson says. "Journalists may not have a reason to cover your restaurant immediately, but in eight months when they are doing a story on Chilean wines, they'll remember you showcased those wines at your dinner."

"Free food remains the tried and proven method of getting publicity," Fortune Public Relation's Walton says.

Lodging F & B, January–February, 2001. Used by permission.

Integrative
Cases

Buying a Piece of Paradise

ROY A. COOK

ROBERT H. WOLVERTON

Their first vacation to the Big Island of Hawaii had lived up to every one of their expectations: warm days, cool nights, bright sandy beaches, sparkling clear water, great accommodations, good food, and friendly people. In fact, the Reynolds had enjoyed their visit so much that they were planning to return the next year and for years to come. That desire to return and the offer to receive discounts at local attractions enticed them to sit through a vacation ownership (timeshare) presentation at The Bay Club condominiums, part of the Waikoloa Beach Resort.

Diana, the Activities Booking Agent at The Shores of Waikoloa condominiums where the Reynolds were staying, said that the presentation would be well worth Cathy and Chad's time. She described The Bay Club, which was less than a mile away, as being just like The Shores, but better, since The Bay Club had been built by the same developer a few years later.

In exchange for listening to a 90-minute presentation on vacation ownership opportunities at The Bay Club, they could receive substantial discounts on luaus, scenic cruises, helicopter rides, and a variety of other attractive activities. The Reynolds had attended timeshare presentations before and the offer sounded interesting, especially since they had been considering buying a condominium in a warm, salt-water location for their retirement.

The Reynolds were like many other baby boomers who had been attracted to timeshare ownership. These owners number over 3.2 million and grow at an annual compounded rate of 9% (Lodging, 1997). Purchasers have a very common profile: married, children, well-educated, average household income of $103,000, and travel at least three times more than the general population (Yetzer, 2000). "From its beginnings in the French Alps in the late 1960s, vacation ownership has become the fastest growing segment of the U.S. travel and tourism industry, increasing in popularity at the rate of nearly 16 percent each year since 1993" ("The Growth of an Industry," 2002).

By purchasing one week (1/51) interest in a timeshare property, owners receive the right to return year-after-year to the unit they purchase or to exchange for a similar unit in another resort location. Exchanges may take place within properties operated by management companies such as Disney, Hilton, Hyatt, or Radisson; or, for a small fee, through ownership exchange companies such as Resort Condominiums International (RCI) or Interval International (II).

ABOUT WAIKOLOA BEACH RESORT

The Bay Club is located in the Waikoloa Beach Resort. This resort is "a planned community of resorts, vacation condominiums, golf courses, restaurants, and a shopping center. Waikoloa Beach Resort is one of the four master-planned destination resorts on the Kohala Coast. The others are Mauna Lani Resort, Mauna Kea Resort, and Hualalai Resort" (*Owner's Manual*, 2001). The resort is located approximately 45 minutes north of the Kohala-Kona Airport. After leaving the airport, visitors are greeted with miles and miles of stark lava flows until they reach the lush emerald green landscaping and brilliant flowers at the entrance of the resort.

"Located at the Waikoloa Beach Resort, The Bay Club is within strolling distance of Hilton Waikoloa Village, two championship golf courses, numerous tennis courts, and the white sand beach at 'Anaeho'omalu Bay. Built on the highest elevation in the resort and surrounded by the greens and fairways of both the Waikoloa Kings' and Beach 18-hole golf courses, The Bay Club offers ocean, Mauna Kea, Mauna Loa, Hualalai, and Kohala mountain vistas" (*Owner's Manual*, 2001).

THE PRESENTATION

After a cup of coffee, a brief overview of the timeshare ownership concept, and pre-qualification questions related to vacationing patterns and annual income, the Reynolds were off to a formal sales presentation. If they had chosen not to attend the full 90-minute presentation, or if they had not "qualified" to attend the presentation, they would not have been entitled to receive their incentive gifts.

Bob Bergstedt, the salesperson in charge of their presentation, could best be described as a low-key, no-pressure source of information. After finding out that the Reynolds were in their mid-fifties, owned their home (but no other property), made over $100,000 a year, and typically took two to three one-week vacations to warm weather sun-and-surf locations, he presented the advantages of the vacation ownership concept.

The Bay Club is part of the Hilton Grand Vacations Club (HGVC) system and ownership benefits included

- A lifetime of annual vacations;
- Assured spacious accommodations;
- A one-time purchase price;
- Privileged club membership;
- Worldwide resort exchange privileges;
- Tomorrow's vacations at today's prices;
- The option to vacation with family and friends; and
- The ability to will ownership to heirs.

In addition to The Bay Club, other destinations in the HGVC system included

- Seven properties in Florida;
- One additional property in Hawaii;
- One property in Las Vegas, Nevada;
- One property in Colorado;
- Two properties in Mexico; and
- Three properties in Scotland.

Based on their discussion of vacationing patterns and desires, Bob presented Chad and Cathy with the option of purchasing one week in either a one- or two-bedroom unit. This fractional ownership purchase would allow the Reynolds to stay at The Bay Club or any one of the other units in the system for one week each year during prime vacation times. Or, they could choose to stay for longer periods if they selected non–prime time weeks. Their choices would be based on the number of HGVC points that were attached to their unit purchase.

Membership in timeshare exchange organizations such as RCI made it possible for owners at one resort to trade for accommodations at another resort in the system. To participate in an exchange program, owners deposit the time they own into an exchange system each year. They then request reservations through the exchange system specifying a desired destination and dates. Reservations are then confirmed subject to availability and the trading power of the unit. If owners do not want to exchange their time, they may return each year to the resort where they own property, their home resort.

Trading power is based on one of two systems. The classic system is based on demand. When units are purchased, they are assigned a color signifying the level of demand for the week purchased. Red weeks are the highest demand, followed by white and then by blue. The higher demand weeks command higher purchase prices since they can be exchanged for red times or any other color at other resorts. Lower demand color periods cannot be exchanged for higher demand color periods. Newer purchase arrangements are allotted point values for exchanges rather than being color-coded. This system allows owners more flexibility in planning their vacations, but it may become very confusing.

With the purchase of a standard one- or two-bedroom unit for one week at The Bay Club, the Reynolds would receive 4,800 or 7,000 points, respectively, per year, if they chose to convert their week to points. Each year, Chad and Cathy had the option of returning to The Bay Club or converting their ownership interest into points. If they converted to points, they could select any of the options shown in Table 1 as well as many others to meet their vacation needs. Gold and silver designations are similar to the classic red, white, and blue system with gold indicating higher levels of demand than silver.

The points accruing to the unit would allow them to reserve and use the same type of unit; for example, a one- or two-bedroom unit, at any HGVC location at any time of the year. The flexibility of using points provided a multitude of opportunities. For example, with the purchase of

Table 1	ClubPoint Use Chart						
	Gold			Silver			
	Nightly		Weekly	Nightly		Weekly	
	Mid-Week (Mon–Thurs)	*Weekends (Fri–Sun)*	*Points per 7-night stay*	*Mid-Week (Mon–Thurs)*	*Weekends (Fri–Sun)*	*Points per 7-night stay*	
Accommodations	*Points per Night*			*Points per Night*			
Studio	160	320	1600	110	220	1100	
1 Bedroom	340	680	3400	240	480	2400	
2-Bedroom	500	1000	5000	350	700	3500	

a two-bedroom unit (7000 points), the Reynolds could select a variety of vacationing options:

- By choosing Gold week options, they could vacation in a two-bedroom unit for one week (5000 points) and a studio for one week (1600 points), yet still have points available for a two-night mid-week getaway in a studio (320 points).
- By choosing Silver week options, they could vacation in
  - a two-bedroom unit for two weeks in the same or different locations (7000 points); or

- a one-bedroom unit for two weeks (4800 points) and two weeks in a studio (1200 points).

At each resort in the HGVC system, a 52-week color-coded demand based reservation calendar was used. The coding system started with bronze, the lowest demand period, and moved up through silver, gold, and platinum. Choosing platinum weeks would limit the Reynolds to one week in a two-bedroom unit or two weeks in a one-bedroom unit during all high demand periods. A sample of demand periods for resorts in the reservation system is shown in Table 2.

Table 2	Resort Demand Periods (Weeks of Year Numbered Consecutively Starting January 1)			
Resort	*Platinum Weeks*	*Gold Weeks*	*Silver Weeks*	*Bronze Weeks*
Breckenridge, CO	115 26–35 47–52	20–25	37–46	16–19
Cancun, Mexico	4–18 51–52	1–3 26–34 40–48	19–25 35–39	None
Captiva Island, FL	7–13 51–52	1–6 14–18 24–33 43–48	19–23 34–42 49–50	None
Fort Myers Beach, FL	10–13 51–52	7–9 26–33	1–6 14–18 24–25 40–48	19–23 34–39 49–50
Las Vegas, NV	9–20 37–42 51–52	5–8 21–35 44–48	1–4 49–50	None
Perthshire, Scotland	1 14–15 21–35 40–42 51–52	6–13 16–20 36–39	5–6 44–47	2–4 48–50

In addition to the fee simple (deeded interest) timeshare purchase, other one-time incentives were offered to entice the Reynolds to commit to the purchase. These included

- 100,000 Hilton Honors Points (the equivalent of a one week stay at any Hilton Hotel or longer stays at Doubletree Hotels or Hampton Inns);
- Lifetime Silver VIP Membership in the Hilton Honors Program (additional bonus points with each stay and preferential treatment during each stay);
- Three years' membership in the HGVC which included membership in Resort Condominiums International (RCI); and
- A five-year membership in the International Cruise & Exchange Gallery (ICE). By exchanging one timeshare week, cruises can be purchased at discounted rates on Carnival, Norwegian, Royal Caribbean, Holland America, Princess, Disney, and others for set daily fees. Per person rates on these cruise lines range from $50 in the Caribbean to $80 in Alaska. There is no exchange fee for this service.

Owners at The Bay Club are members of the HGVC. This membership gives owners the opportunity to trade for similar quality accommodations at thousands of vacation destinations around the world. For example, HGVC points could be exchanged for RCI reservations as shown in Table 3. As an added benefit HGVC members make their reservations through HGVC service representatives rather than dealing directly through RCI. However, RCI exchange fees of $124 for domestic reservations and $162 for international reservations are still applicable.

The total purchase price for these non-negotiable packages was:

- $16,490 for a one-bedroom (approximately 800 square foot) unit, or
- $22,990 for a two-bedroom (approximately 1200 square foot) unit.

The annual maintenance fees for either of these units would be $641. After the first three years, membership in the HGVC can be purchased for $85 per year or $225 for three years.

The Reynolds were also presented with several options to complete the purchase:

- Paying the full purchase price,
- Making a 10% down payment and financing the remaining 90% at 13.9% for seven years,
- Making a 20% down payment and financing the remaining 80% at 10.4% for five years, or
- Making a 30% down payment and financing the remaining 70% at zero interest for six months with a balloon payment at the end of six months for the balance of the loan.

The developer would carry the "paper" on the financing and would reduce the rate by 0.5% if the purchaser agreed to automatic withdrawals for the monthly payments.

Table 3	HGVC Values for RCI Reservations (For One Week)	
	RCI Exchange Reservation	*HGVC Points Required*
Two-Bedroom	Red Time	4,800
	White Time	3,400
	Blue Time	2,400
One-Bedroom	Red Time	3,400
	White Time	2,400
	Blue Time	1,700
Studio	Red Time	2,400
	White Time	1,700
	Blue Time	1,200

Red Time = Greater Demand; White Time = Average Demand; Blue Time = Lesser Demand

THE DECISION

The Big Island of Hawaii was definitely a destination the Reynolds planned to visit again and again for several years. The other locations in the HGVC were also very attractive vacation destinations. The added incentives of cruise discounts, Hilton Honors Points, and upgraded status to Silver VIP membership all fit within their current travel patterns and future vacationing plans.

Based on these plans and desires, they agreed to purchase one week in a two-bedroom unit. Since the Reynolds owned only one piece of real estate (their home), they selected the 20% down payment financing option with the intention of making payments for three years and then repaying the balance with no penalties at that time. Timeshares are treated as second home purchases under federal tax regulations and the interest on these purchases is tax deductible.

While the sales documents were being completed, Cathy and Chad headed off for lunch. They returned about an hour later to sign the required legal documents to complete the purchase. Chad placed the down payment and closing costs of $5,196 on his credit card and selected the automatic payment option. At the closing, the Reynolds were informed that, under

Table 4	Weekly Rental Rates at The Shores
One bedroom (1-4 people)	
High demand periods	$1900
Low demand periods	1500
Two bedrooms (1-6 people)	
High demand periods	$2200
Low demand periods	1700

Table 5	The Bay Club at Waikoloa Beach Resort Units Available for Resale* (Prices Rounded to Nearest Thousand)
One-Bedroom/One Week	$12,000
Two-Bedrooms/One Week	$19,000

* Closing Costs = $380.00
Source: Timeshare Resales, U.S.A.

Hawaiian law, they had seven days to reconsider their purchase and change to another type of unit or cancel the contract for a full refund.

Over dinner that night, Cathy and Chad decided to do a little research to see if they had made the right decision. A telephone call and a few minutes on the Internet yielded the information contained in Tables 4, 5, 6, and 7. They could afford to purchase a unit at The Shores, but did

Table 6	The Shores at Waikoloa Condominiums Available for Resale (Prices Rounded to Nearest Hundred)
One-Bedroom/One-Bathroom Average sale price	$325,000
Two Bedrooms/Two Bathrooms Average sale price	$420,000
Annual Expenses (Costs rounded to nearest hundred) Property taxes	2,000
One Bedroom	2,400
Two Bedroom	
Association Fees (including property insurance)	3,600
One Bedroom	4,400
Two Bedroom	
Utilities including cable television (Same for both)	5200
Liability/Contents Insurance (Same for both)	500
Remodeling Reserve Every 30 years (approximate in current dollars)	35,000 to 45,000

Sources: C. J. Kimberly Realtors, Steve Hurwitz, R. E. Agent, and MLS data

Table 7	Inflation Rates
Average annual inflation rate from 1980-2000: All categories	3.5%
Average annual inflation rate from 1980-2000: Lodging away from home	5.5%

Source: U.S. Dept of Labor/Bureau of Labor Statistics/Consumer Price Indexes

they want to be tied to just one location? They knew the purchase was not an investment, but did it provide enough flexibility to make financial sense? Was the two-bedroom unit a better vacationing choice than a one-bedroom unit? Based on their combined state and federal marginal income tax rate of 34%, had they selected the best financing option? These and many other questions raced through their minds, but they knew they had seven days to evaluate their decision.

REFERENCES

Consumer Price Indexes. (2001). Bureau of Labor Statistics, U.S. Department of Labor.

Hurtiz, Steve. (2001). Interview. C. J. Kimberly Realtors, Kona, HI.

Lodging trends, buying into timeshare. (1997, October). *Lodging*, 23(2), 13.

Owner's Manual. (2001). The Bay Club at Waikoloa Beach Resort, Waikoloa, HI.

The Growth of an Industry. (2002, July 5). *A Consumer's Guide to Vacation Ownership.* http://www.arda.org,consumer.guide.guide.htm.

Yetzer, Elaine. (2000, May 1). Timeshare surveys reveal mobile sector, *Hotel and Motel Management*, 215(8), 3, 68.

Plotting a Course in Uncharted Waters

Consider the following challenges. Your business is positioned in the middle of the supply chain and your major suppliers are trying to drive you out of business by continually assuming your value-added functions and cutting the amounts they pay you for providing these services. Your competitors, both large and small, are merging, acquiring others or being acquired at an increasing rate. Your customers are experimenting with and rapidly adopting electronic venues that could significantly reduce your revenues. Welcome to the turbulent, competitive environment faced by travel agencies every business day. The competitive landscape is not only extremely fragmented and cutthroat, but as Scott Barry, an industry analyst, has noted, "Wall Street has historically viewed [the travel services industry] as one with low barriers to entry, not particularly technologically sophisticated, and (with) deteriorating returns."[1]

This case originally appeared as "Fasten Your Seatbelts—Turbulence Ahead for Travel Agencies," by Roy A. Cook, J. Larry Goff, and Laura J. Yale, all of Fort Lewis College, and Janet Bear Wolverton, Oregon Institute of Technology, in Annual Advances in Business Cases, 1999. The present version of the case was updated in 2004.

 ## TRAVEL AGENTS ENTER THE NEW MILLENNIUM

Traditionally, the channel of distribution for tourism services involved a supplier (e.g., airline, hotel, or tour wholesaler) and a travel agent. The travel agent filled many important functions as a channel member. Prior to the Internet, agents served as a vast sales force for suppliers, having local knowledge of and access to consumers. Travel agents were viewed by buyers as experts in travel planning and relied upon as the best source of travel information. They provided suppliers with a matchmaking service, answering questions, making suggestions, and placing supplier brochures into the hands of those consumers most likely to purchase. These agents facilitated the tourism service transaction by accepting payment and maintaining the client interface for the transfer of reservation confirmations, tickets and other pertinent information.

From these small beginnings, travel agents located in storefront locations grew to be important intermediaries for tourism suppliers. In fulfilling their intermediary role, they simplified the routine booking reservations processes for consumers and increased the marketing efforts of suppliers who were attempting to reach a broad cross section of consumers dispersed over wide geographic areas. They furnished a wide range of services to these customers ranging from providing information and making reservations to ticketing and preparing itineraries. These services were secured from a host of suppliers including airlines, car rental companies, hotels, cruise lines, and tour operators and then sold to retail customers.

From humble beginnings until the dawn of the 21st century, the importance of travel agencies to tourism service providers exploded. Yet this apparent upward trend in the total number of travel agencies (see Table 1) that had been exhibited in the past stopped and is now in question. This dramatic change can be attributed to new and improved forms of technology allowing travelers to access service providers directly and growing commission cuts which are squeezing already thin travel agency profit margins.

Up until the early 1990s, travel agents could earn 10% on all domestic airline ticket sales and 15% on international ticket sales with a potential of additional overrides which are extra commissions paid by airlines to travel agencies who meet sales targets. Then, in February 1995, the commission structure on airline ticket sales was radically altered as the airlines first began by capping commissions and then, in 2002, completely eliminating commissions. Although commissions have dropped to zero, large agencies and smaller agencies that are members of consortia still earn override commissions based on volume and the capture of market share.

Faced with these revenue restrictions, large agencies and especially mega agencies such as American Express Travel Services, Rosenbluth

International, Uniglobe, Maritz Travel, Professional Travel, and Morris Travel continue to grow in importance and capture additional market share while the number of smaller agencies continues to shrink. Although the risks of failure remain high, many individuals are still attracted to the opportunity of opening a travel agency since the process is fairly easy and inexpensive.

AN INDUSTRY IN TRANSITION

No matter what their size or marketing focus, travel agents almost never take title to the services they are selling. Instead, their task is to expedite the flow of information, payment and delivery of services from tourism service suppliers to the final consumer efficiently.[3] Tourism service suppliers have traditionally relied upon a combination of internal sales forces and the assistance of travel agencies to reach potential customers. Nowhere in the industry has this been more noticeable than with the airlines. Until 1995, travel agencies booked 85% of all domestic airline reservations. However, this number will soon reach the 30% range.[4,5] With the rise of Internet connections and direct access promotions by tourism service providers, especially the airlines, many transactions are bypassing travel agents.

Most travel agencies work with a wide array of suppliers. However, larger agencies often focus their marketing efforts on selected preferred suppliers in each industry segment to improve service delivery through conversion privileges and to improve profitability through override commissions. For example, conversion privileges which are often referred to as "waivers and favors" in the industry allow travel agents to enhance customer service to airline passengers by converting full fare economy-priced airline reservations to a discounted price when all discounted seats are sold out. Override commissions are additional commissions paid to travel agencies as a bonus for increased productivity. Overrides, which usually peak at 6% to 8% for peak producers, can enhance profitability when targeted sales volumes and/or market share shifts are achieved.[6] By achieving targeted levels of sales or shifts in market share, travel agencies gain the

Table 1[2]	ARC Accredited Travel Agencies
Year	*Number of Agencies*
1988	32,947
1994	45,168
1996	47,286
2002	29,522
2003	25,620

privilege to upgrade or confirm preferential schedules and/or services for their own preferred high-volume customers.

Tourism service suppliers still rely on intermediaries such as travel agencies and tour wholesalers and operators to help sell and market their services, but they are also becoming tenacious competitors as they strive to minimize controllable expenses. This competitiveness is being exacerbated by consolidation within the industry, rapid proliferation of technology which is providing easy consumer access to suppliers, and cost cutting measures which are continually being implemented by suppliers.

In the face of real or perceived threats to continued profitability, travel agencies have taken several steps from searching for economies of scale and scope to embracing new technologies and implementing service fees. In addition, the merger and acquisition activity in this industry segment has continued to increase.

IS BIGGER BETTER?

As agency owners and managers search for profitability through economies of scale and scope, many are seeking affiliations through franchises and memberships in consortiums. By 2001, 59% of all agency locations were affiliated with a leisure-oriented consortium or marketing group such as Vacation.com, Mast Travel Partners, or Giants.[7] This is in stark contrast to the 36% who were affiliated with a consortium in 1987.[8] The large dollar volume of transactions generated through these contractual combinations allow these affiliations to increase profitability by obtaining preferred vendor status and access to override commissions while, at the same time, lowering costs on everything from advertising expenses to supplies and materials.

Size can make a difference if travel agencies generate enough revenue to achieve preferred vendor status. The dollar volume increases gained through preferred vendor status is becoming more and more important as agencies search for new ways to serve customers who have new choices for acquiring travel services. Preferred vendor status allows agencies to offer lower rates for hotels and cruise lines as well as availability

at locations and on dates that are not available to the general public. The sales or market share targets that must be achieved to gain preferred vendor status are pushing many smaller travel agencies to seek some type of affiliation to remain profitable and provide expected levels of service.

Initial public offerings of companies such as Galileo International, Navigant International, Preview Travel, and Travel Services International during the late 1990s point to yet another change that occurred in the industry. Travel services companies which were once subsidiaries of other companies or operated as privately held companies joined the ranks of publicly traded companies.

Travel Services International (TSI) provides an excellent example of an emerging trend in travel services. TSI, which went public in 1997, pursued an acquisition strategy that has become increasingly common in the industry. This strategy, referred to as a roll-up, is a situation where a company "rolls up" or combines several synergistic companies such as corporate, leisure, and cruise agencies under one management umbrella to gain economies of scale and enhance shareholder value. By bringing several agencies together, back office accounting and other administrative functions can be combined. In addition, cross marketing of services can enhance potential revenues. After going public, TSI bought several smaller competitors in different sectors of travel services such as cruise only agencies and quickly became the market leader.

COPING WITH TECHNOLOGY

Rapid developments in technology are already occurring in the travel industry with many companies beginning to promote and sell their products and services over the Internet. Travelers can access tourism service suppliers through the Internet, and travel agencies are learning that they can continue to fill their traditional intermediary role by facilitating this new group of information and service seekers. As travelers become more comfortable booking reservations through the web, it has been projected that travel agents could facilitate this process through their own web sites. From almost indiscernible sales during the mid 1990s, the volume of travel spending on the Internet is projected to explode to 50–70% of all travel sales by 2015.[9] Other Internet services, such as Priceline.com, are proving to be popular with travelers shopping for bargain fares and airlines wanting to hold anonymous sales of excess inventory.

Purchasing airline tickets has been the primary focus of Internet use by travelers. This has not gone unnoticed by travel intermediaries that control the movement of airline ticket sales through sophisticated computer reservations systems such as Sabre and Galileo. These reservation systems link the airlines to travel agents. Another powerful reservation system, Orbitz, is owned by the five largest U.S. airlines: American, Continental, Delta, Northwest, and United. Other Internet agencies such as Expedia and Cheaptickets are enhancing services and breadth of travel options to gain market share by creating a direct link between suppliers and the final consumer.

According to Travel Industry Association research, 114 million adults in the U.S. were using an online service on the Internet in 2003. Of these, 44% actually booked a trip with the majority of activity being focused on airline ticket purchases. Frequent business travelers in particular have been drawn to this information source as they search and make travel plans. It is expected that this trend will continue to grow for the general population and frequent travelers in particular.[10] According to the results of the survey shown in Table 2, the majority (65.8%) of Internet users were between the ages of 21 and 45, married with no children, college educated and earned $30,000 or more per year.[11]

Technological advances not only provide convenient booking options for business travelers, but companies can also monitor and enforce travel policies through fully automated travel functions. These technological advances are threatening to greatly lessen the need for travel agents by allowing companies to access tourism services directly as well as monitor travel patterns and enforce cost-saving travel policies.

■ SEARCHING FOR PROFITABILITY

Travel agencies, like most members of the tourism industry, are faced with peaks and valleys in demand, resulting in significant cash flow fluctuations due to the seasonality of their business.

Table 2[12]	Age of Internet Users		
Age	*Frequency*	*Percent*	*Cumulative Percent*
5–10	1	.0	.0
11–15	49	1.0	1.0
16–20	251	5.0	6.0
21–25	627	12.5	18.5
26–30	808	16.1	34.6
31–35	684	13.6	48.2
36–40	571	11.4	59.6
41–45	612	12.2	71.7
46–50	496	9.9	81.6
51–55	393	7.8	89.4
56–60	215	4.3	93.7
61–65	103	2.1	95.8
66–70	79	1.6	97.4
71–75	33	.7	98.0
76–80	11	.2	98.2
Over 81	6	.2	98.3
Not Say	83	1.7	100.0
Total	5,022	100.0	

Table 3[3]	Comparative Common Sized Balance Sheet Data*				
Year Ended	*3/31/99*	*3/31/00*	*3/31/01*	*3/31/02*	*3/31/03*
			ASSETS		
Cash & Equiv.	26.1%	27.2%	25.5%	28.7%	29.1%
Trade Receiv.	24.6	23.6	25.2	22.3	21.9
Inventory	0.9	0.5	0.9	0.9	0.7
All Other Current	3.2	4.2	4.2	6.9	4.3
Total Current	54.9	55.4	55.7	58.9	56.0
Fixed Assets	20.1	19.1	19.2	15.6	19.0
Intangibles	10.4	10.2	11.3	11.6	8.0
All Other nonCur.	14.5	15.3	13.9	14.0	17.0
Total	100.0%	100.0%	100.0%	100.0%	100.0%
			LIABILITIES		
Notes Payable ST	14.2	9.4	11.6	15.1	11.1
Cur.Mat.-L/T/D	6.4	3.7	6.0	3.5	3.4
Trade Payables	18.0	20.9	18.9	15.2	24.6
Income Tax Pay.	0.4	0.3	0.8	0.5	0.5
All Other Current	31.0	28.1	27.3	35.5	27.9
Total Current	70.1	62.3	64.6	69.8	67.5
Long Term Debt	13.9	13.3	19.8	12.6	9.7
Deferred Taxes	0.4	0.6	0.3	0.0	0.1
All Other nonCur.	9.4	3.4	10.4	5.4	25.2
Net Worth	6.3	20.3	4.8	12.2	(2.6)
Total Liabilities & Net Worth	100.0%	100.0%	100.0%	100.0%	100.0%

* Although technically totals on common sized statements must equal 100%, rounding adjustments may result in slight internal variations. The percentages presented in these exhibits are as reported in Robert Morris Associates.[14]

[1] The conversion of financial statement absolute dollar amounts to percentages enables the users of the statements to perform a number of comparisons. This process is frequently called common-size analysis because all the years are reduced to a "common size" in that all the amounts are expressed in percentages of some common number and always add up to 100%.

The travel industry is extremely seasonal and, as is true in most service industries, profit margins for travel agencies have traditionally been low. In recent years, the before tax net profit margin has been steadily declining. As can be seen in the common sized data presented in Tables 3 and 4, a low level of fixed investments and high level of operating expenses can characterize the industry. The most significant operating expenses for travel agencies are salaries and benefits, rent, and computer reservations system expenses.

In the face of tightening profit margins, travel agencies have employed several tactics from seeking affiliations through franchises and memberships in consortiums to instituting service fees to improve profitability. In response to commission caps and cuts by airlines, one tactic that has been adopted by a wide range of agencies has been to add service fees to customer transactions. "Travel agencies that have achieved the greatest success over the past several years have been those that take advantage of opportunities created by the Internet to sell certain types

Destinations

The breathtaking ceilings and statues of the Vatican attract visitors of all faiths.
Photo by Janet Wolverton

Enjoying one of life's simple pleasures east of Cape Town, South Africa.
Photo by John W. White.

Economic and Political Impacts of Tourism

The historic mining/lumber town of Leavenworth, WA, transformed itself into a Bavarian village to gain tourism's economic benefits. *Photo by D. A. Yale.*

Pilgrims to Jerusalem continue to arrive even in times of political unrest. *Photo by C. E. Yale.*

Cultural and Environmental Impacts of Tourism

Nature's wonders at Bora Bora, Leeward Islands, are worthy of our preservation efforts. *Photo by John W. White.*

Slow tourism will increase in demand as more travelers seek solace. *Joe Cornish © Dorling Kindersley*

Tourism's Future

Innovative forms of transportation will allow access to fragile environments.
Photo by C. E. Yale

Tourism, like Australia's Ayers Rock, dominates the horizon of the 21st century.
Photo by C. E. Yale.

of travel and have used Internet marketing enticements to bring business into the retail agency."[13]

Caution should be exercised when analyzing sales revenues for travel agencies. Total sales will appear to be very large, highlighting the dollar volume of transactions processed by a travel services company; however, the more important financial target in this industry grouping is not gross sales revenues but net sales revenues. Net sales revenues reflect actual receipts from standard commissions, mark-ups, volume bonuses, overrides commissions, and service fees. For example, a travel agency may produce an airline ticket valued at $400 (sales), but only receives $28 (net sales revenue) in override commission for that transaction.

Eroding profit margins may be traced to commission caps that were first instituted by all major airlines during 1995. When overrides are included, commissions on domestic airline tickets averaged around 7% which compares to pre-cap averages of 11%. Prior to the caps, agencies could earn a base rate commission of 10% on all sales.

LOOKING TOWARD THE FUTURE

With the exception of short downturns during times of war, tourism activities have demonstrated a general upward trend in numbers of participants and revenues. However, there is nothing like a little uncertainty about the future to create concern and a good debate. A hotly debated area in the tourism industry is the future role of the travel agent and agencies. Travel agents have historically played an important role

in tourism distribution channels, performing valuable intermediary service by bringing together tourism service suppliers and the traveling public. Will the role of the travel agent remain the same in a world that appears to be turning in ever-increasing numbers to new information sources such as the Internet?

The technology provided through the Internet has the power to make travel planning more exciting. Computer users will become more informed consumers as they explore travel and other leisure time options ranging from transportation and accommodations to attractions and entertainment. As networking capabilities continue to increase in availability and speed, computer terminals, serving as electronic smart agents that utilize sophisticated software and networks, will develop that can meet travelers' specific needs. Booking a preferred flight time, reserving accommodations that meet specific criteria such as price range, level of service or driving distance from the airport, and reserving tickets for the evening play are all future possibilities. For other people, the personal service and professional expertise provided by a travel agent will continue to be the travel department store of choice.

Some experts say that the role of the travel agent will become unimportant in a world where everyone has access to travel related information and reservation sources through personal computers. Other experts say that the role of the travel agent will become more important and specialized as people have access to more data and less time to sort through this sea of information. Some people may use the information and reservation capacities provided through the

Table 4	Comparative Common Sized Income Statement Data*				
Year Ended	3/31/99	3/31/00	3/31/01	3/31/02	3/31/03
Net Sales	100.0%	100.0%	100.0%	100.0%	100.0%
Op. Exp.	98.2	97.3	97.0	98.7	99.5
Op. Profit	1.8	2.7	2.9	1.3	0.5
All Other Exp.	68.4	0.1	(0.3)	0.2	0.0
Profit Bef. Tax	(66.6)	2.6	3.2	1.1	0.5

* Although technically totals on common sized statements must equal 100%, rounding adjustments may result in slight internal variations. The percentages presented in these exhibits are as reported in Risk Management Association.[15]

Internet to book simple travel arrangements such as traveling from point A to point B. However, as travel needs become more complex and the management of business travel expenses becomes more important, the services of travel professionals may prove to be invaluable. Rapid technological changes and the need to possess detailed knowledge may force more and more travel agents to focus on one particular part of the industry such as cruises or business travel.

In the face of these real or perceived threats to continued profitability, travel agencies have taken several steps from searching for economies of scale and scope to embracing new technologies and implementing service fees. Will the role of the travel agent remain the same in a world that appears to be turning in ever-increasing numbers to an expanding array of Internet services and sites that allow users to not only book individual services, but also construct entire travel packages? You be the judge in this debate.

▮ ENDNOTES

1. Whitney, Daisy. (1998). "Travel Expenses Trimmed." *The Denver Post,* December 5, p. C8.
2. Airlines Reporting Corporation, 2004.
3. Cook, Roy A., Laura J. Yale, and Joseph J. Marqua. (2002). *Tourism: The Business of Travel,* Second Edition. Upper Saddle River, NJ: Prentice Hall.
4. McGee, William J. (1997). "Reshaping the Relationship." *Air Transport World,* 34(12), December: 57–59.
5. Upheaval in Travel Distribution: Impact on Consumers and Travel Agents. (2002). National Commission to Ensure Consumer Information and Choice in the Airline Industry. Report to Congress and the President.
6. Gebhart, Fred. (2002). "Consortiums: Commission Clubs No More." *Travel Weekly,* 61(42), October 21:81.
7. Gebhart, Fred. (2002). "Consortiums: Commission Clubs No More." *Travel Weekly,* 61(42), October 21:81.
8. "Agency Affiliations." (1998). *Travel Weekly,* 57(68), August 27: 88.
9. "Click to Fly." (2004). *Economist,* 371(8375), 8-9.
10. Pfenning, Art. (2004). "Have Internet Bookings Reached Their Pinnacle?" *Travel Weekly,* 63(2), January 12: 12.
11. http://www.cc.gatech.edu/gvu/user_surveys/survey-1998-10/graphs/graphs.html.
12. http://www.cc.gatech.edu/gvu/user_surveys/survey-1998-10/graphs/graphs/html.
13. Miller, Jeffrey. (2004). "Storefront or Internet?" *Travel Agent,* 316(10), May 10: 16.
14. RMA Annual Statement Studies 2001/2002 and 2003/2004, Philadelphia, PA: The Risk Management Association.
15. RMA Annual Statement Studies 2001/2002 and 2003/2004, Philadelphia, PA: The Risk Management Association.

PART 111

The Hospitality Environment

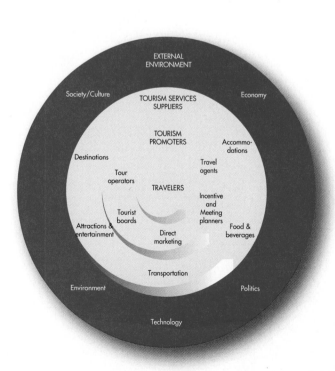

■ An integrated model of tourism.

LEARNING OBJECTIVES

After you have read this chapter, you should be able to:

- Identify and explain the economic benefits of tourism.
- Identify and explain the potential economic problems that can be created by tourism.
- Explain why tourism revenues are considered an export.
- Explain what is meant by the tourism multiplier concept.
- List the various organizations that help promote tourism.
- Explain how convention centers are used to generate tourism in a city and how these centers can be funded and managed.
- Explain the steps involved in tourism planning.
- Explain why tourism development can lead to political tugs of war.

CHAPTER OUTLINE

CHAPTER 11

Economic and Political Impacts of Tourism

Nobody goes there anymore; it's too crowded.

—Yogi Berra

■ Anchorage, Alaska welcomes the world.

CHAMBER DIRECTOR HEADACHE #1456

Maria Sandoval, Executive Director of the Ocotillo, Arizona, Chamber of Commerce, tossed two extra-strength pain relievers into her mouth and washed them down with the lukewarm remains of her second cup of coffee. This was a day she had been dreading. Today, six advertising agencies were making presentations to the Board of Directors of the Chamber of Commerce in attempts to receive the $450,000 annual contract for promoting Ocotillo as a tourism destination.

The selection of which six agencies (out of the 45 that had submitted written proposals) had been a political nightmare. Most citizens, businesspeople, and government officials agreed that tourism was an economic engine for the local economy and that the Chamber of Commerce, in its role as development leader, had an obligation to coordinate tourism promotion. However, many locals, including the editor of the *Ocotillo Times,* believed the promotion contract should be granted to a local advertising agency. Maria had received dozens of calls from irate citizens when they learned that four of the six finalist firms were from outside the Ocotillo area.

Maria sympathized with these dissenters. If the agency selection goal was to generate additional jobs, revenue, and tax dollars within the community, it would be easy to understand why folks would feel that local companies should receive the marketing business. But still, if the primary goal was to bring an increasing number of tourists to the region, and get them to stay longer in the area, shouldn't the most capable firm receive the contract, no matter where that firm was located?

Maria sighed and gathered up the proposals from the six finalist advertising agencies, placing them in her briefcase. It was going to be a long day and a tough decision. But that's why they pay me the big bucks, she chuckled, as she hurried off to the meeting.

INTRODUCTION

How important is tourism to your county or geographic area? What percentage of the jobs available in your city or town is in tourism-related businesses? How much tax revenue is raised through taxes paid by tourists on goods and services they purchase during their visits to your region? Whatever the answers to these questions, the worldwide economic impact of tourism is massive (see Table 11.1). "According to the World Tourism Organization, an important indicator of the role of international tourism is its generation of foreign exchange earnings. Tourism is one of the top five export categories for as many as 83 per cent of countries and is a main source of foreign exchange earning for at least 38 per cent of countries" (p. 2).[1]

International travelers are a large and growing segment of tourism consumers. Travel to

Table 11.1	Top Ten in International Tourism Receipts	
Rank	*Country*	*Billions (U.S. Dollars)*
1	United States	81,680
2	Spain	47,891
3	France	42,276
4	Italy	35,398
5	United Kingdom	30,669
6	China	29,296
7	Germany	29,204
8	Australia	16,866
9	Austria	15,467
10	Greece	13,731

Based on information provided by the World Tourism Organization (WTO), 2005. Available at: http://unwto.org/facts/eng/pdf/indicators/

international destinations has been growing at a rapid pace. However, the popularity of the United States as an international travel destination is interesting, because less money is spent per capita promoting tourism in the United States than in any other industrialized nation. According to tourism industry officials, the United States continues to fall in the top-of-mind awareness among international travelers as lawmakers fail to allocate marketing dollars to attract these visitors.[2] As might be expected, the largest number of visitors to the United States come from its neighbors to the north, Canada, and the south, Mexico. These countries are followed in numbers of visitors by Japan, Great Britain, Germany, France, and Italy. As can be seen in Table 11.2, Europe is the major international destination region. Even though the United States is a major international destination, citizens of the United States travel less internationally than their counterparts in other industrialized countries.

As we pointed out in Chapter 1, there are several factors that can influence the level of tourism activity. The current growth and importance of travel into Canada and the United States by foreign visitors, especially Asians and Europeans, help to highlight several of these factors. First, disposable income continues to rise in these industrialized countries. Second, European workers have longer vacation periods than their American counterparts, usually five weeks. Asian workers are now beginning to have more leisure time and disposable income. Third, these travelers are seeking new adventures away from their traditional vacation spots. Fourth, international airfares have become very

competitive and are enticing increasing numbers of travelers to head to Canada and the United States.[3] Bring all of these factors together and international tourism receipts in the United States are expected to almost triple between 2000 and 2020.[4]

These same factors are important for other developed and developing countries and should be considered as plans are made for attracting or maintaining visitors. The level of disposable income, available leisure time, destination attractiveness, relative travel costs, and local exchange rates should be kept in mind as countries seek to attract even more individuals to participate in international travel and tourism activities. According to the World Tourism Organization, the number of tourist arrivals is projected to grow on every continent and reach a total of 1.6 billion by the year 2020 (Table 11.2).[5]

How do researchers arrive at these estimates of tourism activity? They typically take two steps. First, they estimate the number of "arrivals" at a destination (a city, a state/province, a country). Second, they estimate average expenditures per visitor by surveying samples of travelers or through estimates based on hotel and other tourism-related taxes. Then they multiply these two estimates together to arrive at a total amount of tourism spending in the specific destination. You will find that tourism activity estimates vary widely owing to the differences in the methods used to approximate the number of travelers and their expenses, as well as the different definitions used to determine just who is a tourist. Some agencies define tourists as individuals who travel more than 50 miles away from home, whereas other

Table 11.2		International Tourist Arrivals		
Rank		*Country*	*In Millions*	*Market Share*
1		France	75.1	9.8%
2		Spain	52.4	6.9%
3		United States	46.1	6.0%
4		China	41.8	5.5%
5		Italy	37.1	4.9%

Source: World Tourism Organization (2005). Available at: http://unwto.org/facts/eng/pdf/indicators/ITA_top25

agencies may use 100 or even 200 miles. Some require that the person stay overnight at his or her destination, whereas others do not. So, when you see statistics like those cited in Tables 11.1 and 11.2, realize that other numbers might be quoted from other sources of information, with the difference in the numbers depending on the different methods and definitions used.

LOOKING TO TOURISM FOR ECONOMIC GROWTH AND VITALITY

The people of every country around the world survive or thrive on the income-producing possibilities of the country's resources. Citizens all over the world need income to provide the necessities of life for themselves and their families. Income options may range from subsistence farming to investment banking. More and more countries are finding that the development of tourism offers an effective means of increasing economic well-being. Debate over the appropriate level of tourism development for an area results in political action by individuals, special-interest groups, and governing officials and bodies. In this chapter, we begin by discussing why and how tourism activities affect the economic vitality of a region. Then, we look at some of the many ways that politics comes into play to affect and shape the tourism industry.

Economics is the "social science that seeks to understand the choices people make in using their scarce resources to meet their wants" (p. 27).[6] For tourists, these scarce resources are money, available time, and the physical energy to travel. A small amount of any of these three resources will decrease tourists' ability to travel, whereas a large amount of these three resources will increase tourists' ability to travel. Scarce resources for promoters and suppliers of tourism businesses are human resources (the availability and quality of tourism service employees) and **financial resources** (the amount of money that the developer can raise by borrowing money or by selling stock). Scarce resources

New Orleans

City officials in New Orleans use an unusual measure to determine the success of the annual Mardi Gras festival. They look at the additional tons of garbage collected during the weeklong festivities to estimate the number of visitors to the city!

for communities or countries are the amount and variety of their natural resources and the pool of human resources available at differing skill levels. Scarce resources for governments are primarily tax revenues that can be used (1) to develop natural and human resources productively and (2) to pay for the many services that governments can provide their citizens.

Comparative Advantage

Many towns and cities, states/provinces, even entire nations, have determined that development of their visitor-inducing resources can add to the economic well-being of local residents. Economic decisions are often based on a concept called **comparative advantage.** Tourism can be said to have a comparative advantage over other industries if it yields a better return from the region's human and natural resource inputs than another industry would. Leaders of many communities believe this comparative advantage exists because of the many economic, social, and environmental benefits tourism offers. Let's take a closer look at how comparative advantage might favor tourism development.

Tourism may have a comparative advantage over other industries in two ways. First, the region may be especially appealing to tourists because (1) it has features that are highly attractive, (2) it may be easily accessible to many potential tourists, and (3) it has the necessary **infrastructure** and an abundant labor force to serve in the tourism industry. In other words, the area may have the necessary ingredients for both the demand and the supply of tourism.

Second, tourism, may also be the best industry to develop if there are no other alternatives. For example, many island economies are based on tourism because these small nations have little else of economic value to offer the world. Its citizens, therefore, are best able to achieve a better standard of living through employment in tourism businesses. Owing to very limited natural resources (other than beauty), the islanders have few, if any, industrial alternatives. So, tourism has the comparative advantage because the island country is at a comparative disadvantage for all other industries.

Tourism and Foreign Exchange Rates

One of the most important factors influencing the level of international tourism to a country is the relative **exchange rate** of its currency for other currencies. When international travelers decide to visit a foreign land, they need to trade their currency for the currency of the nation they will visit. For example, if a U.S. citizen were to take a trip to Spain, he or she would need to trade U.S. dollars for the euro. A Spanish traveler would do just the reverse if he decided to visit the United States.

Most currency exchange rates vary daily depending on the supply and demand for each currency. The exchange rate of a nation's currency greatly affects the amount of international tourism that a country will experience. For example, during the last part of this decade, the United States has been a very reasonably priced destination for European travelers as the dollar has fallen in value, whereas travel to Europe has become a more expensive destination for United States travelers to visit as the euro and the pound have risen in value.

The power of a single currency, such as the euro, can have tremendous impact on tourism expenditures. Three of the five most popular international destinations now use the euro as a common currency. With 27 member states and more wanting to join, the European Union is the world's largest trading power; and with border crossings now easier for both Europeans and non-Europeans alike, tourism is thriving.

■ THE MULTIPLIER CONCEPT

Why are tourism expenditures important to an area? And just how big a benefit do they have? One of the most common ideas of the economic impact of tourism is called the **multiplier concept.** Money is added to an area when someone from outside its borders buys a good or service produced within the area. In addition, this new money to the area is re-spent, generating additional value. Tourism is usually a very good source of new money for an area because visitors travel to the area and "leave" their money behind as they buy goods and services during their visit.

Realizing Tourism's Export Potential

Let us first focus on the multiplier concept of tourism expenditures from an **export** point of view. An export is defined as a good or service manufactured or provided in one country that is purchased by a person or business from another country. Exports therefore "add" money to one economy and "deduct" money from another economy. Most countries desire international visitors because tourism services sold to foreign travelers are considered exports.

For example, when an Irish businessman travels to Toronto and spends money on restaurant meals, taxicabs, and hotel rooms, some of the money and purchasing power he earned in Ireland becomes part of Canada's economy. In this way, the tourism receipts from his visit add to the Canadian economy the same way that selling a Canadian manufactured good in Dublin would. Likewise, his tourism expenses represent an **import** in Ireland the same way that a manufactured good does because the traveler's money left Ireland and was gained by Canada.

Here is a more detailed example of a tourism export. Imagine that an Australian family decides to vacation in California, taking in all the entertainment attractions and recreational activities that it has to offer. They arrive at LAX airport and then spend seven fun-and-sun-filled days experiencing southern California. Think of all the expenses they incur during their weeklong visit: meals, rental car and gasoline, admissions, souvenirs, accommodations, and a host of other services. The family pays for all these services and goods by spending the money they brought with them from Australia to cover all these expenses. This money represents "new" money for the U.S. economy and for California in particular. This exchange is an export for the United States and represents an import for Australia because the family purchased foreign goods and services with their Australian money rather than spending their money at home.

What Goes Around Comes Around

The multiplier concept also applies to domestic travel. Imagine you have a friend, Sam, who goes to college and works in Bloomington, Indiana. Sam decides to spend spring break vacation in Fort Lauderdale, Florida. She takes her hard-earned money and "leaves" it in Florida as she pays for her travel needs there. In other words, the purchasing power Sam earned in the Bloomington economy is transferred to the economy of Fort Lauderdale, and the businesses and citizens there benefit from it (see Figure 11.1).

But how does this money "multiply"? The multiplier effect occurs when some of this new money is re-spent within the local economy. For example, while in Fort Lauderdale, Sam had dinner at a local hot spot, dining, dancing, and having a wonderful evening. Her total bill for the evening of fun came to $85. The lion's share of the $85 she paid was then used to pay Joe, her server, as well as the bartender, the dishwasher, the city's local taxes (sales, property, and income), the manager's salary, the local bakery for that delicious bread—you get the idea. In this way, the purchasing power of Sam's $85 is multiplied because it then becomes Joe's purchasing power, which he can use to purchase goods and services he needs. When Joe spends "Sam's share" of his paycheck on a haircut, Sam's purchasing power multiplies again and now becomes purchasing power to be used by the hairdresser. And so on.

However, all of that new purchasing power that has been added to the Fort Lauderdale economy does not stay in the local economy forever because of **leakage.** Just as Sam took some of her purchasing power from Bloomington to Fort Lauderdale, that purchasing power will eventually leak out of the Fort Lauderdale area. For example, Joe's hairdresser could purchase gasoline for her car. Relatively little of the money she pays for gasoline gets to stay in the local economy, because the gas station owner needs to purchase gasoline made from oil from another country. The purchase of this import causes the purchasing power to "leak" out of the Fort Lauderdale economy, so it is no longer available for locals to use within the area. The faster the leakage, the lower the output multiplier concept.

Economists derive multiplier values for a number of important economic variables:

1. Income
2. Employment
3. Output or sales or transactions
4. Government revenue (taxes)
5. Imports[7]

The multiplier effect is the sum of three levels of impact created by tourism purchases. These effects are called *direct, indirect,* and *induced* effects. Together they create the total multiplier impact on the area. Direct effects, also called first-round effects, come directly from tourist spending, such as the increase in the number of employees and the amount of wages paid to restaurant employees owing to tourist eating/drinking at the restaurant.

Indirect effects, also called secondary effects, are created from the increase in purchases by tourism suppliers to serve tourist needs, such as the increase in food and beverages purchased from suppliers by a restaurant. Suppliers in turn will need to increase their purchases and so on. These "ripple effects" are all indirect effects from tourism expenditures.

Induced effects are other increases in economic activity, employment, taxes, and so on generated within the area's economy at large owing to the existence of tourism. For example, the community will see higher expenditures on health care because of the increased number of residents drawn to the area for employment in the tourism industry.[8]

1. Sam leaves her home in Bloomington, IN, with $500 dollars. She is going to Fort Lauderdale, FL, for spring break.

2. Sam pays way too much for a lobster tail at an expensive restaurant on the intercoastal waterway. But what the heck – she's on vacation. Sam's waiter Joe goes the extra mile for her, recommending a few great night spots and even draws Sam a walking map. Sam is so grateful she tips Joe $25.

3. Joe worked 7 days a week for the past 3 weeks. He hasn't had time to get a haircut, do his laundry, or even visit the bank. He decides to go see his hairdresser Sarah and get a haircut – $25 with tip.

4. "Good thing Joe came in today," Sarah thinks. "His $10 tip was the only tip of the day. I've got to start cutting a better class of hair." Sarah looks down as she is driving and notices she's almost out of gas. She pulls over and puts the $10 in her tank.

5. The owner of the gas station lets out a sigh of relief as Sarah pays him. He was just shy $10 to cover his payroll deposit – he can go to the bank now and then go home and relax for the rest of the weekend.

And the [money] continues to move through the economy increasing the multiplier effect.

■ **Figure 11.1**   Multiplier concept.

Tracking the Impact of Tourism Expenditures

How big or small can this multiplier concept be? Tourism researchers and economists have tried to estimate the tourism multiplier concept for countries, regions, and even cities. For example,

Adrian Bull reported that the tourism multiplier concept for Canada is approximately 2.5: For every new dollar injected into the Canadian economy from an international visitor, $2.50 of purchasing power is generated over time before that original dollar is leaked out through expenditures on imports coming into Canada.[9]

Multipliers are an indicator of the economic independence of a country. The higher the multiplier, the more economically self-sufficient the country. Some countries such as Ireland, Turkey, the United Kingdom, and the United States have multiplier factors of approximately 2 or more. Other countries experience much lower multiplier concepts, for example, 0.64 for Iceland and 0.39 for Western Samoa.[10] Although island countries tend to depend on tourism for economic growth, they also have very quick leakage and, therefore, very low output multipliers, because almost all goods associated with tourism need to be imported to the area. These imports may be as simple as the food and beverages served to visitors or as complex and costly as the steel to build the hotels.

Determining tourism's impact on an area's economy is not an easy task. It takes a great deal of information collection and highly skilled researchers to undertake the process. To learn more about tourism research in general and economic impact analysis (EIA) specifically, turn to Appendix B.

■ OTHER ECONOMIC IMPACTS

In addition to the multiplier concept, tourism offers other positive economic benefits. First, tourism can provide stability in an economy. Although recessions affect virtually all industries, tourism historically has seen relatively minor declines in revenue during recessionary times. As we mentioned in Chapter 2, business travel remains relatively constant during changes in economic cycles; and even though people may cut back on the amount they spend on travel during harder economic times, citizens of most industrial nations have come to view vacationing as a necessity of life.

Second, tourism provides economic diversity. A stable economy is one that provides jobs and revenues from a variety of industries. Tourism can be added as another economic engine to the industry mix. Obviously, the addition of any industry to a community will increase the employment opportunities of that community. However, unlike many other industries, tourism provides a wide variety of job possibilities, such as:

1. Entry-level employment for relatively unskilled and semiskilled workers
2. Positions for highly skilled craftspersons, such as chefs and artists
3. Many professional-level career opportunities for well-educated decision makers

Third, tourism often provides the economic incentive to improve infrastructure that can be enjoyed by residents as well as tourists. For example, state-of-the-art airports are built by communities primarily to increase accessibility, thereby enticing more visitors and increasing business activity; but the airport can also be used by locals to meet their travel needs.

Tourism offers a fourth additional positive impact that you may find particularly appealing. Unlike most manufacturing-based enterprises, a tourism business can be started in the form of a small business. In this way, the tourism industry can be used to encourage **entrepreneurial** activity. Have you ever considered developing your own business? Many people today like the idea and challenge of being their own boss. Tourism provides plenty of chances for creative, motivated individuals to start their own businesses. Small retail shops, restaurants, bed-and-breakfast

NYC Walking Tours

Tourism can offer the opportunity to make income from a personal interest or special skill. For example, two Columbia University graduate students developed a business based on their love of urban history. Seth Kamil and Ed O'Donnell started Big Onion Walking Tours in New York City to earn income to pay for school expenses. Seth's major in urban and ethnic history has really paid off. The company now has a staff of guides with advanced degrees in American history and related fields. Columbia, CUNY, and Stratford have joined forces with the New York Historical Society to provide guests with the best from these licensed guides.

homes, and guide and taxi services are just a few of the many tourism-related small business opportunities.

So, tourism has many economic benefits but, unfortunately, the development of tourism is not without drawbacks. Up to this point, we have been looking at the economics of tourism through rose-colored glasses. Next we will consider some of the not-so-positive economic effects tourism can yield.

Potential Problems in Tourism-Based Economies

Like all industries, tourism has the potential for negative as well as positive impacts. Overdependence on tourism can lead to a dangerous lack of economic diversity, so that a major event affecting tourism can threaten an area's economy. Tourism revenues can be quickly and severely diminished by a variety of crisis events. Five of the most common and influential types of crises are:

1. International war or conflict
2. Acts of terrorism, especially those involving tourists
3. A major criminal act or crime wave, especially against tourists
4. A natural disaster that causes substantial damage to natural resources or tourism infra- or superstructure
5. Epidemics of diseases that are highly contagious[11]

In recent years, countries and regions around the globe have felt the economic pain associated with one or more of these events. In 2001, Great Britain suffered a substantial decline in tourist volume when foot-and-mouth disease was discovered on British farms. The British government restricted access to many rural areas, including tourist sites, and the media intensely covered moves made to control the spread of the disease. The head of the British Tourist Authority estimated that international tourism to Great Britain dropped by 22% owing to the disease outbreak.[12]

Even mild winters and health warnings can have harmful effects on economies supported by tourism. In North America, the winter of 1999–2000 started off as one of the mildest in history with snow totals only half of normal by the Christmas vacation period. Towns throughout North America that depend on holiday-skier dollars saw tourism service suppliers slashing prices to try to entice skiers and salvage the season.[13] The outbreak of severe acute respiratory syndrome (SARS) in 2003 brought tourism traffic in Canada and throughout all of Southeast Asia to a screeching halt. In the summer of 2004, forest fires in Alaska darkened its skies and caused air quality warnings to be issued, which kept tourists away during the state's high season.[14] Wars, weather, disease, and political unrest continue to pose challenges for the tourism industry.

The Caribbean islands are suffering now more than ever because of their tourism-only-based economies. When the cruise industry began to flourish, cruise ships brought thousands of eager spenders to the islands and boosted the economy. However, the trend in the cruise business now is to provide more onboard shopping and recreational opportunities. For example, although cruise passengers to the U.S. Virgin Islands represent 80% of all visitors, they generate only 25% of tourist revenue. Many cruise lines, such as Holland America Cruise Line and the Disney Cruise Line, have even acquired their own private islands where their guests can play. Because these islands are owned by the cruise lines, no local island economy gains much benefit from tourism revenues generated on them. Finally, terrorism and the threat of terrorism can wipe out tourism demand. Witness the devastating impacts that the September 11, 2001, terrorist attacks on New York City and Washington, D.C., had on the United States and, indeed, the whole world. Similar devastation of the Indonesian tourism economy occurred after the October 12, 2002, terrorist bombings in Bali, a country that relies on tourism for half its income.

The terrorist attacks on the United States in September 2001 have had the largest and widest effect on tourism since its mass development in the 1950s. The U.S. tourism market was estimated to have declined by 25% at the end of 2001. However, the global impact of these attacks is what sets them apart from previous terrorist actions. Virtually all the world's airlines saw double-digit declines in passenger numbers, which resulted in the worldwide loss of hundreds of thousands, even millions, of jobs in all sectors of the tourism industry and its supplier industries, such as aircraft manufacture.[15] The good news is that, in the aftermath of these attacks, tourism has proven its resilience, and both the number of travelers and the amounts spent on tourism activities haves exceeded pre-2001 levels.

Tourism can also highlight too much of a good thing and bring too many visitors to an area. By showcasing the beauty and other tourism resources of an area, tourism marketers can increase the popularity of the area and bring in many more people interested in playing and living there. This increase in demand frequently leads to increased prices for goods and services as well as higher housing and land values. Occasionally, this problem becomes so severe that workers can no longer afford to live near their work. Such an impact has occurred in the beautiful central California beach towns and many mountain towns of the Rocky Mountain states and provinces.

Large increases in the number of tourists to an area usually increase costs of providing services for both the increased number of tourists and the increased number of residents. Services such as police and fire protection can be strained by the numbers of visitors, and school systems can be strained by new residents who decide to move to their favorite travel destination. Utilities, and other infrastructure resources such as roads, can also feel the strain from increases in the numbers of visitors and residents and the development required to serve their needs.

Tourism in the Economic Balance

Determining whether the total economic impact of tourism will be positive or negative is not an easy task. Many decision makers are turning to **cost–benefit analysis** for help. In cost–benefit analysis, dollar values are assigned to the benefits of tourism (such as increased tax revenues and increased employment opportunities) as well as the costs associated with tourism (such

as the increased need for utilities, schools, and police protection). If the value of the positive impacts (the benefits) is greater than the value of the negative impacts (the costs), the total economic impact of tourism is positive. If the costs are larger than the benefits, then tourism may not be the economic engine it is often believed to be. Recently, to be as thorough as possible, decision makers have tried to quantify difficult-to-value pluses and minuses (such as increased entertainment options for residents and increased crowding and traffic jams) to include these benefits and costs in the equation.[16]

So, as you can see, tourism can have both positive and negative economic impacts. How, then, are tourism development decisions made and who is involved in the decision-making process? In the next section, we will look at how governments and citizens try to make choices concerning the development and growth of tourism.

■ | TOURISM AND POLITICS

Remember, economics is all about decisions concerning scarce resources. Politics is about how decisions concerning the public are made. In a democratic society, economic decisions that can affect large groups of people are likely to involve some political process. An easy way to define politics is "[P]olitics is about power, who gets what, where, how, and why."[17] So, politics is about decision making: how decisions are made, who is involved in the process, and how decisions are implemented. The politics of tourism is usually about how decisions concerning use of scarce resources are made. In a way, economics is about the *quantity of life,* whereas politics involves debates over the *quality of life.*

Often, decision making about promoting and developing tourism does not happen through a rational decision-making process in which all interested parties have a chance to voice their opinions or vote for their favorite alternatives. Frequently, the most influential "players" in tourism are outsiders—developers from other areas, even other countries, who see profit opportunities from developing tourism-related businesses. Development of tourism in an area frequently leads to heated political debates over the benefits and costs of tourism, creating political tugs of war among constituent groups (covered later in the chapter).

The Role of Government in Tourism

Governments, from the local to the national level, can and often do play an important role in tourism development. Why do governments devote scarce funds to the promotion and development of tourism? As we discussed in the first half of the chapter, tourism can provide many economic benefits. First, a wide variety of jobs are created through the development of the hotels, restaurants, retail shops, and other facilities and services required to satisfy the needs of travelers. Second, additional jobs are generated to serve the needs of the employees of the tourism industry. These jobholders earn wages that, in turn, are re-spent in the local economy, creating the multiplier concept. Third, and maybe most important from a government perspective, revenues are boosted by taxing the goods and services that visitors buy. Taxing visitors shifts a portion of the tax burden from local residents to tourists (see Table 11.3). As can be seen in this table, auto rental companies have

become especially concerned about what they consider to be "hidden taxes," because cities, counties, and states have frequently added additional taxes to rental agreements to fund projects from building major league stadiums to subsidizing operating budgets.

For example, the small country of Monaco receives virtually all of its tax revenues from taxes paid by tourists, primarily through Monaco's famous gaming casinos.[18] Communities and other governmental units commonly tax hotel rooms, restaurant meals, and gasoline, and often add **passenger facility charges** on departing flights from the local airport. These tax revenues can then be used to further develop and promote tourism or, as is common, to improve the quality of life by funding services for local citizens.

Green Bay

Did you know that the citizens of Green Bay, Wisconsin, own the National Football League team the Green Bay Packers? Unlike so many other teams, the Packers won't be leaving their city for greener pastures!

Table 11.3	Examples of Tourism-Related Taxes					
					Auto Rental	
City	Hotel/ Lodging Tax	Restaurant Tax	Gasoline Tax per Gallon	Base Tax Rate	Dollar Surcharge	Off Airport Fees
Baltimore	12.50%	5.00%	$0.374	11.50%		
Chicago	14.90%	9.75%	$0.484	18.00%	$2.75/rental	
Houston	17.0%	8.25%	$0.384	15.00%	$1.12	8.15%
San Francisco	14.00%	8.50%	$0.450	8.65%	$1.95	7.00%
New York	13.25%	8.25%	$0.413	13.25%		
Miami	12.50%	8.50%	$0.476	6.9%	$2.05/day	9.00%
Seattle	15.6%	8.20%	$0.414	18.3%	6.9%	10.00%
Washington, D.C.	13.00%	10.00%	$0.384	8.0%	$2.00/day	10.00%

Note: Although many in the tourism industry believe these tax revenues should be used for travel/tourism programs, much of it goes directly to the general fund or to programs unrelated to travel. Airline taxes collected from travelers are significant revenue sources for the federal government. Consumers pay a 10% federal air ticket tax on each airline ticket sold in the United States. Additionally, many airports impose a passenger facility charge (PFC).

National and state/provincial governments can support tourism development by performing many activities. These can include the collection of tourism information, regulation of tourism-related businesses such as airlines, international promotion of tourism, encouragement of development of tourist areas (especially by funding infrastructure or providing government-backed loans), and development of tourism **policy**. In a bid to reshape its economy, the government of Taiwan is shifting its development effects away from manufacturing to tourism. Its "Challenge 2008" plan, backed by $75 billion in financing, is designed to double the number of tourists visiting the country.[19]

In some countries, the national government actually takes part in the tourism industry through government ownership of certain businesses such as hotel chains, tour companies, and airlines. In the United States and Canada, government agencies are an integral part of the management of a valuable tourism resource—the national park systems. However, more and more national governments are getting out of the tourism businesses through **privatization** and limiting their roles to tourism promotion and regulation. For example, in the mid-1980s, the government of New Zealand owned hotels, tour companies, and the national airline. Since then, the New Zealand government has privatized virtually all of these tourism enterprises.

Governments can also aid tourism development by financing necessary infrastructure such as roads and airports and by offering government-backed low-interest loans to private developers who develop **superstructure** facilities. For example, travelers are often surprised to learn that they must pay a departure tax in many locations to fund airport operations and improvements. In other instances, many local governments, aided through state funds, have attempted to revitalize inner-city areas and turn them into leisure, entertainment, and shopping meccas. Local governments can also sponsor "hallmark tourist events" such as the Super Bowl or a World's Fair to generate increased visits and gain publicity for the region that can pay off in the future.

Think of the international awareness that is gained by cities and countries when they host Olympic Games! A primary goal of the Chinese government in hosting the 2008 Summer Games was to showcase China and its people and resources to encourage tourism and investment in China in the coming decades.

Tourism in Action

Tourism Policy

Although by no means universal, some governments (national, state/provincial, or local) formulate a **tourism policy** to aid in guiding the development of a sustainable tourism industry in their jurisdiction. A formal statement of tourism policy serves as a "master plan" that lists the parameters for development and stewardship of tourism resources within the region. Specifically, a tourism policy has the following features:

■ It is written at the macro level and offers a long-term perspective.

■ It delineates the critical resources needed to develop and sustain tourism in the area.

■ It explains the relationship of tourism components to the greater societal and economic systems of the region.

■ It outlines the information inputs that will be needed for decision making.

The tourism policy should provide a **destination vision**, which is defined as an "inspirational portrait of the ideal future that the destination hopes to bring about in some defined future (usually 5, 10, 20 or 50 years)" (p. 154). From this vision, tourism decision makers can formulate a destination image to strive for, both by developing resources and via marketing efforts.

Source: Ritchie, J. R. Brent, and Crouch, Geoffrey I. (2003). *The competitive destination.* Cambridge, MA: CABI Publishing.

Tourism Promotion Agencies

Many governments have an agency that is charged with promoting tourism. At the national level, this agency is called a "national tourism organization/office," or the NTO. National and state/provincial governments fund such offices to fulfill two primary functions. First, the government agency collects visitor and industry information that can be used by tourism businesses to become more successful and grow, employing more citizens and generating more tax revenues. Visitor information is often gathered at welcome centers run by states, provinces, cities, and towns. Second, government agencies promote entire areas as destinations. Tourism businesspeople are usually unable or unwilling to fund advertising that does not expressly sell their individual businesses. But we know that tourists are first sold on a destination area and then look to buy specific services to fulfill particular travel needs, such as hotel accommodations, restaurant meals, guide services, and so forth. So, national and state/provincial governments engage in destination marketing to generate sizable numbers of tourists. Individual tourism-related businesses are rarely able to afford ad campaigns large enough to create a distinctive destination image.

Destination image is simply the detailed impression an individual or target segment has of a specific destination. This impression is composed of three parts. The first, called *cognition*, is the sum of all that the potential traveler knows and believes about the destination. These bits of information and beliefs may be from past experience with the destination or may have been acquired through a variety of information sources, from word of mouth from friends to magazine articles to movie settings. The second part of the destination image impression, called *affect*, represents the consumer's feelings—favorable, unfavorable, or neutral—about the destination. From these two components of impression comes the third, called *conation*. Conation is the likelihood of the potential traveler to visit the destination in the near future.[20]

Closely related to destination image is the concept of a destination's position. Whereas a destination's image can be described by itself, a destination's position relates the image of one destination to those of its competitors. So, destination positioning is all relative. Through consumer research on the amount of important attributes that make up a destination's image and then "mapping" of a destination with its likely competitors, decision makers can see how their destination "stacks up." Destination positioning is a strategic tool used to "reinforce positive images, correct negative images, or create a new image" for a destination (p. 334).[21] Once the position is determined, an ideal position can be decided and then tactics can be developed to move the destination's image to the new, improved position.

PUBLIC/PRIVATE ORGANIZATIONS

Decisions concerning tourism promotion are complicated and raise many questions. Should more be spent on leisure travelers, or should the bulk of funds be spent trying to attract conferences and other meetings to the area? Should a mass-marketing strategy be used, trying to attract any and all comers to the area, or should segmentation and targeting be used to attract a specific group? In addition, organizations need to determine how much money should be spent on attracting tourists from their own region, from outside their region, and from outside the country.

A common way for tourism promotion and development decisions to be made and funded is through **public/private organizations** or partnerships. A public/private partnership is an organization whose members include government officials as well as private citizens. A tourism-related public/private organization usually has a membership composed of local or state government officials, tourism business owners and managers, and local citizens. These partnerships are being used more and more to fund the promotion and development of tourism. Often, the government partner funds infrastructure improvements; the private enterprise partners fund the superstructure (often with the help of tax incentives); and then together the government and private business partners fund tourism promotion through contributions and the collection of special tourism-related taxes, such as a room tax.[22]

Chambers of Commerce and Convention and Visitors Bureaus

Two common examples of local public/private tourism promotion organizations are chambers of commerce and **convention and visitors bureaus.** As suggested in the chapter opener, in smaller communities, chambers of commerce often perform the tourism promotion role (as well as many other economic and business developmental roles). Frequently, as communities grow, the tourism promotion role is conducted through a special organization called a convention and visitors bureau. In very large cities, Chicago, for example, responsibility for attracting tourists is further divided. Promotion to leisure travelers rests with the Chicago Office of Tourism, whereas attracting professional travelers is the concern of the Chicago Convention and Tourism Bureau. A priority of all of these types of organizations is literally to put their area on the map by educating prospective visitors and meeting planners about the destination.

Convention Centers

Convention centers are also frequently public/private organizations. An increasing number of cities worldwide have been developing and renovating convention center facilities to attract the professional traveler segment of tourism. As you learned in Chapter 2, a major portion of the professional traveler segment involves meetings. This "meetings" market is composed of two subsegments: conventions and trade shows. Convention centers are designed to serve the special needs of conventions and trade shows, and range from tiny facilities that are little more than a single large room to immense complexes that can hold tens of thousands of conventioneers (see Figure 11.2).

Cities continue to engage in a "space race" with more and more cities expanding or building centers, trying to edge each other out to be the biggest and newest. Nowhere is this growth more evident than in China, where there was only one large convention center in 1992 with 50,000 square meters of space (538,196 square feet), but by 2003, there were 16 with 1,288,000 square meters of space (13,863,917 square feet).[23] Beijing and Shanghai now boast convention centers of 220,000 and 364,000 square meters (2,368,000 and 3,918,063 square feet), respectively.[24] The reason for this convention center building frenzy? Lots of revenues and some bragging rights too! See Table 11.4 for a sample of other large convention facilities.

Marketing to attract convention and trade show business is very different from efforts used to entice leisure travelers. Single decision makers or, more commonly, a small committee of decision makers, decides where to locate their group's convention, meeting, or trade show. This decision process usually begins years before the event takes place, requiring the coordination of many tourism-related businesses in developing a proposal presented to the site selection committee. Key determinants for these site decisions are price, size, and quality of facilities, and a wide variety of amenities or add-ons that will likely encourage prospective attendees to sign up for the convention or trade show. Convention centers need a staff of knowledgeable and efficient people to sell the center and ensure that conventioneers/trade show participants are satisfied with their experience and will return in some future year.

Convention centers are funded and managed in a variety of ways. Some are funded and managed by local governments. Some are public/private **joint ventures,** whereas others are completely financed and managed as nonprofit private associations of tourism-related businesses. Often, the convention center facilities are built with public money, usually a combination of city and state funds. The annual marketing and operating costs are covered through tourism-related taxes, membership fees, and revenues generated directly from services provided at the center and sold to attendees. But most centers lose money.

■ TOURISM PLANNING

Another major function of government and **nonprofit tourism associations** is **tourism planning.** Planning involves predicting the future, setting **objectives** to attain future outcomes, and then outlining and implementing the actions

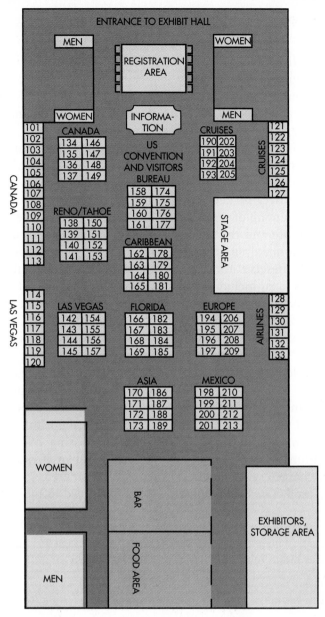

All booths are 10'x12' and all aisles are at least 10' wide
Booths =

■ **Figure 11.2** Example of a trade show layout.

Table 11.4	A Sample of Large Convention Facilities	
Site/Location		Total Meeting/Exhibition Space (in millions of square feet)
Las Vegas Convention Center, Las Vegas, NV		3.2
McCormick Place, Chicago, IL (2008)		3.1
Georgia World Congress Center, Atlanta, GA		2.9
Beijing International Convention Center, Beijing, China		2.3
Orange County Convention Center, Orlando, FL		2.1
The Venetian, Las Vegas, NV		1.9
Berlin Exhibition Grounds, Berlin, Germany		1.7
Metro Toronto Convention Centre, Toronto, Ontario		0.6

Space estimates approximated from information obtained from the website of each convention center.

needed to attain these objectives. You now realize that tourism is a conglomeration of many industries and needs the coordination of a wide variety of enterprises and agencies to thrive. However, because so many organizations are involved in the industry, planning is not easy.

Tourism planning is a continuous process and involves many steps to develop and sustain tourism revenues. A wide variety of decisions must be made, including the timing of development, size of the infrastructure and the superstructure, targeting of promotional campaigns, and efforts to enhance and preserve attraction resources. In addition, plans must include studies of the increased burdens on resources such as water, roads, and police and fire protection, and how the strains on these resources can be met or minimized. Table 11.5 provides a list of the steps that must be included in a comprehensive tourism plan.

Usually, tourism planning rests with a government agency, typically at the state/provincial and local levels, although many countries have strong national organizations as well. Government agencies are often charged with conducting research and making predictions concerning

likely tourism industry trends. Based on research results, plans can be drawn up to achieve the desired level of tourism activity to maximize benefits and minimize the costs that can occur.

A tourism planning organization, whether at the national, state/provincial, or local level, needs to modify and refine its plan continually. First, research to learn the changing trends in market segments needs to be conducted regularly, along with studying emerging economic impacts of tourism (both positive and negative). Second, planners must constantly gain and enhance the cooperation of the industry sectors to ensure effective promotion and delivery of high-quality tourism services to visitors. Third, planners need to determine whether changes in priorities for tourism marketing are needed. For example, research may show that the area has successfully developed the domestic tourism market and now should start developing international promotion campaigns; or maybe the idea of hosting a hallmark event, such as a World's Fair or Olympic Games, should be seriously considered. Last, but certainly not least, planners need to monitor and preserve the very

Table 11.5	Phases in the Tourism Policy and Planning Process

Phase 1 Definitional phase
Definition of the tourism destination system (geographical boundaries and the stakeholder groups and their relationships)
Specification of the tourism destination philosophy (the values to be followed)
Crafting of a destination vision
Specification of objectives and constraints

Phase 2 Analytical phase
Internal analysis (review of existing policies and programs, resources)
External analysis (analysis of current and future demand, competition, and promotion)

Phase 3 Operational phase
Strategy determination
Predictions regarding future demand and competitive environment
Policy and program recommendations

Phase 4 Implementation phase
Strategy for development, promotion, and stewardship
Assignment of responsibilities for tactical implementation
Identification of funding sources
Specification of timing of tactics

Adapted from Ritchie, J. R. Brent, and Crouch, Geoffrey I. (2003). *The competitive destination*. Cambridge, MA: CABI Publishing.

resources that attracted visitors in the first place. Often, these resources are fragile natural or heritage sites, so plans must include ways to protect them from erosion and harm so that they are preserved for future enjoyment.

A fine example of tourism planning is the Banff National Park Management Plan. The plan started with a vision statement that provided direction for the preparation of a detailed plan that will guide decision making about development and operations in the Canadian park for the foreseeable future.[25]

POLITICAL "TUGS OF WAR" OVER TOURISM

Under "Tourism and Politics," we defined politics as power and about who gets what. Whenever a finite amount of resources, especially financial resources, needs to be allocated, there will always be tugs of war among providers and users of these resources. In politics, groups with common needs or wants are called **constituent groups**. In the world of tourism, these constituent groups include:

- Tourism business owners
- Employees of tourism businesses
- Other business owners/managers/employees
- Government officials
- Government employees
- Taxpayers
- Local community/region citizens
- Tourists

Each of these constituent groups has its own set of priorities concerning how resources, especially tax dollars, should be used. In addition, these groups also have differences in opinion concerning issues such as the quality of life. For example, some people believe jobs and higher incomes (quantity of life) are the basis for attaining quality of life for citizens, whereas others believe environmental and cultural aspects are equally or even more important.

Tourism business owners want the number of tourists traveling to their area to increase so that their investments generate more income and profits. Employees of these businesses want secure employment with fair wages and safe working conditions. Business owners, managers, and employees in other industries want the continued growth and success of their businesses. Government officials want strong economies and to be reelected, whereas government employees want job security and good wages. Taxpayers want a wide variety of government services and a bearable tax burden. Local residents want a clean, safe community with a high quality of life. Tourists want enjoyable and safe places to visit that offer a full range of services to meet their travel needs.

How Friendly Is Your Town?

1. Are the main routes into the area equipped with visitor information centers?
2. Does the airport have a full range of visitor information resources?
3. Do front-line visitor contact personnel, such as taxi and bus drivers, receive formal hospitality training?
4. Do hotels and motels offer in-house television channels with information about local sites, transportation, restaurants, and special events?
5. Is a single organization responsible for generating visitor business to the area?
6. Does that organization have a marketing profile of visitors, and is this profile used in developing marketing activities?
7. Does the area accommodate international visitor needs?
8. Is there a range of accommodations provided to match the range of visitors expected?
9. Are attractions and events easily available and affordable?
10. Do visitor service personnel and the local citizens welcome visitors and accommodate their needs with flexible hours, parking availability, and the like?

Adapted from Kotler, Philip, Haider, Donald H., and Rein, Irving. (1993). *Marketing places*. New York: Free Press, p. 228.

Unfortunately, with all of these differing objectives, it is difficult for decision makers to please all constituents. Frequently, a decision for the benefit of one group is often seen as negative by another group. Local taxpayers may welcome the tax revenues generated by visitors to the area but then fight additional tourism development because it would change the landscape of the region and add to the industrialization of the community. Tourism business owners strongly support the promotion of their industry by governments, but owners of businesses in other industries often believe that their industry should receive equal government support. Rarely is there enough tax revenue to promote all industries, so priorities must be established. Determining priorities is where the political tug of war among constituent groups occurs.

You may live now (or have lived) in an area that has experienced a tourism development political battle. We hope you now have a better understanding of the economic and political impacts of tourism development and promotion and how different perspectives can lead to debate. The words of tourism writer Uel Blank may give some food for thought concerning tourism development: "Citizens' rights to enjoy amenities of lakes, cities, and facilities away from home carry with them the responsibility to also share local amenities with travelers from elsewhere."[26]

The international tourism arena is also affected by political tugs of war. Since the terrorist attacks in the United States in 2001, attacks have escalated around the world, including globally publicized attacks in Bali (2002), Kenya (2003), and Madrid, Spain (2004). The chief executive of Spain's tourism promotional body estimated that the number of overseas visitors fell 20% within the two months following the attack.[27]

SUMMARY

Economics and politics are forever linked, and the economics and politics of tourism are no exception to that rule. The use of scarce resources by the tourism industry can lead to a variety of positive economic impacts, as well as some not-so-positive effects. Virtually everyone has an opinion about tourism, and the process of deciding the role tourism will play in the economic development of an area gives rise to a great deal of political debate.

As you learned in this chapter, the tourism industry is often used to bring added economic vitality to an area and frequently has a comparative advantage over other development alternatives. A primary reason for tourism's popularity as an industry is its ability to generate new money for a region, especially in the form of exports.

Tourism revenues enter an economy and then are re-spent, creating additional revenues until the added money finally leaves the economy through leakage—money spent on imports to the area. This increased economic activity is called the "multiplier concept," and its size depends on the amount of imports a region needs to utilize to provide goods and services for visitors and residents alike.

Even though tourism adds diversity and stability to an economy and provides a wide variety of employment, business opportunities, and increased tax revenues, it is not without its costs. Large numbers of visitors strain utilities, public services, and natural resources. Often, these tourists also put upward pressure on prices, which increases the cost of living for local citizens. Researchers use cost–benefit analysis to try to determine whether, all things considered, tourism brings substantial economic gain to an area.

Given the importance of the tourism industry to most countries, states/provinces, and cities, governments often become involved in tourism development. The most common role for government is collection of data on tourist activity and promotion of the area as a destination. A recent trend is for government and private tourism associations to join together to help sustain and increase the tourism industry. Building and promotion of convention centers are just one function of these public/private organizations.

A continuing challenge for government officials and tourism industry members will be to balance the special interests of constituent groups who have conflicting opinions concerning the development of tourism that lead to political tugs of war. Tourism, like any industry, has benefits and costs, and these impacts will always be viewed and prioritized differently by different members of communities.

YOU DECIDE

The following two letters to the editor appeared in a resort town's newspaper.

To the Editor:

Summer is approaching again and, as in every year, I am dreading it. By the middle of June, our town will be inundated with tourists. The price of gasoline will jump and all of the "local appreciation" specials at restaurants will disappear. The traffic jams will start and the number of car accidents will escalate. All of the stores and restaurants will be mobbed and service will suffer. And forget trying to park downtown. All the spaces will be filled by out-of-state cars. Our policemen will find it harder to protect us because they will have all of these "foreigners" to watch. And our fire departments will begin their annual campaign against forest fires started by careless transients. And now our chamber of commerce wants us to celebrate tourism and be extra nice to the "guests" to our area?

Frankly, I am sick and tired of some of my state tax dollars (and I'll bet some of my local taxes, too!) going to promote our state as a tourism destination! All these new people in the area just serve to increase my taxes in order to pay for the increased costs they lead to! Enough is enough already. This area is losing its small-town feel and its small-town security. Why should we pay to decrease the quality of life of our community?

Signed, Jack Smith

To the Editor:

After reading the letter from Jack Smith, who sees only the negatives of tourists to our community, I felt compelled to respond. Without these "foreigners" that he decries, he may not even be able to live here. Many of us, either directly or indirectly, owe our livelihood to the money that tourists spend here every year. And, contrary to Mr. Smith's opinion, the tourists to our town and state actually reduce our taxes by paying taxes on the goods and services they purchase here.

In addition, do the people of this town think we locals by ourselves could support the number of restaurants and shops we have, let alone the jet-capable airport we enjoy? Instead of cursing out tourists, we should smile, wave, and thank our lucky stars that we get to live where they can only visit.

Signed, Linda Jones

With which letter do you agree? Why?

NET TOUR

To get you started on exploring Internet links for this chapter, please see

> http://www.world-tourism.org
> http://www.tourismtrade.org.uk

http://www.tia.org
http://www.occc.net
http://www.oanda.com/convert/classic

DISCUSSION QUESTIONS

1. In what ways can tourism benefit the economy of an area?
2. Why are tourism receipts from international visitors considered exports?
3. How does the multiplier concept work? Why do island countries have small tourism multipliers?
4. What are some of the negative effects that can come from tourism development?
5. What are the various roles that governments can play in supporting the tourism industry?
6. How do convention centers add to the economic activity of an area? How can they be funded and managed?
7. What steps are needed to develop a tourism plan?
8. Why can political tugs of war arise over decisions concerning tourism development?

APPLYING THE CONCEPTS

1. Look at Tables 11.1 and 11.2. Why are these countries top in international tourism receipts and arrivals? In other words, what is it about these countries that enables them to attract so much international tourism?
2. Visit a chamber of commerce, convention and visitors bureau, or a state welcome center in your area. Interview one of the managers about the visitor friendliness of your city/town, using the FYI visitor-friendliness test as your discussion guide.
3. Research the taxes that are added to visitor services in your city/town and your state/province. How do they compare with the examples provided in Table 11.3?

GLOSSARY

Comparative advantage The benefits of one alternative relative to another.

Constituent groups Subgroups of citizens with a set of common needs or wants.

Convention and visitors bureau An organization whose mission is to develop tourism to an area by attracting both professional and leisure travelers.

Convention center A property developed to serve the special needs of groups, especially regarding meetings and trade shows.

Cost–benefit analysis A method used to determine the relative impact of a development, in which total costs and total benefits are estimated and then compared.

Destination image The detailed impression an individual or target segment has of a specific destination.

Destination vision An inspirational portrait of the ideal future that the destination hopes to bring about at some defined future time (usually in 5, 10, 20, or 50 years).

Economics The study of the choices people make in using scarce resources to meet needs.

Entrepreneurial Assuming the risks of a personally owned business.

Exchange rate The number of units of one currency necessary to be exchanged to obtain a unit of another currency; for example, 121 Japanese yen for $1.00 U.S.

Export A good or service produced in one country and purchased by a resident of another country; the opposite of "import."

Financial resources The amount of money available for a given project through the use of debt and equity.

Import A good or service purchased in one country but produced in another country; the opposite of "export."

Infrastructure The foundation utilities and other systems necessary for an economy, such as roads, electricity, and water and sewage systems.

Joint venture Combined efforts of two or more partners, usually organizations.

Leakage Purchasing power that is spent on imports to an area, resulting in a transfer of income out of the local economy.

Multiplier concept The additional economic activity that results when money is spent and re-spent in a region on the purchase of local goods and services.

Nonprofit tourism association An organization that exists to support the tourism industry of an area and often promotes the area as a destination.

Objective A specific target for which measurable results can be obtained.

Passenger facility charge A charge added to airline tickets for enplanement. The monies collected are to be used for airport improvements.

Policy A general statement that provides direction for individuals within an organization.

Privatization The action of converting a government-owned business to private ownership.

Public/private organizations Organizations made up of private and public members, usually to coordinate efforts between government and private businesses.

Superstructure The facilities needed to serve the specific needs of tourists, such as hotels, restaurants, and attractions.

Tourism planning A continual process of research-and-development decisions to create and sustain tourism in a region.

Tourism policy A master plan formulated by a government (national, state/provincial, local) to aid in guiding the development of sustainable tourism industries within its jurisdiction.

REFERENCES

1. Thomas, Sarah. (2003, October 27). Receiving mixed messages. *Travel Weekly,* p. 40.

2. Haussman, Glenn. (2007, June 19). *U.S. ceding world tourism market share.* Available at: http://www.hotelinteractive.com.

3. Parker, Penny. (1999, March 21). Bigger is better. *Denver Post,* pp. 1K, 26K.

4. Plunkett, Jack W. Travel statistics. (2003, January). *Plunkett's airline, hotel, & travel industry almanac.* Houston, TX: Plunkett Research.

5. World Tourism Organization. (2008). Madrid, Spain. *Facts & figures: Tourism 2020 vision.* Available at: http://unwto.org/facts/eng/vision.htm.

6. Lundberg, Donald E., Stavengaand, Mink H., and Krishnamoorthy, M. (1995). *Tourism economics.* New York: John Wiley & Sons, Inc.

7. Fletcher, J. (1987). Input–output analysis and tourism impact studies. *Annals of Tourism Research,* 16(4), 514–529.

8. Fletcher, J. (1987). Input–output analysis and tourism impact studies. *Annals of Tourism Research,* 16(4), 514–529.

9. Bull, Adrian. (1991). *The economics of tourism.* Melbourne, Australia: Pitman Publishing.

10. Bull, Adrian. (1991). *The economics of tourism.* Melbourne, Australia: Pitman Publishing.

11. Beirman, David. (2003). *Restoring tourism destinations in crisis.* Cambridge, MA: CABI Publishing.

12. Beirman, David. (2003). *Restoring tourism destinations in crisis.* Cambridge, MA: CABI Publishing.

13. Keates, Nancy. (2000, January 7). Flake out: Ski season off to slow start. *Wall Street Journal,* p. W7.

14. Gay, Joel. (2004, July 4). Getting burned. *Anchorage Daily News.*

15. Beirman, David. (2003). *Restoring tourism destinations in crisis.* Cambridge, MA: CABI Publishing.

16. Lundberg, Donald E., Stavengaand, Mink H., and Krishnamoorthy, M. (1995). *Tourism economics.* New York: John Wiley & Sons, Inc.

17. Lasswell, H. D. (1936). *Politics: Who gets what, when, how?* New York: McGraw-Hill.

18. Bull, Adrian. (1991). *The economics of tourism.* Melbourne, Australia: Pitman Publishing.

19. Dean, Jason. (2002, August 8). Taiwan is turning to tourism in bid to boost economy. *Wall Street Journal,* p. D5.

20. Pike, Steven, and Ryan, Chris. (2004). Destination positioning analysis through a comparison of cognitive, affective and conative perceptions. *Journal of Travel Research,* 42(4), 333–342.

21. Pike, Steven, and Ryan, Chris. (2004). Destination positioning analysis through a comparison of cognitive, affective and conative perceptions. *Journal of Travel Research,* 42(4), 333–342.

22. Kotler, Philip, Haider, Donald H., and Rein, Irving. (1993). *Marketing places.* New York: Free Press.

23. Kay, Andrew L. K. (2005). China's convention and exhibition center boom. *Journal of Convention and Event Tourism,* 7(1), pp. 5–22.

24. So-hyun, Kim (2007, December 31). Seoul to give boost to convention industry. *Korea Herald.*

25. Ritchie, J. R. Brent, and Crouch, Geoffrey I. (2003). *The competitive destination.* Cambridge, MA: CABI Publishing.

26. Blank, Uel. (1989). *The community tourism industry imperative.* State College, PA: Venture Publishing, Inc.

27. Zoreda, Jose Luis. (2004). Keynote address. World Travel and Tourism Council Summit, Doha, Qatar.

LEARNING OBJECTIVES

After you have read this chapter, you should be able to:

- Describe how tourism can aid the preservation of nature as well as harm it.
- Describe how tourism can benefit or undermine cultural preservation.
- Describe the impact of tourism activities on host community resources.
- Explain the factors that determine an area's carrying capacity.
- Explain how carrying capacities are determined.
- Describe the positive and negative impacts tourism can have on societies and cultures.
- Identify the potential unintended consequences of tourism.

CHAPTER OUTLINE

CHAPTER 12

Environmental and Social/ Cultural Impacts of Tourism

[T]he long-term viability of the [tourism] industry in any location depends on maintaining its natural, cultural, and historical attraction.

—Edward Manning/T. David Dougherty

■ Italy uses the nostalgia of the Roman Empire to attract tourists

REFLECTING ON THE FUTURE

As the sun set slowly in the western sky, the tribal council paused in its discussion to take in the beauty of the moment. This was not the first day of their discussions and it surely would not be the last.

Some of the younger tribal members had brought up the idea of developing a golf, tennis, and ski resort in the heart of the reservation. The area would be perfect—great views, optimal weather conditions, and easy access from several large metropolitan areas. There was even talk of adding a casino to the mix and creating a series of activities and events with year-round appeal.

Development of any of these ideas sounded exciting to some members because of the variety of jobs that would be created, but there were other concerns. The tribal council was familiar with the economic benefits of tourism because the tribe already operated a motel and other small-scale attractions to encourage visitors to the reservation. However, extensive tourism development was a completely different story. Questions were raised about how many new visitors would be attracted and what effects these additional visitors would have on the natural environment and the cultural traditions that tribal members cherished. The lands of the reservation were fragile and untouched in an environmental sense. Some members of the council believed that an influx of tourists would forever damage the lands on which a hundred generations had lived. Other members expressed dismay about allowing tens of thousands of outsiders into the heart of the reservation. Would these outsiders show respect for the ways of the tribe? Could the tribe keep visitors out of the sacred areas, or would four-wheel drive vehicles be racing everywhere, ignoring any restrictions the tribe might impose?

As the council members settled back into their discussions, they reached one decision. Before a final conclusion was made on the matter, they would need a professional analysis of the potential environmental and social/cultural impacts of each alternative.

INTRODUCTION

In the previous chapter, you learned about tourism's many economic and political impacts. While reading Chapter 11, as well as many of the other chapters, you may have thought of other benefits and problems that tourism can bring. For example, in Chapter 10, we considered the range of commercialization that exists at different types of resort locations. But what impact does commercial development have on the cultural, social, and natural environment? Can the attractiveness of an area that drew tourists in the first place be preserved when tourism development occurs? How are residents affected by the creation and growth of tourism in their area?

As the chapter opener suggests, the economic impacts of tourism are not the only important impacts that must be considered when tourism development is proposed. Effects on nature, peoples, and cultures of a region are just as important to study and predict as the economic effects of tourism. In this chapter, we will discuss the environmental pluses and minuses of tourism as well as the benefits and costs of tourism to a society and its culture.

TOURISM AND THE ENVIRONMENT

How can tourism be used to enhance and preserve the environment? Management, education, and appreciation are probably the most important ways. When visitor numbers are managed, and they see firsthand the wonders of the attraction or the beauty of the natural setting and are educated about visitor impacts and nature's fragile balance, they are more likely to understand the importance of preservation efforts. In addition to its educational role, tourism can be used to help finance the preservation of attractions and natural areas. Revenues generated from taxes, memberships, entrance fees, and other guest services can be used to preserve and improve the very attributes that attract tourists.

Think about the hundreds of thousands of acres of national parks and preserves, nearly

Table 12.1	Worldwide Examples of National Parks and Preserves
Location	*Park or Preserve*
Australia	Great Barrier Reef Marine Park
China	Sanjiangyuan National Nature Reserve
Ecuador	Galapágos National Park
Guatemala	Laguna Del Tigre National Park
India	Gir National Park and Wildlife Sanctuary
New Zealand	Auckland Islands National Nature Reserve
Saudi Arabia	Ar-Rub'-Al-Khali Wildlife Management Area
South Africa	Kruger National Park
Tanzania	Serengeti National Park
United States	Arctic National Wildlife Refuge

12% of Earth's land surface, that have been set aside all over the world primarily to preserve them for future generations to enjoy.[1] North Americans and visitors from around the globe owe U.S. President Theodore Roosevelt a great deal of thanks for his foresight in instituting the U.S. National Park System. Similar systems, public and private, as shown in Table 12.1, exist in countries on all continents, from Asia to South America.

But how can tourism managers and planners determine just how much tourism a natural site, an attraction, or any destination can handle? What types of positive and negative impacts does tourism have on culture, society, and the environment? The first question can be answered by determining the **carrying capacity** of a location. After we discuss the concept of carrying capacity, we will then consider some of the particular environmental benefits and costs tourism yields.

Defining Carrying Capacity

Just how many visitors are too many? The answer is, It depends, and what it depends on is the carrying capacity of an area. Carrying capacity is a key concept in analysis of the potential environmental impacts of tourism. Different people mean different things when they use the term *carrying capacity*, but essentially there are three elements to the concept.

1. **Physical capacity**—the limit on the actual number of users that can be accommodated in a region. Such things as the number of roads, the size of parking lots, and the amount of water resources influence the physical carrying capacity of an area. Acadia National Park in Maine is frequently marred by bumper-to-bumper traffic during the height of tourist season.

2. **Environmental capacity**—the limit on the number of users that an area can accommodate before visitors perceive a decline in the desirability of the area. This capacity is more subjectively defined and varies depending on season, and so forth. The beaches of St. Tropez in France are uncomfortably crowded in August.

3. **Ecological capacity**—the maximum level of users that an area can accommodate before ecological damage is incurred. For example, the alpine flora of Waterton-Glacier International Peace Park spanning the Canadian/U.S. border has suffered from the tens of thousands of hikers swarming the park. Ecological capacity will vary depending on the type of use made of the area. Backpackers will have less impact on a national park than campers who travel through the park on horseback or in four-wheel-drive vehicles. In addition, different types of environments are affected more or less by use. Beaches and other dunelike areas tend to be even more fragile than mountainous areas.[2]

Britain's National Trust

The United Kingdom boasts a private organization whose mission is preservation—The National Trust for Places of Historic Interest or Natural Beauty. Started in 1895, it is the largest private landowner in Great Britain (Scotland also has a National Trust). Along with a huge portfolio of stately homes and gardens, the Trust owns or controls 600 miles of coastline.

Determining Carrying Capacities

As you can see from these definitions, preserving the physical and natural features that attract visitors requires managing the carrying capacity of a location. To determine the carrying capacity, planners must look at a variety of factors, including:

- The number of visitors;
- The amount of "use" by the average visitor;
- The quality of resource management and facility development/design;
- The number of area residents and their quality-of-life needs; and
- The number of other users of the area and its resources; for example, industrial users and farmers/ranchers.[3]

The historic old town area in Charleston, South Carolina, provides an excellent example of destination management. The numbers of people, both tourists and residents, who flock to see and enjoy this well-preserved charming southern city could soon overwhelm and destroy its very character if limits were not in place. The city has taken proactive steps to preserve this charm by limiting things such as the number of carriages (a popular way to enjoy the architecture and history of the area) that are allowed in the historic district by the use of a restricted number of medallions. At the entry point to the district, carriages wait in line to be issued a medallion before entering. This medallion must be displayed on the rear

of the carriage as long as it is in the district. Once the carriage leaves the district, the medallion is returned at the entry point to be used by the next carriage in line. Not only are the number of carriages limited, but the drivers must also alert cleanup crews to pick up after their horses when they stop to relieve themselves.

Wyoming's Grand Teton National Park provides another good example of capacity control in practice. About 3.5 million visitors arrive each year to play and marvel at the mountain majesty of the area. At the same time, the nearby town of Jackson Hole has exploded with new full- and part-time residents. The area also supports its traditional agriculture-based industries such as cattle ranching. And the amount of "use" by visitors has increased. In the past, use was primarily hiking and low-impact sports of nature (such as fishing), but visitors now bring all the comforts of home—and more—with them. Dan Burgette, chief of the Colter Bay subdivision of the park, states:

> The toys people bring to the park have changed. Twenty-five years ago they would have a car and a tent. Now they come with a motor home, a boat, trail bikes, and a car in tow. Parking lots built in the 1960s just aren't big enough. One of our biggest chores is getting people to turn off their TV sets and gas-powered electric generators at ten o'clock at night. (p. 136)[4]

The preceding quotation suggests that the carrying capacity of an area changes when any one or more of capacity's determining factors change. For example, if a town begins to see an increase in permanent residents, it will not have as high a "visitor" carrying capacity as before because the additional residents "use up" some of the finite carrying capacity of the area. On the other hand, the carrying capacity of a site can be increased by reducing the amount of "use" by each visitor. Constructing visitor walkways allows more foot traffic in a fragile natural area; busing visitors from remote parking lots cuts down on air pollution within a park; and creating viewing platforms allows many more visitors to view the scenery without endangering the pristine site. Another

Density

"Take nothing but photographs, leave nothing but footprints." You probably have seen this statement on signs in many natural areas including North America's national parks. Surely these simple activities—looking and walking—are harmless? Unfortunately, they can be harmful.

1. At a density of 1 person per square kilometer, little of the natural environment is likely to be lost.

2. At 10 persons per square kilometer, the likelihood of being alone and of seeing wildlife is likely to be sacrificed.

3. At 100 persons per square kilometer, most wildlife will depart; in the absence of any management intervention, there will be visible pollution of the site and noticeable ecological degradation.

4. At 1,000 persons per square kilometer, urban densities are reached, and the experience is no longer a natural one; human-created values are found; and intensive management is needed to maintain the site and to remove trash and human waste.

Source: Manning, Edward, and Dougherty, T. David. (1995). Sustainable tourism. *Cornell Hotel & Restaurant Administration Quarterly*, 36, 29–42.

suggestion that has been mathematically modeled and appears to hold promise for allowing increased use while increasing a sense of solitude is to stagger entry lines. Park managers at the Athabasca Falls site in British Columbia have used all of these means—walkways, buses, and view platforms—to decrease the erosion and vegetation trampling that had threatened its natural beauty.[5]

As you can see, identifying the carrying capacity of an area requires thorough research. The management of a natural attraction demands careful environmental planning and creative carrying capacity design to balance visitor enjoyment and education with the well-being of the flora and fauna of the location.

ENVIRONMENTAL IMPACTS OF TOURISM

To provide services to visitors, a tourism area must first develop the necessary infrastructure to support these services. Infrastructure is the underlying foundation or basic framework for a system or organization. In the case of tourism, infrastructure includes roads, ports and airports, and utilities such as electricity and water and sewage systems. In addition, superstructures will also be needed. The superstructures of tourism are the facilities directly associated with serving visitors' needs such as welcome centers, hotels, restaurants, car rental facilities, tour company offices, and retail establishments.

Obviously, the development of the infrastructure and superstructure necessary for tourism will have an impact on the environment of an area. However, the impact can be minimized with good design and planning. For example, the use of underground lines for utilities can retain the more natural look of vistas, whereas appropriate design of buildings, in terms of colors, height, signage, and landscaping, may even enhance their beauty. Many resort communities have ordinances that require harmony in architecture, color, and signs so that human-made structures blend into the natural setting. For example, in Sedona, Arizona, architecture, color schemes, and signs must follow design restrictions so that the community fits into its awe-inspiring red-rock formation setting.

Unfortunately, such design foresight does not always occur. In the earlier days of tourism development in Hawaii, hotels were built along the beautiful beaches of Oahu with little regard to the "scenic impact" they would have. Today, these hotels completely block the view of the ocean. Developers of the other islands of Hawaii have learned from the mistakes made, and regional planners and developers are now more careful with their designs.[6]

A substantial increase in the number of people using an area's resources is likely to have a detrimental impact on the environment. This impact may simply be annoying, such as increased traffic or crowded parks; but the impact may be severe enough to cause harm to a fragile natural

Venice

Environmental and cultural issues are not restricted to natural destinations. One of the world's most beautiful and historic cities—Venice, Italy—is suffering from tourism's success. This cradle of European civilization, 1,500 years old, includes incredible riches in terms of art, architecture, and history. Ten million visitors each year travel to it and marvel at its beauty. So what's the problem?

The problem for Venice is its location and its size. Venice is an island city, constructed on pilings sunk into the sea and connected by causeway to the rest of Italy. The ancient city is a mere three square miles in size, with a permanent population of only 70,000 residents. And the streets were built hundreds of years ago, which virtually prevents the use of cars, buses, and trucks. Its famous canals and gondolas are a prime form of transit, but they, too, are small. Each day between 50,000 and 150,000 tourists descend on the city and crowd the streets to the point that simply walking across a town square becomes nearly impossible.

This overcrowding is taking its toll on more than just citizens' blood pressures. The amount of garbage and trash is massive and difficult to dispose of due to the city's size, location, and lack of transportation options. And the crowds of visitors are taking their toll on the ancient churches, palaces, and other historic places. Solutions that are being considered include selling tickets and limiting the number of guests who can visit the city each day, as well as allowing only tours that follow differing itineraries so that the crowds are more evenly spread through the streets and the city's monuments.

Source: Zwingle, Erla. (1995). Venice. *National Geographic,* 187(2), 70–99.

area. For example, the Taman Negara National Park in Malaysia is suffering from the impacts of human intervention as visitor numbers have exploded. This astounding increase in tourists has made wildlife scarce, and the forests' floors have become littered with garbage.[7] Likewise, Banff National Park, Canada's oldest national park, continues to suffer from the millions of visitors it receives annually. Many places in its tundra wilderness have been "trampled by so many hikers that in places the route resembles a boggy, 20-foot-wide cattle trail" (p. 50).[8]

Air pollution can become a problem with the increased level of vehicle traffic in an area, along with other activities that cause air-quality problems. For example, the congestion of cars through Yosemite Park causes the very air pollution that visitors try to escape by fleeing to national parks. Some communities have taken serious steps to try to reduce the other forms of air pollution that can be caused by tourism's success. In the mountain valleys of the Rockies, it is now common for towns to prohibit hearth fires on many winter days, because wood smoke is so dense and dissipates so slowly.

In addition to air pollution, noise pollution is becoming a new problem in many communities, especially with the relocation and/or expansion of airports. Noise pollution is even a problem at the Grand Canyon. Each year, about 80,000 scenic flights take tourists low over the canyon, creating an airplane buzz that disrupts the tranquility of its splendor.[9] In 2000, to restore peace and quiet, Utah's Zion National Park became the first park outside Alaska to ban nearly all cars. Tourists now take shuttles from the visitor center to experience the natural sights in the canyon.[10]

Possibly most damaging, however, is the impact that can occur to vegetation, wildlife, and precious historical attractions. Unplanned or poorly planned development can lead to the endangerment of flora and fauna species and to the erosion of the very sites that are the destination's "reason for being." For example, the government of Egypt is excavating more of the dozens of pharaoh burial sites in hope that by providing more sites, they can reduce the amount of tourist traffic to the Great Pyramids in Giza. Each year, millions of visitors troop through the most famous pyramids, worsening the water vapor problem that causes salt to leach from the stones and weaken the structures.[11] Other countries, such as Mozambique, which is recovering from years of civil war, have demonstrated the power of tourism's economic benefits for enhancing culture and the environment.[12]

■ The USS *Arizona* (center), at the bottom of Honolulu, Hawaii's Pearl Harbor, is a sobering historic attraction. Photo by D. A. Yale.

Historic site deterioration can occur in more modern locations as well. Many historic towns in the United States have applied the brakes to tour buses rolling through their streets. For example, New Orleans officials stopped all tour bus access to the French Quarter owing to the damage inflicted on the delicate architecture by the vibration of hundreds of buses passing through the narrow streets. Other cities are considering similar restraints.[13]

Virtually every year, the National Park Service considers limiting the number of people into Yosemite National Park. In the meantime, roads have been upgraded to allow better bus access through the park to try to encourage visitors to leave their cars outside. Mesa Verde, a world-famous archaeological site of early Native American settlements, limits access to the more popular ruins by utilizing tickets. As the market for tourism grows, carrying capacity and means to enhance it will be a major concern for planners and managers.

The United Nations Educational, Scientific and Cultural Organization (UNESCO) is attempting to preserve many of the world's historic cities and natural and cultural properties for future generations. For example, UNESCO has declared Lunenburg, Nova Scotia, Canada, as having unique value to be preserved for the education and enjoyment of future generations by declaring it to be a World Heritage Site.

To try to preserve the environment and still gain the economic benefits of tourism, **ecotourism** has evolved. Although protection of the natural environment is the key component of ecotourism (sometimes called "green tourism" or "alternative tourism"), protection and appreciation of the native peoples of an area are also two of its guiding principles. We will take a closer look at ecotourism and other sustainability efforts in the next chapter.

■ SOCIAL AND CULTURAL IMPACTS OF TOURISM

The concepts of society and culture are closely linked. A **society** is a community, nation, or broad grouping of people who have common traditions, institutions, activities, and interests. **Culture** represents the practices of a society; its customary beliefs, social roles, and material objects that are passed down from generation to generation. As we saw in the chapter opener, tourism's potential effects on the culture of a society are often major concerns when tourism development is being considered. Tourism's impacts on a society can be both positive and negative. Because tourism brings "outsiders" into a society, it has the possibility of influencing that society by changing its culture.

Host Community

Tourism, by its very definition, takes place at a location distant from one's hometown. The community a tourist is visiting is often termed the *host community*. Local residents of the host community share facilities and services with the guests to the area. In this way, the town and its inhabitants become "hosts" to the visitors.

A host community is composed of four resources (see Figure 12.1). The most obvious resource is the local residents, the hosts themselves. They interact directly or indirectly with tourists on many levels: for example, serving tourists at restaurants or in retail stores, enjoying the local parks with them, or talking with visitors while waiting in line at the local amusement park. The community's economic system is also a resource of the host community. The economic health and wealth of the area are created and used by both residents and the community's guests. The infrastructure and basic government services are the third resource of

the host community. The residents of the community literally share the roads, the sidewalks, the water system, and police and fire protection with the guests to their area.[14] Finally, the natural resources of the community are also shared among residents and visitors. Residents and visitors often enjoy the same beaches, rivers, lakes, and mountains. This blending of local people and their resources with outsiders can have many social and cultural impacts, some positive and some not so positive.

Social and Cultural Benefits of Tourism

In addition to economic gains, tourism can provide many social and cultural benefits. By bringing people from a wide variety of places and cultures together, visitors and locals learn about each other, their differences, and their similarities. They also become aware of new tastes and ways of thinking, which may lead to increased tolerance among the hosts and the visitors. After 18 years, the United States lifted the travel ban on Libya in February 2004 because of its progress in fighting terrorism. In April 2004, a Dutch firm signed a $2 billion contract to develop four new tourism resorts on the coastline of Libya. Libya now has a Tourism Ministry to oversee its infant tourism industry. Only time will tell whether citizens of the world will feel comfortable traveling in the previously controversial region.[15]

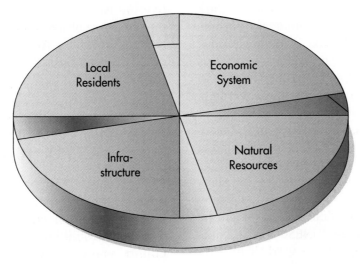

■ **Figure 12.1** Host community resources.

Traveler's Code for Traveling Responsibly

Guidelines for Individuals

Cultural Understanding

- Travel with an open mind: Cultivate the habit of listening and observing; discover the enrichment that comes from experiencing another way of life.
- Reflect daily on your experiences and keep a journal.
- Prepare: Learn the geography, culture, history, beliefs, some local language; know how to be a good guest in the country or culture.

Social Impacts

- Support the local economy by using locally owned restaurants and hotels, buying local products made by locals from renewable resources.
- Interact with local residents in a culturally appropriate manner.
- Make no promises that you cannot keep (sending photos, helping with school).
- Don't make extravagant displays of wealth; don't encourage children to beg.
- Get permission before photographing people, homes, and other sites of local importance.

Environmental Impacts

- Travel in small, low-impact groups.
- Stay on trails.
- Pack it in, pack it out; assure proper disposal of human waste.
- Don't buy products made from endangered animals or plants.
- Become aware of and contribute to projects benefiting local environments and communities (a social benefit as well)!

Source: Partners in Responsible Tourism (PIRT), San Francisco, CA.

Another important cultural benefit of tourism is the attainment of the "critical mass" of interest necessary to maintain the viability of a society's culture, especially the culture's art forms.[16] The opportunity to sell native crafts or to perform to an enthusiastic audience can entice local artisans to continue traditional art forms that otherwise may no longer be seen as a viable means of income. For example, in Fiji, islanders have turned their crafts of palm mats and shell jewelry into lucrative tourist businesses. They also earn additional income by performing folk dances, including fire walking.[17]

In many cases, the growth of tourism in developing countries has led to improved standards of living and greater educational opportunities, especially for women and young people who were formerly "enslaved" by tradition. In Spain, for example, growth in tourism led to the employment of many young women outside the home and gave them lifestyle choices other than the homemaker role that had been their only option in the past.[18]

At the same time, tourism provides the opportunity to preserve the region's historical and natural sites. Revenues from tourist fees and taxes afford the host area the ability to produce income and create jobs from lands and historic sites that would otherwise have to be industrially developed to achieve a higher standard of living for the local people. It is the influx of tourist *piastres* (the currency of Egypt) that is providing Egypt with the funds necessary to uncover and preserve that culture's ancient past. Spain has similarly used tourism demand to aid in historic preservation. The Spanish government developed a system of inns—*Paradores de Turismo*—that utilizes the room capacity of many of Spain's historic castles, monasteries, and convents. By generating revenue from these classic buildings, Spain can afford to maintain them, preserving them for the future.

Using Culture to Attract Tourists

Remember that culture includes the practices of a society, including its material objects. These practices and objects, listed in Figure 12.2, can be grouped into three categories: material goods of culture, daily life activities of culture, and special

■ The culture of Europe, represented in its abundant museums, may be its greatest appeal to tourists.
Photo by D. A. Yale.

expressions of culture (that is, special events or sites of special historical value). The material goods of a culture include its distinctive arts and crafts. Daily life activities of a culture include its food and dress forms, its language, and its special ways of playing, living, and working. Special expressions of culture are found in a culture's unique history, architecture, and special traditions. One of the most well-attended cultural expressions in the world is the daily changing of the guard at Buckingham Palace in London.

Look at Figure 12.2 again and think of the many destinations that attract visitors based on one or more of these elements of culture. Many destinations experience a substantial influx of tourists who are attracted by the local handicrafts and traditions of the area. The American Southwest, for example, is world renowned for its beautiful Native American crafts. The Bahamas are famous for the variety of straw goods produced by its people. Spain attracts tens of thousands of students each year who are studying Spanish. France attracts visitors eager to partake of its renowned cuisine and to view the wealth of art exhibited in its museums and galleries. Greece is a popular tourism destination because of its important historical role in the evolution of Western civilization. And the

United States and Canada have turned into the world's playgrounds, attracting millions of international visitors who participate in the vast array of leisure activities available on the North American continent.

Need more examples of the importance of cultural elements in attracting visitors? The Middle East is the cradle of three of the world's most prominent religions—Christianity, Judaism, and Islam. Literally millions of people trek to various sites in the Middle East as a form of pilgrimage. Salt Lake City serves a similar role for members of the Church of Jesus Christ of Latter-day Saints. Italy, Mexico, and Peru provide unique opportunities for visitors to see the architectural marvels of past civilizations.

Even industry and education can attract visitors. You have probably toured "industrial attractions" yourself. How about the Hershey chocolate plant in Pennsylvania? How about wineries in California, New York, or Washington State? And many colleges and universities are popular sites—Oxford and Cambridge in England, Yale and Stanford in the United States, the Sorbonne in France, and many more.

The list of destinations and attractions (see Table 12.2) that are based on culture is almost

1. Handicrafts
2. Language
3. Traditions ✈
4. Gastronomy ✈
5. Art & Music
6. History & Visual Reminders ✈
7. Work & Technology
8. Architecture ✈
9. Religion & Its Manifestations
10. Educational Systems
11. Dress
12. Leisure Activities ✈

✈ Indicates the most common elements for attracting tourists

■ **Figure 12.2** Elements of culture that attract tourists.
Source: Ritchie, J. R., and Zins, M. (1978). Culture as a determinant of a tourist region. *Annals of Tourism Research*, 5, 252–270.

Table 12.2	Places to Experience America's History
To Experience	*Visit*
Pre-Columbian	Mesa Verde (Cortez, CO). Explore 700-year-old cliff houses.
Colonial	Williamsburg (VA). Mingle with aristocrats in powdered wigs.
Revolutionary War	Boston Freedom Trail (MA). A walking tour of historic sites.
Lewis and Clark	Fort Clatsop (OR). The locale of a long, wet winter for the pair.
Southern Plantations	Cane River Historical Park (Natchez, LA). Stroll through a cotton planter's big house.
Gold Rush	Sutter's Mill (Coloma, CA). Pan for gold where it began in 1848.
Civil War	Gettysburg (PA). Walk the battlefields where thousands died.
Westward Expansion	Little Bighorn (MT). Hike the plains of Custer's last stand.
Industrial Revolution	Lowell (MA). Ride a trolley through this town of textile mills.
Immigrant Life	Tenement Museum (New York City). Step into cramped apartments.
Prohibition	Green Mill (Chicago, IL). Listen to jazz at this former speakeasy.
Depression	Steinbeck Center (Salinas, CA). Visit a re-created "Hooverville."
World War II	Pearl Harbor (HI). Watch oil continue to bubble from the USS *Arizona*.
Civil Rights	Little Rock Central High (AR). Visit the school where black students made history.
Cold War	Strategic Air & Space Museum (Ashland, NE). See parts of the old U.S. nuclear arsenal.

Source: Curry, Andrew. (2003). Blast from the past. *National Geographic Traveler*, 20(5), 26.

infinite. The cultural resources of a society provide many opportunities to generate tourism revenues. Often, the society also gains by meeting and sharing with people from other cultures, each one learning and appreciating the other. But sometimes tourism brings problems to a culture.

UNINTENDED CONSEQUENCES OF TOURISM ON CULTURE

Although we have provided a long list of benefits that tourism can offer, there can be some unintended negative effects of tourism on a society and culture.[19] The term **social carrying capacity** is sometimes used to label the amount of people that a society and its land area can bear without substantial damage to its culture. Newcomers or visitors to a society may cause problems owing to overcrowding or by bringing unfamiliar behaviors.[20] Once tourism in an area becomes successful, it is common for local residents to resent sharing "their" resources and facilities with visitors. Frequently, the residents of the area forget that many of the facilities in the area (both infrastructure and superstructure) were developed to serve the tourist market and would not be available for locals' use if the tourists did not return year after year. As we saw in the "You Decide" of Chapter 11, communities can split apart by the debate over the effect of tourism on the area.

The Demonstration Effect

A more serious societal problem can occur in lower-income areas. In some locations, tourism has caused what is termed the **demonstration effect**. Compared with their own lifestyles, the local residents often see the visitors as uniformly wealthy and in possession of all the "good things" in life. This display of material goods and affluence may lead to envy and resentment from the locals. This effect can happen in developing island countries, such as Jamaica, as well as in industrialized countries. In Great Britain, many locals resent the large number of wealthy Arabs who visit that country each year.[21]

Tourism's effect on young people may have a detrimental effect on the culture of an area. The youth of a region are the most likely to seek the jobs created by the tourism industry, which are often higher-paying than the traditional work available, for example, farming. It is common for a young man or woman in a developing nation to be able to earn much more than his or her elders and to flaunt this disparity through the purchase of material goods. This apparent casting away of the society's traditional ways can cause rifts in families. The younger generation is also the most likely to copy behaviors of the tourists that may be considered improper in the region's culture.

> The advent of a substantial [tourism] industry in an area tends to diminish the traditional ways and inject the styles, tastes and behaviors of the tourists into the local people. Tourism tends to increase the standard of living of those involved in it but also transforms the very fiber of the community, frequently separating a formerly homogeneous group into classes and divergent generations. (p. 143)[22]

Developing countries can experience a subtle change in their class system from tourism. It is common for ownership of the tourism businesses to rest with foreigners, who also frequently bring **expatriate** managers to fill the higher-skilled, higher-paying jobs created. In these instances, tourism can be viewed as a modern form of colonialism, in which the host country is "exploited" for its natural beauty but does not participate in the most lucrative return from the industry. This foreign ownership resentment can also occur in industrialized countries as investments are made by those considered to be outsiders.

External Influences and Internal Problems

Many areas find that tourism development is the only viable "export" industry and therefore change their political and economic structures to accommodate the needs of tourism developers and tourists. To encourage tourism, the local governments often waive taxes, import restrictions, and environmental safeguards on tourism investors and develop infrastructure that is mainly available to tourists and not the native population. In this way, the natives see the trappings of a better life but do not participate in it. In 2004, factions within (and outside of) the Dominican Republic were arguing about denationalizing parklands to allow new tourism developments, thus expanding the tourism industry within the island country.

Crime also can become a serious societal problem when tourism succeeds. Researchers believe this phenomenon is due to both the increase in number of potential victims and the resentment and envy of the apparent wealth and carefree attitude of the tourists. Milman and Pizam found a relationship between tourist season and crime season: Crime increased at the height of the tourist season but was lower during the off-season.[23] Researchers suggest that the larger number of people in an area increases a criminal's potential gain from crime and decreases the chances of being caught. This increase in crime becomes a social and economic burden on the local area because it raises fear and necessitates funding a larger police force.

Unfortunately, another social ill that sometimes occurs with the development of tourism is a decline in the moral conduct of the local people. This moral decay—promiscuity, prostitution, alcohol, and drug use—is particularly damaging to a society that had few of these behaviors owing to a strong religious or cultural taboo against them.

Finally, some cultures have balked at the effect tourism has had on their language. Because so many tourists and business travelers use English as a common communication means, the native tongue loses its value and is replaced by English owing to employment qualifications and the demonstration effect. The French seem especially sensitive to threats to the French language. One of the biggest fears concerning the development of Disneyland Paris was the effect that English usage in the park would have on the native language.

Many of these unintended consequences can be seen in the once isolated country of Nepal. Each year, more than 20,000 visitors arrive at the base of Mt. Everest in Nepal. The Sherpa, a native people of the region, have flourished from this influx of international travelers.

> Strong, congenial, and adept at business, Sherpas play a role in the tourist trade rivaled by few indigenous peoples in the world. Sherpas own most of the 300-plus lodges and hotels and many of the companies that organize the treks. Tourism has made the Sherpas of Khumbu rich, or at least considerably richer than most of their neighbors. (p. 54)[24]

Sherpas involved in tourism earn incomes five times the average for Nepal as a whole. Recently, the Sherpas have begun "subcontracting." The Sherpas organize and guide the mountain treks but now subcontract the "heavy lifting" (of gear and supplies) to less well paid members of other area natives.

This increased prosperity for the Sherpas has not been achieved without problems. This new dependence on tourism means that world events now affect the Sherpas' lives. For example, the Sherpa community saw a reduction in the number of visitors after the September 11, 2001, attacks. Owing to recent Maoist insurrections within greater Nepal and the armed security that is required, tourist numbers dropped nearly 40% in 2002. Interaction with peoples from around the globe has also led young Sherpas to leave their native mountain home for the outside world, primarily Kathmandu, for an easier life, better education, and a variety of jobs. And the Sherpa people now are experiencing irritants from modern technology. In an area where telephone service was nonexistent, the cell phone has arrived and signal disruption is a new irritant that the Sherpas now share with the rest of us![25]

The examples just mentioned are only a few instances of the unintended consequences that tourism can have on a society and its culture. Most of tourism's negative impacts on the physical environment are also unintended. The influx of thousands of visitors to a region is often too much for the environment and the host community to withstand without stress. Tourism to an area in large numbers is called *mass tourism*.

SUMMARY

In addition to potentially positive economic benefits, the tourism industry can have negative impacts on the environment, cultures, and societies. When visitor numbers are planned for and capacities are managed, the revenues generated through taxes, memberships, and entrance fees can be used for marketing and educational efforts to create awareness and minimize the potentially negative impacts of visitor activities. By preserving and maintaining the attractiveness of an area or destination, economic vitality can also be maintained. Achieving this balance has been a proven success, as many of the world's precious historical and cultural sites have survived because of visitors willing to pay to view treasures of the past.

Carrying capacity is a key concept in determining the impact that tourists may have on an area. Both the physical and social carrying capacity of an area can be analyzed by considering factors such as number of visitors, type of use, and number of residents. The carrying capacity of an environment or host community will be increased or decreased by changes in the situation such as better planning or increased intensity of use by visitors. The increase in visitors to tourist destinations, whether natural or human-made, has heightened the need for managers to expand carrying capacity through creative facility designs.

For hundreds of years, communities have utilized natural and cultural resources to attract visitors. However, as tourism continues to grow, additional attention and efforts will need to be focused on planning, management, and preservation efforts. History has taught that failure to do so can lead to a variety of unintended consequences from what should be positive economic benefits. When tourism grows unchecked, locals may not only become resentful and even envious of visitors, but they may also witness increases in crime, congestion, and what many consider to be a "way of life," or a desire to return to "the way it was," before tourists arrived.

YOU DECIDE

Alaska, population 600,000—the last frontier of the United States. Far away, difficult to get to, inhospitable. Not today's Alaska. Thanks to the cruise industry, anyone can visit the distant sights of Alaska, even the far interior Denali National Park. In the past, Mount McKinley, at the heart of Denali park, was visited by relatively few hearty backpackers. With the influx of dozens of cruise ships each summer season, over 100,000 visitors view the majesty of the tundra of the park. Carnival Corporation alone moved 110,000 cruisers from its ships onto its trains and to its hotels on the outskirts of Denali.

The 800,000-per-summer cruise passengers have most affected the tiny coastal towns of Alaska, such as Skagway (year-round population 862). On a typical summer day, 9,000 passengers descend from their "floating hotels" to the buses that whisk them off to several dozen shore excursions, including the White Pass & Yukon Railway or Broadway, the shopping district of Skagway. Some are local shops offering Alaskan souvenirs, but many are shops transplanted from the Caribbean, like Diamonds International. The cruise lines "get a cut from stores . . . in exchange for recommending the establishment and mentioning a money-back guarantee on items" (p. 98).

What do the residents of Alaska think of the growth of tourism to the state? They see the massive increase in visitors as good news and bad news. The bad news? Pollution, congestion, noise. The good news? "The cruise industry spent $900 million into Alaska, mostly in wages and retail sales. Three-quarters of Skagway's $80 million in revenues came from [the cruise industry]" (p. 98). Former railroad conductor, now day-tour operator Steven Hites says, "If it weren't for the cruise industry, my little town of Skagway would have been boarded up" (p. 98).

In the oil-supported state, where there is no income, sales, or property tax, some towns have tried to tax the cruise lines. For example, Haines passed a 4% organized-tour tax in 2001. Cruise lines dropped the port from their future itineraries, and the decline in the town's revenues resulted in a 40% increase in the unemployment rate (9% to 12.5%). In 2003, Haines repealed the tour tax, hoping that the cruise ships would return.

What does the future hold for Alaska? The emerging issues for tourism in Alaska are the same as those for tourism anywhere in the world. More development? More environmental protection? More taxes? More jobs, more entrepreneurial opportunities?

Kroll, Luisa. (2004). Cruise control: Carnival Corp. is leading the charge to open up the last frontier to the vacationing masses. *Forbes*, 174(4), 96–102.

NET TOUR

To get you started on exploring Internet links for this chapter, please see

http://www.nps.gov

http://www.nepalhomepage.com/travel/firstpage

http://www.esok.org

DISCUSSION QUESTIONS

1. How can tourism aid in the preservation of societies, cultures, and natural environments?
2. What host community resources are shared by both visitors and local residents?
3. What are the major factors that determine an area's carrying capacity?
4. How can culture be used to attract tourists?
5. What negative effects has tourism had on cultures and the natural environment?
6. How can tourism be used to benefit a culture? What are some of the cultural problems that can result from large numbers of visitors?
7. What are the potential unintended consequences of tourism?

APPLYING THE CONCEPTS

1. Find an article in a recent magazine (for example, *National Geographic*) that discusses how some host communities manage the demands of tourism. Be prepared to summarize the article for the class.
2. Using the Internet, find an environmental impact study conducted on one of North America's national parks. What steps are suggested to alleviate any problems found?
3. Conduct a cultural inventory, and document what might attract tourists to your area or another area in which you are interested.

GLOSSARY

Carrying capacity   A key concept in environmental impact analysis that relates to the amount of use an environment is capable of sustaining under certain circumstances.

Culture   The practices of a society; its customary beliefs, social roles, and material objects.

Demonstration effect   Display of material goods and wealth by tourists leading to envy by local residents based on either the perception or the reality of being less fortunate.

Ecological capacity   The maximum level of users that an area can accommodate before ecological damage is incurred.

Ecotourism   A form of tourism that focuses on environmental and cultural preservation.

Environmental capacity   The limit on the number of users that an area can accommodate before visitors perceive a decline in the desirability of the area.

Expatriate   A citizen of one nation who lives in a nation of which he or she is not a citizen.

Physical capacity   The number of users that can be accommodated in an area.

Social carrying capacity   The number of outsiders to an area that can be accepted without having damaging psychological effects on the locals of the area.

Society   A community, nation, or broad grouping of people who have common traditions, institutions, activities, and interests.

REFERENCES

1. Quammen, David. (2006, October). An endangered idea. *National Geographic*, pp. 62–67.

2. Lavery, Patrick, and Van Doren, Carlton. (1990). *Travel and tourism.* Suffolk, U.K.: St. Edmundsbury Press.

3. Blank, Uel. (1989). *The community tourism industry alternative.* State College, PA: Venture Publishing, Inc.

4. Hodgson, Bryan. (1995). Grand Teton. *National Geographic,* 187(2), 136.

5. Manning, Edward, and Dougherty, T. David. (1995). Sustainable tourism. *Cornell Hotel & Restaurant Administration Quarterly,* 36, 29–42.

6. Ayala, Hana. (1995). Ecoresort: A "green" masterplan for the international resort industry. *International Journal of Hospitality Management,* 14(3–4), 351–374.

7. Roy, Ranjan. (1999, October 19). Tourists trash famous Malaysia rain forest. *USA Today.* Available at: http://www.usatoday.com/life/travel/leisure/1999/to323drhtm.

8. Krakauer, Jon. (1995). Rocky times for Banff. *National Geographic,* 188(1), 50.

9. Noisy skies over the wilderness. (1996). *National Geographic,* 190(2), 139.

10. Wolfson, Hannah. (2000, May 24). Nature's sounds audible again in popular Utah park. *East Valley Tribune,* p. A10.

11. Powell, Eileen Alt. (1996, June 12). Forgotten pharaohs being remembered. *Durango Herald,* p. 4B.

12. Cohane, Ondine. (2007, December). A once and future Eden. *Condé Naste Traveler,* pp. 176–178, 185–187, 248.

13. Coleman, Calmetta Y. (1996, July 12). Quaint towns apply brakes to tour buses. *Wall Street Journal,* pp. B1, B6.

14. Blank, Uel. (1989). *The community tourism industry alternative.* State College, PA: Venture Publishing, Inc.

15. First tourism contract for Dutch firm. (2004). *Middle East Economic Journal,* 48(16), 18.

16. Mathieson, Alister, and Wall, Geoffrey. (1982). *Tourism: Economic, physical and social impacts.* New York: Longman, Inc.

17. Vaughn, Roger. (1995). The two worlds of Fiji. *National Geographic,* 188(4), 114–137.

18. Lever, A. (1987). Spanish tourist migrants—The case of Lloret de Mar. *Annals of Tourism Research,* 14(4), 449–470.

19. Mathieson, Alister, and Wall, Geoffrey. (1982). *Tourism: Economic, physical and social impacts.* New York: Longman, Inc.

20. Catton, William R., Jr. (1980). *Overshoot: The ecological basis of revolutionary change.* Urbana, IL: University of Illinois Press.

21. Kotler, Philip, Haider, Donald H., and Rein, Irving. (1993). *Marketing places.* New York: Free Press.

22. Mathieson, Alister, and Wall, Geoffrey. (1982). *Tourism: Economic, physical and social impacts.* New York: Longman, Inc.

23. Milman, A., and Pizam, Abraham. (1988). Social impacts of tourism on Central Florida. *Annals of Tourism Research,* 15(2), 191–205.

24. Reid, T. R. (2003). The Sherpas. *National Geographic,* 203(5), 42–71.

25. Reid, T. R. (2003). The Sherpas. *National Geographic,* 203(5), 42–71.

LEARNING OBJECTIVES

After you have read this chapter, you should be able to:

- Explain how ecotourism differs from mass tourism.
- Explain how tourism service providers can fulfill the principles of ecotourism.
- Describe the benefits that may be achieved through the use of ecotourism practices.
- Describe how confusion can be removed from the use of the sustainability terminology.
- Explain why tourism service suppliers are embracing sustainability practices.
- Describe why it is so difficult for tourism service suppliers to achieve sustainable operations.

CHAPTER OUTLINE

CHAPTER **13**

Sustaining Tourism's Benefits

There are no passengers on Spaceship Earth. Everybody's crew.

—Marshall McLuhan

■ Can a tourism destination become too popular?

GREEN'S THE DREAM

It didn't seem possible, but five years had passed since Tyla purchased the Lakeway Resort. She and her staff had accomplished so much in their goal to achieve sustainability, yet there was much more to be done.

When Lakeway had come on the market for sale, Tyla jumped at the chance to buy it based on positive recommendations from her accountant and close friends in the tourism business. She had vacationed at the resort with her family since early childhood and would return anytime her hectic career had allowed. The peace and tranquility of the resort in its pristine location along with numerous water and winter sports activities made it an ideal getaway destination.

Stepping away from a successful career in the hotel industry was a major life change, but she never regretted her decision. Lakeway Resort had been well-maintained, and the 40 cabins clustered on 21 acres had been thoughtfully placed to take full advantage of the natural setting.

As soon as Tyla signed the papers and took possession, she began to make changes that would lead to creating a sustainable operation. Long before people talked about carbon footprints or compact fluorescent lightbulbs were the norm, earth-friendly decisions were being implemented throughout the resort. The small rental fleet of outboard-motor fishing boats had been replaced with kayaks and rowboats. All disposable service ware and cups had been eliminated; linens were now changed only at guests' request regardless of the length of their stays; no pesticides were in use; and the laundry used only recycled water and biodegradable detergents.

Through wise purchasing and an extensive recycling and composting program, waste had been reduced to a minimum. In addition to implementing numerous environmentally friendly programs, Tyla had also worked with neighboring property owners to improve wildlife habitat as well as creating trails with numerous wildlife viewing venues. To her delight, every time she made a change and implemented a new program, the feedback was mostly positive from the resort's guests. They seemed to enjoy being part of the sustainability efforts.

Her efforts were even catching the attention of the press, and last year she had won the Governor's Award for "Sustainability in Hospitality." Still, there was much to be done to meet her dream of creating a truly sustainable operation.

Following the management practices she had implemented from day one, she scheduled a daylong retreat with her full-time staff to discuss possible future actions. It was time to make plans for some major renovations including new furnishings. To preserve the environment and create a truly sustainable operation, what type of furnishings should be purchased? Could they be purchased from sources that used locally produced products? Should any of the carpeting be replaced, or would natural or even textured concrete flooring be more appropriate? What should be done about the disposal of the old mattresses? These were just a few of the questions posed at the beginning of what would launch the next phase of Tyla's dream of serving guests while enhancing the environment.

INTRODUCTION

The tourism industry has exploded in recent decades, and the number of travelers continues to grow each year as quicker, cheaper, and safer transportation to almost every corner of the globe becomes available. A second reason is the explosion in the number of the world's citizens who now have the leisure time and money to travel. The longer lives and better health of many of the world's peoples is a third reason. Finally, global communications make people more aware of the wondrous sites of the world and the endless activity options available to them.[1]

This boom in tourism has given rise to millions of new jobs and increased economic prosperity in countries across the world; but as we began to see in Chapter 11, tourism can usher in problems along with economic benefits. The millions of additional tourists have strained the resources of many destinations, sometimes straining natural resources to the point where the initial appeal of an area is diminished and visitation to it declines. Figure 13.1 provides

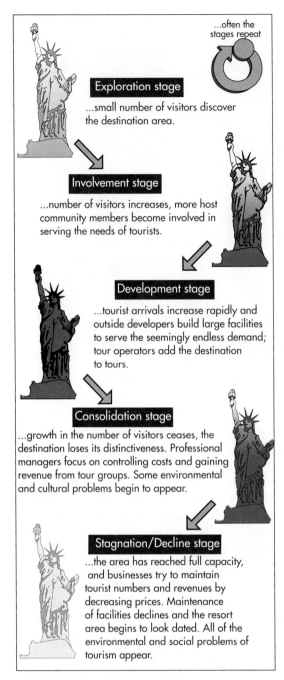

...often the stages repeat

Exploration stage
...small number of visitors discover the destination area.

Involvement stage
...number of visitors increases, more host community members become involved in serving the needs of tourists.

Development stage
...tourist arrivals increase rapidly and outside developers build large facilities to serve the seemingly endless demand; tour operators add the destination to tours.

Consolidation stage
...growth in the number of visitors ceases, the destination loses its distinctiveness. Professional managers focus on controlling costs and gaining revenue from tour groups. Some environmental and cultural problems begin to appear.

Stagnation/Decline stage
...the area has reached full capacity, and businesses try to maintain tourist numbers and revenues by decreasing prices. Maintenance of facilities declines and the resort area begins to look dated. All of the environmental and social problems of tourism appear.

■ **Figure 13.1** Stages of tourism development.
Source: Butler, R. W. (1980). The concept of a tourist area life cycle of evolution: Implications for management and resources. *Canadian Geographer,* 24, 5–12.

one tourism expert's idea of the stages that a destination may go through from beginning to decline. As tourism numbers have increased, questions about future sustainability of these activities have grown.

WHEN IS TOURISM TOO MUCH OF A GOOD THING?

The costs of tourism, especially its environmental, social, and cultural costs, have led many destination residents and tourists alike to become disillusioned with **mass tourism**. Mass tourism, the rise of large numbers of working- and middle-class travelers, to these critics of tourism's continued growth includes:

■ The architectural pollution of tourist strips;

■ The herding of tourists as if they were cattle;

■ The disruption of traditional cultural events and occupations;

■ The diminished natural environment and beauty of the area; and

■ The low priority paid to local needs with funds used instead to increase tourism amenities to keep the community competitive in the marketplace.[2]

Many of the gains realized from tourism are economic and have often been short term in nature. The costs, however, especially to the beauty and natural resources of an area, are more likely to be long-lived or even permanent. Too many times, nonlocal developers relying on "outside money" are the biggest winners, and when the area has become saturated and starts to decline, these developers move on to the next trendy destination with no concern for the damage that may have been done.

Tourism researcher George Doxey studied the effects that "outsiders" have on destination residents and developed an index of these sentiments called the *Irridex*. The Irridex describes the levels of irritation that locals may feel with the influx in the number of tourists and the changes brought about by this growth. Stage One is Euphoria. In the first phase of tourism development, locals welcome both tourism investors and travelers, recognizing the economic boom tourism can generate. Stage Two is Apathy, as residents begin to take tourism for granted, contacts with tourists become businesslike, and communications focus on marketing. Stage Three, termed Annoyance, develops when residents become "saturated"

■ Native peoples can be harmed by the demonstration effect of tourism. Photo by J. B. Yale.

with the number of tourists in their area and begin to see the downsides of sharing their home area. Antagonism, the final stage, is achieved when residents reach their boiling point and overtly treat visitors with verbal or even physical abuse. Tourists are viewed as the root cause for the area's problems. This stage sets off a vicious cycle requiring increased promotional efforts to attract visitors and offset the deteriorating reputation of the region.[3]

So far, we have presented quite a list of problems, both environmental and cultural, that can result from tourism. What can be done to minimize these problems? In areas where tourism activities are still developing, long-range planning will address some of the potential problems in developing tourist destinations. In developing areas and in already popular tourist locations, many efforts can be taken that will help safeguard the environment and the people. These efforts are encompassed in a variety of initiatives ranging from **ecological tourism,** or as it is more commonly known, ecotourism, to more broad-based initiatives such as **sustainable tourism.**

■ ECOTOURISM

The first efforts to reduce the impacts of tourism, especially on fragile areas, were called ecotourism, which primarily involves travel to sensitive natural and cultural environments to observe and learn about a very different culture and environment and participate in low-impact (on nature) sports activities. In addition, **ecotravelers** generally desire to mingle with the local culture and have their travel needs filled by locals in their traditional ways (such as dining on the local gastronomical delights). Compared with other travelers, **ecotourists** tend to be wealthier, college educated, and willing to spend large amounts of money on extended trips.[4] They also tend to participate in active yet nature-focused sports such as climbing, canoeing, and kayaking.[5]

The seed of ecotourism was planted within the burgeoning environmental movement of the 1960s. It grew during the 1970s and 1980s, fed by increased concern for the environment, dissatisfaction with the urbanism of mass tourism, and entry into the tourism marketplace by less developed countries with nature as their primary attraction;[6] and ecotourism continues to explode, having gained the designation as the fastest growing segment of tourism. Ecotourism is experiencing double-digit growth that should accelerate as concerns over the environment and global warming rise.[7] The importance of ecotourism, its size, and its influence on economies, environments, and peoples were recognized by the United Nations when it declared 2002 as the International Year of Ecotourism.[8]

The term *ecotourism* originally was used to label a form or philosophy of tourism that emphasizes the need to develop tourism in a manner that minimizes environmental impact and ensures that host communities gain the greatest economic and cultural benefits possible. The foundation of ecotourism is the preservation of the environment. Ecotourism seeks to minimize travelers' impacts on the social, cultural, and physical environments of communities and locations. The goal is to "integrate tourism development into a broader range of values and social concerns" (p. 11).[9]

There are five basic principles to ecotourism development.[10] The central guiding principle is that tourism should be blended with, or assimilated into, the environment and the local culture of an area. The boundary between the tourism industry and the host community should not be startling: Tourism should fit into the community and share in its ways. This blurring can occur, for example, by matching architecture to the existing local structures and using the area's natural vegetation for grounds landscaping.

A second principle of ecotourism is that the tourist experience should focus on the host community's existing scenic and activity opportunities. In other words, tourism should evolve from the area's natural and historic/cultural attractions. Third, ecotourism is associated with local ownership and management of all or most services. Tourist needs should be filled by local businesspeople and local employees rather than by foreign investors or managers. In this way, more of the economic benefits of tourism flow to the local citizens and their local governments.

To further benefit the host community economically, the fourth principle is that a high proportion of local materials should be used to fulfill

■ Use of local foods and other locally produced goods increases the benefits of tourism. Photo by John B. Yale.

tourists' needs, from construction materials to foodstuffs. For example, in Zambia, there is a unique resort called Tongabezi. The architecture of the "hotel" is a sight to behold. Most of it is built from native lumber and grasses, and many of the guest rooms are open air. One suite, called the Bird House, is built high in a huge tree, and neither the bedroom nor its private bath needs to have walls for modesty's sake. The height of the rooms alone provides all the privacy needed.

Finally, the fifth principle highlights the importance of conservation of resources. By using what are called "ecotechniques," local utilities such as water, heat, and electricity can be stretched to accommodate the needs of both the tourists and the local population. Ecotechniques include use of solar power, rainwater collection, and bioclimatic design of structures to aid in heating and cooling.

Mass tourism, as opposed to ecotourism, tends to strain the environment through the development of more and more infrastructure and superstructure and the increasing wear and tear from the presence and actions of more and more tourists.[11] It is probably obvious to you that building lots of hotels, restaurants, roads, and airports can cause serious problems for an area's environment. For example, the construction of ski resorts in the Alps has led to mudslides and landslides that are damaging the mountainsides.

How do individual tourists threaten the natural environment? One way is simply by blazing trails while walking through nature. One person walking through a wilderness area may not have any significant impact on the area, but 10,000 people within a short period certainly will. The simple action of trampling grass multiplied by 10,000 can lead to erosion of land. For example, several of New York State's Adirondack Mountain peaks are now bare owing to hiker traffic. And driving through a natural area can cause more damage. The manufacture and promotion of "off-road" vehicles may be the biggest threat to nature. To view ever more remote areas, travelers and tour operators are venturing farther into our national forests and parks, scaling fragile rock formations, and converting dirt paths into rutted mud holes. Left unchecked these actions can cause irreparable harm.

Wilderness Act

In addition to national parks and national forests, the United States has wilderness areas. In 1964, realizing that the growing population would strain the natural resources of the country, U.S. Congress enacted the Wilderness Act, which set aside large pieces of land to be retained in their primeval state: "areas where man himself is a visitor who does not remain."

Use of these areas is highly restricted. Although there have been exceptions made, in general, the following are not allowed in federal wilderness areas:

- Commercial enterprises;
- Permanent or temporary roads;
- Motorized or mechanical vehicles, including boats, snowmobiles, and bicycles; and
- Landing of aircraft.

■ ESTABLISHING STANDARDS

The term *eco* has been adopted and abused so widely that a new term has been coined to apply to tour operators who make dubious ecological claims—*greenwashers*. Recently, several governments have created national certification programs to verify the ecoworthiness of tour operators, hotels, and other tourism suppliers. In October 2003, Kenya was the first African nation to introduce such ratings. The private, nonprofit Ecotourism Society of Kenya sends independent inspectors out, armed with a list of criteria that range from environmental measures (water recycling) to economic benefits (purchasing locally grown produce).[12]

However, with so many different uses and misuses of the term *ecotourism*, many industry groups have begun to establish guidelines and standards to define ecotourism operations. As with all standards, the goals are to:

- Provide clear definitions,
- Establish measurable criteria,
- Measure and report compliance,
- Promote consistency in use of terminology, and
- Create defined marketing programs.

Once agreement can be reached on terminology and measurements for agreed-upon standards,

Hogan and Breakfast

One of North America's best examples of ecotourism development can be found on the Navajo Reservation. Navajo families welcome overnight guests who are interested in experiencing the unique Navajo way of life. Visitors sleep in octagon-shaped structures called hogans, made of rough-cut logs, which are heated with wood. Breakfast often features traditional Navajo food such as blue corn mush. The real attraction that keeps guests coming, however, is the opportunity to experience Navajo culture and traditions directly from tribal members.

Source: Rushlo, Michelle. (1999, No. 28). The Navajo way. *East Valley Tribune,* pp. G1, G3.

Table 13.1	Common Terms Used to Describe Ecotourism and Related Activities

Adventure tourism	Green tourism
Low-impact tourism	Nature-based tourism
Rural tourism	Sustainable tourism
Wilderness tourism	Responsible tourism

clarity in meaning and application of ecotourism concepts can be achieved.

Ecotourism in the 21st Century

Since its birth, ecotourism has been defined in various ways and used as a marketing term with growing popularity for any number of tourism attractions and tours. It has come to encompass a wide variety of nature-based activities, from hard to soft. This explosion in the use of the term makes some tourism experts now maintain that the word *ecotourism* "has been applied so widely that it has in many regards become meaningless" (p. 1168).[13] Table 13.1 provides some examples of the common terms that have been adopted as descriptors and lumped together to describe ecotourism and related activities.

David Weaver says such dismay over what many consider to be indiscriminate use is not necessary and suggests today's ecotourism should be defined as "a form of **nature-based tourism** that strives to be ecologically, socio-culturally, and economically sustainable while providing opportunities for appreciating and learning about the natural environment or specific elements thereof" (p. 105).[14] Weaver suggests ecotourism now encompasses the following three core elements:

1. Attraction of natural environments, so ecotourism is nature based
2. Emphasis on learning as an outcome of ecotourism for the tourist that differentiates ecotourism from other more hedonistic forms of "nature-based" tourism, such as sun, sea, and sand; skiing, trekking, or rafting
3. High desire for sustainability of the natural attraction and the native people of the region[15]

As mentioned previously, 21st century ecotourism covers a range of tourism experiences on a continuum of hard to soft activities. As shown in Table 13.2, these descriptions of the end points of the ecotourist spectrum provide clues to participants' views on ecotourism activities. For example, a **hard ecotourist** might travel to coastal sea turtle nesting areas to aid these gentle giants in propagating their species. A **soft ecotourist** might be a passenger on a

Table 13.2	Ecotourist Spectrum

Hard Ecotourist	*Soft Ecotourist*
Strong environmental commitment	Moderate environmental commitment
Specialized trips	Multipurpose trips
Long trips	Short or day trips
Small groups	Large groups
Physically active	Physically passive
Physical challenge	Physical comfort
Emphasis on personal experience	Emphasis on interpretation
Makes own travel arrangements	Relies on guides and tour operators

Source: Weaver, David, and Lawton, Laura. (2002). Overnight ecotourist market segmentation in the Gold Coast hinterland of Australia. *Journal of Travel Research,* 40(1), 270–280.

cruise ship that stops in Costa Rica and takes a guided day trip to the Cloud Forest.

Hard ecotourism activities (rugged and uncomfortable) are enjoyed by a relatively small proportion of environmentally conscious ecotourists. Soft ecotourism applies to short-duration trips often incorporated into a longer multidestination or multipurpose trip. This "side-trip" form of ecotourism is thus tacked on to trips that would largely be considered mass tourism. Estimates of the size of the ecotourism segment have ranged from 2% to 25% or even 50% of the tourism market. The low estimates likely represent the original concept of ecotourism and are the proportion of the market we might term *hard ecotourists*. The larger figure represents soft ecotourists, or those whom Weaver calls mass ecotourists.[16]

Whereas a few of you may have been a hard ecotourist on a past trip, most of you, like the majority of tourists, would probably be classified as a soft ecotraveler based on the activities in which you participated on a recent trip. For example, if during a spring break trip to Florida you spent a day on a guided tour of the Everglades, you would have been considered a mass ecotourist that day. Or you may have taken a whale-watching boat trip off the coast of California. Incorporation of ecotourism activities within trips like these examples has become commonplace, as people around the globe have developed keen interest in the often-fragile natural world around them.

Ecotourism and ecotechniques can be used by both newly developed and fully developed tourist destinations to try to minimize the negative impacts that large numbers of visitors can have on host communities and the environment. As tourism numbers continue to grow, more and more nations and communities need to apply the principles of ecotourism and conservation to ensure that the tourism industry remains viable.

What can we conclude about ecotourism as we see it today? Though use of the term has strayed from its original intent, the key to the idea of ecotourism remains the same: sustaining the natural and cultural elements of fragile environments. Whereas natural and cultural preservation are definitely appropriate for some areas, sustainability is needed in all areas and

operations. So let's turn our attention to the concept of sustainability.

WHAT'S IN A NAME?

Another term that has seen increasing usage by tourism organizations is *sustainability*, a term that is much broader than *ecotourism*. By many accounts, sustainable tourism is the fastest growing segment of the industry, especially when you realize that ecotourism is part of sustainable tourism. When one considers all the related terms that have been attached to and arbitrarily used to describe sustainable tourism, there should be no doubt about this claim. It seems as though everyone finds marketing appeal in describing its service offerings as green, sustainable, or ecologically friendly.

Pick up a copy of any popular travel or tourism magazine and you will be hard pressed not to find at least one article dedicated to sustainability somewhere in the issue. It has become very popular for almost everyone in the tourism industry to tout its efforts at sustainability. Sustainability appears to be just as popular in the academic community, with entire journals dedicated to the subject. Usage of the term *sustainable* has become so prevalent that the concepts and practices of sustainable tourism are beginning to be lost in a semantics jungle.

Just as there is confusion about the use of the term *ecotourism*, so is there a great deal of confusion about what sustainability means. There is a wide variety of associations providing certifications and governmental agencies setting forth guidelines for use of this title, but there are no universal standards for usage. For example, "a vacationer looking to spend time and money in an environmentally conscious manner might run across names such as Sustainable Travel International, Conservation International, Rainforest Alliance, the International Ecotourism Society, Green Hotels Association, and EcoClub, as well as regional associations such as Eco-tourism Australia and Travel Green Wisconsin" (p. 51).[17] "To confuse matters even more, many not-so-green businesses are jumping on the bandwagon for economic benefit, duping good-hearted tourists with their murky promises" (p. T3).[18]

Identifying Tourism Operators Dedicated to Conservation and Preservation

With all of the potential confusion about terms such as *ecotourism* and *sustainability*, the best bet for travelers is to ask some very pointed questions to identify those operators who are dedicated to conservation and preservation. The following questions are a good starting point for initiating the conversation:

- Is there a published environmental policy?
- Are construction materials and supplies provided from local sources?
- How are resources conserved?
- How is gray water used?
- What types of renewable energy sources are used?
- How are local flora and fauna protected?
- Are locals hired as employees and guides?
- What is given back to the local community?
- Are ecotourism education programs provided to employees and offered to guests?

Source: Oko, Dan. (2006, June). Four questions on ecotourism. *Budget Travel*, p. 51.

Creating sustainable tourism operations is more than just words; it requires action and commitment. As environmental issues have become popular discussion points in political, business, and social settings, it seems as though almost everyone is becoming environmentally conscious. As early as 1987, the World Commission on Environment and Development defined sustainability as "[m]eeting the needs of the present without compromising the ability of future generations to meet their own needs" (p. 8).[19] However, as Table 13.3 demonstrates, achieving sustainability requires a great deal of effort.

As the chapter opener demonstrates, even Tyla faced this same dilemma as the decisions about what she and her staff could do to reach her dream of sustainability covered a broad continuum of decisions. These decisions ranged from relatively inexpensive and easy-to-implement changes to costly, time-consuming, and complex actions. What should be apparent as we begin to explore sustainability in the context of travel and tourism is that it is a concept that is still developing.

PUTTING SUSTAINABILITY INTO PERSPECTIVE

If the motives behind these actions have created questions, let's look at the words and phrases that have been spawned by the sustainability movement without verification or certification. For example, any organization can purport to be "sustainable," and use related terms such as *responsible*, *carbon friendly*, and *green*, yet not be held accountable for documenting these claims. Add other related terms such as *ecotourism*, *nature-based tourism*, and **wildlife tourism** to the mix, and the confusion only grows.

To understand more about how this confusion has developed, we need to explore not only the terms that are associated with and used to describe sustainability but also the very broad concepts and practices of sustainable tourism. Take a look at Figure 13.2, which places the many different sustainability efforts into perspective. As industry participants adopt practices designed to maintain or achieve sustainability, the number of visitors that can be accommodated decreases. So, if sustainability is to be achieved, there is a limit to the number of tourists that can be accommodated in any setting.

Now, think back to Chapter 1 and our discussion of the many different definitions and approaches that have been taken to describe the tourism industry. Do you remember how difficult it has been for industry participants to agree on a singular focus? It seems to be just as difficult to describe sustainable tourism. Yet, as difficult as it may be to define, sustainability is critical to the industry as "tourism contains the seeds of its own destruction; tourism can kill tourism, destroying the very environmental attractions which visitors come to a location to experience (p. 27)."[20]

Table 13.3	Sustainable versus Conventional Lodging Operations	
Attribute	*Sustainable*	*Conventional*
Host community	Maintain social and cultural diversity while educating and engaging community members in sustainability activities.	Collect and pay taxes.
Project location and design	Build on previously developed land, and design buildings to blend in with natural setting while incorporating energy-efficient features.	Locate and build on a site with beautiful views or outstanding natural attributes.
Building materials and operating supplies	Use natural materials in construction that do not have to be shipped in, and encourage development of local suppliers for operating needs.	Utilize standard designs to minimize construction costs and centralized, low-cost procurement processes.
Transportation	Promote ride sharing and the use of mass transportation, using electric and hybrid vehicles while limiting the use of fossil-fuel vehicles.	Locate without regard to transportation infrastructure.
Staff	Recruit, train, and develop local employees for all positions.	Import skilled labor and hire local unskilled labor for entry-level positions.
Food	Build menus around local cuisine and crops, encourage sustainable farming practices, and purchase from local sources.	Utilize standardized menus based on popularity and centralized purchasing and distribution programs.
Energy	Utilize passive cooling and solar sources, avoid fossil fuels, utilize renewable energy sources, and use energy-efficient appliances and practices.	Utilize available power sources.
Water	Conserve, utilize natural water sources and gray water, capture runoff, desalinate, and avoid chemicals.	Utilize available commercial or community water sources.
Waste management	Reduce, recycle, and dispose of waste so as not to harm the environment.	Utilize available commercial or community waste management facilities.
Marketing	Provide information on the benefits of sustainability practices and encourage respect for the environment.	Utilize all available marketing channels to increase visitor traffic and occupancy rates for maximum profitability.

Going Green

As you read the following quote about why boutique hotels are embracing sustainability, think about how other tourism service suppliers might embrace similar actions:

Good for the planet, good for people, good for profit—the trifecta of sustainability explains why boutique hotels to big guns are going green. And it's not just greenwashing. Forward-thinking hospitality executives are investing in maintenance makeovers, system

Mass Tourism

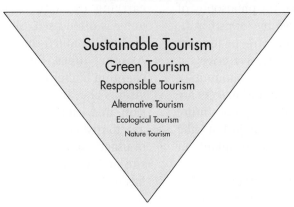

- **Figure 13.2**   Degrees of sustainability.

overhauls, and new green-from-the-ground-up construction. They're choosing renewable materials and earth-friendly supplies, energy-efficient technologies, and management practices that reduce environmental impacts. (p. 24)[21]

Possibly the greatest benefit of ecotourism has been the transfer of the ecotourism philosophy to the preservation of many practices that support mass tourism markets. This extension is represented in the concept of *sustainable tourism* (also called *responsible tourism*). This concept is "broadly conceived as tourism that does not threaten the economic, social, cultural or environmental integrity of the tourist destination over the long term" (p. 80).[22] One simple starting point that is often adopted for identifying sustainable practices is the promotion of the four Rs: Reuse, Recycle, Reduce, and buy Recycled products.

Tourism in Action

The King Pacific Lodge, a 17-room super-luxury barge resort, is towed from Prince Rupert to Prince Royal Island each spring. This uninhabited British Columbian archipelago creates a perfect starting point for wilderness hiking and fishing for affluent guests who want the best of everything. Operating in this pristine location has made owner Hideo Morita keenly aware of his resort's potential for environmental impacts. In an effort to preserve the environment the resort calls home, Mr. Morita has pledged to reduce the resort's carbon dioxide emissions by 50% by the year 2012.

This will be no easy task, as guests reach the lodge in chartered float planes and have the use of a helicopter and a fleet of a dozen high-powered fishing boats. In addition, the resort relies on two 110-kilowatt diesel generators for power.

As a start toward reducing carbon emissions, the all-electric kitchen was converted to use propane as fuel; hot water temperatures were lowered 13 degrees; governors were installed on outboard motors to reduce fuel consumption; and restrictions were placed on boats as to the minimum numbers of passengers required before they can leave the dock. The resort is even exploring the possibility of installing a small hydroelectric system in a nearby stream.

Even the chef has been asked to make sacrifices. He can no longer fly in fresh organic vegetables each week to produce stocks from scratch. Now he must bring aboard stock at the start of the season and keep it in the freezer.

How have guests who are accustomed to getting what they want no matter what the price reacted? According to Mr. Morita, "It's a concern. We're asking our guests to make those sacrifices in hopes that a little bit will do a lot for us. But I can't guarantee that all of the guests will understand that."

Source: The carbon-neutral vacation. (2002, July 28–29). *Wall Street Journal*, pp. P1, P4–P5.

To sustain the viability of destinations, ecotechniques, developed under the philosophy of ecotourism, are now being used by tourism suppliers to sustain the positive benefits of tourism and reduce and minimize the negative effects it can have on destinations and host communities. In addition, more destination decision makers are using formal planning processes to guide future development and operations to sustain both the marketability of the destination and the quality of life of its residents.

From the five ecotourism principles discussed earlier, you can see how host communities can gain many potential benefits from incorporating the concepts into sustainable practices rather than simply chasing mass tourism by:

- Generating more income for more local community members;
- Promoting understanding between locals and members of different cultures;
- Educating local populations on matters of health, education, energy use, business, and environmental conservation; and
- Providing a financial incentive to protect and conserve a globally significant natural/cultural resource.[23]

Many of the techniques just described can also be used in already developed tourism areas to improve or sustain the existing tourism industry. Although applying one or two techniques will not change an area from a mass tourism to an ecotourism destination, simply to adopt efforts such as water conservation and sign codes (limiting their size, height, and lighting) can help alleviate problems that may have arisen.

As you saw in Chapter 12, there are other means of managing the physical and social carrying capacity of developing and developed tourism areas. For example, to eliminate crowds, policies of dispersion have been used. Rather than allowing one area of a destination to become the center of all tourism activity, the infrastructure and superstructure can be spread throughout the region to force visitors to be more evenly distributed. Zoning can also be used to limit the amount of development that can occur in any one place.[24]

To promote sustainability and manage the carrying capacity of specific sites, restrictive entry is often used. Sometimes to the number of visitors is limited through reservations or tickets. At other times, the number can be limited by charging higher fees, thus limiting the number of visitors able and willing to pay the price of admission, and usually reducing the number of times any tourist chooses to visit the site. Limiting types of usage can also reduce the number of users of a site or the impact to the environment any user has on it.

A Future of Sustainability

Thanks to the efforts of Jonathan Tourtellot, the Senior Editor of *National Geographic Traveler* magazine, a new form of tourism, **geotourism**, which combines all of the prominent features of a destination, from natural resources and culture to lodging and shopping, has found its way into the tourism vocabulary. Geotourism is a relatively new form of tourism that focuses on the unique culture and heritage of a location while attempting to help visitors enrich these qualities. Geotourism is all about making a place better by encouraging tourists to visit and spend money with preservation in mind.

Destinations are encouraged to showcase those things that set them apart as unique. The geotourism designation should ultimately attract more tourists, but at the same time, it should motivate both locals and tourists to preserve the cultural and/or natural resources that make the place special. Efforts like this and others, such as increased emphasis on volunteering while on vacation, are increasing awareness, preservation, and protection of all of our resources. **Voluntourism,** a trip that combines travel activities with charitable work, allows tourists to give back through service projects while they take time to experience a destination.[25,26] Geotourism, voluntourism, and other efforts targeting the sustainability of tourism will build a positive foundation for the enjoyment of travel experiences, for both business and leisure, for generations to come.

One thing is for sure: No matter what these efforts to preserve resources are called, maintaining the positive benefits of tourism is in everyone's interests. Unchecked and unplanned tourism growth can lead to the eventual destruction of the very assets that originally served to attract visitors. Taking steps to preserve and protect tourist attractions will create a legacy for future generations. Achieving these benefits begins with awareness and education, and ends with actions!

SUMMARY

The tourism industry has exploded in recent decades as the number of travelers continues to grow. Quicker, cheaper, and safer transportation to almost every corner of the globe and an increase in the number of people who now have the leisure time and money to travel have made this possible. Many of the gains that have been realized from this increased level of travel have been economic, but there have often been costs to the environment and the people in visited areas. In response to these impacts, many initiatives from ecological tourism to sustainable tourism can be taken and have been taken.

The seed of ecotourism was planted with the environmental movement and continues to explode. The term *ecotourism* was originally used to label a form or philosophy of tourism that emphasized the need to develop tourism in a manner that minimizes environmental impact and ensures that host communities gain the greatest economic and cultural benefits possible. Now, ecotourism involves travel to sensitive natural and cultural environments to observe and learn about very different cultures and environments and participate in low-impact sporting activities.

On a broader scale, members of the tourism industry are attempting to ensure the long-term survival and prosperity of travel-related activities by embracing sustainable practices. As the use of terms such as *ecotourism* and *sustainability* has grown in popularity, many industry groups have begun to establish guidelines and standards to define and set apart these terms. There seems to be a great deal of confusion about the definitions and usage of both of these terms, as well as of other related terms that have found their way into the tourism vocabulary. It seems as though everyone finds marketing appeal in describing its service offerings as green, sustainable, or ecologically friendly. However, creating ecologically friendly or sustainable operations is more than just words; it requires actions and commitments.

YOU DECIDE

The chief executive officer of Xanadeaux Hotels and Resorts had been studying the marketing and economic benefits of adopting sustainable practices and decided it was time to act. Failure to adopt sustainable practices at the company's properties would not only put it at a competitive disadvantage; it would also result in lost profits. Therefore, to begin this process, he asked the director of marketing to survey the sustainability actions the company was currently taking and then develop a marketing plan that could be used to highlight the company's best practices and leadership in these efforts.

A quick inventory revealed that many standard practices such as energy and water conservation were in use throughout the chain, but it also revealed that each of the general managers had different ideas about what it meant to run a sustainable operation. These differences appeared to be the most pronounced between those managers who were located in resort settings as opposed to those who were located in major metropolitan areas. What soon became apparent was that there was no organization-wide sustainability program.

Having been charged with developing a marketing plan to showcase and promote the sustainable posture of the chain, it was time to make a decision. It seemed as though most competitors were using terms like *green, sustainable, earth-friendly,* and *environmentally friendly* in their advertising and publicity programs; so why not take the same tack for Xanadeaux, and let practice catch up with reality in the future? Because most of the properties already had programs in place to reduce waste, conserve energy, and recycle whenever possible, wasn't Xanadeaux in fact embracing sustainability?

■ NET TOUR

To get you started on exploring Internet links for this chapter, please see:

http://www.ecotourism.org
http://www.ecotourism.org.au

http://www.ec3global.com
http://www.dep.state.fl.us/greenlodging/

■ DISCUSSION QUESTIONS

1. When can tourism be too much of a good thing?
2. What are the major principles of ecotourism?
3. Why is it important to establish standards for the use of terms such as *eco*?
4. How can hotel and resort operators create sustainable practices?
5. What benefits may be achieved by a host community through the use of ecotourism practices?
6. How can destinations move from mass tourism to sustainable tourism practices?

■ APPLYING THE CONCEPTS

1. Interview a travel agent about the ecotraveler market segment. How many of his or her clients would be part of this segment? What destinations does he or she consider ecotourism destinations? Collect information on one of these destinations to bring to class.
2. How would you describe yourself based on the "Ecotourist Spectrum" shown in Table 13.2?
3. Make an appointment to visit a local hotel or resort. Using the information presented in Table 13.3, "Sustainable versus Conventional Lodging Operations," classify how the property measures up.

■ GLOSSARY

Ecological tourism (more commonly called ecotourism)   A form of tourism that focuses on environmental and cultural preservation.

Ecotourists   Leisure travelers who prefer to visit less popular, more primitive destinations.

Ecotravelers   Travelers who visit sensitive natural and cultural environments to observe and learn about a very different culture and environment and participate in low-impact sports activities.

Geotourism   Tourism that sustains or enhances the geographic character of the place being visited, including its environment, culture, aesthetics, heritage, and the well-being of its residents.

Hard ecotourist   Physically active travelers with a strong environmental commitment who seek specialized trips with an emphasis on personal experiences.

Mass tourism   Twentieth-century phenomenon whereby the working and middle classes began traveling in large numbers for leisure purposes.

Nature-based tourism   Travel to unspoiled places to experience the natural world.

Soft ecotourist   Physically passive travelers with moderate environmental commitment who seek mulipurpose trips with an emphasis on interpretation and physical comfort.

Sustainable tourism   Tourism activities and development that do not endanger the economic, social, cultural, or environmental assets of a destination.

Voluntourism   A trip that combines travel activities with charitable work.

Wildlife tourism   Travel to observe animals, birds, and fish in their native habitats without altering their behaviors.

■ REFERENCES

1. Smith, Valene L., and Eadington, William R. (1992). *Tourism alternatives: Potentials and problems in the development of tourism*. Philadelphia: The University of Pennsylvania Press.

2. Smith, Valene L., and Eadington, William R. (1992). *Tourism alternatives: Potentials and problems in the development of tourism*. Philadelphia: The University of Pennsylvania Press.

3. Doxey, George V. (1975). A causation theory of visitor–resident irritants: Methodology and research inferences. In *Sixth Annual Conference Proceedings of the Travel Research Association* (pp. 195–198). San Diego, CA: Travel Research Association.

4. Chipkin, Harvey. (1994). Tracking the green traveler. *Travel Weekly*, 53(73), 8.

5. Wight, Pamela. (1996). North American ecotourists: Market profile and trip characteristics. *Journal of Travel Research*, 35, 2–10.

6. Blarney, R. K. (2003). Principles of ecotourism. In David B. Weaver, ed., *The encyclopedia of ecotourism* (2nd ed.). New York: CABI Publishing.

7. Kiplinger, Knight. (2007, April 27). *Kiplinger Letter*, 84(17), 2.

8. Butcher, John. (2006). The United Nations International Year of Ecotourism: A critical analysis of development implications. *Progress in Development Studies*, 6(2), 146–156.

9. Smith, Valene L., and Eadington, William R. (1992). *Tourism alternatives: Potentials and problems in the development of tourism*. Philadelphia: The University of Pennsylvania Press.

10. Ayala, Hana. (1995). Ecoresort: A "green" masterplan for the international resort industry. *International Journal of Hospitality Management*, 14(3–4), 351–374.

11. May, Vincent. (1991). Tourism, environment and development. *Tourism Management*, 12(2), 112–118.

12. Lovgren, Stefan. (2003). "Just how green is it?" *National Geographic Traveler*, 20(3), 28.

13. Higham, James E. S., and Carr, Anna. (2002). Profiling tourists to ecotourism operations. *Annals of Tourism Research*, 29(4), 1168–1171.

14. Weaver, David B. (2001). Ecotourism as mass tourism: Contradiction of reality? *Cornell Hotel & Restaurant Quarterly*, 42, 104–112.

15. Weaver, David B. (2001). Ecotourism as mass tourism: Contradiction of reality? *Cornell Hotel & Restaurant Quarterly*, 42, 104–112.

16. Weaver, David B. (2001). Ecotourism as mass tourism: Contradiction of reality? *Cornell Hotel & Restaurant Quarterly*, 42, 104–112.

17. Oko, Dan. (2006, June). Four questions on ecotourism. *Budget Travel*, p. 51.

18. Hoag, Hannah. (2007, June 23). Green to go. *Globe and Mail*, p. T3.

19. World Commission on Environment and Development (WCED). (1987). *Our common future*. Oxford, U.K.: Oxford University Press.

20. Glasson, J., Godrey, K., and Goodey, B. (1995). *Toward visitor impact management*. Aldershot, U.K.: Ashgate Publishing, p. 27.

21. Tierney, Robin. (2007). Going green, sustainable practices take root in hospitality. *HSMAI Marketing Review*, 24(3), 24–33.

22. Weaver, David B. (2003). Ecotourism in the context of other tourism types. In David B. Weaver, ed., *The encyclopedia of ecotourism* (2nd ed.). New York: CABI Publishing.

23. Gurung, Chandra, and De Coursey, Maureen. (1994). The Annapurna Conservation Area Project: A pioneering example of sustainable tourism? In Erlet Cater and Gwen Lowman, eds., *Ecotourism: A sustainable option?* Chichester, U.K.: John Wiley & Sons.

24. Ryan, Chris. (1991). *Recreational tourism: A social science perspective*. London: Routledge, Chapman and Hall, Inc.

25. Rosenthal, John. (2008). Lending a hand at home and abroad. *National Geographic Traveler*, 25(8), 76–78.

26. Kuo, Iris, and Fowler, Geoffrey A. (2008, June 28–29). "Voluntourism" 2.0. *Wall Street Journal*, p. W7.

LEARNING OBJECTIVES

After you have read this chapter, you should be able to:

- Describe emerging trends that will affect future tourism marketing decisions.
- Describe how emerging market segments will affect the future of the tourism industry.
- Describe how tourism service suppliers will be affected by changing consumer needs.
- Describe how and why tourism service suppliers are becoming larger through mergers, consolidations, and alliances.
- Describe how technological changes will affect the future of the tourism industry.
- Explain why the human touch will remain important to the future success of tourism service suppliers.

CHAPTER OUTLINE

CHAPTER 14

The Future of Tourism

The more things change, the more they stay the same.

—Alphonse Karl

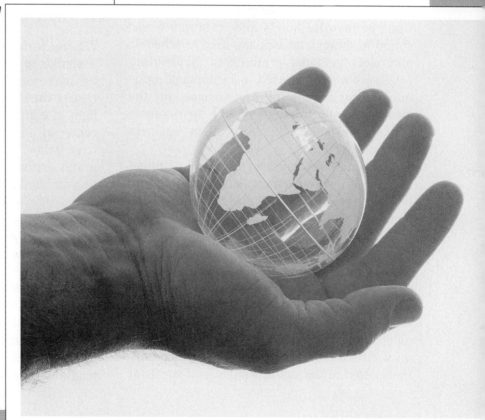

■ The future of the world's largest industry is in all of our hands.

ON THE ROAD AGAIN

Look into the future with us to this imaginary setting. The scenario facing Myra was a familiar one. She had completed and transmitted all of her sales reports and was ready to head out "on the road again." Once a month, she followed up on her webcam calls with personal visits to the primary contacts on each of her key accounts. Webcam calls had improved customer service and made it easier to handle some of the day-to-day details of her job, but the personal touch of regular meetings with her clients was what kept them coming back. Although a routine trip, it would be hectic. She had scheduled 15 sales calls in three cities on Tuesday, Wednesday, and Thursday followed by some well-deserved rest and relaxation in the Miami area.

Setting the itinerary for the business portion of her trip would be easy, as she had called on these clients many times in the past. Technology took a lot of hassle out of the business travel experience. Her profile information was stored in relevant service provider databases, taking the guesswork out of scheduling business travel and making reservations. Everything from the preferred color and style of rental cars to the room types and locations of favorite hotels and restaurants was stored in these databases and used to schedule and meet personal preferences. Scheduling programs were also used to recommend optimum client scheduling and to map out the most efficient routing along with approximate travel times for each sales call or business meeting.

Although she relied on the travel planning databases for the business portion of this trip, leisure decisions were a different story. Like many business travelers, Myra took advantage of her time away from "home" to combine business and pleasure on some occasions. On this trip, she decided to have some fun and do a little exploring. Once again, the technology to plan and dream about a fun-filled weekend was as close as her fingertips. After giving her computer a simple voice command, she was taken on a virtual tour of Miami. She was instantly transported to the sights, sounds, and smells of

the city on a virtual reality site maintained by the city's convention and visitors bureau.

There were so many things to do and see that the choices would be difficult. However, the opportunity to sample before selecting made the decisions a little bit easier. The Bayside Marketplace and the Miami Metrozoo were definitely on her list of things to do, along with a round of golf and a little sun and scuba diving off Miami Beach. After quick virtual tours through a couple of boutique hotels in the heart of Miami, she selected the perfect spot to unwind. Life on the road was still hectic, but it was a lot more fun than it used to be.

Only one more decision to make and then she could pack her bags. The final stop on her business trip would be Atlanta, and she still had to get to Miami and back to Atlanta for her flight home. Which would be more fun: the peace and quiet of a train ride with speeds of over 300 miles per hour or a shuttle flight in one of the new wide-body jets with 1,000 other weekend travelers? Technology was definitely changing, but the planning, adventure, and fun of traveling were still the same.

INTRODUCTION

Peering into the future of travel and tourism is similar to looking into a cloudy crystal ball. We may not be able to bring the future into a clearly focused picture for you, but the bright light of a growing industry is glowing from the center of our crystal ball. The knowledge you have gained through studying the information in this textbook has given you a sound foundation for thinking about the future. Based on this knowledge, you can begin to see some of the challenges and opportunities the tourism industry will face. As you look to the future, can you see yourself becoming a professional member of this industry?

In this chapter, we gaze into the future by considering some of the emerging trends in the tourism industry. These trends may shift and new ones may emerge, but thinking about the future allows you to plan for it. As you read about each of the trends, think about the changes you see happening around you and imagine what the world of tourism might be like 5, 10, or even 20 years from now. No matter how much uncertainty the future holds, there is good news. There will always be the need for talented professionals to tackle the management, marketing, and financial challenges of this growing industry.

THE SHAPE OF COMING TOURISM MARKETS

You read about many of the important tourism market segments of today in Chapter 2. Will these segments still be as important in the future? There is no question that tourism markets will change, but what will these markets look like? Two possible scenarios are beginning to unfold. One scenario points to mass markets and a "one-size-fits-all" approach to delivering tourism services; the other points to highly focused services that are targeted toward meeting the needs of specific market niches.

In countries growing in economic strength, such as Poland, Hungary, China, Vietnam, and Brazil, many tourism services will be developed to meet the needs of mass markets. We will see this type of development as levels of disposable income, leisure time, and infrastructure improvements in these countries encourage tourism growth.

Increased economic activity will lead to increased levels of leisure travel both domestically and internationally. As more citizens of the world discover the enjoyment that comes from tourism activities, increasing participation in travel will drive the development of new facilities and services. The highly populated, newly affluent countries of China and India will become the top two countries for outbound tourists, supplying the world with a huge demand for travel services. There will also be a large flow of VFR tourists to these countries as former emigrants return to visit relatives in the "homeland" and to learn more about their heritage. Unlike their Western counterparts, who seek action and experience in travel, Chinese and other Asian-born tourists are most likely to be motivated to

travel by the cultural values of group engagement, learning, and status elevation.[1]

Tourism markets will probably take a very different path in developed countries such as Canada, Germany, Japan, the United Kingdom, and the United States. In these countries, we will continue to see mass-market tourism, but marketers will continue to refine their service offerings to meet the needs of increasingly sophisticated travelers.

Demographic Shifts

One of the biggest changes that will occur in the tourism market in the 21st century will be the increasing size of the mature traveler segment. The baby boom generation, those tens of millions of post–World War II babies born between the years 1945 and 1964, will retire. As you learned in Chapter 2, mature travelers are a very important tourism segment because of their affluence and ability to travel at any time of the year. By 2050, 34.9% of the U.S. population will be 55 or older, compared with 26.7% in 2010.[2] According to *Statistics Canada* and the U,S, Census Bureau, Canada will see an even larger increase in its mature traveler group. This explosion in the number of senior citizens is happening in virtually all the industrialized countries of the world. Consider the potential effects on tourism of the demographic age pyramids represented in Figure 14.1.

Baby boomers are already the most likely **age cohort** to travel.[3] As retirees, they will be even more likely to travel than their parents and grandparents were, and they will be somewhat different in their tourism interests. Senior baby boomers will be healthier, better educated, and wealthier than seniors of previous generations. Many will have already traveled throughout their country and in foreign lands, often as students or businesspeople. Therefore, they will be seeking new adventures in their future travels.

So what can we predict about baby boomers' travel needs once they achieve senior citizen status? First, they will use computers as a source of travel information and booking. Although they may not be as "connected" as their children and grandchildren, most baby boomers have owned and used computers for decades. Second,

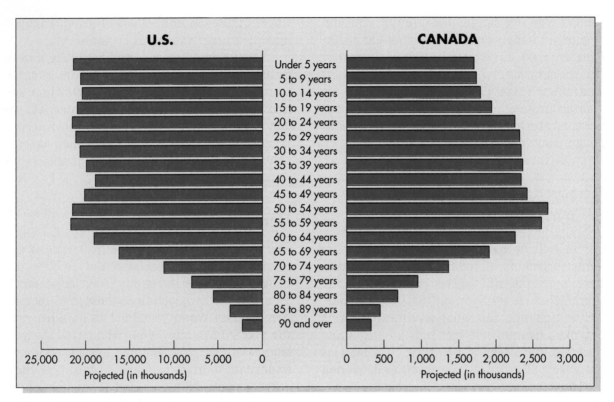

U.S.   **CANADA**

Under 5 years
5 to 9 years
10 to 14 years
15 to 19 years
20 to 24 years
25 to 29 years
30 to 34 years
35 to 39 years
40 to 44 years
45 to 49 years
50 to 54 years
55 to 59 years
60 to 64 years
65 to 69 years
70 to 74 years
75 to 79 years
80 to 84 years
85 to 89 years
90 and over

25,000 20,000 15,000 10,000 5,000 0   0 500 1,000 1,500 2,000 2,500 3,000
Projected (in thousands)   Projected (in thousands)

■ **Figure 14.1**   Population projections—2016.
Sources: Statistics Canada and U.S. Census Bureau.

they are likely to be interested in vacations that include a big dose of healthy food, exercise, intellectual stimulation, and the great outdoors. Because they have been health conscious all their lives, the baby boom generation will be a very physically active group of senior travelers. They will probably place more importance on doing rather than simply seeing attractions. Many will have already "been there and done that" during trips when they were younger, so baby boomer seniors will want to go to new destinations that offer different things to experience and learn.

Many baby boomers will want to travel with their children and grandchildren. Because so many families live far away from relatives and have so little common leisure time, vacations have already become family reunion time, and this trend should pick up steam as the baby boomers enter the ranks of grandparents. Cruises, timeshares, resorts, and extended-stay and all-suite hotels are well suited to meet the needs of extended family getaways. In addition, second homes will become more common as a form of accommodations at destinations as baby boomers retire and can afford seasonal homes. Unlike in

the past, retirees not only will flock to warm climates (snowbirds) but also will purchase in adults-only communities in other resort areas such as the Ozark and Rocky Mountain regions. Many of these second-home communities will offer assisted-living services.

More baby boomers will be single in their golden years because, as a generation, they have been less likely to marry and more likely to divorce. By 2010, it is projected that 25% of all households will be composed of single persons. Combine this with the fact that singles spend more on themselves than those living with others, and the future looks bright for leisure markets.[4]

A **single traveler** is defined by the Travel Industry Association of America as a person who lives alone and travels with or without a companion. Single travelers literally come in all shapes, sizes, and life circumstances. An 18-year-old college student on spring break in Fort Lauderdale, Florida, qualifies as a single traveler, as does an 80-year-old widow enjoying a luxury barge tour on the great rivers of Europe.

Single travelers may not travel alone because traveling alone can be extra costly. Most tours, all-inclusive resorts, and cruise lines charge a **single supplement** that ranges from an additional 25% to 100% more than the per-person price a couple would pay. The Internet is now making it possible for single travelers to find acceptable roommates so they can avoid the single supplement premiums and meet new friends.

Baby boomers will continue to use travel to meet other single people and to fulfill social needs. Savvy tour companies and travel agents will set up travel companion matchmaking services so that boomers do not forego travel for lack of a travel buddy or owing to expensive single supplement prices for cruises and tours. Grand Circle Travel, a tour operator, has already taken steps to aid the single traveler by offering shoulder season tours that have no single supplements.

Another demographic shift, which will have an impact on international travel especially, has been the shift in the ethnic mix of North America. During the 19th and first half of the 20th century, most immigrants to the United States and Canada were Europeans by birth. These ethnic groups enjoyed traveling to their mother countries and fueled transatlantic tourism in the 20th century. But the majority of immigrants during recent decades have come from Latin and Central America, Asia, and former Soviet Union nations (see Figure 14.2). These individuals, as they become more affluent, will also want to visit the lands of their heritage, generating a substantial increase in travel to their homelands.

These demographic shifts are bad news for some tourism suppliers. Snow holiday resorts will experience a double negative effect. Baby boomers and their parents who have been ski resorts' mainstay market segment are giving up skiing as they age, and unfortunately, many did not turn their children on to the sport. In addition, winter sports have been primarily the pastime of Northern and Western European ethnic groups. These ethnic groups are shrinking as

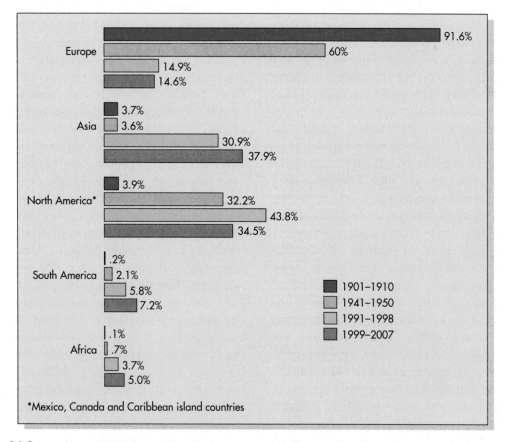

■ **Figure 14.2** U.S. immigration countries of origin through the 20th century.
Sources: 1998 Statistical Yearbook of the U.S. Immigration and Naturalization Service. Washington, D.C.: U.S. Government Printing Office; and *2007 Yearbook of Immigration Statistics.* Washington, D.C.: U.S. Department of Homeland Security.

a percentage of the population of the world. Unless members of the growing Asian and Hispanic ethnic groups can be enticed to learn and participate frequently in winter sports, substantial shrinkage in participation rates will occur in the next 25 years.

Although skiing has decreased in popularity in the traditional ski countries in North America, Europe, and Japan, investment in ski resorts continues, and there is development of ski domes at retail malls. The future may see partnerships between North American and European ski companies to bring the classic resorts of Europe into the 21st century. Resort developers are hoping the snowboarders of today will convert to skiers as they age. Future challenges for snow holiday resort developers will be primarily environmental. Growing concerns about human pollution and traffic congestion are being raised whenever and wherever resort expansion is proposed. In the future, resort management and developers will need to develop more environmentally conscious operations. Whistler Resort in British Columbia, Canada, already has an environmental manager as part of its full-time staff.[5]

The focus will be on development of winter sports resorts, not limiting the market to skiing and snowboarders, as well as the development of winter theme parks that offer plenty to do for the expanding nonskier market. Traditional winter season resorts will also expand their entertainment and sports offerings during the other three seasons of the year. There is a need to look at the mountain as a year-round tourism resource and add other desirable alternatives, such as guided nature hikes and paragliding.

Other members of the tourism industry that will need to change to sustain revenues are theme and amusement parks. The likelihood of visiting a theme park goes down after age 44, so as the average age of the industrialized countries' populations increases, either theme parks will see reduced attendance numbers, or they will need to modify their offerings to appeal to older visitors. Rather than adding faster and more terrifying rides and attractions that appeal to younger crowds, experts suggest that future parks need to become more balanced, still offering high-tech thrill rides but also adding more garden settings and fountains and featuring relaxing themed

restaurants and lounges.[6] You can expect to see theme park growth in some expected locations such as China as well as in unexpected locations such as Dubai as visitors seek to travel, but maybe not as far away from home, to experience new adventures in comfortable surroundings.

Travelers with Disabilities

Physical ability is an important determinant of travel. Travelers with disabilities might have minor limitations, from slight hearing impairments to major mobility obstacles such as confinement to wheelchairs. The United States took the lead to increase accessibility substantially for all by passing the Americans with Disabilities Act in 1990. Since that time, access to most major tourism resources and services has greatly improved within the United States. However, access is still a major issue in other countries of the world and seriously restricts the ability to travel for tens of millions of people. The proportion of the world's population that has disabilities will surely grow as the average age in industrialized countries continues to rise.

The Society for Accessible Travel & Hospitality estimates that about 70% of adults with disabilities travel at least once a year. With the increasing size of the mature traveler segment, accessible travel will become more and more of an issue. Although seniors the world over are likely to continue their interest in travel and new sights and experiences, they will begin to have special needs owing to changing health.[7]

Some forward-thinking organizations are already stepping up to better serve those with special physical needs. By 2005, Avis had introduced Avis Access in its top 100 markets. This program features a variety of specially equipped cars and vans that make renting a car a possibility for many who have not been able to rent in the past. These special cars offer such useful additions as swivel entry seats and hand (as opposed to foot) controls. Microtel Inns and Suites has started a new training program called Opening Doors to enhance service to those with disabilities. Most cruise ships, either by their new designs or through retrofitting, now afford the use of mobility scooters so that those with limitations can easily traverse the huge decks.

The Internet will be an excellent way for those with special needs to find suppliers who will accommodate them. Sites such as wheel-chairsonthego.com (which includes a list of accessible fun places in Florida) will become more common in the future. Hotels, attractions, and other suppliers will feature virtual tours of accessible areas to convince the physically challenged that they too are welcome to enjoy the services of the tourism operator.

Changes in Business, Professional, and Conference Travel

What will happen to the ever-important business and professional travel segment of the tourism market? That is where our crystal ball becomes particularly cloudy: Current trends support the possibility of a decrease or an increase in business and professional travel. Trends in communications, such as computer networking and satellite video image transmission, seem to indicate that business travel will become less necessary. Technological advances will allow businesspeople to see each other and share information as if they were in the same room.

For example, technological improvements in **virtual conferencing** could slow the rate of growth in business and professional travel. Improvements will allow virtual conferencing to be conducted with the same convenience and ease as today's telephone conference call. It will be possible to link participants at multiple sites without loss of picture quality, creating the sensation that they are present. These advances will reduce some travel needs, but they may create other needs.

Think about the potential for an international media company such as Pearson, the publisher of this textbook. Sales representatives from each of its geographic regions within the United States, for example, could gather at a designated virtual conferencing center within their region. They could then share ideas and participate in training programs with others throughout North America or even the world. Travel would still be involved, but by gathering its sales force at regional sites, Pearson could increase efficiency by saving on both travel expenses and time. Where will these virtual conferencing centers be located? The logical locations are those properties—conference centers, hotels, and resorts—that can afford to build and equip quality virtual conferencing facilities. This may in turn lead to more travel, although it may be for shorter distances and durations.

Even though virtual conferencing may help to control travel expenses, more and more companies will be doing business with firms across the world. Representatives of these organizations may feel the need for face-to-face meetings to build trusting relationships that can come only from sharing time together. North American businesspeople in particular are being forced by economic necessity to work with other businesspeople from Asia, the **Pacific Rim**, Central and South America, and former Soviet Union nations. In all these locations, trust is the primary foundation for business transactions. These relationships can be developed only by spending time together, sharing meals, and getting to know one another. Because this type of relationship building requires time and face-to-face interactions, it is unlikely that technology will override these cultural factors and the need for relationship building.

Our best guess is that travel for business and professional reasons will continue to increase in spite of further advances in communication technology. Doing business in the future will involve more, not less, collaboration with others. Some of this increased need for interaction among businesses will be satisfied with telecommunications. However, as Myra noted in our chapter opener, there is no substitute for the personal contact that requires physical travel and meeting with others face-to-face. Yet, business travelers will increasingly find opportunities to tack on a little personal rest and relaxation with their business duties.

We predict that the most popular types of conferences in the future will not be business related but instead will focus on personal lifestyles and interests. Growth in number of conferences and attendees will most likely come in the form of meetings on organized religion, self-improvement/education, hobbies, civic topics, alumni reunions, and politics. This trend began in the 1990s when 20% of U.S. citizens traveled to nonbusiness conference events.[8]

■ Preserving the past becomes more challenging as the number of visitors increases. Photo by D. A. Yale.

■ EMERGING TOURISM MARKETS

What tourist activities will be the favored pastimes in the future? We have already mentioned several of the broad tourism trends shaping the face of the industry in previous chapters. Now we will turn our attention to some specific segments that hold promise for future growth. As one travel professional noted, "[r]ather than sit on a beach and sip a mai tai, there is a move among travelers to engage themselves in the people and places they visit."[9] In a world where many travelers have "been there and done that," there is a growing desire to do something special or participate in life-changing activities.

Slow Tourism

Slow tourism vacations will develop as an important niche segment of the tourism industry to meet the need of travelers looking for a very different experience. To escape the 21st-century "accelerated" life, more and more travelers will opt out of high-activity vacations, instead preferring trips with a slower pace than they experience in everyday life, allowing time and opportunities for immersion. These vacations will involve all the five senses and be designed with the goal of experiencing people and places.

This trend suggests that health spas, "zones of tranquility," rural destinations, and cultural tourism in general will see an increase in popularity. In addition, single-destination, as opposed to multidestination, trips will be preferred by travelers seeking the immersion of the slow tourism experience.[10] A preferred slow tourism vacation might be a two-week cottage stay in a rural Irish town, walking the green hills and ocean bluffs, soaking in the ambiance of local pubs, and meeting and mingling with the townspeople.

Adventure and Extreme Tourism

Adventure travel is defined as a "trip or travel with the specific purpose of activity participation to explore a new experience, often involving perceived risk or controlled danger associated with personal challenges, in a natural environment or exotic outdoor setting" (p. 343).[11] Like ecotourism, adventure travel focuses on experiencing, not sightseeing. Adventure travel is often split into hard and soft forms, and participants

Walkabout Tours

The preferred guided tour of the future may not be conducted via motorcoach but instead via the oldest form of transportation: on foot. Recently there has been a boom in the number of tourists taking walking tours. What is driving this phenomenal growth? One reason is that walking is now the most popular form of exercise among adults. Another is that walking tours can run the gamut from extreme tourism for serious trekkers to "soft adventure" tourism for families or mature travelers. Walking tour packagers also offer a variety of accommodations and meal plans: rustic for the ecotourist segment through luxurious for the walker who wants to be pampered at the end of the trail.

What better place to find this type of tour than Australia? Blue Mountains Walkabout, founded in 2000 by an Aboriginal Discovery Ranger, takes guests into the bush of Dharug country for an immersion experience. On this daylong program that involves about four hours of walking, participants are encouraged to use all of their senses, meditate, and slow down. Discussions about culture bring everything they see, touch, hear, smell, and taste to life.

Sources: Eastwood, Ken. (2007, October–December). Blue Mountains Walkabout, NSW. *Australian Geographic* (88), 79; Gonzalez, Isabel C. (2004). Taking a head trip. *Time,* 163(113), 84.

are called hard and soft adventure travelers (see Table 14.1).

Hard adventure tourism encompasses activities that involve above-average elements of physical challenge and risk. Because of the potential danger involved in many of the hard adventure activities, such as mountain climbing, highly experienced guides often "choreograph" much of the trip for the tourist group.[12]

Recently, researchers have tried to describe the breadth of adventure travelers. Table 14.2 highlights the results of one such attempt that resulted in the psychodemographic description of six "types" of adventure travelers. Note that three of the segments are primarily soft adventure

tourists, whom we might call the mainstream of adventure travel. Many of the hard adventure tourists in the general enthusiast and active soloist categories are probably GRAMPIES, a term for men "who are growing, retired, and moneyed, in good physical and emotional health" (p. 208).[13]

It is estimated that by 2040 over half of the population in the developed world will be over fifty. This means more people in good health with a more informed global perspective—more GRAMPIES—thus more adventure tourists. The lines between adventure and mainstream tourism will become less clearly defined. Adventure will become more accessible and achievable for more people. Moreover, adventure holidays will become more attractive as the collection of experiences begins to undermine the more materialistic elements of consumer society.[14]

During the next decade, the softer adventure activities will increase in popularity to the point that most mass tourism trips and tours will include at least one of the activities listed in Table 14.1. Think back on your last vacation. In which of the listed activities did you participate? As you can see, using this more relaxed definition of **adventure tourism**, a family skiing in the mountains of Alberta during a school vacation week would be classified as adventure tourism. Cruise lines have already found that mixing laid-back relaxation with more adventurous activities has allowed them to reach a broader market of potential cruisers.

Extreme tourism (a subset of adventure tourism) encompasses activities that involve above-average elements of physical challenge and risk. Growth in extreme sports and other extreme activities will continue in the future. Although younger, professional/managerial, single men are most likely to seek extreme thrills, baby boomers and young women are fast-growing subsegments for this market.

Why are these more dangerous activities gaining in popularity? One reason offered by industry leaders is that these sports have been spotlighted and glamorized in the media, including motion pictures. Another reason suggested is that we are so coddled in our everyday world—from tamper-resistant packaging to automobile

■ Tomorrow's travelers will look for new extremes.

air bags—that people want to feel that physical rush of danger, even if the rush comes more from the appearance of living on the edge than from actual terror. Growing demand for extreme activities is also driven by increasing affluence and the increased safety and better equipment of many of the sports. To some extent, tried-and-true activities and attractions have become boring because they are so familiar to so many.

Table 14.1	Adventure Travel Activities
Examples of Soft Adventure Travel Activities	*Examples of Hard Adventure Travel Activities*
Camping	Rock climbing
Hiking	Skydiving
Canoeing	Mountain climbing/trekking
Bicycling	Rapids rafting/kayaking
Walking	Sea kayaking
Snorkeling	Ice climbing
Horseback riding	Scuba diving
Snow or water skiing	Mountain biking
Bird/animal watching	Cave exploring
Off-road driving	Cliff skiing/snowboarding
Sailing	
Photo safaris	
Dude ranching	

Table 14.2	Segments of Adventure Tourists

General enthusiasts (about 25%)—Most likely to take experiential/participatory adventure trips. Mostly male, college educated, with above-average income. Prefer hard challenge activities.

Budget youngsters (about 20%)—Young, single, with low income. Most likely to take adventure trips with friends instead of family.

Soft moderates (about 10%)—More likely to be older, well-educated women. Prefer soft adventure activities such as hiking, nature trips, and camping. Most likely to take package trip.

Upper-high naturalists (about 15%)—Middle-aged and married with the highest incomes of any type. Prefer softer forms of adventure travel with emphasis on more distant exotic locales, such as Africa and Asia. Most likely to travel on long-duration trips and spend a lot per trip.

Family vacationers (about 15%)—Heads of households from dual-income families who travel with entire family. Prefer carefree vacations at least partially planned by operators.

Active soloists (about 15%)—Both young to middle-aged men and women who prefer traveling alone or with members of some organization. The most likely to travel on an all-inclusive package and pay the greatest amount for trip.

Source: Sung, Heidi H. (2004). Classification of adventure travelers: Behavior, decision making, and target markets. *Journal of Travel Research,* 42(2), 343–356.

Adventure and extreme sports are typically outdoor or wilderness sports and go hand-in-hand with ecotourism. A sea kayaking trip off the coast of Costa Rica qualifies as both ecotourism and adventure tourism. Tourism suppliers, especially tour operators, will create at least two different ecotourism packages. One ecotourism package will be more educational and observational, whereas the other will be more physically challenging, including one or more extreme sports.

Medical Tourism

Medical tourism, travel to other countries to receive treatments, is becoming very popular. Many already travel for low-cost cosmetic surgery or dentistry, experimental drug/surgical treatments, or because treatment is either unavailable or untimely in the country of their residency. This type of tourism is likely to increase as a free-market alternative to the rising costs of medicine and the rising trend toward medical rationing, where medical services are withheld from individuals in countries with socialized medical care. With a growing number of health travel agencies, it is becoming easier for travelers to schedule everything from complete physicals to complex surgeries more confidently.[15]

In Singapore, some hospitals and hotels are partnering to offer packages that combine a hotel stay with a treatment package. Thailand's Tourism Ministry has aided the development of packages marketed to rich Arab patients. These packages feature shopping, sightseeing, and other activities for family members who are traveling with the loved one who is receiving treatment. In an interesting twist, Indian nations in Canada are developing private hospitals so fellow Canadians can circumvent the Canadian ban on private-pay medical services by traveling to tribal lands where such laws do not apply.[16]

Vocation and Real Estate Tourism

Very specialized niches are being served and should grow as tourism service suppliers strive to meet ever-changing needs and expectations. Culinary and heritage tourism definitely fit the concept of travel with a purpose, but new niches are appearing that do more than fulfill physiological and psychological needs. For example, **vocation tourism** and **real estate tourism** are being marketed to meet travelers' needs seeking to combine pleasure with accomplishment.

Vocation and real estate vacations are beginning to catch on as travelers seek personal and often tangible benefits by combining relaxation and new experiences into practical leisure-time packages. On a vocation vacation, travelers take time to experience possible new careers before actually making career changes. You can think of these trips as being mini-internships. On a real estate vacation, travelers spend their time gaining in-depth knowledge and perspectives about the area from scheduled meetings with local experts while searching out potential investment opportunities.

Space Tourism

Someday in the not too distant future, we may be able to fly halfway around the globe in four hours. We have already witnessed the advent of space tourism as civilians have joined the ranks of astronauts on space voyages, but the numbers of space travelers will surely grow in coming years as hypersonic travel becomes a commercial reality. Just think, hypersonic travel made possible by scramjet engines will allow passengers to travel from New York to Tokyo or Sydney in two hours at an incredible speed of 10,000 miles per hour. This is not science fiction, as Australia, China, and the United States are all working on perfecting scramjet technology.[17]

Space travel and the future of space tourism became a reality in October 2004 when famed aircraft designer Burt Rutan and his team became the first to launch a privately developed manned spaceship successfully, winning the $10 million Ansari X PRIZE granted to the first team to launch two successful manned space launches within two weeks of each other. The goal of proponents of space tourism is that by 2015, adventure travelers will be able to fly into space for the same price as a cruise vacation.[18] Space Adventures is planning Russian-based spacecraft missions to the International Space Station. And plans are on the drawing boards for full-blown resorts on the moon.

■ | MEETING FUTURE TOURISTS' NEEDS

All of the changes that have been mentioned will lead to two common forms of market segmentation. **Microsegmentation** and **mass customization** have been used for several years, but these two concepts will gain further use in the future. **Subsegments**, also called "microsegments," are market segments that represent a relatively small group of consumers such as Californian young professional Asian Americans or Manitoban back-country fishing enthusiasts. As companies attempted to lure customers from competitors, they began developing product offerings to meet the needs of smaller and smaller market segments.

Mass customization is the extreme of microsegmentation. A company mass customizes when it produces a good or service to fulfill the unique needs of an individual buyer. For example, several computer manufacturers build personal computers to individual customer specifications. The consumer chooses all the components, including the size and number of hard drives, storage options, and the amount of RAM, from a menu of options, and then the manufacturer assembles the pieces to deliver exactly what the buyer

Mass Customization = Personalization

The Ritz-Carlton luxury hotel chain is taking the concept of mass customization seriously. Guest preferences are entered into the hotel database so that service during return visits can be more personalized. For example, if a guest requests a hypoallergenic pillow, for her next stay, housekeeping will make up her bed with that type of pillow without waiting for a request. And if a guest eats only the complimentary peanut butter cookies (foregoing the chocolate chip and sugar cookies), he will receive more peanut butter cookies during subsequent stays. A guest checking into the Orlando Ritz-Carlton receives an empty glass to be filled with his or her favorite citrus juice courtesy of a Citrus Concierge. Talk about making a guest feel at home!

Sources: Brown, Tom. (1996). Efficiently serving customers uniquely. *American Management Association, 85,* 60–61; Braley, Sarah J. F. (2002). The new concierge. *Meetings and Conventions, 37*(11), 14.

needs. Tourism businesses in the future will use both microsegmentation and mass customization to attract guests.

Mass customization will allow travelers to customize their service packages and travel itineraries. Hotels specializing in the business and professional segments are building rooms that can be **configured** to suit individual guests' needs for multimedia presentations, conference calling, telecommunications links, and so on. Tour companies will use mass customization to allow more flexibility in touring. As the tourism market becomes more competitive, the empathy component of service quality you learned about in Chapter 3 will become more and more important. Both microsegmentation and mass customization can add the personal touch of empathy to a tourism service.

TRAVEL AGENTS' CHANGING ROLES

There is nothing like a little uncertainty about the future to create concern and cause a good debate. One of these hotly debated areas in the tourism industry is the future role of the travel agent. As we discussed in Chapter 4, travel agents have been important intermediaries in the industry, performing a valuable service by bringing together tourism service suppliers and the traveling public. Will the role of the travel agent remain the same in a world that appears to be turning in ever-increasing numbers to nonpersonal information sources such as the Internet?

The technology provided through the Internet has the power to make travel planning more personal and exciting. Computer users will become more informed consumers as they explore travel and other leisure-time options ranging from transportation and accommodations to attractions and entertainment. As networking capabilities continue to increase in availability and speed, computer terminals, serving as electronic smart agents that utilize **artificial intelligence,** will develop to meet travelers' specific needs. Booking a preferred flight time, reserving accommodations that meet specific

criteria such as price range, level of service, or driving distance from the airport, and reserving tickets for the evening play based on real-time reviews are all possibilities.

Some people may use the information and reservation capacities provided through the Internet to book simple travel arrangements such as traveling from point A to point B, but as travel needs become more complex, the services of travel professionals may prove to be invaluable. For example, group travel will increase markedly as people look to travel as a means of building social relationships. As leisure time becomes scarcer, families fragment, and quality social time diminishes around the world, people will use trips to squeeze the most out of the precious time they have with family and friends. Family reunion and extended family travel will become the norm for long-distance family vacations, and specialty tours focused on a variety of "hobby cultures" will begin to dominate adventure travel. Travel agents will be more frequently used to develop and coordinate these forms of group travel rather than arranging routine travel for individuals or couples.

Although some may prefer the do-it-yourself freedom of the Internet, for other people, the personal service and professional expertise provided by a travel agent will continue to be the travel department store of choice. According to one respected travel research company, travel professionals who can provide the following benefits can succeed in retaining and attracting customers:

- The best choices and prices,
- Money savings,
- Product knowledge,
- Safety/security information, and
- Time savings.[19]

You be the judge in this debate. Some experts say that the role of the travel agent will become unimportant in a world where everyone has access to travel-related information and reservation sources through personal computers. Other experts say that the role of the travel agent will become more important and specialized as people have access to more data and less time to sort through this sea of information.

TRANSPORTATION TRANSFORMATIONS

Significant changes will be noticed in all forms of transportation. Speed and efficiency will increase thanks to advances in technologies and materials. Every form of transportation from automobiles to ferries will see change. For example, ferry transportation, which has been an old standby, should become more prevalent and popular as gasoline prices continue to rise around the world owing to the ever-increasing demand for oil. New high-speed ferries cut down on travel time by taking shorter across-the-water routes. For example, introduced in 2004, the *Lake Express* ferries across Lake Michigan from Milwaukee to Muskegon in just two and one-half hours.

Expanded rail service will also provide additional relief to crowded transportation corridors. Proliferation of high-speed rail service will be the hallmark of this transportation mode for years to come. Although speeds of 100 miles per hour are commonplace, plans are already being tested to produce trains that travel at much higher speeds. Magnetic levitation (Maglev) trains, especially on shorter high-traffic routes, will replace traditional track-based trains. Maglev trains generate their own energy from the friction created over their magnetic lines and will travel at speeds in excess of 300 miles per hour. As the convenience and comfort of magnetic levitation technology spreads from its experimental status to the norm for high-speed rail travel, more and more passengers will be drawn from the airports to the ground.

To get an idea of how efficient train travel could be, think about the following proposal. Brad Swartzwelter, a conductor for Amtrak, has suggested that the solution to transportation problems within the United States could be solved by underground trains. He proposes that tunnels be dug, connecting points A and B, and a magnetic levitation system be installed to carry travelers between these points at speeds up to 900 miles per hour. Future technological advances could lead to a transcontinental trip that could be completed in approximately three hours.[20]

In the meantime, in the United States and throughout the world, you can expect that more high-speed trains will be put into service as demand continues to be fueled by the efficiencies of point-to-point service in high-demand corridors prompted by fuel costs, security delays, and continuing customer-service problems at crowded airports. Noticeable increases in this type of service in China and India should be seen as the appetite for travel explodes.

Connector trains will become the norm for mass transit in densely populated corridors and as connectors for newly built airports. As you will see next, there will be a boom in new airport construction. In these new facilities, ticket counters, parking, and baggage checking will be located substantial distances from the airports, which will be built far outside of urban areas to alleviate noise, road traffic, and airspace congestion. These new airports will become destinations in themselves, featuring a wide variety of entertainment options for locals and travelers alike.[21]

The future of air travel presents a picture that at first seems to be incongruous. As airline fleets are upgraded, these new planes will be larger or smaller, faster or slower, and be designed to fly more direct routes. First, you will see more of the double-decker superjumbo jets, the 555-seat A380, serving long-haul trans-Pacific and trans-Atlantic routes. These extremely large aircraft can serve routes only between airports that have made infrastructure investments to handle the weight of the planes on the runways, and the large number of passengers during arrivals and departures. At the same time you will also be seeing smaller planes, like the regional jets, as airlines are finding that it is also more profitable to serve many markets through direct routes that can produce passenger traffic to fill planes with fewer than 100 seats. In an effort to conserve fuel, more and larger turboprop aircraft, with lower operating costs, will be placed into service, replacing jets.

Because of new technology, air traffic control centers may become a thing of the past. Pilots in the future will determine their own routes, aided by computers calculating their planes' and other air traffic positions each second. As a matter of fact, planes may fly without pilots. Most commercial aircraft already fly "pilotless" from just after takeoff to just prior to landing. Another new concept, tilt-rotor planes, may make it possible for aircraft to take off and land with little to no runway.

Increases in size and speed of aircraft will be absolutely necessary to satisfy future demand for air travel. Both the U.S. National Aeronautics and Space Administration and aircraft manufacturer Airbus predict air passenger traffic worldwide will triple by 2025. For the United States alone, "[p]rojections of population growth suggest that the [U.S.] will need about 25 more large airports in 2028" (p. 13).[22]

Finally, even with all of the improvements in other forms of transportation, automobiles will still be the most popular means of getting from one place to another, but they will definitely be more efficient. Even if fuel prices remain high, leisure driving will still be in reach of most travelers as new technologies will make it possible for cars to get 100 miles per gallon or more, and some of the stresses of driving will be relieved as newer cars, combined with "smart highways," provide collision avoidance devices, hands-free driving, and computer routing to the driver's destination of choice.[23]

MOVING INTO AN ERA OF COMPETITIVE COOPERATION AND CONSOLIDATION

The tourism industry has historically been fragmented, with many different suppliers serving an ever-growing market. This fragmentation has resulted in varying levels of service, quality, availability, and pricing. At the same time, the traveling public has become more knowledgeable and demanding about tourism services, forcing managers to search for new ways to control costs and improve quality. As organizations respond to the converging demands of improving quality and controlling costs, we will witness an era marked by an increasing number of mergers, acquisitions, alliances, and cooperative agreements.

Manufacturing and other services have led the way by consolidating to gain market share and increase operating efficiencies and profitability. In the early 1900s, there were hundreds

of automobile manufacturers in the United States alone. Now there are only about a dozen worldwide. Smaller, less efficient manufacturers were overtaken by larger, more efficient, and better-capitalized companies that could respond to changing consumer demands. The same type of trend is emerging in the tourism industry as suppliers continue to consolidate. Several airlines have been acquired by larger rivals; hotels, casino operators, cruise lines, and car rental companies are merging as well. Similar combinations will continue and become more common as organizations seek economies of scale and broader name recognition across national and international markets with one notable exception. The exception will be the disaggregation of the megacasino entertainment enterprises that will be spun off into separate enterprises with similar foci: casino operations, hotel operations, and food and beverage operations.

Another trend that will move through the tourism industry is **cooperative alliances**, a concept that was pioneered by airlines to gain greater brand recognition and operating synergies. For example, the alliance between British Airways and American Airlines signaled the importance of gaining dominance in high-traffic corridors such as those serving the North Atlantic marketplace. However, the benchmark for airline alliances is the Star Alliance. This alliance, which was created in 1997 by six airlines with the intent of being the airline of the Earth, has since grown into a global giant, as can be seen in Table 14.3.

Airline alliances meet customer needs by delivering "'seamless service'—simplified ticketing, better connections, thorough baggage checking, and frequent flyer reciprocity" (p. 73).[24] They also provide another important economic benefit by allowing airlines to gain access to landing slots and gates at already crowded international airports. More changes are on the horizon as the number of major participants in the airline industry continues to shrink and the remaining organizations increase their levels of cooperation.

As we discussed in Chapter 8, the move toward industry partnering is also accelerating in the foodservice segment of the tourism industry. Every link in the supply chain, from manufacturers

Table 14.3	The Star Alliance
Member Airlines	*Major Hub Airports*
Air Canada	Toronto, Montreal, Vancouver
Air China	Beijing, Chengdu
Air New Zealand	Auckland, Los Angeles, Sydney
ANA	Tokyo, Osaka, Nagoya
Asiana Airlines	Seoul
Austrian Airlines Group	Vienna, Salzburg, Innsbruck
bmi	London Heathrow, Manchester
LOT Polish Airlines	Warsaw
Lufthansa Aviation Group	Frankfurt, Munich
Scandinavian Airlines	Copenhagen, Oslo, Stockholm
Shanghai Airlines	Shanghai
Singapore Airlines	Singapore
South African Airways	Johannesburg
Spanair	Barcelona
Swiss International Air Lines	Zurich
TAP Portugal	Lisbon
Thai Airways International	Bangkok, Chiang Mai, Phuket, Hat Yai
Turkish Airlines	Istanbul, Ankara
United Airlines	Chicago, Denver, San Francisco, Los Angeles, Washington, D.C.
US Airways	Charlotte, Pittsburgh, Philadelphia, Phoenix, Las Vegas

and distributors to operators and customers, is being brought closer together to improve service and reduce operating costs. These efforts have been dubbed **efficient foodservice response,** or **EFR.** The partnership agreements that are evolving through EFR are providing lower food costs, fewer inventory errors, and higher levels of customer satisfaction and value.[25] Foodservice operators, especially franchise operators, will take advantage of the social networking capabilities facilitated by Web 2.0 through enterprise-level networking to share information targeted at improving purchasing and operating efficiencies.

There is no doubt that the airline industry will also continue to cooperate as well as consolidate with more mergers between rival carriers both inside domestic boundaries and across country boundaries. The trend that began in the United States has already spread to Europe and Asia and will only pick up steam in the future. The "Open Skies" treaty between Europe and the United States set in motion the consolidation wave among previously competing airlines.

With this treaty, consolidation between airlines no longer means losing lucrative international markets. The combined companies can keep their trans-Atlantic routes and they can fly out of any European city to the United States, not just from airports located in their home country. With these artificial barriers to competition being lifted, the urge to merge will definitely grow.

There will also be an increase in **subcontracting** many functions needed to support guest services. Operations such as cleaning, laundry, and food service will be performed by outside contractors. In some situations, the operating company will own the facilities and equipment and rely on the expertise of outside contractors to provide and manage labor. In other situations, space will be leased to subcontractors, who in turn will make the investments in equipment as well as manage the entire operation. This trend is already becoming evident in the number of fast-food outlets that are appearing in hotels, airports, theme parks, service stations, and food courts in malls.

SERVICE ENHANCEMENTS

One thing is for sure, future service enhancements will revolve around technological advances, and the rate of change in these advancements will continue to increase. To get some idea of future technological changes, think back to the computers you used at home, work, or school just five years ago. How fast could they operate? What software did they run? How were they linked to information sources around the world? What you thought was fast and efficient back then is slow and cumbersome by today's standards; and computer technology is just one facet of the technological changes that will shape the future of the tourism industry. Maybe the changes in service delivery won't come quite this fast, but change will definitely come. As we saw in Chapter 5, operators pursue increasing efficiency and effectiveness in everything they do from service delivery to customer connectivity. Although every effort will be made to enhance the guest experience, the human touch will remain the hallmark of hospitality.

Amplifying Guests' Experiences

A glimpse of what may be in store for hotel guests in the future can be seen at the Fairmont Vancouver Airport hotel, where it is no longer necessary for guests to check in at the hotel's front desk. Check-in takes place in the airline baggage claim area, and the hotel arranges for bags to be delivered straight to the guest's room. Guests are greeted with a comfortable and cheery room as check-in also activates room lighting and temperature controls that stay in an energy conservation mode until a room is occupied. In-room motion detectors make "Do Not Disturb" signs a thing of the past, because the housekeeping staff can now time their cleaning activities for maximum customer convenience and satisfaction when guests are out of their rooms.[26] And, there are even more changes on the horizon. According to Tad Smith, Senior Vice President, E-Commerce, for Starwood Hotels & Resorts Worldwide, Inc.,

> In [the future], your credit card will also have your frequent guest information imbedded in a computer chip. When you walk through the door of our hotels, you'll be automatically checked in, and your credit card will become your key. You won't have to stand in any lines at all. You're going to have an entirely personal experience in your hotel. Your computer screen will already be configured to your homepage with your e-mail waiting for you. (p. 64)[27]

Travelers seeking new adventures will have the opportunity to participate in a real Jules Verne experience as they enjoy an underwater odyssey. Jules' Undersea Lodge in Key Largo, Florida, currently provides the only underwater accommodations for undersea adventures. However, if architects and developers have their way, larger nautical hotels could be built at offshore sites in Hawaii, Mexico, and Sicily.[28]

Safety and Security Strides

Realistically, the threat of terrorism will continue, so travelers will likely accept a decrease in their privacy in exchange for greater security. Security will pervade but almost go unnoticed as technologies improve in all aspects of the tourism industry from attractions and sporting events to accommodations and transportation. Surveillance will also become common for all future events and many tourism attractions/congregating sites. In some locales, the future has arrived. "The average visitor to London . . . is now captured on video 300 times in a single day" (p. 16).[29]

As you saw in Chapter 5, biometrics will become the common form of identification. Most countries will move to globally standardized electronic national identification cards in place of passports. These ID cards may also include driver's license information along with fingerprint and/or retinal scan data. In addition, by choice, to achieve better connectedness and better service, travelers will carry individualized computer units (ICUs) that contain a wealth of information such as medical records, bank account information, foreign language translation, and service loyalty program membership numbers and preferences.[30]

As security has tightened, airlines have restricted size and weight of baggage to conserve fuel and space. In response, specialty freight companies will enjoy substantial increases in revenue as more and more travelers elect to ship their luggage and adventure "toys."

Owing to the dominance and immediacy of global media, crisis events will have even greater impact on tourism revenues. In response to hyped 24-hour coverage of natural disasters and terrorism attacks, organizations, especially National Tourism Offices and their lower-level counterparts, will develop restoration and recovery programs with specialists who communicate through the broadcast and print media and use the power of the Internet to inform travelers about the condition of tourism resources and steps being taken to ensure the safety and security of visitors.[31]

To guard against lost or stolen cash or traveler's checks, we will move to a truly cashless society. In all venues, making tourism purchases will be easier. Everything from your credit/debit card to your cell phone will be used to make purchases. Making purchases easier for customers means more revenues for service providers.

Keeping the Human Touch

There is no doubt that the business of travel is adopting technology at an advanced speed, and travelers are embracing the movement. The personal touch still provides the basis for the reassurance and experience travelers seek, but technology is revolutionizing the way service providers are staying attentive and engaged with their guests. To help reduce labor costs, many tourism-related businesses are automating services that until recently were provided by people. More and more businesses within the industry are making greater use of computer terminals and interactive screens to allow travelers to "do it yourself." Although this step depersonalizes service, a growing number of travelers prefer speed and efficiency to the more personal interaction with hospitality service employees. Tourism operators, just like other service providers, will find a balance between the power of technology and human interaction. Customers enjoy the freedom of technology but want to know that when needed there is someone available to serve their needs.

With the shrinking number of available workers owing to the aging populations of industrialized nations, tourism suppliers will offer better pay and benefits to employees. Greater efficiency will partially compensate for these higher human resource costs. Automation and robots will replace human workers in most back-of-the-house operations. Employees will be seen as the most important asset for delivering high-quality, highly customized customer service, so service training and employee empowerment will become the norm industry wide.[32]

THE GREEN FRONTIER

The coming decades will see the rise of mandatory recycling, water and energy conservation, and use of environmentally friendly building products and supplies. The industry will rise to

L.L.Bean

Retailer L.L.Bean encourages visitors to its destination retail outlet in Freeport, Maine, to engage in a little adventure travel. During the summer months, it offers visitors "Walk-on Adventures" including kayak touring, fly-fishing, and clay shooting for the affordable fee of $15. The adventures include bus transportation, equipment use, instructions, and guides. To encourage interest in water sports, the premier outdoors retailer sponsors its Paddlesports Festival in mid-June during which thousands of visitors are given the opportunity to learn to paddle, take tours of the region's waters, and test out various water sports vehicles, such as kayaks and canoes. In addition, L.L.Bean has developed a sport tourism division, called its Outdoor Discovery School, which attracts novices and experts alike to learn or fine-tune fishing, paddling, shooting, and photography skills.

FYI

Modular Hotels

They go by many different names—capsule hotels, modular hotels, and pod hotels—but they all have one thing in common: very efficient use of space in a small footprint. The concept of modular hotels was pioneered by the Japanese, but the idea is sweeping across the world. Priced well below most competitors in high-cost real estate markets such as airports and downtown locations, these small, 75- to 100-square-foot rooms don't waste any space. Most modular units include the basics: private bathrooms, beds that are designed for two, flat screen televisions with integrated technologies, and a small work space. Weary travelers looking for nothing more than a place to sleep are finding that pods "fit the bill." Thanks to their sleek design and small footprints, these new hotels are opening up a new subeconomy category of lodging properties.

Sources: Christine Sarkis. (2007, October 17). Modular hotels: Tiny space, big experience, low price. *USA Today*; Glen Haussman. (2007, February 8). "Pod" hotel changes NYC lodging dynamic. *Hotel Interactive.*

this challenge by focusing on energy efficiency coupled with new energy technologies such as solar, wind, and geothermal energy. New Zealand serves as a good example of what is to come, as sizable quantities of thermal energy from hot springs are already used throughout the major tourism city of Rotorua. The lodging industry will increasingly build or convert to "smart rooms" that sense and adjust climate conditions and can be cleaned at least in part with robot technology.

According to a recent survey, business travelers expect lodging facilities to be environmentally conscious in their daily practices. The results of the survey indicate that these travelers expect them to:

- Recycle (77%);
- Use energy-efficient lighting (74%);
- Have energy-efficient windows (59%);
- Place cards in rooms to let guests request that sheets/towels not be changed (52%); and
- Use environmentally safe cleaning products (49%).[33]

Many of these practices are already in place in the restaurant industry, as the National Restaurant Association reports that more than

In the 21st century, China will become a top tourist destination for, and source of, tourists.

seven out of ten operators purchased products made from recycled materials, and roughly three out of four operate recycling programs.[34]

However, the road to becoming green will not be easy, as we saw in the previous chapter. Even though customers are demanding more environmentally sound practices, achieving this goal will be difficult. There are numerous products that claim to be "green," but there are no accepted standards or reliable guidelines for use in any segment of the industry.[35] When such universal guidelines are accepted across international boundaries, environmentally safe practices will become the norm.

CONCLUSION

It seems that the more things change, the more they stay the same. Think back to that old custom of hospitality we introduced in Chapter 1. We may not follow that practice of sticking a fresh pineapple on the front fence, as the old New England ship captains did as a symbol of hospitality, but the welcoming touch provided by service employees will remain a key factor to service success in this growing industry in which the number of jobs created by tourism organizations is projected to continue increasing for years to come.

You have made a great start in developing a sound foundation for becoming a professional member of the tourism industry or an informed consumer of tourism services. There will always be new things to do and learn in our rapidly changing world. We hope you decide to become a part of this excitement. You can build a bright professional future by dedicating yourself to lifelong learning and a never-ending desire to improve your knowledge, skills, and abilities continually. If you would like to become a part of the growing cadre of tourism professionals, take a look at Appendix C and learn more about how to conduct a successful job search. We hope that you have enjoyed the journey through our exploration of the tourism industry, and we hope to see you in our future travels.

YOU DECIDE

Microsegmentation, grouping consumers into smaller market segments than those more commonly used in the past, has been employed by more and more companies as markets have become saturated. Many companies have found sales growth difficult to come by: To gain increased sales, consumers must be won away from competitors. The best way to win a customer is to satisfy the customer's unique needs better than a competitor does.

By grouping customers into more specific groups, firms can better fulfill customer needs. As the tourism industry becomes more competitive, tourism suppliers have begun focusing on the needs of less traditional segments of potential travelers. For example, instead of targeting the business segment, a hotel company might target the young, technologically savvy, traveling saleswoman subsegment of the business and professional market.

A subsegment that is being targeted more and more is the less affluent counterpart of other segments, such as the low-income mature traveler or the low-income young-family subsegment. Lower-income travelers represent potential growth for travel providers because they have not been able to afford many of the travel services that other, more affluent travelers have been purchasing. To appeal to these lower-income segments, some tourism suppliers are offering special financing services.

The Princess Cruise Line is now offering its own "Love Boat Loan Cruise Financing" plan. Its slogan for the plan is "Bringing Your Dream Vacation within Reach." Prospective passengers unable to afford a cruise owing to a lack of savings are encouraged to "spread the cost over two, three, or four years, into very manageable monthly payments." Clients can even include onboard spending for drinks, shore excursions, and shopping as part of the loan. Interested customers simply call an 800 number to apply: "There is absolutely no paperwork to fill out and you will communicate by phone directly with the bank." Interest rates vary from 15 to 27%, depending on the individual's credit history and desired payment schedule.

For decades, travelers have been able to play before they pay. Banks have long offered vacation loans and credit card companies encourage purchasing travel services on credit. Tourism company–based financing is just one more means that customers can use to gratify their vacation desires now and pay later. Should tourism service suppliers encourage customers to "travel now and pay later"?

NET TOUR

To get you started on exploring Internet links for this chapter, please see

http://www.spaceadventures.com

http://www.sath.org

http://adventuretravel.com

http://lake-express.com

DISCUSSION QUESTIONS

1. Based on your knowledge of the tourism industry, what future services do you think will be developed to serve mass markets or specific market niches?

2. Based on your knowledge of the tourism industry, which of the following groups holds the most promise for future growth—mature travelers, international travelers, or business and professional travelers?

3. What roles do you think travel agents will play in the future of the tourism industry?

4. As speeds and efficiencies in trains and airplanes increase, do you think that travelers will shift their trips to one or the other of these transportation modes?

5. Why will the number of suppliers in the tourism industry decrease, and how will this consolidation of suppliers take place?

6. Will advances in technology replace the need for the human touch in the tourism industry?

APPLYING THE CONCEPTS

1. Using the resources of your local library or the Internet, access either the *Statistical Abstract of the United States*, *Statistics Canada*, or another governmental source. What recent trends have occurred in tourism-related activities? Do you think these trends will continue? Why or why not?

2. Arrange an interview with an experienced travel agent. Ask what changes he or she has observed in the tourism industry in the past five years. Some areas you might ask questions about include changes in business and professional travel, ecotourism, international travel, and technology.

3. Choose any one of the tourism service suppliers that has been discussed in this course. With two or more students, brainstorm ways that mass customization and microsegmentation could be used to improve customer service and revenues.

4. Interview a friend or relative who you think is a member of the adventure tourism segment. Ask about his or her most recent vacation. Also ask why he or she participates in extreme activities and what benefits he or she derives from these activities.

5. Interview a manager of a tourism business to determine what he or she thinks will be some of the major challenges facing his or her sector of the industry in the future. Are any changes being made to meet these challenges, such as EFR, greater automation, subcontracting, and so forth?

6. Find an article that discusses the future of tourism. Summarize the changes that are predicted.

■ GLOSSARY

Adventure tourism   Tourism that involves activities with an above-average element of physical risk.

Age cohort   A generation affected by common experiences.

Artificial intelligence   A segment of computer sciences devoted to the development of computer hardware and software that is designed to imitate the human mind.

Configured (rooms)   Rooms with a well-planned design developed to meet user needs for efficiency and effectiveness.

Cooperative alliances   Long-term relationships that enhance operating efficiencies, profitability, and market share for all parties.

Efficient foodservice response (EFR)   Partnership agreements created among manufacturers, distributors, and foodservice operators to lower food costs and improve the quality of service.

Extreme tourism   A subset of adventure tourism; encompasses activities that involve above-average elements of physical challenge and risk.

Mass customization   The production of a good or service to fulfill the unique needs of an individual buyer.

Medical tourism   Travel to other countries to receive medical treatments.

Microsegmentation   The process of identifying and serving small subsegments of the market.

Pacific Rim   The land masses that have a Pacific Ocean coastline.

Real estate tourism   Travel time spent gaining in-depth knowledge and perspectives about the area from scheduled meetings with local experts while searching out potential investment opportunities.

Single supplement   The additional charge added to the price of a tour or cruise when a traveler does not share accommodations with another traveler; often, 25% to 100% of the double occupancy rate is added to arrive at a single occupancy rate.

Single traveler   A person who lives alone and travels with or without a companion.

Slow tourism   Trips with a slower pace during which travelers step back from everyday experiences, allowing time and opportunities for immersion.

Subcontracting   The hiring of another organization to perform one or more operational functions or services.

Subsegments   A group within a larger market segment; sometimes called a "microsegment."

Virtual conferencing   Meetings among geographically dispersed individuals using video, sound, and data transmission technologies so participants can see and interact with each other.

Vocation tourism   Trips during which travelers take time to experience possible new careers before actually making career changes.

■ REFERENCES

1. Ap, John. (2004). Intercultural behavior: Glimpses of leisure from an Asian perspective. In Klaus Weiermair and Christine Mathies, eds., *The tourism and leisure industry: Shaping the future.* New York: Haworth Hospitality Press.

2. Projection of U.S. Population, by age, 2010–2050, (2008). *The World Almanac Book of Facts 2008.* New York: Author.

3. Ap, John. (2004). Intercultural behavior: Glimpses of leisure from an Asian perspective. In Klaus Weiermair and Christine Mathies, eds., *The tourism and leisure industry: Shaping the future.* New York: Haworth Hospitality Press.

4. Morrow, James. (2003). A place for one. *American Demographics,* 25(9), 24–29.

5. Hudson, Simon. (2003). Winter sport tourism. In Simon Hudson, ed., *Sport and adventure tourism* (pp. 89–123). New York: Haworth Press.

6. Blank, Christine. (1998). Parking it for fun. *American Demographics,* 20(4), 6–9.

7. Blum, Ernest. (2003, January 27). SATH: Disabled travel coming of age. *Travel Weekly,* p. 25.

8. Travel Industry Association of America. (2000). *Travel poll.* Washington, D.C.: Author.

9. Roberts, Alison. (2007, September 9). Several options for walking tours. *San Antonio Express-News,* p. 4L.

10. Woehler, Larlheinz. (2004). The rediscovery of slowness, or leisure time as one's own and as self-aggrandizement. In Klaus Weiermair and Christine Mathies, eds., *The tourism and leisure industry: Shaping the future.* New York: Haworth Hospitality Press.

11. Sung, Heidi H. (2004). Classification of adventure travelers: Behavior, decision making, and target markets. *Journal of Travel Research,* 42(2), 343–356.

12. Beedie, Paul. (2003). Mountain guiding and adventure: Reflections on the choreography of the experience. *Leisure Studies, 22,* 147–167.
13. Beedie, Paul. (2003). Adventure tourism. In Simon Hudson, ed., *Sport and adventure tourism* (pp. 203–239). New York: Haworth Press.
14. Beedie, Paul. (2003). Mountain guiding and adventure: Reflections on the choreography of the experience. *Leisure Studies, 22,* 147–167.
15. Mecir, Anthony, and Katherine Gruder. (2007). Traveling for treatment. *AARP Bulletin,* 48(8), 12–16.
16. Ingebretsen, Mark. (2004, June 22). Medical tourism comes of age. *Wall Street Journal Online.*
17. The hypersonic age is near. (2008). *Popular Science,* 272(1), 36–41.
18. Schwartz, John. (2004, October 4). Private rocket ship earns $10 million in new space race. *New York Times,* p. 1A.
19. Sain, Gary C. (2004, June 23). Top 5 reasons in choosing a travel agent. *Society for Accessible Travel & Hospitality.* Boca Raton, FL. Available at: http://www.sath.org.
20. Underground trains across America. (2004, May–June). *Futurist,* p. 14.
21. Pizam, Abraham. (1999). Life and tourism in the year 2050. *International Journal of Hospitality Management,* 18(4), 331–343.
22. Klesius, Michael. (2003). The future of flight. *National Geographic,* 203(12), 2–32.
23. Transportation. (1999). *Kiplinger Letter,* 76(51), 3.
24. Pine, B. Joseph, II. (1993). *Mass customization: The new frontier in business competition.* Boston: Harvard Business School Press.
25. Malchoff, Kevin R. (1996). The future is spelled E-F-R. *Restaurant Business,* 95(16), 229.
26. Korn, Irene. (2000). Super smart rooms. *Successful Meetings,* 49(2), 29.
27. Garrett, Echo. (1999). Tad Smith, futurist. *Management Review,* 88(11), 64.
28. Dash, Judi. (2000, January 2). Future treks. *Denver Post,* pp. 1T, 6T.
29. Pizam, Abraham. (1999). Life and tourism in the year 2050. *International Journal of Hospitality Management,* 18(4), 331–343.
30. Pizam, Abraham. (1999). Life and tourism in the year 2050. *International Journal of Hospitality Management,* 18(4), 331–343.
31. Beirman, David. (2003). *Restoring tourism destinations in crisis.* Cambridge, MA: CABI Publishing.
32. Pizam, Abraham. (1999). Life and tourism in the year 2050. *International Journal of Hospitality Management,* 18(4), 331–343.
33. Survey takes close look at traveler's green practices, expectations. (2008, May 19). *Green Lodging News.*
34. National Restaurant Association. Available at: http://www.restaurant.org.
35. Audi, Tamara. (2007, September 11). Hotel chains grapple with meaning of green. *Wall Street Journal,* pp. B1, B2.

PART 111

Readings

The Four-Season Challenge

BY TRACEY ARIAL

Whistler's a perfect case study of how an individual region can meet Canada's tourism industry mission and lead one step closer to the vision developed by the industry. It has successfully operated on a year-round basis for more than a decade. Whistler is so successful at meeting the four-season challenge it now attracts more visitors between May and October (1.1 million) than between November and April (942,000).

Whistler attracts visitors without ignoring either the environment or local residents. Innovative displays interpret nature for guests. Employees scoop litter from the trails. Ski run widths have been cut in half. New development budgets include the cost of flood and habitat protection. And anyone who owns land close to Whistler village receives automatic membership in the regional marketing division, Tourism Whistler (formerly The Whistler Resort Association).

"We want a long-term sustainable product," said Tourism Whistler president Suzanne Denbak. "Whistler is unique because it was created to be a tourist destination, but that said we have a strong and vocal community here, and they are an important part of the guest experience. All the visitors interact with the locals, so we want to work well with the community."

Whistler's success didn't just happen; people created it. Innovative operators in the region worked together in a never-ending rotation of building infrastructure, promotion, product extensions, activity creation, and diversification from leisure into business. Any tourism business can follow Whistler's lead. As Denbak says, no matter where you start, you have an uphill battle convincing the markets of your broader offerings.

■ FOUR-SEASON GOAL

When it comes to four-season travel, Whistler has several advantages. One is a solid infrastructure and a long-standing goal to develop four-season business. More than $2.7 billion has been invested in developing Whistler since municipal creation in 1975. That includes lots of accommodation, ski lifts, retailers and restaurants. Leaving all those beds sitting empty over the summer doesn't make sense.

When Lynne Perry, executive director of Nova Scotia's South Shore Tourism Association ran into a similar situation three years ago, she decided to create a guide to winter product.

In it, Perry identified the light-houses, museums and historic architecture of Lunenburg that most people knew, but she also included surfing, sleigh rides or horse and buggy wagon tours, snowy owl viewing, an open lobster season, winter storm watching, beach-side cabins and genealogy research.

Interest in her publication has grown, not only from the advertisers who pay for printing and distribution, but also from potential visitors and the local tourism industry. "Bed and breakfasts stay open longer now," said Perry. "Things that used to close before are now staying open longer because we're telling people we're open."

■ SMALL OPERATORS GO FOUR-SEASON

Four-season operation is possible for even the smallest of operators.

When Richard Shockley took over as director of Lethbridge, Alberta's, Fort Whoop-Up Interpretive Centre in November 1993, the site had a 26-year habit of opening between May and September, even though permanent staff worked year round. "We opened in May 1994, and we've stayed open ever since."

Although the 20,000 visitors the Fort Hamilton replica attracts are far from the number who visit Nova Scotia's South Shore, Shockley's experience tells a similar tale. He's increased his visitor numbers by 40 per cent and he's found that visitors who come between October and May tend to spend more per capita and stay longer.

Unfortunately, Shockley's growth potential is limited by a now-stretched budget. He wants other area attractions to consider opening year round so they could work together. "We had two visitors from Germany here yesterday. The art gallery is open and we're open, but no one else is.

"Maybe if some of the other attractions in Lethbridge were open, we'd get more visitors in the winter."

Or perhaps Shockley could partner with a tour operator who would promote his product for him. Experienced tour operators have the expertise and resources to handle the expanded administrative demands and workload that four-season operation can bring, and they often have the client contacts to make the venture work.

That's what happened to a group of Yukon tour operators in 1998 when Nahanni River Adventures decided to start selling dog sledding trips to winter clientele. "My main product is river expeditions," said Nahanni president Neil Hartling. "When CTC adventure research came out and said that the most profitable adventure companies operate in more than one season, I realized that we could have greater potential with partners."

Once he thought of it, Hartling had no problem finding suitable partners. "It's been a very natural fit." We've been very strategic—our clients chose us for a non-motorized ecotourism product in the summer, so that's what we chose to sell in the winter."

Pampering is also important. Hartling's winter clients stay in quality accommodation and they're supplied with very high-end menus. "After dinner, there's five types of single malt scotch to choose from." Hartling is pleased with his success so far. This spring he's testing a North Pole expedition, and he plans to keep searching for partners to develop a non-ski winter product for his Jasper operation. He's also thinking about ideas for fall.

■ MOTHER NATURE'S HELP NEEDED

Sometimes, though, nature interferes with the best winter ecotourism products.

As this winter season began, Charles Roberge, tourism spokesperson for the UNESCO world biosphere reserve of Charlevoix, in Quebec, faced the possibility of canceling his caribou-viewing tours.

Three spring fires, including a big one last spring, destroyed the caribou's winter feeding grounds in Parc des Grands-Jardins. Roberge wasn't sure they'd be able to find the caribou's new sites in time for the tours. Caribou or not, cross-country skiers will be welcome. Charlevoix has two mountains and a very diverse ecosystem. While hikers and bikers need only three days to travel between lodges, cross-country skiers need six. There's also dog sledding and ice fishing.

Nevertheless, Roberge finds it a challenge to build a stable four-season industry. "Fall, April and May are difficult because the parks are closed. Spring weather conditions are not good because the ground is still frozen and we get rain, so the roads are not safe. The lakes are too dangerous while the ice is melting."

Roberge continues to try. After all, whales are still visible in the autumn and spring and he plans to partner with local agriculture to sell cheese, lamb and veal from the region to larger markets.

That kind of imaginative thinking builds four-season successes like Whistler, although even Whistler claims to have a long way to go yet. As Denbak puts it: "Are we there yet? No. We need to make investments in all four seasons."

Source: Communique, January–February, 2000, p. 3.

Coyote Pass Hospitality

BY WILLIAM L. BRYAN, JR.

"A unique experience awaits you. A very special doorway is now open for you. This entry leads to a remarkable cultural experience—something that has not been available at any other place or at any other time. This is your opportunity to participate in a once-in-a-lifetime journey into the world of the Navajo People."

This is the opening paragraph describing Coyote Pass Hospitality, the brainchild of Will Tsosie, a traditional Navajo and devoted ambassador of the Navajo culture. Will, with his extended family, wants his guests to experience his way of living, culture, and environment—and to do so on his terms.

Coyote Pass Hospitality has been in operation since 1992. Totally dedicated to appropriate cultural tourism, Will Tsosie and his family work hard to establish situations where there are cross-cultural understandings. They first get to understand the guests' perspective and then assist them in learning and integrating the traditional Navajo view into their world of thought and life. As their brochure says, "Your guides (Will Tsosie and family) will shepherd you through many facets of Navajo life—oral tradition, ethnographic interpretation, ceremonies, herbology, and philosophy. Sit with a rug weaver while she works or watch a silversmith at his craft. You may expand your knowledge to include neighboring tribes; our guides are most knowledgeable about other Native American cultures in the Southwest."

Coyote Pass Hospitality explores the countryside, visiting many archeological sites and learning about the Anasazi, from whom some believe the Navajo descended. This is done by visiting various ruins in the vicinity of Chinle. At the same time, the traveler also experiences the scenic vistas of the immediate area in which Coyote Pass Hospitality works, including the spectacular mountains and hills of Lukachukai. One can even spend time with part of the Tsosie family, who raise sheep during the summer in the mountain country. When appropriate, Will wants the visitor to experience life as a Native American. Often he and his guides will allow the visitor to experience Navajo traditions such as dances, songs, food, and even staying as guests in hogans. Coyote Pass Hospitality also is willing to take a client to visit Zuni, Hopi, Acoma, or Rio Grande Pueblos. One also has the opportunity to have a traditional meal with Will's family. Sometimes guests are encouraged to venture forth with family members, collect various edibles found growing in the nearby area, bring them back, and help in food preparation for the evening meal. Blue corn pancakes, fry bread, berries, and various meats and legumes are specialties. At all times, Will engages guests in conversation, trying to draw them out so they can have the opportunity to learn about Navajo religion, politics, ceremonies, economic development strategies, and even the premises and intentions of cultural tourism as practiced by Coyote Pass Hospitality.

Although most of Coyote Pass Hospitality's activities involve cultural interactions and sightseeing, the Tsosies are very careful not to overly impact fragile environmental areas and cultural sites. They are particularly concerned about sharing with guests why it is important to leave artifacts as they are and why certain areas can't be visited; however, an important issue is, what is the appropriate size of the group with which it is best to work? Will prefers to work with groups in the four- to fifteen-person range. Nonetheless, he is frequently asked to be a step-on guide for larger groups that want to spend part of a day or more learning about Navajo history and culture.

Also, the Tsosies feel constant pressure about the issue of money. Currently Will's price is $100 a night, double occupancy. He then charges $20 per hour for his time. Larger groups often can offer a better price to Will than his small-group daily rate.

Will struggles with issues related to how he allocates portions of his fees to other members of his family and to the community. On the other hand, some consumers suggest that perhaps he is charging too much. So, what price guidelines are there? Who helps Will come up with a fair rate? There aren't other operations like Coyote Pass Hospitality in the nearby area—let alone on Navajo lands or in southwestern Indian country. There are large commercial tours, but nothing like the cultural immersion Will tries to provide his guests. Pricing, for all intents and purposes, is solely a somewhat extraneous marketplace factor rather than the issue of providing a livable wage for the Tsosie family. However, if the market targeted is on a tight budget, does this livable wage get compromised?

A particularly sensitive topic is that the Tsosie family is financially benefiting from a willingness to share their knowledge about tribal community and customs, which is a Navajo communal resource and not the exclusive property of the Tsosie family. One must inevitably ask the question, is this an extractive service? Can one realistically incorporate into a "per person price" the appropriate costs of using communal resources owned by the Navajo Nation?

Another dilemma Coyote Pass Hospitality faces is that guest agendas often are inconsistent with their own views and standards concerning cross-cultural experiences and education. Some guests want to go to ceremonies when non Indians aren't allowed. Others want to do Vision Quests under the guidance of a Navajo. The "wanna-be" mentality is often quite prevalent among those who wish to visit tribal members. Frequently confronted with these aspirations, Will finds himself tested—should he be accommodating to such requests or hold firm to his own standards? A short article in *National Geographic Traveler* titled "Native for a Night" states, "If you ever wanted to be a Native American, Will Tsosie, a Navajo, gives you an overnight opportunity." It can be very tempting to let customers dictate how you present yourself when they are willing to pay good money for a contrived entertainment-type experience. It is easy to ask, "Why not?" especially given the modest existence that sustains the Tsosie family and the fact that there is no formal peer accountability process among those tribal members involved in cultural tourism.

Continually confronted by guests wanting to take away something—an experience, a picture, an artifact, a one-way interaction—Will often asks, what do we Navajo get in return? What does the Tsosie family get in return? As one writer said of the Coyote Pass Hospitality experience, "Few visitors will come away without an intimate view and deepened respect for the profoundly esthetic and spiritual nature of Navajo life. And, for himself and his clan, Will Tsosie reminds you, 'It is a two-way street, the world also comes to us.'" Will wishes the "two-way street" was an easier concept for all in the cultural tourism business to grasp. But it is a lonely path to follow, as there isn't an organized group of cultural tourism suppliers in southwestern Indian country where one can talk through these dilemmas or where opportunities exist to help one another be accountable to such standards. The Arizona Indian Business Association can be supportive and even honored Coyote Pass Hospitality in 1997 as the outstanding Indian-owned business in Arizona. The Native American Business Resource Center at Northern Arizona University has been particularly helpful as well. Nonetheless, the demands of larger groups, intermediaries demanding lower prices, and the incessant demands for Anglo-type amenities are and will continue to be difficult pressures associated with cultural tourism.

Since there are no operating standards or codes of ethics for sustainable cultural tourism among the Navajo, it is up to Will and his family to decide from what standards they wish to work. Cultural and environmental accountability is something that is theirs alone with which to reckon. When actions stray, it is family pressure and Will's traditional way of life that provide the proper balance.

"Appropriate Cultural Tourism—Can It Exist? Searching for an Answer, Three Arizona Case Studies." "Coyote Pass Hospitality." by William L. Bryan, Jr., in *The Culture of Tourism, The Tourism of Culture*, Hal K. Rothman, editor. Albuquerque, NM: University of New Mexico Press, 2003, pp. 148–151.

Preserving the Landscape of Cinque Terre

BY DANIELLE MACHOTKA

Ercole is a spry septuagenarian in shorts leading us up a slope outside of Vernazza, in Cinque Terre. His job this morning is to rebuild part of a dry-laid stone wall that is holding up half the mountain we're standing on. We're here, for better or worse, to help.

Ercole sounds just enough like Hercules to work for me. In fact, as I watch his labors, he seems very much like a Hercules. Ten of us eagerly try to supply him with the right size stones at just the right time, but a partial language barrier and a total experience gap keep us always a step-and-a-half behind him. He lifts, places, adjusts and changes his mind, not slowed by the heat radiating off the wall or the glare of the sun on the local rock. The master plan for each stone evolves as he works, yet is buried in tradition.

Vernazza is one of five towns in Cinque Terre ("Five Lands"), a dramatic, romantic stretch of coast at the top of the shin of Italy's boot, facing the Mediterranean. The town winds down to the sea, following the path of the riverbed it covers and opening up to the sea at the river's former mouth, now a sheltered harbor with colorful dinghies and small cruising boats that moor for the day. Vernazza, like all five lands, has layers of buildings stepping up the hillsides and separated by narrow, winding, footpath-streets.

Transportation between towns is limited to train, boat or foot, the last meaning hiking the roller-coaster trails, with the promise of one postcard view after another. The seaside mountains afford unforgettable views of sapphire water, snaking valleys, slopes that have been sculpted into washboard orchards, and the five hamlets that seem to defy gravity to hug the terrain. Everyone lands in Vernazza at some point.

I've come for a three-day program to help protect the landscape of Cinque Terre. It doesn't look particularly fragile, but it turns out to be threatened by the very activity that brought me to Europe—tourism. Tourists are loving Cinque Terre to destruction, and the organizers of our program are trying to find ways to involve travelers in the preservation of a landscape and way of life they treasure.

The working holiday program, *Protect the Landscape of Vernazza,* is actually an experiment in sustainable tourism run by the Italian Environmental Impact Assessment Center (EIA) and the Municipality of Vernazza. Participants devote four hours of each morning to repairing the landscape and participating in the work that locals do daily. In exchange, they get a deeper understanding of local culture while working, eating, and conversing with *Vernazzani.*

Our hosts, guides, and soon-to-be friends, Alessandro Villa and Olga Chitotti, both work for the EIA. Alessandro is a sixth-generation *Vernazzano* with a passion for preserving his

town. Yet he understands that tourism is a reality, that a place as lovely as Cinque Terre will only draw more and more visitors, and that he and his colleagues will have to develop creative ways to address the impact of that pressure.

Alessandro and Olga conceived this program and worked alongside us the whole time, lifting stones while commenting on life in Vernazza, hiking the trails and discussing the condition of the landscape, sipping a glass of wine and sharing their hope for Cinque Terre's future.

Several of our conversations took place over remarkable dinners prepared by townspeople eager to parade the local gastronomy. The first evening began with olives, anchovies and deep-fried pumpkin flowers—more addictive than French fries—followed by pasta with basil and tomato, cheeses, salad, frittata with vegetables, and fruit. We drank local wine and a liqueur called Persechino that Alessandro had made, with white wine, grappa, pear leaves, almonds and alcohol.

The next day, under gray skies and foggy brains, we donned gloves and grabbed large plastic garbage bags as we headed up the path to Monterosso, north of Vernazza. Our task was trail cleaning, and we didn't have to look far to find the refuse of our fellow hikers. Heavy green rubber gloves pulled up as high as they would go, I set to the task of picking up piles of used tissues, water bottles and caps, plastic bags, sandwich wrappers, and items too unpleasant to mention. "Pack Your Trash" is not a mantra in Cinque Terre. How easily people can detach the beauty of their surroundings from their responsibility to keep it that way! Our heads were as full of grumblings about messy tourists as our bags were full of their mess when we headed down the mountain. We met the edge of a rainstorm as we passed the last of the vineyards before town.

That evening, we sat under large umbrellas in the Piazza Marconi and continued our explorations of the cuisine. Ristorante Gianni prepared anchovies with lemon, pepper and olive oil; linguine with pesto (native to Liguria and made better than anywhere); ravioli with tomato and anchovy sauce; fried assorted seafood; stuffed mussels; and a dish layered with potato, anchovy and tomato sauce. We were too full for the tiramisu, but who was going to say no? Between bites, we met Alessandro's family and friends as they wandered by on their evening walks.

Overnight, the rain and clouds blew away, leaving our third day saturated with color. The town was a kaleidoscope of red, orange, yellow, pink and green, slowly sinking below us as we climbed the terraces to Bartolo's vineyards. Bartolo is Ercole's son, another link in the chain of continuity that characterizes life and labor in Cinque Terre. Slowly our work party grew to include Ercole, Bartolo's wife, Lise, and his brother, Paolo, and several local characters who spoke to us in rapid, jovial, chat-while-you-work Italian, not caring that few of us understood.

I crouched to get under the odd vineyard that sloped gently away from me on the narrow terrace. Grapevines in Cinque Terre are trained to grow up about four feet and then horizontally, forming a canopy under which the grapes grow, protected from the ocean winds. What looks like an unruly vine from the top shelters a bounty of grape clusters, future Nectar of the Gods, underneath. As I settled into the dark underbelly of the vineyard, I was enveloped by the musty smell of soil and the heady aroma of ripe fruit. The wet earth slowly soaked my seat as I sat, clippers in hand, and loaded basket after basket with Chardonnay grapes.

Snipping away at their harvest, Bartolo and Lise, who both speak excellent English, told us about wine making in Vernazza. They make all their own, of several varieties, selling some and trading what they don't drink for other locally-produced goods. And they still do most of it by hand, using methods that have been used for generations.

One exception is the way they take the grapes into town. After hours of clipping and picking out the spoiled grapes and raisins, the bulging baskets have to get from the terraces to the crushing vats below. These days, they coast down in motorized carts on tracks or pulleys. In earlier times, it was more difficult. Bartolo and Alessandro bravely demonstrated how workers used to carry the bins of grapes on the back of the neck with a rolled-up T-shirt underneath for padding. I made a point of extolling the fabulous pulley system.

In celebration of a good harvest and the completion of our work, Alessandro and Olga prepared the dinner for our last evening: ravioli filled with vegetables and cheese, macaroni with a fresh tomato sauce, salad, cheeses, stuffed vegetables, and local wine. Another home brew of Alessandro's, Vin Santo, topped off the night.

Over the course of the three days, we learned about the impact that tourism has on a small town like Vernazza. The population of 800 doubles on a typical summer day. Tourists glide in on boats, zoom through town for a couple of hours, buy gelato, post cards, and t-shirts, and leave for the next town. Others hike in, using the well-worn trails that connect each of the five lands. Some stay for a night or two, some return every year.

All create waste. The cost of solid waste disposal in Vernazza goes up almost six-fold from January to August. Sanitary sewer lines and water treatment plants are extended to capacity. Nature-loving hikers increase the potential of erosion with every footstep. Invariably, someone gets injured on the trails, necessitating a local rescue effort. Volunteers with a stretcher have to hike to the injured tourist and carry him to town—budgets don't allow for helicopters and Med-Evac teams.

None of this is immediately fatal to the well-being of Vernazza, but it is eating away at the landscape of the surroundings and the resources of the town. Tourism and agriculture are the primary industries; neither creates great financial surpluses. Alessandro and Olga hope that the working holiday program will take the first step towards solving the problem by raising awareness.

It worked for me. One stone wall is repaired, a stretch of trail is cleaned, and the grapes we picked are crushed and aging in bottles. But I can see there's still much to do. And Ercole would love a few good helpers.

Source: Danielle Machotka traded in a career as a landscape architect for one as a freelance writer, but still combines her passions for travel and the interaction of the landscape and culture whenever she can.

Resorts Go Up . . . and Down

BY ANDREW NEMETHY

Destruction is usually associated with unexpected natural disasters. But, according to futurist August St. John, "destruction" is perfectly natural—indeed, inevitable—for resort and tourist towns.

St. John is a professor of marketing and future studies at Long Island University in New York. He has developed a comprehensive theory on the life and death of tourist towns, which he says go through a cycle of five stages: Welcome, Development, Resentment, Confrontation, and, finally, Destruction.

It's the last stage, not surprisingly, that has raised eyebrows. By "destruction," St. John doesn't mean a physical catastrophe, but the ruin or disappearance, as growth overwhelms a resort area, of the things that were the original attractions: neighborliness and sense of community, a rural landscape, small-town atmosphere, friendliness, low traffic and low taxes.

As this occurs, he says, communities break into hostile camps over development. Growth moratoriums, lawsuits and contentious hearings often ensue. Many residents find they can no longer afford to live and shop in their town. Faced with constant irritants to remind them of their situation—traffic jams, soaring rents—locals wear resentment on their sleeves.

And on their bumpers. In the resort community of Manchester, Vermont, where St. John has had a home since 1962, cars sport stickers saying, "Welcome to Manchester. Now Go Home."

This is obviously no way for a resort to greet tourists, but St. John says Manchester is in the Destruction Stage and this kind of animosity is typical. Not surprisingly, local powers-that-be vehemently disagree. They call him names, such as "Professor Gloom-and-Doom." St. John has been branded everything from pro-development to anti-development, and accused of having a "hidden agenda" by the president of nearby Bromley and Magic Mountain ski areas.

He takes it all in stride, insisting he isn't taking sides, just telling it like it is.

"Everything has patterns," St. John says. "Everything changes if you wait long enough. If something is hot you wait long enough, it's cold. That's all I'm saying. It's not better or worse. It's just different."

Though his tourism cycle is based on five years of studying Manchester, he says it applies to resort communities everywhere. Manchester has been an ideal guinea pig, St. John says, because it has virtually every facet of a tourism-based economy. The town has a business sector dependent on tourists, imported workers who service the resort trade, old-wealth summer residents, affluent newcomers, developers, assorted professionals, and long-time natives.

It has a historic, 150-year-old resort village dominated by the sprawling, restored Equinox Hotel. It's also home to a booming commercial center with the upscale fishing and clothing company Orvis, all manner of outlet stores and boutiques, and grand development schemes.

And three ski resorts are nearby—Stratton, Bromley and Magic Mountain.

Most of the flak St. John faces comes from his use of the word "destruction," but he says this stage isn't all negative. It can also be "creative" and a "rebirth," once a community realizes its original draw has disappeared and "something else has to be put in its place." But if negative attitudes toward tourists do not change and conflicts remain, "there's no guarantee once you hit bottom that you can come back."

St. John, 62, a tanned, animated man with a neat salt-and-pepper moustache and a vague resemblance to Sean Connery, is an unlikely lightning rod. He has spent most of his career teaching or consulting quietly behind the scenes, using his background in economics, sociology, psychology and marketing.

Cycles fascinate St. John, much as statistics thrill a baseball fanatic. He points out that as far back as 500 B.C., his favorite Greek philosopher, Heraclitus "The Obscure," said everything is always in "flux," and that "one cannot step twice into the same river."

Tourism communities must realize their business is in a state of flux and not immune to cycles, says St. John. Sitting underneath the dark, exposed beams of an old, restored carriage barn that is his home, he predicts many changes for ski and resort areas:

■ "There are only going to be two types of ski resort: The very expensive and the very cheap." Ski resorts in the middle face difficulty and some will go bankrupt.

■ "People today want their money's worth." Ski areas have to deliver value to survive, whether it's a decent hamburger or coupons that give a discount at local restaurants.

■ Fancy resorts that cater to the cream of the market have to "savor the customer" and concentrate less on capital investment and more on service. "They've got the apple: They better start shining it."

He points out that 20 years ago no one ever imagined going to a ski resort and "never putting on skis." But a long list of activities and amenities now provide plenty of diversions to attract non-skiers.

"The concept is wider. It's not just skiing," he says.

Some communities fail to recognize that as growth occurs, the local economy becomes

Figuring a Resort's Stage

Professor August St. John devised a survey, excerpted below, to pinpoint the development phase of a resort town. Respondents rate the accuracy of the following statements on a scale of 0 (never happens) to 5 (always happens) for any small resort town. The total points categorize the town in one of the five stages.

1. *Name-verbing.* Residents of other areas turn the town's name into a verb (as in Freeport, Maine). *Example: "Don't 'Freeport' our town."*

2. *Teflon officials.* Difficult or confusing to place responsibility for a town's growth pattern on elected or appointed officials. *Example: "Who's in charge around here?"*

3. *Growth backlash.* Growth reaches a point where a town's development no longer pulls people in, but pushes people out. *Example: The rural simplicity, historic character, charm, or mystique is eroded by pockets of glitzy adornment and clutter.*

4. *Character flip-flop.* The character of a town no longer affects growth decisions; rather, growth decisions affect the character of the town. *Example: Commercial projects such as malls, shopping centers, strip development, subdivisions, etc., dominate the townscape (overall visual impression), not the other way around.*

5. The *"window effect."* New arrivals view the town as it is, not what it was or should be.

Example: As historic architectural heritage is consumed by a contemporary motif, the new arrivals see the present townscape and adapt accordingly. As this process of "dwindling architectural heritage" continues, changing profiles of the town unfold.

6. *From feverish to sick.* The "have nots" will "never have." *Example: Land values soar and/or affordable housing becomes prohibitive.*

7. *Departure of posh.* Quality market replaced by a quantity market. *Example: Clutter, retail glitz, and fast-food restaurants dominate the town; "upscale" shoppers depart and "middle/low-end" arrive.*

8. *A new template.* A general consensus that the town has changed. *Example: The town's new look is better to some, worse to others, different to all.*

9. *A bitter pill.* Present "high" prices of real estate make past "lower" prices, to most previous sellers, a resentful memory.

10. *Wishful thinking.* Traffic activity does not equal business activity. *Example: Roads choked with day-trippers bound for other destinations.*

Total: 0–10 = Welcome stage; 11–21 = Development stage; 22–32 = Resentment stage; 33–43 = Confrontation stage; 44–50 = Destruction stage.

driven less by tourism than by development and a phalanx of architects, lawyers, planners, contractors and engineers. When development runs out of steam, the community is forced to confront how to maintain its economy.

While he insists that going from the "welcome" to "destruction" stage is inevitable, St. John says active planning can prolong and control the progression by helping preserve a resort town's appeal and character.

"It's like the difference between two people. One of them stays fit and takes care of himself, the other drinks and gets dissipated," he says.

St. John has developed a way to rate local attitudes so communities can find out where they fit in his five-stage cycle (see accompanying box). Using the information, a community can look ahead and plan.

"The future of the future," he says, sounding like a modern-day Heraclitus, "is in the present."

A freelance writer/author living in the hills near Montpelier, Vermont, Andrew Nemethy has witnessed 20 years of changes in Green Mountain resort towns.

Source: Nemethy, Andrew. (1990, November). Resorts go up . . . and down. *Snow Country,* pp. 149–150.

Integrative Cases

Coping with Crisis

West Marin: A Case-Study
of Responsible Tourism

Coping With Crisis

■ INTRODUCTION

Imagine a company celebrating 120 years of continuous service. With uniformed conductors, engineers, and authentic coal-fired steam engines, the historic Durango & Silverton Narrow Gauge (D&SNG) Railroad, Inc. fully expected to continue delighting tourists by providing this historic and scenic ride for years to come. As the number one tourist attraction for both Durango and Silverton, Colorado, the train had become a mainstay for both economies. Now, imagine being in charge of this operation and facing a crisis decision in the midst of poor economic times and soft tourism demand.

For most tourism-related industries, 2001 was a dismal year. Even prior to 9/11, many companies were experiencing both declining revenues and increasing operating expenses. Unfortunately, the end-result for most service providers in the tourism industry was worse than projected revenue and visitor numbers. It was a simple case of supply and demand; the supply of tourism venues continued to expand, while the uncertain economy and terrorism fears caused travelers to scale back their plans for venturing out. The stock market peaked in March of 2000 and tumbled dramatically to multi-year lows, making consumers even more financially conservative with their leisure expenditures. People with extra cash were reluctant to part with it.

The tourism industry in Southwest Colorado was feeling the economic pains of the slow-down in tourism like the rest of the country. In the midst of this gloomy scenario, some good news came to the local tourism economy. Newspaper headlines screamed the news: "Thomas the Tank Engine is coming to Durango, June 15–23 to

This case was prepared by Edwin C. Leonard, Jr. of Indiana University–Purdue Fort Wayne and Roy A. Cook of Fort Lewis College and is intended to be used as a basis for class discussion. The views represented here are those of the authors and do not necessarily reflect the views of the Society for Case Research. Authors' views are based on their own professional judgments. Copyright © 2003 by Edwin C. Leonard, Jr. and Roy A. Cook.

travel on the historic D&SNG Railroad, Inc." With records set for lack of snow and rainfall, the drought-conscious Durango business owners needed a shot in the arm that increased tourism could bring. Thomas's popularity, due to its own web site, books, toys, videos, movie, Public Broadcasting System (PBS) and Nickelodeon television features, was expected to draw thousands of new visitors to Durango. For $14 per person (nonrefundable tickets), visitors could experience "A Day Out With Thomas." Every forty-five minutes, the D&SNG coaches were expected to transport thousands of visitors on a thirty-minute ride.

Since the train was the main destination attraction in the region, this added venue came at a good time for many of the local tourism businesses that were starving for customers. Train riders typically stayed in Durango, the largest town in the region, while participating in other activities, such as visiting Mesa Verde National Park and enjoying a variety of outdoor activities. While Durango served as the station for the train, one town in the region was even more dependent on the train than any other—Silverton.

■ SILVERTON AND THE D&SNG

The small mountain town of Silverton, population 720, was especially dependent on the day-trippers that flooded into the town with each scheduled train. These passengers had two and a half hours to sightsee, eat, and shop in this historic mining town before boarding for the return trip to Durango.

In its continuing efforts to promote tourism, the Silverton Chamber of Commerce hailed 2002 as The International Year of the Mountains. Noted events included the 31st Annual Iron Horse Bicycle Classic where riders from all over the world come to race the D&SNG as it chugged along the 45 scenic miles of twisting mountain tracks passing through the San Juan National Forest between Durango and Silverton. An announcement from the Silverton, Colorado,

Chamber of Commerce extolled the virtues of Silverton.

> Nestled high in the heart of the San Juan Mountains, the Town of Silverton's unique mining history, Victorian charm and unequaled natural beauty provide an ideal base for your summer or winter explorations. Accessible by the scenic Narrow Gauge Railroad, this old west town sits at an elevation of 9,318 feet, surrounded by public lands waiting for you and your family to discover (http://www.silverton.org).

Because Silverton was never the victim of a major fire, as so many mining camps were, the buildings have been preserved, many of them with original furnishings, fixtures, stamped tin ceilings and polished, mirror back bars. It's a friendly place to visit (Retzler, 2002).

The town provided visitors an opportunity to see how miners and their families lived over a hundred years ago in this 9,318 foot high mountain valley. The Mayflower Gold Mill, a National Historic Landmark, allowed tourists to see how miners got gold out of the hard rock ores. While accessible by a winding drive via U.S. Highway 550, most visitors took the three to three and a half hour trip via the D&SNG. According to some, the train is Silverton's bread and butter.

Operating daily from May to October, the D&SNG offered riders the opportunity to enjoy views of unparalleled beauty and an unforgettable steam train experience. The train hauls over 200,000 people a year from Durango to Silverton with nearly 40% of those passengers traveling in June and July on four daily trains. The average round-trip fare was about $65.00 per person. In addition, the railroad employed 80 full-time and 145 seasonal employees. While hundreds of thousands of visitors choose to drive the 50-mile high alpine road linking Durango and Silverton, the train experience has continued to serve as a major tourism attraction.

THE SPARK

The drought had become so severe that the moisture content in live trees had dropped to less than would be found in kiln-dried lumber

found in a lumber yard. What started as a spark in the tinder-dry forests north of Durango changed into a roaring inferno as a wildfire jumped control lines and raced towards the top of Missionary Ridge to the northeast of Durango, consuming 6,000 acres in the first day. Silverton lies due north of Durango, and if the fire continued to burn out of control, both the rail and road links between the two towns would be engulfed in smoke. Everyone intently watched the skies as a shift in wind could bring the fire towards Durango (Clay, 2002).

Because of the heavy smoke produced by the fire, air quality in parts of the San Juan Basin, which included Durango, became unhealthy for the sensitive—the elderly, children under seven and those with respiratory problems (Aguilera, 2002). Other attractions also began to suffer. Instead of playing golf at Tamarron Resort (ranked in the top 50 resort courses in the nation by *Golf Digest*) just north of Durango or playing in the river (kayaking, tubing, or rafting), most tourists took their activities inside as dense smoke obscured the sun. Tourism activities and expenditures were evaporating as the fire and smoke spread, and concerns over additional fires in the tinder dry region flared.

THE CRISIS

The chance of accidental fires was all too real. Several small fires had already been started by stray cinders from passing D&SNG trains. In response to this threat, water tankers with small fire fighting crews were scheduled to travel behind every train as a precautionary measure.

By mid-afternoon, Wednesday, June 19, 2002, D&SNG railroad Chief Executive Officer Allen Harper found himself caught between a rock and a hard place as the fire danger increased. See Figure 1 for a timeline of events. Continuing to run the coal-fired trains in the isolated tinder dry mountains could cause additional fires, and fire fighting resources were already stretched. Yet business owners who feared lost revenues if the trains were idled urged management to keep the trains running. At the same time, managers of the San Juan National Forest

January 1–June 15, 2002–Serious snow or rain clouds wanted. The area known as the Four Corners (bordering Colorado, New Mexico, Arizona, and Utah) was in the midst of a severe record-breaking drought.

June 8–August 8, 2002–The peak tourist season for the towns of Durango and Silverton, Colorado.

Sunday, June 9, 2002, Day One–A spark ignited dry timber north of Durango and the soon to be "Missionary Ridge fire" began burning out of control, consuming over 6,000 acres in less than six hours.

Saturday, June 15, 2002, Day Six–The fire has consumed almost 20,000 acres.

Tuesday, June 18, 2002, Day Nine–A spark from the D&SNG started a fire just north of Durango. The fire burned about an acre of land before being put out by two water-carrying helicopters pulled away from the Missionary Ridge fire. This fire was controlled within a couple of hours (Schober, 2002), but the main fire races ahead uncontrolled for four miles, reaching a size of over 50,000 acres by the end of the day.

Wednesday, June 19, 2002, Day Ten–The Second Annual Adventure Xstream scheduled on the Animas River paralleling the D&SNG for Saturday, June 22, was cancelled due to the wildfires raging north of Durango.

Thursday, June 20, 2002, Day Eleven–President Bush declared a major disaster for Colorado, thereby making funds available to help homeowners, renters, business owners, and employees affected by the Missionary Ridge fire (Greenhill, 2002).

Friday, June 21, 2002, Day Twelve–Summer officially arrives. The Missionary Ridge fire near Durango continued to rage out of control, burning almost 60,000 acres.

Structures burned: 33 residences and 26 other structures
Evacuations: 1,760 homes
Percent contained: 25
Firefighters: 1,263
Firefighting costs: $8.01 million (*The Denver Post*, 2002).

■ **Figure 1**   Timeline of Events

were considering closing some or all of the 2,107,554 acre forest.

Harper had spent several hours talking with Silverton business owners who were dependent on train passengers for tourist dollars. They urged him to keep the train running. In addition, business owners from hotels and restaurants to jeep tour companies, fly fishing outfitters, and others in Durango also attempted to persuade him to keep the trains running. Yet, many residents who had no apparent interest in tourism and local officials urged him to close operations.

Earlier in the day, Harper and senior vice president Jeff Jackson rode a pop car (a small two-person rail vehicle) behind the morning train to Silverton to observe first-hand the railroad's expanded fire prevention measures. On that trip, Harper had seen four small fires that were ignited by smokestack cinders and personally stomped one out himself. By noon, the mountain valley close to the railroad's main line between Durango and Silverton was filled with smoke from the advancing Missionary Ridge fire (Schober, 2002). Harper, who had flown in from his office in Florida when the fire started, returned to his hotel room and weighed his options.

He knew he had to make a decision and announce it soon. Should he listen to local businesses, stay fully staffed and keep the trains running? Should he listen to concerned citizens and fire fighting officials and temporarily cease all operations and lay off employees? Should he limit service to only the Thomas the Tank runs that stayed close to Durango in open areas away from the forests? If he did decide to suspend operations, how should he deal with customers who had already made reservations and planned their vacation travels around a ride on the D&SNG? Could local, state, or federal officials pre-empt his decision and order a shut down for safety reasons?

◼ | REFERENCES

Aguilera, E. (2002, June 21). Homes fall victim to sudden flare-up. *The Denver Post*, p. 18A.

Clay, Allen, Deputy Chief of Operations, Durango Fire and Rescue Authority, Durango, Colorado. (2002, July 9). Interview.

Greenhill, J. (2002, June 20). 21 subdivisions now threatened, *The Durango Herald*, p. 1A.

Retzler, K. (2002, Spring). Spectacular Silverton, Colorado. *San Juan Silver Stage*, p. 23.

Schober, B. (2002, June 20). Train will suspend trips to Silverton. *The Durango Herald*, pp. 1A, 10A.

The Denver Post. (2002, June 21). Pp. 1A, 16A, 18A. http://www.silverton.org.

West Marin: A Case-Study of Responsible Tourism

BY BONNIE BERG MACLAIRD

"Responsible tourism is not a tourism product or brand. It is a way of doing tourism."[1] Tourism, by definition, offers experiences that entice visitors to come, play, spend, and/or explore the unfamiliar. Responsible Tourism takes the concept of tourism to another level by saying that those who plan, manage and/or practice tourism ought to do it in a way that minimizes the environmental impacts, balances visitors' needs and desires with the local residents' needs and desires, and does so without compromising the needs of future generations.[2] Responsible Tourism takes the "long-term" rather than the short, typically profit-driven, view of how tourism should be planned and managed. In fact, the concept of planning tourism is fundamentally what responsible tourism is all about.

To ensure tourism is developed according to the principles of Responsible Tourism, both government and the local community need to be wholly involved in the process. Stephen Wanhill, in the article "The Economic Aspects of Location Marketing,"[3] makes the following observation.

The spillover benefits of tourism in terms of income and employment creation are well known, and, more than any other industry, tourism deals with the use of natural and cultural resources, which in outlying regions are often their major asset. The lessons of the past indicate that it is unwise for the state to abandon its ability to influence the direction of tourism development either through the

provision of finance or through legislation. The short-term gains sought by capital markets are often at odds with the long-term sustainability of tourist environments. With tourist movements set to increase both nationally and internationally, there will be a need for more regulation, direction and improved management of tourism resources to prevent environmental degradation and implement tourism development plans in a sustainable manner.

Responsible tourism is a process, a way of developing tourism, and a considerate method of practicing tourism . . . considerate of the environment, considerate of the locals not involved in the business of tourism, and, equally importantly, considerate of future generations of both humans and wildlife who will appreciate and depend upon the same natural resources. Responsible Tourism needs a vision of the future, the input of the locals, and the guiding hand of a forward thinking government to ensure the resources are protected and the benefits are shared equitably.

◼ | THE WEST MARIN EXAMPLE

Anyone who has driven out to Point Reyes National Seashore has seen the enchanting land that lies less than an hour from the San Francisco Bay Area. Forty percent of Marin is still agricultural land. Rarely does the visitor to West Marin understand the economics behind maintaining this pristine wonderland against the pressures of development.

Back in the early 1970s, a grass-roots preservation movement fought and defeated developers who were poised to build a four-lane highway and housing subdivisions in the Point Reyes and West Marin countryside. A zoning regulation was imposed which now allows no more than one house per 60 acres to be built on its agricultural land. Additionally, thousands of acres have been forever preserved in the Point Reyes National Seashore, and 30,000+ acres have been preserved as permanent agricultural land, thanks to preservation easements purchased by the Marin Agricultural Land Trust (M.A.L.T.). M.A.L.T. was founded in 1980 by another grass-roots group of local ranchers and environmentalists and has since created numerous programs to educate people on the need to preserve agriculture, as well as fund-raising to purchase preservation easements from farmers and ranchers in need of capital. These farmers and ranchers still own their property and can farm and ranch it as usual. The only thing they, and their successors, cannot do is develop it for anything other than agricultural purposes.

West Marin is a popular day-trip destination, as well as a growing over-night destination for residents of the Bay Area. It is popular as a day-trip destination for hiking, beachcombing, bicycling, motorcycle riding, kayaking, rustic dining, picnicking and Sunday drives. The Point Reyes National Seashore receives an average of 2.6 million visitors a year, who all together spend on average $100 million each year in the West Marin area. On average only 23% of these visitors spend the night.[4]

In recent years, the economics of maintaining a family-run farm on land that is more valuable for its real estate than the product it produces has created another pressure on this region. Ellie Rilla, Director of the University of California Cooperative Extension for Marin and Sonoma Counties, points out that the high cost of land, and the economic slowdown in the dairy and beef industry, has hurt the local farmers and ranchers.

Half of Marin County, approximately 167,000 acres, is still farm and ranch land. There are 204 small or mini-farms with an annual gross income of less than $100,000. The average size of a farm in Marin is 588 acres, and the majority, are third and fourth generation family-owned operations. Agriculture contributes over $53 million annually to the Marin economy, with milk production dominating at 65 percent.[5] These revenue figures do not represent agriculture's contribution to the local economy in associated areas, such as clothing, groceries, etc.

Dating back to the Gold Rush days, Marin was the dairy producer for California, well known for its milk and butter. Now small family-run farms are in danger of being purchased by wealthy "gentlemen farmers" who know nothing about farming and ranching. To stay on their land, West Marin farmers and ranchers are looking at their land and their trade with a creative eye. There is a movement towards more environmentally friendly enterprises such as organic milk, organic vegetables, and organic or natural beef and sheep ranching. As Bliss mentioned in an article on agriculture and agritourism, "Conventional agriculture has done considerable damage to the earth and needs to be replaced by farming which restores rather than depletes resources."[6] The movement to do just this has been in place for years in Marin and Sonoma counties, and is growing each year.

This is where agri-tourism comes into play. Agri-tourism is "the economic activity that occurs when people link travel with agricultural products, services or experiences. . . . Agritourism has recently emerged as an opportunity for many farm families to diversify their agricultural operations. . . . On-farm diversification is income generation, as well as increased awareness and education of the non-farming public about farms and their products."[7]

Agri-tourism covers a wide spectrum from the U-pick-it farm operations to farm visits by classes of children to overnight farm stays, and everything in between. In Europe, Australia and New Zealand, agri-tourism is plentiful. In the European Union countries, the governments have spent $2 billion since 1991 to support agritourism projects. "European funds go to restoring dilapidated buildings, training farmers in hotel skills, promoting traditional products and trades, and helping to market farm holidays through travel agencies or websites."[8] European political leaders have recognized the importance of keeping farmers on the land as a way to halt "unfettered urban development."[9] In an interesting comparison, the Virginia Tech website states, "agri-tourism can be viewed much like eco-tourism in that it is small-scale, low impact, and, in most cases, education-focused."

West Marin offers an interesting case study of responsible tourism development, specifically in the area of agri-tourism. West Marin residents are friendly, happy to share their beautiful landscape, but not at all interested in an increase in population or allowing their countryside to be disturbed or turned over to outsiders.

Since agri-tourism is by definition small-scale and low impact, it is perfect for West Marin. The County of Marin and the UC Cooperative Extension Office are equal supporters of what agri-tourism could mean to the local farmers and ranchers. The State of California signed a bill in 1999, AB 1258, the California Agricultural Homestay Bill, and the County of Marin is currently developing a code for a sustainable economy that includes provisions for responsible tourism as it relates to Marin in general, and agri-tourism in specific.

The California Agricultural Homestay Bill, AB 1258, exempts farmers from requirements that before had been a barrier. "The law allows working farms to host a limited number of overnight visitors and permits farm families to serve meals cooked in the farm kitchen to visitors, consistent with the Federal Food Code definition of a family home kitchen."[10] To help promote agri-tourism in West Marin, M.A.L.T. offers farm tours and hikes nearly every month, and has created and marketed an entertaining audio driving tour of the history of the countryside, narrated by Peter Coyote.

■ AGRI-TOURISM

There are a number of interesting examples of agri-tourism taking place in West Marin. In 1990 Sharon and Steve Doughty renovated an old home near the main road on their 800-acre dairy ranch and are supplementing their ranch income by operating it as a bed & breakfast as

well as an operating winery. Sharon's grandfather was one of the original settler ranchers in West Marin and Sharon wants to ensure the land is preserved and profitable for her children. As she says, "Farming is a way of life, it is not a way to make money." With the inn, the Doughtys not only have another stream of income and a diversification for their four adult children, they recognize the need to educate the public about farming. As Sharon says, "Ignorance about how our food is grown is widespread. Most guests at our inn come away with some understanding of the strict rules under which food is grown and the need to preserve farms for farming."

The Chileno Valley Ranch is another excellent example of planning, managing and operating a bed and breakfast on a family farm according to the principles of Responsible Tourism. Sally Gale inherited the 586-acre family farm from her mother. In 1850, Sally's great-great-grandfather, Charles Martin, emigrated from a poor town in Switzerland. In 1856, he purchased the 586-acre ranch and, in 1883, built a beautiful Italianate home, the same home that Sally and husband Mike renovated in 1993 after it had sat vacant and vandalized for seven years. They raise and direct market 130 head of natural, grass-fed beef. Their cattle feed naturally on the abundant grass and are slaughtered and sold direct; their beef does not travel anywhere prior to reaching the customer. They also grow and direct market apples.

The economics are such that this enterprise does not generate enough income to sustain the ranch, its land and its taxes. What's more, they entirely renovated the 110-year old home in 1993 and the process ate up five years and all of their resources. Thus was born the idea of operating a bed and breakfast for additional income.

The Chileno Valley Ranch has four double occupancy rooms and a cottage for rent on a two-night minimum basis from Thursday through Sunday, from the month of March through the middle of December. All rooms have private baths, and the price of the room includes breakfast and almost free rein to roam the 586 acres. They point out that guests can wander anywhere, except the fields where the cattle are grazing, or to the top of a hill on their property that would allow the hikers to look down on a neighbor's house. Mike and Sally are very sensitive to not impinge on their neighbors' privacy.

Guests are invited to participate in whatever is happening at the ranch, including the birthing of baby calves. The Gales willingly share their acquired knowledge of the stewardship of the land, the cattle, and the wildlife on their land.

The Gales received a grant from the Marin Resource Conservation District to fence off and replant one-half mile of the Chileno Creek running through their property. This has resulted in a total re-growth of the native trees, and, as an added bonus, they now have a large population of neo-tropical migratory songbirds coming to their property each year to feed on the insects at breeding time. Word of this has spread and many of the guests now come specifically to bird watch.

For a while, visitors to the ranch had to dip their boots in a disinfectant wash to ensure hoof and mouth disease was not being transmitted. The other concern is the Sudden Oak Death Syndrome. The Gales recycle everything they use. They no longer buy the small bottle of room amenities to avoid throwing out bottles.

Mike and Sally are sensitive to what tourists do to the feel of the area. As Sally says, "Tourists change the feel of the place." They try to not overburden the valley they live in by limiting the number of guests they have, by requiring a two-night stay, and by being very selective of the big events they host. Sally mentions they could host weddings every weekend if they wanted because the demand is so high (which they obviously could because of the sheer beauty of their location and the privacy their home affords).

But the Gales thoroughly enjoy their guests. As Sally says, "Guests become part of our community in ways that preserve not only our ranch but also our whole community. We give out literature on M.A.L.T. and a high percentage of them become dues paying members. Guests buy direct (beef and apples) and thus they support

family farms." The only caveat, they say, is it's best to schedule the bed and breakfast activities together (Thursday through Sunday) and focus on the ranch from Monday through Thursday afternoon.

FUTURE DIRECTIONS

Agri-tourism can be the perfect example of responsible tourism: small numbers, low impact, and education focused. To achieve these benefits what must be done? Can this same model be used in other areas?

About the author: Bonnie Berg MacLaird holds an MBA and is a Certified Travel Consultant (CTC). She spent 20 years in the cruise industry as a marketing executive before assuming her most recent duties as Executive Director of Partners in Responsible Tourism (PRIT) as well as owning and operating an independent bookstore, Habitat Books in Sausalito, California.

REFERENCES

1. *Practicing Responsible Tourism: International Case Studies in Tourism, Planning, Policy and Development,* John Wiley & Sons, Inc. 1996, page 2.
2. Archer and Cooper, 1994.
3. Wanhill, Stephen, "The Economic Aspects of Location Marketing," *Economic and Management Methods for Tourism and Hospitality Research,* 1999.
4. Park Service research conducted in 1998.
5. Rilla, Ellie, "Amazing But True . . . Facts about Agriculture in Marin County." January 2001.
6. Bliss, Shepard, "Eco-Farming; Community Supported Agriculture and Agritourism." May/June 1999.
7. Manitoba website, June 2001.
8. *New York Times,* "Preserving a Heritage Via Bed and Barns," 8/13/98.
9. Ibid.
10. "Navigating Legal Constraints," Agritourism and Nature Tourism in California, Small Farm Center, UC California.

Appendices

Appendix A
Geography: Your Window to the World

As a future tourism professional, you may find yourself working in a position requiring more than just a basic understanding of geography. Careers in travel agencies, tour operations, airlines, car rental companies, rail and bus companies, cruise lines, travel publishing, and cartography are just a few examples of where geographic knowledge may be considered important. If you see yourself in any of these careers or just want to be a more informed traveler, join us as we journey through this section and learn how geography provides a window to the world.

Take a look at what *National Geographic Traveler* calls the world's greatest destinations (see Table A.1). How does geography play a role in defining these special places? Are they the same or different? Are they near or far? Are they rural or urban? Let your imagination roam, and take a moment to locate each of these distinct destinations on a map. What makes these destinations special?

Now that you have located these destinations, see whether you can answer these basic questions. How do you get to these locations? Based on climatic conditions, when would be the best time to visit? What would you see and experience once you arrive? A thorough understanding of geography gives you the confidence to answer these questions and meet travelers' needs.

◼️ MAPS

What better place to start studying geography than with *maps*? For centuries, maps have played a role in traveler's plans and adventures. But, what are maps?

"Since classical Greek times, curiosity about the geographical landscape has steadily grown, and ways to represent it have become more and more specialized. Today there are many kinds of mapmaking, . . ." (Robinson, Morrison, Muehrcke, Kimerling, & Guptill, 1995, p. 10). Globes, photo maps, trail maps, topographical maps, and street

guides should come to mind when you think of maps. However, these are only a few examples; other types of maps are also commonly encountered. Mall diagrams, airport layouts, and even stadium and concert seating diagrams are all forms of maps. "Like a model automobile or ship, a map is a scale model of the real world, made small enough to work with on a desk or computer" (Rubenstein, 2005, p. 6).

No matter how large or small, maps show you where you are and how to get to where you want to be. Today, maps serve a variety of tourism purposes, as they are created to depict scale models of reality and convey important information to users. For smaller locations such as airports, theme parks, and historic districts, mapmaking (technically plans) is fairly simple. However, for expansive areas such as continents or countries, mapmaking is not quite as simple.

The Earth is a sphere, so the most accurate map of the world is a globe; but carrying around a sphere that is big enough to provide any level of detail is a physical impossibility. So, although these spheres make attractive conversation pieces and let us visualize the complexity of our world, they are not very practical travel companions. For practical purposes, maps must be flat, which results in distortion, meaning features don't appear exactly as they are when large areas are involved no matter how they are drawn. The most common of these representations is the *Mercator projection* (see Figure A.1), and like most early maps, it was developed for navigation purposes.

In addition to the Mercator projection, two other representations of the world are also used. One is the *Robinson projection* (see Figure A.2) and the other is *Goode's homolosine projection* (see Figure A.3). No matter what approach is taken to represent the Earth in a two-dimensional format, some distortion will occur. The Mercator projection distorts the Arctic and Antarctic regions, making them appear larger than they really are. For example, Greenland appears to dwarf

Table A.1	Fifty Places of a Lifetime

African Continent
Pyramids of Giza
Sahara
Serengeti
Seychelles

European Continent
English Lake District
Coastal Norway
London
Paris
Loire Valley
Barcelona
Amalfi Coast
Vatican City
Tuscany
Venice
Alps
Greek Islands

South American Continent
Tepuis
Amazon Forest
Machu Picchu
Rio de Janeiro
Torres del Paine

Antartica
The entire continent

North American Continent
Canadian Rockies
Boundary Waters
Canadian Maritimes
San Francisco, CA
Big Sur, CA
Mesa Verde, CO
Grand Canyon, AZ
Vermont
New York
British Virgin Islands

Oceania
Papua New Guinea Reefs
Outback
North Island, New Zealand
Hawaiian Islands
Galápagos Islands

Asian Continent
Istanbul
Acropolis
Jerusalem
Petra
Great Wall of China
Japanese Ryokan
Taj Mahal
Hong Kong
Danang to Hue
Angkor
Kerala

Outer Space
An infinite frontier

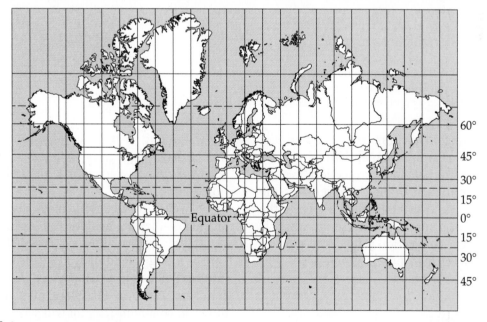

■ **Figure A.1**   Mercator projection.
Source: Semer-Purzycki, Jeannie, *Travel Vision: A Practical Guide for the Travel, Tourism, and Hospitality Industry,* 1st, © 2000. Electronically reproduced by permission of Pearson Education, Inc., Upper Saddle River, New Jersey.

Australia, when in fact, Greenland is only about one-fourth the size of Australia, having a landmass of 2,175,600 square kilometers compared with Australia's landmass of 7,617,931 square kilometers. The Robinson projection provides a more accurate view of the world, but it, too,

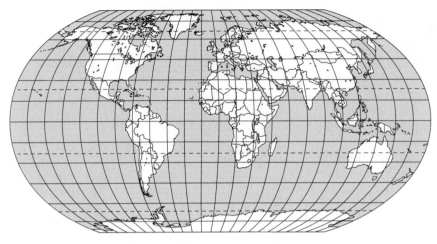

■ **Figure A.2** Robinson projection.
Source: Semer-Purzycki, Jeannie, *Travel Vision: A Practical Guide for the Travel, Tourism, and Hospitality Industry*, 1st, © 2000. Electronically reproduced by permission of Pearson Education, Inc., Upper Saddle River, New Jersey.

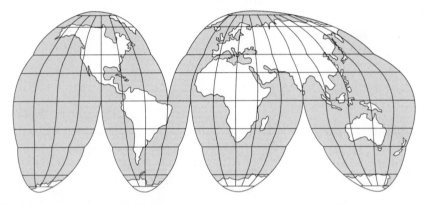

■ **Figure A.3** Goode's homolosine projection.
Source: Semer-Purzycki, Jeannie, *Travel Vision: A Practical Guide for the Travel, Tourism, and Hospitality Industry*, 1st, © 2000. Electronically reproduced by permission of Pearson Education, Inc., Upper Saddle River, New Jersey.

results in some distortion, especially at the poles, which appear to be larger than they really are. Goode's homolosine projection, which resembles a flattened orange peel, creates the most accurate view of the Earth and creates the least amount of distortion. Because the world is round, whichever projection is used, the shortest distance between two points is not a straight line, but a curved one.

Reading Maps

As the previous representations of the world show, not all maps are created alike. However, once you master the basic language of map-making, *cartography*, you can interpret any map. Unlocking this information requires

understanding of basic cartographic notations, that is, geographic grids (*longitude* and *latitude*), legends (symbols and colors), and indexes (location guides).

"Twenty-first-century maps are more than just maps—they are analytical tools referred to as geographic information systems (GIS) and are part of a larger field of study called geographic information science (GIScience)" (Clawson and Johnson, 2004, p. 8). Every map has several things in common. They all will serve as a means of location. The most common means of determining location is via latitude and longitude. Every place on Earth can be located by knowing these two pieces of information.

Finding a location's latitude and longitude relies on two imaginary lines that divide the

Earth. One is the *equator* located halfway between the North and South Poles. Distances moving north or south from this line are measured in degrees of latitude. The other imaginary line is the *prime meridian*, running north and south through Greenwich, England, and connecting the two poles. Distances moving east and west from this line are measured in degrees of longitude. These lines intersect at right angles, forming a grid (see Figures A.1, A.2, and A.3). So, you could locate Christchurch, New Zealand, on a map by knowing the coordinates, 43°32′S and 172°38′E; or if you were given the coordinates 44°57′N and 93°16′W, you would find Minneapolis, MN.

On the opposite side of the Earth from the prime meridian is the *International Date Line* separating east from west. This line is not a straight longitudinal line, but it corresponds fairly closely to 180° longitude, and just like the prime meridian, it extends from the North to the South Pole. This line has been set by international agreement and separates one calendar day from the next. Areas to the west of the International Date Line are always one day ahead of areas to the east. Therefore, Pacific Rim and Asian countries are one day ahead of the United States, Canada, and Western European countries.

Indexes and Locators

Some maps, such as diagrams of specific locations like road atlases, may not be so sophisticated as to have latitude and longitude. These maps may simply have indexes of locations listed alphabetically with map-specific grids or location indicators. Specific map locations are identified through the use of two index points such as A and 12. You would find A by looking down the left- or right-hand side of the map and 12 by looking across the top or bottom of the map. If the location is small, specific points of interest may be identified only by letters or numbers that correspond to locators on the outside border of the map. An airport layout is an example of a small-place diagram providing all the information travelers need to find their way around as they check in, change flights, or locate available services.

Second, maps will have locator information. These locators may be cardinal directions or compass points such as north, south, east, and west. If you are directionally impaired, it may help you to remember that up is north and down is south when using the North Pole as a reference point. The same holds true for left and right. Left is west and right is east. However, anytime your look at a map, always remember to orient (place) the map facing north so that you will have a common sense of direction.

Scales

Maps are replicas of reality, so they must be smaller than the area depicted. Therefore, everything shown on a map must be proportional, which requires a map scale. The scale will be indicated on the map. Examples of scales may include notations such as 1″ equals one mile or 1″ equals ten miles. Scales may also be shown as graphic or bar scales. Figure A.4 provides several examples of how scales may be used on maps.

Legends

Symbols or icons are often used on maps to indicate points of interest, services, and attractions. These legends save space, locating and drawing attention to everything from capital cities, roads, airports, marinas, and waterways to restaurants, museums, roadside parks, points of interest, and campgrounds. When searching for the legend, also take a look at the date the map was produced. The more recent the date, the more accurate the map should be. Finally, you may find several maps using similar notations grouped together in atlases.

Maps are important tools in geography, but there is more to geography than spinning a globe and placing your finger on Tibet or locating the home of the Taj Mahal. For tourism professionals, geography includes knowledge of the physical and human characteristics that influence travel activities.

PHYSICAL GEOGRAPHY

Physical geography describes natural features of the Earth including landforms and vegetation, water, and climate. These features create an

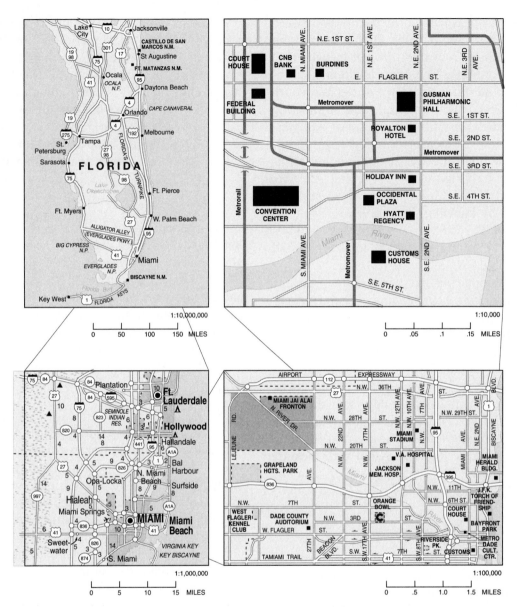

■ **Figure A.4**   Map scale. The four maps show Florida (upper left), south Florida (lower left), Miami (lower right), and downtown Miami (upper right). The map of Florida (upper left) has a fractional scale of 1:10,000,000. Expressed as a written statement, 1 inch on the map represents 10 million inches (about 158 miles) on the ground. The bar line below the map displays the scale in a graphic form. Look what happens to the scale on the other three maps. As the area covered gets smaller, the maps get more detailed, and 1 inch on the map represents smaller distances.
Source: Rubenstein, James M., *Cultural Landscapes: An Introduction to Human Geography,* 8th, © 2005. Electronically reproduced by permission of Pearson Education, Inc., Upper Saddle River, New Jersey.

environment that can either encourage or discourage tourism activities.

Landforms and Vegetation

Landforms refer to the surface features of the Earth. *Relief maps* showing elevation changes provide quick clues to the many different types of landforms that may be encountered. Everything from continents and islands, to mountains and valleys make up our physical world. Mountain ranges, the most significant landforms, not only create impediments to travel but also affect weather. As mountains stop moisture-bearing winds, one side will be wet and the other dry.

Vegetation or the lack of it (based on rainfall) creates the mantle that covers landforms. Whether it is a barren desert landscape, deep-dark forest, verdant grassland, or the stark reality of arctic tundra, the variations capture imaginations and attract visitors.

Water

Most of the world (over 70%) is covered by water, and most of this water is saltwater; so it should come as no surprise that tourism professionals should know something about oceans, seas, gulfs, lakes, and rivers. These bodies of water are the playgrounds for today's cruise lines and river barges, but they were once the primary corridors of transportation. Because water transportation was the first means of moving large numbers of people and cargoes, it is easy to see how cities formed as people congregated around and along major bodies of water (see Table A.2).

Even today, water, and especially water currents, can have dramatic impacts on land temperatures and the amount of moisture that falls. Ocean currents rotate clockwise in the Northern Hemisphere but counterclockwise in the Southern Hemisphere. Thus, the warm Atlantic currents of the Gulf Stream and the North Atlantic Drift keep Ireland and England green almost year-round even though both are located far north of the equator. Likewise, the cold waters of the Indian Ocean are still cool as they move north up the west coast of Australia (the West Australia Current). Even large inland bodies of water can significantly affect weather patterns. For example, the warmer temperatures of the Great Lakes produce large amounts of snow in the winter as warmer moisture from the lakes collides with the cold landmass. In addition to bodies of water, levels of precipitation (see Figure A.5) also affect population densities as well as tourism activities.

Climate and Seasons

Meteorologists can fairly accurately predict short-term weather patterns. However, travel and tourism professionals should be able to describe general weather patterns for any location at any time of the year. Will it be rainy or snowy, sunny or cloudy, humid or dry, hot or cold? Geography provides the answers to these important and specific climatic questions.

Location, combined with season, will dictate long-term weather patterns. For example, a Caribbean cruise would make sense in December but would be questionable in September, the height of hurricane season. Likewise, an Alaskan cruise would be enticing in August, but would be a frosty if not an impossible nightmare in December. Or, a trip to China during the cool-dry

Table A.2	Major Bodies of Water
Largest Oceans (square miles) Pacific Ocean—64,186,300 Atlantic Ocean—33,420,000 Indian Ocean—28,350,500 Arctic Ocean—5,105,700	*Largest Seas (square miles)* South China Sea—1,148,500 Caribbean Sea—971,400 Mediterranean Sea—969,100 Bering Sea—873,000
Largest Gulfs (square miles) Gulf of Mexico—582,100 Persian Gulf—88,800 Gulf of California—59,100	*Largest Lakes (square miles)* Lake Superior—31,700 Lake Victoria—26,820 Lake Huron—23,000 Lake Michigan—22,300 Lake Tanganyika—12,350 Lake Baikal—12,200
Longest Rivers The Nile—4,145 miles The Amazon —4,000 miles The Yangtze—3,900 miles The Mississippi-Missouri—3,740 miles The Huang—3,395 miles	

season in October would be a pleasure rather than in July or August, the hot and humid season.

Seasons may change, but climates remain constant. The world is divided into five basic climatic zones, which are based on distance from the equator, 0° latitude. This imaginary line splits the world into the Northern and Southern Hemispheres. The tropical regions extend to the Tropic of Cancer to the north and the Tropic of Capricorn to the south. The north temperate climate extends from the Tropic of Cancer to the Arctic Circle, and the south temperate climate extends from the Tropic of Capricorn to the Antarctic Circle. Above and below these lines are the North and South Polar zones.

In tropical zones, temperatures are mild, with little variation throughout the year. In contrast, the temperate zones are noted for their four-season temperatures. Polar zones are the exact opposite of the tropical zones, staying below zero degrees Fahrenheit most of the year.

■ HUMAN GEOGRAPHY

In addition to natural features, location and accessibility are also key factors that will influence the level of tourism activity. But geography is more than just landforms, water, vegetation, and climate. It also includes people. Whereas physical geography sets the stage for travelers, human (cultural) geography brings the stage to life through people and their cultures, languages, religion, foods, beverages, arts, and crafts. Every place on Earth will be just a little bit different as each of these factors creates a unique blend. Travel writers create visual and mental pictures of what visitors might expect to encounter in any given location.

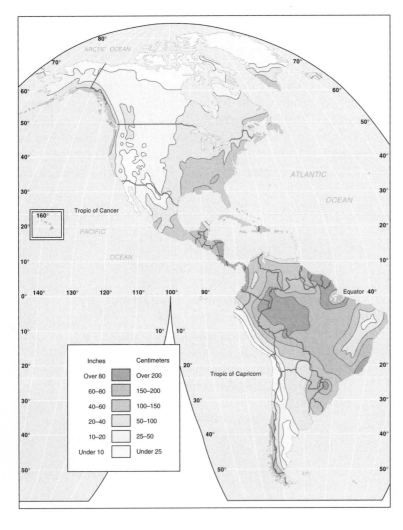

■ **Figure A.5** World mean annual precipitation. Precipitation varies greatly from one part of the world to another. Moreover, there is considerable variability in precipitation from one year to the next. Variability is usually greatest in areas of limited precipitation.
Source: Clawson, David L.; Fisher, James; Aryeetey-Attoh, Samuel A.; Theide, Roger; Williams, Jack F.; Johnson, Merrill L.; Johnson, Douglas L.; Airriess, Christopher A.; Jordan-Bychkov, Terry G.; Jordan, Bell, *World Regional Geography: A Development Approach*, 8th, © 2004. Electronically reproduced by permission of Pearson Education, Inc., Upper Saddle River, New Jersey.

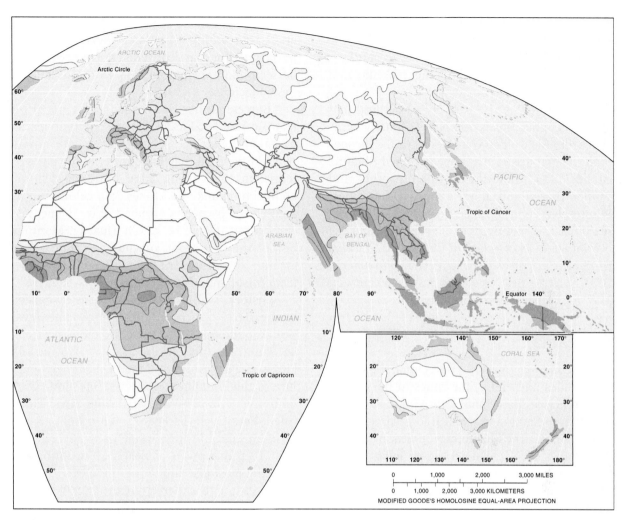

■ **Figure A.5**   (continued)

Consider the rich tapestry of human existence, past and present, that can be experienced in just two destinations that are eight time zones apart and on two different continents. The first destination is San Francisco, California, a metropolis of over 744,000 people. The other destination is Barcelona, Spain, a city of 4,805,000 similar to San Francisco, yet different in many ways.

San Francisco, California

Located in the temperate zone on the Pacific Ocean, San Francisco enjoys mild weather year-round. This truly is a cosmopolitan city. Depending on where you are in the city, you may hear English, Cantonese, Spanish, Italian, or a variety of Asian dialects being spoken. The foods served in San Francisco are as varied as the languages. The many

sights and sounds to be found among the hills create a mosaic that comes together making one very special city.

Although the English were the first to explore the area, it was the Spanish who first settled the Bay area. Their historic footprint can be seen in the mission district. But San Francisco is a true melting pot of cultures. Chinatown grew from early immigration during the gold rush and the building of the transatlantic railroad. Although not an "ethnic" influence, free-spirited "hippies" enlarged their circle of influence in the city and gave rise to "free love," "flower power," and world-renowned musical groups such as the Grateful Dead and Jefferson Airplane.

Not unlike the marketplaces of old, garage sales and sidewalk sales are a hallmark of San Francisco; but the city is also noted for upscale shopping in Union Square, which is served by its famous cable cars. A trip down one of the city's winding hillside streets on these cable cars will find you in another shopping, museum, and tourist delight—Fisherman's Wharf.

In addition to the panoply of cultural and artistic delights, this is also a city of many wonders, from the Golden Gate Bridge to the escape-proof federal prison that once occupied Alcatraz Island. "San Francisco is full of sights and sounds that simply don't exist in other cities. Where else could you hear foghorns, barking sea lions, the ringing of cable car bells, and the continuous clackety-clack of the cable car pulleys winding underneath the streets?" (*Frommer's*, 2004, p. 102). Best of all, no matter where you look, the scenery is breathtaking.

Barcelona, Spain

The second destination, Barcelona, Spain, is 5,967 miles and eight time zones to the east of San Francisco. Barcelona, a thriving metropolis, is similar to San Francisco. It is located in a temperate zone on the Mediterranean Sea. Barcelona covers an area of about 38 square miles to San Francisco's 46 square miles. The scenery and activities of both cities are expansive, but the similarities stop there.

In Barcelona, you can expect to hear mostly Castilian Spanish and a bit of English. A stroll along La Ramblas, the colorful and vibrant walking boulevard running from the harbor to the Placa de Catalunya, showcases the diversity of the city. This is a pedestrian shopping area with living statues, mimes, and booths selling almost everything from lottery tickets to birds to jewelry to food and beverages. And, what can be seen and experienced runs from the tame to the bodacious.

Barcelona, like San Francisco, is noted for its history of lewdness, from the red light district to gambling dens. Although these are quaint relics of the past, they have shaped both cities as icons on the cutting edge of food, fashion, architecture, and good times. "Barcelona can be approached by neighbourhood or by theme. You can set out to see the Gothic Quarter, Montjuïc hill, or the waterfront; or you can create a tour around the works of Gaudí and his fellow *modernista* architects" (*Berlitz*, 2003, p. 23).

History is alive in Barcelona, as evidenced in the *Barri Gotic* containing many medieval Gothic buildings. A taste of the city's past can be found in the *Museu Picasso* showcasing Picasso's early works and the medieval architecture of this prominent port city. Barcelona contains five UNESCO World Heritage Sites: Palau Guell, Parc Guell, La Pedrera (Casa Mila), Palau de la Musica, and Hospital de la Santa Creu i de Sant Pau, making it a unique destination for even the most discriminating traveler.

A visitor to either city can quickly experience a combination of physical and human geographic features that make these cities truly unique destinations. Other destinations and special places await those who understand the importance of geography. The more you learn about geography, the more you and those you serve will enjoy the journey.

■ REFERENCES

Barcelona. (2003). *Berlitz pocket guide* (11th ed.). Singapore: Berlitz Publishing.

Bergman, Edward F., and Renwick, William H. (2005). *Introduction to geography* (3rd ed.). Upper Saddle River, NJ: Pearson Education, Inc.

Clawson, David L., and Johnson, Merrill L., eds. (2004). *World regional geography: A development approach* (8th ed.). Upper Saddle River, NJ: Pearson Education, Inc.

50 places of a lifetime. (1999, October). *National Geographic Traveler.*

Frommer's irreverent guide to San Francisco (5th ed.). (2004). Hoboken, NJ: John Wiley Publishing, Inc.

Robinson, Arthur H., Morrison, Joel L., Muehrcke, Phillip C., Kimerling, A. Jon, and Stephen C. Guptill. (1995). *Elements of cartography* (6th ed.). Hoboken, NJ: John Wiley Publishing, Inc.

Rubenstein, James M. (2005). *Cultural landscapes: An introduction to human geography* (8th ed.). Upper Saddle River, NJ: Pearson Education, Inc.

Appendix B
Tourism Research

If we just had more data, decisions would be easier. This is a common refrain heard from decision makers in every organization. But, **what** is involved in gathering these data? The answer is research. Research is a simple idea. It is the systematic investigation of a topic, often including the collection of information for a set goal. The term *research* is used to describe both a process and the product of that process. Research means to design, gather, analyze, and report information; and it also means the output of that process.

Key to the conduct of research is the attempt by the researcher to be objective, systematic, logical, and empirical. This objectivity is necessary to ensure (it is hoped) that conclusions derived are based on fact rather than hearsay, opinion, or emotion. The bits of information collected during the research process are called *data,* a plural Greek word. So, when using the word *data*, always use it with a plural verb form. For example, you would say, "The data reveal a tendency, **not** the data reveals a tendency."

The term *research* thus encompasses a mind-boggling array of data and methods that can be used in decision making. Differing information needs require differing methods of data collection and analysis. Some data are routinely collected and readily available, such as sales and cost information or census information collected by governments. This routinely and readily available information is called *secondary* data. However, most needs for information are very specific and data need to be gathered for a unique purpose. This type of data is called *primary* data.

Some research is called *applied* and other research is called *basic.* Applied research is used as input for making specific decisions. Basic research is conducted to expand knowledge on some subject, not to use the information directly for problem solving. Much of the applied tourism research done is what we call *proprietary* research, meaning an organization funds the research and holds onto the information, not sharing it. Most of the basic research conducted in the field of tourism is published and therefore shared and is termed *public* research. With this background in mind, let's take a look at the **what, who, when, where,** and **how** of research.

■ TYPES OF TOURISM RESEARCH

Research comes in four forms: descriptive research, experimental research, prescriptive research, and simulative research or modeling. We describe each type of these briefly next.

Descriptive research This involves the collection of information to describe aspects of the tourism industry. Such aspects include the size and positive and negative impacts of tourism, the number of tourists at different locations and during differing seasons, the number of jobs within each sector of the industry, the amount of taxes directly paid by tourists and industry members, inventories of the tourism industry in terms of number of sector members, list of attractions and recreational resources; the possibilities for descriptive research are endless. Data collected by individual tourism enterprises are a form of descriptive research: for example, number of rooms rented, length of stay, table turnover rate, and so on.

Experimental research When you hear the term *experiment*, you probably think of laboratory science experiments, but tourism organizations can and do conduct experiments to learn about the effect of one variable on one or more other variables. How will a price change affect demand for rooms or airline seats? Will running an ad in one magazine result in more inquiries to the visitor center than the same ad in a different magazine? We will discuss experimental research a bit more later.

Predictive research Because in many tourism businesses demand varies greatly, predicting or forecasting demand is critical, especially to smooth operations. Most operational decisions are based on the demand expected for any time period. Staffing, purchases, and cash flow needs are all dependent on service demand. Therefore, predictive research is necessary to ensure cost-effective, quality operations whether we are thinking of a restaurant, a hotel, a museum, or an amusement park. Tourism managers and researchers try to predict the future by looking at patterns of the past and making best guesses about the future.

Simulative research/modeling To help in making longer-term decisions about the future, some tourism organizations try to model or simulate it. By making certain assumptions based on data descriptive of the past and educated guesses about likely occurrences in the future, managers can simulate times to come, particularly with the aid of computer technology. Using spreadsheets and other computer-assisted, awe-inspiring number-crunching powers, decision makers can generate specific levels of demand and other information that they then use to aid them in making longer-term decisions. For example, simulation would help determine the wisdom of investment and development of land tracts contiguous to a ski resort, addition of another tower to a hotel property, or relocation of the regional airport.

WHO CONDUCTS TOURISM RESEARCH?

Research can be conducted by three different types of researchers. Much of the day-to-day information gathering and analyzing activities that occurs is conducted by employees of tourism suppliers, and government or public/private entities. We call this *in-house* research. However, some research requires special high-level skills that often are not available within most tourism organizations. In these cases, tourism suppliers, governments, and other entities will hire research consultants or research firms to conduct the research for them. These specialists utilize a formal research process to focus their efforts and help ensure that the information and reports they provide clients will be objective, accurate, and unbiased. See Figure B.1 for the flowchart of the research process.

Basic research, with the goal of furthering knowledge about the entire process of tourism, is most often conducted by academic researchers

Step	1—Establish the need for research.
Step	2—Define the problem.
Step	3—Establish research objectives.
Step	4—Determine research design.
Step	5—Identify information types and sources.
Step	6—Determine methods of accessing/acquiring data.
Step	7—Design data collection forms.
Step	8—Determine sample plan and size.
Step	9—Collect data.
Step	10—Analyze data.
Step	11—Prepare and present the final research report.

■ **Figure B.1**   Sequential Steps in the Research Process[1]

and is sometimes funded by tourism companies or trade associations. Your tourism professor and other faculty at your school likely conduct research of this type, using the 11-step process listed in Figure B.1. Results of this basic tourism research are published in research journals and therefore made available to all who are interested in reading them. If you go to your school's library, you will find many of the tourism research journals that were used in the development of this textbook: the *Journal of Travel Research, Annals of Tourism Research*, and *Journal of Hospitality and Tourism Research* to name but a few. Articles within these journals are the most important and varied source of information about the human phenomenon and massive industry of tourism.

WHO NEEDS AND USES TOURISM RESEARCH?

Public policy makers, those who make decisions in governmental bodies or in public/private organizations, use tourism research because they are entrusted with making informed decisions about spending tax monies. Tourism research provides them with important information so they can decide (1) how much to invest in infrastructure to encourage/support tourism development; (2) how much money to spend on marketing to attract tourists to the community, region, or nation; (3) whether to make public/private investments to generate more tourism, such as investments in stadiums, convention centers, and/or events (fairs, festivals, tournaments, hallmark events);

and (4) the size of positive and negative impacts to the area's economy, natural environment, and culture. One of the most important techniques in this area is called *economic impact analysis* (EIA) and will be discussed in greater depth later in this appendix. EIA methods are used to compare alternative investments and to determine which is likely to yield the most benefit to the community, region, or nation.

Governments also use tourism research in their role as owners/managers of many tourism resources, especially attractions (e.g., national parks, historic sites). Government employees responsible for the stewardship of these precious resources face many of the same challenges of private-sector tourism managers, discussed next.

Tourism supplier firms, whether commercial or nonprofit, use research information for a variety of strategic/planning, tactical, and operational decision-making needs. Examples of these needs are (1) demand forecasting (determining the level of demand for any period of time, whether the hour, shift, day, week, season, or year); (2) marketing decisions (promotion, price, product, and place tactical decisions) used to create and smooth demand throughout the year; (3) management/operational decisions to ensure cost-effective yet consumer-satisfying performance; and (4) financial decisions concerning the use and source of funds.

WHEN, WHERE, AND HOW IS TOURISM RESEARCH CONDUCTED?

Actually, some forms of tourism research are conducted continually. Countries throughout the world collect economic information year after year to track the levels of and changes in tourism activities. To a limited extent, some states/provinces and cities do likewise. Many companies or industry trade organizations, such as the Air Transport Association, routinely collect information on their business or industry and then disseminate this information to decision makers within the company or to their organization members.

The how of tourism research is represented in Figure B.1, but we should go into a little more detail. On rare occasions, tourism researchers

conduct experiments in which one variable is manipulated and the results of one or more other variables are then measured. This form of research is necessary to determine causation of effects. Because of all the variables that interplay in any tourism-related action, experiments are very difficult to conduct and are therefore used infrequently by tourism researchers.

Data collection is sometimes conducted through observation. Human or electronic counters that record the number of visitors to an entry point frequently conduct tourism counts. Most commonly, however, tourism data are collected from tourists directly. Sometimes this information is collected prior to the tourist's visiting an area, sometimes during the trip, and often after the trip is complete. This direct consumer surveying can be conducted in the consumer's home, but in the tourism industry it is frequently conducted at visitor welcome centers or at border entry/departure locations such as border crossing points and international airports.

By using interviewers in person or over the phone or by using paper-and-pencil surveys or online surveys, answers from tourists are acquired to a wide variety of questions of interest to tourism researchers and decision makers. The Internet is playing a greater and greater role in the collection of information because the majority of potential travelers regularly use the Internet today. Surveys can be quickly, easily, and cost effectively developed and distributed over the Web. They can be fun and easy to respond to, and very importantly, answers are immediately translated into bits of data that can be statistically analyzed at any minute in time.[2]

TOURISM RESEARCH IS HARD TO DO

Now that you know more about tourism research, you may realize that the nature of the industry makes tourism research especially challenging to do and to coordinate. Its large number of organizations, both big and small, and its many sectors make a snapshot of the tourism world hard to come by, let alone a full-blown analysis of its many facets. Data collection from so many organizations is a practical impossibility. Few consistent reporting requirements, except for quasi-regulated sectors, such as airlines, exist to make the task easier. Consumer research in tourism is difficult because consumers experience a set of services away from their homes, and frequently on a short-term basis (as opposed to long-term hometown-based service relationships such as those between consumer and bank or consumer and dentist). The breadth of issues to be researched is also mind-boggling because tourism by its nature strongly affects an area economically, culturally, and environmentally.

Because of tourism's wide reach (and frankly its intrinsic excitement), researchers from a wide range of disciplines focus their eyes and efforts on its study. Tourism is studied by academics and others in the fields of marketing and business, sociology and psychology, history and anthropology, geography and political science, planning and design, and even futurism. Even experts from the hard sciences are studying tourism because of its effects on nature and the Earth.

ECONOMIC IMPACT ANALYSIS: A SPECIAL FORM OF TOURISM RESEARCH

Economic impact analysis is an inexact process, and output numbers should be regarded as a "best guess" rather than as being inviolably accurate. Indeed, if a study were undertaken by five different experts, it is probable that there would be five different results. (p. 80)[3]

Much of the government-sponsored research in tourism focuses on the economic impact of tourism to a certain region. These economic impact analysis (EIA) studies are conducted to determine tourism activities' effects on the income and employment of the residents of some region. Usually the studies reflect annual impacts of total tourism visits, but sometimes they are undertaken to measure the effects of visitors on a single entity or event, such as a major zoo or a festival.

On the benefit side, this normally means the study provides estimates of travel spending and the impact of this spending on employment, personal income, business receipts and profits, and government revenue. On the cost side, this means estimating the costs, sometimes nonmonetary, to government and residents of travel activity in the area. (p. 359)[4]

The results of EIA studies are useful to:

1. Public policy makers and the area's residents when determining economic benefits of investment in tourism promotion or expansion/development of publicly funded tourism attractions, such as events
2. Public/private organizations when measuring impact of travel promotion efforts or specific conferences or groups of travelers enticed to visit the area
3. Tourism industry members in educating the public and government officials of the benefits that the industry offers the community or region

Fundamentally, EIA research involves counting the number of area visitors and determining how much they spent during the duration of their visit, usually using sample surveys (although other estimation methods are used). Tourists are usually counted at border entry/departure points, visitor information (welcome) centers, or accommodation establishments. In the past, the surveys used to query tourists differed from country to country. In 2003, the World Tourism Organization (WTO) published a general questionnaire that can be used by countries (and adapted by other organizations as well) to attempt to generate more consistent data that are more easily compared.[5] Since the 1990s, the WTO has encouraged countries and smaller, more local entities to develop Tourism Satellite Accounts (TSA) to track the expenditures and economic impact of travelers to their regions. The purpose of a TSA is to link tourism expenditures spent in the wide array of industries in which they may be made and therefore better enumerate the total amount and impact of tourism.

Although the development of standard questionnaires is a giant step in the collection of expenditure data from tourists, the process is still no easy chore, for either the researcher or the tourist! To demonstrate the daunting task facing the tourist, imagine you have just spent 10 days having fun in the sun in Cancun, Mexico. While you are waiting to board your flight home, a pleasant-looking lady approaches you and asks whether you would take a few minutes to answer some questions about your visit to her country. Because you have nothing better to do, you agree. First she asks you several easy questions: in what country do you live, how many people (including yourself) are you traveling with, how long have you stayed in Mexico, and what was your reason for traveling to Mexico; but then the questions start to tax your memory and your estimation skills. She asks you how much you spent on transportation within the country; how much on accommodations; how much on food and beverages; how much on souvenirs; how much on activities and attractions. Yikes, those are tough questions. At best, you offer decent "ballpark" numbers for your expenditures.

From this imagined scenario, you can see that statistics you read about average tourism expenditures should not be assumed to be totally accurate. The estimates are only as good as the tourists' ability to give accurate answers and the researchers' estimation of total tourism spending based on the answers of sampled tourists. As the saying goes, "garbage in, garbage out," so the quality of the research depends of the skills of the researcher and the accuracy of tourists' memories and ability to estimate.

Once total tourism expenditures have been estimated, researchers then try to determine how these monies are re-spent within the regional economy. EIA expert John Crompton lists six ways a tourism dollar spent in a local establishment could be re-spent.

1. Paid to other local businesses for some good or service (e.g., a local produce farmer)
2. Paid to local-resident employee or owner
3. Paid to local government in form of tax
4. Paid to other business outside of local area (e.g., distant wholesale food distributor)
5. Paid to nonlocal employee or owner
6. Paid to nonlocal government in form of tax (state/province or federal)

The first three ways are called *linkage,* and the latter three are termed *leakage.* The higher the linkages and the lower the leakages within an area economy, the higher will be the total

economic impact of tourism to the area. The size of these linkages and leakages are assumptions (a type of "judgment call") made by the researchers. "As a general rule, a smaller community tends not to have the sectoral interdependencies that facilitate retention of monies spent during the first round of expenditures. Hence, much of the expenditure would be re-spent outside the local region leading to a relatively low local economic multiplier" (p. 22).[6]

The final judgment that needs to be made is a guess concerning the number of rounds of re-spending of the tourism expenditures within the area economy, the multiplier effect we introduced in Chapter 11. So, final EIA numbers, on which so many decision makers rely, are only as good as the research method used and the validity of the large number of assumptions researchers use in deriving them.

EIA: THE SPRINGFEST EXAMPLE

To better understand how an economic impact analysis is conducted, let's look at a small-scale example. Three researchers published a study of the tourism economic impact an annual event called Springfest has on Ocean City, MD. The town has developed Springfest, a four-day festival in May, to attempt to generate tourism business during the spring shoulder season (during the summer millions of visitors flock to the city's shore location). The festival requires about $50,000 of the town's resources, particularly for expenses incurred by the parks and recreation department.

To accomplish the objective of identifying the "bang for the buck" town residents received, the trio first devised a method to estimate the attendance at the festival by counting entrants to the festival at different time periods and different entry points. By sampling in this way they could generate a good educated guess of the total attendance. The researchers developed a short questionnaire that they then used to collect pertinent information from a sample of attendees. The survey used indicates the type of information that is commonly collected during EIA studies.

The team was very careful to collect information that allowed them to derive the economic impact of the Springfest event. First, survey respondents identified themselves as residents or town visitors based on their zip code. Respondents were asked to guess at the amount of money they spent on various categories of services within the Ocean City area. The researchers asked respondents to separate in-city versus out-of-city expenses. "Even though it is not used, this [out-of-city] information is requested because it causes respondents to think carefully about where they spent their money" (p. 84).[7]

Two questions, 5 and 6, on the short six-question survey, are very important to get an accurate fix on the success of Springfest in generating more tourism to the region. Question 5 identifies visitors who are termed "casuals"–folks who would have come to Ocean City anyway and just happened to include Springfest in their activities. These casuals were not drawn to Ocean City because of Springfest. If Springfest had not been taking place, they still would have traveled to Ocean City and likely would have spent the same amount of money in the area. Question 6 allows the researchers to determine the size of a group called "time-switchers"–those who were planning on coming to Ocean City anyway but changed the date of their visit to correspond with Springfest. This group represents visitors who were already planning to come to Ocean City, so although they timed their trip to coincide with Springfest, it was not the festival, in and of itself, that drew them to Ocean City.

After a careful sampling schedule was developed and five interviewers were trained, a sample of over 1,400 attendees was surveyed. Analysis showed that 326 of the sample were local residents. Of the out-of-towners, 705 indicated that they would have visited Ocean City without the lure of the festival. However, 211 of these time-switchers indicated they stayed an average of nearly two days longer because of the festival. These extra days and associated expenses represent economic impact generated expressly from Springfest. The survey answers revealed that 384 visitors came to the Ocean City area specifically because of Springfest. These festival-motivated travelers represent those extra tourists that Springfest generated for Ocean City. The researchers also included the expenses of out-of-area vendors (business travelers) who rented booths at Springfest because they were drawn to the city by the sales potential of the festival.

To calculate an estimate of the total economic impact of Springfest, the researchers utilized a computer model that derives total impact based on assumptions made concerning total attendance at the festival and linkages and leakage in the city economy. After all this number crunching, the team estimated that the Springfest resulted in $1,239,000 in additional personal income for the residents of Ocean City. Given the care the researchers took in filtering out local resident expenditures and those from tourists who would have come regardless of the festival's existence, the taxpayers of the city can be assured that this is a highly accurate number, not one inflated to look good. Springfest certainly appears to be a good investment.

REFERENCES

1. Adapted from Burns, Alvin C., & Bush, Ronald F. (2003). *Marketing research, online research applications.* Upper Saddle River, NJ: Prentice Hall, p. 28.
2. Burns, Alvin C., & Bush, Ronald F. (2003). *Marketing research, online research applications.* Upper Saddle River, NJ: Prentice Hall.
3. Crompton, John L., Lee, Seokho, and Shuster, Thomas J. (2001, August). A guide for undertaking economic impact studies: The Springfest example. *Journal of Travel Research,* 40, 79–87.
4. Frechtling, D. C. (1994). Assessing the economic impacts of travel and tourism: Introduction to travel economic impact estimation. In J. R. Brent Ritchie and Charles R. Goeldner, eds., *Travel, tourism, and hospitality research* (pp. 359–365). New York: John Wiley & Sons.
5. World Tourism Organization. (2003). *Tourism Satellite Account (TSA) implementation project: Measuring expenditure for inbound tourism.* Madrid: Author.
6. Crompton, J. (2004, July 1). Available at: http://rptsweb.tamu.edu/faculty/EconomicImpact.pdf.
7. Crompton, John L., Lee, Seokho, and Shuster, Thomas J. (2001, August). A guide for undertaking economic impact studies: The Springfest example. *Journal of Travel Research,* 40, 79–87.

Appendix C
Choosing a Career and Finding a Job

Choosing a career and finding that first full-time job after graduation is no easy task. "You *should* pursue a career in travel because of the *business* and the *product* itself. Travel and tourism is one of the most dynamic industries anywhere, offering extraordinary opportunities for mobility, creativity, and personal satisfaction."[1]

In fact, most college graduates change jobs several times after they obtain their degrees. It seems as though the grass is always greener on the other side of the fence. As a student studying in the fields of hospitality, travel, and tourism, you have the chance to beat those odds and find a career and job that will fit your needs prior to graduation. Look at Table C.1 at the end of this appendix for the host of job opportunities that await you and strategies you can take to achieve your career goals.

The tourism industry offers many opportunities to gain career-related experiences through part-time jobs and experiential learning activities such as cooperative education programs and internships. Some of you may already be working in the industry and pursuing a college degree for professional growth and development. Taking advantage of any of these options while still in school will allow you to sample a variety of career options and provide you with important workplace experience. Internships continue to set job applicants apart, as they have gained experience in the field.[2]

Many large organizations use cooperative education and internship programs to select future employees. These programs serve as a realistic job preview for the student and a long-term interview for the employer, creating a win–win situation for employers and prospective employees. Such programs help develop professionalism as well as industry- and company-specific knowledge demanded in today's competitive environment.

Whether you are considering a part-time job, an experiential learning activity, or a full-time job, you should not jump at the first opportunity that comes along. Before committing yourself, take some time to find out more about the job and the organization. What will you learn on the job? How will that prepare you for the future? In your first job, your goal may have been to earn some spending money, but later jobs should help prepare you for increased responsibilities in your chosen career field. Therefore, investigate the learning opportunities before you invest your time!

You can start your investigation by visiting your school's career planning and placement center, participating in on-campus interviews, attending job fairs, visiting with alumni and speakers who come to campus, reading trade publications, and talking with friends, family, and professors. Once you have discovered the types of organizations for which you would like to work and the knowledge, skills, and abilities they are seeking in potential employees, you can prepare for the job search process.

PREPARING YOUR RÉSUMÉ

You should start thinking about and preparing your résumé early in the job search process. You will need to send it along with every job-hunting letter you write and take it with you on interviews. You should also share your résumé with references, friends, relatives, and other associates to let them know about your career goals and qualifications.

Your résumé is like a photograph, highlighting your qualifications on one sheet of paper. It is not your life story but a promotional piece that serves as an attention-getter that can be read in 30 seconds or less. Your résumé should show what you have to offer a prospective employer and create enough interest so that the employer will want to learn more about you. One word of caution, don't exaggerate, because most organizations will verify the accuracy of the information you provide.

The format and content of your résumé should be factual and to the point. There are several formats you can use that allow you to highlight or focus on specific information. You can choose from two standard formats, chronological or functional. Stick to one of these formats and leave the creative approaches to someone else. The chronological format presents key information about you in a historical style. The functional format is built in sections around your specific qualifications, those that set you apart as being special for your targeted job.[3]

1. Contact information: Put your name, address, and a telephone number where you can always be reached. (Note: Make sure you have a professional message on your answering machine and tell anyone who will answer the phone while you are away to answer professionally and take detailed messages.)

2. Career objective: Give the reader some idea of where you want to go with your career. If you are too vague, employers may not know whether you will fit in their organization. However, if you are too specific, you might disqualify yourself from related jobs. General statements, such as "seeking an entry level or supervisory position in _____" (you fill in the blank with your desired position such as restaurant operations, passenger services, or hospitality services), are probably best as you enter the full-time workforce. More directed statements can be made in your cover letter. As you gain more experience, it will be appropriate to express more specific career goals.

3. Education and training: List your college degree(s) and major. Highlight your grade point average if it is good. Include any special training or certifications you have received. If your work experience is limited, expand this section by including an explanation of special skills you have acquired.

4. Work experience: List all employers for whom you have worked. Don't forget summer and part-time jobs, internships, and cooperative education placements. Include name and location of the organization, dates of employment, positions held, and a brief description of your skills and accomplishments. You can present this information in a chronological format (the most recent job first) or in a functional format (highlighting specific skills and accomplishments).

5. Activities and honors: Show what you do when you are not in school or working. List such things as professional, social, and civic organizations to which you belong as well as honors, awards, and scholarships you have received. Describe your accomplishments and responsibilities with these organizations such as officer positions, committee assignments, and completed projects.

Use action words, phrases, and quantifiable accomplishments to show that you are a dependable, can-do, take-charge problem solver.

Once your résumé is complete, have several people critique it for you. Your career services office can assist you throughout this process. This will help you find mistakes as well as test whether or not it is painting the picture you want the reader to see. After it has been checked and double-checked for clarity and correctness, you are ready to have it printed. Use either a laser-quality printer or have your résumé professionally printed on high-quality cotton bond paper. Be sure to save some of the paper so you can send your cover letter on the same type of stationery.

For more pointers on how to approach the job search process successfully, see *Guide to Business Etiquette* by Roy A. Cook, Gwen. O. Cook, and Laura J. Yale (Prentice Hall, 2005).

WRITING YOUR COVER LETTER

Your résumé is only one step in the job-search process. You will also need to prospect for jobs by writing cover letters and including your résumé with this correspondence. Cover letters are written in response to advertisements or job announcements, as a follow-up to a telephone inquiry, or when inquiring about possible job openings.

Your cover letter serves as an introduction to prospective employers and entices them to read your résumé and invite you to interview.

Because it is an introduction, personalize it. Do not send a cover letter to "whom it may concern" or "human resource director." Call and ask for the name, title, and correct spelling of the person to whom the letter should be addressed.

There are two basic types of cover letters that you will write. One is a letter of inquiry, seeking to find out whether the organization is looking for employees. The other is a letter of application that is written in response to a known job opening. In either case, because there may be many people corresponding with the organization, be sure to follow up with a phone call after you have sent the letter, and ask for an interview.

PREPARING FOR THE INTERVIEW

Finding a job may be one of the most difficult challenges you will ever face, but it is also one of the most rewarding. Don't get discouraged. You may send out hundreds of letters of inquiries and résumés and make many calls before you obtain your first interview.

Before you land that first interview appointment, take advantage of any on-campus recruiting opportunities, and attend career fairs to practice your interviewing skills and learn more about what employers are expecting from job applicants. Once you have been invited to interview, prepare yourself for success by using the following outline.

1. Research the company: Find out everything you can about your prospective employer. What services does it provide? Primary competitors? How big are they? Where are its offices/properties/outlets located? Does it have a formal training program? What is a typical career path? Your librarian or career planning professional can help you with this task. Be prepared to relate your skills and accomplishments to the organization's needs.

2. Prepare yourself: Arrive at the interview at least 15 minutes before the scheduled time. Be sure that you are neat, clean, rested, well groomed, and dressed appropriately. Be sure to know all of the information in the materials that have been sent to you before the interview.

3. Sell yourself: Stress your achievements and be prepared to answer some typical interview questions in a positive manner.

4. Don't rely on your résumé to answer any of the following questions.

   a. How do you plan to achieve your career goals?

   b. Why did you choose the career for which you are planning?

   c. How has your education prepared you for a career?

   d. What were your favorite subjects in school?

   e. What subjects did you like the least?

   f. What motivates you to put forth your greatest effort?

   g. Why should we hire you?

   h. What have you learned from participation in extra-curricular activities?

   i. What do you know about our company?

   j. What have you learned from your mistakes?

5. Stay professionally engaged: Watch for cues that indicate when an interviewer wants more information or wants you to shorten your answers. Maintain eye contact; don't slouch in your chair; don't wander from answering the question. Watch for signs that the interview is over. If you are not offered a job on the spot, ask whether it would be okay to call back in about 10 days and check on the status of the search.

6. Follow up after the interview: Write a thank-you note to everyone with whom you interviewed. Thank each one for his or her time and indicate whether you are interested in being considered further. Respond quickly to any requests for additional information.

One final reminder: Before you go on that all-important career interview, review the key points on business etiquette that are presented in this appendix. The final choice a recruiter will make between you and another equally qualified candidate may come down to your attention to detail and professionalism.

Table C.1   Tourism, Hospitality/Hotel, Restaurant Administration

What can I do with this degree?

Areas	Employers	Strategies
RETAIL/SITE MANAGEMENT		
■ Property Management ■ Facility Management ■ Rooms Management ■ Beverage Management ■ Kitchen Management ■ Production Supervision	■ Historic, cultural, and natural attractions ■ Lodging: hotel/motel, bed and breakfast, timeshares, and campgrounds ■ Destination areas: amusement centers, theme parks, and resorts ■ Special event and festival organizations ■ Entertainment industry: casinos, theaters, and stadiums ■ Food service: catering, schools, hospitals, military, concessions, and institutions ■ Restaurants, dining clubs, taverns, and fast-food operators ■ Leisure organizations: sporting clubs, recreation centers, fitness facilities, private and/or country clubs ■ Self-employment	■ Develop a strong foundation in food service, administration, and customer service. Courses in communications, marketing, management, law, accounting, and food and beverage controls are a must. ■ Gain an ability to make quick and independent decisions. ■ Check the placement office, faculty members, and professional organizations for employment leads. Create a network in the industry to establish contacts for advancement. ■ Take leadership roles in student organizations. ■ Gain experience working with budgets.
GENERAL SERVICES		
■ Office Operations ■ Reservations ■ Purchasing ■ Customer Services ■ Travel Planning	■ Tour operators ■ Historic, cultural, and natural attractions ■ Lodging: hotel/motel, bed and breakfast, timeshares, and campgrounds ■ Reservations companies ■ Destination areas: amusement centers, theme parks, and resorts ■ Special-event and festival organizations ■ Entertainment industry: casinos, theaters, and stadiums ■ Food service: catering, schools, hospitals, military, concessions, and institutions ■ Restaurants, dining clubs, taverns, and fast-food operators	■ A high interest in working with the public and problem solving is a must. ■ Start in reservations or telephone sales. Master the product line; learn to give excellent service. ■ Understand and use office machines and office systems in your area of expertise. ■ Serve as treasurer or financial officer of an organization. ■ Gain experience working with budgets. ■ Acquire supervisory skills and experience. ■ An orientation toward service and detail is necessary to succeed. ■ Learn state, provincial, federal, and local government job application process

What can I do with this degree?

Areas	Employers	Strategies
GENERAL SERVICES (Continued)	■ Transportation/travel industry: airlines, cruise companies, car rental agencies, travel agencies, airports, motor coach/tour carriers, and rapid transit, e.g., AMTRAK and VIA RAIL CANADA ■ Leisure organizations: sporting clubs, recreation centers, fitness facilities, private and/or country clubs ■ State, provincial, federal, and local government: tourism offices, visitors bureaus, convention centers, and park systems ■ Self-employment	■ Gain an ability to make quick and independent decisions. Prepare interpersonal and public speaking skills. Be creative; have good planning and organizational skills. ■ Gain experience through planning activities/ events for civic/community organizations. ■ Attend conferences for student organizations and professional associations. ■ Include classes in marketing, promotions, commercial recreation, activity planning, resort management, advertising, public relations, and business. ■ Learn how to do fund-raising. ■ Gain experience working with budgets. ■ Learn state, provincial, federal, and local government job application process.
SPECIAL EVENTS ■ Convention/Trade Show Planning ■ Entertainment/Event Planning ■ Activities Planning ■ Recreation Manager ■ Convention Services Management	■ Lodging: hotel/motel, bed and breakfast, timeshares, and campgrounds ■ Destination areas: amusement centers, theme parks, and resorts ■ Special-event and festival organizations ■ Entertainment industry: casinos, theaters, and stadiums ■ Cruise companies ■ Leisure organizations: sporting clubs, recreation centers, fitness facilities, private and/or country clubs ■ State, provincial, federal, and local government: tourism offices, visitors bureaus, convention centers, and park systems ■ Trade and professional associations ■ Public or private corporations and businesses	

Table C.1	Tourism, Hospitality/Hotel, Restaurant Administration (Continued)

What can I do with this degree?

Areas	Employers	Strategies
MARKETING ■ Product Research ■ Communications ■ General Sales ■ Meeting and Convention Sales ■ Incentive Travel Sales	■ Tour operators ■ Historic, cultural, and natural attractions ■ Lodging: hotel/motel, bed and breakfast, timeshares, and campgrounds ■ Reservation companies ■ Restaurants, dining clubs, taverns, and fast-food operators ■ Equipment suppliers and manufacturers ■ Transportation/travel industry: airlines, cruise companies, car rental agencies, travel agencies, airports, motor coach/tour carriers, and rapid transit, e.g., AMTRAK and VIA RAIL CANADA ■ Leisure organizations: sporting clubs, recreation centers, fitness facilities, private and/or country clubs ■ State, provincial, federal, and local offices, visitors bureaus, convention centers, systems	■ Gain competency in a variety of computer programs. Gain experience in customer service and communications skills. Learn about geography and international travel regulations. ■ Take a part-time job in any area and move up. ■ Strive for excellent interpersonal and public speaking skills. Consider a foreign language or business minor. ■ Take classes in marketing, promotions, advertising, public relations, and business. ■ Start in reservations or telephone sales. Learn the product line; deal with travel agents and the customer. Work in a major port city like Los Angeles, Miami, New York, or Vancouver. ■ Learn state, provincial, federal, and local government job application process.
ADVERTISING ■ Product Design/Illustration ■ Media Planning and Development ■ Public Relations ■ Publicity/Promotion	■ Lodging: hotel/motel, bed and breakfast, timeshares, and campgrounds ■ Destination areas: amusement centers, theme parks, and resorts ■ Special-event and festival organizations ■ Entertainment industry: casinos, theaters, and stadiums ■ Leisure organizations: sporting clubs, recreation centers, fitness facilities, private and/or country clubs ■ State, provincial, federal, and local government: tourism offices, visitors bureaus, convention centers, and park systems ■ Trade and professional associations ■ Public or private corporations and businesses ■ Restaurants, dining clubs, taverns, and fast-food operators	■ Gain competency in a variety of computer graphics programs. ■ Strive for excellent interpersonal and public speaking skills. Consider a public relations or marketing minor. ■ Take a part-time job in any area and move up. ■ Volunteer to advertise/promote events for parties, outings, and organizations. ■ Learn state, provincial, federal, and local government job application process. ■ Attend conferences and trade shows, join student clubs and professional associations, and attend field trips.

Table C.1	Tourism, Hospitality/Hotel, Restaurant Administration (Continued)

What can I do with this degree?

Areas	Employers	Strategies
ADVERTISING (Continued)	■ Product and equipment suppliers and manufacturers ■ Transportation/travel industry: airlines, cruise companies, car rental agencies, travel agencies, airports, motor coach/tour carriers, and rapid transit, e.g., AMTRAK and VIA RAIL CANADA	■ Include classes in marketing, promotions, advertising, public relations, and business. ■ Join student organizations in your field of study and join the publicity committee.
HUMAN RESOURCES ■ Personnel Management ■ Training ■ Employee Support Services ■ Recruitment ■ Labor Relations ■ Compensation and Benefits	■ Lodging: hotel/motel, bed and breakfast, timeshares, and campgrounds ■ Destination areas: amusement centers, theme parks, and resorts ■ Entertainment industry: casinos, theaters, and stadiums ■ Food service: catering, schools, hospitals, military, concessions, and institutions ■ Restaurants, dining clubs, taverns, and fast-food operators	■ Take courses in labor relations, industrial psychology, personnel management, public speaking, organizational behavior, business, communications, management, and law. Foreign language or human resources are good minors. ■ Gain experience in decision making, planning, budgeting, and personnel issues through an internship or co-op. ■ Be a leader in student organizations and professional associations. ■ Plan to be flexible geographically.
CORPORATE ADMINISTRATION ■ Property Acquisition and Development ■ Legal Areas ■ Research/Market Analysis ■ Financial Relations	■ Lodging: hotel/motel, bed and breakfast, timeshares, and campgrounds ■ Destination areas: amusement centers, theme parks, and resorts ■ Entertainment industry: casinos, theaters, and stadiums ■ Food service: catering, schools, hospitals, military, concessions, and institutions ■ Restaurants, dining clubs, taverns, and fast-food operators ■ Transportation/travel industry: airlines, cruise companies, car rental agencies, travel agencies, airports, motor coach/tour carriers, and rapid transit, e.g., AMTRAK and VIA RAIL CANADA	■ Take classes in human relations, foodservice production, marketing, law, accounting, food/beverage controls, and resort management. Obtain a graduate degree in business or law. ■ Be prepared to work "up from the bottom" to gain industry experience. Attend conferences and professional association meetings. ■ Study the industry leaders and trends by reading trade journals. ■ Be willing to work long or unusual hours and on holidays. ■ Gain an ability to make independent decisions. ■ Strive for excellent interpersonal and public speaking skills.

What can I do with this degree?

Areas	Employers	Strategies
CORPORATE ADMINISTRATION *(Continued)*		
	■ Leisure organizations: sporting clubs, recreation centers, fitness facilities, private and/or country clubs	■ Be flexible geographically. Create a network of contacts for advancement.
		■ Gain experience working with budgets, details, meeting deadlines, and supervising others.
PUBLISHING		
■ Guides	■ Self-employment	■ Experience living abroad. Gain an understanding of world history, geography, and international travel regulations.
■ Journals	■ Newspapers, magazines, and trade journals	■ Study and gain an in-depth knowledge of industry trends.
■ Books	■ Tour operators	■ Consider a journalism major. Learn writing skills. Emphasize research methods and computer skills. Learn to be objective.
■ News Writing/Editing	■ State, provincial, federal, and local governments: tourism offices and visitors bureaus	■ Work for your student newspaper; write for student organization newsletters; or work in publications areas at your college.
		■ Practice giving attention to detail and meeting deadlines.
		■ Learn about etiquette and social customs.
GOVERNMENT		
■ Community Relations	■ State, provincial, federal, and local governments: tourism offices, visitors bureaus, convention centers, special-event and festival planning offices, historical, cultural, and natural parks/attractions.	■ Take classes in political science, government, social research methods, public polity, marketing, promotions, advertising, public relations, and business.
■ Travel Information		■ Learn state, provincial, federal, and local government job application process.
■ Tourism Bureaus	■ Food service: catering, schools, hospitals, military, concessions, and institutions	■ Seek experience in customer service and planning. Increase skills in public speaking. Learn about etiquette and social customs. Gain sales skills.
		■ Learn grant writing skills.
		■ Understand and use office machines, systems, and computers.
		■ Serve as treasurer or financial officer of an organization or secure experience with budgets.

Table C.1	Tourism, Hospitality/Hotel, Restaurant Administration (Continued)

What can I do with this degree?

Areas	Employers	Strategies
EDUCATION		
■ Teaching/Training ■ Research	■ Lodging: hotel/motel, bed and breakfast, timeshares, and campgrounds ■ Destination areas: amusement centers, theme parks, and resorts ■ Entertainment industry: casinos, theaters, and stadiums ■ Food service: catering, schools, hospitals, military, concessions, and institutions ■ Restaurants, dining clubs, taverns, and fast-food operators ■ State, provincial, federal, and local governments: tourism offices, visitors bureaus, convention centers, and park systems. ■ Trade and professional associations ■ Self-employment ■ Colleges and universities	■ Possess objectivity, an inquiring mind, and an interest in working with both data and people. ■ Determine an area of expertise. Gain an in-depth knowledge of that industry, its leaders, and trends by reading recent books, journals, and annual reports. ■ Obtain a degree in the subject you plan to teach or research. Learn writing and research skills. Consider a graduate degree in research methods or a specialty of the trade. ■ Gain professional industry experience. Attend and speak at conferences, trade shows, and professional associations. Network in the industry for professional contacts.

GENERAL INFORMATION

■ Obtain volunteer, part-time, summer, internship and/or co-op experience.

■ Bachelor's degree qualifies for entry-level government and industry positions.

■ Master's degree qualifies for community college teaching and advancement in industry and government.

■ Ph.D. is required for advanced research or teaching positions in colleges and universities and senior positions in government.

■ Join professional organizations such as the National Tour Association, the American Hotel and Motel Association, or the National Restaurant Association.

■ It may be necessary to move around geographically to get promotions.

■ Obtain computer experience.

■ Develop strong communications and customer-service skills.

■ Be prepared to "work your way up from the bottom."

■ Be willing to work on weekends, holidays, evenings, and long or unusual hours.

Source: Career Planning Staff, Career Services, 100 Dunford Hall, University of Tennessee, Knoxville, TN, 1994.

■| **REFERENCES**

1. Rubin, Karren. (2001). *Inside secrets to finding a career in travel.* Indianapolis, IN: JIST Works.

2. Nasaw, Daniel. (2004, March 30). Unpaid internships can offer graduates entry to paid jobs. *Wall Street Journal,* p. B4.

3. Whitcomb, Susan Britton. (2003). *Résumé magic* (2nd ed.). Indianapolis, IN: JIST Publishing.

Glossary

A

Accommodations Loosely defined as establishments engaged primarily in providing lodging space to the general public.

Accounting A service activity of business designed to accumulate, measure, and communicate financial information to various decision makers.

Actual quality The level of quality a consumer perceives following the consumption of a good or service.

Adventure tourism Tourism that involves activities with an above-average element of physical risk.

Age cohort A generation affected by common experiences.

Airlines Reporting Corporation (ARC) The clearinghouse for receiving commission payments for airline ticket sales.

Airport code A three-letter designation used to identify specific airports.

Air Transport Association (ATA) A domestic association that provides a format for discussing safety and service issues and promotes the advancement of technology.

à la carte A menu in which each item is priced and prepared separately.

All-inclusive Single price for all or nearly all major services provided in a tour, resort, or cruise package.

Allocentrics *See* Venturers.

Amenities Goods and services provided with accommodations that contribute to guest comfort.

Amtrak The marketing name for the National Railroad Passenger Corporation, which is a combination of the passenger rail services of U.S. railroads.

Appropriations Funding provided through governmental entities.

Aquaculture The farming and cultivation of water plants, fish, and crustaceans, such as kelp, salmon, catfish, oysters, and shrimp, in large quantities for human consumption.

Artificial intelligence A segment of computer sciences devoted to the development of computer hardware and software that is designed to imitate the human mind.

Attractions Natural locations, objects, or constructed facilities that have a special appeal to both tourists and local visitors.

Available seat miles (ASMs) The distance traveled multiplied by the number of seats available.

B

Banks of flights The process of coordinating flight schedules so that aircraft arrive and depart during similar time periods.

Banquet A food and beverage function designed, priced, and produced for a client usually for a single event or occasion.

Banquet event order (BEO) A contract for a meeting or other special occasion that details the date, the sequence of events, special needs, foods and beverages, prices, and guaranteed quantities.

Benchmarks Performance measures that are used by similar types of businesses to monitor key operations.

Biometrics Technologies for identifying and verifying an individual's physiological characteristics such as fingerprints, handprints, facial features, and irises.

Blogs Online journals composed of links and postings in reverse chronological order.

Booking A reservation.

Botanical gardens Gardens dedicated to the preservation, display, and study of growing plants.

Break-even The level at which total sales equals total costs.

Brigade A team of foodservice employees, for example, the service brigade (all service personnel) or the kitchen brigade (all kitchen personnel), in which each member is assigned a set of specific tasks.

Bumping The process of denying boarding to airline passengers with confirmed reservations due to overbooking (overselling) the flight.

Business An organization operated with the objective of making a profit from the sale of goods and services.

Business travel Travel-related activities associated with commerce and industry.

C

Call centers Centralized locations designed and managed to handle large volumes of incoming telephone inquiries, in many cases on a 24/7 basis.

CANRAILPASS Allows 12 days of economy class travel within a 30-day period anywhere VIA Rail goes in Canada.

Carrying capacity A key concept in environmental impact analysis that relates to the amount of use an environment is capable of sustaining under certain circumstances.

Cartography The science or art of making maps and interpreting mapped patterns of physical and human geography.

Catering A department within a restaurant, hotel, or resort property that is charged with selling and planning special meetings and food and beverage events.

Chain operations Groups of properties that are affiliated with one another and have common ownership and/or management control and oversight.

Circle-trip flight A flight plan that includes return to city of origin but via different routing or airline.

Code share An agreement allowing a regional/commuter airline to share the same two-digit code of a cooperating primary carrier in the computer reservation system.

Commissary Central storage area where food and supplies are received and kept until requisitioned.

Commissions The percentage paid to a sales agent (travel agent) by tourism suppliers for booking travel arrangements.

Comparative advantage The benefits of one alternative relative to another.

Computer reservation systems (CRSs) Computer hardware and software that allow travel agents to tap into global distribution systems.

Concessionaires Individuals or companies who have been granted the right to provide a particular service, such as food service, guide service, sanitation service, or gift shop.

Concierge services Services provided by employees who specialize in meeting the special requests of guests and provide guest services such as making reservations and supplying information.

Configured (rooms) Rooms with a well-planned design developed to meet user needs for efficiency and effectiveness.

Connecting flight A flight plan that includes a change of aircraft and flight number.

Consolidators Wholesalers who buy excess inventory of unsold airline tickets and then resell these tickets at discounted prices through travel agents or, in some cases, directly to travelers.

Consortium An affiliation of privately owned companies to improve business operations and gain the necessary volume of business that can lead to improved profitability.

Constituent groups Subgroups of citizens with a set of common needs or wants.

Consumer behavior The study of consumer characteristics and the processes involved when individuals or groups select, purchase, and use goods, services, or experiences to satisfy wants and needs.

Contribution margin What is left of the sales price after deducting operating costs.

Convention and visitors bureau An organization whose mission is to develop tourism to an area by attracting both professional and leisure travelers.

Convention center A property developed to serve the special needs of groups, especially regarding meetings and trade shows.

Cooperative alliances Long-term relationships that enhance operating efficiencies, profitability, and market share for all parties.

Cost–benefit analysis A method used to determine the relative impact of a development, in which total costs and total benefits are estimated and then compared.

Cruise director The person who plans and operates passenger entertainment and activities onboard a cruise ship.

Cuisine A French term pertaining to a specific style of cooking (such as Asian cuisine), or a country's food in general (such as Mexican cuisine).

Culinary The creative arts and crafts of preparing foods.

Culinary tourists/tours Travel for unique eating and drinking experiences in the context of the local culture.

Culture The practices of a society; its customary beliefs, social roles, and material objects.

Curator Person in charge of a museum.

D

Data Facts and figures.

Data mining Analyzing information stored in computer databases with the help of statistical techniques to uncover hidden relationships and patterns.

Deck The equivalent on a ship to a floor or story of a hotel.

Demographics Characteristics used to classify consumers on the basis of criteria such as age, education, income, gender, and occupation.

Demographic segmentation Dividing consumer markets based on demographic data such as age, education, income, gender, religion, race, nationality, and occupation.

Demonstration effect Display of material goods and wealth by tourists leading to envy by local residents based on either the perception or the reality of being less fortunate.

Dependables Travelers who seek the comforts of familiar surroundings.

Destination image The detailed impression an individual or target segment has of a specific destination.

Destination resorts Properties that are relatively self-contained and provide a wide range of recreational and other leisure-time activities.

Destination vision An inspirational portrait of the ideal future that the destination hopes to bring about at some defined future time (usually in 5, 10, 20, or 50 years).

Direct flight A flight plan that includes one or more intermediate stops but no change of aircraft or flight number.

Disembark To go ashore from a ship.

Disposable income Household income after paying taxes that is available for personal use.

Distressed inventory Tourism services that have not been sold as the date of use approaches.

Docent A museum guide.

Domestic independent tour (DIT) Customized domestic tour including many elements, designed and planned to fulfill the particular needs of a traveler; may be designed by a travel agent or by a wholesaler in consultation with the traveler's agent.

Dynamic packaging The ability to aggregate multiple tourism service supplier offerings (e.g., air, hotel, and car) in real time into a package.

E

Ecological capacity The maximum level of users that an area can accommodate before ecological damage is incurred.

Ecological tourism (more commonly called ecotourism) A form of tourism that focuses on environmental and cultural preservation.

Economics The study of the choices people make in using scarce resources to meet needs.

Economies of scale Savings in time, money, or other resources organizations enjoy as the result of purchasing and/or selling in large quantities, specialization at a particular job or function, and the use of specialized machinery.

Ecotourism A form of tourism that focuses on environmental and cultural preservation.

Ecotourists Leisure travelers who prefer to visit less popular, more primitive destinations.

Ecotravelers Travelers who visit sensitive natural and cultural environments to observe and learn about a very different culture and environment and participate in low-impact sports activities.

Efficient foodservice response (EFR) Partnership agreements created among manufacturers, distributors, and foodservice operators to lower food costs and improve the quality of service.

Elastic demand A change in the quantity of goods or services used in a proportion that is greater than changes in prices.

Embark To go onboard a ship.

Employee turnover The number of employees who leave their jobs because they intentionally miss work, quit, or are terminated.

Enterprise resource planning system (ERP) A system designed to combine all information sources, subsystems, and processes from various locations into one unified system.

Enterprise system Management information systems that combine data from multiple properties.

Entrepreneurial Assuming the risks of a personally owned business.

Environmental capacity The limit on the number of users that an area can accommodate before visitors perceive a decline in the desirability of the area.

Escorted tour An all-inclusive tour with a structured itinerary and a guide who accompanies the guests.

Eurailpass Allows unlimited travel for non-European tourists for varying periods of time throughout Austria, Belgium, Denmark, Finland, France, Germany, Greece, Ireland, Italy, Luxembourg, the Netherlands, Norway, Portugal, Spain, Sweden, and Switzerland.

Events Special occasions and scheduled activities.

Exchange rate The number of units of one currency necessary to be exchanged to obtain a unit of another currency; for example, 121 Japanese yen for $1.00 U.S.

Expatriate A citizen of one nation who lives in a nation of which he or she is not a citizen.

Expected quality The level of quality that a consumer predicts he or she will receive from a good or service.

Expected script The set of steps and statements that a guest expects to occur during a service encounter.

Export A good or service produced in one country and purchased by a resident of another country; the opposite of "import."

Extreme tourism A subset of adventure tourism; encompasses activities that involve above-average elements of physical challenge and risk.

F

Facilitating goods Tangible items that support or accompany a service being provided.

Fairs Temporary gathering places for the exhibition of products and services, often accompanied by entertainment and food and beverage services.

Familiarization trips (also called "fams" or "fam trips") Trips offered by governmental tourism agencies, hotels, resorts, and tour operators at low or no cost to acquaint travel salespeople (typically travel agents) with the products and services they offer.

Federal Aviation Administration (FAA) Agency within the DOT charged with ensuring air safety and promoting the growth of aviation.

Fee simple Right of ownership evidenced by the transfer of a certificate of title. The buyer has the right to sell, lease, or bequeath the property or interest (as in a timeshare).

Festival A time of celebration, with scheduled activities.

Feudal system A system of political organization, prevailing in Europe from the 9th to about the 15th century, in which ownership of all land was vested in kings or queens.

Financial resources The amount of money available for a given project through the use of debt and equity.

Fleet utilization Percentage of time transportation vehicles are used for revenue-producing purposes.

Focus group An in-depth interview about a topic among 8 to 12 people, with a researcher (called a "moderator") leading the discussion.

Folio Record of an individual guest's charges, including nightly room charge, telephone charges, food and beverage charges, dry cleaning, parking, etc.

Foreign independent tour (FIT) Customized foreign tour including many elements, designed and planned to fulfill the particular needs of a traveler; may be designed by a travel agent or by a wholesaler in consultation with the traveler's agent.

Franchise A license to operate a tourism service business such as a travel agency or hotel with the benefit of trademarks, training, standardized supplies, operating manual, and procedures of the franchiser. A contractual agreement providing for the use of a recognized brand name, access to a central reservation system, training, documented operating procedures, quantity purchasing discounts, and technical assistance in return for royalties and fees.

G

Geographic segmentation Dividing consumer markets along different geographical boundaries such as nations, states, and communities.

Geotourism Tourism that sustains or enhances the geographic character of the place being visited, including its environment, culture, aesthetics, heritage, and the well-being of its residents.

Global distribution systems (GDSs) Worldwide interorganization information systems that travel agencies use in selling tourism services.

Gross gambling revenues (GGR) The amount wagered minus the winnings returned to players.

Gross registered tons (GRT) A measure of the interior size of a ship determined by volume of public space.

Ground transfers Short-distance transportation between service providers, most frequently provided as part of a tour.

H

Hard ecotourists Physically active travelers with a strong environmental commitment who seek specialized trips with an emphasis on personal experiences.

Heritage attractions Places, structures, and activities with historical and cultural significance.

Heterogeneous Having differing characteristics and needs.

Homogeneous Having similar characteristics and needs.

Host communities Towns or cities that welcome visitors and provide them with desired services.

Hosted tour A tour in which a host is available at each major tour destination to welcome guests, solve problems, and answer questions.

Hotel personnel All individuals responsible for the care and service of cruise ship passengers.

Hub-and-spoke system The primary airline route pattern in the United States. By designating primary hubs, airlines are able to funnel traffic into these centers to feed their trunk point-to-point routes between major market cities.

Human (cultural) geography The human activities that shape the face of a location and shared experiences, including the cultural aspects of language, religion, and political and social structures.

I

Import A good or service purchased in one country but produced in another country; the opposite of "export."

Incentive tour operators Tour operators who specialize in organizing, promoting, and conducting incentive tours.

Incentive travel Motivational programs designed to create competition, with the winner(s) receiving travel awards.

Inclusive price A single price for a package of services such as accommodations, food, and activities.

Independent properties Facilities that are owned and operated as single units with no chain affiliation or common identification.

Independent tour A tour that allows the flexibility to travel independently while taking advantage of prearranged services and rates based on volume discounts.

Inelastic demand A change in the quantity of goods or services used that is not in direct proportion to changes in prices.

Information technology Computer systems that provide for the storage and retrieval of data.

Infrastructure The foundation utilities and other systems necessary for an economy, such as roads, electricity, and water and sewage systems.

Intermediary Firms that help tourism suppliers locate customers and make sales to them, including tour operators and travel agencies.

Intermodal A trip requiring the use of two or more forms of transportation.

International Air Transport Association (IATA) Association for airlines offering international air service that provides a means of resolving problems for mutual benefit.

Involuntarily denied boarding A situation that occurs when airline passengers with confirmed reservations are denied boarding on scheduled flights due to overbooking. Passengers may either voluntarily give up their reserved space or be involuntarily denied boarding in exchange for compensation.

Itinerary A detailed schedule of a trip.

J

Joint venture Combined efforts of two or more partners, usually organizations.

L

Leakage Purchasing power that is spent on imports to an area, resulting in a transfer of income out of the local economy.

Learning curve The rate at which people learn over time.

Learning organization An organization committed to identifying best practices and creating systems to achieve high-quality standards.

Leg The segment of a flight between two consecutive stops.

Legacy carrier A carrier offering varying classes of services with global networks that include

alliance partners, which allow passengers to earn and redeem frequent-flier miles across these networks.

Leisure activities Activities performed during one's free time away from work.

Leisure travel Travel for personal interest and enjoyment.

Lifestyle A mode of living that is identified by how people spend their time (activities), what they consider important in their environment (interests), and what they think of themselves and the world around them (opinions).

Limited stakes Legislative limits placed on the dollar amount that can be wagered on any single bet (typically $5).

Line of credit An agreement with a bank in which loans are automatically made up to an established limit.

Load factor The number of revenue passenger miles (RPMs) divided by the number of available seat miles (ASMs).

Lodging Facilities designed and operated for the purpose of providing travelers with a temporary place to stay.

M

Management The distinct processes of planning, organizing, directing, and controlling people and other resources to achieve organizational objectives efficiently and effectively.

Management contracts Operating agreements with management companies to conduct day-to-day operations for a specific property or properties.

Management information systems (MIS) Computer-based systems designed to collect and store data and then provide information for planning, decision making, and problem solving.

Marketing communications Any communication between a marketer and a consumer.

Marketing concept An overall organizational philosophy that is focused on understanding and meeting the needs of customers.

Marketing mix Those things that an organization can do to influence the demand for its goods or services. It consists of four variables, often called the four Ps of marketing: product, price, place, and promotion.

Market segmentation Dividing a broad market into smaller and distinct groups of buyers—each group with similar needs, characteristics, or behaviors.

Market share The percent of the total market for a good or service that a single company has.

Markup Adding a percentage to the cost of a good or service to arrive at a selling price.

Mass customization The production of a good or service to fulfill the unique needs of an individual buyer.

Mass tourism Twentieth-century phenomenon whereby the working and middle classes began traveling in large numbers for leisure purposes.

Mature travelers People aged 55 and older; also called "senior citizens."

Medical tourism Travel to other countries to receive medical treatments.

Meeting planner An individual who specializes in planning and coordinating all the details of meetings, conferences, or events.

Megaresort A destination resort containing multiple facilities and world-class attractions and entertainment venues. Each revenue center at these destinations could operate as a separate business venture.

Microsegmentation The process of identifying and serving small subsegments of the market.

Missionary sales Sales calls made by individuals to retail travel agencies and other tourism industry intermediaries to answer questions and educate them about the company's services so that they may be sold more effectively.

Model A simple representation showing how important features of a system fit together.

Multiplier concept The additional economic activity that results when money is spent and re-spent in a region on the purchase of local goods and services.

Museum According to the International Council of Museums: a non-profit-making, permanent institution, in the service of society and its development, and open to the public, which acquires, conserves, researches, communicates, and exhibits, for the purposes of study, education, and enjoyment, material evidence of humans and their environment.

N

National monument A landmark, structure, or other object of historic or scientific interest.

National parks A large natural place having a wide variety of attributes.

National preserve An area in which Congress has permitted continued public hunting, trapping, and oil/gas exploration and extraction.

National scenic trail A linear parkland.

Nature-based tourism Travel to unspoiled places to experience the natural world.

Night audit Nightly accounting process that reconciles all property income, including rooms, telephone, food and beverage outlets, catering, gift shop, parking, etc.

Nonprofit tourism association An organization that exists to support the tourism industry of an area and often promotes the area as a destination.

Nonstop flight A flight between two cities with no intermediate stops.

North American Industrial Classification System (NAICS) A classification system developed for use by North American Free Trade Agreement (NAFTA) countries, that is, Canada, Mexico, and the United States of America, to collect and report economic and financial data for similar establishments in the same industry.

O

Objective A specific target for which measurable results can be obtained.

Occupancy rate Ratio comparing the total number of rooms occupied for a given time period to the total number of rooms available for rent.

One-level distribution channels The simplest form of distribution, in which the supplier deals directly with the consumer without the services of intermediaries.

One-way flight A flight plan that includes no return to city of origin.

Open-jaw An air travel trip that includes intermediate surface transportation between point of origin and point of destination, often used by cruise and rail passengers.

Overbooking Accepting more reservations than there is capacity to serve those customers making the reservations (e.g., accepting reservations for more passengers than there are available seats on an aircraft or for more rooms than there are in a hotel). Confirming more reservations for rooms than can be provided during a specified time period.

Overrides Additional bonuses offered to travel agencies beyond their usual commission to encourage the agency to sell more tickets.

P

Pacific Rim The land masses that have a Pacific Ocean coastline.

Passenger facility charge A charge added to airline tickets for enplanement. The monies collected are to be used for airport improvements.

Pension A small inn or boarding house similar to a bed and breakfast.

Per diem Maximum travel expense amount that will be reimbursed on a per day basis.

Perpetual inventory A system of tracking inventory on a continual basis so that current information on the level of stock is always available.

Personal selling A communications process that includes discovering customer needs, finding the appropriate services to meet these needs, and then persuading customers to purchase these services.

Physical capacity The number of users that can be accommodated in an area.

Physical geography The natural features of our planet, including such things as climate, land masses, bodies of water, and resources.

Pilgrimage Travel to a holy place or shrine.

Plate presentation The process of arranging menu offerings in a visually appealing fashion.

Point-of-sale systems (POSs) Systems designed to record and track customer orders, process debit and credit cards, manage inventory, and connect to other systems in a network.

Point-to-point Direct travel between two destinations.

Policy A general statement that provides direction for individuals within an organization.

Prime vendor agreements Agreements directing a majority of purchases to one purveyor.

Privatization The action of converting a government-owned business to private ownership.

Product-related segmentation Dividing consumer markets according to characteristics such as the amount of use or benefits consumers expect to derive from the service.

Professional travel Travel by individuals to attend meetings and conventions.

Profits Revenues in excess of expenses representing the financial performance and the ultimate measure of the financial success of a business.

Property management system (PMS) A unified system used to manage sales and marketing, reservations, front office operations, point-of-sale systems, telecommunications, back office operations, and revenue management.

Properties Individual accommodations and lodging facilities.

Psychocentrics See Dependables.

Psychographics Consumer psychological characteristics that can be quantified, including lifestyle and personality information.

Psychographic segmentation Dividing consumer markets into groups based on lifestyle and personality profiles.

Public/private organizations Organizations made up of private and public members, usually to coordinate efforts between government and private businesses.

Purchase order A contract that specifies the item(s) wanted, including a brief description of quality and grade, the number desired, and the price.

Purser A ship official responsible for papers, accounts, and the comfort and welfare of passengers.

Purveyors Food-service supplier.

Push The act of pushing an aircraft away from the gate for departure. The term is used to indicate the

length of time necessary to unload, fuel, service, and reload an aircraft between time of arrival and departure.

R

Rack rate The standard quoted rate for one night's lodging.

Real estate tourism Travel time spent gaining in-depth knowledge and perspectives about the area from scheduled meetings with local experts while searching out potential investment opportunities.

Receptive service operator (RSO) (ground operator) A local company that specializes in handling the needs of groups traveling to its location.

Recreational activities Activities and experiences people pursue for personal enjoyment.

Reduction The result of boiling a liquid (usually stock, wine, or a sauce mixture) rapidly until the volume is reduced by evaporation, thereby thickening the consistency and intensifying the flavor.

Referral organizations Associations formed to conduct advertising and marketing programs and generate reservations and referrals for member properties.

Regional geography The components of geography that focus on regional landscapes, cultures, economies, and political and social systems.

Rental pools Groups of condominium units that are released by their owners for rental purposes and are managed by lodging companies.

Repositioning cruise The transfer of a ship from one cruising area to another to take advantage of the seasonality of demand.

Resort destinations Communities or areas that contain attractions, entertainment, and supporting facilities needed to draw and host tourists.

Resorts Destination locations that are distinguished by the combination of attractions and amenities for the express purpose of attracting and serving large numbers of visitors.

Restitution An amount of money or other item given to make up for some mistake or wrongdoing.

Return on investment (ROI) A measure of management's efficiency, showing the return on all of an organization's assets.

Revenue management (yield management) The process of allocating the right type of capacity to the right kind of customer at the right price so as to maximize revenue or yield.

Revenue passenger miles (RPM) One seat on an airplane, railroad, or motorcoach traveling one mile with a revenue-producing passenger.

Right-to-use A type of lease in which legal title does not pass to the buyer. The buyer has the right to occupy and utilize the facilities for a particular time period.

Rolling hubs Connecting flights are spread over longer periods of time to reduce congestion and facility and equipment demands.

Round-trip flight A flight plan that includes return to city of origin via identical routing.

Royalties Payment (usually a percentage of sales) for the use of a franchiser's brand name and operating systems.

Russian service A style of service in which the entrée, vegetables, and starches are served by the waitstaff directly from a platter to a guest's plate.

S

Seat (table) turnover The number of successive diners sitting in one seat or at one table during each dining period, breakfast, lunch, and dinner.

Secondary seasons Periods when tourism activities are either increasing toward peak levels or declining from peak levels; also called "shoulder seasons."

Service encounter A single episode during which a customer and service personnel interact; often also called a "moment of truth."

Service expectations The quality level of the five dimensions of service expected by a customer.

Service recovery The process of reversing a service problem.

Services The performance of actions or efforts on behalf of another.

Service script Learned patterns of behavior that guide interactions during a service encounter.

Ship personnel All individuals responsible for the safety and navigation of cruise ships.

Shoulder season The period of time between high and low or closed seasons when demand for services decreases.

Single supplement The additional charge added to the price of a tour or cruise when a traveler does not share accommodations with another traveler; often, 25% to 100% of the double occupancy rate is added to arrive at a single occupancy rate.

Single traveler A person who lives alone and travels with or without a companion.

Slow tourism Trips with a slower pace during which travelers step back from everyday experiences, allowing time and opportunities for immersion.

SMERF An acronym for the market comprising social, military, educational, religious, and fraternal groups.

Social carrying capacity The number of outsiders to an area that can be accepted without having damaging psychological effects on the locals of the area.

Social networking Individuals tied together by a common interest or theme who share bookmarked Web links and conversations.

Society A community, nation, or broad grouping of people who have common traditions, institutions, activities, and interests.

Soft ecotourists Physically passive travelers with moderate environmental commitment who seek mulipurpose trips with an emphasis on interpretation and physical comfort.

Spa resorts A resort property dedicated to fitness and the development of healthy lifestyles.

Special-interest tourism (SIT) Tourism undertaken for a distinct and specific personal reason.

Specification A detailed written description of a procedure or ingredient.

Spoke routes Air service provided from smaller secondary markets to feed passengers into primary hub markets.

Sport tourism visitors People who travel to participate in or view sporting activities.

Standard A predetermined procedure or amount of an ingredient.

Station A designated work area or department in a kitchen.

Stock The strained liquid that is the result of cooking vegetables, meat, or fish and other seasonings and ingredients in water.

Strategic grouping Groups that share common interests.

Subcontracting The hiring of another organization to perform one or more operational functions or services.

Subsegments A group within a larger market segment; sometimes called a "microsegment."

Superstructure The facilities needed to serve the specific needs of tourists, such as hotels, restaurants, and attractions.

Sustainable tourism Tourism activities and development that do not endanger the economic, social, cultural, or environmental assets of a destination.

T

Table d'hôte French term referring to a menu offering a complete meal at a fixed price (prix fixe).

Target market (target segment) A group of people sharing common characteristics that an organization attempts to serve by designing strategies to meet the group's specific needs.

Technology The use of new knowledge and tools to improve productivity and systems.

Teleconferencing A meeting that allows people to remain in several locations but come together and communicate through a combination of television and telephone connections.

Three-level distribution channels Distribution channels in which two or more channel members, such as tour operators or wholesalers, serve as intermediaries between the supplier and the consumer.

Timeshare Either ownership or the right to occupy and use a vacation home for a specific period of time.

Tour A product that includes at least two of the following elements: transportation, accommodations, meals, entertainment, attractions, and sightseeing activities. It can vary widely in the number of elements included and in the structure of the itinerary.

Tourism The temporary movement of people to destinations outside their normal places of work and residence, the activities undertaken during their stay in those destinations, and the facilities created to cater to their needs.

Tourism planning A continual process of research-and-development decisions to create and sustain tourism in a region.

Tourism policy A master plan formulated by a government (national, state/provincial, local) to aid in guiding the development of sustainable tourism industries within its jurisdiction.

Tour operator A business entity engaged in the planning, preparing, marketing, making of reservations, and, at times, operating vacation tours.

Tour package Two or more travel services put together by a tour operator, such as air transportation, accommodations, meals, ground transportation, and attractions.

Travel agent A sales specialist in tourism services.

Travel clubs Membership organizations designed to serve the needs of last-minute leisure travelers at bargain prices.

Trunk routes Point-to-point air service between primary hub markets.

Two-level distribution channels Distribution channels in which an additional channel member, such as a travel agent, serves as an intermediary between the supplier and the consumer.

U

Upgrades Receiving a better class of service or facility than was paid for, such as moving from coach to first class.

Urban tourism Tourism that takes place in large cities, where hotels and other facilities and services have become an integral part of urban activities.

U.S. Department of Transportation (DOT) Organization within the U.S. government charged with establishing the nation's overall transportation policy, including highway planning, development, and construction; urban mass transit; railroads; aviation; and waterways.

V

Venue The location of an event or attraction.

Venturers Travelers who seek adventure.

VFR Visits to friends and relatives.

VIA Rail Canada The marketing name for Canada's passenger train network, which is a combination of the passenger rail services of Canadian railroads.

Virtual conferencing Meetings among geographically dispersed individuals using video, sound, and data transmission technologies so participants can see and interact with each other.

Vocation tourism Trips during which travelers take time to experience possible new careers before actually making career changes.

Voluntourism A trip that combines travel activities with charitable work.

W

Wildlife tourism Travel to observe animals, birds, and fish in their native habitats without altering their behaviors.

World Heritage Sites Sites identified for preservation because of special cultural or heritage interest by the United Nations Educational, Scientific and Cultural Organization (UNESCO).

Y

Yield The amount or quantity produced or returned after the preparation, processing, or cooking of a product or recipe.

Index

Page numbers followed by b indicate box; those followed by f indicate figure; those followed t indicate table.